Individual Change
Through Small Groups

Individual Change Through Small Groups

Second Edition, Revised and Expanded

EDITED BY

Martin Sundel
Paul Glasser
Rosemary Sarri
Robert Vinter

THE FREE PRESS
A Division of Macmillan, Inc.
NEW YORK

Collier Macmillan Publishers
LONDON

Copyright © 1974, 1985 by The Free Press
A Division of Macmillan, Inc.

The Free Press
A Division of Macmillan, Inc.
866 Third Avenue, New York, N.Y. 10022

Collier Macmillan Canada, Inc.

Printed in the United States of America

printing number

1 2 3 4 5 6 7 8 9 10

Library of Congress Cataloging in Publication Data

Main entry under title:

Individual change through small groups.

  Includes bibliographies and index.
  1. Social group work. 2. Group relations training.
I. Sundel, Martin, ed. II. Glasser, Paul H., ed.
III. Sarri, Rosemary C., ed. IV. Vinter, Robert D., ed.
HV45.152   1985   361.4   85–6750
ISBN 0-02-911790-9

Contents

Preface to the Second Edition

The University of Michigan approach to work with groups was initiated more than twenty-five years ago. The first papers appeared in mimeographed form for student use. They were put together in a volume, *Readings in Group Work Practice* (Vinter, 1967), which was printed by a local Ann Arbor publisher for student convenience but received wide circulation nationally and internationally, including translations into a number of languages. The first edition of this volume was a much expanded version of those initial efforts. This book maintains the early thrust and orientation but brings much of the material up to date and provides for the many new developments in group work practice that have taken place in the intervening years.

This approach was the center of much controversy because it changed the nature of practice with groups in social work. Now that the debate has subsided, it seems appropriate to review the early history of the innovation in the context of that period.

THE UNIVERSITY OF MICHIGAN APPROACH IN HISTORICAL CONTEXT

Social group work had its origins in the settlement house movement at the turn of the century. Its beginnings were in such agencies as Hull House in Chicago and Educational Alliance in New York City. Its primary focus was on work with the poor and the immigrant populations in the inner city ghettos and included the use of a great many not yet clearly identified methods to help such groups live somewhat more comfortable lives and move up the social class ladder.

Involved in the movement were men and women from many different disciplines and professions—education, sociology, psychology, recreation, home economics, and social work (Wilson, 1976; Siporin, in press). Central to all of their activities was a philosophical ideal that emphasized the use of the small group to teach democratic decision-making as a means to integrate diverse elements of a bureaucratic, industrialized community into a democratic society (Newstedder, 1935). It was part of the "melting pot" doctrine so popular at that time. That philosophy continues to permeate not only social group work but all social work. However, its more practical implications also have been recognized. When group members participate in decisions likely to affect their lives they are also more likely to carry out those decisions willingly (Cartwright and Zander, 1960).

The proliferation of agencies of the settlement house type led many to identify group work as a field of practice as well. These agencies included the Young Men's and Young Women's Christian Associations and Jewish Community Centers. Just prior to and following World War II they gradually shifted their programs from the education of immigrants and the poor to the American way of life to the socialization of mostly middle-class members to particular religious orientations. The large European immigration had ended, and the sons and daughters of these new Americans, who became the chief supporters of these agencies, had different interests. Some of the inner city settlements maintained their traditional orientation, however, working with rural immigrants who moved to the city and the new immigrants—Puerto Ricans, Chicanos, and most recently Southeast Asians. Their programs increasingly made use of a great variety of methods and techniques.

During World War II the use of groups for therapeutic purposes was started by the armed forces as a means to rehabilitate men and women with psychiatric disorders more efficiently. This led to the use of groups in a great variety of settings and fields of practice that previously had focused on one-to-one methods of change. At the same time the traditional settlement houses continued to include social action programs at the neighborhood level, which gradually became identified as a community organization method. Thus agencies could no longer be recognized as "group service agencies," since the large majority of these institutions used multiple methods of change and rarely focused on the use of small groups only to achieve individual or community modifications.

In the midst of these trends social group work as a method of practice became better defined and refined. The classic work by Wilson and Ryland (1949) encompassed at least four distinct functions of professional practice with small groups: (1) an educational and growth-oriented approach to work with normal children and adults, which included socialization into democratic as well as particular religious orientations (The use of program as a tool for this purpose was especially appealing to recreation and socialization agencies.); (2) a treatment service to deviant and/or pathological clients who required behavioral change, and also as a preventive approach for high-risk population groups such as predelinquent groups of children and adolescents; (3) a "tool" for more efficient and effective agency administration, which under the influence of Lippitt and Lippitt (1978) spread from social agencies to business, industrial, and other types of organizations; and (4) one among an array of techniques useful in community organization and planned change (Rothman, 1968).

The University of Michigan approach, as reflected in this volume, was initiated in the late 1950s and early 1960s under the leadership of Robert Vinter. The approach had at least five purposes: (1) to clarify the ambiguity of social group work as a method by providing a coherent framework for practice; (2) to integrate the social group work method into social work at a time when its professional identification was weak, floundering, and without direction; (3) to reorient social group workers to give priority to persons most in need of professional help—deviant, dysfunctional and/or pathological clients and high-risk population groups—(4) to spread the use of the group work method and social group workers into a great variety of new settings, including many of those that traditionally employed social caseworkers; and (5) to integrate the rapidly developing social and behavioral science literature, especially social psychology and group dynamics, into not only social group work practice but all of professional social work. A close inspection of these goals will indicate that they are related to each other, and a review of each of the chapters in the volume will reveal that one or more is reflected in each piece.

The time was right. There was a growing emphasis in social work on therapeutic approaches. The National Institute of Mental Health provided increasingly large amounts of funds for social work training. The University of Michigan School of Social Work was the first to receive funds to educate group workers exclusively, and at one point group work students were supported by seven different federal grants. The school had the largest group work program in the country, reaching a peak of about 150 students in the four-semester curriculum, with more than fifteen faculty.

The emphasis of the University of Michigan approach is, as the title of this book states, *Individual Change Through Small Groups*. The focus is on the use of small groups for cognitive and behavioral change, and has been from the beginning, although cognitive and behavioral therapy were virtually unknown in social work at that time. Although misinterpreted often, it was not meant to be the only small group approach to work with individuals and communities. As a matter of fact, Vinter and his colleagues encouraged others to develop different frameworks for practice with small groups with different goals and purposes and with organizations and communities. Further, the University of Michigan approach was meant to be used not only with those in need of treatment but also as a preventive approach with those likely to display pathological and deviant behavior. Its emphasis has always been on the use of the group *for individual change*. The professional who works with any group having as its purpose personal change for each of its members can appropriately make use of this framework.

THE GENERIC AND THE SPECIFIC

In the 1950s the National Association of Social Workers (NASW) was formed, the first body that represented all professionals in the field. The association maintained sections that represented the previous social work organizations, which were mainly structured according to fields of practice, such as psychiatric and medical social work. The American Association of Group Workers became the Group Work Section of the NASW. This increased the confusion about whether social group work was a field of practice or a method of practice. By the early 1960s the profession was ready to eliminate the sections, and the NASW did so. That laid the foundation for the generic curriculum.

In the 1940s and 1950s schools of social work were accredited by fields of practice. Social group work was considered one of those. By 1960 accreditation was by method and included social casework, social group work, community organization, administration, and research. Group work had moved from a field of practice to a method, so it was no wonder that confusion arose about its definition. With the NASW decision to eliminate sections, faculty at the schools began to talk about the generic social worker. The Council on Social Work Education, the accrediting body, abandoned the accreditation of specific methods in the schools, replacing it with five curriculum areas of values, knowledge, and skills: direct practice, human behavior and the social environment, social services and social policy, research, and community planning and administration. The University of Michigan School of Social Work was one of the first to move in this direction.

Many schools combined social casework and social group work into the same courses, using such terms as social treatment, interpersonal practice, or direct practice to identify them. Some even included community organization and administration in the same course. A few schools, but certainly not all, maintained advanced courses in each of the methods. This had both negative and positive consequences for development of the social group work method.

Social group work faculty were heavily outnumbered by social caseworkers. As a result it became difficult to include group work content in the curriculum. The caseworkers had little knowledge or experience in group work, and there weren't enough group workers to teach all the courses in which such content belonged. In many places not much group work content was taught, and the identity of group work as a method began to be lost.

Nonetheless, many schools of social work required that all direct practice students have field instruction experience in work with groups. Many also claimed that their graduates were qualified to work with groups. That helped to spread the trend initiated by the University of Michigan approach to include some form of group treatment in many different settings and fields of practice. The groups often were led by workers with little or no group work training. They were sometimes successful in their efforts, but in the opinion of the present authors they could have been more successful with adequate training. Still, the use of groups became a fully accepted method in social work practice for the first time. And the University of Michigan approach to social group work practice fitted well in the great variety of traditional casework settings.

Trends run in cycles, in the profession of social work as in any other area. Once again there is interest not only in specialized fields of practice but also in concentrations by methods. Schools of social work once more are offering courses in social group work not only for their regular graduate and undergraduate students but also for professionals through their continuing education programs. Practitioners in many settings are rediscovering the value of the use of groups, often to carry out functions and tasks described in the early group work literature.

Now, however, there is a much broader array of techniques available to make the method more effective and efficient. The University of Michigan approach was one of the first social work frameworks to emphasize behavioral goals and their evaluation, permitting accountability and continuous improvement in practice as well as refinement of the approach. This has continued to be one of the sources of attraction for professionals. In addition, the ability to intervene with several clients at one time has been seen as a way to improve agency efficiency. Changes in service delivery have been conducive to the use of groups in social work as well. Some of those changes are described in the fifth section, on group work in selected fields of practice.

Thus, the University of Michigan approach to work with groups is as viable today as when it was first initiated. The framework has always been open, allowing the introduction of new findings from the social and behavioral sciences as well as practice experience. That is why this second edition is important: It brings much of the material into relevance for the 1980s.

COMMENTS ON THE SECOND EDITION

Much of the material in this second edition is new. Among the thirty-two chapters, fourteen are totally new, eight have had extensive revisions, and ten have undergone only minor changes. A new section has been added, "The Evaluation of Group Services," to reflect the growing technology in research and its influence on group work practice. New chapters of special

FIGURE 1.   Scheme Depicting Contents of *Individual Change Through Small Groups*

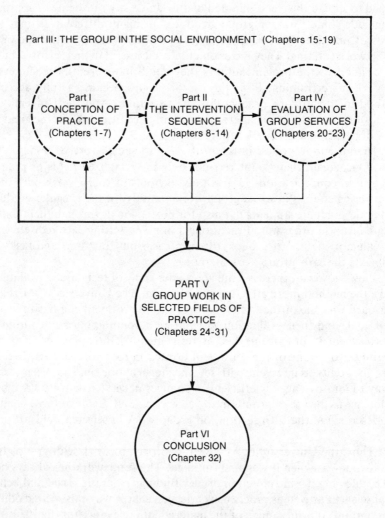

significance today include the ones on gender theory, working with minorities, practice with disadvantaged and oppressed groups, and work with time-limited and open-ended groups. Six of the seven chapters in the "Group Work in Selected Fields of Practice" section are new, reflecting the shift in emphasis in social work as well as social group work.

The basic orientation of the University of Michigan approach remains the same, however. The first two chapters by Robert Vinter therefore required only minor technical editing. Although the volume's authors are now scattered throughout the country, with very few exceptions all have been faculty at the University of Michigan or students in the masters or doctoral programs at the school.

Figure I shows how the six parts of this volume are interrelated. Part I presents the conceptual frameworks, principles of practice, and knowledge bases germane to the Michigan group work model. Part II examines individual components comprising the intervention sequence, which operationalizes the conception of practice presented in Part I. Part III discusses significant aspects of group members' (e.g. ethnicity) and the group's social environment (e.g. organizational context) that impact on their functioning, and which thereby become essential considerations for both the conception of practice (Part I) and the intervention sequence (Part II). Part IV addresses the results of group work intervention, including consideration of outcomes for individuals, salient treatment dimensions, and group-level variables. Part V provides a selected sample of the wide range of applications of the model. Part VI reviews major developments influencing the model and identifies future directions.

The book is organized as a text. The first edition was adopted by a large number of undergraduate and graduate social work programs throughout the nation and was used extensively by many other helping professionals such as psychologists, educators, and pastoral counselors. We are hopeful that this new volume will be accepted as enthusiastically.

The primary responsibility for the revisions was taken by Paul Glasser and Martin Sundel. Our wives, Lois Glasser and Sandra Stone Sundel, were most helpful in making suggestions throughout the process. A special note of appreciation is due to Roberta Dotterer, who went much beyond the typing of manuscripts by providing editorial assistance. It is our wish that this second edition will continue the stimulation the first provided in a way that will increasingly result in better services to people in need.

PAUL GLASSER
MARTIN SUNDEL

REFERENCES

CARTWRIGHT, DORWIN, AND ALVIN ZANDER
  1960   "Leadership and group performance." In Dorwin Cartwright and Alvin
         Zander (eds.), *Group Dynamics: Research and Theory*. Second edition.
         Evanston, Ill.: Row, Peterson & Co., pp. 487–510.
LIPPITT, RONALD, AND GORDON LIPPITT
  1978   *The Consulting Process in Action*. La Jolla, Calif.: University Associates.

NEWSTETTER, W.I.
1935 "What is social group work?" In *Proceedings, National Conference of Social Work, 1935*. Chicago: University of Chicago Press, pp. 291–299.
ROTHMAN, JACK
1968 "Three models of community organization practice." In *Social Work Practice, 1968*. New York: Columbia University Press, pp. 17–47.
SIPORIN, MAX
In press "Group work method and the Inquiry." In Paul Glasser and Nazneen Mayadas (eds.), *Group Workers At Work: Theory and Practice in the 80s*. Totowa, N.J.: Littlefield, Adams & Co.
VINTER, ROBERT
1967 *Readings in Group Work Practice*. Ann Arbor, Mich.: Campus Publishers.
WILSON, GERTRUDE, AND GLADYS RYLAND
1949 *Social Group Work Practice: The Creative Use of Social Process*. Cambridge, Mass.: The Riverside Press.
WILSON, GERTRUDE
1976 "From practice to theory: A personalized history." In Robert W. Roberts and Helen Northen (eds.), *Theories of Social Work with Groups*. New York: Columbia University Press, pp. 1–44.

Preface to the First Edition

This book aims to provide practitioners in the helping professions with methods of serving individuals within and through small, face-to-face groups, to induce desired changes among the participants. It will have use by a broad range of health, welfare, and educational agencies: antipoverty organizations, child guidance clinics and community mental health centers, school social services, juvenile courts and delinquency control programs, mental hospitals and correctional institutions, public welfare agencies, youth development and recreational programs, and others. The methods are useful for the treatment of individuals defined as "deviant" or "psychologically ill" and for the prevention of the development of their problems.

In this problem-oriented approach, problems must be described in concrete behavioral terms to enable the evaluation of individual changes during or following treatment. The practitioner together with the client must plan specifically and use consciously the interaction among group members to change them. Since the individual is viewed in the context of the intervention group and his social situation in the real world, the methods use much material from all the social and behavioral sciences.

The volume is organized as a text. The first section describes the basic approach; the second, the activities of the professional from the beginning to the end of the intervention process in the group; the third, the activities required by the worker in the client's environment outside the group; and the fourth, the application of this approach to a great variety of fields of practice.

The papers in this publication were authored over several years by faculty members and graduate students at The University of Michigan School of Social Work, primarily for use in the group work curriculum. This

School pioneered the development of a problem-oriented approach to group work practice, and teaching materials which were not available in the professional literature needed to be created. These papers are one result of faculty and graduate student efforts to formulate and set forth the major features of group work practice within this general conception.

This is the second such volume; the first, a much smaller and more modest one, appeared in 1967. The six papers from the initial effort also appear in this book, but all have been edited, some completely revised, to bring them up to date. The majority of papers in this volume have not been published before however. This book, much more comprehensive than the first, attempts to provide a great variety of methods and techniques, of the problem-oriented approach developed at the School, for working with groups.

Authors have made considerable effort to integrate theory and findings from the social and behavioral sciences into group work practice. This has been a major orientation of the School since 1955, when the Russell Sage Foundation awarded special funds as part of its attempt to infuse social science into the professions. Some years later the Foundation made a modest but separate grant through Professor Vinter to develop a social science-oriented volume on group work practice. Although the second award supported reviews of literature and curriculum and research development, it did not directly contribute to the present publication. Rather, this volume is a product of the general direction the School has taken as a result of the Foundation's support.

None of this would have been possible without the encouragement and foresight of Fedele F. Fauri, former Dean of the School of Social Work and now University of Michigan Vice-President for State Relations and Planning. He made possible the multitude of major developments in the School, through his organizational abilities and also through his personal allegiance and commitment to the scholarly work of each faculty member. His successor, Dean Phillip Fellin, has continued to move the School in this direction.

The authors of these papers are indebted to many graduate students and to agency field instructors for significant assistance in developing, clarifying and modifying the ideas dealt with here. Several of the papers emerged from classroom discourse and teaching notes, and most have been revised earlier in the light of critical response. The authors also acknowledge with appreciation the contributions and suggestions of their faculty colleagues, a number of whom are not listed as authors of the papers here.

Special appreciation is expressed to Kate Grenholm, who did most of the technical editing for the volume, and to Marian Iglesias and Margaret Lemley, who did much of the typing. Finally, thanks must be given to each of our spouses, who not only took on extra responsibilities during periods of intense activity during the book's preparation, but also participated in the editing process. We are hopeful that all of these efforts will be rewarded through better group work service to people in need.

PAUL H. GLASSER
ROSEMARY C. SARRI
ROBERT D. VINTER

Biographical Notes

MARTIN SUNDEL, Ph.D., is the Roy E. Dulak Professor of Social Work at The University of Texas at Arlington. He has practiced and conducted research in community mental health centers, child welfare agencies, hospitals, family service agencies, neighborhood centers, and community outreach programs. His research interests with groups have focused on behavioral treatment, time-limited approaches, and prevention. A social worker and psychologist, Dr. Sundel is a charter clinical fellow of the Behavior Therapy and Research Society. His publications include *Behavior Modification in the Human Services* (First and Second Editions) and *Be Assertive*, both co-authored with his wife, Sandra Stone Sundel. He is also co-author of *Assessing Health and Human Service Needs*. His current interests include long-range planning and futures research, group processes in community and organizational settings, and the application of general systems theory and systems science to the helping professions.

PAUL H. GLASSER, Ph.D., is now Professor and Dean of Social Work at The University of Texas at Arlington, after serving on the faculty at The University of Michigan for twenty years. He has had extensive social work practice and research experience in child guidance clinics, residential treatment institutions, army hospitals, and family treatment agencies. He has been a Fulbright Scholar in the Philippines, Italy, and Australia. In addition to being author and co-author of more than 100 journal articles, his publications include *Families in Crisis*, completed with his wife, Lois N. Glasser. He has been editor for several social work and social science journals and was senior editor of the 1971 edition of the *Encyclopedia of Social Work*. He continues to be interested in social work practice, the family, poverty, and, most recently, ethical and moral issues of the profession.

ROSEMARY SARRI, Ph.D., is Professor of Social Work and Faculty Associate, Institute of Social Research, The University of Michigan. Dr. Sarri has done extensive research, teaching, and consultation to federal, state, and local governments and internationally in the practice and administration of programs in juvenile and adult criminal justice, child welfare, and school social work. She has taught at several U.S. universities and internationally in the Philippines, Australia, and Hong Kong. Her publications include *Juvenile Delinquency, Brought to Justice, Disruptive Youth in School, Women in Prison*, and *Issues in the Management of Human Services*, which was co-edited with Yeheskel Hasenfeld. She is currently engaged in cross-national comparative research on the feminization of poverty as associated with changes in family structure and social policy.

ROBERT D. VINTER, Ph.D., is Distinguished Professor of Social Work at The University of Michigan. A former social work practitioner, he joined the Michigan faculty to develop the group work curriculum at that School and later served for some years as Associate Dean. Dr. Vinter's research and teaching have focused on professional practice, corrections, and human service organizations. He has written extensively on several areas of professional practice, including group work and, more recently, fiscal and program management. He co-authored *Organization for Treatment* and is co-author of the recent *Budgeting for Not-for-Profit Organizations*. He and Dr. Sarri were Co-Directors of the National Assessment of Juvenile Corrections, and he edited and co-authored several of its publications, including *Juvenile Corrections in the States* and *Time Out: A National Study of Juvenile Correctional Programs.* Dr. Vinter has also served as consultant to numerous state and federal agencies, including the National Institute of Mental Health, the President's Commission on Law Enforcement and Criminal Justice, and Correctional Services of the Ministry of Justice, Government of Jamaica.

MARK D. ALICKE received his Ph.D. in Social Psychology. He is presently doing postdoctoral work at Northwestern University.

HARVEY J. BERTCHER received his D.S.W. from the University of Southern California. He is the author and co-author of many articles and reports, including a volume on group composition. He is Professor at The University of Michigan School of Social Work.

RUTH CAMPBELL is Senior Social Worker, Turner Geriatric Services, The University of Michigan Hospital. After receiving a social work degree at The University of Michigan, much of her practice experience has been in gerontology.

BERYL CARTER (RICE) received her M.S. from Columbia University and her Ph.D. from the Catholic University of America. She is currently Associate Professor at the University of the District of Columbia.

SALLIE R. CHURCHILL received her M.S.W. from the University of Minnesota and her Ph.D. from the University of Chicago. She has authored and co-authored many publications in the area of group work with children and youth, including the recent publication, *No Child Is Unadoptable*. She is Professor at The University of Michigan School of Social Work.

JANE COSTABILE is Associate Professor Emeritus at The University of Michigan. She has had a distinguished career as a social work practitioner, administrator, and educator.

TOM A. CROXTON received both his J.D. and M.S.W. from The University of Michigan, where he is now Professor of Social Work. The author of several articles, he is also a member of the Michigan State Bar.

RICHARD ALLYN ENGLISH received his Ph.D. from The University of Michigan. He is currently on leave from The University of Michigan as the Fred Southerland Professor of Mental Health Policy at The University of Texas at Austin.

LARRY E. DAVIS received his Ph.D. from The University of Michigan School of Social Work and is presently Associate Professor at the George Warren Brown School of Social Work, Washington University, St. Louis. He has published numerous articles on the functioning of minorities in groups.

SHEILA FELD is Professor at The University of Michigan School of Social Work and head of the doctoral program. She has done research and published extensively in the area of mental health.

RONALD A. FELDMAN received his Ph.D. from The University of Michigan and is Professor at the George Warren Brown School of Social Work, Washington University, St. Louis. He has authored and co-authored a number of books and numerous articles on group approaches in work with delinquents.

MAEDA J. GALINSKY received both her M.S.W. and Ph.D. from The University of Michigan and is presently Professor of Social Work at The University of North Carolina at Chapel Hill. She has written extensively on group work practice.

CHARLES D. GARVIN received both his A.M. and Ph.D. from the University of Chicago. As a Professor at The University of Michigan, he is the author and co-author of many professional articles and most recently of two texts, one on group work practice and the other on generic social work practice.

YEHESKEL HASENFELD received his Ph.D. from The University of Michigan and is now Professor and Associate Dean. He has published extensively on administration and practice, including a recent book on human service organizations.

FRANK MAPLE received both his M.A. and M.S.W. from The University of Michigan, where he is now Professor of Social Work. He has taught group work practice for many years and published in the areas of group composition and school social work.

NAZNEEN S. MAYADAS received her M.S.S.A. from Case Western Reserve University in Cleveland, Ohio, and her D.S.W. from Washington University, St. Louis. Currently she is Professor at The University of Texas at Arlington specializing in the field of social group work and interpersonal skills.

ELIZABETH L. NAVARRE is Associate Professor at Indiana University. Her primary interests have been research on social work practice and social work education.

NORMA RADIN is Professor of Social Work at The University of Michigan, where she received both her M.S.W. and Ph.D. She has conducted extensive research on relationships between parental behavior and the school performance of children and recently co-authored, with Sheila Feld, a book on the application of social psychology to social work and mental health.

BETH GLOVER REED is Associate Professor at The University of Michigan School of Social Work. She has done considerable research and consulting in the area of substance abuse.

SHELDON D. ROSE is Professor of Social Work at the University of Wisconsin. His considerable international experience included serving as Deputy Director of the Peace Corps in Nepal. He has published a number of volumes as well as journal articles on behavioral approaches to group work practice.

JANICE HOUGH SCHOPLER received her M.S.W. from The University of Michigan. She is Associate Professor at the University of North Carolina at Chapel Hill and has written much in the area of group work practice and child welfare.

SANDRA STONE SUNDEL is a clinical social worker in private practice in Arlington, Texas, and was previously Coordinator of Social Services at the Jewish Social Service Agency in Fort Worth. Trained in group work at The University of Michigan, she completed her M.S.S.W. at the Kent School of Social Work, University of Louisville. She is co-author, with Martin Sundel, of *Behavior Modification in the Human Services* and *Be Assertive*.

RICHARD TOLMAN received his Ph.D. from the University of Wisconsin at Madison. He is currently on the faculty at the University of Illinois, Chicago Circle Campus. He has worked closely with Sheldon Rose on behavior modification approaches to group work practice.

JAMES K. WHITTAKER received his Ph.D. from the University of Minnesota. He is author and co-author of many articles and several books. He has taught at Boston University and the University of Minnesota and currently is Professor and Director of the Social Welfare Ph.D. program at the University of Washington.

CHARLES WOLFSON received his M.S.W. from Wayne State University. He is Professor at The University of Michigan, having taught group work practice for more than twenty years. During much of this time he served as a consultant on the use of groups for prevention and treatment of delinquent behavior.

I

A Conception of Practice

The University of Michigan approach to work with groups is a systematic, eclectic, integrated set of practice propositions. Its purpose is to make professionals aware of how their actions (or lack of actions) influence the group so that the group will influence both its members and the social environment surrounding the group. The aim of the model is to increase the level of the practitioner's conscious and purposeful behavior so that he or she may more effectively and efficiently help group members achieve the goals agreed upon through contract negotiation. Workers' actions are conceptualized as means of influence, and it is those means that are central to this theoretical orientation. This first section of the volume lays out the core concepts of the approach.

Chapter 1 by Robert Vinter describes the scope of practice with the University of Michigan approach. Its primary focus is on work in groups with persons who are recognized as having social and psychological problems by themselves or others, or on work in groups with individuals who are likely to have such problems because of adverse conditions in their environments. An underlying assumption is that deviance or psychopathy has its sources in interpersonal interactions and the social contexts in which such interactions occur. The group session provides a means for the correction of such dysfunctional behavior through the professional's purposeful intervention. To be most effective the group worker must have a rational change strategy that encompasses a multiplicity of procedures appropriate to different types of clients in a variety of group conditions.

The second chapter by Robert Vinter outlines the fundamental modes of intervention for the problem-oriented approach reflected in this volume. Each part of the outline is expanded upon or illustrated in the remainder of this section and in all the chapters that follow. The orderly sequence of intervention and its relationship to group development is described first, followed by an explanation of how the worker's intervention or treatment goals—the composite or integration of these being named the worker's purposes for the group—each member's personal goals and objectives, and their shared purposes for the group may all be different but can be made consistent through individual and group contract negotiations.

The main portion of the chapter is devoted to the strategy of intervention. "Direct means of influence are interventions to effect change through immediate interaction with a (specific) group member." Such interventions include worker as a central person—object of identifications and drives; worker as symbol and spokesperson—agent of legitimate norms and values; worker as motivator and stimulator—definer of individual goals and tasks; and worker as executive—controller of members' roles. "Indirect means of influence are interventions that modify group conditions which subsequently affect one or more members." These include group purposes, selection of group members, group size, group operating and governing procedures, group development, and program. "Extragroup means of influence include activities conducted on behalf of clients outside the group." In this chapter Vinter provides specific descriptions of the ten direct and indirect means of influence listed above, the nature of individual behavior and group conditions that each may affect, and the techniques that the professional may employ to achieve specified change.

Vinter's second chapter emphasizes that the specification of the indirect means of influence—using the group to achieve individual change—is unique to the University of Michigan approach in work with groups in social work and the other helping professions. The distinctive point is that the professional's power to affect group conditions provides him or her with a potent tool for change not present in other treatment orientations. This emphasis will be repeated often throughout the volume.

Chapter 3, by Garvin and Glasser, reviews and expands upon the material in the two preceding chapters. Personnel issues are briefly discussed at the beginning. It seems clear that social group work is now used in a much greater variety of fields of practice than twenty-five years ago and that the emphasis in graduate education programs on generic curriculum provides a much higher percentage of students with some group work training. However, the extent of these trends is difficult to determine.

The main assumptions of the Michigan approach to work with groups are delineated: (1) The individual is the focus of change; (2) goals for clients are to be expressed in precise, operational terms; (3) a worker–member contract specifying the ends and means of the service is required; (4) emphasis is placed on the use of the group as a means for individual change; (5) the social environment must both reflect and be used to achieve individual change; and (6) practice principles must be derived scientifically and be capable of empirical evaluation. That last assumption refers to the social science bases of the Michigan approach to social group work practice, which include role theory, social systems theory, sociobehavioral theory, cognitive theories, and propositions derived from the social psychology of influence. Much of the remainder of the chapter reviews the treatment sequence, with emphasis on how aspects of group structures and processes can be used to carry out indirect means of influence. Chapter 3 ends with a summary of some of the more important studies that evaluate aspects of this approach.

Because skill in changing group conditions to achieve individual change is central to much of the material in the volume, it is essential that the professional have basic understanding of how small groups operate. Chapter 4, by Radin and Feld, provides this content, focusing on those findings in social psychology most relevant for group work practice.

After defining the small group, the authors discuss group cohesiveness, pointing to the ways it can be encouraged and used to help members achieve rehabilitation goals. They also indicate how too much or too little group cohesion can deter the achievement of such goals. A similar discussion accompanies their review of norms and norm enforcement in groups. For example, they point out that reactance—"a motivational state of arousal that occurs whenever an individual experiences a threat to, or loss of freedom or potential for action"—may take place when extreme pressures are placed on a member to conform to one or more group norms.

Attitudes, which predispose persons to behavior, can often be changed in the group by affecting group conditions. Radin and Feld point out that the worker has at his or her disposal a variety of types of power, each of which and in different combinations can be used to influence different aspects of the group situation and particular persons in the group. The chapter ends with an examination of task and socioemotional functions in groups, how they are related to leadership patterns, and how the professional's knowledge of such material can make her or him more effective.

Studies of groups have revealed regularities in their functioning, a number of which are described by Radin and Feld. Groups, like individuals, have recurrent patterns in their development. These patterns and the ways the group work practitioner can influence them are the focus of Chapter 5, by Sarri and Galinsky. The authors summarize studies of group development, giving particular attention to (1) the social organization of the group; (2) activities, tasks, and operative processes of the group; and (3) the culture of the group. After each of the seven stages is described in detail, the corresponding stages in the treatment sequence are provided. Specific worker actions required to maximize the use of the group for individual change are delineated at each stage. In an interesting way this chapter provides a detailed map of required activities by the practitioner as he or she moves through the intervention process with the group and its members.

Much of the material in the first five chapters assumes that groups have stable compositions or relatively unchanging memberships. The literature suggests, however, that open-ended groups are being used increasingly for both preventive and therapeutic purposes. Chapter 6, by Schopler and Galinsky, addresses the special considerations in practice required in working with groups that have continuously changing members. The authors report that open-ended groups are often used to provide a great variety of persons, many of whom may be in transitional or crisis life situations, with support, treatment, screening, and education. They describe some of the ways to deal with a rapid turnover in membership. Such changes are easier to deal with early in the group's development, although they can be dealt with successfully even at later stages if a core of members remains each time the turnover occurs. The professional provides an especially important and central role in open-ended groups at all stages in their development, since he or she is one of the main sources of continuity.

The final chapter in this section also deals with a special adaptation of the University of Michigan approach to work with groups. Radin observes that in addition to direct service, alternate methods for reaching more people in need must be provided by social group workers. Two such strategies are to offer consultation to caregivers, such as foster parents, nurses, mothers, and teachers, and to provide service before difficulties develop to those who do not now have well-defined problems but are at risk. She calls such groups socioeducational.

Although much of the substance of earlier chapters in this part is applicable, when working as a consultant to caregivers or with high-risk population groups, Radin identifies at least five significant differences: (1) The professional does not focus on problematic behavior but serves more as an educator, building on already available knowledge and skills; (2) the nature of the worker–client relationship is much more equal than in the typical treatment group; (3) group membership is generally much more open and voluntary; (4) there are few intake procedures, and assessments of members usually take place after the group is operating and are often done through observation of behavior in the group; and (5) greater emphasis must be given to the content of the discussion sessions, requiring that the professional have some expert knowledge of the topic. Thus, while the basic core of knowledge and skills remains the same, the Michigan approach can be extended to work with socioeducational groups to serve new priorities when those five considerations are taken into account.

1

An Approach to Group Work Practice

Robert D. Vinter

INTRODUCTION

Group procedures are now given specialized use in a broad range of health, welfare, and educational agencies, including antipoverty organizations, child guidance clinics, school social services, juvenile courts and delinquency control programs, mental hospitals and correctional institutions, public welfare agencies, and youth development and recreational programs. In group work individuals are served within and through small, face-to-face groups to induce desired changes among participants. This practice cannot be distinguished adequately from other helping processes, particularly those in the social work profession, by the types of clientele served, the organizational setting, or the goals set for clients. The essential difference lies in the primary, but not exclusive, reliance on the multiperson group session as the basic form of intervention rather than on the two-person interview, which characterizes casework and individual therapies.

Groups are used widely to solve problems or accomplish tasks, although the existence of a group does not assure that group treatment or prevention work is being practiced. There are diverse service procedures and approaches which center on the use of client groups, even within the profession of social work, and each of these may have utility in pursuing distinct service objectives. The professional service agent should have a full repertoire of alternate procedures from which he or she can select the most appropriate for specific circumstances, resources, and aims (Sarri and Vinter, 1965; Glasser, 1963).

The concern here is to examine social treatment as one major kind of group work practice. The aim in this and in following chapters is to explicate the essential components and the significant dimensions of this particular approach. The objective is to offer a coherent and prescriptive strategy of intervention, which the student or practitioner may adopt or modify as necessary.

5

GROUP WORK AS SOCIAL TREATMENT

Social treatment through group work practice focuses on ameliorating or preventing the adverse conditions of individuals whose behavior is disapproved or who have been disadvantaged by society (Vinter, 1965). It emphasizes manifest personal and social problems and the rehabilitative potentials of guided group processes to alleviate or avert these problems. Persons most appropriate as clientele for such service include the physically or mentally handicapped, legal offenders, emotionally disturbed, isolated, or alienated persons, and those lacking effective socialization.

Recipients of such group work service are individuals who exhibit or are prone to exhibit problems while performing conventional social roles. The behavioral difficulties and the situations which support them are the specific foci of helping efforts; improved performance is the desired change. Behavioral difficulties may be few and appear in only one of the individual's several social roles, as with some malperformers in the public school; or they may be diffuse and pervade broad areas of social life and careers, as with habitual delinquents, psychotics, and others. Social norms provide general criteria of the nature of the problem behavior and the degree of change actually effected.

An Interactional View of Deviance

For an accurate conception of problem behavior attention must be given to the attributes and capabilities of clients, to the nature of their interactions with others, and to the social contexts within which problems are generated, defined, and manifested. This formulation requires no single conception of the etiology and character of personal deviance or pathology. Assertions that group intervention approaches are effective, however, presuppose an *interactional* conception of the genesis and maintenance of problem behavior. Some of the major features of this view can be outlined as follows. All behavior amenable to change is regarded as socially induced, acquired through learning and related processes; it is exhibited, evoked, or constrained within the context of specific social situations. The sources of behavior lie both within the individual (in terms of his or her enduring attributes and acquired capabilities) and within the social situation (in terms of opportunities, demands, and inducements). Behavior, moreover, is judged, encouraged, or sanctioned by others within the person's immediate social situation. These actions between persons constitutes a series of interactions which shape and sustain behavioral patterns (Schafer, 1967). The judgments and responses of others must be regarded as crucial features of all behavioral patterns. Social definitions of deviance are necessarily relative, and those who define behavior as problematic often refer to specialized standards of conduct. In this view, therefore, the targets for intervention include not only the individual whose behavior is judged to be inadequate or deviant, but also the judgments and interactional responses of individuals and groups whom he or she contacts regularly or frequently at the time. This view gives rise to intervention approaches that are centered on the clients' social situations (including relevant others) as well as on clients within and apart from treatment groups.

The interactional view of behavior is hospitable to most schools of thought concerned with client deviance, dependence, or disability. Each of these schools tend to emphasize different sources and facets of problem behavior and, therefore, concentrates on different goals or targets of change. Consequently, the perspective of deviance alters the particular balance of effort under various conditions of professional practice (Rose, 1967). An approach to the treatment group, as a focus of intervention, can be constructed on this general formulation.

The Treatment Group

The treatment group is conceived as a small social system whose influences can be guided in planned ways to modify client behavior. The potency of the social forces generated within small groups is recognized, and these forces are marshaled deliberately in pursuing goals for client change. The composition, development, and processes of the group are influenced by the practitioner in accordance with his or her purposes. The worker attempts to initiate a series of transactions, through the processes of the group and through his or her own interactions with the clients, which can effect behavioral, attitudinal, and other changes. New behavior or other modifications must be stabilized and transferred beyond the treatment process into the spheres of client life that are regarded as problematic or likely to be so.

The group session is of fundamental importance; *the group is both a means of treatment and a context for treatment*. As a means, it constitutes a vehicle through which peer interactions and influences can be used to affect client participants. As a context, it affords opportunities for direct worker-client interactions, which can contribute to change. In order for the group to serve as an effective means of service, the character of the treatment group itself becomes a focus of intervention. The practitioner is concerned with four major dimensions of group development: (1) the social organization of the group, its pattern of participant roles and statuses; (2) the activities, tasks, and operative processes of the group (e.g. modes of decision-making); (3) the culture of the group, with its norms, values, and shared purposes; and (4) the group's relations to its external environment, including the agency in which it is served (Sarri and Galinsky, Chapter 5, in this volume). Each of these refers to an area of interpersonal relations that must develop if the aggregate of client participants is to become a viable group that can generate effective influences upon its members and achieve the purposes set for it. The treatment, or helping, process takes place largely in and through the group, and it is the worker's skill in guiding this process toward desired goals that enables that person to serve the clients.

Not all contact with or assistance to clients is pursued within the confines of the treatment group, however. Practitioners confront their clients outside group sessions and engage in many other activities on behalf of group members. Modification of the problematic social situations in which clients are involved must also be undertaken if the full potential of this strategy is to be realized. The worker must intervene in these situations, directly or otherwise, in order to ameliorate others' (e.g. teachers or parents) interactions with clients, to improve opportunities for clients, or to remove barriers and constraints. The treatment group itself may be helped to change these external patterns that adversely affect its members.

ACTION-ORIENTED INTERVENTION

Our concepts of deviance emphasize patterns of behavior that tend to endure over time, to be sustained by social and personal forces, and to persist unless these forces are changed. The helping practitioner must, therefore, energetically intervene to modify clients' behaviors and situations. Only by direct, active involvement in the relevant processes can practitioners accomplish desired change. Activity must be planned and focused, with optimal involvement of clients. Efforts must be directed toward obtaining information, making assessments, formulating specific objectives, planning the tactics of intervention, and preparing evaluations. Performance of these tasks is instrumental to service but does not in itself accomplish change. The investment of time and development of skill in such activities must therefore be measured against the interventive effort and its outcomes.

These general statements present a rationalistic strategy of service in which group methods and other intervention activities are undertaken in a planned sequence of treatment. Effectiveness is to be assessed in terms of net changes achieved among clients, according to conventional social standards rather than esoteric professional criteria. A treatment strategy must employ known procedures, directed at specified objectives, and must attain objectives at a sufficiently high level to be validated independently outside the helping process. To construct a systematic discipline around such a strategy, codified, decision and action procedures that rest upon a communicable body of knowledge must be encompassed by that strategy. Although these are stringent requirements and numerous difficulties in their realization will be encountered, this volume is an attempt to set forth the essentials of such a discipline (Vinter, 1967).

Serious questions about the effectiveness of procedures, the limits of knowledge, and the uncertainty of accomplishments must be acknowledged. These matters can be neither obscured nor ignored. However, group work as social treatment has several advantages. One, it permits a deliberate, open-ended utilization of empirically validated knowledge about individual and group behavior. For example, knowledge from small group theory and research can be readily assimilated and applied within this framework. Two, it encourages deliberateness in practitioner activity and discrimination in the choice of alternative courses of action. Three, it is receptive to an objective assessment of outcomes and the use of this information in modifying and improving procedures. And four, it provides a basis for systematic teaching and the development of practitioner competence.

This problem-oriented, group work approach lends itself to use in all sectors of the health and welfare fields. Adjustments and modifications are, of course, necessary in keeping with variations in client populations and the program goals of particular agencies. At certain times group work may be the primary method of service, while at others it may supplement various treatment methods. The main limiting condition in the application of this mode of practice has to do with the appropriateness of *any* individual level method for change, rather than with procedures. Many beneficiaries of social welfare programs are confronted with adverse conditions, which must be addressed in the aggregate at community and societal levels. This is especially true when systematic constraints on opportunity or deficiencies in the resources and conditions of life exist. Group work, or any other approach centered on individuals and their behavior, should not be chosen to resolve these broad problems. Nevertheless, even under such adverse conditions particular individuals may need, and benefit from, group work service (Vinter, 1959).

REFERENCES

GLASSER, PAUL H.
   1963 "Group methods in child welfare: Review and preview," *Child Welfare*, 42(June): 312–20.
ROSE, SHELDON D.
   1967 "A behavioral approach to group treatment of children." In Edwin J. Thomas (ed.), *The Socio-Behavioral Approach and Applications to Social Work*. New York: Council on Social Work Education, pp. 39–58.
SARRI, ROSEMARY C., AND ROBERT D. VINTER
   1965 "Group treatment strategies in juvenile correctional programs," *Crime and Delinquency*, 11(October): 326–40.

SCHAFER, WALTER E.

1967   "Deviance in the public school: An interactional view." In Edwin J. Thomas (ed.), *Behavioral Science for Social Workers*. New York: The Free Press, pp. 51–58.

VINTER, ROBERT D.

1959   "Group work: Perspectives and prospects." In *Social Work with Groups*, New York: National Association of Social Workers, pp. 128–48.

1965   "Social group work." In Harry L. Lurie (ed.), *Encyclopedia of Social Work*. New York: National Association of Social Workers, pp. 715–24.

1967   "Problems and processes in developing social work practice principles." In Edwin J. Thomas (ed.), *Behavioral Science for Social Workers*. New York: The Free Press, pp. 425–32.

2

The Essential Components
of Social Group Work Practice

Robert D. Vinter

INTRODUCTION

This chapter presents the essential elements of social group work practice and aims to develop the understanding necessary to help individuals through small, face-to-face groups.[1] As staff members of social agencies, group workers must engage in many activities: They must participate in staff meetings, make referrals, prepare reports, and interpret their functions to the public. But these endeavors, however important, are not immediately necessary to serve people in groups, and the skill and knowledge they require are not distinctive to group workers. The core competencies of group work practice—the methods and techniques directly involved in serving clients in groups—are addressed here.

Concern for brevity requires that there be no discussion of variations in practice that occur within different agencies or in work with different types of clientele. Similarly, in focusing on the essentials of group work, comparisons with other professional treatment approaches that involve group methods are ignored.

THE TREATMENT SEQUENCE

Group work service begins when the practitioner first meets the client, continues through the diagnostic and treatment stages, and ends with evaluation and termination of contact. This entire process is referred to as the *treatment sequence*. The sequence comprises several distinct processes and

---

[1]This chapter outlines the fundamental modes of intervention for the problem-oriented approach reflected in this volume. It was the first piece written about the Michigan approach and provided a seminal framework and foundation for much of the work that followed. For this reason, while it has been edited by the author, the decision was made to retain the basic formulation in its original form.

actions; it includes each client's experiences, the group's development as affected by the worker, and the worker's decisions and overt activities. Since the treatment sequence proceeds through time, the identification of significant events, by locating them along this continuum, will be helpful. For this purpose, the several main stages of the treatment sequence can be defined, along with the events and the practitioners' decisions and activities typical of each stage. The recurrent nature of events and activities, more or less distinctive to each period, permits the identification of the segments of the treatment sequence. However, this presentation should not mislead anyone into supposing that the events and activities are invariant or that one stage is always neatly completed before the next begins.

These stages can be identified only by looking for similarities in a wide variety of actual treatment sequences and by noting the patterns that emerge. Analysis permits a useful but somewhat arbitrary codification of the treatment sequence. The practitioner deliberately intervenes in an extended social process, which would develop in quite different directions (or not at all) if approached differently. Helping people requires that practitioners *do* something; therefore, attention will be given to what it is that workers do as they intervene.

The first stage, the process by which a potential client achieves client status, is customarily termed *intake.* For the client it often involves some kind of self-presentation including the problem or "need," as the client experiences it. On the worker's part, this typically involves some assessment of the client and his or her problem—a preliminary diagnosis—and of the adequacy of resources available to resolve this problem. The intake stage ends in one of two ways: either the worker or the client decides not to proceed, for whatever reasons; or the client commits himself or herself to client status (however tentatively or reluctantly) and the worker makes a personal and agency commitment to provide service (however limited).

The second stage, identified as *diagnosis* and *treatment planning* (see Chapter 8), marks a more comprehensive and exacting assessment by the worker of the client's problem(s), his or her capacities for help and change, and of the various resources that might be useful. This stage involves a preliminary statement of the treatment goal, that is, of the desired changes that can result if the intervention effort is successful. The diagnosis also involves a preliminary plan of the ways the helping process will be undertaken and the direction in which it will be guided. This stage often requires the collection of additional information about the client and his or her situation and the use of consultation or other resources provided by the agency. At the culmination of the treatment planning stage, a concrete statement should be prepared by the worker to crystallize the assessment of the client and to make explicit the objectives the worker will pursue and the ways to implement these objectives.

The third stage is *group composition* and *formation*. During this period the worker assigns clients to groups, gathering the persons who the worker believes can be served together. Under some circumstances—as in work with delinquent street groups—the practitioner may exercise relatively little control over this stage. The worker also sets the purposes for the group, at least within broad limits, in accordance with the treatment groups established for its individual members. He or she begins the establishment of relationships with the group members and helps the group to commence its program. The way the worker initiates the group's process and the roles he or she plays initially with the various members have considerable significance for subsequent phases.

The fourth stage is that of *group development* and *treatment*. The worker seeks the emergence of group goals, activities, and relationships that can render this group effective for the treatment of its members (see Chapter 5). The worker guides the group's interaction and structures its experience to achieve the specific treatment goals established for each of its members. The particular nature and degree of group cohesion, client self-determination, and governing procedures, as well as the type of program, are defined by the individual treatment goals, not by any uniform standards workers have about "successful" or "well-organized" groups. The worker's main concern is that each group become the most potent possible to attain the ends he or she seeks for its members. The worker should not regard the treatment groups as ends in themselves, apart from their contribution to the client members. Since practitioners do not hold the same goals for all groups and because of differences among the members who compose them, no two groups ever appear to have the same experiences or advance along the same developmental path.

The final stage is *evaluation and termination* (Chapter 15). The treatment sequence may last for short or long periods, depending on a variety of circumstances. Obviously, services to clients in groups may be terminated when it is apparent that treatment goals have been substantially achieved. Group services may also be terminated when it appears that maximum benefits for the member clients have been attained or when any anticipated additional gains are insufficient to merit continuation. Groups may also terminate because clients drop out, because pressing commitments arise elsewhere in the agency, or for a variety of other reasons. In any event, the decision to terminate should be made with a view toward the achievement of treatment goals. This decision necessitates a review of the progress made by each of the client members and an estimation of whether continuation of this group would be worthwhile. The worker is compelled, therefore, to return to his or her original diagnostic statements and treatment goals, to evaluate the progress made in terms of them.

The presence of several clients requires a more complex termination decision than with a single case since, as expected, group members will show different degress of achievement. A single termination decision often is not appropriate for all members of the group. Accordingly, the worker may reconstitute the group, keeping those who have not yet shown satisfactory progress (but who may be expected to do so), terminating those for whom maximum benefits have been achieved, and adding new members. Persons also may be transferred to different groups or to other services.

It must be kept in mind that the five stages represent general patterns, not ideal periods that ought to be accomplished neatly. Reality often makes it difficult to determine the end of one stage and the beginning of another. Events and activities identified in a specific period also are likely to be evident in others. The worker does not follow a timetable and must engage in activities that are responsive to the group's process and advance the treatment goals. Activities that may occur during any stage include the continuing search for diagnostic information to enhance understanding of clients, inclusion of a new group member long after the others have been admitted, and evaluation of change at earlier points in the treatment sequence.

Two crucial distinctions must be made in referring to the treatment sequence. As initially stated, this sequence is inclusive of *all* events that occur during the group work process. The first distinction is between the worker's decisions or mental activities, on the one hand, and the worker's overt behavior or social interactions with clients, on the other. Thus, in the foregoing review reference was made to decisions like diagnosis, evaluation of progress, etc.; workers also talk with clients, participate in group programs, and do many other visible things. Practitioners not only participate in significant interactions with clients but also engage in important activities that are not visible to or even in the presence of clients. This leads to the second distinction between the reality of the group's structure and process and the worker's interpretation of and response to its reality.

Although the focus throughout this analysis is on the practitioner, his or her thinking and actions, the individuals' subjective experiences, the unfolding of the group process, and the emergence of group structure must each be seen as independent reality. These events are affected by the presence and activity of the worker, but they should not be regarded entirely, or merely, as consequences of practitioner effort. There are other influences on individual and group behavior, only some of which can be known and affected by the worker. Furthermore, the practitioner can neither observe nor assess objectively all the events that occur, even within the group. It is the worker's dual aim to comprehend sensitively and accurately the group's experience and the experiences of its individual members, and to guide these experiences in accordance with treatment goals. But these distinctions can serve as reminders of the complexities of group process and of the constraints on practitioners' perceptions and actions.

TREATMENT GOALS AND GROUP PURPOSES

As stated, specific treatment goals must be established for each member of the client group (see Chapter 9) since individuals never enter the treatment sequence with identical problems and capabilities. Clients are often discussed in terms of certain broad categories (e.g. delinquents), but this tends to obscure the very great differences characterizing individuals within each category. *Treatment goals* are those specific ends the practitioner pursues in the interests of particular clients within particular groups. This emphasis on the unique and idiosyncratic is referred to as *individualization* in social work literature.

A treatment goal is a specification of the state or condition in which the worker would like *this* client to be at the end of a successful treatment sequence. The concept of social dysfunction is sometimes used to denote all the problematic states of social work clientele. Treatment goals, then, embody more desirable states of social functioning. Several considerations must be introduced at this point. *First*, treatment goals must realistically reflect probable outcomes of group work service. It is impractical to think of ideal but unattainable states of well-being. For example, how to "cure" mental deficiency or brain damage through group work is not known. When working with clients having such problems, therefore, the worker should not suggest their resolution in treatment goals. Group work may, however, seek to ameliorate undesirable secondary effects or to achieve optimum functioning within the limits set by these conditions. Given the present development of the helping professions, workers are obligated to think in terms of limited goals. *Second*, treatment goals must relate directly to the presenting problems expressed by individual clients. While diagnosis is discussed in a later chapter (see Chapter 8), it is necessary to assert here that a treatment goal must anticipate improvement in the client's social functioning as defined by individual assessment and diagnosis. The distinct advantages to defining treatment goals in specific, concrete behavioral terms are that the goals can be more readily derived from clearly stated diagnoses, and movement toward them can be assessed more definitely. *Third*, the treatment goal must be linked to diagnosis in still another way; it should seek reduction of the stress or difficulty *as experienced by the client*. Treatment goals also must bear a relationship to the capacities of the clients, and to their readiness or motivation to change; in this sense, they include prognoses about the likelihood that clients can and will change.

If two clients manifest identical problems yet differ in their personality attributes, attitudes, or social circumstances, these differences would have important consequences for treatment outcomes; some would facilitate treatment (e.g. a high level of discomfort); others would hinder this process (e.g. peer support of problematic behavior). Since treatment goals must be realistic, they should reflect such relevant differences.

Fourth, the treatment goal should refer to improved client functioning outside the treatment group itself. Problematic behavior or conditions exist prior to service and pervade major spheres of the clients' lives. Service therefore should improve these *other* spheres of life. This is referred to as the requirement of *transferability*: gains achieved by clients within the treatment process must be transferable beyond this process. Further, the degree and quality of improvement should be assessed according to conventional standards of the world inhabited by the client. Professional criteria should not subordinate community standards of conduct, achievement, and role performance.

Groups are typically composed of from four to twelve clients and, if unique treatment goals are established for each client, a complex and multiple set of aims must be formulated for every group. The practitioner must seek a composite of treatment goals that can be served simultaneously through a given group's process. Defining and harmonizing goals that serve several clients through the same group's process is obviously no simple task. There are at least two ways that practitioners handle this problem. The worker often has significant leverage in control over the group's initial composition. The worker can attempt to compose a group so that the particular treatment goals are compatible and can be balanced. Although group composition involves more than the compatibility of treatment goals, this is one criterion for selecting persons for a given group. The practitioner, also, defines the *purposes* for the group; i.e., the particular collective ends it will pursue. Since the worker often has considerable control over the concrete purposes the group exists for and the activities it will engage in, he or she can attempt to define group purposes that are consistent with and instrumental to the several treatment goals established for the individual members.

Some aims, goals, and purposes pertain to all groups. The agency and the practitioner have certain ends in mind for each group; in most general terms, they seek to develop groups with strong enough influences to change or move clients toward improved social functioning as defined by specific treatment goals. For the worker, then, the group is intended to serve as the best possible means for achieving the composite of treatment goals. For each particular group, the worker must translate these objectives into more concrete purposes, which in turn lead to variations among group programs, plans, experiences, and processes.

Individual client members also have desired aims or objectives even if they are to "have a good time," to accomplish some task, or to achieve something which lies outside the group itself (e.g. prestige in the eyes of nonmembers). Some of these objectives are crystallized in members' think-

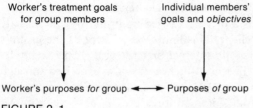

FIGURE 2–1.

ing and aspirations, while some are only latent. In addition, each group tends to develop its own concrete purposes, which can be thought of as a composite of the members' expectations and motives to be fulfilled by the group. Customarily, these purposes are shared and stated, in various ways, and tend to shift over time.

Thus, four different types of ends can be distinguished analytically: (1) the worker's treatment goals for the group members, (2) the worker's functional purposes for the group, (3) the individual members' goals and objectives for themselves through the group, and (4) the shared purposes of the group. These various ends interpenetrate and are interrelated, as we have indicated. Figure 2–1 shows typical relations between such aims and expectations.

The degree of compatibility between these ends always differs among groups and varies through time for the same group. For example, the worker's purposes for a group may differ greatly from the initial expectations and preferences of its individual members. Unless the worker can change these orientations, the worker may have to make his or her purposes more congruent with client preferences, in order to achieve greater member involvement and motivation. Practitioners are confronted with increasing difficulties as the degree of compatibility among these ends decreases. The plausible solution of "let's do what the members want" is seldom effective.

THE STRATEGY OF INTERVENTION

In addition to the assertions that significant help can be given individuals through experience in groups, and that groups provide both the context and means for treatment, the treatment group can be thought of as a deliberately structured influence system to effect change through social interaction. The kinds of changes sought, as defined by treatment goals, range from acquiring new relationship skills, to changes in self-images and attitudes toward others, to behavioral modifications or integration into conventional social structures. Some tendency exists to regard worker–member interactions not only as having special import but as being the essential means by which individuals are helped. This view regards the group merely as the context for treatment, as a process carried on primarily and directly between the worker and each client. This limits the concept of the group's potential. Although practitioners do interact directly with clients to implement specific treatment goals, potent influences are also exercised through interactions between members, through the group's activities or program, and through its structure. The skilled practitioner uses all of these to implement his or her treatment objectives. Frequently the group implements treatment by directly influencing the individual.

The worker must possess a strategy of intervention to make use of these potential resources. Not only must the worker know where he or she wants to go (treatment outcomes) but also the worker must formulate approaches and techniques, taking maximum advantage of every legitimate way to achieve those ends. Besides concern for the group's composition, the worker is concerned also with the group's purposes and major activities. Getting groups "off to a good start," assuming that a well-initiated group can move along successfully with occasional assistance, is not enough. The worker must be concerned with every point in the group's movement and must participate actively to guide it in desired directions. Similarly, the practitioner is concerned with the group's organization and the governing procedures it develops, as well as the quality of interpersonal relations among all the members.

All of these concerns and the way they are made instrumental are the practitioner's *strategy of intervention*. The formal requirements of this strategy are that the worker act (or not act) to "treat" at any given moment throughout the treatment sequence, and to facilitate the long-term development of the group's structure and process to different treatment effects for the client members. As a corollary, the group can be evaluated at any given moment in terms of its immediate treatment effects *and* its long-run potential for mediating treatment outcomes.

Practitioners may employ several modes of intervention or *means of influence* to serve these dual objectives.[2] The worker should direct each action at immediate "treating," setting the conditions for treatment via the group, or both. These are viewed as essentially compatible and mutually instrumental, and the approaches are categorized by whether the practitioner is directly or indirectly influencing an individual member. *Direct means of influence* are interventions to effect change through immediate interaction with a group member. *Indirect means of influence* are interventions that modify group conditions, which subsequently affect one or more members. In the former, worker and client join in face-to-face contact (in or apart

[2]Appreciation is expressed to Edwin J. Thomas for his contributions to the initial formulation of these conceptions.

from the presence of other clients). In the latter, the group mediates the relationship between the worker and the member(s) affected by the intervention. The distinction between direct and indirect provides an analytical reference for the variety of practitioner interventions and emphasizes the immediate context and effects of interaction, that is, whether or not a specific client member is directly interacting with the worker, who is being influenced, when and how. While these means of influence refer to actions engaged in by practitioners, they cannot achieve immediate, full treatment outcomes; instead, they are steps toward outcomes, however minute.

Examples are offered to clarify the distinction between the direct and indirect means. When the worker praises a group member while talking with him or her, perhaps thereby raising his or her self-esteem, the worker directly influences the client (i.e., using direct means). Similarly, when the worker suggests a new solution to a client's dilemma, conducts a marginal interview with him or her or visits him or her at home, the worker is directly interacting with the client. The effects from any of these actions may not have great consequence, but that is beside the point. The distinction between direct and indirect means of influence does not refer to how potent the worker's actions are or how subtle his or her approach is or even how active he or she is. Such variations must be characterized in other terms.

In contrast, indirect means are employed to influence the group so that it in turn influences the members. The worker may modify group governing procedures to encourage more voice in affairs for all participants; this may result in greater satisfaction and acceptance for one or two dissident members. Or the worker may introduce new program activities which gratify most members, perhaps raising the status of one who can succeed now but could not in former activities. All members may be influenced by such worker interventions, some more than others.

A third major means of influence is employed by practitioners when they attempt to affect clients apart from both the group and personal contact. *Extragroup means of influence* include activities conducted on behalf of clients outside the group (see Chapters 16 and 17). Targets of these interventions are nongroup persons whose behaviors affect clients and nongroup situations involving clients (classroom, family). Workers may seek to increase opportunities for their clients in these other situations, to alter attitudes and behaviors of other persons toward their clients, and to restructure elements of clients' social experiences. Parents, employers, teachers, friends, cottage parents (in residential programs), and other agency staff members may be individuals with whom practitioners interact on behalf of their clients. Whereas, through the indirect means of influence, the treatment group mediates the relation between worker and client, through the extragroup means these *other* persons and situations mediate the relation. Both working through the group and working through "significant others" could be considered indirect approaches, but the distinction between indirect and extragroup is preferred.

These terms largely constitute a codification of what group workers seem to do frequently in actual practice. One advantage of this analysis is to order and categorize what otherwise seems to be a confusing welter of worker activities; however, these categories do not encompass all activities employed by practitioners in groups. Only the direct and indirect means are discussed fully here; additional kinds of actions can be employed to exercise influence.

DIRECT MEANS OF INFLUENCE

The four types of direct means of influence presented all involve direct confrontation and contact between worker and client, in or outside the group session. The specific methods, the areas of client behavior affected, and the techniques employed are stated in each case.

Worker as Central Person:
Object of Identifications and Drives

In most circumstances the worker is preeminent in the treatment group, both with respect to position in the structure and in terms of psychological effect on the members. The several sources of this preeminence typically combine and reinforce each other: the worker's activity in initiating the group and beginning its process; the authority vested in the worker by agency and community, which he or she can exercise by controlling resources and facilities available to the group and which enhance the worker's prestige; and the personal resources (competencies, skills, and personality attributes) possessed by the worker. The worker's preeminence is particularly marked in newly formed groups; as the worker may be the only person who knows all the others, he or she is "mobilized" at the outset and free to participate actively without being cautiously passive, and, typically, the worker has personal qualities that are valued by the members. These characteristics, coupled with the clients' knowledge that the worker possesses considerable control over the destiny of the group, render the worker highly significant.

For these reasons the worker serves as a "central person," a focal point for group emotions (Redl, 1955; French and Raven, 1959). Emotional responses of members to the worker constitute ties to him or her; the worker becomes the object of member identifications and drives. The worker serves as the object of identifications when the members want or try to be like him or her. The worker serves as the object of drives when the members are emotionally invested in him or her. Because of the worker's position and attributes, the potentiality of these psychological relationships with client members might be enhanced for two reasons. First, such worker–client relationships provide the basis for continuing service to individuals, for whom the worker has special psychological meaning. The relationships thus formed are crucial conditions for subsequent interpersonal influence, but the difference between actual relationships and those desired or intended by practitioners must be distinguished. Second, such relationships also serve to strengthen member-to-member ties; clients may identify with each other as they experience the similarity of their relationships with the worker. The unity of the group can thus emerge, as common psychological responses among members lead to shared and reciprocated responses between members.

This means of influence focuses on the psychological relationships that are established between the worker and the members. Psychological responses of the members may be manifested in overt behavior (e.g. evidences of liking, affection, compliance with worker requests, or modeling of the worker's behavior), or they may remain at the covert level (changed attitudes toward oneself or others, a shift in values, or resolution of some internal conflict). Covert responses are less readily apparent but may be as significant or real as more obvious behavioral changes.

The specific techniques or actions used by practitioners to exercise this influence are especially difficult to identify. Some of the members' psychological responses are associated with the social or structural position of the worker. Structural sources that might contribute to the technique are the worker's status in the agency and his or her mobilization (initiative and freedom of action); however, these represent *potentialities* for influencing members through exercise of power and through active partcipation in group interaction, respectively. They remain potentialities unless deliberately exercised by the worker; that is, the worker may serve as an insufficient "central person" by abdicating his or her position vis-à-vis the group or by remaining a passive participant in its processes. As indicated above, the worker's personality attributes, competencies, and skills also generate emotional responses from client members. Such attributes may be either instrumental or socioemotional: an instrumental one is useful in achieving some objective or completing some task (e.g. tutoring or teaching a skill), a socioemotional attribute is one for psychological gratification (e.g. friendly responses to another). Who the worker is as a person, and how he or she interacts with clients, however minutely or subtly, has consequences for the worker's becoming an object of identification and drives. A wide range of worker attributes and behavior becomes highly relevant in these terms: cordial and interested responses to others, suggestion of good ideas, capacity for responding to nuances of client feeling and interest, ability to do things clients enjoy, and even personal appearance.

Since groups differ in many respects and clients possess different personalities, obviously specific worker characteristics and behavior will have different psychological consequences for different people. A worker's prowess in swimming will be of little salience in a street gang, and his or her "cool" will not be prized among aged clients. Similarly, a worker's tendency toward repressiveness will have quite different psychological meanings among clients in the same group. The principle of "conscious use of self" directs practitioners to be sensitive to these differences between groups and individuals and to vary appropriately their presentations of themselves and their specific behaviors. As the worker becomes more skilled, he or she can achieve these variations to become the kind of "central person" who will advance treatment for a particular group and client. In general, positive identifications are likely to be increased when workers are friendly, manifest warm and cordial relations, and show sensitivity to the needs and interests of individual members. The issue of negative identification is important but will not be developed here.

Worker as Symbol and Spokesperson: Agent of Legitimate Norms and Values

Many clients served through social group work manifest difficulties with the values and behavioral norms they have internalized. Indeed, for some clients these difficulties may be the essence of their social functioning problems. Client diagnoses may indicate no psychological malfunctioning but an internalization of socially unacceptable values, perhaps through membership in deviant or antilegal groups. Inducing change in these areas is generally termed resocialization. One function of group work service can be socialization, or the acquisition of values and behavioral standards defined by the larger society. Thus children, immigrants from other societies, or persons moving into new sociocultural situations and strata typically need help to acquire conventional orientations and behaviors. Avoiding the extremes of abject conformity and destructive rebellion, the individual must develop a viable interdependence with others by acquiring the basic values essential to community life, and minimal adherence to the norms of conduct required for effective social functioning.

Without imposing his or her own personal value system and standards or those of any particular stratum on clients, the worker must inculcate the essential values of the larger society. The worker is obligated not only by the agency but by the community and by the profession to represent both society and the long-run interests of the client. And the worker must mediate the clients and certain values and norms created informally within the treatment group itself. Thus values and standards are derived from the larger society environing the group (community, agency, etc.) and are developed within the group. Some are specified as laws, rules, or role prescriptions; others appear less tangibly as orientations, patterns of conduct, and generalized attitudes. The worker's task is to determine which of these are crucial, as treatment goals, to individual clients and to the group. Crucial values and norms are then emphasized in practice.

Values and norms may be transferred by the worker in several ways. They may be *personified* by the worker as they pervade his or her total behavior and outlook. What the worker does and does not do, the events to which he or she responds, and his or her views and attitudes toward persons and issues all convey to clients basic values and norms. Thus, as the worker continuously responds to client interests and feelings, he or she "cues" group members to the value of individual dignity and worth and to positive interpersonal norms without having to state explicitly that he or she accepts them. Through member–worker identification and modeling, commitments are inculcated or strengthened among members and become the bases for desirable behavior.

The worker may also be a *spokesperson* for values and norms; that is, he or she must frequently give utterance to both. Even when a large degree of permissiveness is necessary in worker–client relations, the worker must still set limits and voice expectations. What is important is that practitioners act and speak to exemplify a particular set of values and norms that can become operative for clients, rather than interacting in ways that offer few, ambiguous guides (although a "do what the worker wants" attitude should be avoided).

Values and norms within the group may also be informally *created* by workers, especially when the group is newly formed. The creation of such norms and values, whether explicit or implicit, may be facilitated by the worker as personifier or spokesperson. Worker hesitation or inactivity in the creation of group standards can handicap group development and curtail movement toward treatment goals.

As indicated previously, the behavior of the worker itself serves as a model for clients, and the worker may define or strengthen norms by setting limits on the behavior of members by requesting, requiring, or forbidding certain behaviors. The worker may state precepts and rules of conduct. Or the worker may apply various positive and negative sanctions against members, that is, encourage, reward, or chastise group members for their behavior. Rewards and deprivations may be material or social (e.g. praise). Finally, the worker sometimes must use his or her power of coercion and physically prevent a client from engaging in certain behavior (e.g. assaulting another person) or must eject the client from the group. Generally, positive techniques are more effective than negative techniques, and inducements or rewards more helpful than deprivations. The worker must state precepts to define clearly his or her expectations for clients, but by itself this has little utility for enduring change.

Although some workers may be hesitant to act in the area of values and norms, in actual practice they often seem to devote considerable energy to this area. The critical problems are determining which values and norms are crucial and what the effective ways are to implement them. Since the group customarily develops its own values and normative system, which the members then participate in enforcing, the worker has a potent resource at hand. The worker can help the group develop a system of norms and values in accord with treatment goals. Since the primary concern here is with direct means of influence, worker–client interactions should modify an individual client's norms and values in accordance with the specific treatment goals for him or her.

Worker as Motivator and Stimulator: Definer of Individual Goals and Tasks

Throughout the treatment sequence many opportunities occur for practitioners to motivate and stimulate individual members toward specific ends or activities. These opportunities may take the form of encouragement for certain objectives or expectations for individuals, such as undertaking a specific project or acquiring certain skills; or they may enable the stimulation of a member to engage in different behaviors or to act differently in familiar activities or to direct the worker toward new interests. The worker perceives such opportunities within the developing experience of the group and its larger activities, with reference to the immediate social and material environment of the individual and group or with reference to the larger community and society.

For example, a creative adult may see potentialities in the pebbles and sand of a beach or in the repair of an old car; the alert practitioner may see many more significant possibilities in the urban community than the adolescent does. Making the most of such opportunities—whether immediately discerned by the client or beyond his or her horizon—requires that the worker be aware of the potentialities inherent in the social and physical context. Maximizing such opportunities requires that the worker be guided by specific treatment goals.

This means is primarily directed toward individual interests, aims, activities, and skills. Essential is the worker's use of his or her relationship and interaction with members to orient them toward experiences that they might not otherwise engage in and that will facilitate treatment. Regardless of age or problem, clients tend to restrict themselves to conventional and familiar activities, to have limited perspectives, and to be less aware of the full potentialities offered by their social and physical environment. Stimulating clients to use material objects in more creative and satisfying ways is perhaps the most obvious manifestation of this means of influence. But one may also think of motivating clients toward opportunities for the development and different use of their capabilities in social situations (e.g. getting a different job, discovering unknown talents and abilities).

Control over resources permits the worker to use them as "props" or objects to stimulate clients. Introducing or sharing new and unfamiliar materials or using familiar ones in novel ways are customary approaches. Thus a worker can show clients new games that can be played with old objects (e.g. cards, dice, boxes), or the worker may call the client's attention to things and events he or she overlooks in everyday life (e.g. interesting insects or items in the newspaper). Incentives, inducements, and rewards can be employed by the worker to motivate clients. Encouraging, suggesting, proposing, and expressing enthusiasm or excitement are effective interaction techniques. The worker's own interests and responses to objects and situations convey meanings to clients for whom the worker's behavior is especially salient, and the worker may direct or instruct clients in these terms.

Worker as Executive:
Controller of Member's Roles

In addition to the discrete and relatively concrete tasks and purposes discussed above, the practitioner is also concerned about clients' more general orientations and roles. These may be thought of as configurations or sets of specific behaviors. Each group develops its own structure of roles, responsibilities, and positions (see Chapter 5). Within the group each member may be characterized as having distinct positions in these structures, which may be deliberately modified by the worker with regard to his or her treatment aims. For example, tasks or projects undertaken by the entire group require some division of responsibilities among the members (see Chapter 13, "Program Activities: An Analysis of Their Effects on Participant Behavior," and Chapter 14 by Whittaker). Assignment of these responsibilities may refer to the larger task objective, the abilities of members, and the needs of the individual members. The worker must be concerned not only with what is good for the group but also with what is desired for individual clients in terms of the treatment goals.

When the worker develops or modifies those group structures (as when he or she proposes a set of positions or division of labor), he or she is using indirect means of influence. However, when the worker directly interacts to modify an individual's particular role or position within these structures, the worker is using direct means of influence. To continue with the example of task assignments suggested above: When a client is given a specific responsibility, the worker can help the client directly in discharging his or her part of the total task. Such intervention by the worker may have several effects, all different from the effects of allowing the client to "go it alone." Undertaking the task in the way proposed by the worker exposes the client to expectations and experiences he or she might not have had otherwise. The standards and values implicit in this event may have carryover effects for the client in subsequent situations; and the response of the group to the client's performance may be quite other than if the client had not been helped by the worker (e.g. praise for accomplishment rather than criticism). The worker may make the individual assignments, determining the pattern of member tasks as well as helping clients undertake them. The worker may interact directly with clients to affect more general behavior than the mere performance of a specific task. Thus, a worker may assist an individual who holds a particular position in the group's formal structure to perform more effectively or differently in this position. Whether in terms of these positions or of more general roles, the worker can seek to modify the member's behavior with reference to the treatment goals.

As viewed so far, the worker's effort in assigning or modifying membership roles has focused on the behavior and experience of an individual client. Through direct interaction the worker attempts to develop or change a client's personal attributes, thus modifying the client's role performance. The worker may attempt to increase a member's sensitivity to group norms so that the client becomes a less deviant member, perhaps by clarifying the relevant norms for the client or by informing him or her more precisely of other members' expectations as they apply to the client. Or the worker may attempt to change the client member's role behavior by raising the client's self-esteem, giving him or her support, or setting limits on the client's behavior.

The worker can serve as an "executive" by defining new or modified roles for members and by helping the clients to perform differently in their present roles. The emphasis is on interaction with individual clients, in terms of their role behavior, not on the entire role system of the group, which will be discussed later. In the previously discussed means of influence emphasis was on concrete interests and goals. This means of influence can be differentiated by the focus on general patterns of behavior (roles) rather than on specific interests and objectives, and by focus on patterns of client behavior that have particular relevance to other members and to the entire group. All of the techniques previously referred to may also be employed with this means.

These four direct means of influence tend to overlap, particularly with respect to the specific practitioner activities or techniques that may be employed. Distinctions between them mainly have to do with the worker's aims and the consequences for individuals that follow. The range of client experience and behavior that group workers can seek to modify includes attitudes, values, gratifications, tasks, identifications, roles, and so forth. A wide variety of worker–client interactions can be utilized to implement desired change. The similarity of techniques (e.g. praising, encouraging, or setting limits) should not, however, obscure the marked differences in effects for clients when the worker directs activities toward different ends, under varying conditions.

INDIRECT MEANS OF INFLUENCE

Indirect means of influence are those practitioner interventions used to effect modifications in group conditions, which in turn affect the members. The worker acts on and through the group, its processes, and its program. Some of these approaches closely parallel the direct means of influence, and, conversely, certain direct means might implicate changes in the group.

Group Purposes

Groups that persist over extended periods develop distinctive aims. And for all groups that they serve, social workers have purposes in mind that they make more or less explicit to the client members and that have significance for the nature and development of each group and for the experiences of the members. The kind of purposes held by a group and the extent to which they are achieved are important determinants of member motivation to belong to the group and of the satisfactions gained through participation in it. Similarly, the purposes set for the group by the worker are determinant of his or her own actions and these, in turn, vitally affect the group and its members. Diverse group goals and purposes characterize those served by social group workers: planning groups; groups focused on resolution of members' personal problems; activity groups; groups to orient or prepare members for some event (e.g. new clients entering an institution or patients about to be released); diagnostic groups; socioeducation groups for professionals, paraprofessionals, other socialization agents, and adults in role transition; and so on.

The relations between a worker's treatment goals, his or her purposes for the group, member objectives, and purposes of the group have been discussed above. Here consideration is given only to the worker's purposes *for* the group and the purposes *of* the group. Practitioners have considerable control over definition of purposes and goals, although there are wide variations in actual practice. In some instances the worker and agency may set the purposes of the group in advance and select group members with avowed reference to these. Adherence to these purposes may then be a condition for continued participation in the group. At the other extreme the group may have much autonomy in determining its own purposes (but this does not imply that the worker lacks treatment goals). In still other situations, after very broad purposes are set for the group it determines its own specific plans within these limits. Regardless of the source of initial purpose determination, the worker has many opportunities during the treatment sequence to modify group purposes and to alter members' objectives. Thus, even when serving a delinquent street gang, which sets its own purposes, the worker can gradually influence the group toward different aims.

Two specific influences on clients that can be indirectly mediated through group purposes and aims have already been mentioned: Selection of clients for the group can be made explicitly with reference to its established purposes, and a client's attraction to and satisfaction with the group is partially dependent on its purposes (Cartwright and Zander, 1960). The purposes of the group also determine the distribution of leadership functions and member roles within it, thereby significantly affecting the experience of each client member. Similarly, group purposes shape the program and the activities developed in pursuit of these aims. And finally, group purposes will have some implication for the particular kind of decision-making and governing procedures to be employed. In these terms a group of adoptive parents contrasts with a play group of young children. The former may be directed toward consideration of common problems that couples face in adopting children, while the latter is directed toward pleasurable learning experiences, "having fun" in the youngsters' terms. Each will involve quite different activities, group processes, and member roles and will lead to markedly different effects for their members.

Finally, a word about the relation between purposes of the group and worker's purposes for the group. Group purposes have been defined as the composite of members' objectives and motives encompassed in some definite expression of collective purpose. Worker's purposes for the group, written in a specific statement, are the aims a group ought to pursue to achieve treatment goals set for the individual clients. Obviously the worker seeks compatibility between his or her aims and the clients' aims, so that the worker is not oriented in one direction while the group is heading in another. Although both sets of aims tend to change over time and there cannot be perfect identity between them, the worker customarily seeks acceptance of his or her purposes as those of the group. Thus in an institutional context a worker may attempt to gain members' acceptance of the worker's treatment goals and to orient them accordingly. Or with a street gang the worker may gradually seek acceptance of his prolegal purposes in working with the group. In a very real sense, therefore, client objectives and group purposes are targets, not determinants of worker interventions. However, the distinction between worker purposes and group aims should be kept in mind so that the *intentions* of the practitioner are never confused with the *reality* of member interests and motivations.

Selection of Group Members

Selection of group members and size of group (discussed next) are aspects of group composition. As a basic step in group composition, selection of members is one of the most problematic aspects of group practice. Practitioners cannot always select those who join a particular group; sometimes agency circumstances affect group composition, as when a treatment group consists of all the youngsters in the same orthopedic ward or all the inmates about to be released from an institution. Or the group's membership may be set by a decision to serve an existing or "natural group": friends living in the same housing project or all the members of a street gang. By and large the greater an agency's general control over the clients, the more probable will be its determination of group membership (e.g. residential settings as contrasted with other community services).

Before considering the various criteria useful in determining membership, some of the consequences of this indirect means of influence will be examined. The experiences of the members, the interpersonal relations, and even the particular nature of the activities will differ depending on who and how many others there are in a particular group. Thus the capacity of the group to meet the desires and objectives of its members, as well as the goals of the worker, is partially dependent on its composition.

The worker's goals and purposes for the group provide a general guide for group composition: The reason the group is established and served and what it is expected to accomplish serve as determinants of membership selection. For example, if a group were designed to serve children who manifest serious school conduct problems, it would require the identification of such pupils and their inclusion in the group. Obviously a group would have different characteristics if its purpose were to serve parents experiencing difficulties in childrearing or home management practices. The statement that purposes for the group should govern selection of its members may seem to be a truism, but in actual practice this is often ignored, usually because the agency and worker's purposes are too general or too unclear to serve as guides. However, group goals and purposes only point to a category of potential clients and do not indicate specifically which persons within the general category should be selected. Referring to the illustrations cited above, which school children or which parents should be selected for treatment group memberships? To state it differently, what particular attributes or characteristics should the clients possess in addition to their belonging to a general category?

More concrete specification of the type of treatment group and its purposes can point toward particular persons within the general categories of potential clients. Regarding the group to serve pupils manifesting conduct problems, the worker might make two other decisions in advance: (1) that the group will include children manifesting classroom conduct problems and will exclude those who exhibit only academic difficulties; and (2) that the group program will include behavioral retraining as well as discussion of members' problems. These two decisions would provide some concrete direction for the worker in selecting clients from among all the pupils belonging to the general category as described.

The conception of the group as the *means* of treatment suggests another set of criteria. Practitioners would seek groups that have maximum impact or change effects for their client members. To accomplish this, treatment groups must be potentially capable of developing appropriate levels of cohesiveness, solidarity, and mutuality; viable internal structures; and so forth. These requirements in turn direct the selection of members with a view to their similarity of interests, their potentiality of attraction for each other, their adequacy to participate in the general type of activity and group structure planned by the worker, and their capacity to form certain relationships with each other and with the worker. Knowing that the treatment sequence is more likely to be effective if these conditions are met within the group, the worker can attempt to select particular individuals who possess the attributes *with reference to each other* that promise to meet these conditions. Similarity or complementarity is desired with respect to the more important characteristics, however dissimilar the clients may be in other respects (see Chapter 11).

Great incompatibilities in age, interest, problems, interaction style, maturation level, and so forth make it very difficult for group members to form cohesive groups. Reference here is to *compatibility* or complementarity, not identity. Persons may form effective treatment groups because of the compatibility of their attributes even though they vary in terms of the similarity of attributes. For example, in certain circumstances age and sex differences among group members may be essentially compatible. Thus, adolescent boys and girls might be placed in the same group on an orthopedic ward but not be selected for membership in certain sports activity groups.

A number of guidelines can be summarized. First, the types of primary client attributes for which compatibility and complementarity are desired depend on the nature of the group and its program. Second, complementarity is sought with reference to other members of the same group and not with reference to any absolute standards of personality attributes. Third, clients need not be identical with respect to their characteristics but should be potentially compatible. Practitioners find that it is impossible to attain homogeneity with respect to many attributes and must attempt to "match" individuals in terms of primary criteria while expecting considerable difference with respect to secondary criteria.

Size of Group

The size of a group tends to affect members. The worker must determine the appropriate group size for the desired effects for clients as defined by their treatment goals. First, some of the effects associated with differences in size will be examined. *Large* groups (ten or more) tend toward anonymity of membership, less consensus among the members, lower rates of participation, and higher demands for leadership abilities. Larger groups are able to undertake certain tasks beyond the capacities of smaller groups or to engage in certain types of program (e.g. tasks requiring a complex division of effort). Any of these effects may be desired for individual clients under specific circumstances. More mature and more capable clients are better able to cope with the participation requirements of large groups. Older adolescents and adults are probably more able to participate in larger decision-making units than are younger children.

Small groups, in contrast, tend toward high rates of member participation, greater individual involvement, greater consensus, and increased restraint upon members. Relations among persons in smaller groups tend to be more intensive. Effects such as these are often desired by practitioners for treatment groups. It is also easier for workers to cope with serious problems or acting-out behavior in small groups when clients present these patterns.

In some agencies clients may participate concurrently in several different groups; this is especially true for most residential programs—camps, institutions, hospitals, and so on. Under these conditions it is often desirable to vary the kinds of groups in which clients participate so that they can experience the different effects associated with size, type of program, and so forth. Practitioners must guard against a bias toward small groups so that they are not always established, even when clients might benefit from the anonymity or reduced intensivity provided by larger groups. Although workers are not always able to set the initial size of the group, as members drop out or others are added, there are opportunities to influence the size of the continuing group. Workers may find it desirable to vary the size of the treatment group during the treatment sequence.

Small groups effects may be achieved *within* larger groups in many ways. In all larger groups individuals tend to form smaller subgroups, thereby achieving informally many of the effects of small group participation. Practitioners may deliberately design such opportunities and influence the formation and structure of these subgroupings. Ways of doing this include facilitating interpersonal ties among clusters of members, introducing program activities that provide for smaller participation units, or developing a structure of subgroups (e.g. committees) for task and governing purposes.

Group Operating and Governing Procedures

Group workers have been strongly oriented toward democratic leadership and governing procedures because of their high valuation of client self-determination. Permissiveness in guiding the group, and helpfulness and friendliness in contacts with members, have probably characterized most group workers in actual practice. The very strength of this orientation becomes its weakness, however, as permissiveness by the practitioner and high autonomy for the group are widely sought regardless of differences in treatment goals and group member characteristics. Treatment goals and other specific group characteristics warrant deliberate variations in the degree of autonomy granted each group, in its procedures and formal organization, and in worker control practices. Each of these will be discussed briefly.

The degree of autonomy should vary with the type of group and its purpose, the treatment goals of the worker, and the members' characteristics. With younger, less capable, or more disturbed clients the worker may greatly limit the autonomy of the group, at least initially. The location and situation in which the group exists also affect its autonomy—delinquent groups in their own neighborhoods usually retain high autonomy, while institutional groups composed of clients with similar problems often have limited autonomy. High control by the worker tends to induce dependence upon him, reduces the members' assertiveness, and limits the satisfactions they may achieve within the group. The practitioner may vary the *areas* within which groups have autonomy, as well as the degree of self-determination. Thus a group may be granted high autonomy in its program of activities but little choice in its size and composition.

Democratic relations, generally sought within treatment groups, are associated not only with the quality of worker–member interactions and relationships but also with the nature of procedures that are used in governing the group. Governing procedures evolved spontaneously within client groups often reflect and enforce inequalities of power, prestige, and gratification. They can also introduce constraints due to members' unquestioned adherence to tradition or sentiment. In contrast, democratic procedures tend to be more rational, permit more flexible change as circumstances dictate, and provide certain guarantees of channels for individual participation. Unfortunately workers sometimes equate democratic decision-making practices with parliamentary procedures and often introduce an array of "businesslike" patterns. Parliamentary procedures are essentially formalistic and can easily be subverted, and the same positive effects may be achieved by simple norms as "everyone gets a chance to talk," "the majority rules," and "taking turns." The important concern is to increase group-centered decision-making and wide distribution of member gratifications. Group-centered (as contrasted with worker-centered, or clique-controlled) decision-making results in greater member participation, greater consensus, and greater pressures toward uniformity, thus maximizing the impact of the group. The formal organization of a group affects its operating and governing procedures. Along with a predisposition toward parliamentary procedures, practitioners are sometimes inclined to introduce formal systems of officerships within groups. The intent is often to provide members with definite roles within groups and to ensure democratic self-determination. Both aims may be achieved by less arbitrary approaches, however, and a system of officerships often achieves neither. The degree and type of formal structure appropriate for groups vary, and the worker must sensitively create (or circumscribe) patterns within particular groups according to the worker's treatment goals and client characteristics.

Much that has been stated with respect to group autonomy and governing procedures applies directly to worker control practices. In general, group workers attempt to be friendly, responsive, and permissive to the appropriate degree. They can exercise controls and make crucial decisions without being authoritarian or undemocratic. Particularly with newly formed groups and with less capable clientele, workers must be very active in setting group directions, guiding processes, and exercising controls. The degree and method of worker control should vary among different types of groups and over time within the same group.

Group Development

Group workers typically serve groups that exist for extended periods of time. They are concerned with the entire periods as much as with particular sessions. Their intent is to help the group develop through time as an effective treatment or service vehicle, with cumulative impact on its participants. Groups that maintain themselves through time, whether or not they are served by practitioners, develop definite structures, and deal with similar problems. They pass through roughly comparable stages and may develop roughly comparable patterns of organization. The worker's task is to influence the course of a group's development so that it permits maximum attainment of the treatment goals set for clients. Therefore, the worker must act continuously to *effect treatment at any given moment* and to *facilitate the long-run development of a cohesive and viable group.* This dual task requires attention to the immediate events and their treatment potential, and also knowledge of the stages of group development and of the strategic foci for worker intervention. The stages of group development and the implications for practitioner activity as well as additional means of influence will be suggested in subsequent chapters.

REFERENCES

CARTWRIGHT, DORWIN P., AND ALVIN F. ZANDER

    1960   "Individual motives and groups goals." In Dorwin P. Cartwright and Alvin F. Zander (eds.), *Group Dynamics: Research and Theory*. Second edition. Evanston, Ill.: Row, Peterson, pp. 345–69.

FRENCH, JOHN R., III, AND BERTRAM H. RAVEN

    1959   "The bases of social power." In Dorwin P. Cartwright, (ed.), *Studies in Social Power*. Ann Arbor, Mich.: Institute for Social Research, pp. 150–67.

REDL, FRITZ

    1955   "Group emotion and leadership." In Paul Hare, Ed Borgotta, and Robert Bales (eds.), *Small Groups: Studies in Social Interaction*. New York: Knopf, pp. 71–86.

3

Social Group Work: The Preventive and Rehabilitative Approach

Charles D. Garvin and Paul H. Glasser

GROUPS CONDUCTED BY social workers for rehabilitative purposes are located in such varied settings as public schools, mental health clinics, correctional institutions, hospitals, child welfare agencies, settlement houses, community centers, and public assistance agencies. Such groups, like all social work groups, are "a mode of serving individuals within and through small face-to-face groups in order to effect desired changes among the client participants" (Vinter, 1965, p. 715). A rehabilitative approach seeks to make changes that will alleviate specific handicaps to the functioning of individuals in their social roles. Recently the group approach has been used to prevent deviant behavior among groups of children or adults who are known to be highly likely to demonstrate social malperformance.

Although groups were used as early as 1928 (Burrow, 1928), their use for rehabilitative purposes received impetus after World War II, along with similar developments in psychiatry and clinical psychology, through rapid development of programs for the treatment of psychiatrically disabled veterans. In recent years many articles and monographs have been devoted to the practice of group work in rehabilitative settings such as group work with psychiatric patients, the aged, public welfare clients, and delinquents. Work with clients in residential treatment, in the health field, in child welfare, and in the public schools have been described.

The preventive use of groups has been described since the inception of the method in community centers and settlement houses. In these settings group services were seen as helping people cope with developmental tasks and other social stresses so as to avoid deviant adaptations. In recent years specific at-risk populations have been targeted for preventive group services such as single parents, unemployed workers, and children of alcoholics.

An earlier version of this article appeared in the *Encylopedia of Social Work* (New York: NASW, 1971).

PERSONNEL

The highest proportion of group workers were once located in agencies classified as "group services," primarily settlement houses and community centers. Such agencies have usually been thought of as offering socialization services. The use of this category may be deceptive, however, because a number of community-based agencies offer specialized services such as groups for children referred from public schools for help with classroom management problems, for adults with employment difficulties, or for aged persons coping with retirement stresses. While those agencies continue to offer these services, however, they now employ very few social workers with graduate training in direct service positions (Garvin, 1984).

Throughout the 1950s and 1960s writers expressed concern with both the proportion of social workers receiving special training for the practice of group work and the proportion of such group workers being employed to serve the high-risk population who suffer from severe emotional, intellectual, physical, and environmental impairments (Vinter, 1959). Between 1950 and 1960 the number of group workers employed in rehabilitation settings increased slightly. For example, during that decade trained group workers with MSW degrees increased in psychiatric hospitals from less than .5 percent to 2 percent of social service personnel, in public assistance agencies from 2 percent to 3 percent, and in medical agencies from less than .5 percent to 1 percent. The greatest increase took place in child welfare agencies: In 1950 the proportion was 1 percent and in 1960 it was 4 percent in noninstitutional facilities, 10 percent in institutional facilities, and 5 percent in court services (National Social Welfare Assembly, 1961; American Association of Social Workers, 1952).

It is difficult to ascertain what the pattern of group services has been since 1960. During the 1960s a number of developments took place that obliterated many of the distinctions among practitioners who offered services to individuals, families, and groups. Many agencies hired workers who were expected to work with all three entities as the client's situation required. The majority of schools of social work followed suit and created courses in which content on work with individuals, families, and groups was combined in some way. Direct practitioners were referred to as clinical social workers or simply as social workers rather than caseworkers or group workers.

While some schools of social work offer either full method specializations in group work or distinct group work courses, it is impossible to tell the scope of this from the published statistics. In 1982, for example, 53.4 percent of MSW students were specializing in "micro" practice and an additional 20.1 percent in "generic" practice. Of those who had a field of practice concentration, only .8 percent declared this as group services. A slightly larger proportion (1.5 percent) were placed in group service agencies for field work (Council on Social Work Education, 1983).

MAJOR PRACTICE ASSUMPTIONS

The application of group work methods to rehabilitation and prevention has been accompanied by many developments in practice principles and practice theory. Among the principles on which there has been considerable agreement are the following:

1. *The individual as the focus of change.* This principle stresses the notion that the worker tries to attain specified group conditions only as they help achieve relevant goals for *individuals*. Thus to achieve certain individual goals, a highly organized group with an extensive division of labor and other structures is sought. For other goals a loosely organized short-term group is chosen. Autonomy from the worker is an issue in some groups more than in others. Democratic processes of decision-making, while always important, also may be emphasized in some groups more than others.

Concern with individual goals does not mean that the goals are to be achieved only through changes in the behavior of the individual group member. The group worker may decide, on appropriate consultation with group members, to change conditions within the group, agency, or community, and he or she may do this with the group members or on their behalf. In any case, the decision to engage in such efforts is always made with reference to individual goals.

2. *Specificity of goals.* Another proposition of this approach to group work is that client rehabilitation goals are more likely to be attained when expressed in precise, operational terms. Goals consist of "a specification of the state or condition in which we would like this client to be at the end of a successful treatment sequence" (see Chapter 2). Any area of human behavior may be chosen for the establishment of goals, and those goals may relate to the individual's cognitive, affective, attitudinal, or instrumental behavioral repertoires. Goals are formulated by client and worker together, a process that frequently occupies the greater part of a first session with the client individually and/or in the group. The worker may also develop explicit goals for a client, as long as these are communicated as clearly as possible to the client and his maximum involvement is obtained.

There may be one or more goals, depending on the circumstances. As Vinter has stated in "An Approach to Group Work Practice" (Chapter 1):

> Behavioral difficulties may be few and appear in only one of the individual's several social roles, as with some malperformers in the public school; or they may be diffuse and pervade broad areas of social life and careers, as with habitual delinquents, psychotics, and others.

There may be intermediate as well as terminal goals because individual goal accomplishment and worker planning may be enhanced by specific increments prior to termination. Thus a hospitalized mental patient's ability to dress properly, ask questions clearly, and perform other self-care tasks are intermediate goals related to a terminal goal of being able to meet the expectations of a halfway house. Goals are also relevant to people in prevention-oriented groups. These goals relate to either enhancing the social competencies of members or alleviating stressful social conditions or both.

3. *Contract*. The existence of an individual focus and the specificity of goals lead to the concept of a worker–member contract—a set of agreements between the worker and group members regarding the problems to be dealt with as well as the means to be utilized in this process. In some group work frameworks, particularly that of Vinter, the contract specifically covers the goals to be attained by the members as a result of the group experience. In other models the emphasis is more on mutual responsibilities for the development of the group process. The group work contract, in contrast to the legal contract, is not a fixed document; rather, it is a process with many subtle components. Modifications in the understanding between members and workers may occur from session to session and even during a given interaction.

The emphasis on contract has both an ethical and a practical rationale. From an ethical point of view the idea has roots in group work's commitment to the self-determination of the client—that is, the client is not manipulated toward ends he does not seek by means he does not accept. Furthermore, empirical evidence indicates that having a contract increases the likelihood that the goal sought will be reached and that the individual will remain for service (Garvin, 1969).

4. *Group as a means for change*. A distinguishing characteristic of group work as an intervention method directed at individual change, as compared to other group treatment methods, is that the group is used as a means as well as a context for the achievement of goals. Consciously and explicitly, the worker uses peer group pressures, modeling between and among clients, group rules and norms, and the like to obtain and maintain individual change. He or she tries in every way to put the group and its members to work for each other. This conceptualization is highly compatible with a hallowed notion in social group work: that the group should evolve as a mutual aid system in which the mission of the worker is to help the members help each other to attain their goals.

The worker usually must set instrumental goals concerning such matters as group cohesion, decision-making procedures, or group structures and processes that set the stage for and facilitate the accomplishment of terminal goals. Instrumental goals are never seen as ends in themselves; they vary from group to group and are partially dependent on them. It is through the use of such instrumental group goals that the group becomes a viable means for individual change.

5. *Intervention in the social environment.* Goals achieved in and through the group must be maintained in the clients' social environment— their daily living experience. Further, before a decision is made to embark on an intervention method, it must be determined for each client that worker and/or client intervention in the environment alone would be insufficient; and that casework or group work with their emphases on client change would or could be beneficial. Sometimes intervention in the client's life situation must precede small-group interactions. Most often the two approaches must proceed together, because changes in one aspect of the client's life is maintained and reinforced in the other until the client is functioning in a socially acceptable and personally comfortable manner.

6. *Empirical basis of practice.* The stress in this approach to group work on specific operational goals is also related to the contention that practice principles are to be derived scientifically. The existence of such goals makes possible the generation of a series of propositions about the effects of practitioner actions on client and client group outcomes. Particularly pertinent are findings from research in clinical and experimental psychology, sociology, and social psychology, which can be tested for applicability to group work situations.

SOCIAL SCIENCE BASES
OF GROUP WORK PRACTICE

Significant portions of social science theory and research and group work practice share the view that problematic behavior is generated and maintained through interactions between the client and individuals and/or institutions. Vinter has termed this "an interactional view of deviance." All social science efforts that explain either the individual and institutional effects on problematic behaviors or the small-group processes that can modify the individual's response to such phenomena are important to the group worker. Group workers must know about systems other than the small group, because they and their clients' activities are interrelated with those of other systems. The following are some of the principal areas of social science investigation pertinent to group work practice.

1. *Role theory.* Role theory seeks to explain how behavior is elicited and maintained in categories of individuals by the responses of other individuals. A detailed exposition of role theory is contained in a volume by Bruce Biddle and Edwin Thomas (1966). Social reactions to such positions

as "delinquent," "unwed mother," and "hospital patient" are diagnostically important to the group worker, who is also cognizant of such positions in the small group as "task leader," "social emotional leader," and "scapegoat" and their effects on group members who occupy such positions.

2. *Social systems theory.* Social systems theory deals with how systems are created as well as the processes by which they develop and establish linkages with their environments. In the course of their development systems evolve structures to deal with such functions as goal determination, energy inputs, communications, and system maintenance. Because the group is really a small social system, the group worker can utilize this type of knowledge to achieve instrumental group goals by encouraging the development of structures that assist members in attaining individual goals. This knowledge is also useful when the worker, alone or with members, wishes to change his or her own or other community agencies or institutions to maximize benefits to clients. Systems theory applications to group work are discussed by Balgopal and Vassil (1983).

3. *Social-behavioral theory.* Learning theories are now making a strong impact on group work. These theories seek to explain behavior in terms of the conditions that elicit behavior and the consequences that the behavior evokes. Such stimuli and responses may make it more or less likely that behavior will recur. Applications of this approach can be found in Rose (1979). In applying this knowledge, group workers help members behave differently in problematic situations by the manipulation of reinforcements in the group sessions. Group members may be taught how to help each other in a similar manner within and outside the group.

4. *Cognitive theories.* Many conceptualizations of group work have emphasized the vital significance for achieving group work goals through group problem-solving and conflict resolution. Theories dealing with these processes, especially as they occur in small groups, have been advanced by Helen Northen (1969) and Ruth Middleman (1983), among others, and are particularly useful to workers. Since there are important issues regarding the connection between intrapersonal and interpersonal problem-solving and conflict processes, the worker must understand both. The individual's coping mechanisms as he or she is confronted with the need to relate himself or herself to group conflict and problem-solving are also of interest here. Theories of ego psychology, as well as theories specifically dealing with the etiology of social deviance and mental illness, are important in this context.

5. *The social psychology of influence.* Of use to group workers is information about the effects of small-group processes on individual behavior. The attention of behavioral scientists has been called to such phenomena occurring in groups as pressures toward conformity, responses to deviation from group norms, group control mechanisms, socialization processes

in groups, and contagion effects in groups. An understanding of these phenomena is essential to the attainment of instrumental group goals.

GROUP WORK PRACTICE COMPONENTS

Practice approaches in group work deal with (1) the sequential arrangement of the tasks confronting the worker and (2) the appropriate levels of social organization on which the worker seeks to have an effect in order to accomplish these tasks.

The Treatment Sequence

As the client moves from applicant for service to recipient of service, then to group member status and on to the point at which group service is terminated, the worker must take the client's status into consideration. At any phase of this cycle, however, they are concerned with (1) assessing the client's (or applicant's) situation with reference to problems, causal conditions of problems, and goals; (2) planning their own activities in relation to this assessment; (3) executing the plan; and (4) evaluating the outcome and, when necessary, revising the plan based on this evaluation. How the worker engages in these procedures depends on the stage reached in the client's career and the stage reached in the development of the group.

Intake

At the time of intake the worker's assessment will include information on the nature of the applicant's problem, the circumstances in which the problem occurs, and what responses in the environment are evoked by the applicant's means of coping with the problem. This material should be gathered from the client and relevant others, and the objectivity of each source should be evaluated. The worker should observe the client's interactions with the social systems within the organization itself, as well as in the community.

The worker is interested in obtaining reliable and valid information and helping the client develop trust in the agency and the benign attributes of the worker. (Depending on the agency, the intake worker may or may not be the same as the treatment worker.) Workers evaluate the effectiveness of their actions on the basis of how much and what kind of information is produced and on how willing the applicants are to identify with client status and engage themselves with the agency.

During this period the worker must also leave open the question of whether the client will receive individual, group, or family treatment or no service at all from that particular agency. The client should be offered group services only when they are desirable, not just because they are available. To evaluate whether clients can best benefit from group work, the worker must see if they seem ready to engage in group problem-solving, if they are able to accept from or offer to peers information or emotional support, and if they can accept a relationship with a worker in a group rather than in a one-to-one situation. Troubled adolescents, by virtue of their reliance on peers, often make good use of group work, as do psychotics who seek opportunities to relate to others under protected circumstances and parents who wish to find out how other adults are handling behavior problems of children in order to improve their own skills.

Group Composition

Following the intake process, if a decision has been arrived at for group work services, the composition of the group must be determined. Workers obtain information that helps them predict how individuals will behave in the group that they are projecting. Most useful is information on how an individual behaved in a previous group. Even when workers formulate a sound set of compositional principles, they may not be able to act on them if they are working with a group they did not form, such as an adolescent gang or an institutional ward group, or if there are not enough referrals to the group to permit full choice. Workers act, however, with the following two questions in mind: (1) What type of group composition is most likely to enhance the attainment of individual goals and the establishment of a group purpose consistent with those goals? (2) Given a specific group composition, what types of group purposes can evolve, consistent with what individual goals?

Several writers have indicated aspects of group composition relevant to these questions. Arnold Goldstein, Kenneth Heller, and Leo Sechrest (1966) present information regarding the effects of degree of heterogeneity as well as sources of compatibility. Albert and Bernice Lott (1965) have reviewed many different sources of interpersonal attraction in groups. Harvey Bertcher and Frank Maple (Chapter 11 in this volume) have developed a framework for considering both behavioral and descriptive attributes in selecting group members. Helen Northen (1969) comments on considerations of stages of psychosocial development of members, coping mechanisms used by members, and group size in determining membership. She also discusses circumstances for working with such natural entities as those found in residential settings. Baruch Levine (1968) investigated the relationship of social similarity to attraction and indicated implications for group work practice.

Group Development and
the Attainment of Individual Goals

Once the group is formed, the worker assesses the individuals, the group, and environmental situations and, consistent with individual members' wishes, acts to change these situations and then evaluates their consequences.

In describing the workers' treatment interventions, it is helpful for conceptual purposes to discuss separately their actions with respect to different systems. Allen Pincus and Anne Minahan (1970) clarify the existence of four systems: (1) change agency system—"The system concept of the worker is utilized to emphasize that the change agent normally is not a detached professional worker, but is influenced in his or her change efforts by the system of which he or she is part"; (2) client system—who "contracts" with the social worker and is the expected beneficiary of the worker's services; (3) target system—"the person, family, organization, or community (or some subpart or combinations of systems) at which social workers direct their change efforts"; (4) action system—"the system the social worker works with and through in order to influence the target."

MEANS OF INFLUENCE

In the rehabilitation and prevention approach to group work the client system is virtually always the individual who is experiencing or is likely to experience the problem in functioning. (An exception is a group made up of married couples.) In some circumstances the worker may act as if the target, action, and client systems were this individual. Vinter has referred to such interventions as using "direct means of influence." On other occasions the action system is the group, although the target and client systems remain the individual. For Vinter this means using "indirect means of influence." Finally, the worker's action system may be individuals other than group members, his or her own agency, or other institutions in the community. The target system then can be either the individual client or the group. Vinter and Galinsky (Chapter 16) describe such instances as utilizing "extra-group means of influence."

Direct Means of Influence

Vinter details four fundamental types of direct means of influence (see Chapter 2):

1. *The worker as central person: object of identification and drives.* Worker actions appropriate to this category are encouragement, relating to feelings, model presentation, and verbal reward.

2. *The worker as symbol and spokesman: agent of legitimate norms and values.* Some direct actions are clarifying goals of treatment, describing rules and policies, warning, and confronting with long-range consequences of present behavior.
3. *The worker as motivator-stimulator: definer of individual goals and tasks.* Appropriate worker actions include exhorting, interpreting the psychological causes of behavior, exposing client to other organizations, and behavioral assignments.
4. *The worker as executive: controller of membership roles.* Worker interventions in this category are giving responsibility and providing new sociorecreational experiences, subgroupings, and prompting.

Indirect Means of Influence

It is the indirect means of influence—those means used with the group as the action system—that uniquely characterize group work. When workers modify group conditions to help members achieve their goals, they are using indirect means of influence. Group conditions are the group's composition and size, purposes, structures, and processes. Seldom does the composition of a group remain constant. Members drop out, and the worker may add members or encourage members to withdraw when this is appropriate for the attainment of individual goals. Group purposes are more clearly identified as member–member and member–worker interactions that occur around the relationships of group goals to individual goals. After the group has come into existence, however, the worker is in a better position to assess the effects of structures and processes on the achievement of goals.

The use of group structures. Patterns develop and maintain themselves over time in interpersonal situations. In group work these regularities can support or hinder the client and worker in attaining their goals. The worker must learn how to develop, maintain, and modify these patterns, usually termed structures, to attain the instrumental and treatment goals of the group. Among the important structures are the communication, sociometric, power, role, and normative structures. The following are some means by which workers modify group structures.

1. *Program.* A task that requires a specified series of steps for its completion—a program—can be used to establish or change group structures. For example, a game that requires one participant to be a leader can change the power structure of the group. An activity that rewards a participant for communication with others can change the communication structure.

2. *Behavioral modification.* Operant conditioning procedures can be used to modify group structures. Leadership behavior, communication behavior, and task performances, for example, have been modified by these procedures.

3. *Problem-solving, conflict resolution, and logical reasoning approaches.* A group can and often does confront its own structural problems and change such patterns and rules. It may begin with a series of individual behavioral or attitudinal changes, or the group may purposely use programmatic, conditioning, or other interactive methods to change its manner of functioning.

4. *Changes in composition.* Structural changes can also be affected by the addition or subtraction of group members or through a change in the size of the group.

5. *Group development.* When groups exist over time, patterned changes occur in the social organization of the group, the processes of the group, and the group culture. The group worker, by knowing how the group is proceeding with reference to these changes, can enhance the attainment of treatment goals. They can frequently help the members to determine, for example, how far the group must develop for members' objectives to be attained. They can also anticipate changes that are likely to occur in the group and help the members deal with them in a therapeutic manner.

The use of group processes. Group processes—the sequence of behaviors of individuals in interaction with other individuals in groups—may occur within a few minutes as clients and workers arrive at a quick decision, a subgroup identifies itself, or a behavioral norm is enunciated and clarified. A sequence may also occur over several treatment sessions or the life history of the group as purposes are clarified, membership is determined, or complex problems are solved. Changes in structures can be identified as processes, although many group processes have been described (see Chapter 12).

Propositions can be generated about causes of particular processes and specific social events can be described only if clear categories of analysis are used. The concepts presented here are based on a series of dimensions detailed by Rosemary Sarri and Maeda Galinsky in Chapter 5 on group development.

1. *Processes related to changes in the social organization of the client-worker system: Sociometric processes*—those having to do with changes in the affectional choices of some participants for others; *processes of role differentiation*—those that occur as either new positions are created or new participants occupy such positions; *communication processes*—those having to do with changes in the patterns of who communicates with whom and about what.

2. *Processes related to activities and tasks: Program task progression*—that sequence of events set in motion in response to performance requirements of the activity; *problem-solving processes*—processes occurring as problems are identified and solutions attempted.

3. *Processes related to the development of group culture*: changes in the structure and content of norms and values held by participants relevant to their behavior in the treatment system and changes in the goals held by clients, individually and collectively, for the treatment system.

The task of the worker, then, is as follows: The worker, with an awareness of appropriate goals, determines with members which processes enhance or hinder the attainment of goals. The worker develops a series of propositions regarding forces that are maintaining or could maintain such processes. Depending on the goals of the client–worker system, the worker with or on behalf of the clients seeks to increase the occurrence of specified processes or to decrease them.

Extra-group means of influence. The use of "extra-group means of influence" refers to "modification of the behavior or attitudes or persons in the client's social environment, or large social systems within which both clients and other individuals occupy statuses, which may in turn lead to positive changes in the group member's own behavior and attitudes" (see Chapter 17). Such acttivities should be integral to all rehabilitative and preventive efforts. Workers, with or without the help of members or the total group, attempt to change specified others in the client's environment (parent, teacher, employer), their own agency's treatment of group members, or other institutions' responses to those whom they serve. Sociological theory has stressed the need for institutional change to diminish the problems of large numbers of people who seek help from social welfare agencies. Behavior modification approaches have emphasized modification of those behaviors of persons in the client's environment which are antecedent to or consequences of the client's own behavior as a means to achieve client change. In preventive work a special concern is for the creation of social networks to provide support to members in coping with stresses. In some cases the group is continued by members after the termination of professional service as a support system.

TERMINATION AND EVALUATION

An individual may leave the group while the group continues, or the entire group may conclude simultaneously. The decision to discontinue may be made by the worker, the client, or the group; attitudes regarding termination of a given group may differ widely.

Ideally, termination occurs because the treatment goals have been achieved (see Chapter 15). The worker's task, then, is to reduce the nonfunctional attachments that the clients may have formed to the worker and other members and that may prevent them from realizing their new potential. The worker may also attempt to strengthen the changes that have occurred. Evidence that the termination decision was correct lies in the higher value the clients place on leaving the group than on staying, as well as data indicating that they can transfer behavior into contexts other than the treatment group.

When the clients' goals have not been achieved, it is the responsibility of the worker to encourage them to seek help from other sources. For example, they may obtain alternative services from the same agency or different services from other community institutions.

At times the entire group is terminated because the group has developed sufficient resources of its own. It is then able to function without the help of a professional, although members may be referred to community institutions, such as community centers, for less intensive service.

It is incumbent upon workers to evaluate the effectiveness and efficiency of their services periodically throughout the treatment as well as at termination. This allows them to modify their goals and treatment plans and to discard ineffective technologies.

SOME EVALUATION STUDIES

A number of studies have been completed on the practice of group work in rehabilitation and prevention using some or all of the methods described above. Feldman and his colleagues (1983) compared the effectiveness of this approach (which they termed the "traditional" method) with a behavioral method and a nondirective method in work with predelinquent boys. One of the limitations of that study is that it distinguishes between the "traditional" and the "behavioral." We see the behavioral as one of a number of technologies that can be employed in relationship to our approach. Nevertheless, that study advances the methodology for evaluating this approach to group work. Sheldon Rose (1979) describes a number of applications of behavioral methodologies that are compatible with this approach and reports that they were highly effective with children with poor social skills, the elderly, couples experiencing communication difficulties, and unassertive adults, to name a few. Task-centered group work, also highly related to this approach, has also been reported as effective with aftercare patients and the elderly (Fortune, forthcoming). Many new techniques are also emerging for the evaluation of practice, and we have described these in detail elsewhere (Garvin, 1981).

It is evident, however, that these studies are merely a beginning of research on the effectiveness of group work in rehabilitation and prevention. Work should be done to replicate existing studies as well as to determine the precise interrelationships between client variables, composition characteristics, and alternate group work methods.

FUTURE DEVELOPMENTS

Large bodies of research and outcomes of related theory development in the social sciences are now available to the group worker. The main task is the engineering of this knowledge into usable practice theory and the evaluation of these new methods and techniques—particularly in the fields of learning theory, small-group theory, social influence theory, and organizational theory. The application of these theories and findings should help the group worker use his or her methods with greater precision and have more assurance about the results.

Within practice theory in group work itself, new concepts are helping workers to be more specific regarding their activities. Thus they can inform other practitioners about techniques and can better engage in evaluative research. Codifying these concepts to facilitate communications among professionals is still a problem, but the situation has begun to improve. Group work practice knowledge should be accumulated more rapidly and efficiently than it has been up to now.

The effectiveness of rehabilitative and preventive group work depends on how well workers can systematically intervene in many social systems. Until now, either vital systems (for example, the community system) have been ignored or workers with different specializations have operated in the same territory without successfully coordinating their efforts. Social work education and recent conceptualizations of practice appear to be developing resources to cope with this problem.

REFERENCES

AMERICAN ASSOCIATION OF SOCIAL WORKERS
  1952 *Social Workers in 1950.* New York: American Association of Social Workers, Table D-24.
BALGOPAL, R. PALASSANA, AND THOMAS V. VASSIL
  1983 *Groups in Social Work.* New York: Macmillan.
BIDDLE, BRUCE, AND EDWIN J. THOMAS
  1966 *Role Theory: Concepts and Research.* New York: John Wiley & Sons.
BURROW, T.
  1928 "The basis of group analysis," *British Journal of Medical Psychology*, 8, no. III (November): 198–206.
COUNCIL ON SOCIAL WORK EDUCATION
  1983 *Statistics on Social Work Education.* New York: Council on Social Work Education.
FELDMAN, RONALD A.; TIMOTHY E. CAPLINGER; AND JOHN S. WODARSKI
  1983 *The St. Louis Conundrum: The Effective Treatment of Antisocial Youths.* Englewood Cliffs, N.J.: Prentice-Hall.

FORTUNE, ANN
Forthcoming *Task Centered Practice with Families, Groups, and Organizations*. New York: Springer.

GARVIN, CHARLES
1969 "Complementarity of role expectations in groups: The member–worker contract." In *Social Work Practice: 1969*. New York: Columbia University Press, pp. 127–45.

1981 *Contemporary Group Work*. Englewood Cliffs, N.J.: Prentice-Hall.

1984 "The changing contexts of social group work practice," *Social Work with Groups*, 7 (Spring), pp. 3–19.

GOLDSTEIN, ARNOLD P.; KENNETH HELLER; AND LEO B. SECHREST
1966 *Psychotherapy and the Psychology of Behavior Change*. New York: John Wiley & Sons.

LEVINE, BARUCH
1968 "Factors related to interpersonal balance in social work treatment groups." Unpublished doctoral dissertation, University of Chicago.

LOTT, ALBERT J., AND BERNICE E. LOTT
1965 "Group cohesiveness as interpersonal attraction: A review of relationships with antecedent and congruent variables," *Psychological Bulletin*, 64, no. 4 (October): 259–309.

MIDDLEMAN, RUTH R.
1983 "Role of perception and cognition in change." In Aaron Rosenblatt and Diana Waldfogel (eds.), *Handbook of Clinical Social Work*. San Francisco: Jossey-Bass, pp. 229–51.

NATIONAL SOCIAL WELFARE ASSEMBLY
1961 *Salaries and Working Conditions of Social Welfare Manpower in 1960*. New York: National Social Welfare Assembly, Table 28.

NORTHEN, HELEN
1969 *Social Work with Groups*. New York: Columbia University Press.

PINCUS, ALLEN AND ANNE MINAHAN
1970 "Toward a model for teaching a basic first-year course in methods of social work practice." In Lillian Ripple (ed.), *Innovations in Teaching Social Work Practice*. New York: Council on Social Work Education, pp. 34–57.

ROSE, SHELDON
1979 *A Casebook in Group Therapy: A Cognitive-Behavior Modification Approach*. Englewood Cliffs, N.J.: Prentice-Hall.

VINTER, ROBERT D.
1959 "Group work: Perspectives and prospects." In *Social Work with Groups*. New York: National Association of Social Workers, pp. 128–48.

1965 "Social group work." In *Encyclopedia of Social Work*. New York: National Association of Social Workers, pp. 715–23.

4

Social Psychology for Group Work Practice

Norma Radin and Sheila Feld

THIS CHAPTER FOCUSES on social psychological theories and concepts essential for practitioners working with small groups of individuals to reduce or prevent problems in social functioning. The topics to be discussed include the definition of a small group, cohesiveness, norm enforcement, attitude change, bases of social influence, and role theory as applicable to small groups. Other relevant social psychological concepts, such as attribution theory, could not be covered because of space limitations, but a detailed discussion by the authors of these theories and findings can be found elsewhere (Feld and Radin, 1982).

DEFINING CHARACTERISTICS OF A SMALL GROUP

Although some collections of individuals are obviously small groups, for example, members of a blue grass band, and others are not, such as strangers riding in an elevator together, it is sometimes unclear whether a particular aggregate of individuals constitutes a group. The issue is significant, for theories of group dynamics apply only to small groups. Thus the minimal characteristics of a collectivity that warrant calling it a group are a basic question for social psychologists (Cartwright and Zander, 1968; Shaw, 1981). In this chapter we will define a small group as an aggregate of individuals that possesses four elements: (1) The individuals engage in face-to-face interaction. (2) There are few enough of them to notice absences. (3) They are interdependent, that is, they need one another to attain their own goals. (4) They perceive themselves as a group. The first two elements define the collection of individuals as "small" in number and the last two identify them as a unit. When all these characteristics are present, we consider the individuals as constituting a small group and expect to observe the dynamics to be described below. In the remainder of the chapter, small groups fo-

50

cused on problem reduction will be referred to as treatment groups and those with the goal of problem prevention as socioeducational groups. (For a fuller description of the latter category see Chapter 7.)

GROUP COHESIVENESS

Group cohesiveness has been variously defined as the degree to which members of a group desire to remain in that group (Cartwright and Zander, 1968), the attractiveness of a group for its members (Frank, 1957), and the resultant of forces pulling individuals to a group (Cartwright and Zander, 1968). In simple terms, group cohesiveness is the total magnetism a group possesses for individual members. Several sources of this magnetism have been delineated (Frank, 1957; Secord and Backman, 1964). These are group members' liking for one another, interaction among group members that meets members' needs (such as for affiliation), group activities that are inherently rewarding, the group's serving as a means to achieve ends that require group action, and membership in the group as a means to achieve status outside of the group. The first of these factors and, to some extent, the second concern affect and are closely related to the expressive or socioemotional function of groups. The last two factors pertain to group membership as a means to some desired goal and refer to instrumental functions of groups. Thus the main determinants of attraction to groups coincide with the two requirements of all systems that their internal and external needs be met (Parsons, Bales, and Shils, 1953).

Cohesiveness in treatment groups has been described as serving the same functions as a positive transference relationship between therapist and patient in dyadic relationships (Grotjahn, 1981; Lieberman, 1975). A sense of belongingness motivates members to stay in the group, and the pain associated with therapeutic exploration is eased by the feeling of attraction to the group. Cohesiveness in both socioeducational and treatment groups also serves as the "psychological glue" that permits members to reveal themselves and still maintain self-esteem (Lieberman, 1975).

Consequences of High Group Cohesiveness

In conditions of high cohesiveness, groups have a powerful impact on individual members. The most important consequence for group workers is that influence attempts from members are more readily accepted because desire to maintain the group's approval is high; thus group norms are very strong. Other significant outcomes are that the group's boundary becomes clearer and less permeable; membership is maintained and attendance is high; and communication among group members is more frequent, more revealing, and more satisfying. Finally, and particularly relevant for treatment groups, the member's sense of security and self-esteem is enhanced. Several of these outcomes will be elaborated upon below.

Conformity to group norms. The power of group norms is rooted in the fact that members of very cohesive groups have the ability to reward and punish one another, for members wish to belong to the group and win the approval of other members (Thibaut and Kelley, 1959). Thus a group gains compliance from deviant members by giving rewards for conforming to the group's norms, for example, supporting members' efforts to change, and giving punishments for nonconformity, such as ridiculing their problems. But groups cannot force more compliance than their cohesiveness will withstand (Festinger, Schachter, and Back, 1968). If the punishment meted out to deviants exceeds their desire to remain in the group, they will leave, if they can. The corollary is, the more cohesive the group, the more power to modify members' behavior.

Because group norms that are antisocial or antileader can be as effectively enforced by members as those that are prosocial or proleader, the outcomes of high cohesiveness are not always desirable from the point of view of the group worker or of the larger system in which the group functions. It has been found that the likelihood that antisocial norms will develop in cohesive groups is linked to the factors undergirding the group's cohesiveness (Sakurai, 1975). When cohesiveness is based on interpersonal attraction, conformity to the opinions of others will occur regardless of whether the opinions appear to have positive or detrimental consequences for the group's welfare. However, when cohesiveness is based on the interdependence of members for attainment of their goals, there will be less conformity to a norm when it is perceived as having a negative impact on the group's functioning (Sakurai, 1975). Thus it appears that if an individual likes other group members and they feel positively toward a specific norm, for example, complaining about junior high school teachers' lack of fairness, the individual will also feel positively toward the norm, irrespective of what it is, in order to avoid dissonance (Festinger, 1957) with the other group members' attitudes. The effect of conformity to the norm on the group's task performance, which may be to learn how to negotiate with teachers for alternate assignments or class activities, is irrelevant; the individual's main desire is to maintain positive interpersonal relations and to avoid dissonance.

In contrast, when cohesiveness is based on interdependence, the members' satisfactions come from the success of the group as a whole. For example, in the therapeutic use of a program that requires task specialization among group members, as in survival in the wilderness for adolescents of different socioeconomic, ethnic, and racial backgrounds, cohesiveness will be dependent upon the individual achievements of each member's contributions to the group goal. In such situations members will attempt to minimize the costs of obtaining the maximal reward, according to exchange theory (Blau, 1964; Thibaut and Kelley, 1959), and cohesiveness is unlikely to have detrimental consequences.

The implication of these conclusions is that practitioners should attempt to augment cohesiveness based primarily on members' liking for one another with cohesiveness based on the instrumental value of group activities to avoid the danger of enforcement of destructive norms. In treatment groups, for example, emphasizing that members' progress toward more competent social functioning requires help from other members in the form of honest feedback about role plays would be one way to enhance interdependence among group members. And cohesiveness based almost exclusively on interdependence needs to be tempered with more interpersonal attraction, perhaps through some planned social activities, lest scapegoating develop toward members who are seen as disruptive to goal attainment by the group.

Group boundary enhancement. A growth in cohesiveness necessarily entails a stronger delineation of group boundaries, a stronger differentiation between group members and nonmembers; and an increase in the gratifications obtainable only from the group (Guttentag, 1970). Thus associations with other groups can be cut off, and the gratifications that can be provided by alternatives to the group are diminished. This can facilitate commitment to a treatment or socioeducational group, including willingness to attend meetings and to bear the psychological and material costs of group membership. However, it can also cause problems for functioning outside the group, such as a rejection of significant family members, and antagonism toward other groups, especially those perceived as competitors. Rigid group boundaries can also lead to resistance or coldness toward new members.

Enhancement of the members' sense of security. Members' self-esteem is enhanced in highly cohesive groups because of the respect received from others. This factor can be particularly important in groups composed of members with low societal prestige, such as the poor or the handicapped. Members' sense of personal importance is also increased in highly cohesive groups, because they know they have the power to influence others, even when they are absent.

Antecedents of High Group Cohesiveness

Because high cohesiveness is so powerful, practitioners often decide that more or less of it is needed in the group they are leading. One strategy for influencing the group's magnetism is to modify one or more of the factors cited above as sources of cohesiveness, e.g. try to increase members' liking of one another by pointing out the similarities in their problems, experiences, or personal characteristics, because similarity of relevant attitudes or beliefs leads to attraction and liking (Newcomb 1953; Terborg, Castore, and DeNinno, 1976). Another approach to altering the cohesiveness of a group is to influence factors that can affect the magnetism of a group, although they are not directly associated with the defining conditions of cohesiveness. Among these factors are the principle used in allocating rewards, the absence of an attractive alternative to the group, the absence of coercion in composing the group, and sharing of decision-making.

The principle used in allocating rewards to group members. There are two main principles leaders can use in allocating rewards: the norm of equity and the norm of equality (Leventhal, 1976a; Leventhal, Michaels, and Sanford, 1972). If the norm of equity or reciprocity is applied, rewards are given in proportion to the usefulness of members' actions. If the norm of equality is used, the leader gives equal rewards to all members regardless of their activities. Each allocation principle has advantages and disadvantages. The norm of equity tends to maximize the group's overall performance and productivity over a long term, for the individuals who contribute the most to the group's goals will be rewarded the most. The bond between the high contributors and leader will also be strengthened. But the norm of equity can lead to dissatisfaction or antagonistic behavior by members who do not make sufficient contributions to the group. Cohesiveness is therefore threatened. The norm of equality results in better interpersonal relationships, particularly if the group is committed to an egalitarian approach. Productivity may suffer, however, for all members receive the same reward regardless of the efforts they put forth to achieve the group's goals.

A compromise between the two approaches that can avoid the greatest disadvantages of each involves reducing the differences in reinforcements that would be allocated if rewards were completely contingent upon utility of the members' actions (thereby reducing interpersonal problems associated with equity), but not giving everyone equal rewards (thereby reducing deleterious effects on group productivity linked to equality) (Leventhal, 1976a, 1976b). This integration of norms may be the approach of choice for group workers, because both treatment and socioeducational groups usually have dual concerns: about the instrumental goals related to members' social functioning outside the group, and also about the socioemotional goals related to interpersonal attraction among members within the group.

The important issue is that social workers need to be aware of the norms used in allocating reinforcements, be they the opportunity to select the next topic to be discussed or praise for self-disclosure. Further, practitioners should also be sensitive to the allocative principles used by group members as they interact with one another, for these behaviors can also affect the cohesiveness of the group.

The absence of an attractive alternative to the group. When few gratifications are available from alternatives to a group (in other terminology, the comparison level for alternatives is low), members find the group more atractive (Guttentag, 1970; Secord and Backman, 1964; Thibaut and Kelley, 1959). They will remain in the group even when the satisfactions are below their comparison level, that is, the level of gratification they feel is due them based on their past experiences (Thibaut and Kelley, 1959). Further, as groups become more cohesive, the gratifications available from alternative relationships decline (Guttentag, 1970). Thus an initial low comparison level for alternatives contributes to cohesiveness, and once cohesiveness starts to develop the comparison level for alternatives will decline below its initial low level. Practitioners usually have only limited ability to affect the comparison level for alternatives as a means to enhance cohesiveness. The worker cannot eliminate other groups that members find more appealing than the group the social worker is leading, for example, a natural group of friends who engage in attractive activities at the time the group meeting is held. The worker can, however, try to schedule group sessions at times when there is no strong competition, for example, not when elementary school children would ordinarily be having recess or when elderly residents of a nursing home would be watching their favorite soap opera.

The absence of coercion in group composition. It has been found that when individuals have their choices taken away from them, they will react by preferring the opposite of the coerced choice; this phenomenon has been labeled reactance (Brehm, 1972). Thus workers would do well to permit potential group members some degree of choice about joining the group. If treatment is required by external agents, the potential members should have some choice about the service to be received, for example, where the group meets, when it meets, or if possible participation in a second form of treatment.

The sharing of decision-making. Groups in which authority and leadership are centered in a single individual tend to be less cohesive than those in which members share in decision-making and leadership acts. This was found in socioeducational groups focused on parent education with low-income mothers (Wittes and Radin, 1971) and in treatment groups of psychiatric patients, some of whom had been diagnosed as psychotic for many years (Lerner and Fairweather, 1963). In spite of some contrary findings, widespread participation in decision-making usually appears to induce more attraction to the group than situations in which decisions are centralized (Zander, 1979). Consequently, if the theoretical orientation of a group worker requires that authority and decision-making be located in a single person, the practitioner must be certain that other factors are present to foster group cohesiveness; otherwise the members may not be in attendance long enough to benefit from the group experience.

NORMS AND NORM ENFORCEMENT

Definition of a Norm

A norm is a behavioral rule that is accepted to some degree by most members of a group (Thibaut and Kelley, 1959). Norms reduce the need for the exercise of personal influence, which can be costly to both the leader, who has a finite amount of influence, and the member, who loses some self-esteem in acceding to someone else's wishes (Hare, 1982). When there is nonadherence to a norm, conformity can be restored by reference to a rule or value rather than to the desires of a single individual. Because norms are perceived by group members as accepted by most others in the system, behavior that violates a norm is treated as deviant and is typically sanctioned to reduce its recurrence. In most cases sanctions do not have to be exerted frequently or vigorously; the anticipation of sanctions is sufficient to induce conformity. Although group members may seldom discuss them, norms are unwritten social contracts that can be invoked when troublesome behavior arises.

Influences on Norm Enforcement

A group's enforcement of a norm is significantly affected by the importance of the behavior to the group; the greater its relevance to the group's existence or attainment of its goal, the stronger the pressure likely to be exerted (Schachter, 1968). In treatment groups, for example, violation of the norm of confidentiality would typically be more central to the group and hence elicit greater disapproval toward the deviant member than violation of norms concerning tardiness or seating patterns.

Groups where members differ on important dimensions, such as gender or social class, are likely to exert strong pressures toward conformity in order to facilitate goal attainment (Thibaut and Kelley, 1959). This occurs because the heterogeneity in members' experiences makes deviations from some of the group's norms likely. The group therefore becomes particularly sensitive to violations of its agreed-upon rules, such as regular attendance at group meetings. It is noteworthy that conformity with norms is not equally demanded of all group members. Heightened conformity is expected of marginally accepted members if they are to remain in the group and become fully accepted (Thibaut and Kelley, 1959). Yet conformity to central norms is also required of leaders or members who represent the group to the external world, presumably because of the important symbolic value of their conformity. Leaders or high-status persons, however, are given greater freedom in deviating from minor group norms so long as their behavior is not detrimental to the group (Wiggins, Dill, and Schwartz, 1968). When leaders' deviant actions hurt the group, however, the sanctions are greater than when a lower-status person engages in the same behavior.

Members are not helpless in the face of group pressure to conform; they can resist (Cartwright and Zander, 1968; Levine, 1980; Thibaut and Kelley, 1959). Among the techniques that can be used to counteract the onslaught are avoiding exposure to the statement of the rule, misinterpreting what was said, avoiding surveillance, conforming minimally, or conforming so strictly that the actions are destructive although they cannot be called deviations. Further, if there are several deviants in the group, they can form a subgroup and attempt to bring about change in the norms in an effort to make them more tolerable. Deviants can also influence the other members' opinions simply by vigorously and consistently behaving in opposition to the group norm (Moscovici, 1976). Such consistent expression of different opinions can disrupt the certainty of the majority, who may then shift their own opinions and the group norm.

One factor responsible for member nonconformity is reactance (discussed previously in relation to group composition), which is a motivational state of arousal that occurs whenever an individual experiences a threat to, or loss of, a freedom or potential for action (Brehm and Mann, 1975). The goal of this motivational state is to restore whatever freedom has been threatened or reduced, and one way to restore a threatened freedom is to exercise it, that is, to engage in a behavior that is forbidden or not engage in behavior that is coerced. The more important that freedom is to the individual, the greater the magnitude of the reactance; the greater the outside pressure to engage in the behavior, the greater is the tendency not to do so. Thus extreme pressures on a deviant group member to conform to a group norm may backfire if reactance is aroused, and the group may find the least desired behaviors are enacted. Many family battles concerning the adolescent's hair style are likely to stem, in part, from the teenager's reactance.

ATTITUDE CHANGE

Although some practitioners would state that their goal is solely to bring about changes in the behavior of group members, most group workers would add to that changing clients' attitudes about themselves and their environment or changing the attitudes of significant other persons in the clients' environment. To avoid confusion in the discussion of attitudes, we shall define our terms. Variations in favorable or unfavorable feelings toward things, people, or behaviors will be referred to as attitudes. Verbs such as "like/dislike and favor/oppose" convey the affective reactions included in the concept of attitude. The term "belief" will refer to cognitive judgments about things, people, or behavior. Beliefs are perceptions that objects, persons, or behaviors have certain qualities or attributes or are linked to other concepts, objects, persons, or behaviors (Fishbein and Ajzen, 1972). The statement "Drug use leads to crime" is a belief; the statement "I do not approve of drug use" is an attitude.

Attitudes and beliefs are not identical with behaviors (Fazio and Zanna, 1978). There can be myriad reasons for not acting on one's feelings or cognitions, e.g. fear or loneliness. However, to the extent that attitudes or beliefs are stable over time and predispose one to behave in favorable or unfavorable ways to a person, they are of interest to social workers.

Means-End Attitude Theories
of Attitude Formation

One major type of attitude theory is based on a means–end analysis: An attitude toward an object is defined as a composite of the perceived instrumentality (or means) of that object to the person's goals (or ends), weighted by his or her evaluation of those goals (McGuire, 1969). These theories are based on a model of rational human behavior. People are assumed to like those things, people, or actions that they believe are means to achieving satisfactions and, conversely, to dislike things, people, or actions that they believe will lead them to dissatisfactions. Unfortunately, attitudes have not always been found to predict behavior. Consequently, other variables, such as the norms of groups to which an individual belongs, have been investigated to determine when attitudes and behavior would be congruent.

For example, it has been proposed that behavior is typically preceded by an intention to behave in a particular way, and that intention itself is the result of attitudes toward the behavior in question and beliefs about the normative expectations of significant others (Ajzen and Fishbein 1970, 1973, 1977, 1980; Fishbein, 1967). Thus there are personal and social influences on behavioral intentions. Attitudes, the personal influence, are determined by two factors: one's own beliefs about what consequences will ensue from a particular behavior and the values one places on these consequences. The normative or social influences on behavioral intentions, in contrast, are a function of beliefs about how significant others expect the person to behave and the person's motivation to comply with these expectations. According to the behavioral intention model, to predict a specific behavior one should seek out the individual's intention to engage in that behavior. This should be a summation of two principal factors: (1) attitudes based on beliefs about the consequences of that behavior multiplied by the value of the consequences to the individual and (2) beliefs about the expectations of all significant others concerning that behavior (labeled subjective norms), multiplied by the motivation to comply with the expectations of those particular others.

Several independent studies relating to family planning supported the behavioral intention model (Kothandapani, 1971; Werner, Middestadt-Carter, and Crawford, 1975), as have studies about intentions to donate blood (Pomazal and Jaccard, 1976) and attendance at discussion sessions about poverty programs (Rosen and Komorita, 1971). The results of these investigations indicate that overt behavior can be predicted from a knowledge of the personal attitudes and normative components relevant to that behavior.

The implications of these findings and means–end attitude theories for practitioners is that at least four factors can be the target of interventions to change group members' behavioral intentions: members' beliefs that specific objects or events will lead to desired outcomes; the value they place upon those outcomes; members' beliefs about the expectations of significant other people in their lives; and their desire to maintain the approval of those significant others. The last two factors are particularly important to practitioners working with groups. The greater the cohesiveness, the stronger the members' motivation to win approval of other group members. And if group norms develop that are supportive of new behaviors, the social component can become a powerful element in altering members' behavioral intentions. Further, attitudes can also be influenced because discussion in cohesive groups is a powerful tool for changing members' beliefs about the consequences of their own behavior (Kaplan and Miller, 1983; Thibaut and Kelley, 1959). Thus any strategy that fosters cohesiveness, desired norms, and group discussion of the outcomes of alternative actions should promote change in behavioral intentions and, ultimately, change in behavior.

Cognitive Consistency Theories of Attitude Change

Cognitive consistency theories all share the key assumption that consistency among various attitudes, beliefs, and behaviors is a satisfactory psychological state and that inconsistency is dissatisfying or arousing. These theories further assume that attempts by individuals to reduce inconsistencies can lead to changes in attitudes, beliefs, and behaviors. One type of cognitive consistency attitude change theory, cognitive dissonance theory (Festinger, 1957; Brehm and Cohen, 1962; Wicklund and Brehm, 1976), will be described, along with its implications for social work intervention.

Cognitive dissonance exists when two cognitions held by an individual are related to one another but are obverse, that is, there is an inconsistent relation between them; they do not fit together or do not follow from one another (Festinger, 1957). The lack of fit may be due to factors such as logical inconsistencies (for example praying by someone who does not believe in God), choosing one alternative when a second is also attractive, or disconfirmed expectancies (a person working very hard to move to New York City and then finding it is unpleasant). Whenever two beliefs, two attitudes, two behaviors, or an attitude or belief and a behavior, are perceived by an individual to be inconsistent, dissonance is experienced as discomfort, and the individual is motivated to change one of the elements so that it is no longer inconsistent with the second. Most research done within the cognitive dissonance framework has concerned inconsistencies between cognitions about one's own behaviors and relevant attitudes or beliefs. In such situations the behaviors cannot be undone, therefore, the element more likely to change is the attitude or belief.

Modifications of the original theory have specified conditions that must exist for the discomfort of dissonance to occur (Aronson, 1973; Brehm and Cohen, 1962; Festinger, 1964; Wicklund and Brehm, 1976). Among these conditions are that the individual must feel personal responsibility for the behavior, that at least one of the cognitive elements in a dissonant relationship must have some importance to the individual, and that the behavior involved in the dissonance must have aversive consequences for oneself or someone else (Cooper and Worchel, 1970). Anything workers can do to foster these conditions is likely to enhance dissonance and subsequent attitude change. For example, giving a member choices about the behaviors to be changed should increase the feeling of personal responsibility for the decision, and discussing in the group the selection made should enhance its importance to the member.

There is another condition that seems to foster dissonance, although it is not essential to its occurrence: expending effort in a behavior that appears to contradict an attitude. Counter-attitudinal behavior involving a great deal of effort or discomfort to carry out appears especially likely to arouse dissonance. Since the fact of engaging in the act cannot be denied, the negative attitude is highly likely to change to reduce dissonance (Aronson and Mills, 1968; Gerard and Mathewson, 1966; Zimbardo and Ebbesen, 1970). A practitioner applying this concept might foster the expenditure of time or effort by shy or fearful clients to join a group that they do not perceive as very appealing. The result is likely to be a more positive view of the group.

The difference between the cognitive dissonance approach to enhancing members' views of a group and the means–end attitude approach is that if a dissonance strategy is used the behavior change comes first, but for means–end attitude theorists the attitude change comes first. To achieve the same goal of increasing the attractiveness of the group for potential members using the means–end approach, workers might highlight for their shy or fearful clients ways in which the group would help them achieve their own goal of greater assertiveness.

THE BASES OF SOCIAL INFLUENCE

Many conditions have been found that affect an individual's ability to influence others, but one variable that is particularly relevant to social work practice is the characteristics of the source of the influence attempt. It has been found that the most potent predictor of successful influence is credibility of the source of influence (Eagly and Himmelfarb, 1978; Ronis, et al., 1977; Simons, Berkowitz, and Moyer, 1970), and one of the main conditions for the establishment of credibility is expertise or knowledge in a particular area (Corrigan, 1978). Other characteristics of leaders associated with ability to influence group members are the members' acceptance of the legitimacy of the leader, the extent to which the leader exercises control of resources to reward or punish members, and the personal attractiveness of the leader (Kelman, 1965; French and Raven, 1968; Hollander, 1978; Thibaut and Kelley, 1959).

Credibility, attractiveness, and control over rewards and punishments trigger different influence processes (Kelman, 1965). Knowledge of the three types of influence is important, because the conditions in which the induced behaviors or attitudes are expressed differ for the different processes (Kelman, 1965). A process labeled compliance occurs when individuals accept influence because they hope to achieve a reward or approval from another person or avoid punishment. A second process, identification, occurs when members accept influence because they want to establish or maintain a satisfying, self-defining relationship with another person who is perceived as attractive. The third process, internalization, occurs when individuals accept influence because the source of influence is perceived as credible and the induced attitude or behavior is congruent with the value system of the recipient of influence. For compliance, only when there is surveillance, or suspected surveillance, by the source of influence will the new attitude or behavior be evident. In the case of identification, the recipient of influence is likely to perform the induced behavior only so long as the desired relationship remains salient. For internalization, the induced behavior tends to be performed in conditions of relevance of the issue (Kelman, 1965). Because internalization is not dependent upon monitoring of the behavior or on the salience of relationship, the behavior or attitude induced by this process is believed to be the most enduring. However, it is also less controlled by the source of influence, as many parents of radical children learned in the 1960s.

One implication of the findings about the multiple bases of influence is that workers do not necessarily have to control resources to reward or punish group members or possess expertise to exert influence; they may not even be perceived as attractive. Influence can still be exerted if practitioners are seen as legitimately possessing power (French and Raven, 1968; Raven and Kruglanski, 1970). For example, the leader can be perceived as holding an official position, such as probation officer, which grants power to exert influence, or the leader may have been designated by a legitimate authority figure, for example, the director of a mental health clinic, to be in charge of a treatment group. On the other hand, the more bases of influence possessed by the worker, the greater the likelihood of exerting influence. Thus group leaders are in the ideal position to bring about change in behaviors and attitudes when they can demonstrate that they have legitimate power, have credibility in relevant areas, have control over resources, and are perceived as attractive or can become attractive to members through the generous use of rewards (Thibaut and Kelley, 1959).

Although workers need to be influential to be effective change agents, there is danger in the practitioner's having too much power over the group (Kipnis, 1972). This threat is real. The worker often has more education than group members and is therefore usually perceived as possessing expertise. The interaction often takes place in the worker's home base so that the group members are less familiar with the territory and less knowledgeable about what is expected. Further, many workers function in organizational contexts, such as total institutions, where they have control over important resources, such as passes for home visits. The worker's position also has legitimacy in the larger society and in the particular organizational setting, for example, in a psychiatric hospital. All these factors can produce a great deal of power vis-à-vis group members. It is therefore critical that social workers remember the limits of their legitimate influence as defined both by the general value system of their profession and by a contract between the worker and each particular group.

ROLE THEORY AS APPLIED TO SMALL GROUPS

Contextual Roles

Contextual roles are consistent sets of behaviors, and expectations for those behaviors, that develop in certain social settings such as small groups (Biddle, 1979). The concept of contextual roles is congruent with the symbolic interactionists' view of roles as evolving consistencies in the behavior of individuals in informal groups (Bales, 1966; Turner, 1970; Zurcher, 1983). Contextual roles are not necessarily linked to social positions in the larger society, such as female or doctor, which are emphasized in the structural approach to role theory (e.g. Katz and Kahn, 1978; Nye, 1976). The symbolic interactionist approach is more useful in describing roles that arise in small groups composed of unrelated individuals and will therefore be emphasized in this chapter.

Contextual roles tend to be rotated among group members, although over time it is likely that individuals will specialize in certain roles that arise in unstructured social systems because of the requirements of the situation. The two categories of contextual roles that are critical to group functioning are task roles and maintenance roles (Benne and Sheats, 1961). These categories are associated with the two functions that all systems must perform if they are to survive (Parsons, 1955; Parsons, Bales, and Shils, 1953). As was previously mentioned in the discussion of cohesion, one essential function is that they must deal with the world external to the system; this has been called the instrumental function of systems. The second is that of maintaining themselves, that is, having sufficient internal harmony to prevent the dissolution of the system. This has been called the expressive function of a system and refers to the world inside of the system. Some treatment groups and some socioeducational groups appear to have no explicit external goals; however, efforts to reduce or prevent problematic behavior outside of the group can be considered instrumental group goals, especially when the entire group puts forth efforts to help each individual member.

Specific group task roles have been identified by social psychologists. These include seeking clarification of facts or opinions; giving information, opinions, and beliefs; coordinating by showing the relationships among various ideas generated; and energizing the group to action or decision (Benne and Sheats, 1961). Group maintenance roles that have been recognized include encouraging and praising; harmonizing; reconciling or mediating differences between members to relieve tension; compromising or admitting error to maintain group harmony; gatekeeping or attempting to include all participants in a discussion; and providing interpretations of the group's processes for the group's evaluation of its own activities (Benne and Sheats, 1961).

Roles that disrupt the group's functioning have also been described and labeled as individual rather than group roles (Benne and Sheats, 1961). These disruptive roles, which appear to be pervasive in nonvoluntary groups (Newcomb, 1978), include blocking or being negativistic and opposing without reason; trying to call attention to oneself through boasting or acting in unusual ways; dominating or trying to assert authority; aggressing or deflating the status of others; and trying to take credit for the contribution of others. Recognizing and diminishing individual roles when they appear is a skill professional group workers must acquire, especially those with nonvoluntary clients such as incarcerated juvenile offenders.

Theories of Leadership Roles

Extensive observational research has shown that in newly formed groups of peers, two specialists tend to develop, each of whom performs one of the two categories of essential group functions (Bales, 1966). That is, one individual takes over the task functions and becomes an instrumental leader keeping members focused on the goal; the second takes over the maintenance function and becomes the socioemotional leader who is sensitive to the feelings of others and relieves tension. The tendency for the roles to be enacted by different individuals has been hypothesized as the result of social processes common to all social systems (Bales, 1966). As a group attempts to reach a goal through coordinated activity, tension and unequal participation develop. When one person engages in the task, another is denied the opportunity; some ideas are selected and others rejected. The person who is highly active in the task area is the primary source of change, and this individual's actions often force others to adjust their behaviors and ideas. Further, it is difficult to make substantial contributions in small groups without talking a great deal. Yet this may be resented by others as a threat to their own status and a frustration of their own desire to talk. Because the person most active in the task area, the task leader, is the principal source of tension and the main target of hostility, that individual is unlikely to be effective in resolving tension. Someone else must assume that function (Bales, 1966). The result is the development of task and socioemotional role differentiation.

The pattern is not inevitable, however. There is at least one condition in which task leaders are not disliked, and that is when they receive more communications than they send—when they have a high feedback ratio (Bales, 1966). This fact has important implications for social work practice in groups. Should workers observe that an inordinate amount of tension is being generated by task leaders who give far more communications than they receive, the practitioners might discuss the situation with those leaders in private and/or proceed to reinforce any indication of their talking less in the group and listening more. In addition, the importance of the workers' encouraging more feedback to their own behavior should not be overlooked, for the same problem exists for task-oriented practitioners as for task-oriented group members.

CONCLUSION

To summarize, we have tried to present some social psychological theories and research in a fashion that illuminates their relevance to social work practice with groups. As with most social work interventions, the ultimate goal is generalization, that is, use of the new knowledge outside of the setting in which it was first encountered. In this case we hope the fresh insights will be transferred from the classroom or the study to the contexts in which the reader functions as a professional. Further, in those activities we hope the practitioner will go beyond the examples offered in this chapter and will apply social psychological knowledge in areas never considered by the authors.

REFERENCES

AJZEN, I., AND M. FISHBEIN
1970 "The prediction of behavior from attitudinal and normative variables," *Journal of Experimental Social Psychology*, 6: 466–87.
1973 "Attitudinal and normative variables as predictors of specific behaviors," *Journal of Personality and Social Psychology*, 27: 41–57.
1977 "Attitude–behavior relations: A theoretical analysis and review of empirical research," *Psychological Bulletin*, 84: 888–918.
1980 *Understanding Attitudes and Predicting Social Behavior*. Englewood Cliffs, N.J.: Prentice-Hall.
ARONSON, E.
1973 "Dissonance theory: Progress and problems." In L. S. Wrightsman and J. C. Brigham (eds.), *Contemporary Issues in Social Psychology*. Second edition. Monterey, Calif.: Brooks-Cole, pp. 310–23.
ARONSON E., AND J. MILLS
1968 "The effects of severity of initiation on liking for a group." In D. Cartwright and A. Zander (eds.), *Group Dynamics*. Third edition. New York: Harper & Row, pp. 119–24.
BALES, R. F.
1966 "Task roles and social roles in problem-solving groups." In Bruce Biddle and E. J. Thomas (eds.), *Role Theory: Concepts and Research*. New York: Wiley, pp. 254–63.
BENNE, K., AND P. SHEATS
1961 "Functional roles of group members." In L. P. Bradford (ed.), *Group Development*. Washington, D.C.: National Education Association, pp. 51–59.
BIDDLE, B. J.
1979 *Role Theory: Expectations, Identities, and Behaviors*. New York: Academic Press.
BLAU, P. M.
1964 *Exchange and Power in Social Life*. New York: Wiley.
BREHM, J. W.
1972 *Responses to Loss of Freedom: A Theory of Psychological Reactance*. Morristown, N.J.: General Learning Press.
BREHM, J. W., AND A. R. COHEN
1962 *Explorations in Cognitive Dissonance*. New York: Wiley.

BREHM, J. W., AND M. MANN
   1975   "Effect of importance of freedom and attraction to group members on in-
          fluence produced by group pressure," *Journal of Personality and Social
          Psychology*, 31: 816–24.
CARTWRIGHT, D., AND A. ZANDER (EDS.)
   1968   *Group Dynamics*. Third edition. New York: Harper & Row.
COOPER, J., AND S. WORCHEL
   1970   "Role of undesired consequences in arousing cognitive dissonance," *Jour-
          nal of Personality and Social Psychology*, 16: 199–206.
CORRIGAN, J. D.
   1978   "Salient attributes of two types of helpers: Friends and mental health pro-
          fessionals," *Journal of Counseling Psychology*, 25: 588–90.
EAGLY, A. H., AND S. HIMMELFARB
   1978   "Attitudes and opinions," *Annual Review of Psychology*, 29: 517–54.
FAZIO, R. H., AND M. P. ZANNA
   1978   "Attitudinal qualities relating to the strength of the attitude–behavior rela-
          tionship," *Journal of Experimental Social Psychology*, 14: 398–408.
FELD, S., AND N. RADIN
   1982   *Social Psychology for Social Work and the Mental Health Professions*.
          New York: Columbia University Press.
FESTINGER, L.
   1957   *A Theory of Cognitive Dissonance*. New York: Harper & Row.
   1964   *Conflict, Decision, and Dissonance*. Stanford, Calif.: Stanford University
          Press.
FESTINGER, L.; S. SCHACHTER; AND K. BACK
   1968   "Operation of group standards." In D. Cartwright and A. Zander
          (eds.), *Group Dynamics*. Third edition. New York: Harper & Row, pp.
          152–64.
FISHBEIN, M.
   1967   "A behavior theory approach to the relations between beliefs about an ob-
          ject and the attitude toward the object." In M. Fishbein (ed.), *Readings in
          Attitude Theory and Measurement*. New York: Wiley, pp. 389–400.
FISHBEIN, M., AND I. AJZEN
   1972   "Attitudes and opinions," *Annual Review of Psychology*, 23: 487–554.
FRANK, J. D.
   1957   "Some determinants, manifestations, and effects of cohesiveness in ther-
          apy groups," *International Journal of Group Psychotherapy*, 7: 53–63.
FRENCH, J. R. P., AND B. RAVEN
   1968   "The bases of social power." In D. Cartwright and A. Zander (eds.),
          Group Dynamics. Third edition. New York: Harper & Row, pp. 259–69.
GERARD, H. B., AND G. C. MATHEWSON
   1966   "The effects of severity of initiation on liking for a group: A replication,"
          Journal of Experimental Social Psychology, 2: 278–87.
GROTJAHN, M.
   1981   "Group cohesion as a factor in the therapeutic process." In H. Kellerman
          (ed.), *Group Cohesion: Theoretical and Clinical Perspectives*. New York:
          Grune & Stratton, pp. 246–53.

GUTTENTAG, M.
1970   "Group cohesiveness, ethnic organization, and poverty," *Journal of Social Issues*, 26, no. 2: 105-32.
HARE, A. P.
1982   *Creativity in Small Groups*. Beverly Hills, Calif.: Sage Publications.
HOLLANDER, E. P.
1978   *Leadership Dynamics: A Practical Guide to Effective Relationships*. New York: The Free Press.
KAPLAN, M. F., AND C. E. MILLER
1983   "Group discussion and judgment." In P. B. Paulus (ed.)., *Basic Group Processes*. New York: Springer-Verlag.
KATZ, D., AND R. L. KAHN
1978   *The Social Psychology of Organizations*. Second edition. New York: Wiley.
KELMAN, H. C.
1965   "Compliance, identification, and internalization: Three processes of attitude change." In H. Proshansky and B. Seidenbert (eds.), *Basic Studies in Social Psychology*. New York: Holt, Rinehart & Winston.
KIPNIS, D.
1972   "Does power corrupt?" *Journal of Personality and Social Psychology*, 24: 33-41.
KOTHANDAPANI, V.
1971   "Validation of feeling, belief, and intention to act as three components of attitude and their contribution to prediction of contraceptive behavior," *Journal of Personality and Social Psychology*, 19: 321-33.
LERNER, M. L., AND G. W. FAIRWEATHER
1963   "The social behavior of chronic schizophrenics in supervised and unsupervised work groups," *Journal of Abnormal and Social Psychology*, 67: 219-25.
LEVENTHAL, G. S.
1976a "Fairness in social relationships." In J. W. Thibaut, J. T. Spence, and R. C. Carson (eds.), *Contemporary Topics in Social Psychology*. Morristown, N.J.: General Learning Press, pp. 211-39.
1976b "The distribution of rewards and resources in groups and organizations." In Leonard Berkowitz and E. Walster (eds.), *Advances in Experimental Social Psychology*, Vol. 9. New York: Academic Press, pp. 91-131.
LEVENTHAL, G. S.; J. W. MICHAELS; AND C. SANFORD
1972   "Inequity and interpersonal conflict: Reward allocation and secrecy about reward as methods of preventing conflict," *Journal of Personality and Social Psychology*, 23, no. 1: 88-102.
LEVINE, J. M.
1980   "Reaction to opinion deviance in small groups." In P. B. Paulus (ed.), *Psychology of Group Influence*. Hillsdale, N.J.: Erlbaum.
LIEBERMAN, M. A.
1975   "Group Methods." In F. H. Kanfer and A. P. Goldstein (eds.), *Helping People Change: A Textbook of Methods*. New York: Pergamon Press, pp. 433-85.

McGuire, W. J.
  1969 "The nature of attitudes and attitude change." In G. Lindzey and E. Aronson (eds.), *Handbook of Social Psychology*, Volume 3. Reading, Mass.: Addison-Wesley, 3: 136–314.
Moscovici, S.
  1976 *Social Influence and Social Change*. London: Academic Press.
Newcomb, T. M.
  1953 "An approach to the study of communicative acts," *Psychological Review*, 60: 393–404.
  1978 "Use in colleges and in corrections: Institutional influences," *American Psychologist*, 33, no. 2: 114–24.
Nye, F. I.
  1976 *Role Structure and the Analysis of the Family*. Beverly Hills, Calif.: Sage Publications.
Parsons, T.
  1955 "Family structure and the socialization of the child." In T. Parsons and R. F. Bales (eds.), *Family, Socialization, and Interaction Process*. New York: Free Press, pp. 35–132.
Parsons, T.; R. F. Bales; and E. A. Shils
  1953 *Working Papers in the Theory of Action*. Glencoe, Ill.: The Free Press.
Pomazal, R. J., and J. J. Jacard
  1976 "An informational approach to altruistic behavior," *Journal of Personality and Social Psychology*, 33: 317–26.
Raven, B. H., and A. W. Kruglanski
  1970 "Conflict and power." In P. G. Swingle (ed.), *The Structure of Conflict*. New York: Academic Press, pp. 69–109.
Ronis, D. L.; M. H. Baumgardner; M. R. Leippe; J. T. Cacioppo; and A. G. Greenwald
  1977 "In search of reliable persuasion effects: I. A computer-controlled procedure for studying persuasion," *Journal of Personality and Social Psychology*, 35: 548–69.
Rosen, B., and S. S. Komorita
  1971 "Attitudes and actions: The effects of behavioral intent and perceived effectiveness of acts," *Journal of Personality and Social Psychology*, 39: 189–203.
Sakurai, M. M.
  1975 "Small group cohesiveness and detrimental conformity," *Sociometry*, 38: 340–47.
Schachter, S.
  1968 "Deviation, rejection, and communication." In D. Cartwright and A. Zander (eds.), *Group Dynamics*. Third edition. New York: Harper & Row, pp. 165–81.
Secord, P. F., and C. W. Backman
  1964 *Social Psychology*. New York: McGraw-Hill.
Shaw, M. E.
  1981 *Group Dynamics: The Psychology of Small Group Behavior*. Third edition. New York: McGraw-Hill.

SIMONS, H. W.; N. N. BERKOWITZ; AND R. J. MOYER
  1970   "Similarity, credibility, and attitude change: A review and a theory," *Psychological Bulletin*, 73: 1–15.
TERBORG, J. R.; C. CASTORE; AND J. A. DeNINNO
  1976   "A longitudinal field investigation of the impact of group composition on group performance and cohesion," *Journal of Personality and Social Psychology*, 34: 782–90.
THIBAUT, J. W., AND H. H. KELLEY
  1959   *The Social Psychology of Groups.* New York: Wiley.
TURNER, R. H.
  1970   *Family Interaction.* New York: Wiley.
WERNER, P. D.; S. E. MIDDESTADT-CARTER; AND T. J. CRAWFORD
  1975   "Having a third child: Predicting behavioral intentions," *Journal of Marriage and the Family*, 37: 348–58.
WICKLUND, R. A., AND J. W. BREHM
  1976   *Perspectives on Cognitive Dissonance.* Hillsdale, N.J.: Erlbaum.
WIGGINS, J. A.; F. DILL; AND R. D. SCHWARTZ
  1968   "On 'status-liability.'" In D. Cartwright and A. Zander (eds.), *Group Dynamics.* Third edition. New York: Harper & Row, pp. 538–46.
WITTES, G., AND N. RADIN
  1971   "Two approaches to group work with parents in a compensatory preschool program," *Social Work*, 6, no. 1: 42–50.
ZANDER, A.
  1979   "The psychology of group processes," *Annual Review of Psychology*, 30: 417–51.
ZIMBARDO, P. G., AND E. B. EBBESEN
  1970   "Experimental modification of the relationship between effort, attitude, and behavior," *Journal of Personality and Social Psychology*, 16: 207–13.
ZURCHER, L. A.
  1983   *Social Roles: Conformity, Conflict, and Creativity.* Beverly Hills, Calif.: Sage Publications.

5

A Conceptual Framework
for Group Development

Rosemary C. Sarri and Maeda J. Galinsky

GROUP DEVELOPMENT HAS major relevance in social group work. Practitioners who seek systematic control of change in group conditions to attain treatment goals need to understand what group development is and how it relates to specific principles of social work practice.

A frame of reference that limits, focuses, and directs the practitioner's efforts is a prerequisite for the development of systematic practice theory, however modest and limited. In social group work the frame of reference has been largely implicit with the exception of that provided by dynamic psychology, which has affected the perceptions, cognitions, communications, and explanations provided by social workers who focus on the individual level. An orientation specifically addressed to group level efforts is also required. Knowledge from sociology and social psychology, because they deal with precisely such group phenomena, is required for an adequate group work practice theory. The social group work practitioner's goal is to achieve change in individuals who manifest social functioning problems by using the group as the means and the context to accomplish desired changes. Because the group provides the primary situation for change, it is viewed as a "context" for treatment. As a "means" for change the practitioner explicitly uses group conditions to change individuals. Group development is one of these conditions.

Individual member characteristics and environment may strongly influence the development of the group. Here, however, focus is on the regularities and consistencies of group development that can be ascertained, rather than on the total complexity of variables that may impinge on any group.

The concept of group development is based on a number of assumptions, some of which also apply to other areas of concern in social group work. (1) The group, a potent influence system, can be used as an efficient

An earlier versions of this statement was included in *A Conceptual Framework for the Teaching of the Social Group Work Methods* (New York: Council on Social Work Education 1962).

vehicle for individual change. (2) The group is not an end in itself. The aim of social group work is to maximize the potentials of the group for individual change rather than to create an enduring, small social system. (3) Group development can be controlled and influenced by the worker's actions. (4) There is no optimal way in which groups develop. Earlier literature has often asserted that all groups must develop into democratic self-directing entities, embellished with formalized operating and governing procedures. However, in order to attain individual goals for clients, the practitioner must intervene to affect group development in ways that facilitate the pursuit of these goals.

This analysis of developmental phases will refer to all groups, regardless of their objectives, composition, environmental location, and whether or not they are served by a professional or other practitioner. "Worker" will be used to refer to a professionally trained social worker or psychotherapist. "Leader" and leadership" are reserved to refer to group members and aspects of the group structure. The developmental process discussed in this chapter occurs over a series of meetings, not in one meeting. The assumption is made that the group membership would not change frequently. Where membership is more fluid the group would be expected to recapitulate earlier phases of group development (Hock and Kaufer, 1955).

Group development is defined as changes through time in the internal structures, processes, and culture of the group. Three dimensions of group development can be identified: (1) social organization of the group—the group structure, patterns of participant roles and statuses (e.g. changes in the power structure at different stages of development), (2) activities, tasks, and operative processes of the group (e.g. changes in decision-making processes over time), and (3) the culture of the group; *its* norms (that is, expectations of members for one another), values, and shared purposes. These include most of the group dimensions that can be observed and manipulated. What distinguishes them as dimensions of group development is that they change over time and that there are certain regularities which may be noted in their manifestations at different times in the life of the group. It is possible to classify these recurrent patterns into several phases.

Despite extensive research on many aspects of small groups, very few systematic studies of group development have been carried out.[1] Nevertheless, some phase regularities have been identified and reported (Theodorson, 1953; Martin and Hill, 1957). Comparisons between reports are difficult because few observers use the same categories or concepts for describing developmental patterns, and because some studies are the result of relatively rigorous study, while others are less systematic observations of

---

[1]Literature on small groups is voluminous; for an extensive bibliography on small group research, see Hare (1962).

practitioners (Psathas, 1960; Northen, 1958). Furthermore, there are few tools for quantifying degrees of change and only terms such as "increasing," "higher," and "lower" can be relied on. Groups also clearly do not always move through the several phases sequentially—movement backward as well as forward has been observed—and groups spend differing amounts of time in each phase. Despite these and other problems, delineation of the phases of group development and identification of essential elements of each phase are attempted here.

Several authors fail to distinguish group developmental processes from workers' interventions and individual clients' reactions (Weisman, 1953). The range of worker interventions required by each phase of group development will be examined separately in the subsequent discussion of the treatment sequence.

PHASES OF GROUP DEVELOPMENT

Phases of group development and the events that characterize each are presented here in the order in which they typically occur:

1. *Origin Phase* refers to composing the group and is distinguished primarily for analytic purposes, because events that occur precondition later development.
2. *Formative Phase* is characterized by the initial activity of group members in seeking similarity and mutuality of interests. Initial commitments to group purpose, emergent interpersonal ties, and a quasi-structure are also observable in this phase.
3. *Intermediate Phase* is characterized by a moderate level of group cohesion (i.e., interpersonal bonds among members), clarification of purposes, and an observable involvement of members in goal-directed activities.
4. *Revision Phase.* In this phase, a challenge to the existing group structure can be expected, accompanied by modification of group purposes and operating procedures.
5. *Intermediate Phase II.* Following the revision phase, while many groups gradually progress toward maturation, the characteristics outlined in phase 3 may again appear; however, the group generally manifests a higher level of integration and stability than that of the earlier intermediate phase.
6. *Maturation Phase* is characterized by stabilization of group structure, purposes, operating and governing procedures, expansion of the culture of the group, and the existence of effective responses to internal and external stresses.

7. *Termination Phase.* The dissolution of the group may result from goal attainment, maladaptation, the lack of integration, or previous planning to terminate the group.

Each of the phases will be examined in greater detail, using the three dimensions of group development—social organization; activities, tasks, and operating procedures; and group culture—as a basis for analysis.

Phase 1. Origin

As suggested, this phase preconditions or sets limits for possible later development of the group. Regardless of when the worker comes in contact with a treatment group, he or she must obtain knowledge about the beginning of the group. Major variables that affect further group development are size of the group, members' characteristics and initial orientations, and environmental location of the group.

Present knowledge indicates that group size has specific effects upon the development of the group's structural properties, upon patterns of individual participation and performance, and upon individual members' satisfaction (Thomas and Fink, 1963).

Member characteristics influence subsequent activities, tasks, and operating procedures, as well as the culture of the group. For example, urban lower-class children are not likely to respond to activities that require a high level of verbal skill or to be able to participate readily in a group operated under parliamentary procedures.

The initial orientation of members of the group has a significant impact upon its later social organization. For example, voluntary membership affects participants' initial attitudes or orientations toward the group and therefore will influence patterns of relationships among members. Where membership in groups is involuntary, dependence upon the professional worker can be expected to last longer, and the leadership structure within the group can be expected to develop more slowly.

Environmental location, the community and/or agency setting in which the group exists, is of particular concern because it influences the norms and values of members and sets limits for activities and tasks of the group (Miller, 1957). Frequently environmental conditions may allow fluidity in group structure and participation patterns in the early phases of development (for example, an informal hospital ward group).

Phase 2. Formative

The group's social organization during this phase is observable in the emerging interpersonal ties among members and in the appearance of a quasi-structure. As Theodorson observed, this quasi-structure is most often characterized by leadership roles played by the more assertive and aggressive individuals, who give order and direction to the group and who receive some initial deference from other members (Theodorson, 1953). Thus a partial prestige and status structure can be expected to emerge.

In the formative stage members seek common and compatible personal values and attitudes, group purposes, and activities and tasks. During this process norms based on common values and attitudes and relating to ways of behaving in the group are established,[2] frequently through the development of simple operating procedures. Attraction to other members and to the group purposes or tasks is likely to be enhanced, resulting in a basis for group cohesion and for further progressive development of the group (Martin and Hill, 1957; Foulkes and Anthony, 1957; Northen, 1958; Theodorson, 1953).

If these conditions are not satisfactorily attained in this phase, the group most likely will be unable to meet the requirements of subsequent phases and will terminate prematurely. In many groups where membership is voluntary, lack of attendance by members is symptomatic of the failure to establish satisfactory conditions in this phase.

Phase 3. Intermediate

Increasing interpersonal ties with a moderate level of group cohesion characterize this phase. Purposes are clarified, and observable involvement in goal-directed activities and specialized roles gradually emerges; task and socioemotional leaders can be more clearly identified at this time.[3] Cliques and subgroups may begin to form.

Additional norms and values are acquired that specifically relate to group functioning. Social control mechanisms develop, and deviation from norms often tends to be dealt with in a harsh or punitive manner by the group. Because norms and values for a number of areas of attitudinal ex-

[2]See Riecken and Homans (1954) for review of empirical studies where findings support the generalization that while extensive choice changes occur in newly formed groups, a stable social structure emerges early and a given member's relative status tends to remain the same over time. See also Jennings (1950). The acquisition of norms pertaining to ways of behaving in the earliest phases of group psychotherapy is described by Foulkes and Anthony (1957). Hock and Kaufer (1955) also mention the establishment of group norms in the initial stage, which they term the "climate setting stage."

[3]See Bales and Slater (1955). Martin and Hill (1957) describe the development of subgroups and specialized roles in their Phase IV. Foulkes and Anthony (1957) discuss this occurrence during their intermediate phase. During their second phase, that of approach-avoidance, Hock and Kanfer (1955) note how differential roles are assumed by members and also how in this phase and in other phases social control mechanisms and operating procedures are developed. See also Theodorson (1953).

pression and overt behavior are not yet established, member participation may be somewhat restricted in fear of sanctions or because members do not yet know what is expected of them. Pressures toward uniformity and consensus are clearly apparent (Festinger, 1962). Members have now experienced some events in common and are beginning to build up common traditions, sentiments, and values.

The actual emergence of norms, values, and social control mechanisms may be difficult to observe empirically; they are, nevertheless, as necessary to the development of groups as more easily discernible variables such as leadership structure. Considerable evidence shows that crucial norms and values are established during both the formative and the intermediate phases.

Phase 4. Revision

Careful scrutiny of the literature suggests that prior to or following Phase 3, a revision phase (Theodorson, 1953; Martin and Hill, 1957; Foulkes and Anthony, 1957; Bennis and Shepard, 1962) occurs that involves a challenge to and a revision of the leadership structure of earlier stages; it is most likely to occur if the leaders in previous stages are aggressive and attempt to prevent other members from engaging in leadership activities.

Change in group operating procedures is likely to accompany the revision in leadership structure. Increased role differentiation can be expected, with more members assuming leadership functions in their particular areas of competence. A leader who is able to adapt to new group demands for the operation of the group may retain his or her initial status. As members feel more secure in their specialized roles, as they depend more on one another for satisfaction in the tasks and activities of the group, and as they interact more frequently, group members are likely to have more positive feelings toward each other. An increase in negative reactions can also be expected (Bales, 1950; Psathas, 1960; Foulkes and Anthony, 1957). The norms, values, and traditions of the group may change in varying degrees depending upon the extent of the revision. If they do not change, they will at least be strengthened and clarified. Further clarification of group purposes can also be expected both during and following the revision in leadership structure.

Phase 5. Intermediate II

Equilibrium following the revision should be restored early in this phase. A significant proportion of groups appear to manifest characteristics that resemble the earlier intermediate phase, but a higher level of group integration and greater stability in goal-directed activity and in group structure is expected. In addition, because participants have been together longer, there are more traditions, clearer norms, and more collective memories, which can be expected to increase group cohesion and the influence of the group upon members. Many of the problems confronting the group earlier are likely to be resolved by this time. Consequently, specific goal-required activities can be given greater attention, with higher levels of interdependence and cooperation among members in these activities.

As mentioned previously, not all groups experience an identifiable revision in group structure; nevertheless, some modification in structure will be apparent with a more complex division of labor. Leadership becomes more diffused among members, roles are differentiated and increased. These changes are likely to precipitate or accompany changes in operating procedures.

Phase 6. Maturation

Movement into this phase is marked by a relatively high level of group functioning. Maturation is clearly distinguishable from earlier phases of group development. Well-developed group structure is characterized by obvious ranking, specialized and interdependent roles, formalized patterns of interaction, subgroups, and proliferated interpersonal ties. Customary operating procedures include patterns of participation, problem-solving, decision-making, and implementing of decisions. Relatively stable relationships exist with the physical and social environment, and effective procedures for change have been established. Substantial progress along these lines is likely to be found only in well-integrated groups that have existed over a long period of time.[4]

Changes in the group's environment force internal changes; internal conflicts and shifting needs of members generate crises for which the group must develop adaptive mechanisms.[5] Successful groups enter the maturation phase—and remain there—only when they can respond to both extragroup and intragroup pressures for change. Maturation may be viewed as a state of "dynamic equilibrium" rather than one of static maturity.

Phase 7. Termination

There are four general conditions that result in termination of groups. (1) When goals are attained, the group may have no further reason for existence. (2) Some groups are planned for definite periods of time (for exam-

---

[4]Homans's (1950) analysis of W. A. Whyte's "Norton Street Gang" suggests that this group possessed many of the necessary characteristics of the maturation phase.

[5]The final phase described by Martin and Hill (1957), the group as an integrative-creative social instrument, resembles the maturation phase described here. However, Martin and Hill believe that this phase is an important one for treatment groups.

ple, orientation or diagnostic groups). (3) Also, lack of integration occurs if a group is unable to achieve essential conditions for endurance: basic consensus among members about goals, a high level of interpersonal ties, a role system that permits sufficient personal satisfaction and successful completion of major tasks, or effective operating procedures. (4) Maladaptation is most notable when a group has not developed effective means for responding to external changes and environmental pressures. It may never have developed change mechanisms; on the other hand, it may have developed mechanisms that were effective at one time but became rigid or institutionalized and, consequently, would not allow for adaptation to new conditions.

THE TREATMENT SEQUENCE

These phases of group development have disregarded the presence or absence of a professional worker. When a worker is present, his or her ability to recognize, understand, and guide phases of group development can facilitate treatment planning and enhance efforts to attain individual treatment goals within the group. Specific strategies for worker intervention can be related to successive phases of group development.

Practice principles, intervention techniques, and workers' actions are generally formulated within the "treatment sequence," which includes intake, diagnosis, formulation of goals, treatment, and evaluation. Throughout the following review of stages of the treatment sequence, a primary concern will be intervention techniques which the worker uses with groups at different phases of development.

Stage I. Intake, Selection, and Diagnosis

This treatment sequence stage corresponds to the origin phase of group development and occurs prior to the first meeting. Worker actions at this point include intake, diagnosis, and the formulation of treatment goals. Although diagnosis will not be discussed here, diagnosis directly implicates treatment planning, so the two processes must be considered simultaneously.

The use of the group as the means and context for treatment imposes requirements upon the worker for specific actions in this stage. These include the following:

1. Determination of group purposes for the synthesis of individual treatment goals
2. Establishing a "contract" with individual members concerning the particular type of social work service to be provided

3. Determination of the basic mechanics of the particular type of group treatment: frequency of meetings, time and place for meetings, projected length of service, and necessary resources

Stage II. Group Formation

In this stage, which corresponds to the formative phase of group development, the workers' actions are especially crucial, because the conditions must be set for subsequent group development and treatment. From the first meeting, the worker serves as a central person, a psychological core of the group, and intervenes to influence group development in the desired direction.

Specific actions required of the worker at this stage include

1. Fostering members' attraction to the group
2. Initiation and/or support of group norms that facilitate treatment
3. Definition of general purposes and of limits within which members may develop their own goals
4. Maintenance of an open, flexible leadership structure

Initial attraction to the group is fostered through worker assistance to members, individually and collectively, in their search for common values and interests. His or her relationship to each member also serves to increase group attraction potential. Where appropriate, special emphasis is placed on values and experiences related to treatment goals; the worker motivates and stimulates members not only toward activities they enjoy but also toward those which are therapeutically useful. Thus the worker facilitates and enhances commonality among members, including shared recognition of their common difficulties (Foulkes and Anthony, 1957).

The worker's influence on the development of appropriate group norms is particularly important during this stage because norms tend to persist and may be difficult to modify later (Merei, 1958; Hock and Kaufer, 1955). The worker therefore initiates, supports, and stimulates group norms in line with his or her objectives. Simultaneously, the worker deemphasizes and may even suppress those norms which may have negative implications for treatment objectives, but this must be done with caution so that the worker does not jeopardize his or her relationship with members.

The worker defines general purposes for the group, reinforces the contracts established in initial interviews, and sets limits within which members may develop their own goals. The statement of the general purpose will further serve to direct members' activities and tasks.

Groups may develop initial leadership structures with aggressive members predominating. External statuses may be important in their initial prestige, but the worker can expect a gradual shift to prestige based on intragroup performance. During this stage in the treatment sequence the worker influences the structure so that initial leadership will be supportive of the worker's norms, values, and group purposes. The worker is careful not to give positive sanctions to leaders who hinder the treatment process. Primarily through the use of indirect means of influence, the worker attempts to forestall premature formalization or stabilization of the leadership structure in order to preserve opportunities for other members to assume leadership functions later. If the worker does not maintain an open and flexible structure, the group may never attain the level of integration required for viability (Martin and Hill, 1957). One way the worker can ensure more flexibility is to introduce group operating procedures that foster participation by all members to the highest possible degree. These operating procedures will then serve to initiate norms for effective participation by all members.

Finally, the worker can expect considerable "testing" in this stage. Members will evaluate the worker's acceptance of them, concern for them, reliability, and tolerance of their behavior (Northen, 1958; Miller, 1957).

Stage III. Building a Viable and Cohesive Group

At this stage of the treatment sequence, which corresponds to Intermediate Phase I of group development, a wide range of worker interventions may be required:

1. Fostering interpersonal ties among members
2. Planning program activities
3. Assessment of leadership structure
4. Supporting the maintenance or revision of leadership structure
5. Assisting members to fulfill roles
6. Encouraging efforts to develop effective operating procedures
7. Mediating group sanctions
8. Supporting norms and values that facilitate treatment

A moderate to high level of group cohesion is expected during this stage, and the worker facilitates the growth of interpersonal ties among *all* members of the group. While cohesion is necessary if the group is to become a potent and viable influence system, evidence suggests that a very high level of cohesion induces strong pressures for uniformity, which in turn may lead to the rejection of any deviant (Schachter, 1951).

One prime way the practitioner can influence norms and encourage the role structure along the lines he or she desires is through the planning of program activities. The worker must be aware of how activities influence norms and roles. They are planned both to support present, and to develop additional, legitimate norms. For example, the worker can initiate activities that foster considerable cooperation and teamwork (e.g. volleyball). Program activities must implicitly or explicitly underline the problem-oriented focus of the group. If the worker established a treatment contract with individual participants and with the group, the worker will probably find greater receptivity to this problem and change focus, but frequent reinforcement or restatement of the contract is required.

Several observers have noted that a "honeymoon period" occurs in this stage; members may be highly attracted to the worker, to other members, and to the program, Although attraction and satisfaction are required to maintain a viable, potent group, the worker must sense the pitfalls at this time or the group may become static, thus seriously jeopardizing movement toward change goals.

Cliques or subgroups often emerge during this phase; the worker must respond to this process by supporting the structures that have positive consequences for group functioning and treatment. However, if subgroups form factions that pull members in opposite directions, this may lead to dissatisfaction, isolation of members, and disintegration. Depending upon his or her assessment, the worker can support or seek to revise the leadership structure developed in the formative phase. In any event the worker encourages leadership by more and different members. According to knowledge of the developmental processes, during this phase the group is expected to begin to hold different role expectations of members because of their particular skills or other attributes. Direct and indirect means of influence can be employed to place members in positions of therapeutic benefit, so long as such actions do not have negative consequences for other members. Simultaneously, direct means of influence can be used to help selected members meet expectations of particular roles within the groups. Observation of different patterns of behavior provides important information to the worker to support his or her initial diagnostic impressions or to suggest the need for modification of earlier impressions. Corresponding alterations in treatment goals may then be necessary.

More effective operating procedures are encouraged by the worker at this time, but the group should not be expected to develop highly efficient or effective problem-solving or decision-making processes. Premature efforts to formalize operating or governing procedures might hamper treatment objectives and even result in maladaptation. For example, in discussion treatment groups, the worker should avoid establishing rigid participation requirements that block spontaneity.

Because group efforts to develop social control mechanisms are often apparent during this stage, the worker must realize that peer disipline can be harsh and extreme pressures can be exerted on deviant members through the enforcement of group norms. The worker mediates procedures and sanctions so that members are not isolated or made scapegoats. The worker encourages the group to develop appropriate control mechanisms thereby enhancing its potential for influence upon individual members. As in the prior stage, norms and values that facilitate treatment are supported by the worker, who serves as a spokesperson for such norms and also symbolizes them in actions. Special assistance can help members act in accordance with group norms and values.

Stage IV. Maintaining the Group Through Revision

The following worker actions may be required during this stage of the treatment sequence, which corresponds to Intermediate Phase II:

1. Revising group's quasi-structure
2. Modifying group norms, operating procedures
3. Maintaining group cohesion

The worker should expect a challenge to and/or a revision of the quasi-structure established in the formative phase and solidified in the first intermediate phase. Only limited modification may achieve increased participation, or there may be need for rather drastic changes. As pointed out, revision of the initial structures may have been guided by the worker's actions, his or her lack of support for initial leaders, and positive responses to other members who attempt to fulfill leadership functions. Thus, revision of the quasi-structure need not occur suddenly and dramatically but can unfold over a period of time.

If leadership roles are changed significantly, the worker may intervene directly so that former leaders will be retained in the group. The worker may also modify group participation patterns so that all members will continue to derive satisfaction. Direct activity with new leaders can help them assume leadership roles that enhance treatment for all members.

Since this stage is often quite fluid and dynamic, it offers the worker opportunity to modify group norms that he or she could not influence earlier. This task, of course, is much easier if the new leaders are oriented toward desired norms and purposes. Changes in operating procedures can be expected to accompany the revision of leadership structure. The worker supports changes that increase participation, democratic processes of decision-making, and mature approaches to group and individual problem-solving.

During the processes of revision group cohesion equilibrium is upset, so the worker must help reaffirm members' ties to each other and their support for group purposes and tasks. Assisting the group to select a program carefully will be useful at this point. Program activities are directed to provide positive support for the new leaders, to aid role differentiation and specialization so that all members feel like contributing participants, and to provide enjoyable activities so attraction to the group will be enhanced.

Stage V. Guiding Group Processes
Toward Treatment Goals

During this advanced stage, corresponding to the beginning of the Maturation Phase, worker's interventions will be supportive and evaluative:

1. Supporting (modified) leadership structure
2. Supporting group's efforts to cope directly with pressures
3. Assessment of progress toward individual treatment goals

If the group has gone through revision, the worker acts to stabilize the modified leadership structure, helps clarify new norms that relate to treatment objectives, and enables the operating procedures that have developed to lead to greater self-direction by the group. The problem-focused nature of the group is strongly emphasized since equilibrium should be reestablished.

If the group structure has not been revised substantially, the worker fosters the continuation of the developments noted in Stage III—the formation of appropriate norms and effective social control mechanisms, a group structure that encourages maximum participation, an expanded division of labor, and a differentiated role system with most members having the opportunity to fulfill some leadership functions.

During this stage significant movement toward treatment objectives is expected. Periods of progress, however, are often followed by periods of regression. Although the worker acts to prevent serious disruption during these cyclical changes, he or she does not prevent their occurrence because of the valuable learning opportunities provided for group members. Members, individually and collectively, learn to cope with increasingly complex problems and tasks, and thus the group is enhanced as an effective treatment vehicle. Observable increases in the level of integration are expected by this time.

Although the group may experience several "revisions" and appear to revert to earlier stages, different dynamics can be expected in each of these regressions and progressions because of prior experiences. Repeated challenges to the leadership structure often occur, as do attempts to revise norms, purposes, tasks, or operating procedures. If the challenge is negative vis-à-vis treatment objectives, the worker intervenes firmly and directly to constrain the process. Conversely, the worker will intervene to support challenges that have positive implications.

Prior to this stage the worker may have assumed major responsibility for helping the group cope with internal and external pressures to change. Actions should now make the group itself responsible for coping directly with these pressures. Miller has described the dynamics of group development of delinquent gangs, particularly the changes in the gangs' ability to respond to and alter their environment. He has also identified several worker actions that are required if the group is to be successful in this task (Miller, 1957).

Greater use of indirect rather than direct means of influence will be expected in this stage, because worker's actions in earlier stages should have resulted in the development of norms, social control mechanisms, and operating and governing procedures that allow for greater self-direction by the group.[6] The worker's objectives and members' attributes influence the group in establishing norms that support problem-focused actions and lead to treatment goals. Since the danger of reaching a static equilibrium always exists, the worker's interventions should be sufficiently disruptive to maintain that degree of instability required for the group to serve as a continuing vehicle for treatment. In this stage the worker must be especially careful to avoid the danger of perceiving the group as an end in itself. The worker should remain alert and sensitive to group processes so that he or she can intervene to influence norms, purposes, operating procedures, control mechanisms, and group structures to facilitate the attainment of treatment goals for individual members.

Stage VI. Maintaining the Group

Groups can move fully into the Maturation Phase but never reach this stage in the treatment sequence, because individual client goals are likely to be achieved in one of the prior stages, and service is then terminated. This stage is considered briefly because few groups in the Maturation Phase of development are assumed to require the services of a professional group worker.

From the previous review, the following characteristics are expected of a group in the Maturation Phase: a high level of integration, stabilized group structures, consensus of and direction toward goals, customary operating and governing procedures, an expanded group culture, and effective

---

[6]Frequently noted in the literature on psychotherapy groups is the change from a worker-centered to a group-centered group; see Martin and Hill (1957) and Hock and Kaufer (1955). This phenomenon may reflect the worker's inactivity during later states or use of more indirect means of influence. Northen (1958) cites the worker's change from an active to a supporting role.

mechanisms for change. When these characteristics are observed, it is safe to assume that individual members are relatively mature persons who do not require professional group work service. Groups are often terminated at this stage, and members may be referred to agencies for socialization or other services, but generally not for social work treatment. Under special circumstances professional workers might continue to serve such groups for limited periods. The role of the worker would be primarily to facilitate continued group functioning, and indirect means of influence would definitely predominate. The worker's main assistance to the group would occur when crises arise because of internal or external pressures or in especially difficult phases of problem-solving.

A question can be raised whether groups such as street gangs are in the maturation phase at the time of the worker's initial contact and, therefore, do not need the professional services. Many such groups appear to be in the maturation phase at first contact, but the central problem is that they maintain antisocial values and norms. Interventions by the worker are directed toward a drastic revision of existing group conditions to modify norms, structures, and operating procedures. If the worker's efforts are successful, the group can be expected to move back to and through the earlier revision phase. Accurate assessment of such groups is essential, because superficial observation may suggest that the group is in the maturation phase when, in fact, this is not the case.

Stage VII. Terminating the Group

Four reasons were offered for termination of a group: (1) achievement of goals for individual members; (2) predetermined duration of the group by agency policies and/or objectives; (3) lack of minimal integration, and the worker's decision that a satisfactory level cannot be achieved; (4) maladaptation because the group lacks appropriate mechanisms for coping with internal and external pressures. Briefly, the worker's role in each of these termination situations will be examined.

Termination for achievement of goals or objectives results when the worker evaluates his or her original treatment goals for each individual and determines that they have been attained satisfactorily. It is highly desirable that members be engaged in parts of the evaluation and they clearly perceive what has been accomplished. In terminating the group, the conditions of the contract, established in the first phase between worker and members, can be evaluated in a similar manner. Since changes were sought that were stabilized and transferable outside the treatment sequence, careful evaluation prior to termination is essential. Indeed, at this point the worker may help the group to devote special attention to extragroup experiences of its members.

Even when groups are established for specific periods of time (for example, orientation or discharge groups), termination must be carefully considered. Such groups can be expected to have wide variations in the types and degrees of change that occur among individual members. Goals may have been reached at a satisfactory level for some individuals, but others will require referral for additional treatment.

To determine which factors contributed to lack of integration, the worker examines the composition of the group, the members' commitments to group purposes and tasks, pressures from the environment, and the worker's own service to the group. Lack of integration results from inadequacies in one or several of these areas. Whatever the reason, if a decision is made to terminate the group, the worker must do so in a manner that is not harmful to any member. For example, if faulty group composition appears to be the problem, the group may be recomposed with different membership. Other situations also may require dissolution of the group and the referral of members for services elsewhere.

Termination because of maladaptation is likely to result because of inappropriate mechanisms for coping with external and internal pressures or because previously successful mechanisms have become rigid and inflexible. Maladaptation is likely to occur in the later phases of group development. In determining causes and possible solutions, the worker needs to examine factors similar to those for lack of integration. Frequently the worker can intervene to prevent the dissolution of the group.

Termination may take place in any phase for the reasons given or even because of other factors. It is expected, of course, that when termination occurs because of satisfactory goal achievement, the group will be in one of the later stages of development.

REFERENCES

BALES, ROBERT F.
  1950 *Interaction Process Analysis: A Method for the Study of Small Groups.* Cambridge, Mass.: Addison-Wesley Press.
BALES, ROBERT F., AND PHILIP E. SLATER
  1955 "Role differentiations in small decision-making groups." In T. Parsons and R. F. Bales (eds.), *Family, Socialization and Interaction Process.* Glencoe, Ill.: The Free Press, pp. 239–306.
BENNIS, WARREN G., AND HERBERT A. SHEPARD
  1962 "A theory of group development." In W. G. Bennis, K. D. Benne, and R. Chin (eds.), *The Planning of Change.* New York: Holt, pp. 321–40.
FESTINGER, LEON
  1962 "Informal social communication." In Dorwin Cartwright and Alvin Zander (eds.), *Group Dynamics.* Second edition. Evanston, Ill.: Row, Peterson, pp. 286–99.

FOULKES, S. H., AND E. J. ANTHONY
   1957   *Group Psychotherapy*. London: Wyman & Sons.
HARE, PAUL
   1962   *Handbook of Small Group Research*. Glencoe, Ill.: The Free Press.
HOCK, E., AND G. A. KAUFER
   1955   "A process analysis of 'transient' therapy groups," *International Journal of Group Psychotherapy*, 5: 415–21.
HOMANS, GEORGE C.
   1950   *The Human Group*. New York: Harcourt, Brace.
JENNINGS, HELEN H.
   1950   *Leadership and Isolation*. New York: Longmanns, Green, pp. 209–17.
MARTIN, ELMORE A., JR., AND WILLIAM F. HILL
   1957   "Toward a theory of group development: Six phases of therapy group development," *International Journal of Group Psychotherapy* 7: 20–30.
MEREI, FERENC
   1958   "Group leadership and institutionalization." In E. E. Maccoby, T. M. Newcomb, and E. L. Hartley (eds.), *Readings in Social Psychology*. New York: Holt, Rinehart & Winston. pp. 522–32.
MILLER, WALTER B.
   1957   "The impact of a community group work program on delinquent corner groups," *Social Service Review*, 31: 390–406.
NORTHEN, HELEN
   1958   "Social group work: A tool for changing behavior of disturbed acting-out adolescents." In *Social Work With Groups*. New York: National Association of Social Workers, pp. 61–74.
PSATHAS, GEORGE
   1960   "Phase movement and equilibrium tendencies in interaction process in psychotherapy groups," *Sociometry*, 23: 177–94.
RIECKEN, HENRY W., AND GEORGE C. HOMANS
   1954   "Psychological aspects of social structure." In G. Lindzey (ed.), *Handbook of Social Psychology*. Cambridge: Addison-Wesley, pp. 786–833.
SCHACHTER, STANLEY
   1951   "Deviation, rejection, and communication," *Journal of Abnormal and Social Psychology*, 46: 190–207.
THEODORSON, GEORGE A.
   1953   "Elements in the progressive development of small groups," *Social Forces* 31: 311–20.
THOMAS, EDWIN J., AND CLINTON F. FINK
   1963   "Effects of group size," *Psychological Bulletin*, 60: 371–84.
WEISMAN, CELIA B.
   1953   "Social structure as a determinant of the group worker's role," *Social Work*, 8: 87–94.

6

The Open-Ended Group

Janice H. Schopler and Maeda J. Galinsky

THE UNIQUE FEATURE of open-ended groups is their provision for ongoing membership change: New members are accepted on a continuing basis and can attend as long as their needs warrant. This important innovation has evolved from practitioners' efforts to be more responsive to their clients. When groups are open, clients do not have to wait for service, and group attendance can be tailored to the individual requirements of members.

The practice literature suggests a rapid expansion in the use of open-ended groups.[1] This particular adaptation of more traditional group approaches is a productive format for work with a wide range of clients. Once the open-ended group is formed and in place, it can ensure a prompt response to clients in crisis or offer support and treatment as needed to help clients cope with long-term or chronic difficulties. Patterns of implementation and attendance vary from waiting room groups with almost a complete turnover every session to groups that meet for years with only occasional revisions in composition. Despite their diversity these groups all offer an immediate, ongoing response to client needs, and the important theme of changing membership links them conceptually.

Keeping membership open does affect the group system and creates new leadership demands. While practitioners support the benefits of open groups, they frequently express concern about the disruptive impact of members' entering and leaving. Their attempts to deal with membership transitions are promising but rely heavily on their ingenuity and experience. The theoretical literature on groups tends to emphasize long-term groups with stable membership. The existing frameworks are helpful in work with

[1] Our 1981 review of the social work, group therapy, and behavioral science literature revealed almost one hundred articles related to open-ended groups (Schopler and Galinsky, 1984). Since that time articles on open-ended groups have continued to appear in journals and books. The recent *Handbook of Short-Term Therapy Groups* (Rosenbaum, 1983) devoted over half of its chapters to groups with changing membership. Our conceptualization of open-ended groups has also been greatly facilitated by our discussions with practitioners and their response to our research on open-ended groups (Galinsky and Schopler, in press). We appreciate their willingness to share their experiences.

open-ended groups, but the theory often needs to be modified and practice principles given different emphasis. Recently some authors have begun to note the open-ended group as a distinct group form, but only scattered attempts have been made to conceptualize the development of open groups and to consider implications for intervention (Insko et al., 1980; Henry, 1981; Yalom, 1983; Schopler and Galinsky, 1984; Galinsky and Schopler, in press).

Designing and dealing with effective open-ended groups requires special understanding and skills. Practitioners support the need for attention to the purposes, group formation, group development, structure, and processes of open-ended groups. Each of these areas is examined in the light of existing theory and practice experience, and guidelines are suggested for responding to the particular needs of groups with changing membership.

PURPOSES OF OPEN-ENDED GROUPS

Open-ended groups serve a variety of purposes including treatment, support, assessment, orientation, and education.[2] In some cases groups have a single focus such as orienting new residents to a drug treatment center. More often open groups address multiple aims as, for example, an open group meeting in a maternity home that provides education, support, and an opportunity for assessing expectant mothers' strengths and needs.

Clarity and Relevance of Purpose

Whatever form purposes may take, they must be based on the needs of the client population and formulated in clear, concise, readily understandable terms. Clarity of purpose is of key importance in defining expectations for members, maintaining group focus through frequent membership changes, and evaluating member outcomes (Katch, 1983). When the purpose is expressed in a simple, direct statement like "The group helps us understand and deal with our handicapped child," new and potential members know what the topic of meeetings will be and what they can gain from participation. As members come and go, a clear purpose makes it possible for members quickly to identify their common interests and remain productive through transitions.

---

[2]Categorization of purposes and specific group examples are drawn from descriptions of open-ended groups in the professional literature and from the unpublished reports of practitioners to whom we have spoken.

Coping with Transitions and Crisis

Reports from the literature and practitioners indicate that open-ended groups most frequently pursue purposes related to helping clients cope with transitions and crises.[3] Through the open group system, mutual assistance and support are made available to clients who share similar life stresses resulting from a change (1) in status, (2) in physical condition, (3) in the family system, or (4) in the life cycle. Open-ended groups focusing on status changes ease entry into hospitals and nursing homes as well as prepare members for leaving prisons, psychiatric facilities, and residential treatment centers. Those dealing with changed physical conditions are offered to patients with cancer, progressive blindness, emphysema, burns, kidney disease, and rheumatoid arthritis, as well as recent surgery and stroke patients. Family members meet in open-ended groups to obtain help in coping with stresses related to the birth of a normal or handicapped child; remarriage or divorce; the illness, addiction, or emotional disturbance of a relative; or the hospitalization, institutionalization, or death of a loved one. Further, open-ended groups are used to help both adolescents and the elderly in dealing with developmental crises.

Groups formed to deal with particular transitions or crises not only offer members the opportunity to exchange perspectives and obtain information in a responsive, nurturing atmosphere but also stimulate problem-solving and the development of coping behaviors. Members experience relief when they know others share their problem. Expressing pent-up feelings related to the burden of a sick child or the embarrassment of a spouse's addiction reduces members' tensions. Exchanging information provides members with new strategies for dealing with problems such as adjusting to retirement or becoming a single parent. As a result of this sharing of experience, members feel more confident and able to confront their stressful situations. Further, as new members enter and old members leave, the group provides a model for dealing with transitions that can enhance each member's capacity for responding to external stress.

Support, Treatment, Screening, Education

While the most frequently mentioned purposes relate to coping with transitions and crises, many open-ended groups are designed for therapeutic purposes, support, and/or screening and orientation. Therapy may involve a psychotherapeutic examination of the past or refer to a more present-

---

[3]Our conceptualization of these purposes was facilitated by the work of Schwartz (1977).

oriented problem-solving approach. For psychotherapy groups, changing membership is at times excessively disruptive, and there is some indication that a focus on current concerns may be more productive in groups with frequent membership changes (Zabusky and Kymissis, 1983).

Support is seldom the sole purpose for a group but is often listed in conjunction with purposes related to coping, screening, and therapy. Some groups are designed primarily to assess clients or to prepare them for longer-term therapy, but screening groups may also offer information and function as support systems. At times supportive relationships developed during orientation sessions may enable clients to resolve their problems, and no further treatment is needed. Client education and orientation may be the primary purposes, providing information and facilitating the development of coping skills.

Although the purposes of open-ended groups are similar to those of groups with stable membership, open groups seem to be a particularly appropriate response to people facing life crises and transitions. Framing a purpose relevant to the needs and concerns of potential members is the first step in designing an open group. Further, purpose is a critical ingredient in effective group formation and development.

FORMING THE OPEN-ENDED GROUP

Open-ended group formation requires attention to the variables important in forming any group: The purpose based on clients' needs must be defined; optimal group size and the characteristics of potential members must be established; and group arrangements conducive to attendance and productive participation must be made. The differences in open-ended group formation are ones of repetition and emphasis. The decisions made in forming the initial group will provide a framework for responding each time membership changes and a new group comes into existence.

Member Recruitment

The purpose identified by the worker becomes the main criterion for determining group size and member characteristics. Whatever size seems desirable, one of the perennial frustrations of working with groups is uncertainty about how many members will attend any given session. Reports of open-ended groups indicate that workers can typically anticipate about five to twelve members at a meeting but should be prepared for as few as one or two and as many as twenty or more members (Schopler and Galinsky, 1984). Because there usually is no way to predetermine the actual composition of the group at any session, it is particularly important to attract a sufficient number of potential members. This increases the likelihood that attendance at each session will be adequate for group interaction. The optimal number of members recruited will depend on the relative frequency of member turnover. When member turnover is high, it may be desirable to have almost as many possible members as the preferred size of the group. With less frequent membership losses, the occasional addition of one or two new members may serve to maintain the group.

Self-Selection

Criteria for group composition are seldom discussed in the open-ended literature, but self-selection appears to be the predominant mode of composition. Since many groups tend to be voluntary, there seems to be an implicit assumption that if the group meets a need, potential members will come. Relatives of burn patients, for instance, are informed about a support group, and it is anticipated that they will attend if they want to express their concerns or obtain information. Some groups, particularly those established for residents of some treatment centers and inpatient facilities, appear to be less voluntary, and members may be referred, not self-selected. An adolescent entering a residential facility or a patient on a psychiatric ward would seem to have minimal choice about joining a group required as part of the "prescribed" treatment program. Some clients, such as child abusers, are court-ordered to attend.

Excluding Members

Even when group membership is voluntary, there are a number of reasons why individuals may be excluded. People who are negative about becoming involved and those who are denying their problems are not encouraged to attend, particularly when the group's focus is therapeutic. If these individuals have pressing needs, they can be addressed through alternative means, such as individual contacts. Group sessions may induce undue anxiety or resentment in some individuals; the presence of severely disturbed, resistant, or unwilling members may detract from the group's work.

Care must be taken in making the decision to exclude a potential member since there are beneficial results from bringing together people with mutual concerns about impending crises or transitions. As with self-help groups, members dealing with a common experience become peers, and differences in socioeconomic status, education, and occupation often seem unimportant (Sadock, Newman, and Normand, 1968; Levy, 1976). Facing the death of a child or dealing with the aftermath of surgery can be important common denominators. Inviting reluctant individuals to observe or participate in a single session may overcome their negative feelings if the group purpose addresses their needs. For some clients a "trial" session may be an alternative to exclusion (Ringler et al., 1983).

Length of Membership

People become members of open-ended groups for varying lengths of time. Some groups, such as aftercare groups designed to ease the transition from hospitals or residential treatment centers to the community, are often available as long as members feel they have a need or a reason to come. In other groups situational factors may determine attendance. An open-ended group on a psychiatric ward typically has constant turnover because of patient discharge; a waiting-room group involves relatives only for the duration of their family member's stay. In still other groups members may be asked to come for a predetermined number of sessions.

Overall, practitioners emphasize the unpredictable character of attendance in open-ended groups, even when expectations about length of attendance are given to potential members. The general presumption is that members attend as long as they find the experience useful, but there are a number of possible reasons why members terminate. They may leave the group because their needs are met, because they have been discharged from an institution, because they have attended the prescribed number of sessions, because they find group arrangements too inconvenient, or because they do not find the experience helpful.

Membership Transitions

Because changing membership is a dominant force in open-ended groups, practitioners must be prepared to help the group and individual members cope with the arrival and departure of members. Whether members come and go continually or infrequently, the change in composition is often unplanned. According to practitioners' experience and results of research, the impact of membership change can be expected to vary at different points in the group's life.

Groups typically require some time to adjust to any change in composition, whether it involves the loss of a member or worker or the addition of a new member or worker. Ongoing observation of an open-ended therapy group that met for several years, adding and losing members occasionally, indicated that the process of readjustment typically took about six weeks (Scher, 1973). In open groups where transitions are more frequent, the constant change may be accepted as a somewhat normal state—more unsettling to the worker than members who have no basis for comparison (Yalom, 1983). The available theory and evidence do support the assumption that in general groups are most disconcerted by membership change in the middle or later phases, when the members have become cohesive and the group has a defined structure. The antithesis also has some substantiation: Groups incorporate newcomers and deal with losses more easily in early phases before their structure has solidified (Ziller, 1965; Paradise, 1968; Dube, Mitchell, and Bergman, 1982). Before roles have become established, members tend to be less frustrated by change, because they have less attachment to departing members and fewer adjustments to make for newcomers. Further, when newcomers are self-selected and attracted to the group's purpose, they will fit more easily into the existing group structure, filling roles vacated by previous members. In like manner departing members who have had successful group experiences will be missed, but their accomplishments will add to the group's sense of wellbeing.

Establishing expectations and procedures related to change seems to soften its disruptive effects. While members' arrival and departure dates often cannot be predicted, groups can become accustomed to the inevitability of membership change and develop adaptive mechanisms for handling members' orientation and departure. When procedures for responding to member transition exist, change becomes normative and groups appear to have less trouble with assimilation and loss of members, no matter what the group's phase of development.

Entry and Exit Procedures

Although these assumptions about membership change have not been formally tested, they are compatible with what is known about current experience with open-ended groups, and they provide some direction for practitioners. A clear and relevant group purpose can attract motivated members who are easily integrated and who promote satisfaction when they leave. For minimal disruption, it is helpful to maintain a core group or nucleus to pass on group traditions and assist in orientation and termination rituals related to membership change (Hill and Gruner, 1973; Bailis, Lambert, and Bernstein, 1978); the worker must assume this leadership function at points of large turnover. When possible, it is recommended that member additions and departures be paced at regular intervals so the group is able to anticipate change (Singler, 1975). Further, groups need to establish appropriate procedures for dealing with the entry and exit of members (Williams et al., 1978; Yalom, 1983; Galinsky and Schopler, in press). In some groups members share responsibility for "sponsoring" new members and introducing them to the group. When a member leaves, many groups review progress and frequently celebrate the departing member's accomplishments. A restatement of the group's purpose is usually involved in welcoming newcomers and in bidding farewell to the old. Through these rituals the group reaffirms its validity and worth and reinforces expectations for its members, thus easing transitions.

Group Arrangements

In making group arrangements, the worker needs to find a meeting place that is easily accessible and conducive to interpersonal exchange. If the only convenient location is in an open area such as a waiting room then care must be taken so that the group does not invade the privacy of people who do not wish to participate (Bloom and Lynch, 1979; Ringler et al., 1981). The confidentiality of group proceedings should also be protected.

To ensure support for group efforts, individuals who may have significant contacts with potential or active members should be involved. Other staff, such as medical personnel, friends, and relatives, may play a critical role in encouraging or discouraging group attendance. Giving them an opportunity to gain understanding of the group's purpose may win a vote of confidence for the group and result in more active member participation. Member confidentiality should never be violated, although permission may be obtained from members to share selected group information with significant others. Other organizational supports may need to be developed in order to mobilize resources such as educational material, coffee, and meeting areas. Once factors related to formation, such as purpose, size, membership pool, procedures for change, and supportive group arrangements, have been considered, attention must turn to the factors impinging on the group's development.

OPEN-ENDED GROUP DEVELOPMENT, STRUCTURE, AND PROCESS

Practitioners often question whether groups with transient membership ever move beyond the initial phases of group development. Certainly the continual change in composition does provide justification for the concern that some open-ended groups do not move beyond formative issues. There is, however, substantial evidence that these groups progress and change in a cyclic fashion when some continuity is maintained.

Differing Levels of Attachment

In open group systems the group itself can make gains although individual members vary in their identification with the group and its process (Grosz and Wright, 1967; Bailis, Lambert, and Berstein, 1978; Copeland,

1980). Over time the group purpose may be validated by members' accomplishments; expectations for participation may be clarified through experience; and group norms supportive of the group's work and procedures to facilitate transition may become routine. When that occurs, the group is able to operate in an increasingly mature fashion despite fluctuations in membership. At any time, however, newcomers may be caught up in becoming part of the group; other members may be engaged in carrying on the group's work; and members preparing to terminate may have begun to withdraw (Scher, 1973). Thus development in open-ended groups does not have the unitary quality more characteristic of closed groups, where members begin and move through developmental stages together. While these differing levels of attachment to the group place a heavy demand on the worker, they appear to promote members' acceptance of change and ability to cope with transition.

Repetitive Cycles of Development

Because open-ended groups must continuously deal with issues related to beginning and ending during the course of development, frameworks that stress the cyclic, repetitive nature of groups are particularly useful. For example, Schwartz's conception of four phases (tuning-in, beginnings, work, transitions) provides a helpful perspective for understanding development in open systems (Schwartz, 1971). In Schwartz's view these four phases not only characterize the overall process of group development but also occur within a single session. Further, when Sarri and Galinsky's intermediate and revision stages are envisioned as constantly repeating, they provide a sense of the cyclic progress in open group development (see Chapter 5). As new members join or old members depart, the group experiences a period of revision; then, as the group re-forms, a new intermediate level of development is attained.

Continuation Effect

In open-ended groups that have a core of members who remain through periods of transition, there appears to be a "continuation effect" that supports group development (Hill and Gruner, 1973; Bailis, Lambert, and Bernstein, 1978). Through the process of orienting new members and terminating with those who are leaving, the engaged members can preserve and build on group gains. The frequent reiteration and reexamination of group purposes, norms, and expectations coupled with the recounting of group accomplishments builds a tradition that is passed on to newcomers. The group does not have to begin anew each time composition changes. Thus, while groups may experience temporary setbacks during transition, they do not necessarily remain at a beginning level. While a preponderance of incoming and/or outgoing members may slow development, groups with a stable core of members can approximate all the stages of normal development if they continue to meet for a long enough period. Even when such a nucleus is lacking, the worker can intervene and assist the group in its progression. Although each new arrival triggers a new cycle and raises formative issues, the group as a whole gradually develops more mature characteristics.

Impact of Transience

Certain features characteristic of open group systems appear to promote development. There tends to be a sense of novelty and excitement stimulated by the new ideas of incoming members. Frequent turnovers create pressure for members to reach decisions quickly. The focus is then task- and present-oriented, since members know their time together may be brief; for current members to see results, each session must be productive. Because of the transient nature of membership, the primary attachment is to the group and its purpose; relationships among members may be less intense than in closed groups and member roles are less entrenched (Yalom, 1983; Euster, in press).

Centrality of Worker

The fluidity of composition in open groups puts the worker in a more central position. As the only constant in the ebb and flow of member change, the worker has the main responsibility for carrying forward group tradition and providing the structure and information necessary for decision-making. Since members usually share a strong commitment to the group's purpose, they often welcome direction that facilitates their work together. When they are not able to take the initiative themselves, and if a core group is absent, practitioners find members expect and are responsive to a direct approach. Silent members speak up with the worker's encouragement to participate, and groups of relative strangers are capable of dealing with painful emotional content as the worker confronts issues directly and provides the appropriate guidance and support (Ringler et al., 1981; Euster, in press). When such intense interaction occurs, members may quickly form close bonds and even establish supportive networks to assist each other outside the group.

At each session the worker must "tune in" to determine the particular individual and group needs of the members present. If new members are present, the worker needs to ensure that norms and expectations for behavior in the group are repeated in clear and specific terms and that introductions include some statement of each member's stake in the group (Bednar and Battersby, 1976). If members are leaving or have left, accomplishments need to be reviewed and the sense of loss expressed. While these and other tasks may be assumed by "experienced" members or assigned, the worker must stand ready to take responsibility for easing transitions and directing the group's work. Thus the key ingredients for group development in open systems include a meaningful, clearly defined purpose, mechanisms for change, a continuing core of members, and an active, flexible worker who is able to direct as well as delegate.

It must be recognized that some open-ended groups do not move beyond an early stage of development. This may occur especially when there is frequent change and when a core of members is present only for short periods. The worker must then expect to retain the central position of leadership during the group's entire existence.

WORKING WITH OPEN-ENDED GROUPS

Practice wisdom points to the importance of the worker, the group, and the environment. Worker skill, a strong group tradition, and a supportive milieu are required to transform an open group system in a continuous state of flux into a productive, problem-solving network. Practice principles, grounded in experience, theory, and research, need continued refinement.

Worker Demands

The worker(s) must be prepared for ever changing membership; must be attuned to multiple developmental needs within a single session; must be able to define relevant purposes and establish necessary and realistic expectations for members that encompass procedures for dealing with transient membership; and must be able to develop a supportive environment for the group system. Any worker who can meet these demands must have skill in rapid individual and group assessment as well as a leadership style that is adaptive to changing conditions. At any point in the group's development the worker must have the ability to move into a central position to support group purposes, to activate group traditions, or to ensure the effective implementation of procedures for dealing with transition. Further, the leader must be able to play a less active, facilitative role if the group is able to manage its own activites. Because the requirements of conducting open-ended groups may create excessive strains for workers, it is often helpful to have co-leaders.

Group Demands

While open-ended groups can be sustained through formative stages with professional guidance, they cannot be expected to progress beyond this phase unless they develop a strong tradition that includes a sense of purpose, expectations for members' behavior, and mechanisms to respond to continuous change. To ensure that the group's legacy is passed on, it is especially helpful if a core of members is maintained when old members leave and new members enter. When the group's memory fails, the worker must prompt members to engage in rituals related to welcoming newcomers and evaluating the progress of members who are terminating. In any case, through exercises related to members' entry and exit the group reaffirms and clarifies its purposes and expectations.

Environmental Demands

A supportive milieu is essential to an open group system. Membership depends on consistent referrals and reinforcement for participation. Related staff must comprehend the group's purpose and their own relationship to the group if they are to make referrals and promote the group's potential. Friends and relatives of members may also need to be alerted to the group's importance if they are to encourage member involvement in the group. Cooperation of significant people in the group's environment can ensure that members attend and benefit from the experience and that learning, support, and reinforcement begun in the group continue following termination. Even facilitative room arrangements and scheduling may depend on the agency's approval and understanding of the group. Workers need to be sensitive to agency policy and prepared to adjust their plans while advocating for the needs of their clients. The smooth operation of an open-ended group and the achievement of positive outcomes for members require supportive relationships.

CONCLUSION

The dynamic quality of open group systems is an asset in providing service to clients. In an era of societal stress open-ended groups provide a mutual aid system that is adaptive to changing membership demands. They serve a variety of purposes and are especially suited for helping members deal with the crises and transitions that are such a frequent part of life today. Transient membership poses a challenge, but the spontaneous relief and creative solutions produced through members' interactions in open groups seem well worth the effort of structuring these experiences.

REFERENCES

BAILIS, SUSAN S.; SUSAN R. LAMBERT; AND STEPHEN B. BERNSTEIN
  1978 "The legacy of the group: A study of group therapy with a transient membership;" *Social Work in Health Care*, 10 (Winter): 405-18.

BEDNAR, RICHARD L., AND CHARLES P. BATTERSBY
  1976 "The effects of specific cognitive structure on early group development," *Journal of Applied Behavioral Science*, 12 (October–December): 513-22.

BLOOM, NAOMI DAGEN, AND JOSEPH G. LYNCH
  1979 "Group work in a hospital waiting room," *Health and Social Work*, 4 (August): 48-63.

COPELAND, HARRIET
  1980 "The beginning group," *International Journal of Group Psychotherapy*, 30 (April): 201-12.

DUBE, BEATRICE DOROTHY; CAROL ACKERMANN MITCHELL; AND LYNNE ANNE BERGMAN
  1972 "Uses of the self-run group in a child guidance setting," *International Journal of Group Psychotherapy*, 22 (July): 461-79.

EUSTER, SONA
  In press "Adjusting to cancer in an adult family member." In H. B. Roback (ed.), *Group Interventions with Medical-Surgical Patients and Their Families*. San Francisco: Jossey-Bass, pp. 1-34.

GALINSKY, MAEDA J., AND JANICE H. SCHOPLER
  In press "Open ended groups: Patterns of entry and exit," *Social Work with Groups*.

GROSZ, HANUS J., AND CARL S. WRIGHT
  1967 "The tempo of verbal interaction in an open therapy group conducted in rotation by three different therapists," *International Journal of Group Psychotherapy*, 17 (October): 513-23.

HENRY, SUE
  1981 *Group Skills in Social Work*. Itasca, Ill.: F. E. Peacock, pp. 301-18.

HILL, WILLIAM FAUCETT, AND LEROY GRUNER
  1973 "Study of development in open and closed groups," *Small Group Behavior*, 4 (August): 355-81.

INSKO, CHESTER A.; JOHN W. THIBAUT; DEBRA MOEHLE; MIDGE WILSON; WILLIAM D. DIAMOND; ROBERT GILMORE; MICHAEL R. SOLOMON; AND ANGELA LIPSITZ
  1980 "Social evolution and the emergence of leadership," *Journal of Personality and Social Psychology*, 39 (September): 431-48.

KATCH, MICHAEL
  1983 "Commentary," *Social Work in Health Care*, 8 (Spring): 121-24.

LEVY, LEON H.
  1976 "Self-help groups: Types and psychological processes," *Journal of Applied Behavioral Science*, 12 (July–September): 310-22.

PARADISE, ROBERT
  1968 "The factor of timing in the addition of new members to established groups," *Child Welfare*, 47 (November): 524-29, 553.

RINGLER, KAREN E.; HELEN H. WHITMAN; JAMES P. GUSTAFSON; AND FREDERICK W. COLEMAN
1981 "Technical advances in leading a cancer patient group," *International Journal of Group Psychotherapy*, 31 (July): 329–43.

ROSENBAUM, MAX (ed.)
1983 *Handbook of Short-Term Therapy Groups*. New York: McGraw-Hill Book Co.

SADOCK, BENJAMIN; LENORE NEWMAN; AND WILLIAM C. NORMAND
1968 "Short-term group psychotherapy in a psychiatric walk-in clinic," *American Journal of Orthopsychiatry*, 38 (July): 724–32.

SCHER, MARYONDA
1973 "Observations in an aftercare group," *International Journal of Group Psychotherapy*, 23 (July): 166–69.

SCHOPLER, JANICE H., AND MAEDA J. GALINSKY
1984 "Meeting practice needs: Conceptualizing the open-ended group," *Social Work with Groups*, Summer, pp. 3–21.

SCHWARTZ, MARC D.
1975 "Situation/transition groups: A conceptualization and review," *American Journal of Orthopsychiatry*, 45 (October): 744–755.

SCHWARTZ, WILLIAM
1971 "On the use of groups in social work practice." In W. Schwartz and S. R. Zalba (eds.), *The Practice of Group Work*. New York: Columbia University Press, pp. 3–24.

SINGLER, JUDITH R.
1975 "Group work with hospitalized stroke patients," *Social Casework*, 56 (June): 348–354.

WILLIAMS, JAY; CLAUDELINE LEWIS; FLORENCE COPELAND; LANDRUM TUCKER; AND LAURIE FEAGAN
1978 "A model for short-term group therapy on a children's inpatient unit," *Clinical Social Work Journal*, 6 (Spring): 21–32.

YALOM, IRVIN D.
1983 *Inpatient Group Psychotherapy*. New York: Basic Books, Inc.

ZABUSKY, GERRI S., AND PAVLOS KYMISSIS
1983 "Identity group therapy: A transitional group for hospitalized adolescents," *International Journal of Group Psychotherapy*, 33 (January): 99–109.

ZILLER, ROBERT C.
1965 "Toward a theory of open and closed groups," *Psychological Bulletin*, 64 (September): 164–182.

7

Socioeducation Groups

Norma Radin

SEVERAL MAJOR TRENDS with important implications for social group workers emerged in the late 1960s: (1) a burgeoning in the use of paraprofessionals in the helping and educational professions; (2) an increased emphasis on prevention in virtually all the people-serving professions; (3) greater resistance by those with limited incomes and/or minority status to be "treated" by social workers and to the assumption that they are impaired, if not ill, and in need of therapy; (4) rising expectations that all people share in the good life; and (5) the corollary expectations that professionals serve a large number of people rather than a select few. These trends suggest that the time may have come for group workers to examine the ability of their methodology to meet the needs of the coming decade.

Robert Vinter in 1959 took a controversial stand that called for a reordering of priorities of the late 1950s and urged group workers to give prime attention to the poor, the disadvantaged, and those with severe problems in social functioning. In keeping with this, the group work faculty of the University of Michigan School of Social Work developed a methodology focused on group services for these clients and trained hundreds of students in its use. Times and conditions have changed, however, and now there is greater professional commitment to expanding such efforts. The most pressing issue in the profession today is not who should be served first, but which is the most efficient and effective way to deliver service. Today in schools, community mental health centers, public welfare agencies, and residential settings, social workers are being asked to provide in-service training to small groups of paraprofessionals or to offer group consultation to professionals in other fields. Workers are also being asked to help "socializers" (teachers, day-care mothers, ministers, etc.) in their roles to facilitate the development of those for whom they are responsible. Requests are also being made to impart knowledge and skills to youths and adults who function adequately at present but are likely to have difficulties filling important future roles (i.e., as mothers or retirees). Social workers frequently are seen as professionals who can organize and lead these programs. Many accept the assignment reluctantly, because the emphasis in their training has not been on what they perceive as education. In some instances it does not occur to the agency executive or the group worker to take advantage of such opportunities.

Although direct service to the most distressed is still important, group workers must elaborate alternative methods for reaching more people in need; two such strategies are to offer consultation to the "caregivers" (i.e., foster mothers, nurses, parents, teachers) and the "socializers" of those with difficulties, and to provide service to those most in need before problems become severe and affect a network of people around them. These extensions are consistent with the original intent and the purposely open system of the Michigan practice model, as will be shown later.

To prevent the problem of reluctant, unprepared, or unaware social workers, a school can develop an orientation that is distinct from casework, group work, community practice, or administration. Portland State University School of Social Work has developed a program called "Facilitative Services" in which students are prepared for facilitative positions such as teaching, consultation, and supervision positions (Bontje and Longres, 1971). For interested second-year students the program offers courses of study and a practicum experience.

A different strategy is to train people outside the social work profession to serve as consultants, educators, or facilitators. The Community Mental Health Consultant, as described by Gerald Caplan (1969), fits this strategy, as does the Crisis Teacher depicted by Morse (1965).

Another path suggested in this chapter would prepare professionals in other fields for social group work with clients (such as teachers or nurses). This extends the Michigan model of group work to train workers at schools of social work to use the basic methodology of the Michigan model with relatively capable individuals, who would in turn work to improve social functioning of troubled or oppressed individuals. When the Michigan model is used with relatively capable individuals the label *socioeducational* (rather than treatment) *groups* will be used, as it highlights the importance of member interaction and input of knowledge (see Chapter 23) (Wittes and Radin, 1971; Bertcher et al., 1973).

Major changes in the practice model are not required. In work with both treatment and socioeducational groups, the group is perceived as a deliberately structured influence system that effects changes through interaction relationships. In both, the worker attempts to develop a group with maximum potential for influencing its members, and the group becomes both the medium and target for change. The basic principles of social group work that apply to treatment groups apply to socioeducation groups as well. The individual is the focus of change; the goals are specific, capable of being described operationally; and a contract is made between worker and group members specifying the focal areas and means to be used. Social forces within the group such as peer pressures, modeling, and group norms are used to obtain and maintain individual change, and extragroup means of influencing are used to facilitate the attainment of individual goals.

Four major types of direct means of influence are the same: The worker as (1) a central person and the object of identification; (2) a symbol and spokesperson of desired norms and values; (3) a motivator, stimulator, and definer of individual goals and tasks; and (4) an executive and controller of roles and activities. Relatively competent adults usually are able to share in these roles with the worker earlier than in a group composed of members with major social functioning problems. Such participation in the planning and operation of the group facilitates, rather than impedes, goal attainment in all groups.

Further, the indirect means of influence employed are virtually identical. Group, communication, sociometric, power, role, and normative structures are modified to maximize the attainment of individual goals. Group processes such as decision-making and group development are also influenced by the worker to achieve individual change.

An evaluation of the attainment of goals is made at the conclusion of the program, and the group is terminated in such a way as to assure maintenance of these goals. It is more likely that some socioeducational groups may go on to become agents of system change, in Cartwright's (1967) terminology, than do treatment groups. However, the desire for social action that developed in a group of low-income mothers (Wittes and Radin, 1971) is not unlike the desire for more patient self-government that develops out of small-group discussions among hospital patients or residents of group homes.

The major variations in emphasis and application of the Michigan model between work with socioeducational and treatment groups lie in five areas: (1) the worker's orientation, (2) the nature of the worker–client relationship, (3) group composition, (4) intake procedure, and (5) content of group discussions.

Work with socioeducational groups must not imply that the group member is inadequate or ill, or that pathology is involved. The use of treatment labels and terms (often considered generic to the profession) with group members is often dysfunctional to the achievement of individual goals in all groups, and particularly in those with a socioeducation orientation. In describing the nature of family life education Lois Glasser (1971) expressed the matter clearly when she differentiated the role of the family life educator from that of the traditional social worker. In family life education groups, she stated, membership is voluntary, the approach is educational, and the worker views himself or herself on an equal basis with the group members, learning from them as he or she teaches, and "building on strengths by imparting to the student additional knowledge and skills which the student is motivated to learn.'' Many group workers have had a similar orientation, but it clearly cannot be considered universal.

This egalitarian relationship is the heart of the worker–member relationship in socioeducational groups. In pragmatic terms, it is the only type of relationship likely to succeed between social workers serving as consultants-educators to caregivers and socializers such as groups of teachers, nurses, aides, or parents and to others not currently experiencing problems but who require or request help in the transition from one set of roles to another. It is certainly true that skilled and sensitive therapists can have egalitarian relationships with their clients, but Maier (1971), in a plea for a more peerlike relationship, suggests that equality does not typify most therapeutic interactions.

Further, many lower-class and middle-class adults do not view probes into their personal problems or inadequacies with equanimity. Those who have worked with low-income adults have found, on the other hand, that they tend to welcome opportunities to learn new skills and knowledge that will help them reach the goals they hold for themselves and their families. Perhaps the essential difference is that learning new skills is seen as education, whereas exploring personal inadequacies is perceived as therapy and tends to evoke client resistance. The scope of the change to be effected may also be relevant. Almost by definition, learning a new skill implies a minor alteration in one's way of life. Therapy sometimes suggests a major reorganization. Along the continuum between education and therapy, it is suggested here that work with socioeducational groups lies closer to the educational end, whereas work with treatment groups lies closer to the therapeutic end.

Differences in group composition involving the intake and the diagnosis phases are also significant to the practitioner. According to the Michigan model, the first phase customarily is that of intake, when the client presents himself or herself or is presented with his or her problem or need, as he or she and/or others perceive it. In the second phase the worker and client together diagnose the client's problem, his or her capacity for help and change, and then develop a statement of treatment goals, changes that can result if the treatment effort is successful. In the third phase the worker assigns clients to groups, composing them of persons whom he or she believes can be served together. One sentence in Vinter's delineation of the group composition phase suggests that the differences between composing a socioeducational group and a treatment group may not be as great as the following section will imply. "Under certain circumstances—as in work with delinquent street groups—the practitioner may exercise considerably less control over this phase (see Chapter 2). Sallie Churchill, in a personal communication in 1970, suggested that lack of control may exist even more frequently in treatment groups than the literature on the Michigan model suggests.

In composing all groups, the first step is the choice by the worker, and others involved in the program, concerning the target group, that is, the group to be offered a program. This decision involves selecting the nature of the problem to be dealt with and the specific goals to be achieved. The problem may vary from school failure to inability to adjust to widowhood. In reality the type of agency, its location, its resources, and community pressures, tend to highlight the specific problems that are most salient and thus limit the range of choices.

Another decision for those working with socioeducational groups is whether the program required is for individuals who are likely to have problems in social functioning in the future, or for socializers and caregivers of these individuals; for example, day-care mothers, classroom teachers, school aides, ministers, older siblings, and so on. Again, this choice is often limited by the prevailing context of practice. If the worker is employed by a welfare agency, it is often simpler to work with the caregivers, for example, the parent receiving Aid to Families of Dependent Children or the foster mother. If the worker is employed in a school, more options are usually available, such as direct work with children in trouble or likely to get in trouble, work with their tutors, their teachers and teacher-aides, their parents, or even their student teachers.

In composing socioeducational groups for preventive programs, one of three factors is usually given major consideration. The first pertains to demographic information such as the potential member's employment status, age, neighborhood of residence, and so forth. Geismar (1969) used this approach in his primary prevention program. The relevant issue is what data vividly predict future problems. A second variable is that of the potential member's entry into a new role such as that of parent, widow, disabled worker, or caretaker of an aged parent. Difficulties in role performance are likely to occur, according to Duvall (1962), when the role players are unfamiliar with the relevant expectations and knowledge. To gain such proficiencies, socioeducational groups can be very appropriate. The third factor given consideration as a predictor of future problems and an opportunity for prevention is a crisis, such as major surgery or the birth of a handicapped or premature baby. Caplan (1964) has discussed in great depth the opportunities for prevention in such situations. Goode's classic study of divorce (1956) suggests the conditions under which a divorce may also be characterized as a crisis and an ideal opportunity for programs in secondary or tertiary prevention.

In any of the above situations, socioeducational programs should be offered to all who fit the target group description, not merely those who visibly are having difficulties or who ask for help. Through this technique it is likely that the net tossed out will catch some highly skilled members who have little need for group service. These people are not excluded but welcomed into the group, since they can be highly effective as role models and developers of new norms, both in the group and among peers who are invited but refuse to join. A program is then developed around the persons who join the group.

If the characteristics of the target group have been carefully considered before the program is initiated and efforts to reach out to potential members have been made such as provision of transportation, several reminders, and refreshments, the worker should find a high percentage of potential group members who could benefit from the group work service. At the same time the danger of a negative effect from a member's having been especially selected because he or she has a problem is reduced. The group members can feel, justifiably, that they have voluntarily chosen to join a group to improve their knowledge and skills in a specific area.

A different approach can initiate a socioeducational group. An administrator may ask a social worker to conduct a series of in-service training sessions for the staff, professional or paraprofessional. Or the social worker may perceive the need and offer to do such training. Many social workers, for example, conduct in-service training programs for other professionals, such as nurses and teachers and their aides (Churchill and Glasser, 1965; Michigan Department of Education, 1971). Although voluntarism varies widely, membership should be as voluntary as feasible in such groups. It was found in one study (Chesler and Wissman, 1968) that when all teachers were given time off from their classroom duties and required to attend in-service training sessions, considerable resentment developed toward the program, because attendance was not self-chosen. Nonvoluntary groups may be effective where other opportunities for participation in groups or helping relationships are scarce, as with inmates of a correctional institution or children in school, but nonvoluntary membership in socioeducational groups tends to be irritating, if not antagonizing, to adults who perceive themselves as free to make decisions about their own life experiences.

Intake procedures of socioeducational groups may also have to be altered from those of treatment groups. While it may be possible to interview each member prior to organizing the first session of the group, in many situations an invitation is extended to a relatively large target population, such as workers soon to be retired, and the members are seen for the first time at the initial group meeting when a contract or agreement between members and worker is made. On occasion, if a member asks to see the worker individually or if the worker visits a member who missed a session, lengthy individual discussions can take place. Such interviews are not perceived as essential, however. An assessment of each individual's strengths and weaknesses, relative to the preestablished goals, can be based entirely on observations of member behavior during the group meetings themselves and on the informal discussions before and after the sessions. As the individual assessments gain clarity, goals can be specified for individual members. Some of these may pertain to in-group behavior, and others to out-of-group behavior. For example, in a program established for a group of day-care mothers (Green and Valenstein, 1971; Radin, 1970), the initial goals included an increase in the mothers' skills in managing the children and an increase in their perceptions of themselves as professional childcare workers. After several weeks, more specific goals were delineated for individual members. One mother was to increase her repertoire of discipline techniques to include strategies other than punishment; another was to participate more actively in the group discussions so that her creative child management techniques would become known to more women; for a third mother the goal was for greater honesty during the group discussions so that difficulties she was having with some children in her care (which consultants visiting the home had observed) could be discussed and group solutions suggested.

Ideally, after several weeks the worker will be able to determine terminal and intermediate goals for all the members, as well as goals pertaining to group behaviors. The worker must plan carefully to be certain that members who functioned exceedingly well before joining the group play an active part and help support other members in their movement toward the goals. As shown in the Provo study (Empey and Rabow, 1961), such group members are invaluable in creating highly desirable new norms that keep within the worker's goals for the group. Similar procedures have been used extensively with natural groups, such as neighborhood gangs and cottage groups in correctional and psychiatric institutions.

Frequently it has been found that after a series of socioeducational group meetings members feel an enhanced sense of efficacy and wish to use the new-found power to attain new goals for themselves; often the group decides to work as a unit to achieve change in a larger system to meet their needs (Gray and Klaus, 1970; Wittes and Radin, 1971; Badger, 1971) (see Chapter 23). This phenomenon has been observed with populations as diverse as low-income mothers, aged hospital patients, and parents of retarded children. The role of the worker when that stage is reached depends upon his or her own preference and organizational factors. If there is another agency or group available for the members to join, they may be helped to become integrated into the new group. Occasionally the worker may wish to continue working with the group on a reduced basis, decreasing his or her own contacts as the members develop their own leadership and begin to function independently. Under any circumstances it would be impractical and unwise to continue the group indefinitely.

Regarding the program of socioeducation group sessions, here the emphasis differs somewhat from that in treatment groups; the focus is not on the problematic behavior of the group member. Rather, it is only on the needs of the individual in the care of the socializer or on the role demands and potential role conflicts of persons likely to be experiencing a new role. The skills and knowledge needed by the caregiver to foster the development of the person being supervised occupy most of the meeting time. In both types of socioeducational groups specified content serves to guide the worker; for example, the material on childrearing developed by Karnes, Studley, and Wright (1966), Wittes and Radin (1968), Patterson and Guillon (1968), Becker (1971); the material on behavior modification for use by teachers (Buckley and Walker, 1970); or information about problems likely to be encountered in different life stages (Duvall, 1962). In some cases workers conducting socioeducation programs may have to create their own "curriculum" through a review of the literature, talks with experts, and use of their own experiences. The content to be imparted to socioeducational group members is a more important element in treatment groups.

It is possible to combine very effectively the treatment approach with the socioeducational approach. The combination has been highly successful in the cross-age program, developed by Peggy Lippitt (Lippitt and Lohman, 1965). In a cross-age program, students with problems in social functioning were asked to become tutors for younger pupils who were experiencing academic and/or social difficulties. Often some very competent students are included in the group of tutors. The tutors were informed that they were selected for the program because they possessed certain skills that were suitable. Once the program got under way, the tutors met weekly in a "seminar" with a special teacher or social worker to discuss their programs and problems as tutors. In essence the seminar was a socioeducational group for paraprofessionals who were caregivers for malfunctioning individuals.

The essential component of the cross-age program was in placing students with academic or behavioral problems in a new role, that of a helper to someone else in need. The net effect was to raise the tutor's self-image, enhance his or her empathy for other teachers, and stimulate his or her desire to learn so that he or she could be a more effective tutor. This strategy began with a treatment focus, since the members were selected carefully on the basis of their current difficulties as well as strengths. Beyond that criterion, however, the program functioned like any other socioeducational group for paraprofessionals, with the very act of playing the caregiver role being the essence of the helping process. The principle obviously can be extended to many other groups of malfunctioning individuals.

Several problems and unresolved issues related to work with socioeducational groups are evident. Determining which population is likely to encounter difficulties in social functioning based on demographic data, new role entry, or crisis situation is clearly a matter of judgment. No one can know for certain. All that the worker can do is examine the research literature carefully and try to obtain the most specific information possible about the characteristics and condition of those who develop problems. In some cases only correlational data are available from published articles and books. That is, a published report may state that a high correlation was found between characteristic A, such as low income, and behavior B, such as leaving school without a high school diploma. The correlation does not prove causality. It is possible that the behavior in some way caused the characteristic or that a third variable was responsible for both the characteristic and the behavior, for example, racism or the state of the economy. Nevertheless, those who wish to engage in preventive intervention must accept responsibility for formulating hypotheses concerning the type of people who are most vulnerable, and then proceed to design a program for those individuals. It is assumed that other social workers (such as community organizers), other change agents (such as community psychologists), and other groups in society (such as the Welfare Rights Organization, the Urban League, or the National Organization of Women) are working on the environmental factors that contribute to the problem (e.g. discriminatory legislation or employment practices). The group worker will attempt to alter the damaging environment where possible through extragroup means of influence. This may involve efforts to modify school procedures or welfare department regulations. But the group worker, like the caseworker, is involved essentially in modifying interpersonal relations and cannot attempt to effect change on all levels simultaneously. At best, those working on the same problem will cooperate closely so that the efforts of change agents attempting to intervene at the system level, the interpersonal level, and the community level will be coordinated.

Some damage might conceivably result from offering the wrong program to a group; for example, one that stimulates the curiosity of young potential drug users (Stuart, 1973). A more likely consequence of poor judgment in selecting a target group is that money and effort will have been wasted. There is no avoiding this risk, since human behavior cannot be predicted with complete certainty. To reduce disservice to group members, however, the worker about to embark on a preventive intervention program must review the literature as carefully as possible to be certain that he or she has the most recent information and is making use of hypotheses that are strongly supported by data.

Specifying goals for socioeducation groups is also difficult. If one wishes to increase the skills of a mother, classroom teacher, or aide in handling young children who are interfering with the activities of others, a wide array of behaviors might be increased. As mentioned by Sundel and Lawrence (1974) concerning goal setting in a preventive approach, when the objective of the worker is for a group member to add behaviors that are not in his or her current repertoire, it is more difficult to be specific than when the goal is to reduce the frequency of a currently held behavior.

It should be pointed out that group supervisory sessions conducted by leaders empowered to hire, fire, promote, and evaluate group members are not socioeducational groups. The power relationship between members and leaders is too unequal.

An issue that needs exploring is the difference in work techniques of an educator-consultant with individuals likely to experience problems, with paraprofessionals, and with professionals. Thus far, little differentiation has been made among the three groups. In one successful program in Tennessee, where low-income mothers were taught to become teachers to their children, it was emphasized that the women were treated as much like professional teachers as possible (Badger, 1971). Some day-care centers have deliberately created groups composed of parents and teachers to reduce the social distance between the two. Possibly, in this era of increasing community control of schools, day-care centers, and poverty programs, social workers cannot establish two distinct modes of functioning, one for vulnerable populations and one for socializers. The question is rather one of matching the program to the abilities and wishes of the group. At this point in the development of this approach it seems useful to perceive all members of socioeducational groups as competent adults wishing to enhance their knowledge and skills.

Perhaps the most debatable portion of this chapter is the assumption that a more educational approach is more acceptable to many people than treatment is. Potential members of socioeducational groups might be as resentful about the notion that they could benefit from more training as they are about the suggestion that they need treatment. Thus far, those who have used this approach have experienced that it does not engender hostility. Perhaps the voluntary nature of the group filters out those who might be resistant. Undoubtedly some people will refuse to become part of any type of group. For these individuals other programs will have to be developed.

In summary, a pressing need has arisen for those in the helping professions to supplement direct service to malfunctioning individuals with a program of preventive intervention and of consultative service with caregivers and socializers. Social group workers are ideally suited to perform these tasks since they are skilled in using group processes and structures to achieve specified goals for individual group members. Training social work students to use both the treatment approach and the suggested revision, emphasizing work with relatively competent adults, may be an important step in preparing graduates to function more effectively and flexibly in the coming decade.

REFERENCES

BADGER, EARLADEEN
1971 "A mothers' training program," *Children* 18, no. 5 (May): 168–73.

BECKER, WESLEY
1971 *Parents Are Teachers: A Child Management Program*. Champaign, Ill.: Research Press.

BERTCHER, HARVEY; JESSE GORDON; MICHAEL HAYES; MEL LAWSON; AND JEROME MUNSAY
1973 *Group Leadership Techniques: A Self-Instructional Workshop*, Ann Arbor, Mich.: Manpower Science Services, Inc.

BONTJE, AD, AND JOHN LONGRES
1971 "Introducing the social services educator training component within the social work master's degree curriculum." Paper read at the Council on Social Work Education, Seattle, Washington.

BUCKLEY, NANCY K., AND HILL M. WALKER
1970 *Modifying Classroom Behavior: A Manual of Procedures for Classroom Teachers*. Champaign, Ill.: Research Press.

CAPLAN, GERALD
1964 *Principles of Preventive Psychiatry*. New York: Basic Books.
1969 "Types of mental health consultation." In Warren Bennis, Kenneth Benne, and Robert Chin (eds.), *The Planning of Change*. New York: Holt, Rinehart & Winston, pp. 417–33.

CARTWRIGHT, DORWIN
1967 "Achieving change in people: Some applications of group dynamics theory." In Edwin P. Hollander and Raymond G. Hunt (eds.), *Current Perspectives in Social Psychology*. Second edition. New York: Oxford University Press, pp. 520–29.

CHESLER, MARK, AND MARGARET WISSMAN
1968 "Teacher reactions to school desegregation, preparations and processes: A case study," Center for Research on the Utilization of Scientific Knowledge, University of Michigan, Ann Arbor (mimeographed).

CHURCHILL, SALLIE R., AND PAUL H. GLASSER
1965 *Small Groups in the Hospital Community: Lectures and Proceedings*. Lansing: Department of Mental Health, State of Michigan.

DUVALL, EVELYN M.
1962 *Family Development*. Philadelphia: J. B. Lippincott.

EMPEY, LAMAR, AND JEROME RABOW
1961 "The Provo experiment in delinquency rehabilitation," *American Sociological Review*, 26: 678–95.

GEISMAR, LUDWIG L.
1969 *Preventive Intervention in Social Work*. Metuchin, N.J.: The Scarecrow Press.

GLASSER, LOIS
1971 "Family life and sex education." In Robert Morris (ed.), *Encyclopedia of*

Social Work. New York: National Association of Social Workers, pp. 386–92.

GOODE, WILLIAM J.
1956   *Women in Divorce*. New York: The Free Press.

GRAY, SUSAN W., AND RUPERT A. KLAUS
1970   "The early training project: A seventh-year report," *Child Development*, 41, no. 4 (December): 909–24.

GREEN, MELINDA, AND THELMA VALENSTEIN
1971   "The educational day care consultation program progress report," University of Michigan, School of Education, Ann Arbor (mimeographed).

KARNES, MERLE B.; WILLIAM M. STUDLEY; AND WILLES R. WRIGHT
1966   *An Approach for Working with Parents of Disadvantaged Children: Pilot Project*. Urbana: Institute for Research on Exceptional Children, University of Illinois.

LIPPITT, PEGGY, AND JOHN LOHMAN
1965   "Cross-age relationships: An educational resource," *Children*, 12: 113–17.

MAIER, HENRY
1971   "A sidewards look at change," *Social Services Review* 45, no. 2 (June): 132–36.

MICHIGAN DEPARTMENT OF EDUCATION
1971   *Packet: School Social Work Evaluation Study*. Lansing, Mich.: State Department of Education.

MORSE, WILLIAM C.
1965   "The 'crisis teacher': Public school provision for the disturbed pupil." In Nicholas J. Long, William C. Morse, and Ruth G. Newman (eds.), *Conflict in The Classroom*. Belmont, Calif.: Wadsworth Publishing Company, pp. 251–54.

PATTERSON, GERALD R., AND ELIZABETH M. GUILLON
1968   *Living with Children*. Champaign, Ill.: Research Press.

RADIN, NORMA
1970   "Evaluation of the daycare consultation program of 1969–70," University of Michigan, School of Social Work, Ann Arbor (mimeographed).

STUART, RICHARD B.
1973   "Teaching facts about drugs: Pushing or preventing," *Journal of Educational Psychology*, vol. 65, no. 2.

SÜNDEL, MARTIN, AND HARRY LAWRENCE
1974   "Behavior modification with adults in a family service agency." In Paul Glasser, Rosemary Sarri, and Robert Vinter (eds.), *Individual Change Through Small Groups*. New York: The Free Press, pp. 325–47.

WITTES, GLORIANN, AND NORMA RADIN
1968   *Helping Your Child to Learn: The Reinforcement Approach*. San Rafael, Calif.: Dimensions Publishers.
1971   "Two approaches to parent work in a compensatory preschool program," *Social Work*, 16, no. 1 (January): 42–50.

II

The Intervention Sequence

Regardless of the theoretical approach taken and the methods used, the helping process can benefit from a systematic guide. The readings in this section encompass a conceptual framework for the activities of a group work practitioner using a comprehensive approach to interpersonal helping. Those activities can be expressed in outline form:

1. Study and diagnosis (assessment)
   a. Intake and preliminary diagnosis
   b. Tentative service goals
   c. Decision for group service/other modality
   d. Initial helping contract
   e. Assignment to group (composition)
   f. Problem assessment and working diagnosis
   g. Intervention goals
   h. Intervention plan
   i. Helping contract
2. Intervention
   a. Direct means of influence
   b. Indirect means of influence
   c. Extragroup means of influence
3. Evaluation, termination, and follow-up

The outline is not intended to imply that the assessment and intervention processes occur as clearly separate and definable episodes in the course of treatment or service delivery. Although it is useful to distinguish diagnosis from treatment for analytic purposes, in practice neither can be viewed as entirely independent of the other. Any aspect of practitioner activity may have the potential of both eliciting new information and influencing the client. Recognizing this possible interactive condition, the practitioner analyzes intervention activities in relation to assessment data and evaluates their effects as a constant corrective to ineffective or even deleterious treatment.

The first chapter in this section presents diagnosis, or assessment, according to the Michigan group work model. Sundel, Radin, and Churchill describe the practitioner's assessment of the client's situation as a prerequisite to both treatment and preventive intervention. The authors discuss diagnosis as a procedure and statement of the client's present or potential problems at a given point in time, including assessment of variables and events that the practitioner assumes gave rise to the problems, contribute to their maintenance, or are likely to be assets or barriers to the client's successful problem-solving. The client's problems may be located at the personal, interpersonal, or environmental level, and often they exist at more than one of those levels. Use of the group in formulating diagnostic appraisals of members involves the practitioner's observations of the manner in which members participate and interact with others. Role-plays can be structured to observe client responses and compare them with other assessment data. The authors also provide an outline of procedural guidelines for diagnosis in group work.

The formulation of goals is a significant aspect of group work practice addressed by Schopler, Galinsky, and Alicke in Chapter 9. The authors examine goal-setting from both the worker's and the client's perspectives operating within a two-phase process. During the exploratory phase the practitioner and group members explore their common and conflicting interests to establish a basis for mutually acceptable goals. During the second phase the group engages in bargaining to determine which goals will be accepted and how they will be implemented. The specific goals selected guide individual and group efforts, influence member motivation, direct worker intervention, and provide a primary basis for judging the effectiveness of group services.

In Chapter 10 Croxton defines the treatment contract as "an agreement between two or more individuals in which there must be mutuality of understanding concerning the targeted behavioral problems, reciprocal obligations relating to treatment means, and agreed-upon formulation of treatment goals." Drawing from the perspectives of legal history, traditional social work practice, social science theory, and research, the author examines and clarifies the components, negotiation processes, and developmental stages of therapeutic contracts and their use in groups.

Bertcher and Maple, in Chapter 11, explore key elements and issues involved in forming effective treatment groups. The descriptive and behavioral attributes of individuals are considered in relation to the group's objective, as well as how such attributes could be critical for member roles related to group functioning and goal-oriented task performance. Characteristics of effective groups and barriers to group effectiveness are described, based on research findings, behavioral science, and practice knowledge. Using information on potential members of a proposed group, the authors demonstrate how the practitioner's appraisal of critical attributes and decisions about matters of time, place, and size in consideration of specific group objectives can be applied to compose a group of interactive, compatible, and responsive members.

In Chapter 12 Garvin provides a framework for analyzing aspects of group process in relation to selected group problems. Describing group processes, Garvin focuses on the identification of selected group conditions (for example, role differentiation, norm development) and examination of changes in those conditions that take place over time. That conception is contrasted with the traditional global use of the term "group process" as an ambiguous force that positively influences members as they interact with each other and the practitioner in the group. The author describes aspects of group process according to a typology of goal-oriented activities of the group and quality of interactions among the members. Those activities and interactions are considered at both an overt and a covert level. The purpose of the conceptual scheme is to help practitioners target group conditions for change in order to ameliorate a group-level problem or to enhance group functioning.

Chapter 13, by Robert Vinter, describes the use of program activities as an indirect means of influence in which the practitioner can determine the choice and quality of group activities to influence both participants and group processes. Program is defined as "a general class of group activities, each of which consists of an interconnected series of social behaviors that usually is infused with meanings and guided by performance standards from the larger culture." Addressing the problems experienced by practitioners in selecting specific activities to achieve particular treatment objectives, the author presents a framework that can be used in analyzing program activities, making choices among them, and modifying them for particular purposes or situations. Using this scheme, Vinter analyzes two types of activities and suggests how the practitioner can obtain different effects for participants by increasing the level of competence, by altering the rules, or by decreasing participant interactiveness.

Whittaker focuses on the selection and use of program activities for children in residential treatment settings. He identifies eight types of program participants according to the possible combinations of their ratings (low or high) on the individual variables of skill, motivation, and control. Using the six activity-setting dimensions proposed by Vinter, the author provides a rating scheme for analyzing and comparing twenty-three common program activities. The scheme can be used to identify specific activities that may be particularly appropriate or particularly unsuitable for certain types of participants. An ideal activity profile is provided in Chapter 14 for each of the eight types of participants; it indicates the optimal ratings for each in relation to the activity-setting dimensions. Whittaker also discusses specific program suggestions and techniques for childcare workers in residential treatment settings.

In Chapter 15 Mayadas and Glasser examine termination as a significant phase of group development that sets the tone for transfer of knowledge and skill to new and more challenging situations in the natural environments of members. The authors provide a conceptual, interactional model for examining the dynamics associated with group termination, a set of observable criteria to analyze both the phase and processes of termination, and a review of intervention strategies to deal with member reactions to termination. The model can be used in conceptualizing both planned and unplanned group termination for rehabilitation groups, treatment groups, and task groups.

8

Diagnosis in Group Work

Martin Sundel, Norma Radin, and Sallie R. Churchill

THE TERM DIAGNOSIS, or assessment, refers to a professional appraisal
made by a social worker of a client's situation. The assessment is based on
information gathered by the worker and is oriented toward formulation of
specific client goals and an intervention plan. The intervention plan is directed toward attainment of the specific goals. The approach considered
here is based on the Michigan goal-oriented group work model for achieving change at the individual level. Accordingly, the objectives of social work
service are twofold: (1) to solve explicit problems defined by the client, significant others, or a referral source and (2) to reduce the likelihood that
problems will occur by preparing clients lacking requisite skills or knowledge for new roles or for changing demands of old roles. The first objective
describes the treatment orientation; the second, the preventive orientation.
This chapter updates an earlier paper on group work diagnosis according to
the Michigan model (Sarri et al., 1967).

An essential step in both treatment and preventive social work is the
worker's assessment of the client's present or predicted problems. In making a diagnosis the social worker seeks to organize knowledge about the client that can be used to focus interventions effectively. Having organized
this information, the group worker can then use other group members and
the external environment to execute a goal-directed strategy to improve the
client's social functioning. Diagnosis and treatment are elements of an overall process that begins with initial contact between the client and the agency
and ends when service is terminated.

Although it is useful to distinguish diagnosis from treatment for analytic purposes, in practice neither can be viewed as entirely independent of
the other. To determine whether a client will benefit from one specific treatment, the worker must have a clear understanding of the client's problems.
The same information that provides specific direction for intervention and
treatment also serves as a basis for evaluation of change or lack of it.

Historically, diagnosis has involved a continuing search aimed at understanding the problem of the individual within his or her environment.

117

Two contrasting theoretical perspectives have been employed: (1) *the environment* has been viewed as the primary source of problems, with treatment directed at modifying environmental conditions, and (2) *the individual* has been seen as the primary target for change, with the environment serving as a constant against which individual problems could be examined. From the latter perspective treatment has been aimed mainly at changing personality structure. Recent practice and theory emphasize the need to understand the individual in a *specific* environment. The dynamic interaction between the individual and the environment has been recognized and assessed; the individual's problems are assumed to be a function of this interaction.

Social work practice has been eclectic in developing practice principles about individual behavior and environmental influences. Social workers believe that multiple perspectives are necessary to understand human behavior adequately. No single body of knowledge provides this kind of "total" understanding. Social work principles are derived from the various social, behavioral, and biological sciences, including learning theory, ego psychology, social psychology, sociology, cultural anthropology, economics, political science, anatomy, and physiology. Although some theoretical inconsistencies may exist, it is necessary to draw from all of these disciplines, for the social worker assumes that the problematic behavior of clients has multiple causes and influences. Learning theory and the concept of role have been particularly helpful in developing precise diagnoses of clients in ways that lend themselves to relatively effective technologies of change.

An eclectic approach is useful because of the great variety of situations that can hinder or block a client's effective functioning. A client may lack the social, psychological, cognitive, or physical resources required to maintain adequate role performance or to assume new roles. Patterns of performance that are effective in one set of conditions may become problematic when circumstances change. Persons who perform satisfactorily for many years, for example, can face severe stresses when they retire from full-time employment. Similarly, a serious physical illness may lead to social malfunctioning in one or several roles.

Current or predicted problems may be located at an intrapersonal, interpersonal, or environmental level, and often they exist at more than one of those levels. For example, at the intrapersonal level a husband may feel inadequate about his sexual capacity; at the interpersonal level he may be having conflicts with his wife about childrearing; and at the environmental level he may be unable to provide for his family because of periodic unemployment. Each of the husband's difficulties may be unrelated to the others, or the problems may be manifestations of a single problem, the difficulties being interrelated in a complex manner. In developing a treatment strategy, the worker might focus on any one or more of these levels to change the relevant behaviors and conditions.

The focus here is on stresses and difficulties that are manifested in observable behaviors and environmental conditions. To be sure, statements reflecting attitudes and feelings should be considered, especially when they are problematic to clients; however, such subjective states are best described in terms of their behavioral manifestations. Specific behavior is the object of diagnostic concern to the worker; explanations of behavior can be sought at the intrapersonal, interpersonal, or environmental level, or any combination thereof.

The theoretical orientation of the worker will influence the nature of the data that he or she considers necessary to collect. The large majority of clients who reach social work agencies, however, manifest problems of social deviance or are seen as likely to by themselves and others (see Chapter 3). Goals for them must be set in behavioral terms for two reasons. The problems are usually described in behavioral terms, e.g. truanting and fighting, and only with expressed behavioral goals can the community objectively evaluate the professional's effectiveness. Accountability is becoming increasingly viewed as important to demonstrate in practice (e.g. Bloom and Fischer, 1982). Whatever the practitioner's orientation, his or her diagnosis must be related to specific behavior goals.

THE DIAGNOSTIC PHASE
IN THE CHANGE SEQUENCE

The concept of diagnosis was introduced into the literature of social work as early as 1917 by Richmond, and since then it has been employed in a variety of ways:

1. As a procedure in which the social worker and the client collect and synthesize information regarding the client's condition
2. As a statement of the client's condition and the ways in which the client's environment and personality affect it
3. As the assignment of a formal typology to an individual and his or her condition

In social work the first two meanings are used.

Diagnosis is viewed as a distinct phase in the change sequence in the Michigan model. Specific intervention plans such as planned worker activities are produced directly from diagnostic statements. Prior to intervention a worker develops a diagnosis of specific problems or situations in order to form the basis for the worker's activities and for subsequent evaluations of the strategy to elicit change. Data-gathering is focused on contemporaneous influences on the client's situation, as opposed to early historical influences in the individual's life. Past experiences are considered, however, when they exert an influence on the client's current behavior.

The worker's diagnosis provides the basis for planning and implementation of an intervention strategy. In some instances, after diagnosing the client's situation, the worker may conclude that intervention is not indicated or that the appropriate service cannot be provided by the worker's agency. This presents the ethical consideration of determining properly whether a client's situation requires social work services and, if so, by whom is it best offered.

Although diagnosis involves a continuous assessment of the client's situation, the emphasis here is on the *diagnostic phase*, that is, the period from intake to the formulation of the worker's change-directed intervention strategy. The term *diagnostic procedure* will be used to indicate the activities carried out by the worker, which result in a written *diagnostic statement*. The diagnostic procedure includes the "how to" aspects of collecting pertinent information for the diagnosis; the diagnostic statement includes the content of the "what" of diagnosis. This presentation will focus primarily on the content of diagnosis and on the information required in a diagnostic statement, but some attention will also be given to the diagnostic procedure.

Diagnosis as Procedure and Statement

The diagnostic procedure includes client and worker activities aimed at collecting and synthesizing information that will enable them to set specific intervention goals. The worker sets down those goals in writing as part of the diagnostic statement. Interaction of the client and worker with others may be a necessary part of this procedure. Considering the significance and importance of the collected data is essential. During diagnosis the client and worker determine, by careful examination, the nature of the client's problem(s) in relation to the agency's helping resources.

The diagnostic statement represents the worker's judgment of the client's present or potential problem(s) at a given point in time, including assessment variables that the worker assumes gave rise to the problem(s), contribute to the maintenance of the problem(s), or are likely to be barriers to the client's successful problem-solving. The variables are viewed individually as well as collectively to assure that interactive influences are identified. In addition to the known data the worker may specify what additional data are required to assess adequately the client's problems.

The diagnostic statement guides the worker's intervention effort by providing boundaries, relevance, and direction. Essentially, it represents a set of hypotheses about the client's behavior. Necessarily, such a guide is written with an awareness of agency resources, the length of time available for service, and the characteristics and skills of the worker. The importance of the written statement cannot be overemphasized; without it the social worker is likely to lack direction and to be more subject to the influences of immediate events than is desirable.

Diagnosis is a dynamic and continuing process. At any stage in the helping process worker intervention may serve to effect change in client behavior and to obtain additional data in order to increase diagnostic understanding of the client. While the practitioner seeks to prepare an accurate, differential diagnostic statement for initial planning, new circumstances will continue to arise. The worker must continue the diagnosis with the client and frequently may need to modify parts of the diagnostic statement. The diagnostic phase is an arbitrary division of the intervention sequence, useful for analytic purposes only.

Following the initial diagnostic phase, diagnostic activity is no longer the primary focus of the worker; however, frequent evaluation of progress takes place between the client and the worker and, in a group, among members. Such mutual evaluations serve as one important source of new data.

Components of the Diagnostic Phase

Three components of the diagnostic phase are (1) conducting the intake interviews, (2) formulating the initial assessment, and (3) preparing a diagnostic statement. The *intake interview* provides an opportunity for the worker to assess the client's suitability and desire for service from a particular agency and for social group work in general. Factors to be considered are the type of problem presented, agency location, and client attitudes toward the various agencies offering similar service. In addition the worker evaluates the skills of the client that could be used as a model for appropriate behavior by other members of a group. Group work service tends to be most appropriate when the client's concerns are of an interpersonal nature or are related to peer conflicts.

The *initial assessment* is a tentative diagnosis based upon information obtained from the referral source and from the client during the intake interview. It includes the client's presenting problem, tentative goals, and the worker's rationale for group work service. The initial assessment provides the focal point for obtaining appropriate information for the more detailed diagnostic statement.

An early requirement in problem assessment is the examination of the client's present situation. In this effort the *presenting problem*—the verbalized reason given for the client's election or referral for social work service—provides a basis for study of various current role performances. The worker identifies how presenting problems are defined, by whom they are defined, and what aspects of the individual and the environment are involved. Problems may be differentiated by varied perceptions:

1. The client's manifestation of stress or dissatisfaction in role performance
2. Ineffective role performance as viewed by others (e.g. parents, teachers) in the client's environment
3. The practitioner's judgment, based on his or her observations of the client's role performance problems

Intake situations greatly test the skills of the social worker. People who seek help often are overwhelmed by the multiplicity, severity, or confusion of their problems. People who are sent to social workers often fear, deny, and/or are very ashamed of "their problems." Often clients will test the worker's reactions to fantasized problems before trusting the worker enough to reveal their critical concerns. Some clients may try to guess the acceptable symptoms to present in order to receive agency services. To assess significant aspects of the problem, the social worker should observe sufficient examples of the client's behavior during interviews and in the group, that is, how the client sits; the client's tone of voice; when the client changes the subject, smiles, cries, and so on. The worker has the very difficult task of corroborating the problem(s) for which the client seeks (or is sent for) assistance. The starting point is the presenting problem, which is the focal point for initial worker–client interaction but may or may not be the primary focus of treatment at the conclusion of the diagnostic process.

Before gathering specific information during the diagnostic phase the worker might have to concentrate on establishing a trusting relationship with the client. This is particularly important in open community settings such as lower socioeconomic neighborhoods, where workers must reach out to clients in order to provide services. In such situations the worker's actions, languages, mannerisms, and personal qualities should be directed toward establishing a trusting relationship with the client—a prerequisite for any intervention program. Those efforts may take hours or months and may take place in groups or in one-to-one relationships. They are intended to culminate in the client–worker agreement on the goals and conditions for worker services.

In typical situations identifying information is obtained directly from the client in the intake interview, and from significant others and/or from referral sources, prior to or shortly following the first client interview. Pertinent information varies depending on the facts considered critical by the agency. Prior to placement in a formed group an individual intake interview is held to formulate an initial assessment and to determine the client's suitability for group or individual service. In the case of natural groups the worker can observe the group and also interview clients individually in making the initial assessment.

The essential decision at intake is whether the agency and potential client are agreed that the individual will become a client at that agency. Diagnosis then builds on the initial assessment and focuses on goals related to the resolution of presenting and other identified problems and on how social work service can proceed.

Problem Identification

Since social work is directed toward specifying behavioral goals, the diagnostic procedure, as outlined, relies heavily on social role and learning theory approaches. Emphasis is on helping clients change their social functioning by identifying their roles and specifying the behaviors related to the roles that have led to are are likely to lead to the client's difficulty. This method of analysis is not meant to limit or constrain the practitioner's intervention techniques. Rather, the procedure opens up the possibilities of a greater variety of intervention approaches, which can be evaluated responsibly by the client, the professional, and the community.

During the intake interview the worker should record the problem presented by the client in the client's words; the same rule applies to initial interviews with the referral source. A teenager in a training school might indicate failure to get along with friends as a problem, whereas the referring authorities might view the youth's problem as that of physically injuring other children. In order to illustrate the stated problem, examples should be obtained that provide concrete representations of the client's and referral source's perceptions of the situation.

When preventive services are provided, the term "presenting problem" can be misleading, since the focus of service is on improving the knowledge and skills of clients. For example, groups may be formed to help parents foster their children's preparation for school. Parents whose educational background is low might wish to learn more effective ways of guiding, teaching, and communicating with their children. In these cases the term "client's service goals" or "predicted problems" might be more appropriate.

Target Roles and Behaviors

After the problem, present or predicted, has been identified, the most relevant client role is determined. Such a role could be that of parent, spouse, employee, friend, or student. The identification of this *target role* provides a framework for delineating the client behaviors to be acquired, maintained, increased, or decreased in order to attain adequate role performance. Early specification of target roles enables the worker to scan, effectively and efficiently, the domain of possible concerns that the client brings to the agency. This also could save the worker considerable time and effort expended in irrelevant data-gathering and investigation.

After identifying the target roles, *target behaviors*—the behaviors likely to be the focus of intervention—are selected and then ranked in order of their importance. In determining the priority for service the worker should consider the following criteria:

1. The most immediate expressed concern of the client
2. The behavior that has most extensive aversive consequences for the client, significant others, or society, if not handled
3. The most immediate concern expressed by the referral source
4. The behavior that can be handled most quickly and/or effectively
5. The behavior that must be dealt with before others can be handled

In considering these criteria, the worker should involve the client, the referral source, and others whenever possible in determining the priorities for service. Checklists including a variety of roles and problem areas can be used to help the client prioritize the behaviors to be investigated (e.g. Rose, 1981; Sundel and Lawrence, 1974, pp. 341–42; Sundel and Sundel, 1982, p. 83).

Behavioral Specification and Analysis

Analysis of the target behaviors selected for service involves delineation of the client's inappropriate or deficient responses, their antecedents, and their consequences. The client's behavior should be described in terms that clearly specify the client's verbal and motor responses in affirmative, observable terms. Negatively stated descriptions such as "John is not doing his homework" are insufficient, since they fail to describe what the client is doing other than his homework. Therefore, negative statements should be accompanied by descriptions of what the client is doing in the problematic situation. In that example an appropriate description might be, "John is watching television when he should be doing his homework."

Behavior that is judged by the client or others as problematic usually indicates either a behavioral deficit or a surfeit. Behavioral deficits exist when appropriate behaviors are absent or infrequent; behavioral surfeits are inappropriate behaviors. Examples of deficient appropriate responses typically include smiling, talking, attending work regularly, or turning in class assignments that are performed insufficiently; examples of maladaptive surfeit behavior often include lying, stealing, truanting, fighting, or crying. In addition, behavior might be judged as problematic when it occurs under inappropriate conditions, e.g. walking around in one's undershorts might be appropriate in the privacy of one's home but inappropriate in the lobby of a hotel (Staats and Staats, 1964; Ferster, 1965).

Labels such as "hostile" or "passive-aggressive" are insufficient to describe accurately a client's behavior or speech in a specific situation. These terms lack sufficient explanatory value and often are unnecessary when observed descriptions of the client's behavior are made. If such labels are used, they should be accompanied by explicit descriptions of the client's performance that justify their use.

Although levels of specificity vary in describing a response, the basic criterion for description should be that of delineating the response in observable terms. For example, if a mother complained that her son John was "physically aggressive" with his brother, it is unclear as to how he is "physically aggressive." Where did he hit his brother? Was it with his hand or with a weapon? A more acceptable description might be, "John pushed his brother and knocked him to the ground." Thus a stranger reading this description would be provided with a concrete, observable instance of John's "physical aggression" with his sibling.

Determining Behavioral Magnitude and Severity

A useful way to determine the magnitude of a behavior is to count its frequency of occurrence within a given time period or to measure the duration of its occurrence for each incident. This information is referred to as baseline data. For example, "Harold completed two out of three school assignments this week." "Sally cried at the dinner table for fifteen minutes on Tuesday and twenty-five minutes on Friday." Sometimes when a client, a worker, or another individual records and keeps a chart of a behavior that has been labeled problematic, it is found that the behavior occurs less frequently than was originally stated by the client or referral source. This discrepancy can be discussed with the client so that perhaps subsequent attention is given to pursuing other behaviors that in reality give greater cause for concern.

A recording method called *time sampling* is sometimes indicated "where behaviors occur at extremely high rates, are difficult to observe continuously, or cannot be broken down into small discrete units; for example, babbling, nail-biting, or nonattending. Time sampling involves recording behavior at certain times during the day rather than continuously. This method will give an accurate count of behaviors when extended over long periods of time" (Buckley and Walker, 1970). During this sampling an observer records the occurrence or nonoccurrence of a response during a series of predetermined intervals.

The intensity, force, or severity of behaviors, such as punching, screaming, kicking, or crying, are usually difficult or impractical to measure, although instruments that can measure these behaviors in physical units, such as decibels, are available in a laboratory setting. The crucial feature of these behaviors, however, involves the negative consequences or effects these behaviors have for the client, others, or society. Because individuals differ in their tolerance for the behavior of others as well as in their own reactions to stimulation, examining the negative consequences of a client's behavior provides a basis for judging the severity of the behavior. For example, the severity of Sam's "tapping" a classmate is indicated by his victim's bruises or complaints to a teacher. When problems occur infrequently, such as violent arguments between marital partners, the severity of the argument is usually judged by the negative consequences occurring to each person or to others as a result of the argument. Stuart (1980) suggests that higher frequency "microbehaviors" (for example, daily disagreements or insensitivities of one spouse toward the other) also be monitored, since they often can become intensified over time to set the stage for more severe incidents. A client's behavior can produce short and/or long term consequences for the client and/or others, and all possibilities should be considered. For example, Sam's use of obscene language in class might produce the short-term consequence of approval from his classmates, but it might later lead to suspension from school and failure to obtain desired employment as an adult.

Specification of Antecedents and Consequences

After specifying a client's response in a problematic situation, the worker should investigate the antecedent and consequent conditions related to the behavior needing to be changed. *Antecedent* refers to an event that precedes or triggers a specific behavior, so that the existence or onset of the event is related directly to the performance of the behavior. For example, the antecedent for Bob's striking Joe could be Joe's calling him "stupid." A second antecedent might have been urging by two friends, prompting Bob to hit Joe. As indicated by these examples, antecedents should be described with the same degree of specificity as the responses that they preceded. Traditionally antecedents have included early historical events that are presumed to influence the client's current behavior. Inferred socioemotional states such as "low self-image" or "feelings or insecurity" also have been cited as antecedents to problematic behavior. Emphasis is placed on the importance of observable antecedents that are related functionally to the occurrence of specified behavior. If an inferred or hypothetical statement is made, specific behavioral examples are essential. To illustrate, low self-image may be indicated by the client's looking down at the floor when spoken to by peers.

Consequence refers to an event that follows a behavior. *Reinforcement* occurs when consequences increase the probability of that behavior's recurring. Descriptions of reinforcing consequences require the same level of specificity as descriptions of antecedents and responses. For example, if Judy screams when asked to do the dishes and her mother hugs her and does the dishes herself, the reinforcing consequences of Judy's screaming are her mother's hugging her and doing the dishes. These events reinforce Judy's screaming so that the likelihood of Judy's screaming when asked to do the dishes in the future is increased. This assessment of the reinforcing aspects of the mother's behavior could be incorporated in a treatment plan to decrease Judy's screaming and noncompliance when asked to do the dishes by instructing her mother to withhold hugs and not do the dishes.

At times certain reinforcing consequences might be discovered to follow a target behavior intermittently. Then it is important that the worker determine the pattern of when the reinforcers follow the behavior, for the schedule of reinforcement can provide information regarding the maintenance of the behavior (e.g. Ferster and Skinner, 1957). If Judy's mother sometimes did the dishes and hugged her when she screamed but ignored her screaming on other occasions, Judy's screaming would be more resistant to extinction, because it has been intermittently reinforced (Buckley and Walker, 1970, p. 50).

Unless the worker understands the multiple antecedents and consequences of behavior, he or she may have an oversimplified explanation for a client's difficulty. Sarah may be truant from school only when (1) she has failed a test the previous day, (2) she has had an argument with her mother about her poor school performance after returning from school, (3) she interprets her mother's criticism as rejection of her as a person, (4) she meets friends on the way to school who suggest that they skip school together, and (5) there is something attractive to do in the community, like a new movie. Following her absence from school she may regard the criticism from her mother and school officials as further punishment. As the rewards of truancy increase and the punishment of the school experiences increase, fewer antecedents and consequences may be required to lure Sarah into repeating the truant behavior.

In the example above some of the antecedents and consequences of behaviors that are interpreted by others as antisocial involve the client's thinking process. Staats and Staats (1964) refer to these antecedents and consequences as implicit responses that are typical antecedents of most observable behavior. Sometime they can be inferred through observation or confirmed through careful interviewing. In addition, this concept highlights the importance of considering the subjective interpretation of any behavior by the client and others. Many practitioners have encountered children who seek punishment through antisocial behavior in order to get the attention such behavior elicits. What the general community interprets as punishment the child interprets as rewarding, because the child believes that he or she cannot get attention in any other manner.

Sometimes the client and worker wish the client to acquire, increase, decrease, or eliminate certain sequences or chains of responses. Such chains, which occur in learning to talk or to drive, often include both observable and implicit responses in a particular order (Staats and Staats, 1964). In the case of Sarah's truancy, unless each of the five antecedent stimuli and response patterns occurred in the order given, it may have been unlikely that Sarah would have been truant.

Finally, sometimes a client's behavior may have as antecedents a series of behaviors in which the client has not been directly involved at all. The well-known example of the father who gets angry at the mother, who gets angry at the oldest child, and so on until the youngest child kicks the dog, is illustrative. The practitioner may have to trace the stimuli leading to—or the reinforcers of—client behavior to the behavior of others in the client's social environment, such as the actions of family members, for some time before or after the target behavior of the client. For this reason interaction and/or social systems analysis may be useful in understanding and dealing with the client's behavior.

The practitioner is urged to determine the antecedents and consequences of the client's target behavior, although this is not always an easy process. The determination of antecedents and consequences facilitates accurate diagnosis and the development of the intervention plan.

DIAGNOSIS IN THE GROUP

The social group worker's distinctive contribution in diagnosis and treatment grows out of the worker's observation of the individual within the context of the diagnostic or treatment group. When feasible, target behaviors and their antecedents and consequences should be verified by observation of spontaneous behavior in the group. The client as a group member not only interacts with the worker but, typically, does so in the presence of peers. Of equal importance, the client interacts with peers in the presence of the worker. The group worker is able to observe individual patterns of behavior in a context that closely approximates some of the client's usual social situations. The worker observes and confirms patterns of behavior that might emerge slowly or not at all through the client–worker interview situation. The group worker's diagnostic statement includes the worker's observation of clients' attitudes and behaviors within and outside the treatment group. In the diagnostic group the worker also evaluates clients' skills that could be used as models for appropriate behavior by other members of the groups.

In order to determine more accurately the controlling conditions of a behavior, the technique of *behavioral reenactment* can be used in the group situation (Sundel and Lawrence, 1974; also see Chapter 25). Behavioral reenactment is a role-playing technique used to test the adequacy of the description of the response, antecedents, and consequences given by the client before entering the group. It attempts to simulate a client's target behavior in the group. If a male client complains that his foreman at work is always "picking" on him, a member of the group is assigned the role of the foreman while the client assumes his own role. In order to simulate what occurs in the client's work situation, other role players are cued and coached to fill in collateral roles where indicated. The worker or other group members assume the role of the client or a significant other directly involved in the target situation. If the role-play is not congruent with the client's verbal description of the situation, the client would be assigned to gather further information utilizing the knowledge about antecedents and consequences that emerged from the role-play.

For the most part current social work practice is to hold individual intake interviews with each prospective client prior to assignment to any social work service. Many practitioners have found that accurate data can be collected in a formed group and that clients may be more willing to provide personal information in a group setting when the knowledge that others share similar problems detoxifies their own attitudes about themselves as people with problems seeking help (Churchill, 1965; Landy, 1965). In fact, group intake procedures have been used extensively with adoptive parent applicants. In the case of natural groups, families, and gang groups, the worker should observe the group or family if possible. The worker may also interview family or group members individually, if the worker determines that individuals need privacy to express themselves completely.

The diagnostic group is arranged especially to provide a means and context for the assessment of each individual member, not for assessment of the group itself. The group worker plans a series of meetings with several selected clients so that each member is exposed to selected emotional, cognitive, and social tasks and stresses. These experiences simulate situations in which the clients' reported problems occur. The worker can identify the patterns of a group member's behaviors as well as ability to maintain certain behaviors and to perform adaptive behaviors. The group worker sometimes finds it useful to measure the functioning of each member against the expected behavior for people of the client's own age, sex, and cultural group. The diagnostic statement analyzes behaviors in terms of reactive, provocative, and interactive patterns.

In an article describing a diagnostic group of elementary school children referred for services because of problems with peers, parents, and school Churchill lists potential observations:

> For example, in regard to the child's relationship to other children in the initial group meeting: (1) Can he show he wants a relationship? (2) Can he accept friendly overtures? (3) Does he provoke feelings of protectiveness? (4) Under what situations can he relate and to whom? (5) Can he maintain relationships when tension is high? Or in his relationship to an adult in the presence of other children over the period of four meetings: (1) What is his pattern of relating to the group worker? (2) How does a child use the proffered relationships? (3) Is this a child whom adults like in a one-to-one situation yet who shows gross problems in the group when he must compete with other children for the attention of the adult? (4) Do his feelings toward the worker shift when the worker gives to, compliments or supports another child? (5) Do his dependency demands vary with the reality of the situation? In his knowledge of and use of social skills in the context of stress: (1) Can he accept appropriate roles in basic games? (2) Does he quit a game if another child gets a favorite role? (3) Will he disrupt activity when he doesn't want to play? (4) Are his social handicaps caused by lack of knowledge which can be remedied? (5) Do conferred moral attitudes cause emotional reflection of activities? [1965, p. 586]

The social worker plans the activities of a diagnostic group to increase the availability of relevant observations. A craft activity that requires sharing of equipment may be planned to reveal the manner and extent to which members engage in cooperative behavior.

The group worker's special expertise in understanding individual behavior in the context of the group can be put to use for diagnostic as well as treatment purposes through the worker's observations of members in natural and formed groups, some of the latter developed primarily for client assessment. Worker observations and analyses of members' behaviors during group meetings can be facilitated in certain areas by simulation tests, brief questionnaires completed by group members dealing with various group structures, and program activities (e.g. Rose, 1981; Sundel and Sundel, 1980; Toseland and Rivas, 1984; see Chapters 21 and 22). For example, a game requiring cooperation could be used to help the worker assess the social skills of members in handling differences. Similarly, baseline and subsequent measures obtained from members on group-level variables (e.g. communication, affiliation, normative integration) can provide valuable knowledge relevant for intervention planning and evaluation of behavior change of individual members (see Chapter 21).

Validation of Assessment Data

In addition to making direct observations and obtaining a self-report of the client's behavior, the worker should check the accuracy of data reported by interviewing individuals who were present during manifestations of the client's problem—with the client's permission if at all possible. A description of the problem as stated by these individuals should be obtained. Possible sources of validation are parents, relatives, neighbors, teachers, and peers. Such individuals can be used also as monitors to observe and record occurrences of the target behavior and the conditions in which it occurs. Frequently this monitoring procedure effectively points out the monitor's role in stimulating or maintaining the target behavior. In general accurate and reliable assessment of a target behavior can be improved by comparing the descriptions of specific behaviors made by different individuals and adding the information provided by direct observations of the client in the group.

Goal Setting

A full discussion of the variables to be considered in recommending group work rather than casework intervention would be beyond the scope of this paper. However, some factors to be considered include the sensitivity of the client to peer pressure, the availability of other clients with similar or complementary problems, and the possibility that group members will serve as desired models for one another.

After the client's problem has been analyzed and a decision reached that social group work is the appropriate method of intervention, a list of goals is formulated with the client. It is essential that goals be realistic and appropriate to the services offered by the agency. In addition, goals should be agreed upon by worker and client. As a first step they would delineate the desired terminal behaviors. Immediate, intermediate, and terminal levels of goal attainment would then be ordered along a continuum showing progressive changes in the client's behavior. Goal specification at each of these levels involves the same considerations as those in assessment: (1) a precise description of the desired response; (2) its rate or duration of occurrence; (3) the antecedent conditions under which it should occur; and (4) the consequences of the altered behavior.

The priority of choosing one terminal goal over another involves the same criteria used in selecting one target behavior for consideration over another, as indicated earlier. Priorities among goals might be changed in the course of intervention, as some goals are achieved or other problems become more salient.

The following excerpt illustrates the process of assessment and goal setting:

A common problem with which the Hartwig workers had to deal was that of school truancy. One boy, a constant truant from school, attended on the average of once every two weeks. He also had failing grades and conflicts with several of his teachers. From the client's report, the conditions for truancy occurred as he walked to school in the morning with his friends and one peer would suggest that they truant. Consequences maintaining the behavior were the avoidance of academic failure at school and the enjoyment of being "on the streets with his friends." The influence of parents and school officials was insufficient to induce school attendance. The goal chosen for immediate treatment was the reduction of truancy, both because the consequences of truancy would be severe, and because school attendance was a necessary condition for treating the other school problems. The projected terminal goal was attendance at all classes five days a week with intermediate goals such as three days of attendance per week. [Rose et al., 1970, p. 222]

Note that the intermediate goal was stated in terms of the same behavioral dimension as the terminal goal; the intermediate behavior of attending school three days a week was an approximation toward the desired terminal behavior of attending school five days a week.

Behaviors that are prerequisites for attaining the intermediate or terminal goal but are not in the same behavioral dimension are labeled *instrumental behaviors. Instrumental goals* refer to the attainment of skills in these areas. An adolescent boy in a training school might have to gain more skill in talking with strangers before he can apply for a clerical job. In determining the instrumental goals, the worker would go through a procedure similar to that followed in determining intermediate and terminal goals. A clear delineation of the desired instrumental behavior would be made along with an analysis of its antecedents and consequences. The desired frequency or duration of the behavior's occurrence would also be determined.

Goal Attainment: Resources and Barriers

In developing the intervention plan, the worker should consider resources and barriers facilitating and impeding achievement of the goals—immediate, intermediate, terminal, and instrumental. This might require the worker's investigation (with the client's permission whenever possible) of the client's peers, community, school, and/or work situation. Also of significance are personal, interpersonal, and organizational factors. Personal factors might include the client's intellectual ability, personality predispositions, physical handicaps, and financial state. Interpersonal factors include power conflicts between the client and others and the trust the client feels toward others. Organizational factors include such variables as administrative structure of the client's place of business or school, the goals of the service agency, and the worker's legitimate functions within it (see Chapters 18 and 24).

Preparation of the Intervention Plan

After delineation of conditions influencing the client's target behaviors and the formulation of specific behavioral goals—all of which are summarized in the diagnostic statement—the worker plans an intervention strategy. The worker's intervention strategy usually includes steps to modify the client's behavior as well as to influence conditions surrounding the client's situation. Modification of the client's behavior involves interventions directed toward acquiring, strengthening, weakening, or eliminating specific behaviors. The worker may also make plans to increase intermediate and/or instrumental behaviors. A wide range of intervention modalities is usually available to the worker, only one of which is group work.

In order to select the appropriate intervention for a particular target behavior, it is vital that the worker assess all aspects of the problem. If a child has stolen money to replace old school clothes, the worker's intervention might best be directed toward modifying antecedent conditions, that is, increasing the provisions of adequate school clothing, rather than focusing on the target behavior of stealing. The worker's intervention strategy may involve modification of institutional, agency, community, or outside factors related to the client's life. For example, an in-service program for junior high school teachers may be planned in addition to, or instead of, group work with truant students. Such strategies are said to employ "extragroup means of influence" (see Chapter 16).

The intervention techniques used by a worker are influenced largely by his or her theoretical orientation. Whatever techniques are selected, their application must be based on careful consideration of their potential effectiveness in light of client resources and barriers. The worker also should evaluate continuously the effects of his or her interventions on the target behaviors and goals set for the client.

Before an intervention strategy is carried out, the worker should discuss the various procedures to be used with the client as fully as possible, particularly those which involve the client directly. The client should agree to fulfill his or her obligations, and the worker should agree to follow through with the procedures as indicated. This should be done both for ethical reasons and because it serves as an aid in goal attainment. The agreement between the worker and the client prior to implementation of the intervention strategy is referred to as the contract (see Chapter 10).

Diagnosis and Crisis Intervention

Because intervention strategies should be founded on diagnostic statements, interventions made by the worker prior to development of a diagnostic statement are generally inappropriate. In some settings, however, much of a worker's activities consist of on-the-spot or crisis-oriented interventions. In these instances the worker makes rapid judgments of the client's situation and takes immediate action (see, for example, Parad, 1965). The worker might immediately refer clients to agencies that provide special resources such as services for physically handicapped or mentally retarded individuals, housing information, or employment counseling. Such rapid assessments and interventions depart considerably from the more systematic diagnostic procedure considered here. These actions may be necessary but should be taken cautiously (Rose et al., 1970) in order to avoid jumping to inappropriate conclusions. Even when adequate information appears to be available, the worker should avoid two pitfalls in diagnosis: that of premature generalization based on limited information and that of positing false assumptions about problem causality.

RECENT DEVELOPMENTS AND CONCLUSION

The term *assessment* currently appears to be used more frequently in the literature than the term *diagnosis*. The term diagnosis has been associated primarily with the medical use of the term and with psychodynamically oriented practice that labeled clients according to the nomenclature of the *Diagnostic and Statistical Manual (DSM-III)* of the American Psychiatric Association. Concern about the negative effects of labels for clients and greater emphasis on observable behaviors and events rather than on inferred, underlying causes might be responsible for increased use of the term assessment among many human service professionals in the 1970's and 1980's. The term *assessment* is most clearly associated with the practice of behavior modification and behavior therapy (e.g. Gambrill, 1983; Sundel and Sundel, 1982).

During the past decade considerable attention has been given to behavioral assessment, with entire volumes and at least two specialty journals devoted to this topic. Much of this effort has been directed toward identification and development of instruments for use with special populations such as children or the elderly, or to assessment of specific problem areas such as anxiety, depression, marital discord, or assertiveness. Increased emphasis has been placed on the use of multiple response measures such as self-reports, observations, checklists, case records, and reports of significant others as a means of improving the reliability and accuracy of assessment. A number of assessment checklists relevant for social work practice have been developed (e.g. Hudson, 1982; Levitt and Reid, 1981). Rose (1981) has discussed the relevance of these developments to assessment in groups, including his work and that of his colleagues. Toseland and Rivas (1984) also provide an informative review and discussion of recent research findings and approaches to individual and group assessment.

Procedural Guidelines for Diagnosis in Group Work
Preparing the initial assessment
  I. Identifying information about client
 II. Nature of client's initial contact with agency worker
III. Problem presented by client or referral sources
IV. Description of tentative client goal(s)
 V. Rationale for acceptance or rejection of client for social group work
VI. Recommendation regarding further work with client
Preparing a diagnostic statement
  I. Identifying information
     A. State information about individual: age, sex, race, occupation, school grade, length of participation in group, significant others in client's life, etc.
     B. Give information about the group:
        1. Name of agency and group
        2. Member composition
           a. age, sex
           b. voluntary/involuntary; natural/formed
           c. race, ethnicity
           d. occupations
           e. worker goals for individual group members
           f. other
        3. Number of sessions held prior to current diagnosis; frequency and length of meetings.
 II. Problem Identification
     A. State the problem (present or predicted) as given by (1) the client and (2) the referral source. Be as specific as possible.
     B. Briefly state the rationale for social group work as the appropriate intervention strategy for this client.
     C. Specify the client roles that will be the focus for the intervention program, e.g. parent, spouse, employee, friends, student.
     D. Specify the target behaviors that are to be the focus of the intervention program in each role.
     E. Order these target behaviors according to their importance for investigation and state the criteria used to determine priorities among them.
III. Preliminary interventions and referrals
     A. Describe worker interventions that are required prior to fur-

ther analysis of the selected target behaviors and give the rationale for their use.

B. State worker referrals that have been made to other agencies and community resources and/or those that are required.

C. Describe worker contacts with other individuals that have been and/or must be made.

IV. Behavioral analysis and goal setting

A. Select the target behavior of highest priority.

1. Give one representative example of the performance of the target behavior(s) or situation where the desired behavior should occur.

2. Specify the responses made by the client when the problem occurs. These responses should be described precisely in terms of what the client *says* or *does*.

3. Describe the antecedent conditions related to these responses.

4. Describe the consequent conditions that are related to the performance of these responses in terms of (1) reinforcing consequences (or potential reinforcers) for the client and (2) negative consequences for the client, others, or society.

5. Describe measures of group structures (e.g. communication, leadership, affiliation, decision-making) relevant to the target behaviors, obtained through observations in the group and analyses of questionnaires completed by group members.

6. Give more examples of the problem as observed in the group and/or in the natural environment as reported by others and/or by the client.

7. Display graphs or charts completed by the worker, the client, and/or others describing the responses, their rate of occurrence, and the possible controlling antecedents and consequences.

8. Using examples describing the client's responses, organize the antecedents and consequences so that consistencies can be determined regarding their relation to the client's responses.

B. Goal setting

1. Formulate specific *terminal, intermediate*, and *instrumental* goals that are directly related to the analyzed target behaviors in terms of:

a. The responses to be observed and their desired frequencies or duration of occurrence

   b. The desired antecedent and consequent conditions to be present during the performance of desired responses.
   Each of these goals should describe responses to be acquired, increased, maintained, or decreased. If a response is to be decreased, then a concomitant response should be specified for occurrence in its place. An *instrumental* goal should also include specification of its *intermediate* and/or terminal goal(s).]
  2. State the manner and the extent to which the client has been involved and is in agreement with the established goals.
  3. Specify environmental barriers that impede attainment of the client's goals, e.g. economic deprivations, lack of transportation.
  4. Specify personal factors that impede attainment of the client's goals, e.g. speech impediments, rural background, divorced parents.
  5. Specify environmental resources that can be used to facilitate achievement of treatment goals, e.g. interested relatives.
  6. Specify personal resources that can facilitate goal achievement, e.g. a school dropout has good mechanical skills.
  7. Identify group members who could facilitate achievement of the client's treatment goals.
 C. Select the target behavior ranked second highest on the list of behaviors requiring service and establish appropriate goals by following the above procedures.
 D. Continue analysis of all target behaviors and formulation of client goals using these procedures.

REFERENCES

BLOOM, MARTIN, AND JOEL FISCHER
 1982 *Evaluating Practice: Guidelines for the Accountable Professional.* Englewood Cliffs, N.J.: Prentice-Hall.
BUCKLEY, NANCY K., AND HILL M. WALKER
 1970 *Modifying Classroom Behavior: A Manual of Procedures for Classroom Teachers.* Champaign, Ill.: Research Press.
CHURCHILL, SALLIE R.
 1965 "Social group work: A diagnostic tool in child guidance," *American Journal of Orthopsychiatry*, 35, no. 3 (April): 581–88.
FERSTER, CHARLES B.
 1965 "Classification of behavioral pathology." In L. Krasner and L. P. Ullman

(eds.), *Research in Behavior Modification*. New York: Holt, Rinehart & Winston, pp. 6–26.

FERSTER, CHARLES B., AND B. F. SKINNER
1957   *Schedules of Reinforcement*. New York: Appleton-Century-Crofts.

GAMBRILL, EILEEN
1983   *Casework: A Competency-Based Approach*. Englewood Cliffs, N.J.: Prentice-Hall.

HUDSON, WALTER
1982   *The Clinical Measurement Package: A Field Manual*. Homewood, Ill.: Dorsey Press.

LANDY, DAVID
1965   "Problems of the person seeking help in our culture." In Mayer Zald (ed.), *Social Welfare Institutions: A Sociological Reader*. New York: John Wiley & Sons, pp. 559–74.

LEVITT, JOHN L., AND WILLIAM J. REID
1981   "Rapid-assessment instruments for practice," *Social Work Research Abstracts*, 17: 13–19.

PARAD, HOWARD J. (ed.)
1965   *Crisis Intervention: Selected Readings*. New York: Family Service Association of America.

RICHMOND, MARY
1917   *Social Diagnosis*. New York: Russell Sage.

ROSE, SHELDON
1981   "Assessment in groups," *Social Work Research and Abstracts*, 17: 29–37.

ROSE, SHELDON; MARTIN SUNDEL; JANET DeLANGE; LINDA CORWIN; AND ANTHONY PALUMBO
1970   "The Hartwig Project: A behavioral approach to the treatment of juvenile offenders." In Roger Ulrich, Thomas Stachnik, and John Mabry (eds.), *Control of Human Behavior*. Glenview, Ill.: Scott Foresman, pp. 220–30.

SARRI, ROSEMARY C.; MAEDA J. GALINSKY; PAUL H. GLASSER; SHELDON SIEGEL; AND ROBERT D. VINTER
1967   "Diagnosis in group work." In Robert D. Vinter (ed.), *Readings in Group Work Practice*. Ann Arbor, Mich.: Campus Publishers, pp. 39–71.

STAATS, ARTHUR A., AND CAROLYN STAATS
1964   *Complex Human Behavior*. New York: Holt, Rinehart & Winston.

STUART, RICHARD B.
1980   *Helping Couples Change: A Social Learning Approach to Marital Therapy*. New York: Guilford.

SUNDEL, MARTIN, AND HARRY LAWRENCE
1974   "Behavioral group treatment with adults in a family service agency." In Paul Glasser, Rosemary Sarri, and Robert Vinter (eds.), *Individual Change Through Small Groups*. New York: The Free Press, pp. 325–47.

SUNDEL, MARTIN, AND SANDRA STONE SUNDEL
1982   *Behavior Modification in the Human Services: A Systematic Introduction to Concepts and Applications*. Englewood Cliffs, N.J.: Prentice-Hall.

SUNDEL, SANDRA STONE, AND MARTIN SUNDEL
1980 *Be Assertive: A Practical Guide for Human Service Workers.* Beverly Hills, Calif.: Sage Publications.
TOSELAND, RONALD W., AND ROBERT F. RIVAS
1984 *An Introduction to Group Work Practice.* New York: MacMillan Publishing Co.

9

Goals in Social Group Work Practice: Formulation, Implementation, and Evaluation

Janice H. Schopler, Maeda J. Galinsky, and Mark D. Alicke

GOALS ARE CRUCIAL in effective social group work practice. They represent the ends toward which service is aimed and give direction and meaning to the encounter between social group worker and clients. The way goals are defined can determine the acceptability of group work service to clients, agencies, and society.

Social work literature affirms the need for goal setting by client and worker. Although terminology may differ—ends, goals, objectives, foci, and purposes often are used synonymously—the importance of formulating goals is stressed. There is, however, some disagreement as to whether the worker or clients should set goals (Balgopal and Vassil, 1983; Toseland and Rivas, 1984). The position adopted here is simply that both parts of the group system, clients and worker, formulate goals, and goals need to be examined from the perspective of each. In addition, through its institutional agents and values the community determines certain goals or a range of goals for the group system (the collectivity of both worker and members) and affects what can be achieved.

Goal formulation begins very early and continues to affect the activities of the group throughout the treatment sequence. Initially the group's purpose is the single most important factor in group composition (Levine, 1979; Yalom, 1983). After making an assessment of each client's functioning, the worker formulates goals for individual clients. In addition the worker's perspectives on group goals are defined and redefined following the initial assessment of member needs. Each client comes to the pregroup interview or initial session with some notion, however vague and ill-defined, of the individual and group goals that may be pursued. Those goals are verbalized and reshaped as the situation is explored with the worker. In the early stages of group development the worker and members arrive at mutually acceptable individual and group goals. Their ability to set such goals will largely determine the success of the group. The goals selected guide the choice of group activities, influence the worker's strategy of intervention, and serve as a standard for measuring the achievements of individual members and of the group.

Although the goal formulation process differs from group to group, general principles can be derived from small group theory and practice to guide the worker's actions. In this chapter the process of goal formulation and its influence on group activities will be examined, using concepts from both social work and social science. First client and worker perspectives on individual and group goal setting are discussed; then the steps are given that lead to a commitment by group members and the worker to shared goals; and finally the implementation and evaluation of goals are explored.

CLIENT AND WORKER PERSPECTIVES

The client and worker have different perspectives in formulating goals. They enter the group for different reasons, have different roles within the group, and have different bases for formulating goals. However, for success clients and worker must mutually understand and agree on appropriate goals to pursue during treatment.

The Client's Perspective

The client may come to the agency through self-referral, through referral by an organization or concerned person, or in response to worker recruitment. In any case each client comes with some idea of what may be gained from this encounter. Whether or not the goals held by clients at the point of entry are relevant to reasons for referral or group formation, each individual will add ideas about what might be accomplished by the group.

The individual and group goals held by clients stem from each member's self-concept and view of the group and its surroundings (Cartwright and Zander, 1968a). The many internal and external forces that influence client perspectives include personal values, the environment, reference groups, capabilities, and experiences. The communities where clients live and the statuses they have attained determine much of the content of their values; and these values provide clients with a frame of reference for defining the problems that brought them to the group. The expectations held by significant others, such as peers, spouses, employers, or teachers, may also influence client perceptions of their problems and their motivation to do something about them. Each individual's capabilities determine the limits of their potential achievements and contributions to the group. Client expectations, both positive and negative, of the group may be based on prior contacts with an agency, past experiences in school, work, and peer groups, and "grapevine" reports of friends. Thus, various factors determine what goals the client sees as relevant and what goals they consider attainable (Garvin, 1981; Zander, Medow, and Efron, 1965).

The initial goals that clients hold, whether tentative or well-defined, may reflect what is expected in terms of personal gains and outside recognition. The reasons clients have for entering a group do not necessarily relate to their presenting problems but may encompass a variety of motivations (Cartwright and Zander, 1968a, pp. 403–6). Some clients may hope that involvement with the group will help them to meet expectations in systems outside the group; others may view the group as a panacea or a means to escape pressure about solving a problem. A depressed client may have only self-oriented goals for the group, such as, "the group should help me stop crying" or "the group should make people like me." Even when inappropriate, the goals that clients hold define what they want from the group.

Members are able to formulate group-level goals only after each client shares goals within the group and the similarities among group members are identified (Zander, 1968). In the process of accepting and rejecting individual goals for the group, more group-oriented motives develop, and members set priorities about what the group as a whole should and can accomplish. Occasionally client goals may be primarily group-oriented even before a group meets with the worker. For instance, a group of residents from the same housing project may have selected group goals prior to the worker's intervention and may be more clear about the goals they prefer for the group than for themselves. In formed groups, the worker will almost always have some influence on members' initial formulation of individual and group goals. It is important to remember, however, that in both natural and formed groups the clients' and worker's perspectives of appropriate goals may differ.

The Worker's Perspective

The worker begins goal formulation at a very general level; objectives are partially determined by professional orientation, agency affiliation, and the agency's mandate from the community. Professional values support goals related to individual and group functioning and broader social concerns. The agency provides a focus for selecting the specific group of clients to receive assistance, as well as for the methods used to aid them. The agency will also constrain the types of goals that can be formulated. The community may provide the agency with mandates that may specify or reject certain goals and methods (Garvin, 1981; Roberts, 1968).

Profession, agency, and community do not always agree on general goals for the group, and conflicts may arise. The community and profession, for example, may present the worker with disparities. Citizens concerned about teenage vandalism may want youth contained and corrected, while professional values may dictate the development of more employment opportunities and recreational outlets. The worker's personal and professional values also may conflict with community or agency objectives, as when an agency emphasizes treatment of emotional problems and the worker sees the need for parent education.

The social worker performs an important function in mediating between agency and client (Shulman, 1984). If the worker and agency are viewed as holding unitary purposes, however, the worker is ignored as an independent source of purpose or goals. In fact, the worker brings a set of values and experiences that influence his or her view and use of agency purpose. The worker may interpret the agency goal in an idiosyncratic manner and may even disagree with the agency purpose. In a loosely structured setting the agency may leave formulation of group purpose almost solely to the worker. In any case the worker interprets the agency purpose to the group, and worker goals must be considered as independent and significant.

The worker's general goals for the group direct efforts toward a target population with identifiable problems and provide a range of objectives that can be pursued. For instance, a worker composing a group of recently divorced single parents with young children might have the general goal of helping these members cope with the stress related to their roles as single parents. As the worker meets members individually or as a group, goals are formulated for each member. Individual goals for a mother in the group might include increasing her perception of her competence for employment and arranging job training and childcare. A father might want to explore ways he can meet new friends and work on hobbies that won't conflict with his parenting responsibilities. The worker, considering each member's presenting problems and personal goals, discusses individual goals with the group and attempts to reach consensus with the members during goal formulation (Galinsky and Schopler, 1971). In some situations, as with growth groups, the worker's purpose may be to help clients formulate their own goals; in that case the worker may not formulate individual goals and more specific group goals.

Typically, after general group and individual treatment goals are established, the worker engages members in formulating a more specific set of goals for the group to pursue. The worker seeks specific goals capable of steering group action to meet individual needs (Cartwright and Zander, 1968a, pp. 409-10). More specific goals for the group of single parents might be to increase coping skills related to sole management of household and children; to identify social outlets; and to find common childcare arrangements for special situations. Other goals such as support and sharing are more nebulous but will be important to the members, who need this kind of mutual assistance. Over time, goals at both levels may change as clients and worker gain new knowledge of each other's perspectives.

FORMULATION OF GROUP SYSTEM GOALS

During contract formation the worker and clients come to a common working agreement about individual and group goals (Rose, 1973, 1977). Client and worker perspectives continue to influence the degree of acceptance of the individual and group goals, but the shared goals guide the group system and represent an initial common ground.

Goal formulation is a process, not an event; goals are constantly evaluated and reevaluated. At any given moment, however, the goals formulated by the group system should meet certain criteria to be useful in guiding action (Rose, 1973, 1977). To be effective, goals must be formulated in clear, specific, and realistic terms. If these criteria are met, clients and worker can observe and perhaps measure changes as they occur, using the initial situation of each client and the group as a baseline. The goals also must be relevant to the lives of the individuals and the group. Individual goals should pertain to behavior and attitudes desirable outside the group. Group goals should refer to problems the group members are having, tasks for the group to accomplish as a whole, ways of attaining individual goals, or the relationship between the group and the external environment.

When the group first meets, the worker is often the only person who is aware of each member's goals. Members have some idea of the worker's perspectives and of their own goals; also, if they have had pregroup interviews with the worker and prior contact with other members, they may have some notions of the problems and concerns that have brought the other clients into the group. Unless it is a preexisting group, members have not met together to share their perspectives. Before group system goals can be formulated, various client and worker perspectives must become a part of the group's shared reality.

Formulating goals involves both cooperative and competitive processes (Kelley and Thibaut, 1969; Walton and McKersie, 1966). Although the worker seeks to encourage cooperative aspects of group interaction, the competitive feelings of the members must be recognized as they strive to get their own ideas accepted. Group members do not always strive for group success; they have the choice of working for themselves, for the group, or for the benefit of both (Zander, 1977). If group cohesiveness is sufficiently strong, then group-oriented motives should supersede individual motives, and a strong desire should arise for the group to provide a successful experience for all of its members.

Goal formulation can be conceived as a two-phase process: first, worker and members explore their common and conflicting interests to establish a basis for mutually acceptable goals; then the group engages in a bargaining process to determine which goals will be accepted and how they will be implemented. During the first, the *exploratory phase*, cooperation is dominant. Members assess the mutual benefits that the group as a whole can potentially provide and anticipate future exchange of rewards and costs (Moreland and Levine, 1982). The nature of the relationship among members is explored (Kelley and Thibaut, 1978) as are the boundaries that define acceptable and normative group behavior (Mabry, 1975). In the second, the *bargaining phase*, some competition among group members and between worker and group members is expected.

Exploration

In the exploratory phase of goal formulation the worker and members must identify areas of mutual concern, consider different means to pursue these concerns, and discuss the relative values these various alternatives hold for them. An atmosphere of sharing and cooperation is necessary if members are to feel free to state their perspectives, their preferences, and their disagreements. The group must obtain a true and complete picture of common and conflicting interests, concerns, and problems. Only through a sharing of individual perspectives will members be able to sort out their differences and to synthesize their individual interests into common group goals.

The group's ability to formulate effective goals and, ultimately, the group's success depend on how adequately information about problems and goals is exchanged among members and between members and worker during this exploratory phase. Ability to exchange valuable information freely depends on members' abilities, needs, and preferences, and the processes the group develops to solve problems of coordination and disagreement (Thibaut and Kelley, 1959). Self-disclosure among group members is facilitated by reciprocity—the willingness of each member to reveal as much of himself or herself as do the other members (Cosby, 1973; Taylor, DeSoto, and Loeb, 1979). Members must be encouraged to reveal enough about their own personal needs, resources, and interests so that they can establish a basis for commonality—a reason for continuing as a group (Walton and McKersie, 1966).

As members present their own situations, personal values are disclosed as well as expectations of other people and systems that are important. As members interact with each other, they learn that they have mutual concerns. Two girls in a school group may find they both have fights with their mothers about dating. Spouses of cancer patients learn they have experienced the same frustrations in obtaining information from hospital personnel. As members recognize their common situations and similar attitudes, group bonds begin to form, and members begin to see the possibility of common solutions to their problems (Terborg, Castore, and DeNinno, 1976). The worker's responsibility is to help group members perceive their similarities and view their differences with respect.

It is critical to remember that in most cases only the worker has knowledge of all members' interests and goals as exploration begins. The worker must take care not to dominate the group and short-cut the exploration phase, thinking that the interests of all members are being represented. The worker, after all, is backed by the authority of the agency and professional expertise. The members, initially, have little authority, little clarity about what the group should do, and little understanding about their relationship to the group. Unless the worker recognizes the importance of member contributions and exercises skill and knowledge to help members define their roles and express their concerns and interests, the worker may sacrifice member involvement in the group (Gerard, 1957).

While the worker generally is aware of which concerns need to be discussed in order to formulate goals and to prevent future dissatisfactions, the members usually need time to go through the process of getting acquainted and setting goals for themselves as a group (Kelley and Thibaut, 1969). For instance, a worker who composes a group of mental patients who are ready to be released may view preparation and planning for discharge as an essential goal for the group. The members may be ambivalent about leaving the hospital and may resist planning. They may need to learn what each member is like and what problems and plans exist before they are ready to formulate either individual or group goals. When goals are openly determined in the group and not imposed by the worker, they will be more likely to influence the group's activities and individual behavior (Krause, Fitzsimmons, and Wolf, 1969; Raven and Rietsema, 1960).

While the worker should not impose goals on members, worker goals should be clearly communicated to the group members. Some social workers contend that formulation and transmission of goals by the worker divest the client of self-determination, but the opposite is true. Only with open discussion of worker goals does the client have a choice. The worker, as a professional, has objectives to pursue with and for clients. The worker will formulate goals for clients as information is gained about them, whether or not the worker admits his or her role in goal formulation. Clients who come to a worker or who are sought out have problems of concern to them or others in their social environment. The worker must have some ideas about how these problems might be resolved by the conclusion of treatment. If the worker does not explicitly share his or her perspectives with the group, members do not have the chance to consider the worker's goals, and they may wonder why the worker has chosen to meet with them. When the work-er's goals are stated clearly and specifically, clients generally perceive them accurately. When the worker is vague and nonspecific, clients tend to as-sume the worker has a hidden agenda or no purpose at all (Schmidt, 1969; Northen, 1969).

Giving group members an opportunity to examine and explore worker perspectives does not imply that the worker's goals are relinquished. The worker may still try to gain acceptance of and commitment to purposes that will be most beneficial to clients. If the worker's goals are based not only on his or her own and the agency's purposes and values but also on a knowl-edge of each client's wants and needs, the worker's purpose is more likely to be accepted by the group members. It is crucial, however, that the worker be willing to modify objectives as new information is gained through inter-action with group members and while helping members find their common purposes.

The worker must be able to state and restate goals in terms that will be clear to all members of the group. Goal clarity leads to group cohesiveness and mutual attraction (Anderson, 1975). It is not sufficient for the worker merely to enumerate general goals at the outset. In working with a group of parents at a child guidance clinic, the worker has to do more than speak about the improvement of mental health of the children; the worker needs to illustrate problems and goals through reference to the day-to-day prob-lems the parents are having with the children. Parents of a three-and-one-half-year-old child who is extremely dependent may be reinforcing their child's problems by overprotective behavior. Instead of discussing problems in general terms, the worker can encourage the parents to focus on incidents such as mealtime behavior. As the parents describe to the group their exas-peration at spending two hours every meal feeding the child, the worker may suggest that an appropriate goal for the parents would be to teach the child to feed himself with a limit of a half-hour each meal. The worker must elicit members' discussion of specific objectives to make sure that they are understood and accepted.

The problems of clarity relate to goal specificity. General goals tend to be less clear than specific ones. Nonspecific goals may lead to conflict over the appropriate means to pursue specific ends, or what has been called me-taconflict—conflict over how to resolve conflict (Jacobson and Margolin, 1979; Knudson, Sommers, and Golding, 1980). In the process of searching for commonality among members, the worker and members may be tempted to state goals at a general level so that agreement of all members to goals will come easily. For example, the goal for a group of schoolchildren could be "to act better in the classroom." This level of generality may suf-fice when, with agency function and professional mandate in mind, the worker is first considering formation of a group or selecting members. Such a goal merely indicates a broad concern but does not identify problem be-haviors that should be the focus of the group's work together. If the school-children are expressing hostility to the teacher through rude and inappro-priate behavior, goals should be developed to change this specific problem behavior. Specific objectives provide direct guidance for the group's actions, since they indicate exactly which problems need to be resolved (Henry, 1981).

Through mutual exploration of goals the group members and the worker come to an understanding of each other's perspectives. As explora-tion occurs, the worker must help develop an atmosphere of mutual trust, clearly defined roles, and relevant norms. As members begin to feel com-fortable with each other, they can then tolerate the pressures of the bargain-ing phase of goal formulation.

Bargaining

Exploration is a necessary precondition for achieving group consensus about goals. Once the members and the worker understand each other's perspectives and motivations, they must decide which goals to pursue and how to pursue them. The bargaining phase of goal formulation necessarily involves disagreements among group members and the worker. It would be naive to expect all the goals of members and worker to mesh perfectly and be accepted, even when group members have been selected on the basis of compatibility. Members may differ about the goals to select, the goals that are most important, and the most appropriate means for pursuing goals.

Thus priorities must be determined. Individuals enter the group with preferences about goals for themselves and for the group; however, these initial preferences usually are influenced by group membership (Cartwright and Zander, 1968a, p. 405). The group system considers member preference and decides on goal priorities that will guide the group and that each mem-ber will be helped to achieve. The worker helps members set these priorities, taking into account the members' abilities and needs, the environment in which the group is located, and the time the group has to work on problems.

Priority setting may be relatively simple, especially when members have very similar problems. A group of patients who have just learned they have arthritis may immediately decide to focus on coping with this physical dis-ability. In other situations members may have multiple, varied problems, and goal setting becomes a more complex process. The group system will then need to use criteria relating goal preferences to their importance for so-cial functioning, the immediacy of the problem, relationship to the achieve-ment of other goals, accessibility to change, and availability of resources.

A group of low-income mothers who have been asked to meet because their children have behavior problems in school may present a range of problems, including difficulty in communicating with school personnel, lack of money for school supplies, behavior problems with children at home, lack of recreational facilities, and discrimination in the school system. The group may decide to place highest priority on communicating with school personnel, since this problem is most closely related to the reason for forming the group and because success in this area may lead to avenues for approaching discrimination and resolving school supply difficulties. Behavior problems at home may be assigned lower priority because they do not have such immediate social repercussions. The lack of recreational facilities may also be given low priority, because the group has insufficient resources and motivation to deal with this problem.

Group goals and individual goals must, of course, be congruent. A husband entering a group of couples who are meeting to resolve marital difficulties may give budgeting problems high priority, although he and his wife also indicate there is much dissension in their home about disciplining their children, recreation, and their sexual relationship. If the group agrees to focus on communication difficulties between spouses, this husband's initial priority may be unacceptable as a main focus of interest to the group as a whole, and he will be urged to reconsider his goal preferences.

The high-priority individual goal of one member will not necessarily interfere with the specific individual goal setting of another member. In a nursing home group, there is no conflict between one resident's desire to become more articulate in stating her needs to the staff and another resident asking for support in completing a daily exercise routine that will enable him to become more ambulatory. In group goal formulation, however, when the goal of one or more members is accepted as a high priority, another group member's competing goal automatically assumes a lower priority. If most of the nursing home residents agree that group time should be used to develop their self-help skills and two members want the group focus to be on reminiscing and socializing, the group will have to compromise so that these conflicting interests can be represented in the group goals. The group might, for example, decide to have one "social" meeting a month, with other sessions related to skill development (Kelley and Thibaut, 1978). At times it may be impossible to meet all of an individual's identified needs within the group system. When possible the worker should help these clients meet their goals through additional means such as individual or family counseling or membership in another group.

Trust among members can provide one basis for the acceptance of lower priorities. If mutual trust has not been developed during the exploratory phase, bargaining is likely to be conducted almost entirely on the basis of power, manipulation, and prestige (Mencher, 1964; Walton and McKersie, 1966). The worker must be aware of potential conflict in this bargaining phase and must make certain that all members are heard, that consideration is given to all members' views, and that when priorities are set they are fair to all (Cartwright and Zander, 1968b; Thibaut and Kelley, 1959). High-status members should be prevented from dominating the group, and the worker must be careful not to align with apparent leaders or to sanction the goals they promote unless this is beneficial to the group as a whole. In fact, the worker can prompt a reconsideration of goals if emerging priorities do not adequately represent all member needs.

Since use of power is a part of bargaining among members and worker, it is important to note that the worker has the most power in a newly formed group system. The worker has legitimate power by virtue of assignment by the agency. The worker has control over material resources and personal qualities, which provide a basis for exerting positive or negative sanctions. Expert power is gained from prior training, and referent power is achieved from personal characteristics and interest (French and Raven, 1968). The worker is therefore potentially in a position to influence greatly the selection of goals. The worker's power can be a positive force in the group, but it must not be abused. Unless members are directly involved in selecting goals, they will be less likely to commit themselves to the goals, and the goals will be less likely to influence their behavior (Raven and Rietsema, 1960).

The worker will, of course, vary the degree of autonomy allowed to the group in goal selection. The agency may prescribe or proscribe certain goals. A probation group may be required to focus on regulations and rules specified in their court orders. Clients themselves differ in their ability to formulate goals. A group of preschool children in a therapeutic nursery would be allowed less freedom in choosing goals than a group of teenagers in a low-income housing project. In any case, the worker must involve the members in the goal selection process.

No matter how goals are selected, the worker can expect resistance from members, and it may come from a variety of sources. If members have vested interests in particular goals, they may want group priorities to be set in accordance with those interests. Members may be concerned that group goals will not represent what is most important for them, or they may be unsure about which goals would be good for the group to pursue. A man entering a group for spouses of alcoholics may be overwhelmed with his problems. In addition to having an alcoholic wife, he and his family are facing eviction, his oldest son is appearing in court for car theft, and two younger children are ill. As he hears other members discuss their extensive problems, he is confused about which problems the group should handle and which group goals would benefit him. Members may also avoid particular goals because they feel the group does not have enough consensus or enough power to act on them. For example, a group of residents in a halfway house may resist setting a goal to complete all chores prior to special community activities because they doubt that all members will comply and fear the whole group will suffer the consequences. If members lack clarity on any aspect of goal formulation, their concerns may take the form of resistance, which may lead to procrastination in goal setting or conflict among group members (Thibaut and Kelley, 1959).

Group discussion with all members and worker participating provides information and reassurance to resistant members and is more likely to lead to goals that are acceptable to a larger proportion of group members. Open discussion increases the chance that the most widely shared concerns and values will be incorporated in the selected goals. As members exchange information, they may find new bases for agreement and may even change opinions about the value or attainability of certain goals. Members who question the group's ability to achieve goals may have increased confidence in the group as they view members effectively engaging in the decision-making process. The halfway house residents may agree to a group goal of all chores completed prior to group trips after they have heard all members share their concerns and have adopted a system of monitoring each other's behavior outside the group. A fair hearing of all views and open discussion are the worker's responsibility. Commitment of members to common goals, and therefore action on these goals, will be more likely to occur when members discuss the pros and cons of these goals (Thibaut and Kelley, 1959; Horowitz, 1968). Although not all members have to agree on goals, it is necessary for a relatively large number of members, possibly a majority, to reach consensus (Thibaut and Kelley, 1959). Even if members differ in their commitment to group goals, the worker may urge all members to express openly some degree of commitment to work toward these goals. Expressed commitment may provide pressure to persuade reluctant members to go along with the majority and may permit more effective use of group pressures. Once all members have stated their intention of working toward goals, whatever their reservations, the group can influence deviant members to engage in activities that will bring the group closer to achieving its goals. A highly cohesive group is likely to be more successful in exerting these pressures (Cartwright and Zander, 1968b).

Once goals have been selected, they serve as a standard against which members can measure their own and the group's progress. It is important to remember, however, that goal formulation is not a one-time transaction. Goals may be reformulated, and additional goals may be established as new information is received, as member interests and satisfactions change, as pressures from the environment shift, and as some goals are achieved. The worker, while helping members to reach the goals they have selected, should be ready to help members reevaluate and readjust their goals.

IMPLEMENTATION AND EVALUATION OF GOALS

When initial consensus has been reached, the group system can focus on implementing and evaluating their goals. Implementation refers to all activities, worker intervention and group action, that the group system directs toward the achievement of goals. Although evaluation may frequently be regarded as a terminal activity, evaluation and implementation are concurrent and complementary processes. The group system can use goals continually to evaluate the effectiveness of its activities.

Intermediate Goals

At the conclusion of the bargaining phase individual and group goals have been selected and priorities have been set. The sequence in which goals will be pursued must be decided. Some individual goals can be worked on simultaneously. For instance, abusive parents who recognize they may lose custody of their children may have the common goal of finding more appropriate ways of dealing with their anger and frustration. Other goals must be worked on serially, so that at certain points one or several individual goals take precedence over others. In a mental hospital predischarge group, some members may be returning to their previous communities, family problems, and job situations; others may be considering foster care in new communities. Activities and discussion related to the various individual goals would, at times, be difficult to handle simultaneously. Intermediate goals are frequently necessary to achieve long-range goals.

An intermediate goal may constitute a lesser quantity of certain behavior than a long-range goal (e.g. consistent completion of one assignment a week for a pupil who rarely finishes any assignment) or one aspect of the final desired behavior (e.g. respectful listening to a teacher on the part of a student who interrupts, is rude, and disrupts the class). Intermediate goals need to be related logically to long-range goals, and the connections should be stressed by the worker. Intermediate goals also must be geared to the members' current abilities. Different goal levels may affect client motivation. If goals are too low, clients may become apathetic; and if too high, clients may become frustrated. Since intermediate goals are more easily attainable than long-range goals, their achievement provides tangible evidence to members of their competence, motivating them to proceed to the next step in goal achievement (Zander and Wulff, 1966). A client who has been unsuccessful in budgeting can take pride in reporting to the group that he has cleared his gas bill for the first time. Breaking down long-range goals into intermediate goals also facilitates program planning from session to session. In fact, most planned program activities represent means to achieve intermediate goals.

Program Planning

Discussions and activities should of course be planned so that they relate directly to the achievement of goals. Activities such as role-playing that re-create problem situations allow members to reenact their behavior in a supportive environment, providing them with an opportunity to gain insight into their problems and to discuss new ways of coping. A member who becomes aggressive when questioned by her Food Stamp worker can practice more effective assertive responses in the group. Situations structured to elicit problem behaviors can provide members with an opportunity to develop and practice new behaviors. A competitive game may arouse aggressive behavior that a member has been denying and will make this behavior directly accessible to change efforts. Further, the worker can capitalize on problem behaviors that occur during group interaction. In a group of couples discussing marital problems, a wife's dominance over her husband may be apparent; the group and worker may then reinforce her for allowing him to express his opinion.

The relevance of each activity to goal achievement should be discussed before, during, and after group action. This helps members relate their interactions to their reasons for being in the group and serves as a source of stimulation. Individuals who are clear about goals and the means to achieve them have a tendency to show more interest in their personal tasks, to express less hostility, and to have a greater feeling of group belongingness, which is particularly apparent in their involvement with group goals and willingness to accept influence from the group (Raven and Rietsema, 1960). Unless the relationship between means and goals is stressed, members and worker may become so involved in discussions or activities that they lose sight of the ends they wish to achieve (Zinberg and Friedman, 1967).

Worker Intervention and Member Interaction

The worker's direct relationships with members, attention to group conditions, and participation in systems external to the group create a climate in which goal-directed action can take place and facilitate movement toward individual and group goals. It must be remembered, however, that whenever possible members should be encouraged to help each other work toward goals. In their roles as group members they will engage in activities and interaction within the group system and with outside systems in pursuit of individual and group goals. Some groups will be more able than others to engage in a proces of mutual assistance. The degree of autonomy the worker allows the members in implementing group goals should depend on member abilities.

The conditions created within the group system are crucial for goal attainment. Meetings should be planned so that all members can contribute to goal achievement and can receive recognition and support for their goal-directed behavior by other group members and the worker (Zander and Medow, 1965). Effective group treatment also requires interaction where members exert influence on each other. Group cohesiveness, group consensus, group norms, and group structure are all important in developing this system of interaction. A continuing emphasis on commonalities of members and attention to group maintenance are required to facilitate group development and positive relationships among members.

The worker needs to remember that even where consensus on goals has been reached by the group system, individual and worker perspectives continue to influence behavior and interpretation of group system goals. The worker may try to change individual and group goals if it is felt that they are inappropriate or unrealistic by seeking to renegotiate the initial group contract. Members may also try to force changes in goals. The worker should react to these attempts, supportively or negatively, depending on their impact on the group.

Interaction with External Systems

Both workers and members will be involved with external systems as they seek to implement goals. Individual goals always pertain to members' behavior and attitudes outside the group system and may require changes in significant role relationships with spouses, employers, or others. Group goals may focus on the relationship of the group to its environment, as when a group in a center for senior citizens chooses to focus on increasing recreational opportunities for older persons in the community. In addition, the environment in which the group system is located influences group effectiveness and member motivations.

The worker needs to enlist the assistance of persons outside the group to ensure that gains made in the group will continue after the individuals' membership terminates. The worker should communicate goals and member progress toward goals to persons significantly involved in the definition of members' problems (e.g. teachers, parents, staff in residential facilities). The worker should also seek their opinions of member change and gain their cooperation in trying out new ways of handling difficulties or in rewarding indications of individual progress. For instance, a group worker and a childcare worker, after discussing one member's extensive problems with verbal and physical aggression, may agree that the child should be praised for his progress each time he stops at name-calling and resists becoming involved in a fist fight. Changing behavior and perspectives of others in the clients' lives may be essential to goal attainment.

Group members are vitally involved in external systems as they test new behavior. The reactions of persons in the environment help members evaluate their progress toward goals. They may find themselves rejected or rewarded by others for changed behavior. Rewards for new behavior may further motivate members; however, if changes are ignored, members may become discouraged. A child who remains seated during a whole class period for the first time may fail to repeat this behavior unless the teacher comments favorably. Members may find their own perspectives have changed during the group experiences so that their ideas and behavior are no longer compatible with people who are important to them. Youth who have been dependent on drugs may lose face with their former associates as they begin to pursue more constructive goals. In such cases, if the previously relevant external systems cannot be changed, the worker must help the members form new supportive relationships.

Evaluation

All groups need periodic evaluation of movement toward individual and group goals. Systematic evaluation should be structured into group activities and into the worker's feedback to clients on their progress. Clients should be taught to monitor their own progress and to analyze group conditions and individual efforts. Involvement in evaluation activities can help to clarify goals and motivate clients.

Information for evaluation must be obtained from the group system itself and from related systems. When assessment of group goals focuses on the effectiveness of the group as a treatment means, the worker and members together can assess the achievements of the group, members' capacity to help each other, and various members' contributions to group performance. The worker needs to contact significant others about the client's behavior in external situations. Their perceptions are an important source of information in the evaluative process. The group may decide that members should observe each other's behavior in the group and in settings outside the group and provide feedback on what they have noted. Members should also be asked to assess their own progress on an individual basis and share their evaluation with the group.

Final evaluation of the accomplishment of individual and group goals occurs with members' termination from the group. The group may terminate for a variety of reasons, and in open-ended groups individual members leave at different times. Whether or not the group members have been successful in achieving some or all of their goals, they should participate in a final evaluation process. Only if final assessment is a mutual effort will both worker and members have an understanding of their successes and failures. A review of successful individual and group efforts may reinforce members' achievements; discussion of the reasons for failure may make members more amenable to future treatment. The worker's independent assessment of group and individual progress should be shared with group members, and their reactions should be elicited. Members should also be asked to evaluate the impact of the worker's activities. During this process the group worker is able to obtain a more complete understanding of this particular group and to gain information that will help improve his or her own interventive skills. For group members a final summation of successes and failures in meeting goals is equally important, because it clarifies what has been accomplished and what remains to be done when the group no longer exists.

Goal formulation, implementation, and evaluation are critical aspects of social group work practice. Although worker and members enter the group with their own individual perspectives on goals, they come to a shared understanding of what is possible in their work together through a process of exploration and bargaining. The specific goals selected guide group and individual efforts, influence member motivation, and direct worker intervention. As the group experience concludes, the individual and group goals are used by members, the agency, and the community to judge the effectiveness of group service.

REFERENCES

ANDERSON, ALONZO B.
  1975 "Combining effects of interpersonal attraction and goal-path clarity on the cohesiveness of task-oriented groups," *Journal of Personality and Social Psychology*, 31, no. 1: 68–75.

BALGOPAL, PALLASSANA R., AND THOMAS V. VASSIL
  1983 *Groups in Social Work, An Ecological Perspective.* New York: Macmillan Publishing Co.

CARTWRIGHT, DORWIN, AND ALVIN ZANDER
  1968a "Motivational processes in groups." In Dorwin Cartwright and Alvin Zander (eds.), *Group Dynamics.* Third edition. New York: Harper & Row, pp. 403–6 and 409–10.
  1968b "Pressures to uniformity in groups." In Dorwin Cartwright and Alvin Zander (eds.), *Group Dynamics.* Third edition. New York: Harper & Row, pp. 144–47.

COSBY, PAUL C.
  1973 "Self disclosure: A literature review," *Psychological Bulletin*, 79: 73–91.

FRENCH, JOHN R. P., JR., AND BERTRAM RAVEN
  1968 "The bases of social power." In Dorwin Cartwright and Alvin Zander (eds.), *Group Dynamics.* Third edition. New York: Harper & Row, pp. 259–69.

GALINSKY, MAEDA J., AND JANICE H. SCHOPLER
  1971 "The process of goal formulation in social group work practice." In *Social Work Practice.* New York: Columbia University Press, pp. 24–32.

GARVIN, CHARLES D.
  1981 *Contemporary Group Work.* Englewood Cliffs, N.J.: Prentice-Hall.

GERARD, HAROLD B.
  1957 "Some effects of status, role clarity and group goal clarity upon the individual's relation to group process," *Journal of Personality*, 25: 475–88.

HENRY, SUE
1981   *Group Skills in Social Work*. Itasca, Ill.: F. E. Peacock.

HOROWITZ, MURRAY
1968   "The recall of interrupted group tasks: An experimental study of individual motivation in relation to group goals." In Dorwin Cartwright and Alvin Zander (eds.), *Group Dynamics*. Third edition. New York: Harper & Row, p. 444.

JACOBSON, NEIL S., AND GAYLA MARGOLIN
1979   *Marital Therapy*. New York: Brunner/Mazel.

KELLEY, HAROLD, AND JOHN THIBAUT
1969   "Group problem solving." In G. Lindzey and E. Aronson (eds.), *The Handbook of Social Psychology*. Second edition. Reading, Mass.: Addison-Wesley, 4: 35–47.
1978   *Interpersonal Relations: A Theory of Interdependence*. New York: John Wiley & Sons.

KNUDSON, ROGER M.; ALISON A. SOMMERS; AND STEPHEN L. GOLDING
1980   "Interpersonal perception and modes of resolution in marital conflict," *Journal of Personality and Social Psychology*, 38: 751–63.

KRAUSE, MERTON; MARGARET FITZSIMMONS; AND NORMA WOLF
1969   "Focusing on the client's expectations of treatment: Brief report," *Psychological Reports*, 24 (June): 973–74.

LEVINE, BARUCH
1979   *Group Psychotherapy*. Englewood Cliffs, N.J.: Prentice-Hall.

MABRY, EDWARD A.
1975   "Sequential structure of interaction in encounter groups," *Human Communication Research*, 1, no. 4: 302–7.

MENCHER, SAMUEL
1964   "Current priority planning," *Social Work*, 9 (July): 27–35.

MORELAND, RICHARD, AND JOHN LEVINE
1982   "Socialization in small groups: Temporal changes in individual–group relations." In Leonard Berkowitz (ed.), *Advances in Experimental Social Psychology*, Vol. 15. New York: Academic Press, pp. 137–92.

NORTHEN, HELEN
1969   *Social Work with Groups*. New York: Columbia University Press.

RAVEN, BERTRAM H., AND JAN RIETSEMA
1960   "The effects of varied clarity of group goal and group path upon the individual and his relation to his group." In Dorwin Cartwright and Alvin Zander (eds.), *Group Dynamics*. Second edition. Evanston, Ill.: Row, Peterson, pp. 395–413.

ROBERTS, ROBERT W.
1968   "Social work: Methods and/or goals," *Social Service Review*, 42 (September): 360–61.

ROSE, SHELDON D.
1973   *Treating Children in Groups*. San Francisco: Jossey-Bass.
1977   *Group Therapy: A Behavioral Approach*. Englewood Cliffs, N.J.: Prentice-Hall.

SCHMIDT, JULIANNA T.
1969 "The use of purpose in casework practice," *Social Work*, 14 (January): 77–84.

SHULMAN, LAWRENCE
1984 *The Skills of Helping Individuals and Groups.* Second edition. Itasca, Ill.: F. E. Peacock.

TAYLOR, RALPH B.; CLINTON B. DeSOTO; AND ROBERT LOEB
1979 "Sharing secrets: Disclosure and discretion in dyads and triads," *Journal of Personality and Social Psychology*, 37, no. 7: 1196–1203.

TERBORG, JAMES R.; CARL CASTORE; AND JOHN A. DeNINNO
1976 "A longitudinal field investigation of the impact of group composition on group performance and cohesion," *Journal of Personality and Social Psychology*, 34, no. 5: 782–90.

THIBAUT, JOHN, AND HAROLD KELLEY
1959 *The Social Psychology of Groups.* New York: John Wiley & Sons.

TOSELAND, RONALD W., AND ROBERT F. RIVAS
1984 *An Introduction to Group Work Practice.* New York: Macmillan Publishing Co.

WALTON, RICHARD, AND ROBERT McKERSIE
1966 "Behavioral dilemmas in mixed-motive decision making," *Behavioral Science*, 11 (September): 370–84.

YALOM, IRVIN D.
1983 *Inpatient Group Psychotherapy.* New York: Basic Books.

ZANDER, ALVIN
1968 "Group aspirations." In Dorwin Cartwright and Alvin Zander (eds.), *Group Dynamics.* Third edition. New York: Harper & Row, pp. 418–29.
1977 *Groups at Work.* San Francisco: Jossey-Bass.

ZANDER, ALVIN, AND HERMAN MEDOW
1965 "Strength of group and desire for attainable group aspirations," *Journal of Personality*, 33 (March):122–39.

ZANDER, ALVIN; HERMAN MEDOW; AND RONALD EFRON
1965 "Observers' expectations as determinants of group aspirations," *Human Relations*, 18 (August): 273–87.

ZANDER, ALVIN, AND DAVID WULFF
1966 "Members' test anxiety and competence: Determinants of a group's aspirations," *Journal of Personality*, 34 (March): 55–70.

ZINBERG, NORMAN E., AND LEONARD J. FRIEDMAN
1967 "Problems in working with dynamic groups," *International Journal of Group Psychotherapy*, 17 (October): 447–56.

10

The Therapeutic Contract

Tom A. Croxton

INTRODUCTION

Since the original article, written for the "Michigan Collection" in 1964 and later incorporated into the first edition of this volume, much attention has been given to the concept of the "therapeutic contract" (Henry, 1981; Garvin and Seabury, 1984). It has emerged as one of the pillars of the therapeutic process, as it is from these agreements that the worker–client relationships are forged and treatment techniques, processes, roles, and purposes (goals) are defined. Components, negotiation processes, and developmental stages of these "contracts" will be clarified in what follows by an examination of this concept from the perspectives of legal history, traditional social work practice, social science theory, and social science research.

INITIAL CAVEATS

The concept of the worker–client therapeutic agreement has been variously referred to as the social-worker–client contract, the therapeutic contract, the behavioral contract, and so forth. There are several dangers associated with the word "contract" that demand brief exploration. The first is that the meaning of the term varies. For the lawyer it means one thing, while for the economist it may mean something quite different. In the criminal world the word contract has quite a sinister connotation. While we may use the term to connote a very special relationship within the context of professional practice, our clients may well give the idea quite a different meaning, one in keeping with its more widely accepted definition.

The second problem with the word "contract" is that in law it has a quite specific definition, generally understood and accepted by the larger society. The legal definition of the term is quite simply stated: "A contract is a promise or a set of promises for the breach of which the law gives a remedy or the performance of which the law in some ways recognizes as a duty"

(American Law Institute, 1981, p. 5). The complexities are, of course, far greater than these words initially suggest. One complicating result is that the word "contract" may imply to the client a promise to cure. There is not much danger here of a successful legal action should that cure not be forthcoming, but great care must be taken in discussions about "contract" not to mislead the expectations of the client. Of course, if the client has clear proof of an express promise to cure, a successful legal action in contract is much more likely (Schutz, 1982).

The use of the term "contract" may also mislead the therapist into believing that all of his or her obligations and responsibilities toward the client and others are defined by the agreement. This, of course, is not true. The law imposes on any professional relationship the implied *promise to treat with care and skill*. The failure to do so may result in a malpractice action combining both the law of negligence and the law of contract (Schutz, 1982). In addition, the law may impose upon the therapist/promisor and the client/promisee a special relationship with fiduciary obligations running from the therapist to the client. This recognition would infuse the contract to treat skillfully and carefully with the additional obligation of treating the client both *faithfully and honestly* (Feldman and Ward, 1979). Beyond these additive features the law may well attach our professional code of ethics, about which most of us know very little.

Finally, the term "contract" may connote a static, fixed understanding rather than a more fluid, organic agreement. Despite the public's understanding to the contrary, there is a good deal of fluidity of behavioral expectations and outcomes in commercial transactions. The same kind of fluidity must exist to even a greater extent in agreements concerning individual and group therapy. While one can reach general agreement on such logistical elements as time, money, and the physical environment of treatment, contracts with respect to relationships must necessarily be more vague, fluid, and organic in nature.

Based on these caveats, it would seem the better part of wisdom to discard the term "contract" from the therapeutic thesaurus. However, finding an acceptable alternative is difficult at best. If the phrase were not so cumbersome and bound to be misconstrued, the term "organic treatment accord" might best describe the concept, for it is the dynamic, growth-producing qualities of the therapeutic relationship that give the process true meaning and life. Other terms might include covenant, working agreement, concordat, consentient, and so forth. Perhaps each practitioner should be left to his or her own imagination, although further complicating an already confusing professional vocabulary seems counterproductive. So, despite many misgivings and wishing for that artistic inspiration to create the perfect terminology, the phrases "therapeutic contract" and "therapeutic agreement" will be adopted and used interchangeably throughout the balance of this article.

LEGAL AND HISTORICAL PERSPECTIVES

Whenever humans create a community, they enter into an understanding or agreement to abide by certain behavioral expectations in order to obtain a more secure and permanent relationship with their fellow humans. As Macneil (1980) has noted, one of the fundamental roots of contract is society. Without society there can be no contracts, and without contracts there can be no society. The other roots of contract, which have special meaning within the therapeutic context, are (1) specialization of labor and exchange; (2) choice or the concept of at least some freedom to elect from among a range of behaviors; and (3) an awareness of the future. "Once mankind has [this] awareness and with it an increasing sense of himself as a choosing creature, the potential reality for the full development of contract comes into being" (Macneil, 1980). We shall return to these ideas from time to time throughout this chapter, especially when speaking of the limitations of the idea of contract as a pillar in the therapeutic process.

Historically the concept of contract was a primary part of the beginnings of law as a recognized and viable institution. According to Corbin (1963), "That portion of the field of law that is classified as the law of contracts attempts the realization of reasonable expectations that have been induced [expressly or by implication] by the making of a promise." In legal terminology, contract has been defined as a "promissory agreement between two or more persons in which there must be subject matter, consideration and mutuality of agreement" (Corbin, 1963). Generally there must be an offer, an acceptance, and some consideration. In addition the agreement must not be so vague and uncertain that the terms of the contract are not reasonably ascertainable.

These same elements must be present to some extent in the therapeutic contract. However, the problem with these conceptions of contract is that they are largely viewed as fixed, static, undimensional agreements. At the other end of the spectrum are the philosophical perspectives of Locke (Gough, 1946; Barker, 1951), Rousseau (1976), and Kant (1974), which give us a more expansive interpretation of contract. Rawls (1971) carries us to an even higher level of abstraction. However important the ideas of these renowned philosophers, they give us few concrete guidelines in utilizing the idea of social contract in our daily transactions. Somewhere between these two extremes is that enviable middle ground where contract is not so much viewed in its legal or philosophical context as it is seen with all its psychological and sociological manifestations. In its essence contract is not about law; it is rather about people and how they relate to each other as they pursue their individual and collective goals.

Since contracts necessarily involve an exchange between people, to view such agreements in a mechanistic, dyadic fashion is to overlook the essence of such accords, for in effect the contract creates or modifies a social relationship. This function has profound consequences for the parties involved. Ideally such covenants should be viewed as the dynamic interaction of two or more persons arriving at a point of mutual understanding and agreement, which requires a new set of responses and imposes a new set of obligations and responsibilities upon the participants. Such agreements must be viewed as organic in nature, meaning that the specifications and contours of these contracts change as the parties experience their own personal growth in relation to each other and their social environment.

The idea of contract as an integral part of human relationships is emerging as a central theme in this society. While the marital union is not the analog of the therapeutic relationship, there are enough similarities to suggest that a review of the marriage agreement might be instructive. Certainly no other contract has such dramatic implications for the parties involved. Legally, a marriage continues to be viewed as a contractual agreement: the offer consists of some poetic form of "Will you marry me?" and the acceptance is, of course, some form of affirmative response. The consideration, the *quid pro quo* flowing between our two lovers, continues to be viewed optimistically as the mutual benefit the parties receive from the union (Green and Long, 1984; Statsky, 1984). The terms of the marriage contract usually remain ambiguous as the parties, often to their detriment, seldom worry about the more practical aspects of the union until after the ceremony. However, society may resolve certain of the ambiguities, as superimposed upon the contract is a socially and culturally predetermined set of behavioral expectations. The more fundamental aspects of those expectations may have legal sanction. For instance, one can no longer beat one's wife with a stick no bigger in circumference than the husband's thumb. That was the old "rule of thumb" in common law. Economic support by the wage earner continues to be legally enforceable. If certain behaviors are not forthcoming, e.g. sexual intercourse, the contract can be annulled.

With our whirlwind adoption of no-fault divorce, the place of our courts in the enforcement of the marriage contract has all but disappeared. Instead, the courts are now in the business of simply monitoring the dissolution of one contract, that pertaining to the marital union, as it seeks to assist the parties in forging a new agreement, that which focuses on property distribution, continuing economic support, and child custody. In this regard it is significant that the process of forging the new accord is likely to involve third-party negotiation, as states formally adopt mediation as a problem-solving methodology in divorce cases (Haynes, 1981; Irving, 1980). Although there are political forces with which one must contend, it seems logical to assume that social workers will be court-appointed mediators in many of these cases (State of Michigan, 1983). The focus of the mediating role will, of course, be directly on reaching a contractual accord between the parties.

It is also noteworthy that formal, written marital contracts are becoming much more common. Although there may be problems of enforceability, many couples see written agreements as providing an added foundation to the marital union (Clark, 1978–79; Weitzman, 1981). We have also seen the recent increase in the number of "living together agreements," an idea virtually unheard-of twenty years ago (Casad, 1978–79; Weyrauch and Katz, 1983; Weitzman, 1974). The advantage of such agreements, outside the economic aspects of contract, is that the parties may and should include in their precontractual discussions the more interpersonal and essential aspects of their marital expectations. Indeed, one might even recommend that the issuance of a marriage license be conditioned on participation in premarital education, counseling, and "living together" contracts.

There are essentially five basic elements linked to any contract based in promise. The first two elements are the respective wills of two or more people who believe in the power of one or both to affect the future in some respect. The other elements linked to promise are (1) commitment, (2) communication, and (3) measured reciprocity (Macneil, 1980). While these elements may exist to varying degrees in the marital relationship, they lie at the very heart of the therapeutic contract.

CONTRACTUAL RELATIONSHIPS IN SOCIAL WORK

Social agencies enter into a variety of contractual agreements, both express and implied. Harry Bredemeir (1964), in his analysis of social agencies, speaks to the implied tripartite contract between the agency, the community, and the clientele. He writes of the vagueness of the promises and the agency's frequent inability to fulfill its implied contract with both community and clientele. The failures toward community and toward clientele often go hand in hand. The juvenile court, being a *parens patriae* creature of the state, was established with the promise of rehabilitation for children. Yet the court has been accurately described as simply a people-processing organization (Vinter and Sarri, 1965). The United States Supreme Court in somewhat harsher terms has stated, "There is evidence, in fact there may be grounds for concern, that the child [in the juvenile court] receives the worst of both worlds; that he gets neither the protections accorded to adults nor

the solicitous care and regenerative treatment postulated for children"
(*Kent* v. *United States*, 1966).

The concept of the right to treatment is based in a contractual/consti-
tutional analysis (Mascow, Menolascino, and Galvin, 1976). We are told
that in exchange for the security of the community, the *quid pro quo* for the
loss of liberty experienced by the involuntary patient is *treatment* (*Wyatt* v.
Stickney, 1971; *Wyatt* v. *Anderholt*, 1974). If therapy is not forthcoming,
the patient may bring legal action in one form or another against the institution and the state. One of the sad ironies in the therapeutic world is that as
the right to treatment has become recognized in professional practice and
statutory law, the means of securing that right have been severely curtailed
as a result of budgetary cuts in mental health services. This same contractual analysis has been used to vindicate the right to treatment for the developmentally disabled (*Wyatt* v. *Stickney*, 1971; *Wyatt* v. *Anderholt*, 1974)
and those under the solicitous care of our juvenile courts (Pyfer, 1972: *Nelson* v. *Heyne*, 1974).

State social service agencies are in the business of providing resources
for children through protective services, family rehabilitation programs,
and adoption services. On the one hand there is a promise to intervene in
abuse and neglect cases to save families through the provision of therapeutic
and other services. On the other hand there is the promise of adoptive services for families seeking children. To fulfill the latter opportunity the
agency may give priority to the promise of protecting children rather than
concentrate its services on "saving families." It may fulfill its promise to
one client by reneging on its promise to another. Given our current budgetary crisis in human services, the setting of priorities has become an exercise
in the establishment of a hierarchy of promises. All are made equally, but
some become more valued than others.

At a more concrete level explicit written contracts have become a dominant force in the organizational life of most agencies. We enter into
contracts with the federal government or with foundations for research,
training, and demonstration projects. "Contracting out" for services by
governmental units at both the state and local level is commonplace. As a
result of such contracts there is now a blurring effect between public and
private sectors in the human services. Union contracts, health insurance
agreements, and other accords often dominate the administrative life of an
organization. Although we do not often think in these terms, today's social
service agency is often built on a complicated, interlinking, and sometimes
conflicting set of contracts.

At a more individual level there is a set of emerging expectations, or in
some circumstances legal rights, which can be analyzed in contractual
terms. There is, I believe, a new sense of partnership among professionals
and others in at least limited mutuality in the therapeutic relationship. In

strictly contractual terms the idea of informed consent is receiving more serious attention, albeit too often as a consequence of legal opinions (*Canterbury* v. *Spence*, 1971; *Cobbs* v. *Grant*, 1971). If the individual is not fully informed of the purposes, procedures, and risks of treatment intervention, the contract or the exchange may be abrogated in any subsequent action for damages. If the individual cannot intelligently enter into an agreement, or if his or her consent is the product of duress, the contract for treatment is considered null and void (*Kaimowitz* v. *Department of Mental Health for State of Michigan*, 1973). This recognition of mutual obligations and responsibilities between professionals and their clients has resulted in a greater balance of power in the professional relationship.

A second example of emerging mutuality in the therapeutic relationship pertains to record access. The right of our clients to access their own records is being recognized both through legislation (*Washington Law Review*, 1982; Hayes, 1978) and case law (*Cornell* v. *Medical & Surgical Clinic*, 1974; *Emmett* v. *Eastern Dispensary & Casualty Hospital*, 1967; Helfman et al., 1973). This development should be applauded by clinicians, as it promotes equality, mutuality, independence, and ultimately autonomy. It also seems to break down the hierarchic nature of the therapist-client relationship and replaces it with a more horizontal paradigm.

The primary and crucial relevance of the contract considered here lies in the professional relationship between the social worker and the client. As in the doctor–patient relationship, the contract is either explicit or implied by the verbalizations and/or actions of the parties. However, such contracts are perceived too often in simplistic terms as money-for-service arrangements or as a set of behavioral responses for service. Like the marriage contract, the worker–client accord includes many essential terms that are either unperceived, disregarded, or viewed as unimportant. Yet it is when these elements are overlooked or misinterpreted that confusion and hostility may result. To see such arrangements as a qualified partnership agreement or as a joint venture would seem to be a preferable perspective. Physicians, generally, would be horrified at the thought of such a perspective, since they usually see themselves not so much as servants of their patients but as dispensers of technical wisdom. They may or may not tell their patients the source of the problem or for what purpose the treatment is imposed. They may not keep the patient informed during the medical explorations or the treatment process. The physician becomes the dominant and central person of the relationship; the patient, a necessary adjunct, is simply the raw material (Schutz, 1982).

All such professional behavior is rationalized on the premise that "the doctor knows best." Much the same, one fears, is the state of affairs within the social work profession, which too often has imitated or assumed the medical model. The profession until recently has paid little heed to defining the terms of the relationship between the worker and the client. The profession has not seen this as essential to the relationship, despite the fact that the worker–client relationship is taught as one of the primary ingredients in the social work process. One simply does not share with the client the diagnosis, the treatment plan, or the problem focus. The contract thus remains vague, unstructured, and nonspecific; it arises through ill-defined, almost magical processes, or it is part of somebody's "hidden agenda." Since the worker is not sharing—and is often hiding from the client—the real purpose of treatment, such vague contracts may lead toward a basic sort of professional dishonesty. The client may expect and feel that he or she is being treated for a particular problem that is completely outside the intent of the therapist as he or she formulates and implements treatment goals. The essential terms of the contract remain hidden. Frustration, inefficiency, and defeat are frequently the consequences. Or, as stated by Maluccio and Marlow (1974) in somewhat different terms:

> Lack of clarity about the contract, its limited development and its restricted application to social work practice, may be factors that contribute to the clash of worker–client perspectives, client discontinuance and the frustrations that clients and practitioners encounter when they try to work together meaningfully and productively.

SOCIAL SCIENCE PERSPECTIVES

A working agreement or contract does not exist in a vacuum; it presupposes interaction between two or more persons operating within a particular milieu. It is a social transaction. While we can, and indeed do, look at such behaviors microscopically, we must be aware that behavior can be neither understood nor meaningfully evaluated without reference to the environment within which that behavior occurs. Bateson (1958) reminds us that "to increase awareness of one's scientific universe is to face unpredictable increases in one's awareness of self. . . . Such increases are always in the very nature of the case unpredictable. . . . No one knows the end of the process which starts from uniting the perceiver and the perceived—the subject and the object—into a single universe." This lack of mathematical certainty should not, however, serve as an excuse for ignoring social transactions or being imprecise in reference to them.

Alan Watts (1975) has suggested that "in a pattern so mobile and volatile as human society, maintaining consistency of action and communication is not easy. It requires the most elaborate agreements as to what the pattern is, or to put it another way, as to what are the consistencies of the system. Without agreement as to the rules of playing together, there is no game. Without agreement as to the use of words, signs, gestures, there is no communication." It is imperative that there be communication in the typical therapeutic contract and consensus about the rules of the game as well.

Social scientists—theorists, researchers, and therapeutic strategists—have different perspectives on contractual relationships, but they share the conviction that a voluntary and unambiguous contract between observer and observed, psychoanalyst and patient, worker and client, is crucial to the effectiveness of any therapeutic transaction. Erikson (1964) notes that one can study the human mind only by engaging the fully motivated partnership of the observed individual and by entering into a sincere contract with him or her. The dimensions of Freud's discovery are contained in a triad that in a variety of ways remains basic to the practice of psychoanalysis. Freud's triad is, one, a therapeutic contract; two, a conceptual design; and three, a systematic self-analysis (1958). Wolberg (1967), in writing of the working therapeutic relationship, states:

> Unless a cooperative contract is established with the patient, the therapeutic process may come to naught. An effective system must maintain this as a prime objective during the first part of therapy. The techniques of achieving a relationship are rarely formalized, but usually they involve a gaining of the patient's confidence, an arousal of his expectations of help, a mobilization in him of the conviction that the therapist wishes to work with him, and is able to do so, a motivating of the patient to accept the conditions of therapy, and a clarifying of misconceptions. Without a working relationship, there can be no movement into the exploratory and working-through phases of therapy; the patient will be unable to handle his anxieties associated with the recognition and facing of unconscious conflict.

Both Greenson (1965) and Powell (1967) have written of the "working alliance" and have noted the importance of separating the alliance from other transference phenomena. Saul Bernstein (1964) writes: "In several human relations fields, the idea is developing that as service begins, there should be some clarification as to what it involves, mutual expectations, and whether each part wants to enter into the relationship" (p. 84).

Kanfer and Marston (1961) have shown empirically that the effects of ambiguity on learning and transfer in a verbal conditioning situation are that ambiguity may retard learning and that the more ambiguous the messages, the more retardation in learning. Raven and Rietsema (1960) show evidence that the client working toward a clear goal increases his interest in his work; a lack of structure in the situation makes his work less attractive or more threatening and increases group hostility. To a group member a clear group goal and goal path give meaning to membership in the group, increase attraction to one's fellow member, make the member more group-oriented, and increase the power of the group over him or her. Goldstein, Heller, and Sechrest (1966), in an exceptionally fine chapter on message ambiguity, after a review of relevant research, conclude that "reducing ambiguity in therapy will decrease threat and increase the likelihood that the therapist's remarks will be understood and accepted."

Wolpe and Lazarus (1967) seem to suggest a great deal of explicitness in the therapeutic process when they state that the therapist should give the client an explanation of the therapist's theoretical orientation: "The behavior therapist does not moralize with his patient, but on the contrary, goes out of his way to nullify the self blame that social conditioning may have engendered." They illustrate this point with examples in which the theoretical base as well as the process are explained and clarified. In speaking on the contract, Boszormenyi-Nagy (1965) notes that the family therapist must "sell" his approach to the family as a valid treatment approach. It appears that he or she, too, would have a therapist explain his or her orientation and, to some extent, the process. Framo (1965) notes that in the Pennsylvania Project treatment was enhanced by demanding of the families adherence to certain preconditions to therapy. Each member of the family had to sign an application in which the entire family agreed to participate regularly in therapy and to adjust their individual schedules accordingly, to pay a fee, and to demonstrate that they could give more than lip service to the notion that the problems of the designated patient were family problems. Steinzor (1967) writes:

> I think it would be a good idea and quite useful for every patient to obtain from the therapist a concrete description—perhaps even in writing—of just what philosophy he is "selling." The patient does have the right to know what kind of person he is choosing and what he is "buying." And since we therapists prize honesty, we should warn the patient that it does make sense to hesitate before entering psychotherapy. A democratic society is based on the making of choices which grow out of the voter's consideration of as much information as can be obtained. Throwing in one's lot with a therapist is one of the most crucial votes a person can cast. [p. viii]

In social work literature and research there has been more recent attention to the concept of contract than in any other human relations field. While Schwartz (1961) and Fry and Meyer (1973) introduced the concept of contract to the profession of social work, Henry (1981) and Seabury (1976, 1979), among others, (e.g. Kravetz and Rose, 1973; Stein and Gambrill, 1977), have developed the notion of contract much further and placed it as one of the central constructs of social work practice. As stated by Estes and Henry (1976):

> Contemporary emphasis on professional accountability—especially accountability to and with clients—and on client participation in the sequencing and focusing of social work treatment appears to be fostering recognition of the contract as a central dynamic in the therapeutic process.

COMPONENTS OF THE TREATMENT CONTRACT

The following definition of contract is proposed: The treatment contract is an agreement between two or more people in which there must be mutuality of understanding concerning the targeted behavioral problems, reciprocal obligations relating to treatment means, and finally an agreed-upon formulation of treatment goals. Unless all parties to the transaction agree on the purpose of intervention and the means by which treatment goals are to be achieved, there is little likelihood of a successful outcome. It must also be stressed that the terms of the contract must be stated with clarity and specificity if the contract is to impact on both client and worker accountability. To reiterate an earlier point, there are five basic elements in such contracts: *commitment, communication*, and *measured reciprocity* are three of these; the fourth and fifth are the respective *wills* of two or more people who believe in the power of one or both to affect the future in some respect.

PHASES IN THE CONTRACTUAL SEQUENCE

The negotiation of a treatment contract is a gradual and complex process. The stages of that process are not discrete enough so that one can proceed in a "lockstep" manner. Both worker and client must recognize and accept that prior understandings and agreements may have to be reviewed and renegotiated as the dynamics of the relationship change and individual growth occurs. As stated earlier, the professional therapeutic relationship must of necessity be fluid and organic.

Precontractual Phase

A set of prior conditions may affect the freedom within which the therapist operates, and the client must be made aware of these limitations. The protective service worker should not promise the client a total commitment to the therapeutic relationship when the worker is fully aware that his or her testimony against the parents may be called for in future neglect proceedings. As another example, the social work agency may prohibit the counseling of minors without parental consent, though such a policy is shortsighted at best.

In addition to those and many other policy limitations on the freedom to contract, there are both ethical standards and individual value systems that make certain agreements untenable. An agreement to use sexual intercourse between therapist and client as a treatment tool not only violates our ethical standards but constitutes a civil wrong. An individual social worker on the basis of personal religious beliefs may have difficulty discussing the alternative of abortion openly and objectively with a pregnant client. These preconditions may profoundly affect our ability to contract openly and honestly, and it is imperative that we both recognize and acknowledge these limitations.

Exploratory Phase

During the exploratory phase all parties begin to "test out" other members of the transaction and begin to define and specify expected role relationships, behaviors, and goals. For instance, there are certain "sell" tactics the therapist uses. The therapist wants the client to identify him or her as a problem-solving person, as someone who cares and will help in the solution of problems. Thus the therapist, at least initially, presents himself or herself as a benign person; he or she accords the client the usual social amenities. He or she is nonauthoritarian and treats the individual with dignity. In Rogerian terms, he or she presents an image of a genuine, accepting, empathic individual.

During this phase there is a mutual worker–client concern in defining the presenting problem, with the usual information-gathering strategies being applicable. The worker must not be so intent on diagnosis that he or she is inattentive to the client's own "diagnosis" and problem definition. Both the worker and the client must ultimately decide whether the case is appropriate to the agency and to the process that may ultimately be offered. Both members in the relationship must independently or mutually decide on continuance or discontinuance. The worker during this phase explains what the agency is about—its strengths, limitations, and restrictions. If certain terms of the contract are nonnegotiable, they should be made explicit. Time, place, and fee terms may be established through agency policy or norms in rather inflexible, nonnegotiable patterns. The worker may require that significant others must agree to participate in therapy.

During this phase the worker begins to orient the client to the treatment process. Orientation material may be presented in rather generalized terms, but it seems preferable to give the client some case examples of others with similar problems who have been helped and/or to give the client written material that illustrates the process for his or her study and his or her critical response. If one is working with ongoing groups, other members may provide orientation information to new members concerning how they have been helped through their present or prior group experiences. The client must have a fair opportunity to know what he or she is "buying." As well as possible, giving consideration to age, intelligence, and cognitive functioning, the offer must be made in clear, precise terms. The worker must begin to define with the client the elements of the consideration that flow between the participants.

The goal during the exploratory phase is to bring the client to a relatively unambiguous position. Not only does this approach present the therapeutic process on an honest, clear footing, but it also helps the client to determine better whether or not he or she wishes to participate in the process. A secondary but important benefit from such an approach is that it allows the client to test the expertness of the therapist and to ascribe to him or her expert status.

It is important to reemphasize here that in any contract based on promise there must be a meeting of the *wills* of two or more people who believe in the power of one or both to affect the future. One must also be reminded that contract involves choice or the concept of at least some freedom to elect from among a range of alternatives. If there is no choice there is no freedom, and if there is no freedom there is no contract. If the client is forced to participate in the therapeutic process it may well be meaningless to talk of contract. If one *will* is seeking to dominate or manipulate the other, then we have a clash of wills rather than reciprocal exchange. Such conflicts must be discussed openly and honestly during this phase if a meaningful contract is to result.

As an example of the above, the correctional social worker in our prison system may have a difficult time implementing the concept of contract as the result of the great power imbalance between worker and client and the manipulative struggle that is so endemic to our prison system. Clients who agree under the duress of a threat to their freedom cannot be said to be joined in a contract as defined here. To explore the possibility of contract where all the power lies with the therapist in a nonnegotiable state is basically dishonest and counterproductive.

Negotiation Phase

In the negotiation phase it is necessary to become as specific and explicit as the understanding of the client seems to allow. Generally the client's cognitive powers are underrated; workers tend to "talk down" inappropriately and thus alienate clients. If concepts cannot be explained in rather simple, illustrative terms, there exists either a fuzzy grasp of concepts or loss of the ability to communicate. To say merely that the worker is going to "help them with their problems" or will "help them to reconceptualize their roles" is so generalized and nonspecific as to be meaningless. Roles in treatment can be clarified by defining and explicating the treatment process. The expectations of both parties must be specified and conflicting expectations explored. At least minimum norms for performance must be defined.

There must be dialogue concerning goals and goal path, or the immediate and successive tasks in the treatment process. If time, place, and fee terms are negotiable, these must be discussed. Needless to say, many of these terms may be reviewed and possibly renegotiated throughout the treatment process. The traditionalist, using transference phenomena, will refer to the beginning role conceptualizations within the contract; as new role expectations develop during treatment, further clarification and interpretation may be necessary.

Preliminary Contract

The mere proposal of a term does not, of course, guarantee its inclusion in the contract. There must be specific acceptance of the term by the offeree, who may be either the worker or the client. A rule of contract law is that generally the written word takes precedence over the spoken word; in the treatment contract the behavioral agreement should take precedence over the spoken word. That is, if there is verbal agreement, one must seek collaboration in the client's behavior; if that consenting behavior is lacking, then one should assume that there is no agreement. The client may agree to come regularly at appointed times or to pay a specific fee and then not perform the agreed-on behaviors. Agreement may come at once, with major reservations, or never at all.

The preliminary or beginning contract is often no more than agreement to try out the process. The therapist may make this explicit by saying, "Why don't we try out this process and see how it works with no long-range commitments on either side?" Helen Perlman (1957) suggests:

> The initial phase ends, as phase, when a kind of pact has been arrived at in the nature of a "trial engagement" between client and caseworker to go forward together in their problem-solving efforts. This pact may sometimes be reached in a single interview, but sometimes it may take four or five discussions before clarification, mutual understanding, and decision are arrived at. [p. 106]

The client at this point may not have enough information about the therapist or the process. Realizing that he or she can gain that knowledge only through further experience, the client may agree tentatively to participate in the process.

Bertcher (1966) gives an example of a worker who religiously attends to the terms of the initial contract with each individual member in the group prior to their first meeting, and then proceeds to open the first meeting by stating, "Well, I guess we know why we are all here?" only to be met with a group of blank or confused expressions. The worker's initial statement of contract may reflect only his or her own state of mind, and this initial effort too often becomes a monologue; it is the worker's dictate as to the terms of the agreement. Even if the matter is thoroughly discussed, the client may often feel he or she is being coerced or manipulated; the client is unsure of his or her ground, ability to negotiate, and bargaining power. He or she may only agree passively to participate in the enterprise without having negotiated on any terms.

The Reciprocal Contract

The treatment contract is not a static set of agreements. Terms are added and withdrawn with the mutual consent of the parties. Such alterations are made with specific deliberation regarding the relevancy of these modifications to the treatment situation. During this phase client and worker clearly define their roles and expectations and the treatment process, and both parties verbalize their agreement and present behavioral collaboration in that agreement. At this point consensus is reached concerning the nature of the problem and the goals to be pursued. Goal path, with immediate and successive tasks, will be tentatively defined as well. The client and worker must achieve a reciprocal agreement concerning the central issues to be addressed in the therapeutic process. According to Estes and Henry (1976):

> [T]he client shares with the worker his formulation of the problems which compelled him to seek professional help. . . . Responding to the client's understanding of his own problems the worker, in turn, reinterprets the client's statements in light of the worker's diagnostic perspective, shares his tentative conclusions or areas of agreement with the client and if reasonably together, client and worker arrive at an agreement as to the major therapeutic objectives which each will pursue on behalf of the client in the course of treatment.

The contracts are typified by reciprocity or at least limited mutuality, and are the product of at least some choice among alternatives. They are arrived at through the "give and take" of negotiation and emanate from the penumbras of the therapeutic partnership. It is important to note also that such agreements must be both specific and clear. Ambiguities in contractual terms will eventually result in lost time and effort, renegotiation, and possibly client discontinuance.

Secondary Contracts

If all the above were not complicated enough, the situation becomes even more thorny when one is dealing with multiclient systems. In reference to group work Estes and Henry (1976) state:

> From our perspective, the contract mediation process is often ended and moves through a series of increasingly complex stages in the end resulting in not one therapeutic contract but a series of contracts which reflect changing individual and group-as-a-whole priorities over time.

Henry (1981) refers to such agreements as "interdependent contracts," while Churchill (1966) uses the term "secondary contracts." Not only does the individual have a contract with the worker, but each member of the group has a contract with every other member and with the group as a whole with respect to both individual and group goals. In addition the worker has a contract with the group as a whole. In groups the state of the contract formation may well be measured by the developmental stage of the group. It is perhaps the key element in measuring group cohesiveness and consensus.

As one might imagine, contracting in multiclient systems is more complicated and time-consuming than reaching two-party agreements. As a consequence the group worker must be somewhat more assertive in facilitating the process. In families and especially in groups the business of contracting can become so elaborate that the group gets bogged down to the point of destruction. It is extremely important to keep the provisions of the contract clear and simple. It is equally important to make individual and group goals behaviorally specific and measurable. The more global the goals, the greater the likelihood of goal ambiguity and confusion. One should start the process by seeking agreement on simple, short-term procedures and goals. Gaining agreement quickly and achieving short-term goals both facilite the contracting process and reinforces reciprocity, mutuality, and competency within the group.

Contract Termination

Within the contract sequence termination refers to that stage of the treatment process when the parties agree that their goals have been achieved and there is no longer need for the contract. In a sense it is a "letting go." It constitutes, among other things, a review and evaluation by both parties of the goals, the process, and the product. It is not within the purview of this paper to elaborate upon the termination process; however, in addition to currently recommended procedures and techniques, an evaluative process should be undertaken in which the client participates fully with specific reference to and evaluation of each of the contractual terms. The value of the therapeutic contract for research and evaluation purposes should be self-evident.

CONCLUDING CAVEATS

The therapeutic contract is a tool of treatment, not a panacea. In emergency or crisis situations there may be simply little or no time to invoke a deliberative contracting process. Where circumstances demand immediate action, we should not indulge in the fantasy that our response, which is dictated by our own personal and professional concerns, is within the realm of contract, as it is not. Neither can we foresee every condition or contingency in formulating contracts. We may be forced by the behavior of our client to step outside the contract or even to violate its implicit assumptions. If our client threatens the life of some third party, we may be forced to warn that individual despite the assumption of confidentiality (*Tarasoff* v. *Regents of The University of California*, 1976). If our client is a suicidal risk, we may be forced to take action in contradiction of our client's wish.

We also must not lose sight of the fact that the therapeutic agreement is not a contract in the legal sense. It is an agreement that evolves over time and, in a sense, is not final until the point of termination. One might well argue that a constantly changing agreement is no agreement at all, that its very fluidity stands in opposition to the efficacy of any contractual analysis. Contract for the purposes of therapy, however, need not be defined in such narrow terms. In addition we must be warned that the contract is not an end in itself. It is simply a tool used to facilitate treatment and does not encompass the entire process. Neither does it always guide treatment, as the therapeutic process is far too complicated to be embraced by any contract.

Despite all the above, however, a basic contract must be achieved between client and worker, no matter what the sequence, if effective treatment is to result. Failure to negotiate and reach agreement in clear, precise terms leaves both the worker and the client in ill-defined, ambiguous positions. Failure to resolve such ambiguities in the early stages of treatment results in an inefficient, self-defeating process for the therapist and, most especially, for the client.

REFERENCES

AMERICAN LAW INSTITUTE
   1981   *Reinstatement of the Law of Contracts*. Second edition. St. Paul: American Law Institute Publishers.
BARKER, ERNEST
   1951   The theory of the social contract. In John Locke, Jean-Jacques Rousseau, and David Hume, *Essays on Government*. Second edition. Oxford: Clarendon Press, pp. 81–119.
BATESON, GREGORY
   1958   "Language and psychotherapy," *Psychiatry*, 21: 100.
BERNSTEIN, SAUL
   1964   *Youth in the Streets*. New York: Association Press, p. 84.
BERTCHER, HARVEY
   1966   "The influence on field instruction or one approach to the teaching of so-

cial group work." Paper delivered before the Council on Social Work Education, January.

BOSZORMENYI-NAGY, IVAN
1965   "Intensive family therapy as process." In Ivan Boszormenyi-Nagy and James L. Framo (eds.), *Intensive Family Therapy: Theoretical and Practical Aspects.* New York: Harper & Row, pp. 96–98.

BREDEMEIR, HARRY C.
1964   "The socially handicapped and the agencies: A market analysis." In Frank Riessman, Jerome Cohen, and Arthur Pearl (eds.), *Mental Health of the Poor.* New York: Free Press, pp. 88–109.

CANTERBURY V. SPENCE
1971   464 F.2d 771, D.C. Circuit Court.

CASAD, ROBERT C.
1978–79   "Unmarried couples and unjust enrichment: From status to contract and back again," *The University of Michigan Law Review*, 77: 47–62.

CHURCHILL, SALLIE R.
1966   "State of second treatment contract." The University of Michigan School of Social Work, Ann Arbor, unpublished manuscript.

CLARK, HOMER H., JR.
1978–79   "Antenuptual contracts," *University of Colorado Law Review*, 50: 141–64.

COBBS V. GRANT
1971   8 Cal. 3d 229.

CORBIN, ARTHUR LINTON
1963   *Corbin on Contracts.* St Paul: West Publishing Company, 1: 2.

CORNELL V. MEDICAL & SURGICAL CLINIC
1974   315 N.E. 2d 178, Illinois Appellate Court.

EMMETT V. EASTERN DISPENSARY & CASUALTY HOSPITAL
1967   396 F.2d 931, U.S. Appellate Court, D.C.

ERIKSON, ERIK H.
1964   *Insight and Responsibility.* New York: W. W. Norton.

ESTES, RICHARD J., AND SUE HENRY
1976   "The therapeutic contract in work with groups: A formal analysis," *Social Service Review*, 50 (December): 611–12, 615.

FELDMAN, STEPHEN R., AND THOMAS M. WARD
1979   "Psychotherapeutic injury: Reshaping the implied contract as an alternative to malpractice," *University of North Carolina Law Review*, 58: 63–96.

FRAMO, JAMES L.
1965   "Rationale and techniques of intensive family therapy." In Ivan Boszormenyi-Nagy and James L. Framo (eds.), *Intensive Family Therapy: Theoretical and Practical Aspects.* New York: Harper & Row, pp. 146–47.

FREUD, SIGMUND
1958   "On beginning treatment: Further recommendations for the technique of psychoanalysis." In James Strachey (ed.), *The Complete Psychological Works of Sigmund Freud.* London: Hogarth Press.

FREY, LOUISE, AND MARGUERITE MEYER
1973   "Exploration and working agreement in two social work methods." In

Saul Bernstein (ed.), *Explorations in Group Work*. Boston: Milford House, pp. 1-16.

GARVIN, CHARLES, AND BRETT SEABURY
1984 *Interpersonal Practice in Social Work*, Englewood Cliffs, N.J.: Prentice-Hall.

GOLDSTEIN, ARNOLD P.; KENNETH HELLER; AND LEE B. SECHREST
1966 *Psychotherapy and the Psychology of Behavior Change*. New York: John Wiley & Sons, pp. 146-211.

GOUGH, J. W. (ed.)
1946 *Second Treatise of Government*. Oxford: Basil Blackwell.

GREEN, SAMUEL, AND JOHN V. LONG
1984 *Marriage and Family Law Agreements*. Colorado Springs: Shepard's, McGraw-Hill.

GREENSON, R. R.
1965 "Working alliance and transference neurosis," *Psychoanalytic Quarterly*, 34: 155-79.

HAYES, JOHN
1978 "The patient's right of access to his hospital and medical records," *Medical Trial Technique Quarterly*, vol. 24.

HAYNES, JOHN M.
1981 *Divorce Mediation: A Practical Guide for Therapists and Counselors*. New York: Springer.

HELFMAN, DENNIS, ET AL.
1973 "Access to medical records." *Appendix, H.E.W. Secretary's Commission Report on Medical Malpractice*. January. Washington, D.C.: U.S. Government Printing Office, pp. 177-213.

HENRY, SUE
1981 *Group Skills in Social Work*. Itasca, Ill.: F. E. Peacock.

IRVING, HOWARD H.
1980 *Divorce Mediation: A Rational Alternative to the Adversary System*. New York: Universe Books.

KAIMOWITZ V. DEPARTMENT OF MENTAL HEALTH FOR STATE OF MICHIGAN
1973 No. 73-19434-AW, Michigan Circuit Court, Wayne County, July 10.

KANFER, FREDERICK H., AND A. R. MARSTON
1961 "Verbal conditioning, ambiguity and psychotherapy," *Psychological Reports*, 9: 461-75.

KANT, IMMANUEL
1974 *The Philosophy of Law*. Trans. W. Hastie. Clifton, N.J.: A. M. Kelley.

KENT V. UNITED STATES
1966 383 U.S. 541, pp. 555-56.

KRAVETZ, DIANE, AND SHELDON ROSE
1973 *Contracts in Groups: A Workbook*. Dubuque, Iowa: Kendall/Hunt Publishing Co.

MACNEIL, IAN R.
1980 *The New Social Contract*. New Haven: Yale University Press.

MALUCCIO, ANTHONY M., AND WILMA D. MARLOW
1974 "The case for contract," *Social Work*, 19 (January): 28.

MASCOW, BRUCE G.; FRANK J. MENOLASCINO; AND LORIN GALVIN
1976 "The right to treatment for mentally retarded citizens: An evolving legal and scientific interface," *Creighton Law Review*, 10: 124–66.

NELSON V. HEYNE
1974 491 F.2d 352.

PERLMAN, HELEN
1957 *Social Casework: A Problem Solving Approach*. Chicago: The University of Chicago Press.

POWELL, THOMAS
1967 "Two types of superego impediment to the working alliance." Ann Arbor: The University of Michigan, unpublished.

PYFER, JOHN F., JR.
1971 "Juveniles' right to receive treatment," *Family Law Quarterly*, 6: 279–320.

RAVEN, BERTRAM H., AND JAN RIETSEMA
1960 "The effects of varied clarity of group goal and group path upon the individual and his relationships." In Dorwin Cartwright and Alvin Zander (eds.), *Group Dynamics, Research and Theory*. Second edition. Evanston, Ill.: Row, Peterson, pp. 395–413.

RAWLS, JOHN
1971 *A Theory of Justice*. Cambridge, Mass.: Harvard University Press.

ROUSSEAU, JEAN JACQUES
1976 *Social Contract and Discourse on the Origin of Inequality Among Mankind*. Ed. Lester G. Crocker. New York: Washington Square Press.

SCHUTZ, BENJAMIN M.
1982 "Establishing the therapeutic framework: The patient as partner." In Benjamin M. Schutz (ed.), *Legal Liability in Psychotherapy*. San Francisco: Jossey-Bass, pp. 21–43.

SCHWARTZ, WILLIAM
1961 "The social worker in the group." In *The Social Welfare Forum, 1961*. New York: Columbia University Press.

SEABURY, BRETT
1976 "The contract: Uses, abuses, limitation," *Social Work*, 21 (January): 16–21.
1979 "Negotiating sound contracts with clients," *Public Welfare*, 37 (Spring): 33–38.

STATE OF MICHIGAN
1983 Public Act 294, providing for the licensing of social workers in child custody disputes.

STATSKY, WILLIAM P.
1984 *Family Law*. Second edition. St. Paul: West Publishing Company.

STEIN, THEODORE AND EILEEN GAMBRILL
1977 "Facilitating decision making in foster care," *Social Service Review*, 51 (September), pp. 507–13.

STEINZOR, BERNARD
1967 *The Healing Partnership: The Patient as Colleague in Psychotherapy*, New York: Harper & Row, p. viii.

TARASOFF V. REGENTS OF THE UNIVERSITY OF CALIFORNIA
   1976   17 Cal. 30425.
VINTER, ROBERT D., AND ROSEMARY SARRI
   1965   "The juvenile: Organization and decision making." *Juvenile Court Hearing Officers Training Manual*, Ann Arbor: Institute for Continuing Legal Education, The University of Michigan, 2: 173–95.
WASHINGTON LAW REVIEW
   1982   "Patient access to medical records in Washington," *Washington Law Review*, 57: 697–713.
WATTS, ALLAN
   1975   *Psychotherapy East and West*. New York: Pantheon Books, p. 100.
WEITZMAN, LENORE J.
   1974   "Legal regulation of marriage: Tradition and change—A proposal for individual contracts and contracts in lieu of marriage," *California Law Review*, 62: 1169–1288.
   1981   *The Marriage Contract*. New York: Free Press.
WEYRAUCH, WALTER O., AND SANFORD KATZ
   1983   *American Family Law in Transition*. Washington, D.C.: Bureau of National Affairs.
WOLBERG, LEWIS R.
   1967   *The Technique of Psychotherapy*. Second edition. New York: Grune & Stratton, p. 48.
WOLPE, JOSEPH, AND ARNOLD A. LAZARUS
   1967   *Behavior Therapy Techniques*. New York: Pergamon Press.
WYATT V. STICKNEY
   1971   325 F. Supp. 781 (M.D. Alabama).
WYATT V. STICKNEY
   1972   344 F. Supp. 373 (M.D. Alabama).
WYATT V. ANDERHOLT
   1974   503 F.2d 1305, 5th Circuit Court.

11

Elements and Issues
in Group Composition

Harvey J. Bertcher and Frank Maple

THE EFFECTIVENESS of any group is determined partially by the particular attributes or characteristics that each individual brings to the group. Deliberate grouping of clients who have certain attributes can yield benefits for all group members. But what is an optimum mix? And how can the composition of a group influence its effectiveness?

The answers presented here are far from completely satisfying. The prediction of group effectiveness is a complex matter. Many of the studies done in this area pertain to effectiveness in completing some discrete task rather than focusing on the development of a group that is effective in bringing about change in the problematic social functioning of individual social work clients. Useful material has been drawn from studies in small group theory related to member characteristics that influence group effectiveness as well as from research in group psychotherapy.

Many workers underestimate the powerful effect of a group's composition on the interaction that ensues or ignore the potential benefits that could accrue from changing the make-up of a group once it has begun to meet. (The exception to this rule is worker willingness to remove a group's most obstreperous member.) A dearth of empirical data on this subject in reports of research with social work groups and unsatisfactory presentations of material on this topic led to the development of the instructional program on which this discussion is based. We hope it will facilitate learning about group composition and stimulate some definitive research on composition of effective treatment groups.

GROUP CREATION AND GROUP MODIFICATION

Social workers use group composition skills and knowledge to create and modify treatment groups. In group creation members are selected from

This chapter is an exposition of concepts and other teaching material presented by Harvey J. Bertcher and Frank F. Maple, with Henry Wallace (1971).

a collection of people, often strangers, for a group that does not yet exist. In group modification the composition of an existing group is changed by adding new members, either because old members leave or to maintain the size of the group, or by removing present members to enable those who remain in the group to achieve treatment goals more effectively. Both in creating and in modifying a treatment group, the worker's goal is to achieve a situation in which the attributes of each member can have beneficial consequences for every other member, or at least no serious negative consequences for any other member of the group.

A wide range of individual attributes have potential consequences for group members. They include both *descriptive attributes*, which classify an individual as to age, sex, marital status, occupation, or other "positions" that the individual can be said to occupy; and *behavioral attributes*, which describe the way an individual acts or can be expected to act, based on past performance. An individual can be characterized by both descriptive and behavioral attributes with regard to any aspects of his or her life.

Descriptive Attributes	*Behavioral Attributes*
sixteen years old	acts like a two-year-old
ward of the court	conforms well to the expectations of
marijuana user	probation officer
member of high school football team	encourages peers to use marijuana
	plays football aggressively

Descriptive attributes were once thought to be most useful in selecting group members. However, research has shown that behavioral attributes, which indicate how an individual interacts with others, are much better predictors of an individual's behavior in a treatment group.

Selecting Critical Attributes

Every human being can be characterized in terms of an enormous number of descriptive and behavioral attributes. How is it possible to decide which attributes will be *critical* to the effectiveness of a group?

A group of adolescent unwed mothers is to be created within an institution (population: 120; age range of residents: 13–30, with an average of fifteen; residents typically enter the home in their sixth month of pregnancy). The problematic behavior leading to the creation of the group is widespread violation of doctor's orders. The girls can be classified according to such descriptive attributes as race, socioeconomic status, educational attainment, number and age of siblings, place of birth, and so on, and such behavioral attributes as enjoying long walks, knitting skillfully, being very possessive of friends, participating actively in group singing, and so on. Which—if any—of these might be *critical* attributes for *this* group?

Group objective.   The main criterion for the selection of critical attributes is group objective: those activities members should be able to do well as a result of being in the group. Initially a group's objective may be based on an agency's view of the needs and interests of several clients or potential clients. Once the group begins, the members themselves may negotiate a modification of this objective with the worker. Group objective must be stated in measurable terms, or no one can be sure it has been achieved (Goldstein, Heller, and Sechrest, 1966).[1] Helping a group of unemployed men *to secure and hold a job*, or a street corner gang *to avoid antisocial actions*, or a group of classroom malperformers *to improve all of their grades to a passing level* are directed toward *measurable* group objectives.

In the hypothetical home for unwed mothers the group is to be created for several girls who are not following the doctor's orders, thus presenting a definite health hazard for themselves and their babies. A discussion group could be crated with the objective to reduce or eliminate violations of doctor's orders with regard to good prenatal care, e.g. the eating of inappropriate foods, failure to get sufficient rest. Some of the *descriptive* attributes that might be regarded as critical to the achievement of the group's purpose include age, length of time before delivery, and physical condition. Some critical *behavioral* attributes include eating habits, rest habits, and behavior with regard to doctor's orders.

Group development.   A secondary consideration in designating attributes as "critical" is group development. Sometimes particular individuals are selected because they can help a group to grow. Group membership for such individuals, even if it is initially counterindicated, can be appropriate for group development. Behavioral attributes that facilitate the development of an effective group include certain task performance, group maintenance acts, and the ability to model desired behaviors. The task role can help keep the group on target toward its goal or objective. The group maintenance role might keep the group together by effecting compromises, soothing hurt feelings, making members feel important, and so forth. The inclusion of individuals who have demonstrated good task role performances as well as some who have performed maintenance roles effectively will help any group to survive and develop. An exception would be if two strong task specialists are likely to clash.

The kind of task role performance or task leadership needed is related both to the task itself and to the situation in which the task is to be addressed. A person who has the behavioral attributes of being well organized

---

[1]A more thorough examination of group objectives can be found in Robert F. Mager (1962). A shorter (five-page) discussion of objectives is in Robert F. Mager (1968).

and purposeful might be the best task leader for a time-limited group, but an individual who has many community contacts and knows how to use them might be the best task leader for a group that is meeting in order to improve its members' use of community, rather than agency, resources. On the other hand, the type of group maintenance skill needed is a function less of the task than of the behavioral attributes of most group members. In a group with several verbally aggressive members, a calm, friendly member may be able to help the group navigate troubled waters; but in a group whose members are likely to be reluctant to participate, a person with a good sense of humor could ease the situation, thereby fostering participation.

The other kind of behavioral attribute that can be particularly helpful in enhancing group development is the ability to serve as a good model for others to emulate. An individual may be selected for group membership because of a specific skill or personality trait, appropriate for others in the group to imitate and adapt to their own style of behavior. A person who has developed some talent or interests or who can keep his or her temper in an argument may be a potential model. In seeking individuals capable of modeling desired behavior, workers often overlook an excellent source: people who have "graduated" from client status. An appropriate model for a group approaching discharge from a psychiatric hospital could be a former patient who is doing well in a new job.

Obtaining Information About Behavior

When critical attributes have been selected with reference to group objectives and development, the worker must find the potential members who have the relevant descriptive attributes and learn as much as he or she can about the degree to which each individual shows critical behavioral attributes in settings similar to the group treatment setting. Behavioral information may be obtained by developing a list of questions about specific interpersonal behaviors and seeking answers from persons who have seen the potential member function in group situations. Other approaches involve giving the potential member an opportunity to observe an effective group, then eliciting relevant information from the potential member during an individual interview; or placing the potential member in a special diagnostic group (Churchill, 1965).

Obtaining accurate and complete behavioral information is difficult. Someone may tell you that a particular boy is very good at effecting compromises. He sounds like someone who could play a group maintenance role and serve as a model for less patient boys. In your first group meeting you discover that he effects compromises by beating up everyone who disagrees with him. Such crucial behavioral information often is not contained in diagnostic statements.

Developing Behaviorally Specific Objectives

Since they constitute the bases for deciding which attributes are critical, the first step in selecting members for a treatment group is to specify, however tentatively, the objectives of the group. While initial objectives should be tentative, they should also be specific and explicit, not vague. Behaviorally specific group objectives indicate where, when, how well, how often, and/or how much a desired behavior is to be performed. A behaviorally specific objective indicates the conditions under which the desired behavior will occur; it states the desired behavior in terms of observable activity— what people will be able to do, not how they think or feel; and it specifies standards or criteria by which performance of desired behavior is to be measured.

Examples:

GIVEN   In a mental hospital, six patients to be discharged within the next three months

BEHAVIOR   will develop plans for activities regarding family relationships, job, school, etc.,
             which, in the opinion of the group and the worker,

CRITERIA   should make it unnecessary for any group member to return to the hospital.

GIVEN   When presented with any situation in which the individual could violate the law, each member of the gang

BEHAVIOR   will act according to the law

CRITERIA   voluntarily, in a majority of cases.

The "given" conditions, the desired behavior, and the criteria for measuring results should be stated specifically.

Example: When confronted with an opportunity to eat forbidden food, girls who are members of a group in a home for unwed mothers will have a good understanding of the dangers to themselves and their babies.

In the above example, while the conditions under which the girls are to act are specific, the desired behavior is not (what will they *do* with their understanding?), nor are the criteria for measuring behavior specific (how well or how often should they be able to do whatever they should be able to do?).

Not only should initial group objectives be behaviorally specific, they should also be clear to potential members. Potential members should believe that the achievement of objectives is possible. Their achievement should include beneficial outcomes for each individual member. And they should be optional, with potential members having some power to select, create, or modify them.

Client Choice

Should individuals be able to choose whether they or others become members of a particular group? Many social work clients receive service on a quasi-voluntary or involuntary basis. A psychiatric hospital patient is expected to participate in a discharge planning group. A rebellious youngster is brought to a child guidance clinic by his or her mother. An AFDC mother is strongly encouraged by her caseworker to attend meetings of a group with the purpose of orienting her to seek employment. Can a group be effective if some members don't want to be in it?

There are no pat answers, but when an involuntary client enters a group, the client has more chance to like the group if he or she sees that others like it. On the other hand, an individual who feels that he or she has some or total choice about becoming a member will be more likely to accept the group from the start. Since effective groups tend to have members who want to be there, an individual's decision to join or not to join may be regarded as a critical attribute. A group with involuntary members may knit more quickly with voluntary members, and the greater the number of voluntary members the more likely that it will become an effective group quickly.

Determining the potential member's attitude toward entering a particular group requires talking with the individual before the group begins. The degree of choice the individual feels he or she has about joining the group will probably be influenced by the amount of choice the individual has in determining or affecting group objectives. In the same vein, members may feel more positively toward a group if they can exercise some choice about new members who enter the group. Finally, the truly voluntary group member should know who the group worker is going to be, so that the individual can consider this factor when making a decision about joining the group.

Attributes of the worker. Experience has demonstrated that some workers prefer and/or perform better with certain clientele, e.g. children, senior citizens, or hospital patients. Initially certain clients may experience greater comfort with—and thus be more willing to be influenced by—a worker who has descriptive attributes similar to their own, such as age, sex, race, or religion. Although the worker is not a client-member, he or she is a central person in the group, and the worker's behavioral attributes may be crucial to group effectiveness. The worker's ability to perform task, maintenance, and/or modeling roles, as well as his or her ability to function as an advocate of the interests of each potential group member, have to be considered. The likelihood of group effectiveness will be increased by a high degree of client involvement in group creation, including some decision-making power, particularly regarding the group's purpose but also regarding the choice of other group members and even the worker.

Client Pool

If the worker and the clients are to have a choice in determining group membership, an agency must have a pool of potential clients. The worker should play a major role in nominating and selecting group membership in order to maximize the utility of group composition as a means of influencing the treatment process. To maintain a reservoir of potential clients, when referral is appropriate the worker should inform all referring agents of the critical attributes for each prospective group.

Often social workers must rely on others to make referrals, and this can lead to an ineffective referral process. Juvenile court workers may be instructed by their supervisor to refer any of their clients who in their opinion might benefit from group services. The psychiatrist at a clinic may list five patients who are "having trouble with peer relationships" and ask the social worker to work with them as a group. Even when referrals are the only source of potential group members, the worker can increase the likelihood of group effectiveness by clearly specifying to the referring person a definite set of objectives for the prospective group by identifying critical attributes in some detail, and by striving to develop a reservoir of potential clients.

Reliance on others to make referrals usually leads to no referrals at all, unless some supporting administrative procedures are developed.

>*Example:*   A group worker was hired to introduce group work services in a public welfare agency. To acquaint him with the agency's operation, he had been assigned a small caseload.
>Seeking to create a group, he had told the caseworkers that the group's purpose would be to assist AFDC mothers in solving problems of raising children when the children's father was not living at home.
>In order to avoid administrative hassling, the group worker had discussed the group with several caseworkers individually but had not talked about it with any supervisor. Although caseworkers expressed interest in the group work service for their clients, referrals were not forthcoming.

To reduce the caseworkers' resistance to making referrals, the group worker could have stated what he regarded as critical attributes in greater detail; he could have discussed his intentions and cleared his plans with supervisors, so as to gain greater influence; and he might have developed a demonstration group from his own caseload.

EFFECTIVE GROUPS

Group effectiveness is partially determined by the attributes that each individual client and worker brings to the group. Effective groups tend to have interactive, compatible, and responsive members. Interactive members like each other. Responsive members are interested in helping each other.

Research indicates that a group often is more effective if members have homogeneous descriptive attributes and heterogeneous behavioral attributes (Goldstein, Heller, and Sechrest, 1966). Common descriptive attributes help foster interactiveness and compatibility: A young adult in conflict with his or her parents would probably not be very compatible or interactive in a social club for senior citizens. Heterogeneous behavioral attributes, on the other hand, increase the chances that members will be constructively responsive to one another and have something in their behavioral repertoire that will be useful to the group. When all members have similar behavioral attributes and similar descriptive attributes, have faced similar problems, have tried the same solutions and experienced the same failures, the group typically holds little promise for those who are seeking new answers for themselves. Members sometimes talk about "the blind leading the blind" in such a group.

In one study male psychiatric patients in a Veterans' Hospital were observed and scored for their behavioral attributes of "social activity," that is, the degree to which they talked to others, were chosen by others, spoke in group meetings, and were helpful task group members (Fairweather, 1964). Four groups were then created, as follows:

	High Social Activity	Low Social Activity
	Group I	*Group II*
Homogeneous behavior attributes	All above agerage	All below average
	Group III	*Group IV*
Heterogeneous behavior attributes	⅔ above average ⅓ below average	½ above average ⅔ below average

Groups I and II were homogeneous with respect to the composite of behavioral attributes called "social activity." Groups III and IV were heterogeneous. After making sure that there were no significant differences among the four groups as to the descriptive attributes of age, length of stay in the hospital, and living situation prior to hospitalization, the researchers found Group III—the heterogeneous group with a predominance of members having high "social activity" attributes but several having low "social activity"—to be significantly better than any other group at complex problem-solving and general performance.

Barriers to Group Effectiveness

Several compositional factors can hinder the development of effective groups:

1. *Too much compatibility* can enable group members to resist effectively all efforts to modify their behavior.
2. *Too much or too little stress* can result in a surplus of anxiety or a surfeit of apathy.
3. *Negative subgroups* can sabotage group purpose, victimize individual members, and control "democratic" decision-making processes.

Balance

Most effective groups are composed of members who differ with respect to behavioral attributes. In addition, the critical behavioral attributes of members of such groups tend to fall along a "linear continuum." Balance—an optimum mix of critical behavioral attributes—is an important characteristic of effective groups.

Locating potential group members along a linear continuum for a particular critical attribute can facilitate selection of a balanced group.[2] In a residential program for adolescent unwed mothers, experience had shown that unless some anger toward doctors could be openly expressed and dealt with, group interaction did not effectively reduce violation of doctors' orders. At the same time the venting of too much fury had been known to blow such groups apart. The worker decided that the ability to express anger toward authority figures, e.g. doctor, nurse, social workers, was one critical attribute that should be carefully balanced within the group.

Worker's Assessment of Ability to Express Anger Toward Authority Figures

Too Little	In Between	About Right	In Between	Too Much	Much Too Much
−2	−1	0	+1	+2	+3
Bea	Ann	Maude	Sue	June	Cookie
Mabel	Sarah				
Louise					

Although all nine girls were regarded as "eligible" with respect to other critical attributes, the worker decided that a group of six would be more effec-

---

[2]The authors are indebted to their colleagues, Paul Glasser and Sallie Churchill, for the approach used to describe balance in terms of a linear continuum.

tive. Bea's group maintenance skills were badly needed; Mabel, Louise, and Cookie were eliminated from this particular group.

Environment

People continually overlook the effects of a group's immediate environment on the level and quality of interaction among group members. Many variables in the environment or setting of a group meeting can be influential: size of meeting room, arrangement of chairs, place to meet (home, car, agency, ward lounge, and so on), privacy, location of meeting place, and ease of reaching it. Basically, choice of setting should be guided by the group's purpose, by evidence of preplanning and atmosphere.

Evidence of preplanning. Most people like to know that some consideration has been given to their comfort. Meeting at a time that is convenient for all, having ashtrays for smokers, being able to shut a door to ensure privacy, and having coffee available when members arrive are all indications to clients that the worker cares enough about them to have made some preparations.

Atmosphere. The situation in which a group of people find themselves has a definite effect on the mood of the group. A small room can provide a feeling of intimacy for one group, a feeling of crowding for another. For some groups a station wagon can be an exciting, attractive meeting place. Providing an appropriate environment can be a significant contribution to group effectiveness.

Time

Some groups need to meet only once to accomplish their objective effectively; others require a considerable amount of time and many meetings to achieve their goal. Some groups are limited in their time by prior agreement; others are open in terms of the time that individuals stay in the group and the lifetime of the group itself. There is no optimum lifetime for all groups; on the contrary, the duration for a group should be determined by its objective.

Establishing definite time limits helps groups develop quickly. Recent research in psychotherapy indicates that when a worker expects treatment to take about two years, it usually takes that long; if the worker expects that treatment goals can be achieved in only three months, three months often prove sufficient (Goldstein, 1962). Optimistic estimates are well advised.

Groups are more likely to be effective if the worker, perhaps with the group, makes carefully considered decisions about the frequency, length, and time of meetings than if the traditional "fifty-minute hour once a week" is used automatically. Time is viewed differently by different cultural groups. How will the group feel about meeting at the same time, each time?

Number

How large is an effective group? Substantial research has been done on the effects of group size, yielding a plethora of propositions. As groups get larger, participation, satisfaction, consensus, and intimacy among members decrease; subgroups emerge; leadership requirements and the group's ability to tackle more complex tasks increase; opinions are asked of others (Thomas and Fink, 1960).

There is no optimum size for all groups; rather, size depends upon the objectives of the group and the attributes of its members. Many considerations should enter into decision-making about the best size for a particular group: How important is group morale? How complex a program is desirable? How capable are members of helping each other? of sharing the attention of the worker?

If clients need an opportunity to move gradually into group participation without having immediate demands placed upon them, a larger group may be preferable. If members need to be convinced from the start that the group is designed to provide maximum benefit for each individual, a smaller group will permit rapid involvement. If group morale is all-important, a larger group will permit some members to be absent or to drop out without having negative consequences for everyone else. A larger group may be good if it requires members to turn to one another for help. A larger group may be disastrous if members are likely to panic without the immediate support of the worker or to be very jealous of attention given by the worker to other members.

Most treatment groups are composed of individuals who are likely to interact in negative ways from time to time. It would appear that some degree of conflict is inevitable and potentially useful. If a tolerable amount of useful stress is to develop, a group should not be too small (e.g. three) or too large (e.g. fifteen); there should be enough people to interact in resolving conflict.

Composition and Effectiveness

No matter how "good" the composition of a group may be, it cannot assure the achievement of treatment goals. But the skillful composition of a group can enhance its effectiveness. By basing his or her definitions of critical attributes and decisions about matters of time, place, and size upon explicitly stated group objectives, the worker can create a group whose members will be interactive, compatible, and responsive.

GROUP CREATION: A PROBLEM

As a focal point for consideration of issues and difficulties associated with group composition, the following information is offered about a number of boys who are potential members of a group to be sponsored by a juvenile court. Given the following objectives, create the most effective treatment group possible, noting what further information you would like to have and why you need it. When no mention of probation status is made, you should assume that the boy is still on probation.

Group Objectives

Once members have terminated from this group, they will no longer engage in illegal behavior, so that institutional placements will not be necessary for any of them. In addition, they will develop and act on prosocial goals for themselves—e.g. return to and maintain satisfactory performance in school, become involved in training for employment, seeking, securing and holding a job—and will work consistently to achieve their goal(s).

1. *Donald W.* (Age 14). 8th grade. Black. Interests: none known. Lower-lower class. Below average intelligence. Docile, uninvolved in any ongoing activity. No previous group or institutional experience. Little interest in socializing; a "lone wolf." *With gang in breaking and entering.*

2. *Robert T.* (Age 16). 10th grade. Black. Interests: mechanical work. Lower class. Average intelligence. Spent six months in Boys Training School with group experience. Aggressive, domineering, hostile. Loud voice, compulsive talker, pushes own ideas on group but doesn't take responsibility for following through on own ideas. *Broke probation. (His mother stated that he was out of her control.)*

3. *Ray D.* (Age 16). 10th Grade. White. Now living in detention home. Interests: chemistry, athletics. Lower-middle-class family. Well above average intelligence. No previous group work or institutional experience. Independent, somewhat aloof from peers and adults. Seems to be afraid of getting too close to anyone. Won't talk in social groups; remains uninvolved when group takes action. *Stealing cars and reckless driving; incorrigible according to parents.*

4. *Gene R.* (Age 15). 9th Grade. Black. Interests: does good school work; likes fighting, exciting activities. Lower class. High intelligence. Spent eight months in detention home. No group work experience. Leader

of delinquent gang. Effective at controlling group—but not by physical aggression—rather is good at effecting compromises; has a good sense of humor. Has been off probation for several months, doing well in an auto mechanics training school. *Breaking and entering.*

5. *George D.* (Age 16). 10th grade. White. Interests: athletics, cars. Lower-middle class. Above average intelligence. No previous group work or institutional experience. Conforming; a follower. Can become very verbal when cars are discussed; otherwise rarely opens his mouth. *Several drinking violations; drunk and disorderly in public.* Is not now on probation.

6. *John V.* (Age 16). 10th Grade. Black. Interests: track, football. Lower class. Average intelligence. Participated in group work program at Community Center—noninstitutional experience. Blows up, falls apart when frustrated. Gene R.'s close friend; Gene plays an important role in helping John to control his temper. *Breaking and entering.*

7. *Jim S.* (Age 15). 9th Grade. Black. Interests: biology and track. Lower class. Above average intelligence. No previous group or institutional experience. Subtle leader—skillful manipulator—the "cool" type. Distrustful of adults so that he operates behind the scenes. Particularly dislikes social workers but, in their presence, appears to be a conformist. Off probation, doing passing work in school. *Stealing.*

8. *Jerry M.* (Age 15). 10th Grade. White. Interests: hunting, fishing. Lower class. Average intelligence. No previous group work or institutional experience. Very aggressive; assaulted father twice with hammer although provoked each time. Uncomfortable in the presence of blacks. Hot temper; fears he will lose it so avoids group contacts. *Assault with weapon (father).*

9. *George A.* (Age 16). Out of school. White. Interests: metal work, welding. Lower class. Below average intelligence. Eliminated from a previous group work experience because of aggressive behavior. Breaks rules, acts as a "know-it-all." Backs down when confronted by forceful person. *Chronic truancy.*

10. *Robert B.* (Age 15). Out of school. White. Interests unknown. Lower class. Below average intelligence. Unemployed—deemed "uneducable." Docile, quiet, meek. Will follow any leader. *Stealing.*

11. *Joe F.* (Age 16). 11th Grade. Black. Interests: music (drums). Lower class. Above average intelligence. No group work or institutional experience. Follower; small boy, docile. Music teacher indicates he has exceptional talent, but Joe is afraid to try for fear he will fail; others like him because of his musical ability and the fact that he poses no threat. *Stealing.*

12. *Pete S.* (Age 16). Out of school. Black. Unemployed. Interests and skills unknown. Lower class. Below average intelligence. One year in Boys Training School. No group work experience. Aggressive, huge—takes over. Clumsy; covers his embarrassment at being awkward by a "don't care" manner. *Several breaking and entering and car thefts.*

13. *Ralph O.* (Age 17). 9th Grade. Black. Interests: sports, gang activity. Lower class. Average ability. Poor school performance—reading problem. No previous group work or institutional experience. Involved in gang fights. Witty, quick in remarks. Verbally cuts others down. Close friend of Gene R. *Gang activity—destruction of property.*

14. *William C.* (Age 16). 10th Grade. White. Interests: carpentry, woodworking. Lower-middle class. Above average ability. In Boys Training School six months. Quiet, a loner; can be angered if teased. Spends most of his time with one girl. Does not want to be in a group. *Two breaking and enterings.*

15. *Stan W.* (Age 16). 10th Grade. White. Interests: football, basketball. Middle class. Superior ability; poor school performance. No previous group work experience. Plays it smart, wise, initiates action. Pseudo-sophisticated. Aggressive, tense, and nervous. Always on the go; excitement seeker. In previous social contacts has been seen as initiator of antisocial behavior. *Drunk and disorderly.*

A SOLUTION TO THE PROBLEM

Rationale for Group Objective

The purpose of a juvenile court with regard to youth who are adjudicated delinquent is to see to it that those juveniles who violate the law do not continue to do so. We assume that law-abiding behavior is more likely to occur if the individual is "making it" in society in some legally acceptable way. Accordingly, the group purpose must include both restraining aspects (no further law violation) and facilitating aspects (working to achieve prosocial goals).

Time. Ten of the fifteen boys are sixteen or older. It was stated that if they break the law once they are seventeen, they will be placed in an institution. Since it is the purpose of the group to avoid the necessity of such a placement, short duration (three to six months) might be appropriate. On the other hand, it could be useful to make this an "open-ended" group, that is, one in which new members are added as old members leave, because of the prosocial modeling that the remaining older members could provide for newer members. Accordingly, each boy could be told that he would be expected to "graduate" in three to six months, with the understanding that as members leave, new members would be added. (Graduates could retain a quasi-official membership and be involved as helpers.)

Incidentally, note that the given age for the boys, e.g. "16" is quite non-specific. Are they all just about to turn seventeen? Did they just become sixteen? In other words, age might prove to be a critical attribute. If so, you would need to have birth dates for purposes of decision-making.

Meeting time is often a question of convenience; some boys may be in school, others on a job, and so forth. Accordingly, this decision can probably be delayed until some tentative ideas about grouping emerge. For example, if all but one potential member could meet in the late afternoon, that individual might be eliminated from that particular grouping. Again, more specific information is needed—this time with regard to the boy's current situation vis-à-vis school, job, and so on.

For this group a regular once-a-week meeting (always on the same day at the same time) could establish a reliable pattern for adolescents whose world may otherwise be chaotic and unpredictable. Once a week would perhaps be as much contact as the boys would want. However, should the group so decide, frequency of meetings could be altered.

Numbering.   While groups of six to eight appear to be preferred by many group workers (small enough to allow for individualization, large enough to remain a group in spite of absent members), such a group automatically eliminates nine (or seven) other individuals. It is possible that two groups could be created. It is also possible that several of the boys would profit more from a one-to-one contact. Again, let's defer this decision for the moment.

Environment.   For many juveniles, the setting of a juvenile court is not conducive to the kinds of relaxation that might prove necessary for boys to share concerns comfortably in the group. In their city a Community Center is four blocks away from the County Court. It is centrally located and thus easily accessible by car or bus. The center's program is flexible enough for use of the building—e.g. rearrange furniture, serve refreshments. Accordingly, plans are to meet at the center.

Limiting Conditions

Client pool.   In this case the client pool is sufficiently large to allow for choice. Since this is to be an open-ended group, some procedure would have to be worked out so that potential new boys could be routinely referred.

Worker control of intake.   In working out a referral procedure it would be essential to indicate critical attributes, so that boys who would be inappropriate would not be referred for possible inclusion in the group only to be turned away.

Critical Attributes

With regard to group purpose
1. Descriptive attributes
While it may be unnecessary to say this, considerable selection has al-

ready clearly preceded actions in creating a group; all of the potential members share certain descriptive attributes:

    a. All are males.

    b. All are adolescents (although a fourteen-year-old adolescent may be at a very different level of maturation from a sixteen-year-old).

    c. All are now or have been on probation.

    d. All are likely candidates for placement in a correctional institution.

These four factors represent critical descriptive attributes for this group. At this time in the community, racial differences are not as significant as they might be elsewhere, so "race" would not be labeled as a critical attribute. Socioeconomic class differences do not appear to be a significant factor for this group.

    Nature-of-offense might be of importance, e.g. nine boys have engaged in some kind of theft activity—stealing, breaking and entering, car theft—which may be considerably different from truancy or alcoholism but not of sufficient importance to make the actual legal offense itself a critical attribute.

    2. Behavioral attributes

    In only one instance (William C.), is there any information about client voluntarism with regard to group treatment. Nevertheless, it seems that it would be important to know how each boy views the group purposes of eliminating illegal behavior and at the same time "making it" in a prosocial way. Accordingly, client voluntarism would be established as a critical behavioral attribute, with a goal of achieving some balance in the degree of voluntarism. If this information is not available it may have to be done without. Some elimination of illegal behavior is a prime purpose of the group; hence a second critical behavioral attribute could relate to the degree to which the individual has previously been known to initiate illegal acts. Thus, the following continuum based on subjective assessment of available information could be established.

History of Initiating Illegal Acts That Others Follow

None	Little	Average or Unknown	Some	Very Much
−2	−1	0	+1	+2
1. Donald W.	(No one)	6. John V.	2. Robert T.	4. Gene R.
3. Ray D.		8. Jerry M.	7. Jim S.	15. Stan W.
5. George D.		13. Ralph O.	9. George A.	
10. Robert B.			12. Pete S.	
11. Joe F.				
14. William C.				

One is immediately struck by the number of boys who have been seen as "followers." While it would be premature to select or eliminate any boys at this stage, this continuum should be kept in mind when the attempt eventually is made to achieve a balance of behavioral attributes.

A third critical behavioral attribute for group purposes relates to the interests, experiences and abilities individuals have that might be capitalized on in moving boys toward school or employment opportunities.

Possession of Interests and Skills Related to School and Work

Antisocial Interest and Skills	Neither School- nor Work-oriented Interests or Skills	No Known Interests or Skills	Some Interests	Considerable Interest and/ or Skills
−2	−1	0	+1	+2
13. Ralph O.	6. John V.	1. Donald W.	2. Robert T.	4. Gene R.
	8. Jerry M.	10. Robert B.	3. Ray D.	14. William C.
	15. Stan W.	12. Pete S.	5. George D.	
			7. Jim S.	
			9. George A.	
			11. Joe F.	

Again, information is inadequate—although typical of the kind of information most workers have to work from—but it does appear that a number of the boys have interests and/or skills that could be useful in work and/or school.

With regard to group development

1. Descriptive attributes

It was stated earlier that race is not a major descriptive attribute in terms of the purpose of this group. Obviously, were the purpose different, e.g. fostering "black pride," then race would be critical. On the other hand, if many of the boys have strong negative feelings about associating with members of another race, the group's develpment would be hindered. While information here is sparse, Jerry M. might be considered for membership only if the group turns out to be composed predominantly of white boys.

2. Behavioral Attributes:

Task and group maintenance ability, plus the ability to model prosocial behaviors, appear to be critical behavioral attributes in this group.

Ability to Perform Task (Leadership) Acts

None	Very Little	Average	Some	Quite a Lot
-2	-1	0	$+1$	$+2$
1. Donald W.	5. George D.	4. Gene R.	2. Robert T.	(No one)
3. Ray D.	15. Stan W.	6. John V.	7. Jim S.	
8. Jerry M.			12. Pete S.	
9. George A.				
10. Robert B.				
11. Joe F.				
13. Ralph O.				
14. William C.				

Ability to Perform Group Maintenance (Leadership) Acts

None	Very Little	Average	Some	Quite a Lot
-2	-1	0	$+1$	$+2$
1. Don W.	(No one)	(No one)	11. Joe F.	4. Gene R.
2. Robert T.				
3. Ray D.				
5. George D.				
6. John V.				
7. Jim S.				
8. Jerry M.				
9. George A.				
10. Robert B.				
12. Pete S.				
13. Ralph O.				
14. William C.				
15. Stan W.				

Selection of appropriate models would be based on those particular attitudes and/or behaviors that would be desirable to be imitated. In a sense, each continuum developed so far provides potential models and modelers, e.g. a boy who has particular interests and/or skills could model this behavior for those who have no such involvement. However, one further critical attribute should be added since it appears to be a serious deficit for some: the ability to control impulsive, antisocial behavior.

Ability to Control Impulsive, Antisocial Behavior

Very Poor Control	Little Control	Average Control	Good Control	Excellent Control
−2	−1	0	+1	+2
6. John V. 8. Jerry M. 9. George A.	2. Robert T. 5. George D. 10. Robert B. 12. Pete S. 13. Ralph O. 14. William C.	1. Don W. 11. Joe F.(?)	3. Ray D. 7. Jim S. 15. Stan W.	4. Gene R.

Taken together, these critical attributes could all be classified as being prosocial or antisocial in quality. That is, involvement in some interest or skill could be expected to be associated with prosocial behavior while a lack of such skills, although not necessarily associated with antisocial acts, would be less likely to lead to socially acceptable behavior. (The only exception to this is the "initiation of illegal acts" attribute, in which a "plus" score means that the individual has acted this way frequently; in other words, a plus score is associated with antisocial acts. In the summation that follows, the signs of this particular rating have been reversed to bring it into conformity with our prosocial/antisocial dichotomy.)

Summing the ratings each boy received on the five critical attributes produces the following table:

NAMES	INITIATING ILLEGAL ACTS	INTERESTS AND SKILLS	TASK ACTS	SOCIO-EMOTIONAL ACTS	SELF-CONTROL	TOTALS
1. Donald W.	+2	0	−2	−2	0	−2
2. Robert T.	−1	+1	+1	−2	−1	−2
3. Ray D.	+2	+1	−2	−2	+1	0
4. Gene R.	−2	+2	0	+2	+2	+4
5. George D.	+2	+1	−1	−2	−1	−1
6. John V.	0	−1	0	−2	−2	−5
7. Jim S.	−1	+1	+1	−2	+1	0
8. Jerry M.	0	−1	−2	−2	−2	−7

Names	Initiating Illegal Acts	Interests and Skills	Task Acts	Socio-emotional Acts	Self-Control	Totals
9. George A.	− 1	+ 1	− 2	− 2	− 2	− 6
10. Robert B.	+ 2	0	− 2	− 2	− 1	− 3
11. Joe F.	+ 2	+ 1	− 2	+ 1	0	+ 2
12. Pete S.	− 1	0	+ 1	− 2	− 1	− 3
13. Ralph O.	0	− 2	− 2	− 2	− 1	− 7
14. William C.	+ 2	+ 2	− 2	− 2	− 1	− 1
15. Stan W.	− 2	− 1	− 1	− 2	+ 1	− 5

Recasting the totals, the following clusters of scores emerge:

Total		Names
+ 4		Gene R.
+ 3		
+ 2	A	Joe F.
+ 1		
0		Ray D., Jim S.
− 1	B	George D., William C.
− 2		Donald W., Robert T.
− 3		Robert B., Pete S.
− 4	C	
− 5		John V., Stan W.
− 6	D	George A.
− 7		Jerry M., Ralph O.

In an attempt to create a balanced group of eight boys, the total was arbitrarily divided into clusters of 4 (note broken lines) and the decision was made to select two boys from each cluster. Believing that four factors that could lead to an ineffective group (too much compatibility, too much stress, inadequate alternative models, and negative subgroups) an attempt was made to avoid these difficulties in the selection. Also, an effective group consists of members who are interactive, compatible, and mutually responsive.

The selection process went something like this:

1. First Gene R. was seen as a potentially strong, positive group member. In selecting him his two friends were eliminated (danger of negative subgroup), John V. and Ralph O.

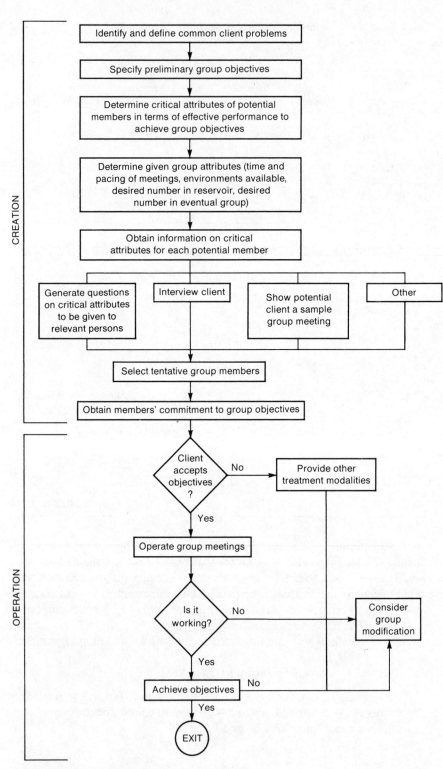

FIGURE 11-1. Group Composition Sequence

2. Since Gene R. had been known to initiate illegal acts, the other "high initiator," Stan W., was eliminated to reduce potential stress.
3. William C. was chosen for his "skills and interests" since this could provide a good model for others.
4. Robert T. and Jim S. were selected because they had demonstrated task ability.
5. The fact that Gene R. and Jim S. were no longer on probation, and were apparently doing well, was an additional reason for wanting them in the group (as potential models for prosocial behavior).

The group then consisted of:

A. Gene R.
   Jim S.
- - - - - - - - -
B. William C.
   Robert T.
- - - - - - - - -
C. Robert B.
   Pete S.
- - - - - - - - -
D. George A.
   Jerry M.
- - - - - - - - -

In addition, Jerry M. was known to be uncomfortable with blacks. Since this was to be a racially mixed group, it was decided to drop him from this group and lower the total to seven boys: Gene R., Jim S., William C., Robert T., Robert B., Pete S., and George A.

Alternatives to the group creation problem are entirely possible. Furthermore, the boys not selected for the first group might be formed into a second group. (How effective would you expect such a group to be? Why?) The boys not selected might be seen individually or regarded as a reservoir of potential members should any of the original group members "graduate," fail (get in trouble again), or prove unworkable in the initial grouping.

The group composition sequence is summarized in Figure 11–1.

REFERENCES

BERTCHER, HARVEY J., AND FRANK F. MAPLE (WITH HENRY WALLACE)
    1971   "Group composition: An instructional program." University of Michigan School of Social Work, Ann Arbor (mimeographed).
CHURCHILL, SALLIE R.
    1965   "The use of the social group work method as a diagnostic tool in the interdisciplinary evaluation of a disturbed child in the Pittsburgh child guidance center," *American Journal of Orthopsychiatry*, 35 (April): 581–88.

FAIRWEATHER, GEORGE W.
1964 *Social Psychology in Treating Mental Illness: An Experimental Approach.* New York: John Wiley & Sons.

GOLDSTEIN, ARNOLD P.
1962 *Therapist-Patient Expectations in Psychotherapy.* New York: Macmillan Publishing Company.

GOLDSTEIN, ARNOLD P.; KENNETH HELLER; AND LEO B. SECHREST
1966 *Psychotherapy and The Psychology of Behavior Change.* New York: John Wiley & Sons.

MAGER, ROBERT F.
1962 *Developing Instructional Objectives.* Palo Alto, Calif.: Fearon Publishers.
1968 *Developing Attitudes Toward Learning,* Palo Alto, Calif.: Fearon Publishers, pp. 13–17.

THOMAS, EDWIN J., AND CLINTON F. FINK
1960 "Effects of group size," *Psychological Bulletin,* 60: 371–84.

12

Group Process: Usage and Uses in Social Work Practice

Charles D. Garvin

ONE OF THE MOST HALLOWED CONCEPTS in social group work practice is the term "group process." The use of this concept, however, is frequently ambiguous, obscure, or even mystical. At the same time, "process" is used to denote a force that can account for all desirable practice outcomes. The significance of group processes, however defined, is well stated by Whitaker and Lieberman (1964, p. 3):

> Processes characteristic of the group as a whole are an intrinsic and inevitable aspect of all groups no matter what their size or function. In a therapy group, group processes not only "exist" but are a major factor influencing the nature of each patient's therapeutic experience. The manner in which each patient contributes to, participates in, and is affected by the group processes determines to a considerable degree whether he will profit from his group therapy experience, be untouched by it, or be harmed by it.

Therefore the clarification of the "process" concept for group work practitioners will enable them to understand and, when necessry, modify processes occurring in treatment groups so as to attain appropriate treatment goals.

DEFINITION OF PROCESS

We conceive of group processes as changes that take place in group conditions. The conception we wish the reader to bear in mind is of the group as an organic entity that changes constantly as members interact with each other and with their environment.

One way of describing group processes is to examine these changes as they occur from moment to moment in the life of the group. Thus as member A speaks, followed by B, followed by C, changes occur in many ways such as in the views A, B, and C have of each other, the views all hold about the subject under discussion, the roles that each enacts in the group, and their very pattern of interaction.

Another way of describing group process is to select some group condition and to examine how it changed over time. Thus we can take the roles played by members and identify how they evolve. When we do so, we are looking at only one aspect of a complex picture. Nevertheless, this is often a necessary way to view the group, because it is difficult for the practitioner to visualize the many ways the group is changing without focusing on one or at the most a few of its aspects. It is possible, then, to use this approach gradually to broaden and deepen one's understanding of the full complexity of a group's process. That is the perspective we take in this chapter.

As we shall describe more fully later, the purpose of this examination of group process is to help the worker and the members to solve group-level problems that stand in the way of their accomplishing their separate as well as mutual goals. These problems are frequently a consequence of the way various aspects of the group's process unfold. The worker and the members can engage in a problem-solving activity to identify group-level problems, relate these problems to group process, modify the process, and ultimately create group conditions that are the most conducive to goal attainment.

A sharp contrast must be drawn between group process and "group structure." Collins and Raven (1969, p. 103) define group structure as follows:

> [T]he regularity of person-to-person and person-to-task relationships observed in many groups has led social scientists to search for a patterning of interpersonal relationships which can be considered in the abstract, transcending the personalities and idiosyncratic relationships of a given group. With perhaps more optimism than is justified, the concept of "structure" has been borrowed from the physical sciences. Social structure may be defined as the relationship among elements of a social unit. The elements may be individuals, or positions for which no individuals have yet been designated as in a formal organization chart. The dimensions of structure (the ways in which the elements can be interconnected) include communication, attraction, prestige, role, power, locomotion, and dependence.

As can be seen, then, the main focus in *structure* is on the existence of a pattern or on the relationship among units. The main emphasis in *process* is on changes occurring in group conditions. At times, of course, an aspect of the group's process is the change taking place in the group's structure.

ASPECTS OF GROUP PROCESS

As we have stated above, we have developed a typology of the aspects of group process that workers and members can target for change in order to enhance group functioning or ameliorate a group-level problem. As shown in Figure 12–1, broadly speaking these aspects are the goal-oriented *activities* of the group and the quality of the *interactions* among the members. The former partially corresponds to the goal attainment and the latter to the group maintenance functions referred to in the small group literature (Bales, 1951, 1965).

We have further ascertained that activities and interactions occur in the group at an *overt* and *covert* level. By overt, we refer to those events that are clearly identifiable through the observable actions and communications of group members. By covert, we mean the feelings and thoughts of group members that are related to such activities and interactions. We refer to these feelings and thoughts as group-level phenomena because *patterns* of thoughts and feelings exist among the members of the group, and these patterns are both causes and consequences of other group events. As we shall describe later, members can make these thoughts and feelings known to each other, and the worker can facilitate this process.

Definitions of these aspects of group process are as follows: The *overt goal-oriented activities* of the group are goal determination and goal pursuit. Goal determination includes all the activities members engage in to decide upon group goals. Goal pursuit includes all the activities members engage in to attain these goals. The associated *covert goal-oriented activities* occur as the values that members place upon the group's goals and the way the group pursues them evolve.

The *overt interactions* among the members are role differentiation, communication–interaction, and conflict resolution–behavior control. A role structure exists in which members hold perceptions and expectations for how each will behave in terms of his or her position in the group. The process of role differentiation refers to the evolution of the group's role structure. Communication–interaction refers to the messages members send to one another as they define and enact their roles. Conflict resolution–behavior control refers to the interactions that occur among members as they seek to maintain the group through constraining tension-inducing or group-

FIGURE 12–1. Aspects of Group Process

	GOAL-ORIENTED ACTIVITIES	QUALITY OF INTERACTIONS
OVERT	1. Goal determination 2. Goal pursuit	4. Role differentiation 5. Communication–interaction 6. Conflict resolution and behavior control
COVERT	3. Values and norms	7. Emotions

threatening behavior. *Covert interactions* consist of changes in the nature of emotions (both caring as well as hostile) among the members.

FRAMEWORK FOR ANALYSIS
OF GROUP PROCESS

In order to analyze each group process, we shall consider the following issues:

1. The function of the specific process within small groups
2. The phases that may occur as the process evolves (These phases for some aspects of process may include only the presence or absence of a single condition, or they may include movement among several different conditions.)
3. Etiological and mediating factors in the evolution of the aspect of process (Specifically included here are the forces that determine its initiation, its content, its maintenance, and its termination.)
4. The character of the process in differing phases of group development (One important aspect of group development is the nature of the changes in group processes over time; this formulation draws upon a definition of group development offered by Sarri and Galinsky (in Chapter 5) as "changes through time in the internal structures, processes, and culture of the group.")
5. Illustrations of the kinds of phenomena, observable events, or circumstances that characterize the process, particularly in the context of group work
6. When and how workers seek to intervene in this aspect of group process

ASPECTS OF PROCESS RELATED TO GOALS

Goal Determination

Goal determination takes place as members interact to select the desired end state to be achieved through group actions. The end state might be a specific event like taking a trip, constructing something, or having a party. Or it might constitute an ultimate and often abstractly defined series of goals. Often the aim is toward achieving changes in group members such as "improved school performance" or "reduction in antisocial activities."

Phases of goal determination. As pointed out by Thibaut and Kelley (1959, p. 256), "group goals are social matters and require some degree of consensus before they can be processed by enough of their members to warrant their being called group goals." They describe consensus as follows:

> [I]t is probably necessary that this consensus rest largely on the acceptance of these goals by a relatively large number, possibly a majority, of the group members. By the acceptance of a group goal it is meant that the individual believes that he will attain good outcomes when the task is put into the state designated by the goal. And for consensus to be based on acceptance, there must be correspondence among the members in this respect: each must believe he will attain good outcomes . . . acceptance of goals implies that the person is dependably ready to enact the behavior thought to put the task in the goal state even in the absence of enforcement by the techniques of gaining compliance: surveillance and sanctioning. [Thibaut and Kelley, 1959, pp. 257–58]

Generally the process of goal determination begins when alternative outcomes for the group are posed. The step that follows consists of discussion of these alternatives in which factual information and evaluative criteria may be introduced. Choices are then made and more specific goals derived. This process follows the same sequence as the more general problem-solving paradigm discussed later.

Another way of examining phases of goal determination is to inspect not only the development of consensus around a goal, but also the succession of goals that occurs when one goal is attained or when the group abandons efforts toward attaining a goal. Goal determination occurs either when intermediate goals are developed or when a new episode of consensus-seeking takes place.

Etiological factors in goal determination. The forces affecting the achievement of consensus on a group goal and progression of group goals may be examined on three levels: (1) the characteristics of individuals, (2) group characteristics, and (3) environmental characteristics. Cartwright and Zander (1968) summarize individual-level forces when they state:

> The attractiveness for any given member of a particular goal for the group is influenced by the nature of the member's person-oriented and group-oriented motives, by his judgment of the rewards and costs involved for him and the group in activities relevant to the goal, and his subjective probability that the group will attain this goal. [p. 405]

On a group level, a range of variables can have an impact on goal determination process: whether cooperative or competitive conditions prevail in the group; whether members have power to *compel* nonconforming members to accept specified goals; whether there be consensus that the group has the resources to achieve the goal; whether the group is cohesive enough to secure behavior consistent with the group goals (Thibaut and Kelley, 1959, pp. 257–61). Structural elements also play an important role: whether the pattern of participation in the group lends itself to securing consensus on goals or not; whether existing group norms and patterns of dealing with conflict are important considerations.

Finally, influences from the environment affect goal determination processes. Cartwright and Zander (1968, pp. 405–6) summarize these environmental variables as the extent to which the group is seen as relevant to furthering or obstructing the objectives of those persons.

Group development and goal determination. The long-term goals of the group are frequently at issue during the formative phase of group development. Members also may seek to select short-term goals to demonstrate that sufficient commonality exists for the group to continue. In the intermediate phase of the group there is less emphasis on the selection of goals and more upon carrying them out. The revision phase is the time when new goals emerge as new leadership is identified (see Chapter 5). Either may occur first: New leadership may bring about a reformulating of group goals, or a reformulation of goals may initiate the replacement of the existing leadership.

Phenomena characteristic of goal determination. The process of goal determination may take the form of a discussion of the kinds of member problems to be dealt with in the group. A group of unwed mothers might spend time discussing whether their greater priorities are to relinquish the child, how to handle the putative father, or how later to pursue their own careers.

Another type of goal decision frequently encountered is whether to change some aspect of the clients' environment or to change the clients' responses to that environment. When this decision is made initially, the subsequent goal decision may be to move on to the alternate decision after attaining the first goal or to give up on it.

Worker intervention in goal determination. Workers will often help members to describe their individual goals prior to identifying group goals. This usually takes the form of helping members to state problems or concerns and what they would like to see different with reference to these. Members then are assisted to choose group goals that will help them attain individual ones.

One problem that workers encounter in this process is a conflict over group goals. If this is because member individual goals are incongruent, workers may help members to negotiate priorities in group goals or even to join other groups that will be more appropriate for them. At times such conflicts arise because members have not genuinely identified their own goals, because they seek to use a goal discussion to resolve power issues, or because they experience the agency as imposing group goals. Each of these causes must be dealt with in ways appropriate to it.

In some groups the worker must be fairly active in suggesting group goals, because members have difficulty in identifying their alternatives. This may be true in groups of young children or of cognitively impaired adults. In other groups members will be highly articulate in describing possible group goals.

Goal Pursuit

The ensuing discussion uses the definition of goal pursuit provided by Thibaut and Kelley (1959, p. 263), "the processes by which actions are chosen as means of attaining [the] goal." The literature describes two types of actions in this respect. One is primarily cognitive and relates to the process of *group problem-solving*; the other may involve cognitive, motor, and affective elements in order to *accomplish a task*.

The concept of task has been defined by Thibaut and Kelley (1959, p. 150) as a "problem, assignment, or stimulus-complex to which the individual or group responds by performing various overt or covert operations which lead to various outcomes." This is, of course, a generic definition. For purposes of analysis the problem component has been identified as a separate process.

Phases of goal pursuit. The work of Bales and Strodbeck (1968) on the phases through which the process of problem-solving evolves is quite definitive. These phases are identified as those in which acts of either "orientation," "evaluation," or "control" predominate. Orientation behaviors include a member's "giving or asking for orientation, information, repetition, clarification, or confirmation." Evaluation activities occur when a member "gives or asks for opinion, evaluation, analysis, expressing of feeling, or a wish." In control activities members "give or ask for suggestions, direction, and possible ways of action."

When the task relevant to attaining the goal is not primarily a cognitive one, the phases have to be described more abstractly. Thibaut and Kelley (1959, p. 151) define such a state at any given point in time "in terms of its yielding a unique repertoire." In his analysis of program activities, Vinter in "Program Activities: An Analysis of Their Effects on Participant Behavior" (Chapter 13) stresses that activities in pursuit of treatment goals may vary in any one of the following dimensions:

1. Prescriptiveness of the pattern of constituent performances
2. Institutionalized control governing participant activity
3. Provision for physical movement
4. Competence required for performance
5. Provision for participant interactiveness
6. Reward structure

Etiological factors in goal pursuit.   An excellent summary of variables that affect group problem solving, provided by Kelley and Thibaut (1969, pp. 1–101), points out that problem-solving behavior is initiated with the receipt of outcomes below the "comparison level" (p. 11). By this they mean that outcomes through individual efforts are perceived to be less desirable than alternate outcomes resulting from group efforts. Subsequent problem-solving events will be determined by such group structures as communications structure, affectional structure, reward structure, and power (or status) structure (pp. 19–41).

The leadership structure of the group will also affect the pursuit of goals. Two types of leadership are task and socioemotional. Each type fulfills a corresponding group function. Task leadership acts are, of course, the relevant behaviors for the process being discussed here.

Similar variables affect all other problem-solving and task completion behaviors. Among those that have been described are the individual's power to determine the stages the task will take (Thibaut and Kelley, 1959, p. 153), the sources of social definitions of reality (Thibaut and Kelley, 1959, p. 155), and the behaviors defined socially as basic and essential to the activity (Vinter, "Program Activities," Chapter 13, below). The structure of the task itself also affects the pursuit of goals. Some tasks are conjunctive (all participants have to make a response to receive the reward), while others are disjunctive (some subset of the small group system can act so that the reward will be secured).

Group development and goal pursuit processes.   The main emphasis in the formative period of group development is on goal determination, not problem-solving or task completion. Activities, if engaged in, are primarily used for members to discover common goal and activity interests. The intermediate phase is characterized by "observable involvement in goal-directed activities." This involvement continues through the period of revision, with shifts in activities made necessary by changes in purposes and in leadership. A higher commitment to goal-oriented activities is found in later intermediate stages as earlier problems are resolved and as group cohesiveness is stronger. Subsequently a termination stage may coincide with the completion of the tasks for which the group was organized (see Chapter 5, by Sarri and Galinsky).

Phenomena characteristic of goal pursuit.   If a group of prisoners discuss how they can overcome the onus of having been in jail when seeking employment, they have begun the process of problem-solving. This process, using the propositions described above, has been initiated because the "comparison level" of undertaking employment without having solved this problem is lower than what may be achieved through the group's solution to their common "problem."

The group of prisoners may then role-play interviews with prospective employers, using a "script" developed through the problem-solving process. The "script" represents the completion of the first task. A powerful individual may seize a particular role because of outcomes he desires. From the point of view of the group worker, the way the role is played may appear dysfunctional, but the prisoners may not object because of their definitions of reality. However, to the degree that a satisfactory outcome depends on the satisfaction of all participants, the task is conjunctive and will not terminate until such satisfaction is attained. This example illustrates a "program activity" to pursue a goal in which elements of the sequence have been pre-structured.

Worker interventions in goal pursuit.   Many skills are called upon to facilitate the group's problem-solving. At times workers train the group members in an approach to problem-solving. This involves explaining problem-solving phases to the members and coaching them in appropriate behaviors. A useful technique to use in the orientation phase is to explain the process of "brainstorming" in which members contribute as many ideas as possible while withholding critical or evaluative comments.

The worker must also identify barriers to the group's problem-solving and help the members to overcome these. This involves helping members who have ideas to contribute to do so; helping members to learn to communicate their ideas clearly; helping members to learn to support each other in this process; and securing resources members may require for problem-solving, such as consultation from experts. The worker also supplies information about the subject under consideration. At times the members' emotional state inhibits problem-solving. They may be anxious or angry, and the worker must help them to deal with these feelings so they can proceed rationally.

Still other skills are required of the worker when the group works on tasks. The worker may have to help members tailor the task to their purposes and abilities. This can be done by modifying the activity dimensions referred to earlier. Thus the worker might help members make the task more interactive or rewarding or less demanding of member competence. As with problem-solving, the worker may have to secure expert consultation for the members. Occasionally opposition to a task is forthcoming from the environment. An example occurred in a group of developmentally disabled young adults who were learning appropriate ways to express their sexuality. Their parents objected to this program, and the worker had to devote time to overcoming this source of opposition.

Values and Norms

According to Mills (1967), norms "help orient persons to each other by providing guidelines as to how certain universal interpersonal issues are to be managed by the parties in question." Since it is impossible to imagine a group without a system of rules to govern the behavior of members, the emergence of norms is a *sine qua non* of group existence. External conditions change, however, and new tasks require new rules. Norms, as a consequence, may be in flux as the group develops. We discuss norms in relation to goals as on a covert level; they strongly influence the group's choice of goals as well as how the members will pursue those goals. Admittedly, norms also relate to interactions, but ultimately this links back to which interactions are necessary in order for the group to accomplish its purposes.

Phases of normative development. Mills draws upon Parsons for a series of categories regarding the phases by which norms evolve in the group:

> Norms in any society or group, he suggests, must provide answers to questions relating to at least four issues: (1) Are relations among members to be based upon the expression of the feelings they have toward one another, or upon the assumption that those feelings are to be suppressed and controlled . . . ? (2) Is involvement with one another to be total and unbounded (as with parent and child) or is it to be restricted and specific . . . ? (3) Is the significance of the other to be due to the unique relation one has with him . . . or is it to be due to the fact that he represents a type, or a class, or person . . . ? (4) Is the significance of the other to be due to his qualities . . . or is it to be due to how he performs . . . ?

Another paradigm is provided by Thibaut and Kelley (1959, p. 24) who described three phases: (1) stating a rule, (2) maintaining surveillance; and (3) applying sanctions.

Mills adds that norms are "cognitive and moral statements which screen, evaluate, prescribe and proscribe feelings and action. As statements they are distinct from feelings and from behavior. They exist in symbolic form in the mind, and are elements of group culture."

Etiological factors in the development of norms. The following list includes some of the principal factors that determine the operation of group norms:

1. "Greater pressure to conform in groups is associated with greater group cohesiveness" (Mills, 1967, p. 77).
2. "When a member in a cohesive group deviates, others will first actively try to convert him to the norms and then, if they fail to do so, will reject him" (p. 78).
3. "Outside agents (which may even be thought of as supernatural forces) may be used to support norms if there is consensus in the group regarding their action and power" (Thibaut and Kelley, 1959, p. 241).
4. "Norms about behavior that are highly important to the life and

success of the group will be more thoroughly publicized, more carefully monitored and more strongly enforced than norms about behavior of little importance" (p. 254).

5. "Good communication in the group permits more accurate transmission of the norm" (p. 254).

6. "For surveillance to be effective, the behavior of the member must
be open to view and individually identifiable" (p. 254).

Group development and norms. The establishment of norms begins
during the formative period of the group as members explore each other's
personal values. In the intermediate period, "Additional norms and values
are acquired that specifically relate to group functioning" (see Chapter 5).
Sarri and Galinsky also point out that social control mechanisms develop,
and deviation from norms often tends to be dealt with in a harsh or punitive
manner by the group. Because norms and values for a number of areas of
attitudinal expression and overt behavior are not yet established, member
participation may be somewhat restricted in fear of sanctions or because
members do not yet know what is expected of them. Pressures toward uniformity and consensus are clearly apparent.

In the revision phase the norms, values, and traditions of the group
may change in varying degrees depending upon the extent of the revision. In
any case the revision stage ends with a strengthening and clarification of the
group's norms. In later phases of group life, because the group has existed
for a longer time, norms can be expected to be more clearly enunciated and
deviation more likely to secure a response from other group members.
Throughout, the worker is aware of the potential of group norms for the
support of prosocial behavior.

Phenomena characteristic of normative development. When deviant
behavior occurs in a group, deviant norms are likely to be operating. The
worker in such groups frequently challenges antisocial norms and reinforces
the expression of socially desirable norms. Discussions take place on the desirability or undesirability of specified behaviors such as stealing, sexual
promiscuity, and rule-breaking in the agency itself.

Worker interventions in normative development. In the formative
phase the worker helps the group to develop norms that are required to accomplish its purposes. They usually include confidentiality, openness regarding ideas and feelings, and commitments to help each other.

As the group moves on to goal pursuit, normative issues arise related to
the goals in question. Thus, discussions occur on values in childrearing,
choice of career, or success in school. The worker will help members identify and communicate their values through such approaches as values clarification. The worker will also state his or her own beliefs when this will help
members in the process of developing and clarifying theirs.

ASPECTS OF PROCESS
RELATED TO INTERACTIONS

Role Differentiation

As Guetzkow (1968) points out, "An important feature in the development of groups is the differentiation of roles into an organizational structure." Differentiation of roles occurs in the emergence and modification of roles necessary for both task and maintenance functions in groups.

Phases of role differentiation. In a general sense the process may involve a change from (1) an undifferentiated condition to one in which roles are clearly defined or (2) a state in which one set of roles exists to a state where a different set of roles prevails. For example, a group may embark upon a new project requiring skills that were not required previously. Behaviors required for this activity will be defined, and roles will be assumed or assigned.

Etiological factors in role differentiation. Guetzkow classified etiological factors under two headings: "those external environmental factors that induce role formation because of the task components and those internal processes involved in the establishment of particular persons in particular roles."

The external factors considered by Guetzkow include task characteristics such as information exchange (patterns of information distribution), solution formation (requirements for satisfactory solutions), and answer exchange (patterns of communication of possible solutions). Other external factors were communication restrictions and group goals. Internal factors included whether individuals withheld information, how individuals perceived the situation, and what kinds of organizational planning were involved. Personal characteristics of members such as intellectual abilities and social ascendance tendencies were also considered as internal variables (Guetzkow, 1968).

Group development and role differentiation. The process of role differentiation assumes different characteristics in each stage of group development. In the orientation stage as described by Northen (1969, p. 116) or the formative phase as described by Sarri and Galinsky (see Chapter 5), roles are relatively undifferentiated, and the process is primarily one of seeking role definitions, including the role of being a member.

Sarri and Galinsky assert that in the next, or intermediate phase, specialized roles gradually emerge; the task and socioemotional leaders can be more clearly identified at this time. They also identify a revision phase in which the existing roles are challenged, particularly the leadership roles. This will lead to an acceleration in role differentiation during this period, again with particular reference to such leadership roles. This process can stimulate divisive reactions among group members, and the resolution of such conflicts will lead to a further differentiation of socioemotional as well as task leadership roles.

When the group moves into later "intermediate" phases and a maturation phase, a continual process of role differentiation can be expected to occur. This process will be affected by changes in goals and other phenomena as the group moves toward a phase that Sarri and Galinsky term "maturity" and Mills (1967, p. 111) calls "growth." In this last phase, according to Mills, a "generative role" emerges that embodies creative experience and is "able to translate it into a communicable form so that it may be either stored for future use or made the basis for the formation of a new group."

Phenomena characteristic of role differentiation. Observable indications that the process of role differentiation is occurring include the planning for group statuses and the assumption by members of roles associated with such positions. Another important indication is the reactions of some members to position planning or role assumption of other members. Those reactions may tend to reinforce the behavior of persons who have assumed roles, to ignore such behavior, or to punish it. Such processes have been described in terms of role conflict (Thomas, 1967, pp. 27–28), role complementarity (Garvin, 1969, pp. 127–45), and role collision (Hare, 1962, p. 19).

In group treatment situations members go through a role differentiation process when they clarify and assume the role of client and when they develop behaviors appropriate to the use of the group as a mutual aid system. This process also occurs when workers try to help members assume roles in activities (e.g. playing the role of teacher in a role-play) that relate to their treatment planning.

Worker interventions in role differentiation. The worker will help members during group formation to understand the expectations they should fulfill in the member role. These may include obligations to attend meetings promptly, notify the worker or other members when an absence is necessary, and invest in accomplishing the purpose of the group. This socialization to the group often begins in pregroup "role induction" interviews.

The worker will subsequently help members to identify positions that the group should create. In some groups this includes formal roles such as chairperson or secretary. In other groups the main emphasis is on identifying the roles that emerge out of the interactions among members such as "mediator of disputes," "leader of the opposition," or "clown". In the case of either formal or informal roles, the worker will help members to consider how occupancy of the roles relates to their goals for being in the group. The worker's objective in this process is to help the group to create roles that will be useful to the members and help members to fulfill roles that are constructive for them and abdicate roles that are not. The procedures of "process illumination" to be discussed later is relevant to this.

Communication–Interaction

We have adopted the concept of communication–interaction process from Collins and Guetzkow (1964, p. 166). As used here, the process of communication–interaction refers to responses to the existing or emerging differentiation of roles in the group. As such, the communication–interaction process fulfills a significant integrative function in small groups.

Collins and Guetzkow (1964) quote Blau and Scott (1962) as stating that processes of communication and interaction

> . . . refer to the same processes but to different aspects of them. The concept of social interaction focuses principally upon the formal characteristics of social relations: such terms as frequency, initiative, superordination, and reciprocity indicate its dimensions. The concept . . . conveyed in the encounter, and its characteristics are described by such terms as flow of messages, obstacles, positive and negative reactions and exchanges.

Phases of communication–interaction.   The phases present as the process of communication–interaction evolves encompass the initiation, maintenance, and termination of message exchanges. A second dimension is that of changes in the content of communications (Bales, 1951).

Etiological factors in communication–interaction.   Six factors determine the course of communication–interactions:

1. The hierarchical status of group members affects the quantity and directions of communications. As Collins and Guetzkow (1964, pp. 171–73) have indicated, high-status persons initiate more interactions and receive more communications than low-status members do. Persons seeking higher status are also more likely to direct interactions to lower-status persons than to other high-status persons.

2. The likelihood of being rewarded affects the communication–interaction process. Reinforcement may well stem from the power of a group member to control the use of his or her expertise, possession of resources, or ability to inflict harm (French and Raven, 1968).

3. The structure of the group affects the communication–interaction process. The structural component may include not only interaction patterns among group members but also their physical location (Collins and Guetzkow, 1964, pp. 177–78).

4. Control problems within the group have important effects upon the communication–interaction process. It has been observed, for example, that "a high number of communications will be addressed to an accepted group member who expresses deviate opinions" and "rejection of the deviate and subgroup formation will result in a low number of communications

addressed to an unaccepted group member who expressed deviant opinions'' (Collins and Guetzkow, 1964, p. 180). The issue of control processes will be discussed later.

5. The characteristics of the message itself will help to determine communication–interaction process. An important issue here is the relationship of the content of the message to the attitudes of group members and the normative structure of the group.

6. Forces in the environment may also have effects, particularly as these interact with or determine the above five factors.

Group development and communication–interaction process. In the group's formative stage, the communication–interaction process occurs as members ''seek common and compatible personal values and attitudes to group purposes and to activities and tasks.'' In the intermediate phase, in order for the group to complete tasks, processes of communication and interaction among persons in various positions must occur. The revision phase, characterized by a challenge to the existing leadership structure, must be accompanied by a change in communications processes for members to meet this challenge. An increase in interactions in general, has also been noted as occurring during this period (see Chapter 5).

When a group reaches ''maturity,'' changes in communication–interaction processes will occur as ''external pressures force internal changes'' (see Chapter 5). These changes are accomplished self-consciously and with minimal conflicts among group members.

Phenomena characteristic of communication–interaction. In group work, after the roles of worker and client have been clarified and assumed, many communications and interactions are initiated in order to fulfill the task requirements of these roles. Communications may be directed at workers to determine their expertise, attitudes, and expectations. Communications also take place among members as they seek to share relevant experiences. Participants may inform each other about role expectations and the nature and quality of role performances. The group worker may describe what he or she intends to do and what he or she expects members to do. Members in turn may tell the workers of life areas they may or may not touch upon or express ideas about the ways they expect the worker and other members to respond to sensitive material.

In addition, maintenance of the group requires that members test how far they can trust each other in the client/group member roles before they share sensitive information. Thus, this second type of communication–interaction occurs when members and workers express or betray emotions regarding role assignments or attempt to respond to emotional expressions when they form barriers to group maintenance. Members may express fear or anger regarding the role of the worker or the roles assumed by other members.

Worker interventions in communication–interaction. The main aspect of worker interventions relevant to communication–interaction is the facilitation of feedback among members regarding their group roles and their interactions related to these. The feedback draws upon information the worker receives from both the verbal and nonverbal communications of the member. By modeling good feedback, as well as describing it, the worker helps the members to provide it to each other. Members in this way are helped to take responsibility for the accuracy of their communications as well as for the way they listen. At times the worker promotes this process by proposing that members provide feedback before adding to a discussion.

A more complex aspect of this intervention is to help the group engage in "process commentary," in which members provide and receive feedback not only on the content of their messages but on the perceived intent of the message and on the effects the message has on the thoughts and feelings of others. This helps members to become more aware of their effect on the group's process as well as the effect of the group upon themselves. This type of activity increases the members' awareness of group processes as well as of how they participate in and affect social situations outside the group. This technique is used only in groups that contract for it and with members who have the strength to deal with the anxiety it can produce.

Conflict Resolution and Behavior Control

These aspects of process are directed at behaviors that can cause the destruction of the group. Mills (1967), while quite critical of a conflict model of groups, describes this as follows:

> To organize, a group must coordinate one part with another, and in doing so must limit the freedom of some parts. So long as persons value freedom, there is an inevitable conflict between their latitude, and demands upon them for conformity and coordination. Too, some members are more competent, more powerful and more prestigeful than others; and since the interest of those on top are opposed to those on the bottom, positional conflict also is unavoidable. And further, groups accept and reward some members more fully than others. [p. 14]

Although Mills correctly points out that assumptions giving primacy to these processes over others are fallacious, the existence of such processes cannot be denied.

The universal quality of pressures in groups toward behavioral as well as attitudinal uniformity has often been commented upon. As Cartwright and Zander (1968) note, "If a cohesive group has developed a standard or a norm, it may exert strong pressures on any member who attempts to deviate. The function of such pressures toward behavioral conformity is to enable group locomotion, group maintenance, and social definintions of reality'' (pp. 141–42).

Phases, conflict resolution, and behavior control. Group phases related to conflict resolution will proceed from conflict among members to the termination of such conflict. This continuum can be described further by the nature of subgroups that embody the conflict, the variance in the content of the conflict, and the mechanisms used to resolve the conflict. Behavioral control, to secure uniformity in groups, has states that vary from (1) the observation of the deviant act by another group member to (2) the initiation of behaviors directed at the deviant to (3) a resolution of the issue. The resolution may be to the satisfaction of the deviant, of the group, or of both.

Etiological factors in conflict resolution and behavior control. The use of conflict resolution and behavioral control techniques may be required by the presence of one or more of the following sources of conflict or deviance:

1. Motives of individual members that differ from either the motives of other members or from the stated objectives of the group
2. Personality traits of some members that conflict with the personality traits of other members
3. The desire of several members to occupy the same group position or the existence of several group positions with ambiguous or overlapping functions
4. Role requirements that conflict with the status attributed by the group to a member or by a member to himself (Collins and Guetzkow, 1964, pp. 88–98).

Additional propositions regarding the resolution of conflict or the attainment of uniformity have been developed by Collins and Guetzkow (1964):

1. The expression of many self-oriented or personal needs by the participants is detrimental to the reaching of consensus.
2. A positive affective atmosphere in a meeting is an important condition for bringing groups in conflict toward agreement.
3. Meetings in which discussion was orderly in its treatment of topics, and without backward references to previously discussed issues, tended to end in more consensus despite large amounts of conflict.
4. Groups that have more expertise available and that utilize this knowledge are those whose substantive conflict ends in more consensus.
5. Chairmen of groups in high substantive conflict that ended in consensus did three times more seeking for information of an objective

factual nature from members of their groups than did chairmen in groups that did not end in consensus.

6. When the members of the group seem to like each other personally, substantive conflict tends to be more easily resolved.

Group development, conflict resolution and behavior control. The general trend is for processes of conflict initiation and resolution and behavior control to increase throughout the life of the group, as the group becomes more cohesive and as task progression and decision-making occur. Conflict is likely to be intensified in revision phases as leadership is changed and tasks modified. In the stage of maturity, however, the group is characterized as possessing the resources to meet both individual needs and group maintenance requirements effectively in a complementary fashion.

Phenomena characteristic of conflict resolution and behavior control. Two principal types of conflict are likely to occur in social work groups, one related to the purpose of the group and the other to the power of the worker. Conflict over purpose may arise because of the existence of behavior defined as deviant. The group worker may try, for example, to help a member with deviant behavior within the group which corresponds to the problem for which help is sought. The entire group, on the other hand, may be defined as deviant by the larger society, in which case the worker often reinforces the behavior of a member whose behavior is "deviant" within the context of the group.

Conflict over the power of the worker is likely to occur in any therapeutic encounter because of the threat to the existing equilibrium that the worker presents. Thus members will often defy the worker's suggestions regarding such relatively innocuous matters as meeting times and places, procedural suggestions, and so forth.

Worker interventions in conflict resolution and behavior control. The worker must recognize that conflict is an almost inevitable aspect of social interaction and that the emergence of it in the group is likely. Consequently the worker must help members to cope with rather than avoid it. This involves helping members to deal with their anxiety about conflict and to communicate with other members involved in the conflictual situation. The worker must create a safe environment for conflict resolution by offering himself or herself as a mediator and by creating "ground rules" such as those against physical force. The worker views conflict resolution as, in part, a problem-solving situation in which members gather information about the sources of the conflict, generate alternative solutions, and implement the one that optimizes gains for each side. At times the worker will help the members to see that their conflicts are displacements from other situations such as ones involving family members and peers who are not group members.

The worker must assess whether efforts at behavioral control in the group are conducive to or destructive of individual and group goals. When efforts at control are antitherapeutic (such as punishing members who self-disclose), the worker must challenge them. On the other hand, one of the most powerful values of the group experience is the support that can be created among group members for achieving individual and group purposes. The worker will often initiate such support and will reinforce it when it occurs. A caution workers observe, however, is to maintain group sanctions within bounds that the group, as a whole, and the individual members can tolerate. Groups can become punitive in the pursuit of their legitimate ends and in this way defeat them.

Emotions

The emotional aspects of group process are the attractions among group members and the attraction toward the group as a whole. The latter attraction includes the development of group cohesiveness and the state of morale among members regarding group tasks.

Phases relevant to emotions. The attractions of group members for each other will change in intensity and direction. The feelings members have for the group will also change over time and may differ among subgroups. Group emotional states, therefore, depend on the intensity of the emotion, the direction of the emotion, and the differences that may exist in the emotions expressed by different members.

Etiological factors in emotions in groups. Extensive research has been conducted into sources and consequences of attraction in groups (Lott and Lott, 1965). Attraction among members is associated with frequency of interaction and similarity among the members on variables relevant to the existence of the group. Dissimilarity can also lead to attraction when members are able to meet complementary needs. Attraction to the group itself, referred to as group cohesiveness, has been found to be associated with the value placed upon group outcomes as opposed to possible outcomes from other sources, the probability attached to the meeting of personal needs in the group, and other rewards available from the group experience.

Other possible sources of attraction to a group include the goals of the group and the nature of the group's activities. The size of the group may also be a factor; small groups are attractive when intimacy is desired and larger ones when members wish multiple opportunities to form emotional bonds with others.

Group development and emotions. Group development is associated with an increase in attraction among group members and for the group itself. The formative period is when members seek the commonalities upon which attraction depends. An increase in interpersonal ties occurs in the intermediate phase after the testing in the formative phase has been completed. The revision phase, according to Sarri and Galinsky (Chapter 5), is one in which "as members feel more secure in their specialized roles as they depend more upon one another for satisfaction in the tasks and activities of the group, and as they interact more frequently, group members are likely to have more positive feelings toward each other."

In the revision phase, as members become more involved with each other, an increase in negative reactions can also be expected. Groups that reach a maturity phase will be well able to resolve tensions among members, thus maintaining the equilibrium characteristic of mature groups.

Phenomena characteristic of emotions in groups. Members often spend time in the first group meetings eliciting information about one another as they search for commonalities. The result of this process then determines subgroup patterns based on interpersonal attraction. Emotional reactions are directed to the group worker as his or her likability is assessed. Members may express verbal or nonverbal concerns that the group's activities be attractive. Members also evaluate the group atmosphere and may attribute it to external factors such as agency receptivity, as well as to internal factors such as friendliness among members. Many emotional responses relevant to this last issue will occur.

Worker interventions in emotions in groups. Members at times have difficulty expressing their emotions toward each other and toward the group. The worker will help members to express these feelings when avoidance of such expression prevents necessary problem-solving, creates misunderstandings among the members, and leads to tension and anxiety in the group. The worker at times models such expression by stating his or her own feelings. On other occasions the worker may ask directly about feelings. When the expression of feelings is anxiety-provoking, the worker can seek to reduce the anxiety by talking with members about their fears of revealing feelings.

The feelings present in the group include those of affection and of hostility. Either one may produce difficulty for members. In the former case members may fear that their positive feelings will be rejected or that they will be interpreted as openly sexual. Members may fear that their angry feelings will go out of control or will provoke more aggression from others than they can handle. These issues must be discussed in the group so that members can learn constructive ways of expressing feelings. They may also have to learn how to be aware of their feelings so these can be consciously expressed.

Because feelings can have sexual overtones, the worker must understand how to deal with sexual expressions in group situations. These can be frightening whether directed at members of the same or the other sex or at the worker. As sexuality is an inevitable part of life, so it is of group experience. Workers will often require consciousness-raising experiences of their own in order to be comfortable enough to deal with these feelings as they arise in group work practice.

CONCLUSIONS

We recognize that this is a complex chapter, resulting from the fact that group process is a complex phenomenon. We have been able to use this conceptualization in our practice by using these steps individually as well as discussing them with group members:

1. Determine the kind of group problem that is impeding individual or group goal attainment.
2. Determine the aspect of the group's process that is contributing to the problem.
3. Work with members, utilizing the ways we have described in this chapter, to modify the group's process.
4. Reassess the group problem and, if necessary, proceed through these steps again.

As a means of helping the reader to utilize these steps, and as a review of this chapter, we present in tabular form some of the aspects of group process we have analyzed in this chapter and the types of group-level problems associated with each aspect (Figure 12–2).

FIGURE 12–2. Relationship of Group Problems to Aspects of Group Process

GROUP PROBLEM	RELEVANT ASPECTS OF PROCESS
Lack of attraction to group	Goal determination Goal pursuit Emotions
Members think group is not helping them achieve their goals.	Goal determination Goal pursuit
Members are in conflict with or hostile to one another.	Goal determination Communication–interaction Conflict resolution Emotions
Some or all members break group rules or are confused about them.	Norms Conflict resolution and behavior control

FIGURE 12-2. *(Continued)*

GROUP PROBLEM	RELEVANT ASPECTS OF PROCESS
Some members say little and/or do not contribute to the group in relevant ways.	Role differentiation Communication–interaction
Members maintain behavior patterns that are self-defeating or hinder others from attaining their goals.	Communication–interaction Conflict resolution and behavior control
Subgroups emerge that are barriers to individual and group goal attainment.	Emotions
Some individuals are isolated from relationships with others in group.	Role differentiation Communication–interaction Emotions

REFERENCES

BALES, ROBERT F.
  1951 *Interaction Process Analysis*. Cambridge: Addison-Wesley.
  1965 "The equilibrium problem in small groups." In A. Paul Hare, Edgar F. Borgatta, and Robert F. Bales (eds.), *Small Group: Studies in Social Interaction*. New York: Alfred A. Knopf, pp. 424–56.
BALES, ROBERT F., AND FRED L. STRODBECK
  1968 "Phases in group problem solving." In D. Cartwright and A. Zander (eds.), *Group Dynamics: Research and Theory*. New York: Harper & Row, pp. 389–440.
BLAU, PETER M., AND W. R. SCOTT
  1962 *Formal Organizations: A Comparative Approach*. San Francisco: Chandler.
CARTWRIGHT, DORWIN, AND ALVIN ZANDER
  1968 "Pressures to uniformity in groups: Introduction." In D. Cartwright and A. Zander (eds.), *Group Dynamics: Research and Theory*. New York: Harper & Row, pp. 139–51.
COLLINS, BARRY E., AND HAROLD GUETZKOW
  1964 *A Social Psychology of Group Processes for Decision Making*. New York: John Wiley & Sons.
COLLINS, BARRY E., AND BERTRAM H. RAVEN
  1969 "Group structure: Attraction, coalitions, communication and power." In Gardner Lindzey and Elliot Aronson (eds.), *The Handbook of Social Psychology*. Second edition, Vol. IV. Reading, Mass.: Addison-Wesley, pp. 102–204.

FRENCH, JOHN R. P., AND BERTRAM RAVEN
1968 "The bases of social power." In D. Cartwright and A. Zander (eds.), *Group Dynamics: Research and Theory.* New York: Harper & Row, pp. 259–69.

GARVIN, CHARLES
1969 "Complementarity of role expectations in groups: The member-worker contract." In *Social Work Practice.* New York: Columbia Univesity Press, pp. 127–145.

GUETZKOW, HAROLD
1968 "Differentiation of roles in task oriented groups." In D. Cartwright and A. Zander (eds.), *Group Dynamics: Research and Theory.* New York: Harper & Row, pp. 512–26.

HARE, PAUL
1962 *Handbook of Small Group Research.* New York: The Free Press.

KELLEY, HAROLD H. AND JOHN W. THIBAUT
1969 "Group problem solving." In Gardner Lindzey and Elliot Aronson (eds.), *The Handbook of Social Psychology.* Second edition, Vol. IV. Reading, Mass.: Addison-Wesley, pp. 1–101.

LOTT, A. J., AND B. E. LOTT
1965 "Group cohesiveness as interpersonal attraction: A review of relationships with antecedent and consequent variables," *Psychological Bulletin*, 64: 259–309.

MILLS, THEODORE M.
1967 *The Sociology of Small Groups.* Englewood Cliffs, N.J.: Prentice-Hall.

NORTHEN, HELEN
1969 *Social Work with Groups.* New York: Columbia University Press.

THIBAUT, JOHN W., AND HAROLD H. KELLEY
1959 *The Social Psychology of Groups.* New York: John Wiley & Sons.

THOMAS, EDWIN J.
1967 "Concepts of role theory." In Edwin Thomas (ed.), *Behavioral Science for Social Workers.* New York: The Free Press, pp. 17–50.

WHITAKER, DOROTHY STOCK, AND MORTON A. LIEBERMAN
1964 *Psychotherapy Through the Group Process.* New York: Atherton Press.

13

Program Activities: An Analysis of Their Effects on Participant Behavior

Robert D. Vinter

CONCEPTION AND USE OF PROGRAM

Social group workers' long understanding that activities have important meanings and consequences for groups and their members has led to a stress on "program as a tool." Since the practitioner may determine the choice and quality of group activities, he or she may thereby influence both participants and group processes. In this sense program affords the worker an indirect means of influencing groups and their members and is deliberately used to achieve desired objectives.

Program is a vague term, seldom defined, that has special uses in the literature of practice. It loses meaning when intended to refer to all the social interactions and processes engaged in by group members. For present purposes, program will denote a general class of group activities, each of which consists of an interconnected series of social behaviors that usually is infused with meanings and guided by performance standards from the larger culture. The social behaviors that constitute any particular activity tend to follow a pattern, unfolding in a rough chronological sequence and sometimes reaching a definite climax or conclusion. A game, an athletic event, and a musical performance are archetypes of program activities, but reference to such clear-cut examples should not result in ignoring other kinds, e.g. group discussions, telling a story or a joke, role-playing, or swimming. Use of and interaction with physical objects are included within the concept of program activity detailed here.

Problems arise in selecting specific activities to achieve particular treatment objectives. Even the comparatively inexperienced practitioner can choose from a vast range of activities in accordance with his or her own skills and the interests and abilities of members in a given group. Experience, intuition, even personal preferences of the practitioner, in combination with expressed interests of participants, are typical bases for making selections from the total range of activities. Conventional perspectives on activities, however, provide few indications of their specific effects for groups. Particular activities may be too indecisive (e.g. boxing calls forth aggression) or may be focused on effects for individuals without reference to group results (e.g. finger painting permits catharsis). Discussions or analyses of activities usually are stated in such unique terms that comparisons cannot be made with a number of alternate activity forms.

The worker's task of selecting activities with maximum impact in the desired direction is made more difficult by the necessity of modifying chosen types of activities. Not only must the worker know when to engage the group in singing rather than discussion, but he or she must also be ready to select the particular form of singing most suitable for the group at that time.

The intent here is to present a formulation useful in analyzing program activities, in making choices among them, and modifications within them. The specific criteria for making a particular choice for a given group must be consistent with objectives for that group and its individual members. The given formulation permits application of such criteria and has the advantage of encompassing both group behavior (i.e., social interactions) and individual responses to activity.

The present formulation draws heavily on one initially conceived by Gump and his associates (Gump, Sutton-Smith, and Redl, 1953). Subsequent field testing has shown considerable utility for the scheme (Gump and Sutton-Smith, 1955a). Gump's original conception has been revised and extended for the following formulation; an important contribution to this revision has been made by Edwin J. Thomas.

ACTIVITY SETTINGS

All activities comprise (1) *a physical field*, (2) *constituent performances*, and (3) *respondent behaviors*. Each of these components can be described generally.

1. *Physical field* refers to the physical space and terrain, and the physical and social objects characteristic of each activity. For example, a relatively flat, unobstructed field, a ball and bat, and a given number of players constitute the physical and social objects of a baseball game.

2. *Constituent performances* refer to those behaviors which are basic and essential to the activity and which are required of participants. Throwing the ball, hitting and catching it, and running are some of baseball's constituent performances. The behaviors required of various players may vary, although there is typically some rotation: The batter does not also catch the ball, and so forth. Constituent performances are of two orders: (a) acquiring the necessities, and (b) executing a method.

Since the physical field and constituent performances are intrinsic to each activity, they may be considered together as the *activity-setting*.

3. *Respondent behaviors* are individual participant actions evoked by, but not essential to, participation in the activity. Many activities require few if any verbal interactions, yet they customarily accompany participation. In baseball "talking it up," cheering and arguing are behaviors that participants almost inevitably manifest in response to the game. Other nonverbal respondent behaviors are also typical: expressional acting from any position, but particularly by the pitcher and batter; patting the successful player; much short running and jumping that are not directly instrumental to playing.

The basic rationale of this analysis may be stated simply. First, different activities *require* different behavior patterns (as "constituent performances") from their participants. Second, different activities inevitably evoke diverse behavior patterns (as "respondent behaviors") of their participants. Third, both types of behaviors are conditioned or determined by the nature of the activity-setting and are relatively independent of the personality characteristics of the individual participants. Fourth, both constituent performances and respondent behaviors have important consequences for the individuals and for the group that are relevant to treatment or service objectives. And fifth, both constituent performances and respondent behaviors may be deliberately achieved or modified by informed selection or modification of particular activities. Practitioners need to know *which* features of an activity are likely to result in *what* behaviors.

ACTIVITY-SETTING DIMENSIONS

Various forms and combinations of the two basic components of the activity-setting (physical field and constituent performances) are distinctive to different activities. A scheme for assessing activity-settings must detail the elements of the two components that evoke or generate respondent behaviors. It must also encompass all possible combinations of the components. These requirements are partially met by identifying the basic *dimensions* of activity-settings. Six dimensions can be specified as relevant to all activities.

1. *Prescriptiveness of the pattern of constituent performances*. For a given activity, this means the extent to which behaviors in which participants must engage do exist and the required order of the behaviors, if any. Prescriptiveness denotes the degree and range of rules or other guides for conduct. The activity-setting of chess is highly prescriptive, with limited movements possible for each piece, rules of silence during tournament play, and so on. Contract bridge is a more prescriptive card game than Old Maid.

Simple children's games have few rules prescribing a limited area of behavior, leaving undefined a great range of permissible behavior. Athletic contests are usually characterized by a greater degree and broader range of prescribed behavior.

2. *Institutionalized controls governing participant activity.* Refer to the form and source or agent of controls that are exercised over participants during the activity. Controls may be exercised by another person, sometimes a fellow participant, or impersonally (as with rules and shared norms relevant to the activity). Umpires, referees, coaches, and team captains are obvious agents of institutionalized controls. They may determine not only how an activity shall be conducted but also who shall participate at a given moment. Often such agents interpret or are guided by general rules commonly accepted for a given activity. The individual who is "It" in many children's games exercises control over fellow players, although he or she is a less obvious agent of control.

Note that the first and second dimensions discussed refer to prescriptions, requirements, and controls. There is an important distinction between them, however. The first focuses on the content and degree of activity prescriptions, while the second focuses on the form and source (or agent) of requirements that are imposed in the activity process.

3. *Provision for physical movement* means the extent to which participants are required or permitted to move about in the activity-setting. Movement may be of the whole body (as in swimming or football) or of any specific parts of the body (as in bridge or group discussion). Activity-settings that have broad physical boundaries and performances allowing for much motor movement may be contrasted to those with limited boundaries, constricting physical barriers, and performances limiting body movement.

4. *Competence required for performance* means the minimum level of ability required to participate in the activity, not the competence required to excel or to win. In some activity-settings constituent performances can be executed by inexperienced persons (as with children playing tag or singing); in others the setting requires special skill or ability (as with playing most musical instruments or water-skiing). Different forms of the same general activity may be distinguished by different minimum competencies. Playing in a string quartet calls for competence far exceeding that needed to play in a rhythm band, yet both activities are classed as "playing musical instruments." The degree of competence required may be assessed with reference to the entire population; or competence may be assessed relatively, with specific reference to the population segment to which the participants belong (e.g. teenage boys).

5. *Provision for participant interactiveness* is the way the activity-setting locates and engages participants so that interaction among them is required or provoked. In group discussions that adhere to formal proce-

dures, most statements are directed to the chairperson. In bridge, players oppose each other in teams of two, bidding and playing follow a strict order, and "table-talk" is often confined within limits. In many types of team sports players are allocated certain portions of the area and even opposing players to "cover." Interaction may be verbal and/or nonverbal.

6. *Reward structure* means the types of rewards available, their abundance or scarcity, and the manner in which they are distributed. All activities are capable of producing gratifications. They may be inherent in the activity-setting, as with winning, or they may be personal rewards such as those intrinsic to making music and creating attractive or useful objects. Gratifications may also derive from receiving praise for excelling, releasing tension legitimately, improving skill, and so on. Each activity provides distinctive types of rewards for its participants.

Rewards may be scarce or abundant; for example, a weekend of group camping may offer more rewards than a chess game for many participants. The distribution of rewards can be distinguished from their scarcity or abundance, although these characteristics are related. Obviously, if there are fewer rewards than participants, rewards cannot be equally distributed. Whatever intrinsic gratifications are derived by all players through participation in competitive play, only one side can win. In many activities certain positions or roles provide greater rewards for their occupants than do others. Thus, in orchestral playing the conductor, first violinist, and solo players gain rewards in addition to those earned by all participants. Similarly, in baseball the pitcher, catcher, and infielders may gain greater rewards than outfielders.

All activities can be assessed with respect to each of these activity-setting dimensions. To illustrate the application of these dimensions, two contrasting types of activities are evaluated in Table 13-1. Ratings are given in terms of high, medium, and low, where such a scale is appropriate. "Arts and Crafts" refers to such activities as woodworking; "Swimming" denotes noncompetitive free-play in the water. The two activities are conceived as occurring in a children's camp situation and involve group participation with an adult.

A number of shortcomings in this scheme must be recognized. The dimensions are not entirely mutually exclusive and tend to overlap at some points. And they are perhaps not inclusive of all relevant activity characteristics. Difficulty arises in rating activities along these dimensions without standard scales on which they can be assessed. Despite its limitations, the analysis provides criteria for determining the kinds of constituent performances that are required by diverse activities. On this basis the practitioner can choose activities or modify selective aspects of them, with reference to certain of the particular behavioral experiences he or she wishes to induce

TABLE 13–1.   Analysis of Activity-Setting Dimensions for Arts and Crafts and for Swimming

DIMENSIONS	ARTS AND CRAFTS	SWIMMING
1. Prescriptiveness	1. HIGH. Patterned sequence of steps. Delayed gratification.	1. LOW. No behavior required. Within limits, one may do as he or she wishes.
2. Controls	2. HIGH. Staff typically control availability of materials, tools, technique, and assistance. Tools and materials impose own constraints.	2. LOW. Staff typically intervene only when behavior exceeds permissible limits of safety.
3. Movement	3. LOW for whole body. HIGH for hands, etc.	3. HIGH. All degrees of movement for all parts of body.
4. Competence	4. VARIABLE. Depends on specific project being made.	4. LOW. Wading requires only ability to walk. Full swimming, diving, etc., require greater competence.
5. Interactiveness	5. LOW to MEDIUM. Individual task orientations and little attraction to others' behavior limits interaction. Close physical contact in small area induces some interaction. High adult control induces interaction with adult.	5. HIGH. No barriers to maximum interaction by all participants. Many people in confined area interact physically while participating.
6. Rewards	6. Types: Mastery of tools, production of valued article, closeness to assisting adult. Distribution: Wide. Everyone has opportunity to gain rewards (if tools and supplies are ample), and some may excel.	6. Types: Maximum freedom of movement, bodily self-expression, mastery of method. Distribution: Wide. Everyone has equal opportunity for basic rewards; greater competence provides greater rewards.

for the client participants. (Consideration of any program activity must, of course, take into account the physical, social, and emotional attributes of the participants.) The dimensions do not immediately lead to predictions about different *respondent* behaviors that may be associated with them, but differences in the dimensions between activities can be noted without one's being able to anticipate which respondent behaviors will vary.

DIMENSIONAL VARIANCE AND RESPONDENT BEHAVIOR

Given specific participants, if the activity-setting of two or more of their activities varies with regard to a single dimension, what differences in respondent behaviors might be expected? A number of predictions are presented below.

1. Prescriptiveness of the pattern of constituent performances
   a. Highly prescriptive activities are likely to be less attractive than less prescriptive activities.
   b. High prescriptiveness is likely to result in a channeling and constricting of behavior.
   c. High prescriptiveness is likely to result in high fatigue and high satiation.
2. Institutionalized controls governing participant activity
   a. The greater the exercise of controls and their concentration in one or a few persons, the greater the interaction of others with and dependence upon the one or few.
   b. Emphasis on formal controls is likely to freeze the form of the activity and to reduce innovation in rules, etc.
   c. Emphasis on informal controls by participants is likely to increase their pressures on each other to conform.
3. Provision for physical movement
   a. If movement is specialized (as in instrument playing), the less the bodily movement, the greater the likelihood of fatigue.
   b. The greater the bodily movement, the greater the likelihood of physical interaction and, perhaps, physical aggressiveness.
4. Competence required for performance
   a. High minimum competence is likely to result in lower interaction among participants.
   b. High minimum competence is likely to shift rewards from interpersonal gratifications to those of task performance.
   c. High minimum competence accompanied by high prescriptiveness is likely to induce a strong task orientation.

5. Provision for participant interactiveness
   a. High interactiveness is likely to result in high involvement and effort.
   b. Highly facilitated interaction leads to cooperativeness, high sentiment, and friendly relations.
   c. Highly hindered interaction leads to competitiveness, rivalry, and hostility.
6. Reward structure
   a. *Type.* The greater the range and variety in the type of desired and expected rewards, the greater the likelihood of attraction for most participants.
   b. *Abundance* or *scarcity.* Scarcity of rewards is likely to result in competitiveness, rivalry, and unequal distribution of power.
   c. *Distribution.* (1) The more broadly and evenly distributed the rewards, the greater the likelihood of cohesiveness, trust, cooperation, productivity, and responsibility. (2) The more unevenly distributed the rewards, the greater the likelihood of rivalry, competition, conflict, factions, and distrust. (3) The greater the discrepancy between expected and actual (earned) rewards, the greater the likelihood of frustration, dissatisfaction, and withdrawal.

The general predictions of respondent behavior provide a tool for differentiating between activities that are similar in most respects. Clearly, the differences between arts and crafts and free swimming are too obvious to require close analysis of their contrasting respondent behaviors. But for a rough test and for illustrative purposes, the predictions may be applied to these activities.

1. Prescriptiveness
   a. Arts and crafts are more prescriptive than swimming and, among children, usually less preferred.
   b. Arts and crafts behavior is manifestly constricted compared to the expansiveness of swimming.
   c. Satiation is probably greater for arts and crafts, with typically shorter periods of involvement than for swimming.
2. Controls
   a. Participant interaction with and dependence upon the arts and crafts instructor is greater than upon the swimming lifeguard.
   b. Emphasis on formal controls may be introduced into either activity (e.g. following the craft pattern, instructor directions; swimming instruction, curtailing of free play).
3. Movement
   a. Arts and crafts permit movement of fewer body parts and less of

the whole body than swimming. Swimming is less specialized and more strenuous, but probably less fatiguing.

b. Swimming involves greater bodily movement and, typically, considerable aggressive play.

4. Competence
   a. The more difficult the arts and crafts project, the greater the individual concentration and the less the interaction. Swimming requires low minimum competence and involves much interaction.
   b. Arts and crafts performance, in contrast to swimming, involves greater emphasis on achievement and production. It is also more frequently engaged in alone than is swimming.
   c. Certain types of arts and crafts performance involve great concentration on technical procedures.

5. Interactiveness
   a. Swimming is characterized by higher activity than arts and crafts and has potential for greater interactiveness.
   b. It seems likely that, by limiting excessive aggression, swimming induces somewhat more liking and friendlier relations than arts and crafts.
   c. Competitive swimming (e.g. water polo) leads to considerable rivalry; rivalry may also emerge in arts and crafts work when participants must take turns with tools and equipment.

6. Rewards
   a. The attractiveness of both swimming and arts and crafts may be increased by extending the facilities and equipment, and the alternatives permitted participants.
   b. Rivalry stemming from limited essential resources (tools and supplies, instructor's time) is more likely to occur in arts and crafts than in swimming.
   c. (1) rewards may be similarly distributed among participants for both activities.
      (2) the greater tendency in arts and crafts to shift rewards to achievement probably leads to more competition.
      (3) discrepancies between the expected rewards of achievement and actual accomplishment are greater in arts and crafts, with frustration and dissatisfaction more commonly observed.

It is apparent on the basis of this analysis that two activities, intuitively known to be different, can be distinguished in terms of specific dimensions and the expected behaviors associated with them. It appears that certain predictions based on these dimensions are roughly supported when tested against common experience with the activities.

Activity-setting dimensions focus attention upon the activities' common features affecting participants. Behavior variations of participants engaged in the same activity may be attributed largely to different positions held in the activity-setting, e.g. when they are on the losing rather than the winning side, or when they play different positions in a softball game. These circumstances subject participants to different conditions and should result in differing responses and experiences. Of course, differences among individuals result in dissimilar behaviors, even within the same activity-setting. Variations in skill, competence, intelligence, and motivation all give rise to differences among participants' behavior patterns. Nevertheless, the behavioral consequences of individual attributes are conditioned or limited by the activity-setting and by the individual's location within it. For example, intelligence is more likely to influence behavior in a game of checkers or chess than in free swimming.

Behavioral differences among individuals participating in the same activity may be identified and assessed in several ways:

1. As variations due to different locations in the same activity (e.g. being on a winning or losing team)
2. As deviations from the required pattern of constituent performances (e.g. ignoring the ball in a baseball game)
3. As permissible elaborations or modifications of the constituent performances (e.g. skipping around the bases after a home run)
4. As specific respondent behaviors manifested while participating in an activity (e.g. high anxiety, passivity)

This list permits the practitioner to identify more precisely which are the *uniquely individual* behaviors, and to attribute these in part to elements in the activity-setting. However, first a focus on the activity-setting and its consequences is required, rather than on the individual differences among participants.

The primary purpose of this scheme is not merely to provide the practitioner with a framework for observation and analysis. Such a framework is necessary to provide a sound basis for the selection of specific activities that are likely to achieve the particular consequences pertinent to treatment objectives. This scheme also directs the practitioner's attention to concrete features of activity that can be deliberately modified to achieve desired consequences. The dimensions outlined suggest that the practitioner can obtain different effects for participants by increasing the level of competence, by altering the rules, or by decreasing participant interactiveness. No attempt has been made here to consider particular client characteristics and interests. However, the practitioner must refer to these just as he or she must design a program with regard to specific treatment objectives. This formulation makes it more feasible for practitioners to "prescribe strategically activities for specific children and groups; it becomes possible to make activity-settings congruent with diagnostic knowledge and with therapeutic aims" (Gump and Sutton-Smith, 1955a; 1955b).

Lest the emphasis on concrete activities be misleading, the practitioner must also remember to be concerned about program sequences: the introduction of activities during each group session and their continuity or variation from one session to the next. The group worker may wish to heighten or offset the particular benefits and limitations of an activity in the next session. Attention must be given to the cumulative effects of several program experiences, to the transition problems of moving from one to another, and to the residual or spillover effects that persist beyond the group meeting. Over several group sessions, the program must be adjusted to the processes of group development and to increased skills and sophistication among participants.

REFERENCES

Gump, Paul V.; Brian Sutton-Smith; and Fritz Redl
   1953   "Influence of camp activities upon camper behavior," Wayne University School of Social Work, Detroit (dittoed).
Gump, Paul V., and Brian Sutton-Smith
   1955a   "Activity-setting and social interaction: A field study," *American Journal of Orthopsychiatry*, 25: 755–60.
   1955b   "The 'it' role in children's games," *The Group*, vol. 17.

14

Program Activities: Their Selection and Use in a Therapeutic Milieu

James K. Whittaker

> A boy, alone, sits on a fence staring sadly, a tear wending its way down his face, at a group of children playing in a yard. This is the lonely isolate, hurting inside to be able to join in but so threatened by relationships with himself and others that he cannot. [DeNoon, 1965]

ANYONE WHO HAS WORKED with disturbed children will recognize the plight of the "empty" child—the child who cannot make friends easily or who considers himself or herself so devoid of marketable skills that nobody would want to be his or her friend. Any treatment plan for such a youngster would have to include participation in carefully selected and supervised activity programs, where the child could begin to learn new peer relating skills and develop his or her own embryonic sense of self-worth. Skilled clinicians have come to think of activity programs not merely as a pleasant adjunct to psychotherapy but as a meaningful and necessary part of a child's treatment. Redl and Wineman (1957) speak of activity program as a "full-fledged therapeutic tool"; they state quite emphatically: "Programming can play a specific role in the clinical task on its own, not only a 'time filling' substitute for psychiatric contacts during the rest of the day" (p. 393).

Theorists have shown that activities have a reality- and a behavior-influencing power in their own right (Gump and Sutton-Smith, 1965, p. 414). Others have pointed out that specific developmental needs of children are met through activities: mastery of skills, release of aggression,

The author wishes to acknowledge Kathleen Whittaker, Barbara Riggs, Ruth Ann Smullin, Winslow Meyers, Bob Bruzzese, John Magnani, Dana Eddy, and Rick Jessel—counselors at The George Walker Home for Children, Inc., in Needham, Massachusetts—who have helped to prove that activities really constitute "full-fledged" therapeutic treatment. A special debt of gratitude is owed to Thomas Gearhart, whose thoughts on the selection of activities provided a partial basis for one of the sections of this paper.

mastery of relationships, and the art of sublimation (Konopka, 1954, pp. 141–46). Play as described by Bettelheim (1950, p. 218), is that area where the child tests and develops his or her independence and where the child learns to hold his or her own with peers. Obviously an important part of the child's world, "play" should not be looked upon as a uniform event or as a totally random activity. Piaget (1950) has given some insight into the complex normative structure governing what at first glance appears to be unplanned activity. Erikson (1950) gives some insight into the potentialities of child's play as a medium for learning: "Child's play is not the equivalent of adult play . . . it is not recreation. The adult steps sidewards into another reality; the playing child advances forward to new stages of mastery" (pp. 194–95). Finally, Redl (1966, p. 87) and others have noted the tremendous impact of the structure of games and activities on those participating in them.

With or without the intervention of helping adults, activities can benefit both the individual child and the group. Activities also provide an opportunity to practice group participation, to experiment with new roles in a small group situation, and to try out newly acquired peer relating skills. Participation in activities may enable individual children to acquire a sense of competency and mastery over their environment.

Activities also may be used as diagnostic tools to assess not only individual children but also group structure and decision-making processes. Most of the case records accompanying children to residential treatment centers have a surplus of intrapsychic evaluative data but a dearth of material pertaining to how the child functions in a group situation. Often there is awareness of a child's learning deficiencies, but the fact is overlooked that many children simply do not know how to have fun, much less how to compete or how to compromise. The mastery of program activities can provide concrete and marketable peer skills. Finally, if it is truly believed that an activity program is not merely a pleasant addition to psychotherapy but functions as a "full-fledged therapeutic tool," then the activity program must be a guaranteed commodity in the therapeutic milieu and not something held out solely as a reward for "good" behavior.

Many of the presenting problems of the youngsters—poor peer relations, aggressive outbursts, and low self-images—can be treated better in the context of an activity than in a fifty-minute office interview. It is therefore important that the use of this "tool" not be limited to those times when children are in good psychological shape.

HOW TO SELECT AN ACTIVITY

The selection of successful and beneficial activity programs involves evaluating such variables as skill and interests of the children, staff coverage, available materials, and the mood of the group. There are other slightly more distant variables that may be crucial to the success of a particular activity, including weather, time of day, and other "atmospheric variables." Nothing can ruin a carefully planned baseball game quicker than an unexpected cloudburst; pity the poor childcare worker who does not have an alternate program available.

One of the questions most frequently asked by childcare workers is, "How do I know which activity to choose?" Every worker knows that he or she can do certain things even before the start of the activity that will influence the course the activity will follow. Group work practitioners know that manipulation of space, time, props, and materials can alter the way in which groups will approach and carry out activities (Churchill, 1959), but the activities themselves also have "built-in" dimensions which have a good deal to do with the behavior of the participants and are less well known to childcare workers than they might be.

Comparison of alternate program activities along the dimensions proposed by Vinter (see Chapter 13) will help the childcare worker to identify activities that can best serve the group's purpose. The worker's evaluation of certain individual and group variables should also influence the selection of a specific activity for a particular group.

Individual Variables

1. *Skill*: the level of the child's competence to participate in activities. Skills include physical dexterity and motor coordination, as well as specific athletic, mechanical or crafts skills. Many children come to social workers with relatively few specific skills, though their interest might be keen in specific areas. Basically, a question focused on this variable asks, "What is this child capable of doing right now?"

2. *Motivation*: the child's willingness to participate in activities. The more complex and difficult the activity, the higher the child's motivation will have to be to ensure successful completion of the activity. Children with relatively low motivation to join in activities may be lured into participation by activities whose rewards are both immediate and abundant.

3. *On-tap control*: the amount of self control available to the child at a given time. One would not recommend a game of chess for a hyperactive child who has been struggling to control his or her behavior in school all day. With hyperactive, aggressive children, there is not always time to wait for them to be completely in control before attempting to engage them in an activity. Rather, they may be engaged in an activity for the purpose of controlling their behavior.

Group Variables

In planning a program, one has to keep in mind certain group phenomena that may influence the course of the activity. Some of the more important variables are group solidarity (cohesion), group composition, and group mood. Given a loosely assembled group with little cohesion and solidarity, parallel activities might be more appropriate than those requiring a good deal of interaction and interdependence among the members (e.g. model building rather than soccer). As for group composition, the more heterogeneous the grouping, the more difficult it will be to find an activity that all members can participate in and enjoy. Finally, the childcare worker must use his or her sensitivity to assess the mood of the group. A spontaneous suggestion for an unplanned hike may be just the solution for youngsters during the latency period who have been using massive amounts of control to complete a project in school and seem ready to "burst out."

The typical childcare worker will not go through all of the activity-setting dimensions, individual variables, and group variables every time he or she plans a program; trying to control all variables before making a program decision would be disastrous. However, careful attention to activity dimensions and individual and group variables can facilitate planning for particularly difficult activity times, and they may be particularly useful as guidelines to dissect and analyze particular successes as well as utter disasters.

The "goodness of fit" between any theoretical model and its "real life" counterpart is at best a tentative union. With this in mind the application of the Vinter material along with the individual variables should represent to the worker a somewhat incomplete framework to help answer the question, "How do I select an activity?" There will inevitably be some disagreement as to the "ratings" assigned to different activities, as well as to the eight types of program participants identified below. If the following exercise provides even a rudimentary framework for the analysis of activities and the people who participate in them, its purpose will have been well served.

The eight "participant types" in Table 14–1 represent all of the possible combinations when one controls individual variables of *skill, motivation*, and *control*.

The following behavioral descriptions will help to illustrate:

Type A. This child has high skill, motivation, and control; he or she is able to participate in a wide range of individual and group activities. The child can perform demanding tasks for moderate reward and is able to postpone gratification. This youngster probably "programs" quite well for himself or herself.

Type B. Highly skilled and motivated, this child is plagued by a poor control structure; any activity for him or her must substitute external controls for the lack of internal control. The child is easily swayed by others, thus should avoid mass group activities, but he or she can certainly function well in small group situations.

TABLE 14-1. Types of Program Participants

Participant Type	Skill	Motivation	Control
Type "A"	High	High	High
Type "B"	High	High	Low
Type "C"	High	Low	Low
Type "D"	Low	Low	Low
Type "E"	Low	Low	High
Type "F"	Low	High	High
Type "G"	Low	High	Low
Type "H"	High	Low	High

Type C. This child has an abundance of natural ability but is unable (or unwilling) to utilize it effectively; rewards for him or her should be abundant and immediate. Controls must be provided externally, but the fewer rules the better. This child will probably work best in a one-to-one situation.

Type D. This youngster presents a real challenge; he or she is poorly motivated, relatively "empty" of skills and has extremely poor control over his or her own impulses. The child needs very simple activities that assure almost "instant success"; a good deal of external support is required to supplement his or her poorly integrated control structure. Finally, a good deal of space should be provided for physical movement and this child should not be expected to stick to any one thing for a very long period of time.

Type E. This child is poorly motivated and unskilled but presents no great control problem. He or she is probably a shy, withdrawing youngster who feels rebuffed by peers and has a very low self-image. The child needs immediate successes and uncomplicated games and projects. Lots of help and praise will enhance the child's development; the rest of the group could help in this respect.

Type F. This child has good motivation and control but a low skill level. He or she is a clumsy youngster, bad at athletics and group games. The child is willing and able to work on mastery experiences and could probably use a plan for skill development so that his or her ego will not be crushed every time he or she misses the basket or strikes out.

Type G. This child has low skills and a faulty control structure but really wants to "do well." He or she must begin with activities that require a low degree of competence and have plenty of provision for physical movement. Probably the most difficult task with this particular child will be getting him or her to accept the fact that skill or control take time to develop and that he or she should not become discouraged in the process.

Type H. This youngster has good ability and control but is poorly motivated to participate in activities. Immediately the thought comes of the sociologically trained delinquent who stands aloof from the "fun and games" of the residence. The key here is, of course, relationship development and finding the most meaningful reward that will enhance the child's entry into the group (peer status, friendship, privileges).

"Typing" specific children according to their level of skill, degree of motivation or willingness to participate, and amount of self-control is tentative at best; skill, motivation, and self-control are difficult to assess. It should be somewhat easier to quantify and compare dimensions of program alternatives according to the extent to which they are *prescriptive*; the degree of *control* to which they subject participants; the extent to which they require or permit physical *movement*; the extent to which they provide *rewards*; the level of *competence* they require; and the degree of *interaction* they require or provoke. In Table 14–2, numerous familiar program activities are analyzed and compared by quantifying all six dimensions of the Vinter scale.

It now becomes possible to identify certain activities as being especially suitable (or inappropriate) for certain types of participants. Monopoly can be seen to be a good activity for Type A and Type H and possibly for Type C; it is clearly not a good choice for Types D and E.

Furthermore, it is possible to project for each type a particularly appropriate set of activity dimensions, an "ideal activity profile," as in Table 14–3.

Thus Type E (poorly skilled and motivated, but presenting no great control problem) would require an activity that has a low degree of prescriptiveness but provides a goodly amount of external control. In addition, the rewards would have to be fairly abundant, but the competency needed to attain them would have to be minimal. Hence, the child might try finger painting or papier mâché, but definitely not origami or copper enameling. In either case it would be good to substitute for the lack of internal control by keeping the group small and the counselor close to the child. Outdoor games might include tag or dodge ball but not Chinese tag or baseball, as they require a higher level of beginning competence.

The ultimate value of such an Ideal Activity Profile depends upon

1. The adequacy of the individual variables on which the definition of participant types is based
2. The manner in which the individual variables are assessed in individual cases

TABLE 14–2.   Activity-Setting Dimensions of Program Activities

Activity	Prescriptiveness	Control	Movement	Rewards	Competence	Interaction
Swimming	Low	Low	High	High	Low	Low
Model building	High	High	Low	High	High	Low
Clay molding	Low	Low	Low	High	Low	Low
Finger painting	Low	Low	Medium	High	Low	Low
Papier Mâché	Low	Medium	Low	High	Low	Low
Origami	High	High	Low	High	High	Low
Copper Enameling	Medium	High	Low	High	Medium	Low
Lanyard making	Medium	Medium	Low	High	Low	Low
Baseball	High	High	Medium high	Medium	High	High
Touch football	Medium	Medium	High	High	Medium	High
Hockey	Medium	High	High	Medium	High	High
Kick ball	Low medium	Medium	Medium	Medium	Medium	Medium
Dodge ball	Low	Low	High	High	Low	High
Red rover	Medium	Medium	High	Medium	Low	High

243

TABLE 14-2. (*Continued*)

Activity	Prescriptiveness	Control	Movement	Rewards	Competence	Interaction
Tag	Low	Low	High	High	Low	High
Chinese tag	Medium	Medium	Medium high	High	Medium high	High
Red light	High	High	Medium	Medium	Low	Low
Simon says	High	High	Medium	Medium	High	Medium low
Hide 'n seek	Low	Medium	Medium	High medium	Low	Low
Checkers	High	High	Low	Medium	Medium	Medium
Chess	High	High	Low	High	High	High
Monopoly	High	High	Low	Medium high	High	High
Chutes 'n ladders	Medium	Medium	Medium	Medium	Medium	Medium

TABLE 14-3. Ideal Activity Profile

PARTICIPANT TYPES	PRESCRIPTIVENESS	CONTROL	MOVEMENT	REWARDS	COMPETENCE	INTERACTION
"A"	High	Low high	Low	Medium	High	High
"B"	Medium	High	High	Medium	High	Medium low
"C"	Low	High	High	High	High	Low
"D"	Low	Low	High	High	Low	Low
"E"	Low	High	Medium	High	Low	Medium
"F"	High	High	Medium	Medium	Low	High
"G"	Low	Low	High	Medium	Low	Low
"H"	High	High	Low	High	High	High

3. The accuracy of Vinter's activity-setting dimensions and of their quantification
4. The manner in which they are applied to specific activities

WHEN TO USE AN ACTIVITY

The maintenance of the rather delicate balance between individual and group psychotherapy, remedial education and program activities is one of the most crucial issues in any good therapeutic residence. Probing the depths of a child's psyche, helping the child to overcome a learning problem, and teaching the child an alternative behavior are all laudable goals, but the milieu must provide some respite from the rigors and pains of psychic change. Skillful use of activities can often initiate and foment real therapeutic progress. For many youngsters activities may constitute the key enhancement of growth and development and may also be immensely useful in managing behavior.

Transition Time Activities

All childcare workers face the problem of moving children through the routines and activities of the day. Children must arise in the morning, go off to school, come to lunch and supper, and prepare for bedtime and group activities; indeed, much of the child's day is spent moving toward or away from the routines of the milieu. If the worker depends solely upon "authority" to move children through the day, the worker soon finds himself or herself making "issues" over fairly simple rules and getting into power struggles where the only goal of the child seems to be, "Whatever you tell me to do, I'm going to do the opposite!" If, on the other hand, the counselor resorts solely to direct appeals, the counselor soon finds himself or herself laying the relationship on the line for every demand and request. Direct appeal also presupposes that the child is motivated to follow the routine (go to school, come to lunch, and so on).

Certain activities are useful management tools. These activities are by definition short-term, since they end as soon as the child is engaged in the routine. Their primary purpose is diversion; if possible, their focus should be on the counselor as the "central figure." Thus, games like "follow the leader" or "red light" have been found to be quite useful in guiding children from the schoolroom to the lunch table. It helps if certain games become associated with certain times of the day, as the child sees the game as a "marker" which indicates the proximity of the particular routine. One counselor made very successful use of a "timing game" with a child who had particular difficulties getting dressed in the morning (Whittaker, 1969).

Waiting for an activity or a routine to begin can often be the source of a great deal of frustration for the impulsive youngster. One therapeutic camp keeps a long rope outside the dining hall to be used for group high jumping if the dinner bell is late. One need not think of elaborate materials for the these diversions. One's own pockets often provide ample props for successful short-term programs. Thus the stopwatch may be used to "see how fast you can run to school"; the penny may be the object of some sleight of hand or the counter in a game of penny-pitch. A few simple card tricks may be enough to keep a group occupied until a broken projector gets fixed. Finally, since these activities are by nature short-term, the counselor might use a whole sequence of them while moving the youngsters from one part of the program to another.

Individual and Group Activities

Activities may be structured around the needs of a particular child or may be designed for the benefit of the entire group. A newcomer to the group might have a particular skill or interest that could serve as his or her inroad to the group if included in a carefully prepared activity by the child-care worker. Generally speaking, it is good to think of activities that tax the control of the individual child only slightly at first; here the depersonalized control of the activity is substituted for the internal control the child is lacking. For example, the counselor might wish to outline the rules for dodge ball rather than leave each dispute to be arbitrated by the children.

The whole question of when to use program activities carries with it a certain aversion to the whole notion of programming. No one likes to think of himself or herself as being "programmed," and the thought of a rigidly designed activity structure (swimming at 2:00, arts and crafts at 3:00) does not take account of the creative abilities of the childcare worker, much less the needs of the impulsive child. The goal should be to weave activities into the fabric of the milieu, taking into account the needs, interests, and limitations of the children, as well as the abilities of the counselor and the resources available.

One way to avoid the problem of rigid programming is through the project method. Here the counselor starts with the kernel of an idea from a child or group of children and builds it into an activity or series of activities that may carry on for days and provide many levels of rewards for the participants. The following group log may help to explain one such program.

Today Bobby greeted me and told me that the class had just concluded the unit on American Indians. He expressed some interest in making a bow and arrow, but said that "it probably wouldn't work anyway." I approached Vince and Rick on the idea and they seemed to be enthusiastic; the four of us set about gathering sticks for the arrows and discovered a natural "teepee" in some large bushes. Two boys began at once to clear the area while Bobby began work on his bow and arrow. By now, Carol [counselor] had become involved and began making Indian bracelets and trinkets out of scraps of leather. I spoke with Linda [teacher] after school and she said she would introduce the idea of an Indian exhibit in school . . .

This project, which began with one boy's idea to make a bow and arrow, culminated in an Indian day about a week later, complete with ceremonial dancing, totem-pole making, and a cookout. Within the general framework of the program there was tremendous room for individual tastes and skills. Thus one child spent most of his time painting shields, while another was engaged in the rather formidable task of "guarding the campsite."

In short, the richest source of inspiration for program may come from the children themselves and may require the childcare worker to refine, modify, and build upon the idea of the child.

USING ACTIVITIES IN A THERAPEUTIC MILIEU

The final section of this paper deals with specific techniques and program hints culled from the collective experience of many childcare workers. These suggestions and observations reflect the goal of every childcare worker in a therapeutic residence to relate the world of fun and activities to the child whose ability to enjoy success is often overshadowed by his or her fear that "I can't do anything right."

1. One of the worker's key tools in executing a successful activity is the worker's own enthusiasm. The counselor, who is actively involved in the game and who is quite obviously enjoying the game, provides a model for the child of how a person relates to an activity. It is no small task to juggle the roles of "helping adult" and "playmate," and counselors should guard against becoming so involved in the activity that they cannot step out from time to time to manage a crisis.

2. Activities should be ended when they are going well and while the children are enjoying themselves. Many counselors have experienced dismay when the activity they have been running all evening crumbles before their eyes when it is left to run out. It is better to leave the child with a positive picture of the activity at its high point rather than with a negative picture of its demise.

3. The timing and sequence of activities are important variables to control. For example, large group activities first thing in the morning usually are not successful because the individual egos of the youngsters are too fragmented and shaky to be exposed to mass group games. Similarly, body contact sports right before bedtime are likely to involve the group in erotic and aggressive play at a time when children are undressing and taking

showers. (By the way, the myth should be exploded for all time that "a few laps around the track" or a "wrestling match" will "tire them out and make them ready for sleep.")

4. Often the counselor must rejuvenate and alter old activities to make them more attractive to youngsters. One counselor changed the old and familiar game of "ghosts" to "rocket ships" and enjoyed a good deal of success with it. Allowance also must be made for the child's inability to delay gratification. A rapid rotation of hitters may be better than a conventional game of baseball.

5. With ego-damaged children whose skill level is often pitifully low, too much emphasis must not be placed on the "finished product." Similarly, the counselor should complement his or her own skills with those of the child and not be overly concerned over "who did what."

6. Despite the most careful planning of an activity, the counselor may be faced with seeing it turn to dust before the counselor's eyes according to the pathologies of the individual youngster or the mood of the group. The counselor must always be ready to switch activities in midstream as the need arises.

7. Many childcare workers ask the question, "How do I start an activity?" The answer is simply, "By doing it!" It is quite easy to fall into the trap of wanting to "get the whole group together" (and quiet) before beginning, when often the lure of the activity itself will do most to interest the youngsters.

8. Generally speaking, with a younger group it is better to begin with parallel activities, that is, those which do not require interaction between the members. Thus it is better to have six individual model ships and not one giant aircraft carrier for "everyone to work on." Participation and facilitative interaction are goals to be sought as the group develops.

9. Similarly, when beginning to work with a younger group, it is wise for the childcare worker to retain the greater portion of decision-making. This somewhat alleviates the problem of each child's having to negotiate with every other child about what the activity is to be.

10. Finally, the childcare worker should not attempt activities in which he or she is not skilled or does not feel comfortable, just because the worker feels a need to be the "complete counselor." It is far better to develop skills and interests that are most important to the worker, for there is usually a wide enough variation among childcare staff members to expose children to a whole range of different activities.

REFERENCES

BETTELHEIM, BRUNO
1950   *Love Is Not Enough*. Glencoe, Ill.: Free Press.

CHURCHILL, SALLIE R.
   1959 "Prestructuring group content," *Social Work* (July): 52–59.
DENOON, BARBARA
   1965 "Horses, bait and chocolate cake." In Henry W. Maier (ed.), *Group Work as Part of Residential Treatment*. New York: National Association of Social Workers, p. 88.
ERIKSON, ERIK H.
   1950 *Childhood and Society*. New York: W. W. Norton.
GUMP, PAUL, AND BRIAN SUTTON-SMITH
   1965 "Therapeutic play techniques." In *Conflict in the Classroom*. Belmont, Calif.: Wadsworth.
KONOPKA, GISELA
   1954 *Social Group Work in Children's Institutions*. New York: Association Press.
PIAGET, JEAN
   1950 *Play, Dreams and Imitations in Childhood*. New York: W. W. Norton.
REDL, FRITZ
   1966 *When We Deal with Children*. Glencoe, Ill.: Free Press.
REDL, FRITZ, AND DAVID WINEMAN
   1957 *The Aggressive Child*. Glencoe, Ill.: Free Press.
WHITTAKER, JAMES K.
   1969 "Managing wake-up behavior." In Albert Treischman, James Whittaker, and Larry Brendtro, *The Other Twenty Three Hours*. Chicago: Aldine, pp. 120–36.

15

Termination: A Neglected Aspect of Social Group Work

Nazneen Mayadas and Paul Glasser

A REVIEW of the literature reveals that termination continues to remain a relatively unexplored area of social group work practice (Johnson, 1974; Lawler, 1980). An inordinate amount of attention is paid to other aspects of group development (Hare, 1976; Shaw, 1976; Tuckman, 1965), such as starting a group, member composition and size, emerging group processes, communication patterns, timing and worker interventions, etc. However the truism of "what begins, also must end" is frequently given only cursory recognition. This may be attributed to factors inherent in the act of termination itself which allegedly signifies a state of mixed emotions for all parties concerned (Hartford, 1971; Klein, 1972; Konopka, 1963; Northen, 1969). As such, the "ostrich syndrome," i.e., "If it is not seen, it is not there," may be a safe avoidance technique to eliminate handling the discomfort and grief associated with parting. Further, termination suggests "taking stock" of what thus far has been achieved. It is the stage for goal evaluation and may entail coming face to face with performance discrepancies which for the worker, essentially, may be better left implicit. In other words, if goals were never explicitly stated, performance contracts not negotiated and an achievement plan not systematically implemented, evaluation becomes a well nigh herculean task. Better to be ignored than attempted!

Finally, termination focuses upon that group stage where there is a cessation of structured interaction. As such it would appear more reasonable to give attention to theoretical explanations and empirical investigations directed at understanding and dealing with those group phases which concentrate on optimizing constructive interaction toward goal achievement, rather than on that phase, when either by design or default, the incentive properties for group continuity are viewed as absent, or at best marginal. Based on this perspective the scales logically weigh more heavily on the side

This chapter is reprinted from *Social Work with Groups* 4, nos. 1–2 (Spring/Summer 1981): 193–204. Used with permission of the journal and The Haworth Press.

of developmental group progression rather than lean towards its ending, which may be viewed as the inevitable aspect of a group's life cycle.

It is the contention of this paper that termination is a necessary and critically important phase of group development, since it sets the tone for learned skill transfer to various other experiences in the natural environment of members. Put within this context termination is viewed as "installation of hope" (Yalom, 1975) for future satisfactory performances of members, rather than a time for sentimental nostalgia, as is often stated in social work literature (Klein, 1972; Northen, 1969). Further the worker's planned interventions from the inception to the fruition of group life integrate termination into the members' structured expectancies of group outcomes and individual rewards. And it is during the termination process that the professional can evaluate his own efforts to improve his or her performance with groups in the future.

Sarri and Galinsky (see Chapter 5) view termination of groups from two perspectives; namely, planned and unplanned group disbandment. Planned termination results either as a function of the group's achieving its avowed goal or due to the expiration of the scheduled time period allotted to the functioning of the group, i.e., an ad hoc committee. Unplanned termination is the consequence of a basic lack in group integration, the inability of the group to adapt to external environmental changes outside its control, or the failure on the part of the leader to maintain equilibrium between the task and members' affective involvement with the task and the task milieu (Kernberg, 1979). Although it is suggested that one or more of these four conditions must prevail at group termination, the specific factors and the worker's interventions related to each of the four conditions are not made explicit. This paper uses the above orientation as the point of departure to provide a structured format for explicating the process of termination in groups, delineate behavioral criteria for termination assessment, and provide intervention strategies for workers relative to the context within which group termination occurs. Presented here are: (1) a conceptual interactional model for understanding the dynamics associated with group termination, (2) a set of observable criteria to analyze both the phase and processes of termination and (3) contingent on the type of termination (Chapter 5; Klein, 1972), a review of intervention strategies to deal with diversified member reactions to terminations, i.e., "what" does the worker "do" to "whom" under "which" specific conditions to achieve the most desirable outcomes for both the individuals and the group.

INTERACTIONAL MODEL

Thibaut and Kelly (1959) theorize that behavior is not idiocyncratic but is based on systematic assessment of group members' actual or perceived satisfactory interactional outcomes. Outcomes are viewed as highly satisfactory if members find that rewards on both the instrumental and socioemotional (Parsons, 1951) dimensions of interactional exchanges are at their perceived optimal levels. If rewards on either of the two dimensions fall below the perceived costs, the group experience proportionately loses its valence (Lewin, 1951) for members. Members then evaluate the group experience against the availability of alternate attractions, which so far had not been explored. The intensity and magnitude of involvement outside of the group situation have an inverse correlation with group cohesion. Thus ideally, the termination phase for the group is arrived at the point where the outcome gains for members outside of the group exceed those within the group. When this process is a planned, mutually negotiated, purposive act, it is most satisfactory for the group and its members, especially if it is viewed in the context of a new beginning following the successful completion of contracted goals. Underlying a successful termination is the assumption that the group experience has served its purpose, and it is time for members to move on to situations other than this particular group.

The model proposed here provides a framework for conceptualizing both planned and unplanned group termination. The two dimensions on which group participation are measured are socioemotional attraction and instrumental interdependence. This paradigm suggests that for a group to be functioning at its maximum level, members must display high scores on both dimensions. Lowering of scores on either dimension activates the members' motive base (Cartwright and Zander, 1968) for seeking affinities outside of the group, thus bringing into effect the possibility of group termination. It is further postulated in this model that planned termination in treatment or rehabilitation groups is designed to occur when group ratings are high on socioemotional attraction and low on instrumental interdependence. That is, goals have been achieved for individuals and the group as a whole, but member attraction remains high, at least partly because of these accomplishments. On the other hand, in task groups (community organization or administration), individual motivation may result in high instrumental interdependence while socioemotional attachments may remain at a moderate level. With rehabilitation and treatment groups, planned termination is required to help members move on to new challenges which maintain and reinforce their new patterns of behavior. Task groups are more likely to end on their own unless new demands are made upon members by the outside environment.

Neither type of group is likely to continue for long periods of time unless it has a moderately high level of both task interdependence and socioemotional attraction. These two factors reinforce each other. High morale associated with group cohesion goes together with high goal orientation associated with task achievement incentive, and both together result in satisfactory group participation for its members.

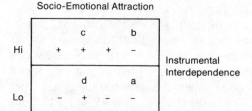

FIGURE 15–1. Interaction of SEA and II During the Group
Termination Plan

THE INTERACTIONAL MODEL: A CONCEPTUAL
FRAMEWORK FOR GROUP TERMINATION

Looking at Figure 15-1 it can be seen that at the pre-group period
(Hartford, 1976), potential group members and worker are in cell "a,"
where there is an absence of both socio-emotional attraction (SEA) and instrumental interdependence (II). This is a stage of decision making when the
pros and cons of the group are weighed, and members decide whether they
wish to continue to meet. Cell "b" indicates a stage when there is high task
interdependency, but interpersonal affinity amongst members is lacking. In
the absence of variables that lead to interpersonal attraction the enforced
task dependency can result in resentment of the group situation. If this is allowed to continue, either conscious or inadvertent attempts may be made by
members to sabotage the group goal. Such groups, due to lack of integration, may really never get started with the task and result in unplanned termination. Also in cell "b" are those groups who originally may have
functioned satisfactorily, but due to a change in environmental support
have suffered a slump in morale, thus lowering their incentive for cohesion
and socio-emotional attraction to the group, leading to unplanned group
termination (see Chapter 5). Cell "c" is not applicable to the phase of termination. It indicates the active working phases of the group where there is
high socio-emotional attraction and high instrumental interdependence.
Cell "d" indicates high group cohesion but there is no further task interdependence. The exception to this statement may be those groups whose primary purpose is the maintenance of close interpersonal friendships.

In Figure 15-2, cell "a" of Figure 15-1 becomes the active cell, suggesting that termination of a group is only the closure on one structured social microcosm, and that members move on to other affective relationships
and task orientations in different environments. This conceptualization of
group phases is based on the following assumptions:

1. For optimal functioning all groups must be in cell "c" (Figure 15-1)
and rate moderately high on both socioemotional attraction and instrumental interdependency.

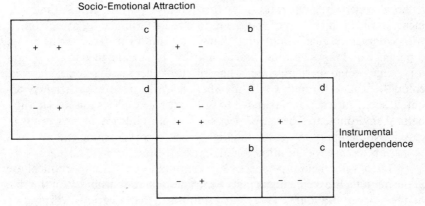

FIGURE 15-2.   Movement from Group Termination to New Group Formation

2. Groups high on instrumental interdependence and low on socioemotional attraction, i.e., cell "b" (Figure 15-1), are either short-term to achieve a specified task, may never move toward displaying group characteristics or result in unplanned termination. Involuntary groups in institutional settings, mandatory task groups in organizations and involuntary treatment groups fall into this category.

3. Groups high on socioemotional attraction and low on instrumental interdependence as indicated in cell "d" (Figure 15-1) usually result in planned termination. While members continue to have positive affinity for each other, since the group has satisfactorily achieved its goals it no longer has a purpose, and its continuation can lead to the loss of gains made earlier.

PLANNED TERMINATION

Social work literature on groups tends to emphasize the negative effects of termination on members, such as regression in behavior and a sense of rejection, anger and frustration at an imposed loss, etc. (Hartford, 1976; Klein, 1972; Northen, 1969). Few references are made to the positive elements in termination (Rose, 1972). Since termination is an inherent part of the total group process it needs to be integrated into the mosaic of group development and viewed as much more than a traumatic act of separation and loss.

In rehabilitation and treatment groups, termination, to some extent, is faced by members and workers at the end of every session. These opportunities can be utilized by the worker to systematically taper the meeting to a closure, thus structuring expectancies (Lennard & Bernstein, 1970) and making termination an integral and normative part of each member's be-

havioral repertoire. Operationally, this requires portioning off time segments in the initial stages of the group to discuss termination, associating it
with satisfactory goal attainment. Viewed within this framework the group
experience no longer becomes an end in itself, but can be seen as a preparatory, time bound learning state, where skills are acquired and tasks are accomplished, and through which members learn to transfer their newly acquired social interactional patterns to other more complex situations in their
natural environment. The use of peer support is an integral part of this process. Termination of the group highlights satisfactory learning and acts as a
point of reference for the initiation and assessment of other challenges.

This developmental perspective of termination as an important phase
in the ongoing life of members places considerable responsibility on the role
of the worker. Bandura (1971) has established that vicarious learning or
modeling is a viable source of growth and change. As such, "how" the
worker "acts" is an important part of the structured intervention plan used
by the worker, the group and its members. In other words, if the worker
portrays termination as a positive graduation process which completes a
preparatory phase of social learning for the members and equips them with
the necessary skills for more effective and varied social functioning, termination will take on the hue of a desirable state to be anticipated with excitement and hope rather than dread and despair as suggested in the social
group work literature (Northen, 1969; Klein, 1972).

In therapeutically oriented groups the worker can build in the expectation of termination in members by being aware of the following points:

1. An essential component of the structural framework of effective
groups is the successful negotiation of the group contract, which required
agreement among members and between members and the workers about
the group's goals and objectives. Implicit in such a contractual agreement is
that once the group's goals have been achieved, the group will be terminated
or continued under a newly negotiated agreement. This is a prerequisite to
successful group activity and helps to structure the role expectations of both
members and workers (Goldstein, 1971).

2. It is necessary to establish contractual plans of action with members
and what benefits accrue to the group as a whole from it. What are the incentive properties of this group for members? This is essential, as members'
covert agendas need to be made overt to minimize sabotage behaviors so
that both group and individual goals can be achieved.

3. It is advisable to build in the "transfer of learning" phenomenon by
introducing home assignments, behavioral rehearsals, and assessment criteria so that reports of members' functioning in their natural environments
becomes an ongoing part of the group's data for analysis. The rationale for
maintaining an outside focus within the group is to allow the members
to develop instrumental interdependency and socio-emotional attraction

within the group while continuing to maintain emotional cathexis where it rightly belongs—in their natural environment. If this is accomplished in the early stages of the group, then the dread of termination is reduced, and the group environment is seen for what it actually is—a unique learning context and a means for the acquisition of desired performance repertoires to be utilized outside the group.

4. Behavioral contracts with members are important to negotiate. If individual performance contracts as well as group goals are clearly stated in behavioral terms with members, they also serve as outcome measures for evaluation and subsequent graduation to other life-space events. Rose (1972) suggests that once contracted goals are achieved to the mutual satisfaction of worker and members, any further reinforcement of behaviors that suggest involvement with the group is a disservice to members. He points out that group reinforcements must be gradually faded out with worker's verbal behavior primarily focused on extra-group activities. If this is done with systematic planning, the challenges of the natural environment become more atractive, and the attraction to the group proportionately recedes into the past, thus making termination a desirable and timely activity.

5. If some members still have questions about leaving the group, it suggests that their goals are not yet satisfactorily attained, and as such, they may need to be placed either in a new group environment or referred to individual therapy. Termination does not preclude follow-up or the possibility of future help if need arises. It merely brings to a satisfactory conclusion one phase of treatment, while taking care of unfinished business for individual members who require it. Thus termination, like other group processes, becomes a mutually agreed upon task in which worker and members participate with equitable interactional exchanges.

Some rehabilitation and treatment groups, due to agency exigencies or other factors, are scheduled for non-renewable time periods. Under these circumstances the goals set by members and worker together must be carefully developed so that they may be fulfilled within the period the group expects to meet. It may be better to set more limited individual and group goals that can be realistically achieved, specifying intermediate objectives along the way, rather than take the chance of terminating the group with unrealized promises. With this caution, the five suggestions reviewed above continue to be relevant.

When planned termination is implemented in task groups, the worker's interventions take on a somewhat different emphasis. While attempts are made consciously to establish both instrumental interdependence and socio-emotional attraction, these generally reach only moderate levels since the group situation is much more structured, with the worker assuming directive leadership throughout the life of the group. The contracted agreement is focused on the task to be accomplished, which is the group goal, and the relative service contribution of individual members vis-à-vis the specified task. The readiness for termination is measured on two criteria: (1) structured time allotment for task and (2) task completion. The worker's planned interventions are directed toward concurrent outcome gains for members on both criteria. The group must try to accomplish the task within the scheduled time. Termination is viewed as a desirable state when members experience the gratification of a job well done. Recognition and reinforcement of the achievement by the worker/leader highlights success and provides the incentive for members to be receptive to other task groups so that the successful experience can be replicated.

UNPLANNED TERMINATION

From both worker and member points of view unplanned termination is probably as significant an event as planned endings of groups. For each it has probably been a negative experience. The worker must take responsibility for making the time spent in the group a learning experience for the members by seeing them singly or together despite both his/her and their disappointments. In addition he/she has a professional obligation to review what occurred to prevent similar errors in the future.

As indicated above, unplanned termination may be due to lack of group integration. Frequently the cause may be poor group composition. Another likely possibility is lack of clarity of goals and objectives by worker, members of the group or both, as well as little consensus on how to achieve these ends. Both overt and covert individual member purposes may not have been dealt with and no true consensus concerning the group goal achieved. It is also possible that there were not a sufficient number of members committed to the agreed-upon goals and means to reach them, and thus the group drifted apart. In each of these situations it is possible that the worker might have acted differently, and only by careful review of his performance, sometimes with the help of his supervisor, can the professional come out of this experience with increased understanding useful for practice in the future.

The second cause for unplanned termination may be the inability of the group to adapt to external environmental changes beyond its control. The conditions surrounding some groups make it impossible for them to achieve desired ends almost from the beginning of the group's history (Glasser and Garvin, 1976). In other situations changes in agency policies, procedures, staffing patterns, etc. may make the group obsolete or prevent its continuation. This too should be of central concern to the professional involved.

But the worker's involvement must go beyond his/her own learning. In rehabilitation and treatment groups he/she must reach out to members in whatever way he/she can to help them understand why premature termination occurred. If there were positive features to what happened, these must be pointed up as well.

However, this is certainly not enough. Each member must be aided in finding a new helping situation, one that is more likely to succeed. Referral and follow-through action must be taken to demonstrate to the client that unplanned termination does not mean the worker is abandoning him/her. Instead his/her interest is greater than before as he/she enables the client to make use of another therapeutic group or alternatively a one-to-one or family helping situation.

It is also important for leaders of task groups to analyze the reasons for unplanned termination. They too have a responsibility to evaluate the experience to prevent future errors. Whenever possible it is helpful to inform members of their thinking about this as well as allow them an opportunity to share their views. While members may be disappointed, most should be sufficiently capable to weather this reversal. The leader should be aware that there are exceptions, however, and go beyond explanations for those who require further help.

SUMMARY

The approach of this paper to termination is unique in that it takes a much more positive view of this process, seeing it in the context of phases of the group's development. As such, the need for the group by the members should diminish over time as individual and group objectives are achieved. This orientation emphasizes that learning in and through the group is internalized by members in making it possible to transfer such learning to new and more challenging situations outside of the group itself.

A conceptual framework organized around this framework is provided for understanding the termination phase of group development. The termination stage is analytically described for rehabilitation and treatment groups as well as task groups. Practice suggestions are made on the basis of this analysis.

REFERENCES

BANDURA, ALBERT
   1971   "Psychotherapy based upon modeling principles." In A. E. Bergin and
          S. L. Garfield (eds.), *Handbook of Psychotherapy and Behavior Change:
          An Empirical Analysis*. New York: Wiley, pp. 653–708.

CARTWRIGHT, DORWIN, AND ALVIN ZANDER (eds.)
  1968   *Group Dynamics: Research and Theory*. New York: Harper & Row.
GLASSER, PAUL H., AND CHARLES D. GARVIN
  1976   "An organizational model." In R. W. Roberts and H. Northen (eds.),
         Theories of Social Group Work. New York: Columbia University Press,
         pp. 75–115.
GOLDSTEIN, ARNOLD P.
  1971   *Psychotherapeutic Attraction*. New York: Pergamon Press.
HARE, A. PAUL.
  1976   *Handbook of Small Group Research*. Second edition. New York: Free
         Press.
HARTFORD, MARGARET E.
  1971   *Groups in Social Work*. New York: Columbia University Press.
  1976   "Group method and generic practice." In R. W. Roberts and H. Northen
         (eds.), *Theories of Social Work with Groups*. New York: Columbia Uni-
         versity Press, pp. 45–74.
JOHNSON, CAROLE
  1974   "Planning for termination of the group." In P. Glasser, R. Sarri, and
         R. Vinter (eds.), *Individual Change Through Small Groups*. New York:
         Free Press, pp. 258–65.
KERNBERG, OTTO
  1979   "Regression in organizational leadership," *Psychiatry*, 42:24–39.
KLEIN, ALAN F.
  1972   *Effective Group Work: An Introduction to Principles and Method*. New
         York: Association Press.
KONOPKA, GISELA
  1963   *Social Group Work: A Helping Process*. Englewood Cliffs, N.J.: Prentice-
         Hall.
LAWLER, M. H.
  1980   "Termination in a work group; Four models of analysis and interven-
         tion," *Groups*, 4: 3–27.
LENNARD, HENRY L., AND ARNOLD BERNSTEIN
  1970   *Patterns in Human Interaction*. San Francisco: Jossey-Bass.
LEWIN, KURT
  1951   *Field Theory in Social Science*. New York: Harper.
NORTHEN, HELEN
  1969   *Social Work with Groups*. New York: Columbia University Press.
PARSONS, TALCOTT
  1951   *The Social System*. New York: Free Press of Glencoe.
ROSE, SHELDON D.
  1972   *Treating Children in Groups*. San Francisco: Jossey-Bass.
SHAW, MARVIN E.
  1976   *Group Dynamics: The Psychology of Small Group Behavior*. New York:
         McGraw-Hill.
THIABAUT, JOHN W., AND HAROLD H. KELLEY
  1959   *The Social Psychology of Groups*. New York: John Wiley & Sons.

TUCKMAN, B.
    1965   "Developmental sequence in small groups," *Psychological Bulletin*, 63: 384–99.

YALOM, IRVING D.
    1975   *The Theory and Practice of Group Psychotherapy.* Second edition. New York: Basic Books.

III

The Group in the Social Environment

Increased interest in the client's natural environment has been accompanied by a growing knowledge base and advances in practice methods. The readings in this section cover a range of topics and issues in the social environments of group members that affect the achievement of individual client goals and group goals. Organizational context, gender, ethnicity, and race are included among the salient factors that influence the roles, statuses, and functioning of the practitioner and group members.

According to Vinter and Galinsky, in Chapter 16, a group's social environment includes "the separate social affiliations and personal environments of the group's individual members . . . and the objects, persons, and other units collectively encountered by the group as a social entity." In their presentation on extragroup relations, the authors discuss four principal areas of outside influence: social roles and relations prior to client status; significant others with whom clients currently maintain association; the social systems of which clients are members; and the social environment of the treatment group. Various intervention approaches pertinent to those areas are discussed, including ways to promote the transfer and stabilization of treatment gains beyond the group.

The authors of Chapter 17, Garvin, Glasser, Carter, English, and Wolfson, extend the Vinter and Galinsky formulation with an analytic framework that includes methods for changing the social environment of the client or client group. They propose a scheme for selecting intervention strategies that involves strategic choices of both the agent of change and the target of change. They suggest that the best strategy is the least conflictual one that can attain the desired objective. The authors describe twenty-one specific intervention techniques, which they group under the twelve headings of intervention strategies included in their analytic framework. The techniques are listed within the headings according to a presumed ascending order of aversiveness to the target. The authors conclude that successful modification of the environment may provide gains besides the achievement of treatment goals, such as greater cohesiveness of the group and increased autonomy and effective participation by clients in the community.

According to Hasenfeld in Chapter 18, the group worker's decisions are affected by various organizational factors, including domain, practice ideologies, resource allocations, dominant technologies, division of labor, and measures of effectiveness. The author distinguishes organizational influences on group work practice according to a classification of social service agencies along two dimensions: the types of clients an agency serves (normal functioning or malfunctioning) and the primary function of the agency's services (people processing, people sustaining, or people changing). The author's analyses of pertinent organizational variables and dynamics imply that effective group work depends on particular organizational prerequisites and that group workers should assume an active role in analyzing the organizational effects of the setting on their clients, on their groups, and on themselves.

Reed focuses on three areas in which knowledge of gender differences is relevant for training group leaders: assumptions about feminine and masculine behavior, the effects of gender composition, and group reactions to women leaders. Chapter 19 presents relevant research and theory to document and elaborate those areas. The author discusses the implications of sex-role bias held by group leaders, including the effects on participation of group members. She indicates that all-men and all-women groups have been found to face different issues in their operation and development, provide different benefits and outcomes for their members, and present different challenges for their leaders. Groups with women leaders have proved more stressful and confusing for both members and leaders than groups with men leaders; however, they also have great potential for promoting learning and change about gender-related stereotypes. Reed discusses the implications of these assumptions and issues for training women group leaders and offers suggestions on providing supervision, feedback mechanisms, and peer support for women trainees. She concludes that attention to gender-related issues is necessary to improve the readiness of women to assume positions of authority, to enable groups to optimize the resources of their members, and to prepare women trainees for leading groups.

Davis, in Chapter 20, addresses the significance of ethnic minorities of color as a factor affecting group work practice, directing his attention to blacks, Hispanics, Asians, and American Indians. The author focuses his analyses on four key areas: the appropriateness of the theoretical orientation of the group work model and practitioner; the importance of practitioners' having a sound understanding of the sociocultural and political history of minority populations; the potential salience of racial group dynamics; and the significance of group leadership style. The author urges group practitioners, before working with minorities, to evaluate the suitability of their theoretical orientations for the intended client population, as well as to make efforts to assess their potential racial or ethnic biases. He cites literature that suggests that negative racial attitudes and biases of practitioners have frequent deleterious effects for minority clients. Greater exposure of practitioners to the history and culture of potential minority client groups is recommended as a strategy to combat underutilization of treatment programs and facilities by minorities, as well as unfair or inappropriate treatment. Davis discusses the racial and ethnic dynamics of groups, including their effects on group composition, communication, trust among the group's leader and members, and member statuses and roles. Ethnic and racial differences suggest that those who work with minorities in groups should recognize that the cultural values of their members may contraindicate the use of certain interventions. The author concludes with a discussion of the effects of differing leadership styles. Stylistic dimensions identified as being advantageous in offering services to minority clients are respect, formality, concreteness, and activeness.

16

Extragroup Relations and Approaches

Robert D. Vinter and Maeda J. Galinsky

EVENTS AND PROCESSES that occur outside the boundaries of the service group, and even outside the treatment sequence, are significant in the treatment group work model explored here. Four major areas of outside influences, termed "extragroup relations," are social roles and relations prior to client status, "significant others" with whom clients currently maintain association, the social systems of which clients are members, and the social environment of the treatment group. Persons and events at issue in one category are also foci in others, although with somewhat different terms of reference. Following an examination of these four areas some practitioner approaches will be proposed, and in conclusion consideration will be given to ways to facilitate the transfer and stabilization of client change beyond the boundaries of the treatment group.

CLIENTS' PRIOR ROLES AND RELATIONS

In keeping with the interactional view of deviance, we have asserted that an individual's problems are generated, manifested, and defined in and through social interactions. The behaviors and events that evidence personal problems or needs occur within these social relations and necessarily *prior* to the provision of group work treatment. They have been characterized in more general terms as problems in role performance, i.e., the failure or inability of individuals to adhere to conventional behavioral standards in one or more of their social roles. This phrasing is not meant to ignore instances where the person's situation or social condition (e.g. orphans) or even the behavior of others (e.g. the abused child), rather than the person's own behavior, constitutes the essence of the problem. The concept of role emphasizes patterns of interactions between persons and, more precisely, of social expectations directed at individuals by persons in association with them.

Persons maintain multiple memberships or statuses in a variety of groups and small social systems within which they are subject to role expectations. It can be within any one or several of these interactional networks that behavior is perceived as problematic.[1] And generally others' definitions provide the terms of clients' "presenting problems" in their initial confrontation with service agencies. Clients typically have their own perceptions and evaluations of what (and whose) the problems are (or are not), but the definitions of others are crucial even in most instances of self-referral.

Standards of conduct and criteria of judgment vary widely among families, social groups, and subcultures. Behavior approved by some may be merely tolerated by others or strenuously proscribed by still others. Readiness to apply a deviant label to behavior and to invoke the formal responses of the community (whether police or social agency) also varies widely. Apart from subcultural differences, critical variations are due to the *kind* of behavior being judged and to the *social contexts* in which its exhibition assumes special meaning. Thus certain behaviors permitted within the family (or in a recreation area) would not be condoned in a classroom. Variations are also due to disparities in the distribution of available services by law enforcement agencies, social services, or whatever. For example, persons are less likely to be labeled and handled as emotionally disturbed if there are few means to respond with these particular definitions of problems.

These variations lead to a critical aspect of the deviance-defining and -coping process. *Private* judgments that another's behavior or condition violates social norms typically and generally have little consequence outside the immediate social context (e.g. between family members), although they may have adverse psychological effects. When such judgments are rendered or confirmed by persons acting in their *official* capacities as agents of professions and organizations, however, they assume special meaning and can lead to very serious results. The action of a court intake worker transposes a neighbor's complaint into a delinquency or neglect case. The assessment of a teacher transforms an indifferent pupil into an underachiever. Such authoritative judgments usually are needed for an individual to acquire formal status as a deviant, indeed, as a certain kind of deviant. Each agent controls access only to particular kinds of deviant statuses; psychiatrists cannot create welfare cases, nor can truant officers create patients. A person cannot become a client of most social agencies, and thereby receive group work or

---

[1] Merton's concepts of role-sets, status-sets, and of sequences of role- and status-sets are particularly relevant. Although Merton's analysis is primarily directed at the sociological implications of deviance, his explication of the processes and mechanisms involved is useful for purposes of the treatment model described. See Merton (1957, pp. 357–86); also Biddle and Thomas (1966).

other services, until some agent has made an authoritative judgment that his behavior and/or social situation violates certain social norms.[2]

These behaviors, these judgments and labels, these agents, and these social norms must be specifically addressed in both diagnostic and treatment processes. Failure to keep them at the center of attention risks defining "problems" and setting treatment goals that are socially irrelevant or inconsequential. Moreover, there is risk in overlooking the extent to which people other than the client must be changed (or merely persuaded) for treatment to be successful.

Implicit in this analysis is the fact that those whose judgment must be reckoned with are not entirely the same as those who were or are involved in the deviance interaction process. The client has had significant interactions with two main sets of actors: those who generated the problematic behavior, and those who observed, evaluated, and officially labeled the behavior. Thus, a boy may fight in school corridors or the playground; to understand the nature and origin of this behavior it is necessary to know which peers he was associating and fighting with. But it is also necessary to know which teachers or other school personnel observed or learned about the incidents, reported them, labeled the youngster as disruptive, and initiated sanctioning procedures or services. In such instances the "presenting problem" is defined as much by the judgments and responses of the school staff as by the peer conflict events. The two interrelated processes of deviance sequences are the one that generates problematic behavior and the one that recognizes, copes with, or otherwise responds to the behavior.

In actual cases the practitioner may or may not wish to study or recapitulate these earlier events and relations leading up to the point of service. Retrospective analysis of the onset and etiology of problems may have little use in either diagnosis or treatment. Apart from the difficulties and costs of obtaining reliable information from the past, it may offer few guides for present intervention. The primary concern is with understanding the nature of individuals' *current* problematic behavior, the forces maintaining it, and the responses of significant others to it.

Before proceeding, the stigmatizing effects of deviance-defining processes should be noted. Negative judgments and labels by salient persons tend to have adverse effects independent of the sanctions that may also be applied. The experience of being judged as a deviant and violator of social norms may harm the self-image, sense of self-worth, and moral value, whether the agent of judgment is a parent, a schoolteacher, a policeman, or any other individual perceived as having moral authority and social power.

---

[2]Merton notes the limited consequences of private responses to perceived deviance. He also emphasizes the significance of responses based on the "moral indignation" and disinterestedness of others who are not directly disadvantaged by the deviant behavior but who may cope with it (Merton, 1957, pp. 361–62).

The defensiveness of clients, the denial of being deviant, and the resistance to service may all be occasioned by an understandable desire to offset the psychological harm from being stigmatized.

INTERVENTION WITH SIGNIFICANT OTHERS

The two sets of persons having crucial relations with clients—those involved in the maintenance of deviant behavior and those involved in coping with the disapproved behavior—exist, for the most part, beyond the boundaries of the treatment group. Practitioners must become informed diagnostically about both and must often undertake intervention efforts directed at both.

The persons toward whom the worker may direct extragroup means of influence are parents, teachers, prison guards, cottage parents, doctors, employers, or anyone else whose influence is important to the client's functioning. The modification of the behavior or attitudes of these persons constitutes a change in the social environment of the client, which may in turn lead to positive changes in the group member's own behavior or attitudes.

Work with significant others in the client's environment can serve two purposes. First, such interventions can make it more possible to ensure that client changes noted in the group will also characterize extragroup behavior. Typically, significant individuals are encouraged to become sensitive to the client's new behavior and to demonstrate new behavior and attitudes in response to the client's changed behavior and attitudes. For example, an adolescent who used his or her fists each time the adolescent was frustrated may have learned to verbalize anger in the group. If the child's parents are alerted to this new behavior as an improvement, they may reward rather than punish the child for venting anger. A mental hospital patient may have expressed increased interest in returning to the community and seeking employment. Both the attendants on the ward and the relatives of the patient may be stimulated to reinforce and to draw out this interest from the patient. A failing student may express to the worker and other members increased motivation and willingness to perform passing work. The worker may then encourage the teacher to take notice of this effort, even though the academic results remain poor. An important point to be noted here is that changes in the client's behavior or attitude may be slight but nonetheless significant in view of the client's past behavior; unless they are alerted to watch for such changes, persons other than the worker may not notice them. If the client receives no outside reinforcement for new behavior, the client may become discouraged and regress to old patterns of action or may display improved behavior only in the treatment group.

A second aim of intervention directed at the attitudes or behavior of significant others is to produce new client behavior. The nature of the desired new behavior may be such that encouragement can take place only outside the group or that first attempts at encouragement from outside the group are specifically advisable. The aim of the worker's intervention is to enable significant others to draw new behaviors or attitudes from group members through their direct interactions. It is most likely that worker intervention will be required to enable the significant other to change his or her behavior or attitude toward the client. For example, parents may have set academic standards for a child that he or she feels unable to live up to. As a consequence the child may do poorly in school and cause trouble there. The worker may seek a relaxation of the parents' standards to enable the child to take a new approach to school. Of course, it may be advisable for the parents to receive independent treatment. But when the parents are unwilling to accept treatment or when treatment is not feasible in terms of resources, it is important for the group worker to intervene with them. To help a withdrawn, reticent child become more verbal, a houseparent in a children's institution may be encouraged to listen to the child's attempts to explain why he or she misbehaved instead of immediately punishing the child. A mental hospital attendant may be requested to give a particular inmate more responsibility for his or her own care. In a training camp for adolescent offenders, a vocational adviser may be asked to give a reluctant client extra encouragement to help the client move toward finding legitimate work possibilities and use of existing skills.

In employing this means of influence, it is important for the worker to obtain the cooperation and understanding of the "significant others." The worker needs to explain precisely what he or she is asking of them and why this action is requested. The worker must express awareness of the extra work and effort involved and recognize the importance of the role these individuals play in the treatment process.

It is necessary at this point to distinguish between extragroup means of influence and collaboration. *Extragroup means of influence* refers only to worker attempts to modify the behavior or attitudes of an individual who has a direct, significant relationship with a client in order to attain treatment goals. *Collaboration* refers to contacts between service personnel where the attempt is not expressly to modify the behavior or attitudes of the other professional but to enlist his or her cooperation or effort in mutual problem-solving. For example, a worker may feel that it is advisable for the wife of a client to change her behavior toward the client. If the wife is in treatment with another practitioner, the worker might then have conferences with that practitioner. Although the worker's objective is to affect the behavior of a "significant other" (the wife) as an aid in reaching treatment goals for the client (the husband), this intervention would be considered collaboration between the group worker and the wife's therapist.

At times the distinction between extragroup means of influence and collaboration becomes blurred. When a practitioner works with a teacher to develop a plan for the teacher's behavior toward a child and also seeks possible modifications in the teacher's interactional behavior, this intervention may be classified as either collaboration (since two professionals are involved together) or extragroup means of influence (since the purpose is also to change the behavior of the teacher). Classification of such activity depends on whether the worker's intent in interacting with the teacher is to engage in mutual problem-solving or to influence the teacher directly.

A distinction should also be made between using extragroup means of influence and information gathering. Where the aim of contacting a significant other is solely to obtain information about the client from that individual (for example, an attendant, a guard, a guidance counselor, a parent) and not to influence the individual's behavior, the activity of the worker would not be regarded as employing extragroup means of influence.

SOCIAL SYSTEM INTERVENTIONS

Clients' associations with significant others are components of large social systems within which both clients and other individuals occupy statuses. Patterns and conditions that prevail within these systems may be viewed as resources or barriers to achievement of treatment goals. For example, the public school constitutes an important social system in the lives of its pupils; it contains the processes of interaction between them and their teachers, classmates, special service personnel, and others. Curriculum structure, grading practices, sanctioning procedures, and instructional resources and methods are among the relevant features of this social system that impinge upon pupil experience. A second type of extragroup intervention involves activities intended to alter such features.

Using this approach the worker attempts to change those parts of the social system that are nonsupportive of or detrimental to the client's change and wellbeing. The worker seeks modifications so that positive features are enhanced and supported, and negative and nonsupportive features are changed or replaced by more positive ones. For example, the group worker may determine that the sanctioning policies in a school curtail a failing student's motivation to continue in school. Not only is the student a failure academically but, because of poor grades, the student is not allowed to participate in extracurricular activities. The worker may attempt to have the policies altered so that the marginal student, on the verge of being a dropout, can find some aspects of school life in which he or she can participate successfully. In a training school setting, if increased responsibility is important for treatment purposes, a worker may try to change cottage routines and regulations to allow more independence for the members of his or her group in their study hours and in their recreational pursuits. In a prison setting practitioners may attempt to develop a work release program for their clients, or, in a mental hospital ward, to increase the degree of decentralization so that treatment effectiveness is enhanced.

In employing this type of extragroup influence, the practitioner interacts with others to modify the social system rather than a specific client's behavior. In order to accomplish changes in the social system it may be necessary to work with a wide variety of persons—administrators, employees, family members, or agency board members. If the worker were to seek changes in the rules concerning extracurricular participation by failing students in a school, the worker would probably have contact with guidance counselors, the principal, the superintendent, and perhaps even the school board. In addition, interpretation of proposed modifications to teachers may be considered part of the worker's task. Alteration of cottage routines in a children's institution would necessarily put the worker into communication with the director and the houseparent staff.

Intervention at this level on behalf of particular clients may also affect others, since changes in a social system typically affect all members of that system. Change efforts focused on social systems are both greater in scope and less immediate in their effects than are interventions with significant others. A change in teacher–client relations may have rapid consequences, whereas the outcomes of modification in grading practices are not realized at once. Both interventions with significant others and social system intervention require the practitioner to work outside the boundaries of the treatment group but with specific reference to the practitioner's goals for individual clients.

In considering extragroup means of influence, only those situations have been considered in which the worker acts with others to move toward treatment goals for individual clients. There are other instances in which the practitioner works for the benefit of persons who are not members of the practitioner's group. The practitioner may interpret a program directly to board members to ensure their understanding and support for it, even though the practitioner may not be serving particular clients at this point. The worker may seek to change the organizational structure of a prison or a mental hospital ward, although the worker is aware that the contemplated changes would have no possibility of being enacted in time to affect current clients. The worker may seek to change policy decisions that affect welfare clients' rights to retain part of their earned income without penalty to their grants, even though this could not be put into practice in the immediate future. In such situations the practitioner becomes a kind of "lobbyist" or community intervener, concerned with the welfare of persons like his or her clients, but not expecting immediate benefits for a particular individual.

SOCIAL ENVIRONMENT OF THE GROUP

To this point practitioner activities have been described that may be undertaken without the participation or even the full knowledge of individual clients. Although it is desirable to inform clients, gain their consent, and even obtain their active assistance before intervening with significant others in their life situations, it is not always possible to do this. However, some extragroup approaches necessarily involve client group members.

The environment of a treatment group has been cited as a source of powerful influences on the group's development and experience. A group's social environment includes the *separate* social affiliations and personal environments of the group's individual members. Influences stemming from these sources have been the focus of most of the discussion in this chapter. Social environment also includes the objects, persons, and other units *collectively* encountered by the group as a social entity. While customarily these two environments overlap, depending on the group's composition and activities, to a significant extent they are mutually exclusive. Treatment groups often occupy places, confront pressures, and develop affiliations that do not characterize the separate, personal environment of any individual member.

Potent demands and constraints are often imposed upon the group by conditions in its external environment. What the group is allowed or expected to do, and the means it is given with which to do it, are often set by the service agency and the surrounding community. The material and resources for group activities are limited to those provided by (if not extracted from) the local context of the group. Responses from salient external persons and other social units often critically shape the group's public identity and its conception of itself.

At the very least, the group's development depends upon how effectively it can cope with critical pressures from the outside, from its social environment. The treatment group need not merely react to or accommodate external persons and events. Spontaneously or with encouragement from the practitioner, the group may undertake active engagement with features of its environment and seek to change, exploit, or redirect environmental forces playing upon it.

Treatment goals can be implemented in important ways through the worker's guidance of extragroup relations. The group itself may be a highly useful mediating vehicle. To supplement his or her own efforts, the worker may wish to stimulate the whole group to confront the "social system" conditions that impinge upon the individual members. As part of its planned program, a treatment group in a residential institution may be involved in proposing (or negotiating) improvements in cottage life, the daily cycle, or discharge procedures. Within the public school, a group of underachievers may be helped to persuade administrative and teaching staff to modify practices that reduce achievement opportunities.

The practitioner may also encourage group attention to focus on the outside experiences of its client members, thus creating opportunities to explore individual behavior, to enhance group problem-solving, and to enlarge the group's perspectives. The worker may encourage such processes when they occur spontaneously, may deliberately introduce them in a group for disruptive pupils, may call upon members to describe concurrent classroom episodes, or may initiate discussion of these events on the basis of his or her outside knowledge. In a group of mothers with childrearing problems, the worker may help members anticipate problematic situations, create and rehearse ways of handling them, and subsequently review members' success in trying out new behaviors. Such outside experiences may have direct relevance for more than one member.

The practitioner ought to plan for and engage in externally oriented activities as a deliberate step taken in the interest of group development and treatment goals. Extragroup activities expand the horizons and experiences of the group; they provide the group and its members with significant opportunities for learning and for problem-solving. Perhaps most significantly, external activities can assure that the treatment process does not become abstracted and disengaged from the social environment. The practitioner and the group must be cautious not to focus on matters only having relevance within the treatment group. Active confrontation and engagement with the social environment facilitate socially meaningful treatment.

TRANSFERRING AND STABILIZING CHANGE

Changes sought through group work service should represent improvements in the client's behavior and/or situation in the social roles and contexts where his or her problems have been identified. Further, such changes should be evaluated as real and significant with respect to accepted standards of conduct and wellbeing.

What are the implications of these requirements for the treatment sequence itself? If the worker has formulated individual treatment goals and plans with specific reference to clients' role performance problems, the ensuing treatment process is less likely to be misdirected. Nevertheless, the task remains of focusing this process directly on the problematic behaviors and, further, of ensuring that changes are not circumscribed by the boundaries of the treatment group. Several lines of effort may be pursued.

1. *Replication of external problem.* The worker can attempt to replicate inside the group the crucial aspects of the interactional situations that manifest client performance difficulties. The treatment group then enables clients to learn more adequate modes of response through direct experience. Suppose, for example, that affect management is a common problem among boys in a group for delinquents. The worker will have ample opportunities to induce familiar stress situations through which the members can explore reaction alternatives, develop personal controls, and rehearse new modes of conduct. Similarly, the treatment group's activities can offer training experiences for clients who lack sufficient social or technical skills to cope with specific role demands elsewhere. In this approach the treatment group affords a protected social environment, partially insulated from but having significant parallels to clients' other social situations, where intensive learning can occur without the usual risks or constraints.

2. *Group discussion of external problem.* The worker can initiate discussion of clients' problematic behaviors or situations, thus enabling members to explore and assess stressful episodes, to gain understanding of cause–effect relations, and to discover alternative courses of action. The group becomes a vehicle for individual and collective problem-solving and provides special advantages in challenging clients' distorted perceptions, in modifying attitudes that may underlie problem behavior, and in generating an expanded range of feasible alternatives.

3. *Initiation and review of external action.* Group members may be encouraged or required to take action between sessions in order to apply, test, or reinforce learning acquired within the group. Individuals in a group for mothers with childrearing difficulties or for disruptive school pupils may be expected to engage in new behaviors in designated situations outside the group and then to report back on their experiences. When used this way, the treatment group provides incentives to try different behavior, serves as a reviewing body to assess results, and provides support and reinforcement for desired change beyond its boundaries.

Needless to say, these procedures can be employed interchangeably or simultaneously. Moreover, the worker may bring (or induce members to bring) tangible evidences, artifacts, or persons into the group from outside. For a group having difficulties in school, it may be advantageous to introduce members' actual grades, to administer and discuss a test, or to bring in for confrontation the school official who handles discipline problems. Similarly, taking groups to various locations for sessions can create opportunities for guided learning in handling physical materials, social engagements, and the like. In all of these instances reference is made to events that have a direct and significant relevance to clients' "presenting problems," and not merely to a regimen of benign experiences.

Worker interventions outside the group with significant others and social systems supplement and reinforce changes induced through the group. Extragroup work should be coordinated with treatment group interventions so both are complementary. Client changes first manifested within the group can be extended beyond its boundaries, while episodes, and events occurring outside can be connected with or exploited for intragroup purposes.

Throughout their efforts to bring about the transfer and stabilization of client behavior, workers frequently recognize that widely held prejudicial attitudes toward "deviants" constitute a major obstacle. Authoritative judgments of deviance have stigmatizing effects both during and beyond the treatment process. It is often more difficult to lose a deviant identity than to acquire one. Limited opportunities and secondary sanctions reduce motivation. Too often, small but significant changes in client behavior pass unnoticed outside the treatment group. With few apparent routes back to nondeviant status and with no rewards in sight, "deviants" become "locked in" deviant careers.

Efforts by the worker can block, or at least reduce the adverse impact of, deviance labeling. Client attempts to change any area of role performance need to be acknowledged. The worker must actively seek to facilitate both the transfer of change into important phases of daily life and the recognition of change when it occurs. In part, such interventions on behalf of clients are advocacy efforts. Their purpose is to obtain positive reinforcement for treatment gains.

REFERENCES

BIDDLE, BRUCE J., AND EDWIN J. THOMAS (eds.)
  1966   *Role Theory: Concepts and Research*. New York: John Wiley & Sons.
MERTON, ROBERT K.
  1957 *Social Theory and Social Structure*. Revised edition. Glencoe, Ill.: Free Press.

17

Group Work Intervention in the Social Environment

Charles D. Garvin, Paul H. Glasser, Beryl Carter,
Richard English, and Charles Wolfson

SINCE ITS BEGINNING the social work profession has emphasized its concern with the client's social environment (Richmond, 1917). That social environment often maintains the client's problematic condition and therefore should be targeted by the worker and client for change. Nevertheless, throughout many of the years of social work history, there was little development of practice theory regarding systematic ways for clients and workers to cooperate together to seek environmental changes despite the availability of a body of social and behavioral science and theory relevant to this issue. Recently a number of efforts have been made to rectify this deficit (Grinnell and Kyte, 1974; Grinnell, Kyte, and Bostwick, 1981) and many current textbooks on social work practice integrate strategies for environmental change with those devoted to individual, family, and group approaches (Hollis and Woods, 1981; Toseland and Rivas, 1984; Garvin and Seabury, 1984).

The history of group work, however, stands in some contrast to the history of other social work modalities in this respect. The early group workers saw social action skills as necessary components of individual socialization. As Coyle stated in the 1940s:

> Group work may contribute to social change in essential and significant respects. Whether or not it will do so in practice will depend on whether group workers adopt *educational objectives which recognize social needs as well as individual growth*. For the fulfilling of such objectives the group worker will require not only a set of techniques—valuable as they are—not only a skill in program making or in organization but, in addition, a social philosophy and the courage to turn his philosophy into action. Only so can he become an adequate group worker or for that matter—which is perhaps more important—an adequate citizen of a new age. [Coyle, 1947, p. 156]

Nevertheless, despite such historical antecedents, caseworkers and group workers have overemphasized the reorganization of client personality as a means to behavioral change. Consistent with an individualistic, competitive society, once such reorganization was achieved, the client was expected to adapt adequately to the social environment or to change aspects of his or her situation to make such an adaptation. Little attention was given to techniques that would enable the client or worker to change the environment more directly.

Now social workers have begun to understand that behavioral change usually cannot be achieved or maintained outside the treatment situation without somehow changing the reinforcing agents or systems in the client's environment. Further, it is sometimes more feasible to make changes in the client's environment that facilitate improved social functioning than to attempt personality change. In any case these two efforts usually must go together.

This is not to deny that considerable social work literature on the social environment is available. The child guidance movement and social work in psychiatric settings generally have emphasized the influence that nuclear family members have on the patient. Sociobehavioral approaches focus more directly on the client's social environment, but they are addressed primarily to the personal interaction level and not to the system level (Thomas, 1971). Traditional approaches in social group work, such as the work of Coyle, emphasized how groups may be used to achieve social change, particularly at the neighborhood level. But no clear strategies of intervention were available (Briar, 1971), although the recent interest in client advocacy procedures is encouraging. Further, this latter approach seems more related to the growing body of literature on community organization rather than to that on rehabilitation methods. Finally, studies of the social organization of agencies and its effect on practice deal directly with the social environment. Nonetheless, like the other approaches, little connection is made between individuals and their problems and strategies to change the social environment that maintains dysfunctional behavior.

An exception is the paper by Vinter and Galinsky entitled "Extragroup Relations and Approaches" (Chapter 16). This chapter seeks to extend their formulation. Vinter's and Galinsky's focus is limited to intervention strategies as part of the treatment plan. A framework for analysis is presented here and, within that, methods for changing the client or client group social situation are developed.

Extragroup relations, as defined by Vinter and Galinsky in their chapter, refer to the behavior or attitudes of persons in the client's social environment or to large social systems within which both clients and others occupy statuses. Modification in extragroup relations may be initiated by the individual client or the group as a unit, directly by the workers themselves, or by some combination of client, group, and worker efforts. Attention may be directed toward persons and/or social systems within which service is being received and the worker is employed, and/or to other institutions in the community.

TARGETS OF CHANGE EFFORTS

Some means for focusing on the environmental context of the client's problematic condition must be developed if the professional is to be effective in his or her use of extragroup means of influence. There are those who play a role in the generation of a problem, others who serve to maintain or exacerbate it, and still others who respond to it. The worker must be able to determine the nature of these interactions and together with the client and group devise strategies that take them into account when working on treatment goals. There are also various useful ways of classifying the social environment to help the worker make choices in responding to those conditions affecting the client. On a general level the impact on the client of specific social situations can be located as:

1. Serving to cause or exacerbate the problematic condition
2. Interfering with the proper pursuit of treatment goals
3. Serving to enhance the attainment of treatment goals

When attempting to achieve modification among persons in the client's social environment, a general rule might be that attention must first be given to those people with whom the client interacts most frequently, for it is likely that deviant or dysfunctional behavior is stimulated or reinforced by them. Further, the type of behavior the worker wishes to modify directs him or her to particular aspects of the client's social environment. When dealing with a child who misbehaves in the classroom, the worker should focus first upon the child's relationship with classmates and teacher. The worker involved with the withdrawn schizophrenic in the hospital ought to give attention to aides, orderlies, and nurses to whom the patient is exposed on the ward. Other patients with whom the schizophrenic is required to interact may be problematic for him or her as well.

Within the service agency two levels of personnel require consideration: (1) those with whom the client has person-to-person interaction and (2) those administrators who have authority over the first level. In some situations administrators may require the worker to behave in ways that are dysfunctional for the client. In other instances the power of the administrator may be required to change the behavior of the worker. In closed institutions clients must interact with large numbers of caretaker personnel— guards, attendants, aides, nurses, doctors, patient workers, childcare staff, houseparents, and so on. In open settings the number may not be so large, but the influence of receptionists, secretaries, and others may be subtle and important, especially during the client's initial contact with the agency.

Too often professionals do not give staff in agencies and other organizations in the community sufficient attention. It is particularly important to remember that institutionalized clients will be returning to the outside community, where they will have to deal with schoolteachers and principals, employment agency staff, the police, and so forth. If the positive changes achieved within the institution are to be maintained, the worker must deal with these personnel.

More frequent contacts during the typical day include other clients, parents, spouse, children, peers, friends, neighbors, co-workers, and so on. It is sometimes possible to pinpoint problematic behavior to particular interaction situations. A child may have temper tantrums only in the presence of an older brother. Violent arguments may take place between a married couple only when the wife's mother is in the home or shortly after she leaves. Sometimes intervention with the relevant other may be easier than with the client.

Once a decision has been made about the person in the client's environment with whom to intervene, workers must be specific about what changes they wish to accomplish. In general the worker is interested in making sufficient change in the other's behavior so that the client's problematic actions will not be stimulated or reinforced, or so that the client's new, more constructive reactions will be maintained. Sometimes specific behaviors can be dealt with. Following each of Johnny's temper tantrums, mother spends a good deal of time holding and loving her son, providing a good deal of secondary gratification. At other times attitudes, feelings, and values must be dealt with, because the stimuli and responses are large in number and broad in scope, reflecting other persons' more generalized predispositions to the client's behavior. The teacher may find every excuse to find fault with and punish Johnny, "for lower-class welfare children do not appreciate an education or the teacher's efforts," as Johnny's previous school record proves. There are also times when the goals of relevant others must be redirected. Despite contrary hospital policy, ward attendants may believe it is more important to maintain strict discipline and control over the patients assigned to them than to permit the type of positive interactions necessary for their rehabilitation.

Social systems are made up of persons. Therefore the distinction between personal and system levels is for analytic clarification. Focus at this level can provide a different set of insights.

Any sizable organization in the community is made up of a number of subsystems. The types of subsystems each organizations develops vary but usually are dependent on the goals of the organization and the training, experience, and technical competence of its personnel (Vinter, 1965; see also

Hasenfeld in Chapter 18, following). Thus the elementary school can be conceived as comprising five subsystems: (1) administrators, (2) teachers, (3) students, (4) special service personnel, and (5) school board. Each subsystem has regularized ways of dealing with other subsystems and defined patterns for dealing with other organizations in the community. To achieve or stabilize client change it is often necessary to intervene in those patterned ways of handling matters within or between subsystems or between organizations. While clients or worker have to deal with individuals in the organization, the focus of their effort is different from that at the personal level.

Changes in organizational or subsystem goals may be required. Efforts are gradually being made to convert mental hospitals from custodial centers to treatment facilities for short periods until the patient can be placed in the community. Middle-class socialization has become an increasingly important goal for schools located in lower-class neighborhoods. Clark (1965) points out that changes in goals are difficult to achieve when (1) they are inadequately defined, (2) the position of the proponents is not fully legitimized, and (3) the values are unacceptable to the "host" population. Without such goal changes, however, the mental hospital patient may have little chance for recovery, or the lower-class child may have little opportunity for upward mobility through education.

Another type of needed intervention may be in the structural relationships within or between subsystems. Communication may be blocked. Most welfare agencies have appeal procedures, but many clients are not informed of these and know of no way to challenge the decisions of the worker. The distribution of power in an agency may be dysfunctional for the rehabilitation of clients. The small amount of power clients possess often has this effect in many agencies. The sociometric structure of an institution may be problematic. Placing large numbers of paranoid patients together on a ward may reinforce their paranoia; certain client roles may increase their disabilities; and labeling clients as criminals, delinquents, school behavior problems, or retarded provides the lay community with sets of expectations for these clients that reinforce their problematic behavior.

A third type of change has to do with the formal and informal rules within and between subsystems and with the procedures used to carry out these rules. High school rules that deny problematic students access to athletic activity also lower their motivation to achieve or reform. The formal bureaucratic application procedures some clients are required to go through in some social agencies discourage them from seeking or continuing service.

Finally, the distribution of resources within and between organizations may prevent maximum utilization of them by the client. Aides in an institution for the retarded who must spend the majority of their time cleaning, toileting, and dressing the residents have little energy left for training them in skills required for community living. Or the provision of expensive athletic equipment in some schools may prevent the hiring of additional teachers needed to decrease class size.

It can be noted that these types of changes in the social system are closely related to each other and at points overlap. However, the concepts and illustrations should make it evident that the focus of effort must be considerably different from that at the personal level and thus leads to differences in intervention methods and techniques. Benefits from changes at the system level often accrue to others as well as to clients in the group. Nonetheless, the initiation of such change grows out of the treatment requirements of members of the group, and the benefits of such system change should be clear to them and the worker.

CRITERIA FOR CLIENT INVOLVEMENT

One of the principal decisions to be made by the worker and by clients is how involved clients should be in obtaining the desired changes within the service agency or other organizations in the community. The position adopted by the authors is that clients should be maximally involved in securing changes in the environments that affect them, so that ultimately they will be able to act on their own behalf without professional help. It is recognized, however, that frequently it is infeasible to involve certain clients in extragroup change endeavors, hence the following criteria were developed to aid in worker decisions regarding such involvement.

Client Motivation

In motivation, the client's preferences for his or her own activity must be considered. Workers must guard against meeting their own needs by developing or limiting the client's participation in the change effort. The client must also wish to act to improve his or her circumstances. The worker, as always, should help the client make as rational a choice as possible by using problem-solving techniques.

Client Capacity

The client must be able to understand the intent of the change effort, perform the actions required, and withstand the anxiety and stress that may be engendered by the effort. It is unlikely, for these reasons, that young children, psychotics, or the retarded will be able to contribute substantially to extragroup means of influence. On the other hand, public welfare clients, inmates of correctional institutions, and parents of schoolchildren may have adequate capacity and motivation for participation in such change.

Strategy Effectiveness

The probability that a particular extragroup means of influence will be the most effective strategy must be considered by clients and worker together. For example, it is unlikely that a teacher will change negative attitudes toward an adolescent who disrupts the classroom unless there is some evidence that the adolescent intends to change the behavior. On the other hand former addicts can demonstrate to prejudiced members of the community that this problematic condition can be given up if treatment is provided and jobs made available, both of which may be necessary for the rehabilitation of drug users.

Risk of Adverse Consequences to the Client

Many clients have suffered severe social stress through unsuccessful change efforts, which may increase their anxiety, reduce their already very limited power, and reinforce their image of the agency as punishing, prejudiced, and destructive. Great caution should be exercised in encouraging client participation in events that may possibly lead to this outcome.

Effects upon Group Conditions

As in any task activity, the effects upon such group conditions as cohesiveness, structure, and intragroup process must be assessed. Successful efforts may add to the attractiveness of the group, may present new structural possibilities for member roles, and may aid in problem-solving activities. Opposite results are likely to ensue from unsuccessful activities in the social environment, unless one includes the attraction to the group created by external threats—a poor basis for long-term treatment planning.

Relationship to Intervention Goals

An important consideration in this type of activity is its relationship to the individual treatment goal and contract with each client in the group. Questions should be asked as to whether the goal is to further assertiveness or to further self-awareness; to further environmental change or individual change; to add to aggressive or assertive behavior directed at particular organizations or to ameliorate it; to add to independence at a given point in the treatment sequence or to stress adaptation to the social situation.

INTERVENTION STRATEGIES

Our set of techniques is suggested by social work literature and by material in the social and behavioral sciences. Interventions concerning work with significant persons in the environment are drawn from interpersonal change theory but applied to nonclients. This includes not only casework and group work but also psychoanalytic theory and methods, behavioral therapy and learning theory, and a variety of interactional approaches, such as the social role framework and the knowledge about cognitive dissonance and attitude change. Interventions concerning work with significant social systems are drawn from community organization and administration theory in social work and analyses of bureaucracies, voluntary associations, and interest groups in the social sciences.

No attempt has been made to provide sets of mutually exclusive intervention techniques. Some overlap may be inevitable and preferable, as long as each is sufficiently different to merit special consideration. It is often necessary to use a number of them together in any particular situation. A repetition of techniques is available to the individual client, the group, and the worker at both the personal and the system level. Finally, this is not intended to be an exhaustive list of interventions but rather suggestive of possibilities that may be used for a large variety of problematic situations.

GROUP WORK INTERVENTION

As can be seen from Figure 17-1, two determinations must initially be made in the selection of an intervention strategy: (1) whether the agent of change will be the individual group member, the entire group, or the worker acting on behalf of the member or group and (2) whether the target of change will be an individual or a system either within or outside of the service agency.

FIGURE 17-1.   Intervention Strategies in the Social Environment

		AREAS OF THE SOCIAL ENVIRONMENT *Target of Change*			
		ATTENTION WITHIN SERVICE INSTITUTION		ATTENTION TO OTHER INSTITUTIONS IN THE COMMUNITY	
		Level of Change			
Change agent		Personal	Social system	Personal	Social system
Client	Individual member	1	2	3	4
Intervention	The group	5	6	7	8
Worker intervention		9	10	11	12

Selection of Intervention Strategy

An important issue in the selection of both strategy and target is the level of risk assumed by the member, group, and worker. We have found that when the target is a service agency with a therapeutic orientation, the client or group is less at risk of punitive consequences than the worker. That is because the agency assumes the client is functioning at the level of which he or she is capable while the worker is "rocking the boat" and should "know better."

On the other hand, when the target is in the community, the client is at greatest risk, because he or she is often seen as attacking an individual or institution that is part of his or her ongoing life situation. This is not necessarily true for the worker in that circumstance, for the worker is often motivated by his or her agency. These risks must be carefully examined by members and workers so that they are not assumed unknowingly.

Another consideration in selecting an environmental change strategy is how much conflict is provoked with the individual or system that is the target of change. In some cases the environment can be changed in ways that the relevant individuals regard as in their own best interests. In other cases those individuals regard the change effort as aversive. We propose, therefore, that the best strategy is the least conflictual one that can attain the desired objective. This approach is usually the least costly in terms of energy and resources; it has the fewest "side effects" in terms of future retaliation; and it still permits an escalation of conflict when required. The least conflictual approach also has the advantage of being seen by many people as a just one. For this reason we present strategies in this chapter in what in our judgment is an ascending order of costs to the target and thus of conflict.

As we noted above, the worker, the member, and the group will have to decide whether the individual will act on his or her own behalf; whether the worker will take action; or whether the entire group will also be involved in the implementation of the strategy. We believe that if the relevant environment is an intimate one for the member (such as his or her family), the member should be helped to implement the strategy on his or her own. If the member lacks the capacity to do so, the worker may act on behalf of the member. We rarely find it appropriate for the group to act in more than a problem-solving capacity with the individual except in joint meetings between the group and a full set of significant others (such as a group of abusing husbands holding a joint meeting with their wives). In this latter circumstance such "special meetings" might momentarily focus on an individual situation.

In contrast, it is always appropriate for the group members to act in concert when they seek to change an individual or system that is oppressing several or all of the members. Examples of this are a group of black parents protesting the discriminatory behavior of a schoolteacher and a group of welfare clients protesting the inadequacy of welfare allocations. Again, the worker will not act on behalf of the group unless they either lack the capacity to take action or would be highly vulnerable to retaliation were they to do so.

Another strategic decision is whether to select a person or a system as the change target (see Figure 17-1). The main issue in deciding whether to direct a change effort at an individual is whether the individual is acting alone or in conformity with an institutional policy. In the former case the group members will usually be helped to develop a strategy aimed at that individual. At times it is difficult to tell whether the questionable action is idiosyncratic or not, in which case the group should interview informants within the system to determine whether an "unwritten" policy exists. In that situation it is often an effective strategy to act as if one wishes to help the individual come into conformity with official policies.

An occasion for personally based strategy was that of a public assistance worker who did not help clients to obtain benefits to which they were entitled because he believed they were immoral people. An occasion for selecting an organizational target was in a welfare department that provided inadequate clothing allowances for children. An occasion of an "unwritten" policy was with regard to an agency that avoided serving people with substance abuse problems by labeling them untreatable even though the official policy of the agency was to offer services to such individuals.

As we have indicated, the principal strategic choices are (1) whether the active change agent is the individual, group, or worker and (2) whether the target is an individual or system. For this reason, we group our description of specific strategies under these headings. We also list the strategies according to our impression of ascending order of aversion to the target.

Individual member intervention at the personal level (boxes 1 and 3). Clients are constantly required to deal with their social environment, and sometimes they make attempts to change it so that it will be less problematic for them. That is usually not done consciously, however, or with a strategic sense of direction concerning the desired change. The techniques below suggest ways for the worker and group to arm the client with means for more effective modification of his or her environment.

1. *Avoidance.* Some situations in which present stimuli lead to problematic behavior can be avoided by the client. If such situations are clearly identified, the worker can coach the client in appropriate avoidance behaviors and even help the client to practice them in the group. The delinquent who performs antisocial acts only in the presence of buddies may be taught how to stay away from them and how to find new friends who are unlikely to get him or her into trouble. This means of intervention presupposes an intermittent or continuous exposure by the client to the problem situation.

2. *Alternate reactions*. Much of the therapeutic literature assumes that one type of treatment goal is for clients to learn to react differently in a variety of interpersonal situations. These situations are rarely defined in explicit terms, however; nor is the alternate reaction specified. Clients can be taught alternate reactions in the group in a variety of ways, such as behavioral rehearsal, role-playing, or model presentation (Frankel and Glasser, 1973). The employee who always responds to his supervisor's criticism by withdrawing can be taught (coached) to be more assertive when he or she believes such comments are unfair.

3. *Manipulation of the social and/or physical situation*. A lower-class elementary school child was evaluated negatively by his teacher because of her stereotype of children with his background, confirmed by his usually not answering her questions. It was discovered that he had an auditory problem and could not hear well in his seat in the back of the room. When he asked to be moved up front his diligence and intelligence became apparent, and the teacher's reaction to him changed radically.

4. *Education of others*. There are many times when the reactions of others to a client are based on incorrect information or lack of knowledge. For example, many employers are reluctant to hire workers diagnosed as having epilepsy. They do not know that both grand mal and petit mal seizures can be controlled well with drugs, and efficient performance can be expected. Epileptics may need to inform potential employers of these facts.

5. *Interpretation*. Sometimes relatives, members of the lay community, and even professionals are not aware that their interpersonal reactions to clients may stimulate their problematic behavior. By having clients bring these responses to their attention, they may readily agree to change their behavior. A mother may be completely unaware that joking about her adolescent daughter's relationships with boys not only embarrasses the girl but makes her feel uncomfortable in coeducational situations. The mother may be quite willing to stop such behavior if her daughter talks with her about it.

6. *Evaluation* is very similar to interpretation but has a different connotation. The emphasis in evaluation is on helping the relevant other see the negative consequences for himself or herself as well as the client. This then serves as additional motivation to change the responses to the client. Each time Don does not complete the class assignment the teacher reprimands him. In turn he gets angry in a way that disrupts the entire class and her personally. On worker's suggestion, Don points this out to her, adding that his previous preparation has been inadequate and this is the reason he does not finish the assignments. From then on, she lowers performance expectations for him and refrains from reprimanding him.

7. *Co-optation* involves making the relevant other a colleague or friend to aid in client change, sometimes even without awareness of the change in relationship or behavior. The negative attitudes of a childcare

worker toward a resident may be changed by having the resident involve the worker in an activity in which they have a strong mutual interest.

8. *In bargaining or negotiation* the client agrees to change or do something for someone in the social environment, and in return the other person agrees to reciprocate in a way helpful to the client. Mother is constantly nagging Bob about how dirty and disorderly his room is, which gets him angry and starts a family argument. Bob agrees to clean his room thoroughly once a week if mother agrees not to mention the matter any more.

9. *Use of influentials.* The client may try to use the aid of others to persuade some important person in his social situation to change. He or she may attempt to enlist other members of the treatment group, the worker, or powerful or expert people in the community.

10. *Confrontation.* If some of the other techniques do not work, the client may have to employ confrontation. The client forces others to face the ways in which their behavior or attitudes are problematic and demands some change. The group worker may help the adolescent girl confront her mother about the large number of household tasks she is required to perform, leaving almost no time for homework or recreation. Sometimes compromise solutions can be worked out after confrontation has taken place.

Group intervention at the personal level (boxes 5 and 7).   Emphasis in this category is on clients working together as a unit. Some aspect of the social environment requires change for the majority of treatment group members, who are both capable and motivated to cooperate to achieve this end. The worker has to be sure that the actions taken will not harm some individuals within or outside the treatment group at the cost of helping others, although sometimes risks must be taken.

Techniques 3–10 above apply to the total group as well. Often they can be used more effectively when the group works together. That is particularly true when modification of organizational personnel, either within their own service agency or at some other agency, is required. In addition, another technique may be useful.

11. *Alliance.* The group may unite with other groups that are experiencing similar problems in the environment to effect change in some person or situation. While this technique may apply more often to system change, it sometimes is useful at the personal level as well. For example, a psychiatric hospital orderly consistently brings the ward patients to the dining room late. As a result they must eat hurriedly and sometimes do not get a full meal. Treatment group patients may enlist the support of other groups on the ward or organize other patients into a larger group to put pressure on the attendant to change his pattern.

Worker intervention at the personal level (boxes 9 and 11).   Techniques 3–11 also can be used effectively by workers. Since workers generally possess considerably more power than an individual client, especially among colleagues in their own agency, they may be more successful than clients acting alone or together in their own behalf. Further, they may often find it useful to form alliances (technique 11) with other colleagues to achieve specified changes. This power that the worker possesses is employed in the additional techniques described below.

12. *Consultation.* The group workers' specialized skills may provide them with an opportunity to serve as consultants to other professionals. This may also allow them to induce changes in the attitudes and behaviors of others who they know have detrimental effects on the clients with whom they are working. Social workers may be asked to consult with teachers on how to handle certain disruptive aspects of classroom behavior. They may deliberately include material on attitudes toward children whose parents are on the welfare rolls, attempting to change negative perspectives of teachers toward AFDC mothers and their children, some of whom are in groups for which they are directly responsible.

13. *Collaboration and/or joint planning.* When the person to be changed is another professional within the service agency or another organization in the community, the worker may attempt to initiate collegial discussion, providing an opportunity to use other techniques. For example, the school social worker may request a conference with the client's teacher to discuss new developments in the case and to initiate some joint planning.

14. *Advocacy.* The worker stands next to and in partnership with the client(s) relative to the problematic condition in the environment (Purcell and Specht, 1965). In many cases this means that techniques 2-11 are used by worker and client or worker and client group together. For example, it is often not enough for adolescents to change their behavior in the classroom to achieve the designated treatment goal of improved school performance. For the teacher to change an attitude toward the student and provide rewards for more positive behavior, the client and worker must often bring these changes to the teacher's attention together.

15. *Supervision.* In some situations the group worker may be in a supervisory relationship with staff who affect clients in the treatment group. This is true for some closed institutional settings, where professionals play a dual role of being responsible for the treatment of a specified group of clients and being responsible for supervision of other staff such as childcare workers, custodial personnel, housemothers, aides, and so on. In these circumstances the supervisory relationship can be used to achieve change in the environment for clients in the treatment group. For example, irrational attitudes toward residents in a training school for the retarded might be handled in this way.

Individual member intervention at the system level (boxes 2 and 4). System change by individuals is extremely difficult. This is especially true for clients, for in many agencies they have low status and power. System change involves patterns of performance that include numerous persons in the environment, often requiring that the change agent have considerable power to be effective. While techniques 1–10 are available to the client, they usually are not potent enough to achieve changes in structure, goals, rules and procedures and the distribution of resources in an institution. There are exceptions, however, and the worker should be alert to this possibility in order to maximize individual client effort. No new techniques are proposed.

Group intervention at the system level (boxes 6 and 8).   Client groups, particularly in alliance with other groups, can be a potent force for system change. Activities in a voter registration drive, the civil rights movement, poverty programs, and the consumer protection area have demonstrated this well.

This category moves into what has often been considered citizen action and community organization. The distinction made in this chapter is that such group action grows out of and is directly relevant to the attainment of treatment goals for the members of the group. For example, when dealing with the very poor or nonwhites, their social functioning problems cannot easily be divorced from their class and caste status. Not all such groups are ready to attempt system change, however. A wise strategy may be to begin with small environmental changes, often at the personal level, and through successful experience work up to broader system changes within and between organizations.

All of the techniques proposed for groups at the personal level are relevant here. In addition, three other techniques will be delineated.

16. *Mass communication.* The spread of the rationale for system change through written or verbal reports (newspapers, pamphlets, radio, television, and so on) can be an effective means of putting pressure on those in positions of responsibility. The presentation of constructive alternatives to present policies is useful in convincing others of the need for environmental modification. The literature on propaganda and attitude change should be used in planning such a campaign.

17. *Passive resistance.* A number of passive resistance techniques involving noncooperation with key authorities in the institutional system have been developed. These include refusal to perform required tasks or to be present at mandatory meetings. Many clients are not sufficiently confident to use such techniques or not in a position to use them advantageously. On the other hand, while they may not be able to begin such actions, they may be able to participate in those initiated by others.

18. *Active resistance.* This means playing an active role against the social system—picketing, marching, and so forth. This also can be difficult for many clients, but they may participate under the leadership of others.

The consequences of using resistance techniques, active and passive, should be evaluated carefully by the worker before he or she encourages clients to initiate or participate in them. The risk of greater damage than benefits to clients or others in the community may sometimes be great. The use of violence, even to pursue justifiable goals, is usually considered unethical conduct in the professions. Many of the other techniques of change proposed may achieve the same end more easily. While workers may not endorse some forms of active resistance, they nonetheless can empathize with those clients who are driven to desperate actions by aversive environments.

Worker intervention at the system level (boxes 10 and 12). Intervention in these categories has to do with social action and policy formation, that is, practitioners as social reformers. They may attempt change as staff members working through the agency bureaucracy, as professionals with other professionals through social work organizations, or as independent citizens with a variety of lay and professional organizations. The focus of this paper points to the practitioner's expert knowledge concerning environmental conditions that are problematic to large numbers of clients, some of whom they work with directly.

All of the worker techniques reviewed at the personal level, plus techniques 16–18, are relevant here too. Three additional ones for the practitioner as social reformer are summarized below.

19. *Planned contagion.* Sometimes the professional can demonstrate the superiority of certain types of innovations by means of special projects (Herman and Rosenberg, 1967). It is helpful if outside financing for these ventures can be found. Planning such projects with other agency staff can lead to contagion of the modifications throughout the agency and to other agencies as well. For example, a demonstration of the use of group work service in a local welfare department led to the continued use of group methods after the project terminated and its spread to other county departments.

20. *Social engineer.* Closely related to the foregoing is the social engineer approach. This technique is particularly useful when one or more aspects of a program seem to be failing and there is a request for help. The practitioner plans in detail some aspect of the institutional program and builds in evaluation procedures to demonstrate its success. This approach has been used effectively in some school systems to initiate behavioral therapy programs in the classroom.

21. *Authority.* A supervisory relationship carries authority with it. However, sometimes practitioners have no formal supervisory role with other staff but do have legitimate power over them. They may use their position in the agency hierarchy to modify goals, values, structural arrangements among personnel, rules and procedures, or the distribution of resources. They should be aware that while this may temporarily change staff

behavior, it will not necessarily change individual attitudes and values, unless the persons involved become convinced that the system changes work better than the old ways and are more satisfying to them.

CONCLUSION

This paper reviews many of the variables to be considered in extra-group means of influences and suggests a number of strategies and techniques to achieve this end. While its focus is clearly on modification of the environment to achieve treatment goals, by necessity it implies relationships between social group work practice, community organization, and administration methods.

Successful modification of the environment may provide gains beyond the achievement of treatment goals. When clients, either singly or in a group, participate in the process, it may help them to attain a new sense of autonomy. Their involvement may have the same benefits as other carefully planned programs and, in addition, provide them with new and satisfying roles in the community. For many it may be excellent training in tactful and strategic assertiveness, a requirement for successful management of their environment. For the group this type of experience may help to clarify goals and norms and lead to greater cohesiveness, which permits more effective use of indirect means of influence.

For too long the concept of "environmental manipulation" has been given lip service only. We hope this paper will stimulate the development of effective intervention strategies at both the personal and system levels in the social field surrounding the client and his treatment group. In that way a more comprehensive and efficacious practice technology may be had.

REFERENCES

BRIAR, SCOTT
    1971   "Social casework and social group work: Historical foundations." In Robert Morris (ed.), *Encyclopedia of Social Work*. New York: National Association of Social Workers, pp. 1237–45.

CLARK, BURTON R.
    1965   "Organizational adaptation and precarious values," *American Sociological Review*, 21: 327–36.

COYLE, GRACE L.
    1947   *Group Experience and Democratic Values*. New York: Woman's Press.

FRANKEL, ARTHUR, AND PAUL GLASSER
    1973   "Behavioral approaches to group work," *Social Work*, 19, no. 2 (March): 163–75.

GARVIN, CHARLES, AND BRETT SEABURY
  1984 *Interpersonal Practice In Social Work*. Englewood Cliffs, N.J.: Prentice-Hall.
GRINNELL, RICHARD, AND NANCY S. KYTE
  1974 "Environmental modification: A study," *Social Work*, 20, no. 2 (May): 313–18.
GRINNELL, RICHARD M.; NANCY S. KYTE; AND GERALD J. BOSTWICK, JR.
  1981 "Environmental modification." In Anthony N. Maluccio (ed.), *Promoting Competence in Clients: A New/Old Approach to Social Work Practice*. New York: Free Press, pp. 152–84.
HERMAN, MELVIN, AND BERNARD ROSENBERG
  1967 "Effecting organizational change through a demonstration project: The case of a youth-work program." In George A. Brager and Francis P. Purcell (eds.), *Community Action Against Poverty*. New Haven, Conn.: College and University Press, pp. 83–103.
HOLLIS, FLORENCE, AND MARY F. WOODS
  1981 *Casework: A Psychosocial Therapy*. Third edition. New York: Random House.
PURCELL, FRANCIS P., AND HARRY SPECHT
  1965 "The house on Sixth Street," *Social Work*, 10, no. 4 (October): 69–76.
RICHMOND, MARY E.
  1917 *Social Diagnosis*. New York: Russell Sage.
THOMAS, EDWIN J.
  1971 "Social casework and social group work: The behavioral modification approach." In Robert Morris (ed.), *Encyclopedia of Social Work*. New York: National Association of Social Workers, pp. 1226–37.
TOSELAND, RONALD W., AND ROBERT F. RIVAS
  1984 *An Introduction to Group Work Practice*. New York: Macmillan.
VINTER, ROBERT D.
  1965 "Analysis of treatment organizations," *Social Work*, 8, no. 3 (July): 3–15.

18

The Organizational Context of Group Work

Yeheskel Hasenfeld

LIKE OTHER INTERVENTION METHODS in social work, group work practice is nearly always embedded in a formal organizational setting. From an organizational perspective group work can be seen as one of the means through which the agency produces its outputs, be they persons with improved levels of social functioning, street gangs with more prosocial behavior, or inmates with higher levels of conformity to institutional norms. More than other service technologies, group work originated as an agency-based practice. Nonetheless, with few exceptions, notably Garvin (1981), the development of group work theory and practice has tended to adopt a "clinical practice" rather than an "organizational practice" model. A clinical practice model focuses primarily (and often exclusively) on client–worker relations and assumes that the clinical decision-making processes are governed by: (1) the information elicited from the client; (2) the body of knowledge against which such information is evaluated, and (3) the prescribed treatment procedures derived from that body of knowledge. Such a model ignores the fundamental fact that the entire helping process is anchored in an organizational context and that every decision made by the worker is influenced by such organizational factors as domain, practice ideologies, resource allocations, dominant technologies, division of labor, and measures of effectiveness. This can be seen in Figure 18–1.

To elaborate briefly, who contacts the agency is determined in part by the definition of agency's domain, namely the population over which the agency claims jurisdiction, the range of needs to which it is responsive, and the type of services it has developed. Such domain is a negotiated product of the relationships between the agency and key elements in its environment such as funding and legitimating organizations (Hasenfeld, 1972). Moreover, the agency cultivates a reputation that selectively attracts different types of clients.

The commitment of the client to a relationship with the worker—engagement—is significantly influenced by the dominant practice ideologies in

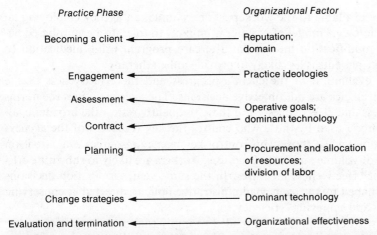

Practice Phase   *Organizational Factor*

Becoming a client ◄——————————— Reputation;
                                  domain

Engagement ◄——————————— Practice ideologies

Assessment ◄——————————— Operative goals;
Contract ◄——————————— dominant technology

Planning ◄——————————— Procurement and allocation
                        of resources;
                        division of labor

Change strategies ◄——————————— Dominant technology

Evaluation and termination ◄——————————— Organizational effectiveness

FIGURE 18–1.   The Interaction between Organizational Factors and
the Phases of the Practice Process

the agency. These encompass moral conceptions about human nature and
causes of behavior. Clients who present "undesirable" moral attributes according to the practice ideologies are less likely to be engaged and more
likely to be discontinued (Roth, 1972).

The assessment or diagnosis of the client needs is highly influenced by
the operative goals of the agency, namely what the organization is *actually*
trying to accomplish. Client needs will be defined in ways that enhance the
attainment of these goals. Second, the service technology of the agency will
define which client attributes are relevant to the organization and the range
of diagnostic options available to the worker. Similarly, the contract options to be negotiated between the worker and the client are constrained by
the operative goals of the agency and the service modalities it sanctions. For
example, in an agency emphasizing short-term treatment, the workers will
avoid contracts involving lengthy time commitments.

The planning process, which includes the formulation of the service objectives, setting priorities, and identification of target systems, is determined in no small measure by the availability of resources and their allocation among different program priorities. In general agency staff will be
constrained to devise service plans that conserve agency resources and are
"cost-efficient." In addition the division of labor in the agency will determine and circumscribe the responsibilities and obligations of the worker to
the client.

The change strategies, such as group work, are dictated by the dominant service technologies of the agency. By declining to allocate resources to
other potential technologies, the agency in effect excludes them from the

repertoire available to the workers. For example, an agency employing an ego psychological model of practice is unlikely to tolerate a group-based behavioral modification model. An aftercare program using medication to manage its patients is less likely to provide milieu therapy.

The evaluation of the client's progress and the effectiveness of the change strategies are not objective decisions. The agency defines the norms of progress and effectiveness, and these frequently reflect the broader evaluative criteria used by those who control the key resources of the agency. For example, when those who control key agency resources evaluate it on the basis of volume and cost of services, workers are likely to substitute efficiency for effectiveness measures. In the same vein, termination decisions may be shaped by the agency administrative policies directed at conserving resources and achieving efficiency.

These examples are not intended to imply that agency policies are inherently in conflict with social work practice norms and values. Quite the contrary—they have significant influence on agency policies. They are simply stated in the negative in order to emphasize the underlying fact that many professional decisions are subordinate to and shaped by organizational policies. These policies in themselves reflect the political and economic realities to which the agency must adapt if it is to survive and thrive.

AGENCY TYPE AND GROUP WORK PRACTICE

Degrees and patterns of organizational influence on group work practice vary from setting to setting. It is essential that types of social service agencies be distinguished along dimensions that have particular impact in shaping the character and function of the intervention methods used. Social service agencies can be classified along two dimensions: the types of clients they serve and the primary function of the services (Hasenfeld, 1983).

The types of clients an agency is mandated to serve will influence the composition of the group and its treatment objectives. An agency whose primary mandate is to maintain and enhance the well-being of persons judged to be functioning adequately in society will use group work to supplement and complement other service technologies directed at bolstering the clients' well-being (Rose and Roessle, 1980). Clients will be perceived as "normal" and motivated to improve themselves. In contrast, agencies which are mandated to control, ameliorate and remedy the ill or deviant status of persons judged as malfunctioning will use group work for control and behavior change (Empey and Erickson, 1971).

The second dimension refers to the type of services provided by the agency or, more generally, the function and purpose of such services. We can distinguish among three service functions: (1) people-processing, in which the agency attempts to transform clients not by altering their personal attributes but rather by conferring upon them a social label and a public status that evoke desirable reactions from other social units. Group work in this context is used for "diagnostic" or evaluation purposes, and for socialization into the new status. For example, an assessment and referral agency may use groups to identify clients' interactional deficits. A juvenile court may use groups to socialize offenders to their new status as probationers. (2) People-sustaining in which the agency attempts to maintain, or to prevent and retard the deterioration of, the personal welfare or well-being of clients. Group work is used to control undesirable behavior, to provide support, and to sustain desirable role performance (Silverman and Brahce, 1979). (3) People-changing, in which the agency aims to alter directly the personal attributes of clients in order to improve their well-being. In this context group work is used for psychotherapy, for the acquisition of new behavioral patterns, and the like.

The cross-classification of the two dimensions results in six distinct organizational contexts for group work practice (see Table 18-1).

Agencies vary in their conception of the role of the "client." Becoming a client, while a common occurrence, not only determines the range of services people receive but also affects their social and moral status. Two dimensions determine the structure of the relationship between agency and clients. The first is the degree of control the agency has over the client. At one extreme are agencies that base their services on the voluntary participation of the client, such as the youth service agency or private family service agency. At the other extreme are agencies that have nearly total control over the client, such as a correctional institution or mental hospital. An important task for group work in the former will be to maintain the client's commitment and attachment to the agency, while in the latter group work will confront the task of maintaining the client's compliance to the organizational regime.

A second dimension of the organization–client relationship is the degree to which the agency transacts with clients as individuals or as groups

TABLE 18-1. Client–Organization Relations

	SERVICE FUNCTION		
CLIENTS	*People-Processing*	*People-Sustaining*	*People-Changing*
Normal functioning	Admissions office	Retirement home	Youth club
Malfunctioning	Juvenile court	Nursing home	Mental health clinic

(Wheeler, 1966 pp. 60–66). In an agency that regularly deals with clients individually (child guidance clinic or a welfare department), the deployment of group procedures runs counter to the basic work structure. Group work practice in such settings tends to be marginal and confronts the problem of formulating a common basis for clients to interact as a group. For example, group work practice with AFDC mothers tends to occupy a marginal position in the total service program of the agency. The group worker and the clients are constantly preoccupied with identifying and maintaining a common basis to justify the existence of the group (Zander and Kendy, 1980). In an agency where clients often function collectively, group work encounters competition from other organizational units that transact with clients collectively in the pursuit of the unit goals. These patterns of interaction may neutralize or negate the group processes instituted by the worker. In a juvenile correctional setting an internal conflict may exist between cottage parents, educators, and social workers vis–à-vis the inmate groups (Street, Vinter, and Perrow, 1966). Similarly, the relationship of a teacher to the classroom may differ radically from the relationship of a social worker to the same group of pupils.

While in an individual-oriented agency the group worker encounters forces reducing the potential attraction and cohesion of the group, in a group-oriented agency, the worker encounters powerful group forces, such as the inmate subculture or peer group, over which he or she has limited control. The cross-classification in Table 18–2 highlights the various combinations of organization–client relations that impinge directly on the content of group work practice in different settings.

Becoming a Client

Upon entry to the organization, clients undergo a process of assessment, classification, and categorization that prescribes their access and routes to various services in the agency. Several decisions are made in this process, including the client's moral worth, amenability to change, and ca-

TABLE 18–2.   Client–Organization Relations in Various Agencies

| | | AGENCY CONTROL OVER CLIENT | |
		Low	High
MODE OF TRANSACTION WITH CLIENTS	Individual	Child guidance clinic Adoption service	Probation Parole
	Collective	Summer Camp Street gang work	Correctional institution School

pacity to participate in the treatment process. These decisions emanate from the cultural and normative context of the organization. More important, the typification process of the client reflects the political economy of the agency, in the sense that the process is greatly influenced by both external and internal political and economic exigencies such as relations with funding agencies, monitoring organizations, the influence of dominant professional groups in the agency, and the like (Hasenfeld, 1983).

The culminating result is that the clients the group worker is asked to serve have been prescreened and preselected, and the problems and attributes have been partly defined by the organization's intake procedures. That is, the initial status of the clients and the preliminary assessment of their problems and attributes are presented to the worker in the first stage of the treatment sequence. In the private family service agency clients referred to a worker are likely to have been selected by criteria such as the nature of the client's problem, social class, place of residence, and the like (Cloward and Epstein, 1965; Teele and Levine, 1968). Such criteria become crucial constraints in the decision-making processes of the worker during intake, for they define *a priori* the key variables in the diagnosis process. The organization itself is a very "significant other" whose definition of the clients and their problems constitutes a basic building block for the diagnostic process.

Furthermore, client problems presented to the group worker may have been partially induced by the organization itself, particularly in "total institutions." In such organizations the worker may be asked to deal with problems generated by the clients' isolation from their natural environment or with problems of maintaining the compliance and acquiescence of the clients to institutional requirements for control and order or with problems generated from the client's interaction with other inmates. Group services are often called upon to deal with organizationally induced problems in other settings as well. Winters and Easton (1983) suggest that group services in school settings, for example, can effectively facilitate the ability of students to cope with the multiple and often conflicting demands placed on them by teachers and peers. Organizational factors can induce similar problems for welfare recipients, probationers, and aftercare patients, among others. The probability that the diagnosis will find organizationally induced problems increases as the control of the organization over the client increases and/or as the organization interacts more with clients collectively.

ORGANIZATIONAL GOALS, TREATMENT OBJECTIVES, AND GROUP GOALS

The relationship between the diagnosis and the formulation of treatment objectives is mediated not only by the change or treatment theories adopted by the worker but also by the operative goals of the organization itself. Following Mohr (1973) we distinguish between two types of goals: (1) transitive goals, which refer to the projected impact of the organizational outputs on the environment, and (2) reflexive goals, which refer to the organizational efforts to provide sufficient inducements to evoke adequate contributions from all members of the organization. These goals are arrived at through a complex process of negotiations among various interest groups, both internal and external, which form the dominant coalition in the organization. An organization's operating goals reflect five interdependent policy issues:

1. The service ideologies of the executive elite
2. The availability of the technical means to achieve various service objectives
3. The costs involved in pursuing different service alternatives and the availability of resources
4. The need to maintain a stable internal work and authority structure
5. The constraints placed on the organization by external regulatory groups such as legislature, funding agencies, professional organizations, and so on.

Decisions and choices made by an agency in these areas are expressed in its operative goals. They influence the definition of worker treatment objectives in ways similar to, although more intense than, the manner in which organizational goals influence the intake process. In the choice of treatment objectives the group worker, as a member of the organization, incorporates into the decision-making some of the following considerations:

1. *The extent to which alternative treatment objectives conform to the dominant service ideologies of the agency.* The greater the congruency between a worker's treatment objectives and the agency's operative goals the greater the likelihood of mutual support. For example, if the predominant service ideology of the welfare department is to encourage AFDC mothers to get off welfare, the worker's treatment objectives are more likely to include encouraging the mothers to seek employment, enter training programs, and use day-care facilities for their children rather than increase their welfare grants, develop self-esteem as welfare recipients, and the like. Similarly, if the predominant treatment ideology of a juvenile correctional program is based on education and training rather than the development of self-awareness and insight, the treatment objectives of the group worker are more likely to reflect the former, rather than the latter.

2. *The degree to which the organization has the necessary resources to pursue alternative treatment objectives and plans.* The worker will be constrained to choose those treatment objectives for which necessary organizational resources can be marshaled. Needless to say, resources such as the availability of personnel, equipment, and facilities necessary for the treatment plan play an important role in the unfolding of the treatment process.

The very selection of treatment goals is affected by the degree of control the organization has over crucial elements in its environment that potentially or actually influence the functioning of the client. The greater the control or influence the organization has over such elements, the wider the range of treatment goals the worker can pursue. For example, treatment goals for a group of mental patients being prepared for reintegration in the community are likely to reflect the referral options most available to the hospital. A group worker in an employment services agency will be influenced by the jobs available to the agency. Similarly, group work with socially deprived youth to introduce changes in their relations with school personnel, parents, and police, as advocated by Empey and Erickson (1972), is preconditioned by the social service agency's relations with and influence upon parents, police, and school personnel.

3. *The degree to which alternative treatment objectives conflict with the tasks of other organizational units.* It is most likely that the group worker will be asked to formulate treatment goals that are congruent with the tasks of other staff members vis-à-vis the clients. Yet to do so may pose various dilemmas to the worker, particularly in settings that relate to clients collectively and maintain a high level of control over them. In a school, for example, the worker will be pressured to formulate treatment goals that complement the needs of the teachers rather than the children. In a youth service center the group worker may be discouraged from pursuing treatment goals for maladaptive behaviors displayed by the youth, if such goals are seen to conflict with the agency's recreation functions. In a correctional institution the worker may be prohibited from formulating treatment plans that raise security problems.

4. *The extent to which alternative treatment goals can be legitimated by the organization.* The worker is not likely to obtain the support of an agency if the treatment goals call for activities perceived as undermining the legitimacy of the organization or endangering its relations with important external units. This issue becomes particularly problematic when the group seeks to achieve social change. When the target of change is the organization itself or an external unit essential to the survival of the organization, the worker may face considerable sanctions. Consider, for example, the problem the welfare worker will encounter from the agency when organizing welfare recipients to change departmental policies.

ORGANIZATIONAL MEANS OF CONTROL, CLIENT MOTIVES AND TRUST, AND GROUP GOALS

The foregoing discussion points to specific ways in which organizational factors influence the formulation of treatment objectives and therefore group goals. Group goals are also influenced by the client motives for joining and being in the group and client trust. These are also greatly affected by the organization's choice of its means of control over the clients. Those means may range from persuasion to promises and threats (Gamson, 1968). Clients may enter the agency with positive, neutral, or negative attitudes toward it. The interaction between clients' initial motives and trust and the agency's control mechanism they experience will influence their subsequent motives and trust, as shown in Table 18-3.

Thus a child who joins an activity group with positive and trusting anticipation, only to be subjected to promises and threats, is likely to lose some of the initial trust. In contrast, an inmate in a correctional program who reluctantly joins a counseling group but finds that the predominant means of control are not coercive is more likely to develop a more positive motive and a more trusting orientation. The dynamic process through which group goals develop and the impact of the organization on the process are presented in Figure 18-2.

The structure of the agency will determine the range of resources at the disposal of the group worker and consequently his or her ability to influence group processes. The position of the worker in the organizational power structure will therefore determine (1) the worker's sources or bases of power; (2) the amount of power that can be mobilized, and (3) the conditions in which such power can be used. The worker's position in the power structure is dependent on two conditions: first, the extent to which the worker's skills are central to the agency's operations, and second, the extent to which these skills are not easily replaceable (Pfeffer, 1981). This may explain why it is often so difficult for social workers to start groups in host institutions such as hospitals or correctional programs. Often in such settings the skills of the social workers are perceived to be tangential to the overall services of the agency, and the workers themselves are viewed as replaceable by nurses or guards.

As noted above, the bases of power—persuasion, promises, or threats—available to the worker will be a critical factor in affecting the cli-

TABLE 18-3. Effect of Means of Control on Client Trust

	Agency's Means of Control		
Client's Initial Orientation	Persuasion	Promises	Threats
Positive	M	–	–
Neutral	+	M	–
Negative	+	+	M

M = maintained current level of trust.
+ = increased level of trust.
– = decreased level of trust.

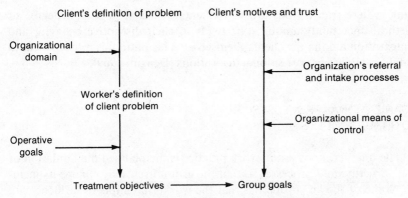

FIGURE 18-2. Organizational Structure and the Worker's Role

ent's behavior and in maintaining the desired behavioral changes. A group worker in a correctional setting will have very limited access to persuasive means of influence, simply because the institution does not sanction them.

The quality of the relationships the worker develops with the clients is strongly affected by the quality of his or her relations with other staff members in the organization. A process of "isomorphism" occurs in which worker-group relations come to reflect the same structural properties of worker relations with staff members in the agency. Three interrelated dimensions that may characterize the quality of staff relations can be identified:

1. *The use of authority and supervision.* The discharge of authority and patterns of supervision influence the use of authority by the worker in the group. The more formalized and rigid the authority relations among staff, the more formalized and rigid the worker's role in the group is likely to be. And the basis of the authority relations—coercive, utilitarian, or normative—is also likely to be reflected in the relations between the worker and the clients (threats, promises, or persuasion).

2. *The level of conflict among staff.* The greater the level of conflict between the worker and other staff, the more likely it is that the consequences of this conflict will be reflected in the worker's relations with the clients. The worker, on the one hand, brings into the group the uncertainties of his or her role definition; and the group, on the other, reacts negatively to such uncertainties and the probable precarious position of the worker.

3. *Morale and communication among staff.* When the morale among staff is low, when communication channels are broken, and when there is a high rate of change among staff, the worker is likely to function with a low level of motivation and a high degree of uncertainty. The capacity of the worker as a change agent under such circumstances is clearly curtailed. In

settings where transactions are with clients collectively, a high degree of structural uncertainly among staff tends to elicit disruptive behavior and disintegration among the clients themselves. This pattern is most evident in mental hospitals and correctional institutions (Denzin, 1969).

ORGANIZATIONAL PROCESSES
AND GROUP PROCESS

The uniqueness of group work practice is the planned manipulation of group structure and processes so that the group itself may change its members. Some of the key properties that the worker attempts to influence are group composition and size, group goals, group problem-solving procedures, leadership structure, and group development. The properties of the group reflect both its external and internal systems (Homans, 1950). Here focus is on the external system, and examination is given to the emergence of group properties as a response to the group's external environment, of which the agency is a crucial segment.

Group Composition and Size

The extent of agency control over the composition and size of the group is reflected in the position of the worker. Studies indicate that factors such as conflicting patterns of interpersonal personality traits among members, status incongruency, and heterogeneity of personalities and backgrounds may produce obstacles to the effectiveness of the group. As indicated by Shaw (1981, pp. 167–68), individual characteristics affect groups in two critical ways: (1) the members' behavior in the group and how others will react to them, and (2) the group's behavior, which is a consequence of the particular constellation of individual characteristics. The less control the worker has over the composition of the group, the greater the probability that such obstacles will arise. Although the agency may not determine who should belong to the group, it usually defines the "pool" from which the worker must draw the clients, thereby limiting the ability of the worker to minimize obstacles to group effectiveness.

Studies on group size indicate that as size increases, participation by members declines, the group has a lower level of attraction, the leadership is more centralized, and there is less group consensus (Shaw, 1981). Thus the greater the pressure from the agency to include more clients in the group, the less control the worker has over such group characteristics. In agencies that transact with clients collectively or define fixed career phases for them, the control of the worker over group composition and size is likely to be small. In such diverse settings as the youth service center and the correctional institution, the worker must either accept every client who wishes to join the group or work with an already well-defined population. If group work is used to deal with problems arising from the adjustment of clients to fixed career phases in the agency such as entry or exit, the worker's choice of clients is limited.

Another dimension of group composition determined by the agency is the degree to which group membership is voluntary or nonvoluntary. In the latter instance the group is likely to develop apathy, self-aggression, frustration, and inability to adapt to "free situations," which could undermine any treatment objective (Thibaut and Kelley, 1959, pp. 169–87).

Ecological Base

Probably the greatest impact the agency has on the group after its initial formation is in determining its ecological base. The *ecological base* of the group refers to its organizational location, the space and time allocated to it, and the resources available for carrying out its various functions. Unfortunately the least knowledge has been accumulated about the effects of these variables on the performance of the group. A pioneering study on the effects of the ecological base on group processes was done by Gump, Schoggen, and Redl (1957) and Barker and Gump (1964). Ecological factors such as the physical environment of the group, its space or territory, interaction distances, density and crowding, spatial arrangements, and communication networks have significant effects on group processes (Shaw, 1981). They are often organizationally determined.

Studies on the social organization of inmates in juvenile correctional settings indicate that when staff discourage and disrupt the interaction among inmates, the latter are likely to form very unstable relations among themselves (Street, Vinter, and Perrow, 1966, pp. 222–54). Likewise, the capacity of the group to develop well-defined boundaries and identity is partly determined by its ability to establish and shape its own "territory" according to its needs. Development of the group requires a space that provides some insulation from the environment and protection from excessive external disturbances. The space must also facilitate rather than hamper interaction and communication among members. Restrictions on the group in the use of time and space are likely to generate problems that must be solved by the group and that divert energies from its main tasks.

Most important are the resources provided by the agency to the group. Basic to group work practice are the resources necessary for program activities. The activities selected by the worker for the group are an important tool to achieve changes in group processes and the behavior of individual members (Garvin, 1981). The choices of activities and the resources necessary to implement them are organizationally determined in two ways: (1)

The resources available to the agency itself will determine the repertoire of activities available to the worker, and (2) the ability of the worker to use these resources in accordance with the needs of the group will be determined by the existence of organizational mechanisms to distribute them.

Finally, the ecological base of the group includes the reaction of other organizational units, including other staff members and other clients to the group itself. Their attitudes and actions may facilitate or disrupt group processes. In general the group's ecological base as structured by the agency will determine whether the group can develop in a nurturing environment or whether it must expend most of its energies to protect its survival. It is not surprising that one purpose of street gang work is to move the ecological base of the group from the street to the youth-serving center so that the new base will enable the group to pursue more legitimate goals.

Problem-Solving Procedures

The agency also influences the group's problem-solving procedures, partly through its control over the type and amount of information available to the group for solving its problems. The agency may withhold information about the purpose of the group, information about the attributes of each member, information about treatment decisions, and so on. The most extreme example of information control can be noted in the Provo experiment (Empey and Erickson, 1971). The amount and type of information needed vary according to the nature of the problems to be solved. The group's effectiveness therefore depends upon the degree to which the agency provides the proper information when needed. For example, a group of underachievers attempting to develop new learning skills will find the task extremely difficult without knowledge of the evaluative criteria used by teachers. Similarly, inmates preparing for exit from the correctional institution cannot function properly without knowledge of the parole board's decision-making processes.

On the other hand a group may encounter a great deal of "noise" in its communication network if the agency fails to provide adequate buffers to the group from external stimuli. This situation may occur when the group lacks an appropriate meeting place, when other staff persons interact freely or randomly with the members of the group, and when the group receives conflicting messages about the agency's policies, procedures and regulations, and expectations from the group. Both information deficit and noise can seriously impair a group's problem-solving capabilities.

Leadership Structure

The agency also affects the group's leadership structure through the resources it provides. This aspect of the ecological base of the group is directly related to the division of labor within the group. When the resources are scarce, the group's ability to develop an elaborate division of labor will be limited, and its leadership functions will tend to be concentrated among few. Scarcity of resources also increases competition within the group; strategies to resolve competition and conflict, such as cooperation, domination by a few members, or disintegration, have direct consequences for the structure of leadership in the group. The worker's ability to influence the leadership structure depends on the resources available to him or her. The stability of the emerging leadership also depends on the support it receives from outside the group—from other units in the agency, for example. Again, the presence or absence of such support is more critical in agencies that transact with clients collectively or have control over them. Thus, for example, when the leaders of a treatment group in a mental hospital are not supported by the nurses or psychiatrists, their position in the group is likely to be precarious, and vice versa.

Group Development

The reward structure of the agency must be mentioned again in this context. The ability of the group to develop and influence the behavior of its members in accordance with treatment plans is dependent, to a large measure, on the reward structure of the agency vis-à-vis the group. Relations between the two are mediated, by and large, by the worker. The effectiveness of the worker is a function of the ability to reward the group processes that enhance the attainment of the treatment objectives. One important aspect of the reward structure, besides its magnitude, is its internal consistency. The agency's reward structure may simultaneously reward conflicting behaviors or fail to reward appropriate behavior. Such inconsistencies can occur when the structure of an agency is highly differentiated and when various units are likely to transact with the same clients. In this situation the group worker is only *one* of the mediators between the agency's reward structure and the clients, and a continuous source of conflict in such agencies is the application of conflicting reward schedules by various staff members to the same clients. The group worker may discover that while he or she encourages a certain type of behavior among the members of the group, other staff may discourage such behavior or even punish it. Thus, unless effective patterns of coordination exist in the agency, group development toward treatment goals may be retarded or jeopardized.

CONCLUSION

The common failure of group work theory to recognize the organizational forces that shape the nature of group work practice may help explain the endemic gap between group work theory and practice. An alternative to the clinical model has been adopted through a perspective on group work as a subsystem within a larger organizational system that defines what goes in and comes out of group work practice and also predetermines group work processes.

Analyses of organizational variables that influence group work practice and of the dynamics through which these variables affect the worker and the group imply that the effectiveness of group work is dependent upon certain organizational prerequisites, and that the group worker cannot assume a passive role in the agency but must engage in the analysis of the effects of the setting on the group. As a result workers may find that they need to induce and stimulate changes within the organization itself before they can effectively achieve changes in their clients.

REFERENCES

BARKER ROGER G., AND PAUL V. GUMP
1964 *Big School, Small School*. Stanford, Calif.: Stanford University Press.
CLOWARD, RICHARD, AND IRWIN EPSTEIN
1965 "Private social welfare's disengagement from the poor: The case of family adjustment agencies." In M. Zald (ed.), *Social Welfare Institutions*. New York: Wiley, pp. 623–44.
DENZIN, NORMAN
1969 "Collective behavior in total institutions: The case of the mental hospital and the prison," *Social Problems*, 15: 353–65.
EMPEY, LAMAR T., AND MARCENE L. ERICKSON
1971 *The Provo Experiment: Evaluating Community Control of Delinquency*. Lexington, Mass.: D. C. Heath.
GAMSON, WILLIAM
1968 *Power and Discontent*. Homewood, Ill.: Dorsey Press.
GARVIN, CHARLES
1981 *Contemporary Group Work*. Englewood Cliffs, N.J.: Prentice-Hall.
GUMP, PAUL; P. SCHOGGEN; AND FRITZ REDL
1957 "The camp milieu and its immediate effects," *Journal of Social Issues*, 13: 40–46.
HASENFELD, YEHESKEL
1972 "People processing organizations: An exchange approach," *American Sociological Review*, 37: 256–63.
1983 *Human Service Organizations*. Englewood Cliffs, N.J.: Prentice-Hall.
HOMANS, GEORGE
1950 *The Human Group*. New York: Harcourt, Brace & World.
MOHR, LAWRENCE
1973 "The concept of organizational goal," *American Political Science Review*, 67: 470–481.

PFEFFER, JEFFREY
1981 *Power in Organizations*. Marshfield, Mass.: Pitman.

ROSE, SHELDON, AND ALISON ROESSLE
1980 "Social skill training in a group for fourth and fifth grade boys." In S. Rose (ed.), *A Casebook in Group Therapy*. Englewood Cliffs, N.J.: Prentice-Hall, pp. 169–85.

ROTH, JULIUS
1972 "Some contingencies of the moral evaluation and control of clientele: The case of the hospital emergency service," *American Journal of Sociology*, 77: 839–56.

SHAW, MARVIN E.
1981 *Group Dynamics: The Psychology of Small Group Behavior*. Third edition. New York: McGraw-Hill.

SILVERMAN, A., AND C. BRAHCE
1979 "As parents grow older." *Journal of Gerontological Social Work*, 2: 77–85.

STREET, DAVID; ROBERT D. VINTER; AND CHARLES PERROW
1966 *Organization for Treatment*. New York: Free Press.

TEELE, J., AND S. LEVINE
1968 "The acceptance of emotionally disturbed children by psychiatric agencies." In S. Wheeler (ed.), *Controlling Delinquents*. New York: Wiley, pp. 103–26.

THIBAUT, J., AND H. KELLEY
1959 *The Social Psychology of Groups*. New York: Wiley.

WHEELER, S.
1966 "The structure of formally organized socialization settings." In O. G. Brim and S. Wheeler (eds.), *Socialization after Childhood*. New York: Wiley, pp. 51–116.

WINTERS, W. G., AND F. EASTON
1983 *The Practice of Social Work in Schools*. New York: Free Press.

ZANDER, T., AND P. KENDY
1980 "Behavioral group training for welfare parents." In S. Rose (ed.), *A Casebook in Group Therapy*. Englewood Cliffs, N.J.: Prentice-Hall, pp. 85–113.

19

Gender Issues in
Training Group Leaders

Beth Glover Reed

UNTIL RECENTLY, most small group research and theory have ignored gender as a major variable. Researchers and group workers have now begun to recognize and explore the effects of different proportions of men and women, their perceptions and behaviors, and the impact of leader gender in different types of groups. The results thus far are complex, needing replication and further exploration to determine how regularly and under what circumstances the effects related to leader and member gender occur. That gender issues are important in understanding group behavior is undeniable, however, and attention to these issues must become a regular part of training programs for those who plan to work with groups. This is especially the case for women who intend to work with groups, because the current literature will only partially prepare them for the group leadership roles they will be assuming.

This article will focus on three areas in which a knowledge of gender differences is important in training group leaders: assumptions about feminine and masculine behavior, the effects of gender composition, and group reactions to women leaders. In a short article a thorough review of the available literature is impossible, but I will cite some relevant research and theory whenever possible. *Gender* rather than sex is used deliberately to include the sociocultural (and not just biological) meanings associated with *male* and *female* in this society. *Leader* refers to various positions of formal responsibility and authority within groups—facilitator, trainer, consultant, director, chair, and so forth.

ASSUMPTIONS ABOUT GENDER DIFFERENCES

1. While men and women often behave in groups in ways consistent with societal stereotypes about gender, wider ranges of behaviors are possible

From the *Journal of Specialists in Group Work*, 6, no. 3 (August 1981): 161–70. Copyright 1981 American Association for Counseling and Development. Reprinted with permission.

and desirable. Group leaders need to understand that gender-related behaviors are functions of the group and its environment and not simply reflections of the individual characteristics of its members.

The concept of androgyny (Bem, 1974, 1975, 1976, from the Greek *andro*, male and *gyn*, female) has evolved to indicate a flexible and less limiting integration in a single person of characteristics usually associated with women and men (cf. Kaplan & Bean, 1976). "Masculine" behaviors are typical of those with higher status in a society (Lockheed & Hall, 1976; Meeker & Weitzel-O'Neill, 1977), while those with lower status and without access to advancement and sources of power and influence behave in ways usually considered to be "feminine" (Kanter, 1977a, 1977b, 1977c).

Group leaders who assume only a sex-role of biological basis for women's and men's behaviors are likely to perpetuate role divisions, stereotypic behaviors from both women and men, and related group dynamics that can prevent the full participation of group members in the work of the group and limit the potential for learning and change. Those engaged in training group specialists must examine their own assumptions about gender, be informed by some of the new research and thinking in this area, and create similar opportunities for trainees. This should include opportunities to explore both the masculine and feminine components of themselves and whatever limitations are residuals of their gender-role socialization. If women do not have formal authority, real influence, and chances for advancement within the larger organization, confronting and modifying stereotypically femine or masculine behaviors within a subsystem is much more difficult.

ISSUES OF GENDER COMPOSITION

2. *All-men and all-women groups face different issues in their operation and development, provide different benefits and outcomes for their members, and present different challenges for their leaders.*

All-men groups tend to be characterized by stable dominance patterns and hierarchies, strong and often counterproductive strivings for status, intellectual discussion of issues, and low levels of expression of feelings and personal information (Aries, 1977; Farrell, 1975; Stein, 1981). Competition can interfere with task performance (Hoffman, 1965; Ruhe, 1978), and status within the group is often influenced by a member's prestige in positions outside the group rather than on the basis of performance and relevant skills demonstrated in the group (Ward, 1977; Wheelan, 1975).

Group leaders, then, must learn skills in developing more flexible status structures and encouraging more personal sharing among members. Some (e.g., Farrell, 1975) feel that men's groups need strong leaders who can be role models for behaviors that are not competitive or dominance-seeking and who can confront a group's tendency to intellectualize and avoid exploration of personal feelings and meaningful topics. Ways in which members contribute to or are assigned tasks in groups need to be examined by the group to ensure maximum assessment and use of the resources of all members. Training in collaborative decision making and working strategies should be useful.

All-women groups have more flexible status and leadership patterns; members share both task behaviors and feelings and often explore topics in some depth (Aries, 1977; Carlock & Martin, 1977). They may be less motivated by any group task and more concerned about accommodating for different points of view among members (Hoffman, 1965; Maier, 1970). Work on intimacy issues and norms related to self-disclosure and closeness may be present from the beginning of the group, although disagreements and attempts to influence the group may be handled much more indirectly than in groups of other compositions, that is, they may be "saved" for later, avoided, or denied. In some cases conflict can be faced more directly after a network of interpersonal relationships is present to provide support, but it is not uncommon for the norms of avoiding conflict and denying power issues in the group to become so strong that any disagreements become harder and harder to address directly. This may lead to considerable uneasiness, interpersonal antagonism, and even group fragmentation. Making decisions under time pressure and doing concrete tasks together may be particularly problematic. There also may be a tendency to devalue work done or things learned in a group without higher status men.

A group leader of an all-women group will need to attend carefully to developing procedures for handling disagreements early in the group and in helping members establish norms that promote active statements of personal needs and priorities. Skills and training in giving and receiving feedback (both positive and negative) and conflict-management skill training should be useful. Exploration of the ways in which women express power (Johnson, 1976) and issues vis-à-vis women leaders will also be important, as will learning to think about the group as a social system rather than to attribute all behavior to the intentions and personalities of individual members.

3. *Groups in which women are outnumbered lead to token dynamics that heighten gender stereotypes and lead those who are outnumbered to be treated as outsiders.*

This topic is addressed elsewhere as it relates to racial differences in groups (Davis, 1981, and Chapter 20). Kanter has written extensively on this topic (Kanter, 1977a, 1977b, 1977c; Kanter & Stein, 1980) as it relates to women and has described some of the stereotypes commonly assigned to token women (i.e., "earth mother," "sex object," "mascot," and "iron maiden"). This dynamic is hard to change and might best be avoided in small groups by recruiting sufficient members of each gender to ensure more equal composition.

4. *Groups composed of roughly equal numbers of women and men tend to limit women to more circumscribed behaviors and relatively powerless roles.*

With women in a group, men are more able to be personal and self-disclosing than in all-men groups, and they initiate and receive more interactions from others (a measure of status) (Aries, 1977; Carlock & Martin, 1977; Rubin, 1975). Women, in a group with men, compared to those in all-women groups, exhibit more restricted behaviors (e.g., they talk less, talk primarily to the men, share less personal information, and are less involved in topics and instrumental tasks associated with masculinity). There seems to be more tension, nervousness, and excitement that may promote conformity (Shaw, 1981), interfere with task performance (Clement & Schiereck, 1973), and decrease personal change in the women (Carlock & Martin, 1977), although Hoffman (1965) found that groups with both men and women were most effective in problem-solving tasks. Like all-men groups, these groups tend to develop relatively stable patterns of dominance and use external status rather than current performance to evaluate members' leadership potential and competence (Ward, 1977; Wheelan, 1975). Apparently, men's higher status means that male "cultural" norms strongly influence the way women behave in the group.

Group members are often unaware of these dynamics. Tower's (1979) findings are similar to those in the Aries study with trainees who had chosen to attend this training program because of their concern about providing nonsexist and useful services to women. They knew of the Aries results, yet when presented with their own data expressed surprise, reporting that they had been generally unaware of the pattern. Apparently, women and men peers may not be perceived or behave as equals, even when group members (and leaders) are aware of these phenomena and are working to change them.

Thus, information about gender and work on one's own assumptions about gender, although important, are unlikely to be sufficient to change the dynamics that limit the behavioral range of women and perpetuate gender-stereotyped behaviors and status relationships. Use of tools to collect and examine group interaction data can be useful (e.g. video or audiotapes, research tools, observers). Alternating single gender groups with groups composed of both men and women can also be helpful. Women and men can analyze their experiences in both types of groups, give each other feedback about their behaviors in the different situations and work to change their behaviors and interactions. This is a common model in other intergroup training designs (e.g., cross-generational, cross-racial), but has been less discussed regarding gender (Bernardez & Stein, 1979, is an exception). As described in the next section, use of a woman leader (not coleader) also seems to promote an exploration of gender-related dynamics and related assumptions and behaviors.

Finally, those who train group specialists must recognize that at the current time all-women groups may be the only way for women to receive some benefits from a group experience. They can validate women's styles and experiences apart from situations largely governed by norms more comfortable for men. Removed from the need of male approval, women can explore relationships with other women and work on task and leadership skills largely unavailable to them in groups with both men and women (Bernardez-Bonesatti, 1978b). Attention to many issues that are important for men if they are to develop an awareness of gender-dynamics is also unlikely to occur in mixed groups.

5. *Groups with women leaders are likely to be more stressful and confusing for both members and leaders than groups with men leaders—especially for male group members—because they can lead to a disruption in members' gender-related expectations and behaviors. They also have great potential for promoting learning and change about gender, related stereotypes, and "traditional" modes of male and female behavior in group situations.*

Only a few studies have examined explicitly the effects of women leaders in group situations, although their results are largely consistent with a larger body of research about the perceptions and evaluations of competence in women and men. The results are complicated but suggest that gender of group leader is related to how the leader is perceived and responded to by group members (Eskilson & Wiley, 1976; Mills, 1964; Reed, 1979; Wright, 1976), how the group develops and does its work (Mayes, 1979; Perlman, 1977; Reed, 1979), and how group members feel about themselves, each other, and the group (Eisman, 1975; Yerby, 1975). The results can be mediated by the style of the group leader (Wright, 1976), the gender composition and task of the group (Eskilson & Wiley, 1976; Maier, 1970; Yerby, 1975), and member and leader perceptions of how and why a particular leader was chosen (Eskilson & Wiley, 1976). In general, groups with women leaders appear to be less comfortable and more confusing for members; behaviors of women leaders are evaluated differently from similar behaviors exhibited by men; and the group seems to need to deal with different issues over the course of its development. A number of theoretical formulations have been proposed to account for these differences, and knowledge of these will be important to include in any training program for group leaders.

Kiesler (1975) proposes an actuarial prejudice toward women in her review of evidence about society's biases toward women's abilities and "proper" place in life. While all conceptions of masculine and feminine behaviors and roles are not negative, many views of women are incompatible with conceptions of leadership. Thus, behaviors expected of leaders would be viewed as role discrepant when exhibited by women and therefore evaluated differently, often more negatively, from the same behaviors exhibited by men. The woman leader is also likely to receive conflicting messages about how members expect her to behave (leaderlike but feminine). Because many of these expectations are incompatible, she will be unable to meet them all, thus producing some level of dissatisfaction and discomfort among members.

Laws (1975) proposes that a woman who occupies a role that is not consistent with women's socially defined roles is doubly deviant. She deviates as do all women from the dominant culture of the society because she is not male; she also deviates from female culture by not being appropriately female. Thus, a woman leader may face the dilemmas of the token described by Kanter, even when she is not the only woman in a group. As leader she occupies a role more commonly occupied by men and is thus different from the other women.

The concepts of diffuse status characteristics and associated role expectations (Berger, Cohen & Fisek, 1974; Berger, Cohen, & Zelditch, 1972; Berger, Fisek, Norman, & Zelditch, 1977) suggest another interpretation. Role expectations associated with *masculine* and *feminine* are linked to different status rankings with the male state more valued. Thus, a woman occupying a leadership role is both role- and status-incongruent. She simultaneously occupies two positions: female, the lower status position of the two genders, and leader, a higher status position than member. Since gender is a basic organizing concept in this society, expectations associated with gender affect our perceptions in a wide range of situations and are very powerful. *Leader* is more likely to be an earned or achieved status with expectations associated primarily with the particular situation in which one is to lead.

Status incongruence usually leads to conflicting expectations and confusion about how to interact with the person whose status characteristics are inconsistent. It is stressful both for the woman and those who must interact with her. Group members are likely to try to find ways to avoid the situation or the person, or to maintain consistency among the different levels of status by distorting information about one of the other positions.

Bernardez-Bonesatti (1976, 1978a) discusses unconscious beliefs about women and their effects in groups, most notably a general dread of the potential destructiveness of a woman's anger. There is now a body of literature, most of it arising from psychoanalytic perspectives, that discusses ambivalence about and fear of women, the personal, social, and cultural implications of these fears, and the ways in which individuals and the culture defend against them. These theories suggest that more fear, anger, and intense primitive feelings would be generated in a group with a woman leader.

A psychoanalytic approach seems quite incompatible with more social-role and sociological, status-related approaches. There are some areas of strong agreement, however, although the language and underlying assumptions differ. For instance, social psychologists would agree that, in group and other social situations, especially when the situation is new, ambiguous, or stressful, people tend to rely on past experience and stereotypes to organize their perceptions and guide their behavior. If they have less experience with women in leadership positions, except early in their lives, the patterns of responses they have learned in these situations may be less adult, or they may behave as if the woman leader was occupying some other female role with which they have more experience, such as mother, daughter, wife, sexual partner, or friend. In fact, the "stereotyped informal roles" described by the sociologist Kanter as ways people deal with token women are very comparable to those described by psychoanalytically oriented writers exploring the ways in which the "dread" of women is handled.

All the theories and most of the available data suggest that groups with women leaders are likely to be more stressful and confusing for both members and the leader. Women leaders are less familiar, to the leader, group members, and the literature. If members avoid a woman leader or the group situation, the development of a cohesive productive group is less likely. Devaluing her leadership abilities or acting as if she is occupying other female roles incompatible with her leadership responsibilities is not helpful if she is to use her skills optimally. Dependency behaviors and ambivalent reliance on the leader to provide structure and direction is one possible outcome. The often uncomfortable and frustrating early stages of group development may be greatly prolonged because the processes of clarifying leadership and developing stable group norms are much more difficult. The high levels of tension, aggression (much of it covert), and anxiety reported in many groups with women leaders are probably a result of these processes occurring simultaneously among different group members.

Because *female* encompasses a wider range of expectations and life areas than *leader*, members are first likely to try and ignore or distort a woman's leadership or competence as a way of maintaining status consistency. If this is impossible because her leadership is inescapable or she is clearly proved to be competent, the use of gender as an indicator of status may be discarded. This would disrupt the role expectations associated with the two status-states of gender and shift the power balance between men and women. Gender stereotypes would be challenged and customary roles for women and men within groups disrupted. Two studies (Mayes, 1979; Reed, 1979) suggest that a shift in gender roles does occur in groups with women authority figures, while those with men largely reinforce stereotypic gender behaviors and perceptions.

Mayes (1979) suggests that resistance to changing sex-role behaviors involves fear that this will lead to chaos and collapse in the norms and behaviors that govern our everyday life, most notably concerning the family and sexuality. She suggests that men especially will struggle to regain control. While some may perceive this view as a bit extreme, gender identity and role conceptions and behaviors are acquired and learned very early and reinforced continuously. While some people have developed more androgynous orientations and skills associated with both masculinity and feminity, many will not know how to behave if gender role expectations are disrupted. Because many people confuse issues of gender identity (identification as a male or female), gender roles (expectations about appropriate masculine or feminine behaviors), and sexual preference, a challenge related to role expectations can be felt as a threat to one's identity or imply that one must prefer as sexual partners persons of the same gender as oneself.

Reed (1979), while suggesting that groups with women leaders are more stressful for men, also finds that members of both genders felt they learned more in self-study groups (designed to learn about group dynamics by examining their own process) with women leaders than did those in groups with men leaders. There were indications that women felt more empowered and that members of both genders were confronting issues related to gender roles.

These dynamics can be controlled and are often not noticed in groups with more concrete tasks or more structure; but they may emerge at times of stress or change in a group, or when particularly difficult or ambiguous tasks are undertaken. A more reciprocating leadership style seems to decrease the discomfort in a group experience with a woman leader, although it doesn't seem to make much difference in groups with men leaders (Wright, 1976).

Leader style and behaviors are fraught with dilemmas for the woman wishing to work with groups. If she behaves in ways that reduce role incongruence (i.e., develop a more "feminine" leadership style), her behavior is likely to perpetuate the perceived status incongruence. If her behavior continually reminds group members that she is a woman, their tendency to discount her authority and competence is likely to remain strong, as is their discomfort with the status discrepancy. If she is too giving or nurturing, she may acquire aspects of the "mother" stereotype and promote unhelpful dependency. If she is tough and perceived as uncaring, she may elicit fear or anger. She may also behave inconsistently, trying to respond to different group and member needs, and because of the ambivalence and increased confusion in the group, she is likely to get more distorted feedback than a man leader about how she is perceived and what members think and feel about the group and its task accomplishment.

There is also great potential for learning and change in groups led by women, precisely because they are less familiar and challenge our expectations and usual modes of behaving. Such learning is very important if women and men are to move towards more coequal roles within society, and if we are to learn how to change the very powerful dynamics that now tend to restrict women's behavior in groups with men.

IMPLICATIONS FOR TRAINING
WOMEN GROUP LEADERS

In training group leaders, recognition of the differences that are likely to characterize female-led groups is essential. Otherwise, a woman trainee is likely to blame herself for not being able to make groups work the way "the books say they should," and the way they do when she coleads with a man. Coleadership models are common in training programs for group leaders; first, the trainee is paired with a more experienced leader, then with a peer, and may finally train others by coleading with less-experienced trainees. Coleadership experiences will only partially prepare a woman for what she will experience leading a group by herself. There is some evidence that male–female coleadership situations strongly perpetuate gender-stereotypic behaviors in groups, even when both leaders are behaving in nonstereotypic ways for their gender. Members commonly misattribute particular behaviors to the leader of the gender from whom they most expect that particular behavior. Even female–female pairing may elicit stereotyping, with one being perceived as more masculine and one more feminine. Much more research is needed on these dynamics.

Thus, other ways of providing supervision of and feedback to women trainees will need to be developed. Using observers as well as video- and audio-taping can be useful. Regular discussion and peer supervision among women leading groups will also be important to provide support for each other, to identify commonalities in their groups, and to share and develop problem-solving and intervention ideas and strategies together. Such support, coupled with regular supervision and other feedback mechanisms, is likely to be especially important if further research confirms the indications that women leaders are more likely to be isolated from the group, experience more covert hostility and distorted feedback from the group, and therefore have fewer ways to monitor and evaluate their own performance. Being an effective woman leader is likely to be more difficult than being a man leader because of the lack of knowledge about these types of groups and the complexity of the events that appear to be occurring. Feeling alone and struggling to understand complex dynamics on the basis of less clear data can only make it more difficult and more likely that both leader and members will feel less good about the experience and their work.

Having strong women with status equivalent to the men involved as part of the training and supervisory team will also be important. Using different combinations of men and women as trainers, single gender, and combined gender groups, and exchanging leaders may all be very effective learning tools. Those doing the training must examine their own reactions to women in authority in order to understand what group members may be experiencing and to train and supervise women students with greater sensitivity.

Women trainees should be encouraged to experiment with different types of leadership styles: to discover ways in which their individual characteristics influence group stereotypes and to develop a balance between being appropriately supportive (without encouraging dependency) and optimally responsible for leadership tasks (without engendering unnecessary hostility and confusion). Probably the clearer a woman can be in her self-presentation (who she is, what she expects, why she is doing what she is doing), the more she can control the dynamics related to her gender. Attention to the status of women in the larger organization and ensuring that women leaders have as much legitimate power as the men in a given situation will be useful.

A group's early phases are likely to be the most problematic because they are likely to be more confusing and stressful; resolution into accepted and effective working routines is likely to take longer. Trainers should consider teaching trainees to raise gender as a potential issue with their groups and to build in education about gender issues, especially in learning, therapy, or growth groups. In task groups this may be less acceptable but still necessary to identify and work through some gender-related dynamics if they become problematic. In many cases, outside consultation may be useful, as can separating men and women into single-gender subgroups to identify issues and to solve problems together. Separate skill-building sessions for men and women may also be necessary to help them work better together. In all-women groups, work on stereotypes, dividing into subgroups, and discussion of issues and concerns related to leadership, power, and other topics mentioned earlier can be helpful.

All of this will be difficult, but it is my belief that the consequences of violating gender role expectations, although not always pleasant, can lead to a productive struggle within groups about gender issues and, if the group has sufficient time, can allow both men and women members a chance to learn and develop new behaviors and perspectives. Moreover, attention to these issues will be necessary if women are to assume positions of authority more willingly and less painfully, if groups are to have the advantage of the full resources of their members, and if the training program intends to provide opportunities for women trainees to learn about these issues before they must face them.

There are also great opportunities to add to the literature. If the dynamics of women-led groups are as different as I believe, examination of them will be rewarding for members, leaders-in-training, and supervisors alike. How they vary with leader style, type of task, and group composition needs to be examined via an ongoing program of research. They may also change over time as the entire society struggles with changing gender roles, and we learn more about the situational factors that influence people's perceived status and behavior.

REFERENCES

ARIES, ELIZABETH
    1977   "Male–female interpersonal styles in all male, all female and mixed groups." In A. Sargent (ed.), *Beyond Sex Roles*, St. Paul, MN: West Publishing Co., pp. 292–99.
BEM, S. L.
    1974   "The measurement of psychological androgyny," *Journal of Consulting and Clinical Psychology*, 42: 155–62.
    1975   "Sex-role adaptability: One consequence of psychological androgyny," *Journal of Personality and Social Psychology*, 31: 634–43.
    1976   "Probing the promise of androgyny." In A. G. Kaplan and J. P. Bean (eds.), *Beyond Sex-Role Stereotypes: Readings Toward a Psychology of Androgyny*. Boston: Little, Brown,
BERGER, J.; B. P. COHEN; AND M. ZELDITCH, JR.
    1972   "Status characteristics and social interaction," *American Sociological Review*, 37: 241–55.
BERGER, J.; T. L. COHEN; AND M. H. FISEK (eds.)
    1974   *Expectation Stages Theory: A Theoretical Research Program*. Cambridge, Mass.: Winthrop.
BERGER, J.; M. H. FISEK; R. Z. NORMAN; AND M. ZELDITCH, JR.
    1977 *Status Characteristics and Social Interaction: An Expectation-States Approach*. New York: Elsevier.
BERNARDEZ-BONESATTI, TERESA
    1976   "Unconscious beliefs about women affecting psychotherapy," *N.C. Journal of Mental Health*, 7, no. 5: 63–66.
    1978a   "Women and anger: Conflicts with aggression in contemporary women," *Journal of the American Medical Women's Association*, 35, no. 5: 215–19.
    1978b   "Women's groups: A feminist perspective on the treatment of women."

In H. Grayson and C. Lowe (eds.), *Changing Approaches to the Psychotherapies.* New York: Spectrum Publications, pp. 55–67.

BERNARDEZ, T., AND T. S. STEIN

1979   "Separating the sexes in group therapy: An experiment with men's and women's groups," *International Journal of Group Psychotherapy*, 29: 493–502.

CARLOCK, C. J., AND P. Y. MARTIN

1977   "Sex composition and the intensive group experience, *Social Work*, 22: 27–32.

CLEMENT, D. E., AND J. J. SCHIERECK, JR.

1973   "Sex composition and group performance in a visual signal detection task," *Memory and Cognition*, 1: 251–55.

DAVIS, L. E.

1981   "Racial issues in the training of group workers," *Journal for Specialists of Group Work*, 6: 155–60.

EISMAN, E. J.

1975   "The effects of leader sex and self-disclosure on member self-disclosure in marathon encounter groups." Doctoral dissertation, Boston University. *Dissertation Abstracts International*, 36 (3-B): 1429 (University Microfilms No. 75-20, 974).

ESKILSON, A., AND M. G. WILEY

1976   "Sex composition and leadership in small groups," *Sociometry*, 39: 183–94.

FARRELL, W.

1975   *The Liberated Man.* New York: Bantam Books.

HOFFMAN, L. R.

1965   "Group problem solving." In L. Berkowitz (ed.), *Advances in Experimental Social Psychology*, Vol. 2, New York: Academic Press.

JOHNSON, P.

1976   "Women and power: Toward a theory of effectiveness," *Journal of Social Issues*, 32: 99–110.

KANTER, R. M.

1977a   *Men and Women of the Corporation.* New York: Basic Books.

1977b   "Some effects of proportions in group life: Skewed sex ratios and responses to token women," *American Journal of Sociology*, 82: 965–90.

1977c   Women in organizations: Sex roles, group dynamics, and change strategies." In A. Sargent (ed.), *Beyond Sex Roles.* St. Paul, Minn.: West Publishing Co., pp. 371–86.

KANTER, R. M., AND B. A. STEIN

1980   *The Tale of "O": On Being Different in an Organization.* New York: Harper & Row.

KAPLAN, A. G., AND J. B. BEAN (eds.).

1976   *Beyond Sex Role Stereotypes: Readings Toward a Psychology of Androgyny.* Boston: Little, Brown & Company.

KIESLER, S. B.

1975   "Actuarial prejudice toward women and its implications," *Journal of Applied Social Psychology*, 5: 201–16.

LAWS, J. L.
1975 "The psychology of tokenism: An analysis," *Sex Roles*, 1: 51–67.
LOCKHEED, M. E., AND K. P. HALL
1976 "Conceptualizing sex as a status characteristic: Applications to leadership training strategies," *Journal of Social Issues*, 32: 111–24.
MAIER, N. R. F.
1970 "Male versus female discussion leaders," *Personnel Psychology*, 23: 455–61.
MAYES, S. S.
1979 "Women in positions of authority: A case study of changing sex roles," *Signs: Journal of Women in Culture and Society*, 4: 556–68.
MEEKER, B. F., AND P. A. WEITZEL-O'NEILL
1977 "Sex roles and interpersonal behavior in task oriented groups," *American Sociological Review*, 42: 91–105.
MILLS, T. M.
1964 "Authority and group emotion." In W. G. Bennis, E. H. Schein, D. E. Berlew, and F. I. Steele (eds.), *Interpersonal Dynamics*. Homewood, Ill.: Dorsey, pp. 94–108.
PERLMAN, L.
1977 "The management of hostility in female-led vs. male-led self-study groups: The fear of women." Doctoral dissertation, City University of New York, 1977. *Dissertation Abstracts International*, 38 (3-B): 1414 (University Microfilms No. 77-18891).
REED, B. G.
1979 "Differential reactions by male and female group members to a group experience in the presence of male or female authority figures." Doctoral dissertation, University of Cincinnati, 1979. *Dissertation Abstracts International* (University Microfilms No. 8002133).
RUBIN, S. A.
1975 "The effect of sex composition on selected process and outcome variables in adolescent counseling groups. Doctoral dissertation, American University, 1974. *Dissertation Abstracts International*, 35 (12-A): 7660–61 (University Microfilms No. 75-05456).
RUHE, J. A.
1978 "Effect of leader sex and leader behavior on group problem solving," *Proceedings of the American Institute for Decision Sciences, Northeast Division*, May, pp. 123–27.
SHAW, M. E.
1981 *Group Dynamics: The Psychology of Small Group Behavior*. Third edition. New York: McGraw-Hill.
STEIN, T. S.
1981 "Men's groups." In K. Solomon and N. B. Levy (eds.), *Men in Transition: Changing Male Roles—Theory and Therapy*. New York: Plenum.
TOWER, B.
1979 "Communication patterns of women and men in same-sex and mixed-sex groups." Unpublished paper, Women's Training Support Program, Harrisburg, Pa.

WARD, J. M., JR.
1977 "Normative determinants of leadership." Doctoral dissertation, Oklahoma State University, 1976. *Dissertation Abstracts International*, 37 (5-B): 4710 (University Microfilms No. DBJ-77-05106).

WHEELAN, S. A.
1975 "Sex differences in the functioning of small groups." Doctoral dissertation, University of Wisconsin-Madison, 1974. *Dissertation Abstracts International*, 35 (9-B): 4712-13 (University Microfilms No. 74-26, 518).

WRIGHT, F.
1976 "The effects of style and sex of consultants in self-study groups," *Small Group Behavior*, 7: 433-56.

YERBY, JANET
1975 "Attitude, task, and sex composition as variables affecting female leadership in small problem-solving groups," *Speech Monographs*, 42: 160-68.

20

Group Work Practice with Ethnic Minorities of Color

Larry E. Davis

TO A GREAT EXTENT the significance of race as a factor affecting social work practice has been ignored in the group literature. Although social workers have occasionally mentioned race as a notable descriptive attribute, few have attempted to address the issue with other than perfunctory or superficial consideration. Inattention to the salience of race has characterized not only social group workers but group practitioners and theorists in general (Yalom, 1975; Cartwright and Zander, 1968). Fortunately, an increasing number of researchers and practitioners are, with greater sincerity, focusing upon the importance of race and its effects on group dynamics and treatment (Bednar and Kaul, 1978; Sattler, 1977; Shaw, 1976). The focus of attention here will be limited to a discussion of group work as it pertains to members of the majority group—whites—and members of minority groups of color, e.g. American Indians, Hispanics, Asians, and blacks. Specifically the discussion here will address the appropriateness of the theoretical orientation of the group work model and practitioner; the importance of practitioners' having a sound understanding of the sociocultural political history of minority populations; the potential salience of racial group dynamics; and the significance of group leadership style.

A discussion of group work practice with ethnic minority groups of color is worthy of our attention for two principal reasons. First, skin color has had historically, and continues to have, great significance in American society. Despite claims by some who suggest that color may be declining in its significance (Wilson, 1980), it continues to be one of the best predictors of the quality of life for a great many Americans (Hopps, 1982; Ozawa, 1971; Glasgow, 1980). Second, skin color is important to consider because the percentage of Americans who are nonwhite is growing. For example, in 1980 the U.S. Census estimated the numbers of black Americans to be 26.5

The author wishes to thank Professors Melvin Delgado and Man K. Ho for their helpful comments and criticisms of this chapter in manuscript.

million or 11.7 percent of the total population. By the year 2000 this number is expected to be 35.2 million or 13.1 percent of the total population. The Hispanic population in 1980 was estimated to be 14.6 million or 6.4 percent of the population and by the year 2000 has been projected to reach 30.3 million, or 10.8 percent of the total American population. Similar percentage increases are projected by the year 2020, at which time the nonwhite population—blacks, Hispanics, Asians and other persons of color—is expected to exceed 35 percent of the total American population (Davis, Haub, and Willette, 1983). Thus it is reasonable to expect that a third of all individuals in need of social work services in the future will be minority persons of color. Such a significant growth in the numbers of nonwhites as clients has profound implications for those who are expected to provide social services. The implications are perhaps even more profound for group workers as declining fiscal resources, coupled with increasing need for assistance, will probably necessitate grater use of groups as a means of service delivery.

The Appropriateness of the Theoretical Orientation and the Practitioner

Despite an abundance of literature attesting to the significance of race and ethnicity as mediating factors in the helping relationship (Griffith and Jones, 1979; Sattler, 1977; Siegel, 1974), we continue to hear the argument that certain modalities or orientations are racially or culturally generic. In contrast, the present discussion takes the staunch position that those practitioners who believe their particular group work orientation transcends race and culture would perhaps do best by minorities to refrain from working with them. It is posited here that all practitioners, regardless of their theoretical orientation, should give strong consideration to the fact that race and culture are powerful factors that significantly affect the lives of minorities. Consequently they must consider the potential mitigating effects those factors have upon the employment of their interventions. For example, before employing a specific orientation with minority clients, practitioners should first ask themselves a number of questions: Has the theoretical orientation been employed successfully with minorities in the past? What, if any, criticism has it received, especially from minority clients and practitioners? If in fact the theoretical orientation has received criticism, how does their intended employment of it differ from prior use? What are the potential strengths and weaknesses of their chosen theoretical orientation in working with a given minority group? Finally, is the theoretical orientation in or out of congruence with the values, customs, and culture of the intended client population?

Of concern also is the degree to which the theoretical orientation pays attention to the environment. In general the consensus among minority practitioners seems to be that problems of minorities are frequently systemic and fostered by the environmental context. That is, many problems that minorities experience are believed to be due to an unresponsive social system (Brown and Arevalo, 1979; Davis, 1984; Ryan, 1971). The argument for a strong environmental focus in group work with minorities is not to suggest that all problems that minority clients experience are environmentally induced. However, it should be noted that minorities do, more than whites, perceive casual events in their lives as a consequence of factors that reside outside their personal control (Lefcourt and Ludwig, 1965; Lessing, 1969; Duke and Lewis, 1979). Hence, while a treatment model employed to treat minorities should not overlook possible intrapsychic or interpersonal aspects of the client's problem, neither should it overlook the importance of the social environment, which is frequently hostile and sometimes acts to initiate and exacerbate their social and psychological difficulties.

Along with inspecting the racial and cultural appropriateness of the theoretical orientation of a given group modality, practitioners should also take inventory of their racial attitudes. Group practitioners, before working with minority clients, should make efforts to assess their potential racial or ethnic biases. Such soul-searching as it pertains to treating minorities appears from the literature to be sorely needed. There exists a wealth of evidence suggesting that the negative racial attitudes and biases of practitioners have frequent deleterious effects for minority clients (Sue et al., 1974; Gary, 1978). One good assumption with which to begin this self-exploratory process is that "we are all ethnocentric" (Pinderhughes, 1973). Moreover, in general we are most attracted to those individuals whom we perceive to be most similar to ourselves (Byrne, 1971). It may be some comfort to those preparing to work with racially dissimilar others to accept the fact that despite their educational training and professional preparation, they will probably always feel most comfortable when working with clients who are racially similar to themselves.

THE SOCIOCULTURAL POLITICAL HISTORY OF THE POPULATION

"If mental health professionals who plan programs, make policy, and offer direct treatment do not understand the special needs, values, and cultures of minorities then their programs and treatment will be ineffective and thus continuously underutilized even when they do exist" (Bush et al., 1983, pp. 99–100). This statement suggests what many believe to be a typical scenario: that those responsible for providing social work services to minorities frequently have little familiarity with or knowledge of minority client populations (Tseng and McDermott, 1975; Sue and McKinney, 1975; Karno and Edgerton, 1969; Henderson, 1979). This general lack of familiarity with and knowledge of the client population appears to have had two important consequences for minorities: (1) underutilization of available treatment programs and facilities and (2) receiving unfair or inappropriate treatment when they do seek services (Sattler, 1977; Yamamoto et al., 1967; Cafferty and Chestang, 1976; Gary, 1978). Both situations argue strongly in support of greater exposure of practitioners to the history and cultures of those clients with whom they have a reasonable probability of working.

Clearly, one of the most important facts that all who work with minorities of color should know is that skin color has played a large role in majority–minority relations in this society. This fact is best supported by the reality that American Indians (Blanchard and Unger, 1977; Deloria, 1969), Asians (Daniels, 1971; Kitano, 1969), Hispanics (Grebler, Moore, and Guzman, 1970), and blacks (Ginzberg, 1962) have all experienced extensive and prolonged racial confrontations and strife. To a significant degree, members belonging to these groups have been segregated into ghettos, barrios, reservations, and "towns or districts." The once prevalent notion that America is an ethnic melting pot (Glazer and Moynihan, 1963) has been replaced with the recognition that our society is more interethnic than intraethnic. This typical pattern of in-group–out-group partitioning has been especially true for minority groups of color. Consequently Americans in general receive little, if any, formal education pertaining to the history, culture, and life-styles of minority groups. Moreover, frequently what little they do receive is both incorrect and negative. By the same token, most minority group members are equally unfamiliar with individuals who belong to other minority groups.

It is not possible in this brief discussion to provide an adequate sociocultural-political-historical backdrop of each of America's principal minority groups of color. There are, however, a number of references we strongly recommend to group workers who are attempting to prepare themselves to work more effectively with minorities: American Indians (Red Horse, 1983; Deloria, 1969), Asians (Ho, 1976; Murase, 1977), Hispanics (Ghali, 1977; Meier and Rivera, 1972), and blacks (Franklin, 1969; White, 1984). An in-depth review of materials such as these should provide the worker with a rudimentary understanding of the "minority experience" as perceived by the respective groups. As pertains to group treatment with minorities, practitioners have a yet insufficient, but growing body of literature upon which they can draw (Brayboy, 1971; Brown and Averaldo, 1979; Davis, 1979; Delgado and Delgado, 1984; Edwards and Edwards, 1978; McRoy and Oglesby, 1984). While this literature has given insufficient attention to providing workers with prescriptive interventions, it does provide group leaders with some helpful guidance.

In addition to a cognitive component, preparation for work with ethnic minorities of color should also include affective experience and training. It has been suggested that those being trained as group workers should be afforded the opportunity to experience, through actual interracial role-play and rehearsal, the positions of both client and group leader (Davis, 1981). If at all possible, the worker's first contact with members of a racial or ethnic group different from his own should not occur in an actual treatment situation. Group leaders need an opportunity to get in touch with their feelings regarding interracial treatment before being thrust into a situation where they are simultaneously required to feel and act. Such affective training, along with the informational component, may be especially valuable to white group workers who have had very limited exposure to actual contact with minority individuals.

THE RACIAL DYNAMICS OF GROUPS

Race, as noted by skin color, has been observed to have profound effects upon the dynamics of small groups. A sound understanding of these dynamics is of considerable benefit to those who hope to lead viable groups containing members of different racial backgrounds. Hence the following pages outline what appears to be some of the most powerful racial dynamics as indicated by their ability to modify and influence group processes.

Group Composition

The issue of group composition is of considerable importance to those who lead groups. However, despite the wealth of information available to guide practitioners in composing treatment groups (Yalom, 1975; see also Chapter 11), very little exists that addresses the issue of race in composing groups. Perhaps one of the first questions to be asked is, "Should the group be racially homogeneous or heterogeneous?" That is, what general theory of group composition should be employed? Should groups be composed of racially similar persons in an attempt to enhance and foster group cohesion, or should they be composed of racially diverse individuals in hopes that the racial heterogeneity will add a greater sense of external reality to the group process?

Group compositions of both types have been intentionally constructed by practitioners (Delgado and Siff, 1980; Edward and Edwards, 1978; Sommers, 1953). By and large, group purpose has been at the root of these divergent constructions. Characteristically, those groups which have been composed of racially similar individuals have had as their goal the enhancement of ethnic identity of the group members. Such groups are composed with the assumption that racially similar individuals will be more attracted to each other and therefore will be more cohesive. It is also believed that these groups are more likely to engage in greater in-depth disclosures about themselves (Cobbs, 1972; Toldson and Pasteur, 1975, 1976). In contrast, some groups have been intentionally constructed to include members whose racial and ethnic backgrounds differ. Most groups of this type commonly have the reduction of racial prejudice as their goal (Samuels, 1972). The underlying assumption of these group compositions is that intergroup strife is best reduced by experiencing or engaging in positive interracial contact. Both types of group compositions appear suitable, given the nature of their goals.

Most practitioners who lead groups, however, will have neither ethnic identity enhancement nor the reduction of racial tensions as their group purpose. The more common question to confront group practitioners is, "What strategy of group composition should be employed when race *per se* is unrelated to the group's purpose?" Specifically, as it pertains to blacks and whites, there would appear to be no simple answer to this question. Indeed, there is evidence which indicates that blacks and whites prefer different racial compositions in mixed groups. Blacks, for example, have been found to prefer racial compositions in which they are approximately half of the population. In contrast, whites in the same condition appear to prefer compositions in which blacks are approximately 20 percent or less of the total population (Davis and Burnstein, 1981). This clear difference in racial preference for group composition has the potential to lead to group member dissatisfaction, discomfort, and conflict.

It has been posited that whites, because of their customary numerical racial dominance, may feel themselves to be psychologically outnumbered in groups where blacks are present in numbers greater than 20 percent (Davis, 1980). This phenomenon is believed to occur even if blacks remain in the numerical minority. Davis refers to this mental state as being in the "psychological minority": It is characterized by a disproportionate sense of loss of power and control, which in this instance is brought on by members of the minority group being present in numbers greater than is customary or expected. It is also postulated by Davis (1980) that minorities in these situations may experience a reciprocal sense of psychological majorityness. That is, they may feel themselves to have a disproportionate sense of power and control as a function of being present in numbers greater than are customary.

While the foregoing conceptualizations are based on research findings that employed blacks and whites, it is believed that the dynamics outlined may be applicable to any composition of minority–majority group members. In any case, the issue of racial balance is one that appears salient for all groups, whatever the race or ethnicity of the group members involved. For example, it has been suggested that Asians may be initially disadvantaged in racially heterogeneous groups (Chu and Sue, 1984). It is argued that because of a strong adherence to the cultural value of politeness, Asians may fail to participate in the group process for fear of interrupting others. By contrast it is suggested that an all-Asian group may offer a verbally less competitive situation in which Asians might express themselves more adequately. Of course, differences in cultural styles are apt to be less pronounced and hence less problematic for second- or third-generation nonwhite Americans who are more familiar with Western culture and language. In addition, it has also been suggested that because of the importance of language (e.g. Spanish), some groups may be more effective when all its members speak the same native tongue (Boulette, 1975; Ho, 1984; Martinez, 1977).

Moreover it has been noted that even homogeneous compositions of certain minority groups—e.g. Asians, Hispanics—may be problematic because of various in-group cultural differences (Ho, 1984; Werbin and Hynes, 1975; Acosta and Yamamoto, 1984). That is, heterogeneous cultural subgroups within racial groups may have negative implications for group processes. Hence, in addition to possessing awareness of potential interracial difficulties, it is also incumbent upon group leaders to be aware of potential problems that may result as a function of combining certain racially or linguistically similar but culturally diverse individuals.

Consistent with the above discussion, there is evidence that indicates that both minority and majority group members resist being outnumbered in small groups (Brayboy, 1971; Davis, 1979). Therefore it would seem wise, when composing racially heterogeneous groups, to attempt to avoid large racial imbalances. Furthermore, empirical and anecdotal evidence suggests that being "one of a kind" in a group, e.g. the only female or minority, is a difficult position to occupy, as it has the tendency to put too much pressure on the "different member" to represent and defend a given population (Davis, 1979; Kanter, 1977). Certainly the practitioner must consider both group and individual member needs. At the same time the group leader should be cognizant of the potential pressures that might be experienced by the minority client in such a situation. When such racial compositions do occur, they must always be accompanied with considerable leader awareness and sensitivity to the uniqueness of this situation for the client.

The race of the group leader is also important when considering a group's composition. There is evidence to suggest that the leaders of racially heterogeneous groups may experience more difficulties than leaders of racially homogeneous groups (Samuels, 1972; Triandis, 1976). For example, minorities who find themselves leading groups containing whites may experience challenges to their leadership. Since minorities as a group are ascribed a lower social status than nonminorities, a position of leadership for them (minorities) is inconsistent with their ascribed lower status. Indeed, it has been argued that because of the minority therapists' lesser status, they may be more subject to displaced aggression than are white therapists (Kadushin, 1972). Quite similar dynamics have also been discussed by others as they pertain to women in group leadership roles (Kanter, 1977; see Chapter 19; Martin and Shanahan, 1984). At least one means of dealing with this situation would entail the leader's fostering a discussion of the significance of social statuses and their possible implications for the group.

The potentiality of group leadership problems are not limited to the racially heterogeneous group. A number of minority practitioners have noted that the internalization of lower-status ascriptions by some minority clients has resulted in their having negative attitudes toward practitioners who belong to the same ethnic group as themselves (Acosta and Sheehan, 1976; Davis, Sharfstein, and Owens, 1974; Sue and Sue, 1971a). Given the societal changes since the 1960s, it is probably true that such minority biases on behalf of minorities are less prevalent today than when some of those practitioners made their initial observations. However, some resistance by minority clients to the minority group leadership is still likely to occur.

White leaders of minority clients are also subject to race-related challenges to their leadership. Some minorities have been found to resist the efforts of white practitioners for philosophical, political, or personal reasons (Sattler, 1977; Samuels, 1972). It is also probable that minority client resistance to white group leadership is due to minority clients' perception of the white practitioner as insufficiently knowledgeable about them as minorities. Hence, while minority clients may accept the white group leader as a "good person," he or she may be rejected as a source of relevant information. In short, while minority clients may like the white group leader, he or she may be viewed as an inappropriate source of guidance.

Finally, before leaving the topic of group composition, let us address a frequently asked question: "When is race an important attribute to consider when composing groups?" The answer to this question is "virtually always." The race of the group members and leader is always of importance, even when race *per se* is unrelated to the goals of the members. Despite even the best of intentions race, covertly if not overtly, acts to mediate the interactional processes within groups. That is, it affects the group processes by influencing both the behavior of and communication among all individuals in the group. Social psychological and therapeutic evidence indicates that the racial composition of a group influences the communication and interactions that take place in the group (Katz, 1955; Katz and Benjamin, 1960; Shaw, 1976). Thus while the relationship between the significance of race and treatment outcome is not yet clear, race consistently influences the interactional process. Race is notably of more importance in some groups than in others. As a general rule it appears that race becomes more important as an issue as the intimacy of the group increases (Davis, 1979). It is also probable that those composing and leading groups are sometimes afraid to acknowledge race as an issue in the group for fear that it suggests that they are racists—it does not! Acknowledging race does not make one a racist; how one behaves, whether race is acknowledged or not, determines the extent of one's racism.

Culture and Communication

The style of communication within any group is strongly influenced by the culture of its members. While it is not possible to review the multitude of cultural effects on communication, some note of their influence is worth while.

It is well known that the expression of affect is a valued style of communication in Western culture. This cultural value is reflected in many therapeutic orientations—that is, great significance is attached to such factors as catharsis, ventilation, and, frequently, overt expressions of sexuality. The cultural values of some minority groups are at odds with these behaviors. Consequently, client resistance to certain interventions may indicate that the intervention is inappropriate, rather than that the client is pathological. As an example, Asian culture places high value on restraint of the expression of strong feeling and of overt behaviors that may have sexual overtones (Ching and Prosen, 1980; Kaneshige, 1973). Hence group leader interventions designed to produce affective expressions may place some Asian clients in direct conflict with their cultural values. Similarly, confrontations and member problem disclosure, as they occur in groups, may result in the creation of cultural conflicts for Asians, who value humility (Ching and Prosen, 1980; Chu and Sue, 1984; Ho, 1984).

In contrast, some minority groups, notably blacks, pride themselves on their ability to engage in heated boisterous confrontation (Kochman, 1981). Indeed, individual confrontations are valued as an activity in that they are used to test the validity of one's point of view. At the same time self-flattering comments are taken lightly and viewed as jesting behavior. Either group members or leaders who are unfamiliar with the cultural style of black communication would misinterpret such highly affective communication between blacks as being vitriolic, overly confrontational, and aggressive (Kochman, 1981; McNeely and Badami, 1984). Pointing out these differences in cultural orientations is not to suggest that two or more minorities cannot be seen successfully in groups, as there is evidence to the contrary (Sommers, 1953). It does suggest, however, that those who work with minorities in groups should be cognizant of the fact that the cultural values of their members may make certain interventions inappropriate.

Trust

Many who have written on the topic of group work have also written about the importance of establishing trust among the group's leader and members (Corey, 1981; Yalom, 1975; Konopka, 1983). Establishing a basis of trust is especially important when working with groups with minority members. As was mentioned earlier, the history of nonwhite minority contact with the larger white majority group has witnessed extensive betrayal, neglect, and abuse. Not surprisingly, the resulting legacy of mistrust toward persons and representatives of the majority culture manifests itself even in small treatment groups. Indeed, it has been suggested that one reason for the low utilization of mental health services by many minorities may be the perception that the white professional is an agent of society and thus of questionable trustworthiness (Sue and Sue, 1971a).

Despite a sociopolitical history replete with minority–majority group strife, those who lead groups containing minorities must attempt to establish trust within the group. There are no prescribed ways of establishing the trust needed for open and honest group interactions, but it is probably a good first step to view minority group members' resistance or reluctance to disclose information about themselves as a sign of health rather than a sign of pathology. Resistance or caution when expressed by nonwhites has sometimes been referred to as healthy paranoia (Grier and Cobbs, 1968). That is, it is the healthy individual who has learned to shield himself from those who might cause him harm. Consistent with this notion, Edwards and Edwards (1984), in referring to the treatment of American Indians in groups, have suggested what is probably a good rule of thumb for working with minorities in general—"avoid asking too many personal questions too early in the professional relationship."

Thus far the issue of trust has focused upon the possibility that minority group members will suspect the group leader of having ill intentions toward them. That is perhaps the most common type of mistrust experienced by minority clients. However, there are also two other bases of client mistrust about which leaders should be cognizant. First, there is the issue of professional mastery or expertise (Sue, 1981), an issue of primary concern to minority group leaders. As we noted earlier, minorities have characteristically been ascribed a low social status; part of the low status ascription has included being portrayed as cognitively deficient and inept, e.g. dumb Mexicans, lazy blacks. To the extent that minority clients themselves have adopted this racial image, they will question whether a minority practitioner is competent to lead their group.

The other basis of leader mistrust is of primary concern to white leaders. As was outlined above, whites frequently have little or no experience with or exposure to minorities. In light of this fact, minority clients may feel that white group leaders are ill prepared to advise them. Hence guidance offered by white group leaders to minority clients may be viewed by the clients as inappropriate and/or unsuitable.

There are no quick and easy roads to the establishment of trust with minority clients. What is helpful is time spent with clients. However, group leaders must be sensitive to the fact that trust in the early phases of group work with minority clients will probably be in shorter supply than in groups that do not include minorities. Consequently group leaders should anticipate that the dynamics within the group may reflect a more guarded stance on the part of minorities; members of these groups must have sufficient time to make their assessments of the trustworthiness of both the leader and the group members.

Status and Roles

There is considerable evidence to suggest that the group behavior of nonwhites is significantly altered by the presence of whites (Katz, 1955; Katz and Benjamin, 1960; Lefcourt and Ladwig, 1965). Much of the literature indicates that when minorities interact with whites in groups, they frequently behave in a manner consistent with their ascribed second-class social statuses. Shaw (1976) has characterized the general behavior of nonwhites interacting with whites as akin to that of subordinates interacting with superiors. It should be noted, however, that much of the group research in the area of minority–majority group interactions was conducted prior to the social revolts of the late 1960s and early 1970s. Since that time minorities have made tremendous social and political strides and no longer behave in the obsequious ways of the past. Much of the literature in this area may now be inaccurate and dated. Indeed, minorities since the 1950s have altered their social roles significantly.

Unfortunately, majority conceptions of minorities in many instances have not kept pace with minority conceptions of themselves. While the majority of nonwhites have taken on a more assertive posture in society with respect to their legitimate roles, many whites may view this new posture as uppity, out of place, and in some cases aggressive (Cheek, 1976). In situations where whites and nonwhites hold divergent perceptions of what is acceptable behavior for minorities, conflicts may occur. In groups, such conflicts may manifest themselves in the attempt by some members to limit the participation of nonwhite members to subordinate group roles. Such efforts to relegate minorities to second-class positions or statuses in the group have a number of potentially harmful consequences for the group. The most immediate is that the group may breakup. It is also possible that the group, even if it stays intact, will faction off along racial lines, thereby terminating meaningful group interaction. Consequently those who lead groups containing minority members should pay attention to the status and roles occupied by members in the group. Leaders should remain alert to potential negative role ascriptions to minorities and resist such efforts if they do occur.

LEADERSHIP STYLE

There is now some evidence to suggest that certain practitioner styles may be more attractive to some clients than to others (Fiedler, 1962; Hill and Ruhe, 1974). A review of the literature in this area also suggests that minorities of color may in general prefer group leadership styles that vary somewhat from those of whites (Cobbs, 1972; Hardy-Fanta and Montana, 1982; Werbin and Hynes, 1975). These differences in leadership style can be classified along four behavioral dimensions: respect, formality, concreteness, and activeness.

First and foremost, leaders of minority client groups should have a style that clearly and unmistakably emphasizes respect for the client. As has been pointed out, nonwhites on the whole are afforded less social status from society than are whites and are the recipients of less respect. In order to establish a warm and accepting group climate, minority clients must be shown all possible indicators of respect. The group leader's first contact with his or her minority client should assure the client that he or she (the client) is welcome and will be treated in a professional and courteous manner. The leader's ability to convey to the client a sense of respect has potentially long-term effects upon his or her future group interventions. It is believed that first impressions in interpersonal contacts establish the tone of future contacts and that subsequent behaviors at odds with the first impressions are discounted (Mizio, 1972; Newcomb, 1947). Leaders must therefore exhibit respect from the outset when working with minorities.

Clients, for example, should be referred to by their last names. Mrs. Mary Jones is not Mary or Mrs. Mary but Mrs. Jones. If a minority client explicitly asks to be called by his or her first name, this request should be granted. However, the group worker should not assume *a priori* that it's appropriate to be "familiar" with clients. If clients wish to deformalize the treatment relationship, they, not the practitioner, should do so. In time most clients will perhaps ask to be referred to by their first names; but some will not. There is little risk in addressing clients by their last names, as few are offended by demonstrations of respect. In any event the option to retain or relinquish a title of respect should be left to the client. In sum, as a group leader, it is probably unwise to "cut corners" with those persons whom society is already cutting short. The group leader must attempt to make the group experience one where the minority client receives clear messages that in all aspects they are being treated with respect.

Formality is another aspect of leadership style to which group leaders of minority clients ought to pay attention. Formality, while similar in some ways to respect, is subtly different. For example, virtually all cultures value personal respect, but not all cultures value formality as a means of conveying respect; some value formality more than others. Customarily American society values informality over formality as a form of interacting. Many nonwhite cultures attach greater importance to formal interaction. Such cultural differences in styles of interacting have important implications for those who lead groups containing minority members.

Those who lead groups of Asian clients, for instance, should expect to establish a relationship with the group members in a manner that clearly places the leader in a leadership role (Ching and Prosen, 1980; Chu and Sue, 1984; Ho, 1984). Such a formal demarcation of roles may be in striking contrast to the "most experienced member" style of leadership advocated by some contemporary treatment modalities, such as Gestalt. It is believed that a style of leadership which fails to establish a clear "leadership role" by the leader can expect a high dropout rate among its Asian members (Ho, 1984). Indeed, the quintessential American "slap on the back" style of relating to people may be inappropriate as a style of interacting with some minorities.

Concreteness as a style of leadership is another dimension that has been identified by practitioners as desirable in working with minorities (Brown and Arevalo, 1979; Sue, 1977; Comas-Diaz, 1981). Minority clients frequently want guidance and directiveness from workers (Ho, 1984; Sue, 1977). Treatment strategies that are vague appear to many minority clients as unprofessional. Certainly some of the need for greater practitioner concreteness is a function of immediate environmental stressors commonly experienced by minority client populations. That is, minorities frequently identify more immediate and tangible problems that are in need of immediate and tangible resolution. Therefore it should not be surprising that on the whole minorities prefer concrete directives.

Finally, minority clients appear to prefer active leaders over passive ones (Kaneshige, 1973; Hardy-Fanta and Montana, 1982; Sue and Sue, 1971b; Chu and Sue, 1984). Therefore, leaders of groups containing minorities should consider employing leadership approaches in which the leader has considerable involvement and input. Passive, noninvolved, "laid back" styles of group interventions may be less well received by minority group members. Naturally, the extent to which a leader needs to be active is mediated by factors such as age of clients, type of client problem, and so forth. In general, however, it would appear that minorities want a style of group leadership that engages them as members in the group process and in which the leader actively provides ideas, advice, and direction.

SUMMARY

Although race is known to be an important element in helping relationships, it has received slight attention from group workers. However, by the year 2020 it is anticipated that more than 35 percent of the American populace will be nonwhite. It is therefore reasonable to expect a sizable proportion of all persons who seek social work services to be nonwhite. Moreover, diminishing fiscal resources with which to provide these services will cause greater numbers of persons who receive assistance from social workers to do so via small groups. In an attempt better to prepare practitioners to meet this apparent challenge, this discussion has identified group work topic areas of which practitioners should have cognizance if they wish to work effectively with minorities.

First, it is suggested that the theoretical orientation of the group work models employed be appropriate for working with minority populations, that is, the model's theoretical tenets should be in congruence with the basic values and customs of the client population. By the same token, it is recommended that group practitioners inspect their own racial attitudes in an effort to rid themselves of biases that may retard their treatment effectiveness.

Second, an argument is made for practitioners' acquisition of a sound understanding of the sociocultural-political history of the population with which they plan to work. It was beyond the scope of this chapter to provide an in-depth discussion of the sociocultural-political backgrounds of the four principal nonwhite groups: Native Americans, Asians, Hispanics, and blacks. However, a number of possible sources of information about these groups was provided.

Third, factors believed to be most important in affecting pertinent group dynamics were reviewed: group composition, communication as affected by culture, trust, and status and roles of group members.

Finally, the discussion identified leadership style as having considerable significance in working with minorities. Those stylistic dimensions identified as being advantageous in working with minority clients were respect, formality, concreteness, and activeness.

REFERENCES

ACOSTA, FRANK X., AND JOE YAMAMOTO
    1984   "The utility of group work practice for Hispanic Americans," *Social Work with Groups*, 7, no. 3: 63–73.
ACOSTA, FRANK X., AND JOSEPH G. SHEEHAN
    1976   "Preferences toward Mexican-American and Anglo-American psychologists," *Journal of Consulting and Clinical Psychology*, 44: 271–79.
BEDNAR, RICHARD L., AND THEODORE J. KAUL
    1978   "Experimental group research: Current perspectives." In A. E. Bergin and S. Garfield (eds.), *Handbook of Psychotherapy and Behavior Change*. New York: Wiley.

BLANCHARD, EVELYN, AND STEVEN UNGER
1977   "Destruction of American Indian families," *Social Casework*, 58: 312–14.

BOULETTE, THERESA R.
1975   "Group therapy with low-income Mexican Americans," *Social Work*, 20: 403–4.

BRAYBOY, THOMAS
1971   "The black patient in group therapy," *International Journal of Group Psychotherapy*, 21: 288–93.

BROWN, JOHN, AND AVERALDO, RODOLFO
1979   "Chicanos and social group work models: Some implications for group work practice." *Social Work with Groups* 2, no. 4: 331–42.

BUSH, JAMES; DELORES NORTON; CHARLES SANDERS; AND BARBARA SOLOMON
1983   "An integrative approach for the inclusion of content on blacks in social work education." In J. D. Chunn, P. J. Dunston, and F. Ross-Sheriff (eds.), *Mental Health and People of Color: Curriculum Development and Change*. Washington, D.C.: Howard University Press.

BYRNE, DONN
1971   *The Attraction Paradigm*. New York: Academic Press.

CAFFERTY, PASTORA, AND LEON CHESTANG (eds.)
1976   *The Universe Society: Implications for Social Policy*. Washington, D.C.: National Association of Social Workers.

CARTWRIGHT, DARWIN, AND ALVIN ZANDER (eds.)
1968   *Group Dynamics: Research and Theory*. Third edition. New York: Harper & Row.

CHEEK, DONALD
1976   *Assertive Black–Puzzled White: A Black Perspective on Assertive Behavior*. San Luis Obispo, Calif.: Impact Publishers Inc.

CHING, WAYNE, AND SELINA PROSEN
1980   "Asian-Americans in group counseling: A case of cultural dissonance," *Journal for Specialists in Group Work*, 6, No. 2: 229–32.

CHU, JUDY, AND STANLEY SUE
1984   "Asian/Pacific Americans and group practice," *Social Work with Groups*, 7, no. 3: 23–36.

COBBS, PRICE M.
1972   "Ethnotherapy in groups." In L. N. Solomon and B. Berzon (eds.), *New Perspectives on Encounter Groups*. San Francisco: Jossey-Bass.

COMAS-DIAZ, LILLIAN
1981   "Effects of cognitive and behavioral group treatment on the depressive symptomatology of Puerto Rican women," *Journal of Consulting and Clinical Psychology*, 49, no. 5 (October): 627–32.

COREY, GERALD
1981   *Group Counseling: Theory and Practice*. Beverly Hills, Calif.: Brooks/ Cole.

DANIELS, ROGER
1971   *Concentration Camps USA: Japanese Americans and World War II*. New York: Holt, Rinehart & Winston.

DAVIS, CARY; CARL HAUB; AND JOANNE WILLETTE
1983 "U.S. Hispanics: Changing the face of America," *Population Bulletin*, 38, no. 3: 38–41.

DAVIS, LARRY E.
1979 "Racial composition of groups," *Social Work*, 14: 208–13.
1980 "When the majority is the psychological minority," *Group Psychotherapy, Psychodrama, and Sociometry*, 33: 179–84.
1981 "Racial issues in the training of group workers," *The Journal for Specialists in Group Work*, 6, no. 3: 155–60.
1984 "The essential components of group work with Black Americans," *Social Work with Groups*, 7, no. 3: 97–109.

DAVIS, LARRY E., AND EUGENE BURNSTEIN
1981 "Preference for racial composition of groups," *Journal of Psychology*, 109: 293–301.

DAVIS, MACK; STEVEN SHARFSTEIN; AND MAUREEN OWENS
1974 "Separate and together: All-black therapist group in the white hospital," *American Journal of Orthopsychiatry*, 44: 19–25.

DELGADO, MELVIN, AND DENISE DELGADO
1984 "Hispanics and group work: A review of the literature," *Social Work with Groups*, 7, no. 3: 85–96.

DELGADO, MELVIN, AND SHIRLEY SIFF
1980 "A Hispanic adolescent group in a public school setting: An interagency approach," *Social Work with Groups*, 2: 83–89.

DELORIA, VINE
1969 *Custer Died for Your Sins*. New York: Avon Books.

DUKE, MARSHALL, AND GAYLE LEWIS
1979 "The measurement of locus of control in black preschool and primary school," *Journal of Personality Assessment*, 43: 479–96.

EDWARDS, E. DANIEL, MARGIE E. EDWARDS ET AL.
1978 "Enhancing self-concept and identification with 'Indianness' of American Indian girls," *Social Work with Groups*, 1, no. 3: 309–18.

EDWARDS, E. DANIEL, AND MARGIE E. EDWARDS
1984 "Group work practice with American Indians," *Social Work with Groups*, 7, no. 3: 7–21.

FIEDLER, FRED E.
1962 "The effect of leadership and cultural heterogeneity on group performance: A test of contingency model," *Journal of Experimental Social Psychology*, 65: 308–18.

FRANKLIN, JOHN
1969 *From Slavery to Freedom: A History of Negro Americans*. New York: Vintage House.

GARY, LAWRENCE E.
1978 "Mental Health: The problem and the product." In L. E. Gary (ed.), *Mental Health: A Challenge to the Black Community*. Philadelphia: Dorrance.

GHALI, SONIA B.
1977 "Cultural sensitivity and the Puerto Rican client," *Social Casework*, 58: 459–68.

GINZBURG, RALPH
1966 *One Hundred Years of Lynchings*. New York: Lancer Books.

GLASGOW, DOUGLAS
1980 *The Black Underclass: Poverty, Unemployment, and Entrapment of Ghetto Youth*. San Francisco: Jossey-Bass.

GLAZER, NATHAN, AND DANIEL MOYNIHAN
1963 *Beyond the Melting Pot: The Negros, Puerto Ricans, Jews, Italians, and Irish of New York City*. Cambridge, Mass.: MIT Press.

GREBLER, LEO; JOAN MOORE; AND RALPH C. GUZMAN
1970 *The Mexican American People*. New York: Free Press.

GRIER, WILLIAM H., AND PRICE M. COBBS
1968 *Black Rage*. New York: Basic Books.

GRIFFITH, M., AND E. JONES
1979 "Race and psychotherapy: Changing perspectives," *Current Therapies*, 18: 232–55.

HARDY-FANTA, CAROL, AND PRISCILLA MONTANA
1982 "The Hispanic female adolescent: A group therapy model," *International Journal of Group Psychotherapy*, 32, no. 3 (July): 351–66.

HENDERSON, GEORGE (ed.)
1979 *Understanding and Counseling Ethnic Minorities*. Springfield, Ill.: Charles C. Thomas.

HILL, WALTER A., AND JOHN A. RUHE
1974 "Attitudes and behaviors of black and white supervisors in problem solving groups," *Academy of Management Journal*, 17: 563–69.

HO, MAN K.
1976 "Social work with Asian Americans," *Social Casework*, 57: 195–201.
1984 "Social group work with Asians/Pacific Americans," *Social Work with Groups*, 7, no. 3: 49–61.

HOPPS, JUNE
1982 "Oppression based on color," *Social Work*, 27, no. 1: 1–5.

KADUSHIN, ALFRED
1972 "The Racial Factor in the Interview," *Social Work*, 1972, 17, 88–98.

KANESHIGE, EDWARD
1973 "Cultural factors in group counseling and interaction," *Personal and Guidance Journal*, 51: 407–12.

KANTER, ROSABETH M.
1977 *Men and Women of the Corporation*. New York: Basic Books.

KARNO, MARVIN, AND ROBERT B. EDGERTON
1969 "Perception of mental illness in a Mexican-American community," *Archives of General Psychiatry*, 20: 233–38.

KATZ, IRWIN
1955 *Conflict and Harmony in an Adolescent Interracial Group*. New York: New York University Press.

KATZ, IRWIN, AND L. BENJAMIN
1960 "Effects of white authoritarianism in biracial work groups," *Journal of Abnormal and Social Psychology*, 61: 448–56.

KITANO, HARRY
  1969   *Japanese-American: Evaluation of a Subculture.* Englewood Cliffs, N.J.: Prentice-Hall.
KOCHMAN, THOMAS
  1981   *Black and White Styles in Conflict.* Chicago: The University of Chicago Press.
KONOPKA, GISELA
  1983   *Social Group Work: A Helping Process.* Third edition. Englewood Cliffs, N.J.: Prentice-Hall.
LEFCOURT, HERBERT, AND GORDON LADWIG
  1965   "The American Negro, problem in expectancies," *Journal of Personality and Social Psychology,* 1: 377-80.
LESSING, ELISE
  1969   "Racial differences in indices of ego functioning relevant to academic achievement," *Journal of Genetic Psychology,* 115: 163-67.
MARTIN, PATRICIA Y., AND KRISTINE A. SHANAHAN
  1984   "Transcending the effects of sex composition in small groups," *Social Work with Groups,* 6, nos. 3-4: 19-32.
MARTINEZ, CERVANDO
  1977   "Group process and the Chicano: Clinical issues," *International Journal of Group Psychotherapy,* 27, no. 2: 225-31.
McNEELY, ROBERT, AND MARY BADAMI
  1984   "Interracial communication in school social work," *Social Work,* 29, no. 1: 22-26.
McROY, RUTH, AND ZENA OGLESBY
  1984   "Group work with black adoptive applicants," *Social Work with Groups,* 7, no. 3: 125-34.
MEIER, MATT S., AND FELICANO RIVERA
  1972   *The Chicanos: A History of Mexican-Americans.* New York: Hill & Wang.
MIZIO, EMELICIA
  1972   "White worker-minority client," *Social Work,* 17: 82-86.
MURASE, KENJI
  1977   "Minorities: Asian Americans." In *Encyclopedia of Social Work.* Washington, D.C.: National Association of Social Workers, pp. 953-60.
NEWCOMB, THEODORE
  1947   "Austistic hostility and social reality," *Human Relations,* 1: 69-87.
OZAWA, MARTHA
  1971   "Social welfare: The minority share," *Social Work,* 1: 69.
PINDERHUGHES, CHARLES
  1973   "Racism and psychotherapy." In Charles Willie, Bernard Kramer, Bertram Brown (eds.), *Racism and Mental Health.* Pittsburgh: University of Pittsburgh Press.
RED HORSE, JOHN
  1983   "Indian family values." In G. Powell, A. Morales, and J. Yamamoto (eds.), *The Psycho-Social Development of Minority Group Children.* New York: Brunner-Mazel, pp. 258-72.

RYAN, WILLIAM
  1971 *Blaming the Victim*. New York: Pantheon Books.
SAMUELS, ARTHUR S.
  1972 "The reduction of interracial prejudice and tension through group therapy." In H. I. Kaplan and B. J. Sadock (eds.), *New Models for Group Therapy*. New York: E. P. Dutton, pp. 214–43.
SATTLER, JEROME M.
  1977 "The effects of therapist–client racial similarity." In A. S. Gurman and A. M. Razin (eds.), *Effective Psychotherapy: A Handbook of Research*. Oxford, England: Pergamon, pp. 252–90.
SHAW, MARVIN E.
  1976 *Group Dynamics: The Psychology of Small Group Behavior*. New York: McGraw-Hill, pp. 225–36.
SIEGEL, JEROME
  1974 "A brief review of the effects of race in clinical service interactions," *American Journal of Orthopsychiatry*, 4: 555–62.
SOMMERS, VITA
  1953 "An experiment in group psychotherapy with members of mixed minority groups," *International Journal of Group Psychotherapy*, 3: 254–69.
SUE, DERALD W.
  1977 "Counseling the culturally different: A conceptual analysis," *Personnel and Guidance Journal*, 55: 422–25.
  1981 *Counseling the Culturally Different: Theory and Practice*. New York: John Wiley.
SUE, DERALD W., AND STANLEY SUE
  1971a "Ethnic minorities: Resistance to be researched," *Professional Psychology*, 2: 11–17.
SUE, STANLEY, AND DERALD W. SUE
  1971b "Chinese-American personality and mental health," *Amerasia Journal*, 1: 36–49.
SUE, STANLEY, AND HERMAN McKINNEY
  1975 "Asian Americans in the community mental health care system," *American Journal of Orthopsychiatry*, 45: 111–18.
SUE, STANLEY; HERMAN McKINNEY; D. ALLEN, AND J. HALL
  1974 "Delivery of community mental health services to black and white clients," *Journal of Consulting and Clinical Psychology*, 41: 794–801.
TOLDSON, IVORY L., AND ALFRED B. PASTEUR
  1975 "Developmental stages of black self-discovery: Implications for using black art forms in group interaction," *Journal of Negro Education*, 44, no. 2 (Spring): 130–38.
  1976 "Beyond rhetoric: Techniques for using the black aesthetic in group counseling and guidance," *Journal of Non-White Concerns in Personnel and Guidance*, 4, no. 3 (April): 142–51.
TRIANDIS, HARRY C.
  1976 "Interpersonal behavior across cultures," in H. C. Triandis (ed.), *Variations in Black and White Perceptions of the Social Environment*. Chicago: University of Illinois Press, pp. 11–25.

TSENG, WEN-SHING, AND JOHN F. McDERMOTT
   1975   "Historical roots, universal elements, and cultural variations," *American Journal of Psychiatry*, 132: 378–84.
WERBIN, JORGE, AND KATHLEEN HYNES
   1975   "Tranference and culture in a Latino therapy group," *International Journal of Group Psychotherapy*, 25, no. 4 (October): 396–401.
WHITE, JOSEPH
   1984   *The Psychology of Blacks: An Afro-American Perspective.* Englewood Cliffs, N.J.: Prentice-Hall.
WILSON, WILLIAM J.
   1980   *The Declining Significance of Race: Blacks and Changing American Institutions.* Chicago: University of Chicago Press.
YALOM, IRVIN
   1975   *The Theory and Practice of Group Psychotherapy.* Second edition. New York: Basic Books.
YAMAMOTO, JOE; QUINTON C. JAMES; MILTON BLOOMBAUM; AND JACK HATTEM
   1967   "Racial factors in patient selection," *American Journal of Psychiatry*, 124: 630–36.

IV

Evaluation of Group Services

Although accountability in the helping professions has been a growing concern during the past decade, in practice it is often determined in a superficial manner. Cutbacks in social programs have made group services appear advantageous to administrators eager to find ways of providing more services for the same dollars. While this propensity might stimulate the expansion of group services, the public might be better served by greater attention to the quality or effectiveness of services than to appraisals based only on quantity of services and economic costs. The field of practice is so diverse and complex that knowledge-based advancement involves consideration of the multidimensional question: What types of interventions, performed by what types of practitioners, under what conditions, can produce particular outcomes for specific problems of particular types of individuals or groups, at what personal, social and economic costs? Finding the answers to this question requires a serious commitment to evaluation research, as well as formative and summative evaluations of group services by practitioners, program evaluators, and consumers. Such knowledge could help program sponsors, administrators, and the public to make more informed decisions regarding the allocation of resources to achieve particular results and to recognize the consequences of failing to address various aspects of evaluation.

The focus of the Michigan group work model has been on delineation of individual and group goals in behaviorally specific terms, so that evaluation is based on improved client functioning measured by goal attainment. It requires careful assessment of client concerns and establishment of group conditions designed to provide an optimal environment for achieving individual and group goals. The chapters in this part pursue the issues raised here in terms of examining group-level variables and treatment dimensions, as well as measurement of goal attainment using differing evaluation designs.

In Chapter 21 Feldman argues that the evaluation of group work interventions requires attention to significant group structures and processes that lead to individual behavior change, as well as consideration of outcome measures. The author examines seven aspects of group work evaluation: (1) the definition of pertinent group-level variables; (2) the clarification of longitudinal processes of development; (3) the specification of relationships between group change and individual behavior change; (4) the assessment of interactive relationships among group-level variables; (5) the evaluation of treatment implementation; (6) the establishment of control and comparison techniques; and (7) multiple evaluation strategies. Research on group integration and power dispersion is discussed from these perspectives.

Feldman's research focuses on the social integration of small groups and the patterning of social interaction among the group's members. Time series analyses are performed to make comparisons of various group structures at periodic intervals, including the form of the members' indirect influence upon one another and related changes in the target behaviors of clients. Feldman recommends periodic evaluations by independent judges of the group worker's implementation of treatment, based on his finding that the treatment method might be effective but inadequately applied. The author encourages more use of baseline procedures, control groups, and comparison groups in evaluation studies. The use of multiple evaluation techniques is considered advantageous in terms of the increased breadth, reliability, and validity of the information obtained.

Based on analysis of his field research, Feldman examines hypothetical cases involving group work practice with scapegoats and antisocial youths treated in groups of prosocial youngsters. His longitudinal research shows that the group worker's interventions and program activities shape the extent of functional integration, normative integration, interpersonal integration, and power dispersion that emerges, as well as the overall patterns of prosocial and antisocial behavior within the group. The author concludes that longitudinal evaluations of group-level variables and their interactions provide the only hope for determining and refining the quality of group work practice.

Rose and Tolman present in Chapter 22 a framework for group work practitioners which can guide their attempts to evaluate individual change. The authors define the purposes of evaluation and explain how to involve clients and significant others in the specification and measurement of identified concerns. Various measurement procedures are discussed, including role-play tests, self-rating checklists and inventories, self-monitoring, goal attainment scaling, and observations by trained observers within and outside the group. A self-monitoring form and a stress diary form are provided, along with guidelines for their use. The authors discuss the pre-post design, which allows the practitioner to make judgments regarding the magnitude and direction of change. The repeated A-B design is considered more practical for group treatment, since threats to internal validity are reduced and the design allows the worker to determine on an ongoing basis if the intervention is proceeding successfully. The authors also describe designs that permit causal inferences, including A-B-A-B or reversal designs, withdrawal designs, multiple baseline designs, and changing criterion designs.

Rose and Tolman used a pre–post follow-up design without a control group to evaluate a ten-week stress management group. Their measurement procedures included the use of goal attainment scaling and checklists on symptoms, hassles, and depression. A postsession questionnaire was distributed to measure member self-disclosure, satisfaction, and usefulness of each session. Data were also collected on the rate of participation and assignment completion. At termination and at a three-months follow-up, members were retested on the checklists and inventories and also interviewed to determine the degree to which their goals were achieved and maintained. Total cost of the evaluation activities was eight hours of professional time. The authors conclude that failure to design such a program is the most costly approach, because without evaluation estimates of progress, failures, and successes cannot be obtained.

Using objective measures of change and a control group, Navarre, Glasser, and Costabile evaluate a group treatment project involving AFDC mothers with children having learning and behavioral difficulties. The four-year project was designed to facilitate the healthy development of children by improving the attitudes and behavior of their mothers. The authors present in Chapter 23 a summary of the group work methods and techniques used, a review and interpretation of the statistical findings of the evaluation study, and implications for future research and practice. Prior to initiating the group program, three subgoals were established: the provision of additional resources, such as clothing and medical care related to the children's achievement and attendance in school; changes in the mothers' attitudes toward the school system; and changes in the mothers' attitudes toward their children's behavior and school achievement. The authors describe the recruitment, diagnostic, and group leadership procedures, as well as the conceptual basis for the group problem-solving approach. Social and demographic characteristics are given for the four types of populations used as experimental and control subjects.

Measures used to evaluate the effectiveness of group service with the client population included ratings by group leaders of each member's goal progress and participation in the group; an anxiety test that measured initial anxiety as well as change over the demonstration period; an instrument that measured general childrearing attitudes; a test to assess how tasks were performed in four family areas and one school-related area; an inventory used to evaluate classroom behavior; and school grades and attendance.

The experimental group showed significant changes in many of the target areas, including reduction of anxiety and increased responsibility toward children's adjustment at school, while the control group showed change in the opposite direction. Goal achievement scores, as rated by group leaders, were positively and significantly related to attendance and participation in group treatment. Cross-comparisons were made to identify relationships among the variables. The authors discuss the difficulties of treating clients with multiple, interrelated problems and point out that the short-term nature of the groups as well as the measures used might have limited additional client change.

In the final chapter in this part, Chapter 24, Sarri and Vinter report on their research and demonstration project employing group service methods to reduce malperformance among junior and senior high school students. Their research design specified four main areas: (1) student characteristics, behaviors, and perspectives related to both educational achievement and malperformance; (2) school policies and practices for identifying and handling student malperformance; (3) interactions between student characteristics and school practices; and (4) the processes and outcomes of group service methods. The study design involved a series of before-and-after measures, in addition to comparisons between experimental groups and both matched and random control groups. Measures included teacher assessment of student behavior, objective indices of school performance, and student self-reports of behaviors and attitudes. School organization and practices were assessed through several direct and indirect procedures, including classroom observations and administration of questionnaires to professional personnel. Group intervention with students focused on specific academic skills and abilities, skills of social interaction with teachers and peers, and student values, goals, and motivations.

Over the three-year project period, school organization, curriculum design, and staff behavior emerged as significant factors related to student malperformance. No significant changes were found for either the experimental or the control groups in grades, absences, truancies, suspensions, or leaving school. These findings indicated that student malperformance can be viewed in terms of adverse school–student interactions, and that malperformance may be maintained and even generated by certain school policies and procedures. After the project ended, four of the five school systems in the study attempted to make organizational changes based on the findings. The authors conclude that effecting innovation and change in the public school requires attention not only to attributes of individuals in the system but also, and perhaps more importantly, to the behavior of the school itself.

21

Evaluating Group Work Interventions

Ronald A. Feldman

THERE HAVE BEEN NUMEROUS debates about the proper definition and measurement of outcomes in group work and about the preferred junctures at which outcome measures ought to be applied. Indeed, the existing literature about the evaluation of group work treatment remains prodominantly a literature about client outcomes. Useful and necessary as this knowledge may be, however, it does little to inform either the practitioner or the researcher about the particular group-level variables and processes that ultimately lead to observable changes in clients' behavior. Yet, if group work practice is to advance significantly beyond its current stage of development, practitioners must understand the crucial intervening processes that lead to individual behavior change. This requires us to extend our conception of "evaluation" beyond the mere assessment of distal treatment outcomes for individual clients. Hence it becomes necessary to evaluate, and therefore comprehend, crucial group structures and processes at every phase of treatment. Accordingly, the focus of the present discussion is upon the evaluation of group work interventions rather than group work outcomes. While the latter topic necessarily is subsumed under the former, it represents only one aspect, howsoever important, of the evaluation enterprise in social group work.

Most evaluative measures in group work focus only on individual outcomes. Few studies examine the outcomes among group-level variables. This represents a supreme irony—if not an embarrassment—for a profession that claims to promote behavior change by employing the small group not only as the context for treatment but as the means for achieving it. Hence, the present discussion seeks to rectify partially a neglected area of group work evaluation. It concentrates primarily upon group-level variables

The research cited in this paper was supported by grants from the National Science Foundation (GS-790); Center for Studies of Crime and Delinquency, National Institute of Mental Health (MH18813); Office of Prevention, National Institute of Mental Health (MH35033); and Youth Development Bureau, Administration on Children, Youth and Families (90 PD 86517). Grateful appreciation is expressed to the staffs of these agencies for their generous support.

rather than individual client outcomes. Seven aspects of group work evaluation will be examined. In order, they are (1) the definition of pertinent group-level variables; (2) the clarification of longitudinal processes of development; (3) the specification of relationships between group change and individual behavior change; (4) the assessment of interactive relationships among group-level variables; (5) the evaluation of treatment implementation; (6) the establishment of control and comparison techniques; and (7) multiple evaluation strategies. Pertinent research regarding group integration and power dispersion will be viewed from these perspectives. Finally, the practice implications of knowledge about these variables will be examined by referring to pertinent field studies.

ISSUES IN THE EVALUATION OF GROUP WORK INTERVENTION

While numerous issues must be considered in the evaluation of group work intervention, the present discussion focuses primarily upon the assessment of group-level variables. Moreover, emphasis is placed on the assessment of intervening variables in group treatment as well as outcome variables.

Definition of Pertinent Group-Level Variables

Over the years certain terms have become integral components of the group work lexicon. "Group climate," "group cohesiveness," and "group work programming," for example, frequently appear in the literature of group work and in the oral and written reports of group work practitioners. Yet it is painfully obvious that little consensus exists about the meaning or measurement of such terms. Indeed, the extant literature reveals virtually no attempts whatever to operationalize these constructs and thence to evaluate either their presence or their effects upon group members. This is somewhat disconcerting, for efforts to influence group climate, group cohesiveness, and group work programming constitute central features of group work practice. Yet, given the paucity of scholarly work concerning these variables, one wonders if they might not be incapable of operationalization in their current form.

Potentially an infinite array of group-level constructs can be articulated for group work practice. However, the present discussion will focus primarily upon group-level variables that already have been subjected to empirical research and that appear to be relatively potent for group work practice. Specifically, this means that they possess relatively high predictive potency and variable potency and also that their referent features are relatively identifiable, accessible, and manipulable at reasonable cost (Thomas, 1967).

The concept "group cohesiveness" provides an obvious example of the difficulties that inhere in the measurement of group-level variables. It has been the subject of numerous articles concerning group treatment, including a now classic treatise by Jerome Frank (1957). Yet, most definitions of the concept have been set forth in terms that do not lend themselves readily to operationalization. Consider, for example, Cartwright's and Zander's (1968) widely accepted definition of group cohesiveness as "the resultant of all the forces acting upon all the members to remain in the group." While this definition may be satisfactory on a conceptual basis, it is virtually incapable of operationalization in group work practice. As a result, most studies of group cohesiveness have operationalized the construct narrowly by employing measures that focus solely upon group members' interpersonal attraction or reciprocal liking for one another.

While this approach simplifies efforts to evaluate the extent of cohesiveness in a group, it mistakenly implies that a group is bound together only by the liking, or friendship, relations among its members. Such a perspective seriously neglects the functional interdependencies and normative constraints that influence group members' behavior. It also fosters the illusion that substantive variations in a group's cohesiveness, to the extent that they are related to interpersonal liking, necessarily lead to corresponding changes in a group's overall cohesiveness or to concomitant variations on other dimensions that are presumed to promote group cohesiveness. Yet it does not necessarily follow that changes in interpersonal liking will result in uniform variations along other dimensions of group behavior or even in a group's overall cohesiveness. Rather, a variety of countervailing tendencies may be set in motion by changes in a single group-level variable. It is possible, for example, for one or more of the various bases of group cohesiveness, such as members' reciprocal liking, to be negatively correlated with other bases of the phenomenon or to manifest no systematic relationship with the larger phenomenon.

Accordingly, a major challenge for group work evaluation rests upon the ability of the field to articulate important interrelationships among the chief dimensions of small group behavior. This must be done, however, in a manner that examines such dimensions in a relatively standardized fashion and recognizes their common and uniform features while also identifying their respective differences. Employing this perspective, the author has conducted several programs of field research, which have attempted, among other things, to examine the regularity and coordination of behavioral patterns among group members. Emphasis is placed in particular upon the social integration of small groups or upon the patterning of social interaction among the group's members. Three important bases of group integration have been subjected to study: normative integration, functional integration, and interpersonal integration. As explicated in the case illustrations that appear below, variations in these dimensions of small group behavior seem to exert important influences upon the behavior of individual group members. Furthermore, each of these variables can be operationalized both at the group level and at the individual level of analysis, thus enabling the group worker to consider parsimoniously the reciprocal influences between the group and the individual, and vice versa.

Normative integration. Norms are behavioral rules that are accepted by all or most members of the group. At the group level normative integration refers to the degree of consensus among group members concerning any number of group-relevant behaviors. At the individual level it refers to the extent to which any given member shares the norms of his or her peers in the group. Normative integration, as one basis of group integration, does not necessarily presuppose the existence of either strong affectional or strong functional ties among members. Depending on the amount of time available for evaluation, the intellectual capabilities of the group members, and the group worker's desire for detail and reliability, the normative integration of a group can be measured by either a "long" or "short" method. The former technique employs an index based on group members' responses to a questionnaire consisting of twenty normative items. A five-point Likert scale, in which response categories vary from "strongly agree" to "strongly disagree," is used. Detailed examples of this measurement procedure appear in a variety of sources (cf., for example, Feldman, 1967, 1968, 1969a, 1969b, 1972, 1973b, 1976a, 1976b). Depending on which particular norms are considered most relevant, the group worker can prepare, evaluate, and apply specifically tailored questionnaires that examine behaviors particularly central to the group. If that procedure is not feasible, however, either the group worker or a trained nonparticipant observer can rate individual members by means of a short form that reflects their adherence to important group norms (for a detailed explanation of this procedure, see Feldman, Caplinger, and Wodarski, 1983, p. 87). The resultant data then can be used to calculate the extent of norm consensus within the group itself. Measurements should be made at periodic intervals so that the group worker can monitor alterations in the group's normative integration and in the resultant effects on individual group members.

Functional integration. Functions are regularly performed specialized activities that serve one or more requirements of a group. At least three functional requirements must be satisfied by most small groups, namely, goal attainment, pattern maintenance, and external relations. Goal attainment refers to the ability of a group to progress toward the goals that have been explicitly selected by its members. Pattern maintenance refers to the ability of a group to maintain harmonious and consistent intragroup relations. External relations refers to the ability of a group to maintain viable relationships with other groups. An individual's functional integration into a group refers, then, to his or her effectiveness at performing the functions of goal attainment, pattern maintenance, and external relations for the group. The functional integration of a group refers to the effectiveness of group members in performing the three foregoing functions and also to the extent of complementary specialization that exists among the group members as they perform these crucial functions. Hence, effectiveness alone is not the sole criterion of group functional integration. It also is necessary to consider the extent to which responsibility for the performance of key functions is distributed among the group's members. In an activity group, for example, high functional integration exists when certain members effectively suggest the ideas for group activities or assist the group in attaining its objectives (goal attainment), other members effectively prevent or resolve interpersonal conflicts within the group (pattern maintenance), and several others effectively represent the group in its relationships with other groups or with the larger agency (external relations). Here, too, the members can be asked to rate one another's functional contributions to the group. A functional integration table can be employed to calculate an index of group functional integration (for a detailed explanation, see Feldman, 1967, 1968, 1969a, 1969b, 1973b). Or again, the group worker or a nonparticipant observer can briefly evaluate each member's functional integration into the group (see, for example, Feldman, Caplinger, and Wodarksi, 1983, p. 87).

Interpersonal integration. Interpersonal integration refers to that mode of group integration which is based on the group members' reciprocal liking for one another. An individual's interpersonal integration into a group depends not only upon the extent of his or her liking for groupmates but also upon the extent to which they reciprocate that liking. Interpersonal integration can be measured by requesting each group member to rate others in the group according to the question, "How much do you like him (her)?" Response alternatives can range along a five-point Likert scale from "like very much" to "dislike very much." The interpersonal integration of a group refers, then, to the average of all such ratings for any given group. In contrast, an individual's interpersonal integration into the group refers to the mean liking score that the individual assigns to all the other group members and in turn receives from them (for more detail, see Feldman 1967, 1968, 1969a, 1969b, 1973b). Again, however, either the group worker or a nonparticipant observer can rapidly rate each member in lieu of administering a sociometric questionnaire to the entire group (see Feldman, Caplinger, and Wodarski, 1983, p. 87).

Power dispersion. Social power refers to the ability of a group member to exert influence over others within the group, and power distribution is one of the most fundamental concerns of the group worker. The power of individual group members can be evaluated by asking each member to rate each of his or her peers according to the latter's ability to get others in the group to do what he or she desires. Again, a five-point Likert scale can be employed. Power dispersion within the group as a whole can be evaluated by calculating the mean score for all respondents (for a more detailed discussion of measurement procedures and interpretative considerations, see Feldman, 1973b, 1976b).

Space limitations require that more detailed explanations about the measurement and operationalization of group normative integration, functional integration, interpersonal integration, and power dispersion be found in the references cited, but it is obvious that the pertinent procedures are not beyond the capabilities of most professionally trained group workers. Indeed, either a "long" or a "short" method can be employed. Depending on the practitioner's requirements for rigor and detail, many features of the requisite measurement procedures can be tailored specifically to the needs of the worker's own group. The measurement procedures yield data that can be applied readily to assessment at both the individual and group levels of analysis. Most important, fundamental processes of group behavior are evaluated, to wit, when high base rate behaviors are the target of intervention. In group settings, it is difficult to assess low base rate behaviors accurately, to influence them effectively, and to identify the consequences of related interventions.

Far more challenging than the evaluation of either group-level or individual-level constructs alone, however, is the problem of assessing the effects of the former upon the latter. Indeed, it is difficult to infer causality even in highly controlled casework studies that focus on the treatment of merely one or two behaviors of a single client. Because many casework procedures, such as treatment reversals, are not very feasible in group work, time-lag analysis is one of the few techniques available to the group worker for inferring sequential relationships between changes in group variables and individual behaviors. Essentially it entails the assessment of intercorrelations between group and individual variables at successive points in the treatment process (for a detailed explanation, see Feldman, Caplinger, and Wodarski, 1983, pp. 248–67). Other procedures require control groups or limitations upon group treatment that may be impractical or unacceptable to the group worker.

Assessment of Interactive Relationships Among Group Variables

The assessment of interactive relationships among group-level variables is an area of analysis that requires particularly close cooperation between the researcher and the practitioner. While many group workers intuitively recognize such relationships, a sound grasp of research methods and statistical analysis is necessary in order to understand their subtleties fully. The interrelationships among group-level variables can be examined by techniques that vary from simple product-moment correlations (see, for example, Feldman, 1968, 1973b) to multiple regression and discriminant analyses (see, for example, Feldman, Caplinger, and Wodarski, 1983, 95–102, 130–31).

Studies of children's groups, for instance, show a strong product-moment correlation between the functional integration and interpersonal integration of small groups (r = .51). In contrast, the product-moment correlation between group normative integration and interpersonal integration is .24, while the product-moment correlation between group normative integration and functional integration is only .14 (Feldman, 1967). Several practice implications can be derived from even these very limited findings. Thus, to enhance a group's functional integration, it is far more useful to promote members' reciprocal liking for one another than to strive for norm consensus. Indeed, the latter approach may prove fruitless. Second, members' mutual liking can be strengthened more readily by enhancing functional integration than by strengthening norm consensus. However, both approaches are warranted if the group worker seeks to maximize his or her interventive potency. Third, it is probable that functional integration and interpersonal integration are reciprocally reinforcing within a small group. That is, effective group work with either of these variables is likely to have a salutary effect on the other. However, the same cannot necessarily be said for other combinations of the above-cited variables. Hence, to the extent that these empirical findings are generalizable to other groups, the worker's knowledge about such interrelationships will enable intervention priorities to be selected more judiciously.

In similar fashion it may be useful for group workers to realize that high levels of normative integration and functional integration are likely to generate relatively high levels of conformity in a group, while on the other hand high interpersonal integration may enable members to withstand undue conformity pressures (Feldman, 1967; Feldman, Caplinger, and Wodarski, 1983). Social power is distributed more equally and at higher levels within a group when it attains high functional integration (r = .52) or high interpersonal integration (r = .64). High group normative integration, however, contributes much less to power dispersion (r = .28). Moreover, since directionality cannot be inferred from product-moment correlations, the converse possibilities also are of practical interest. Equal and high dispersion of power within a small group, for instance, is less likely to promote norm consensus among the members than are high functional integration or high reciprocal liking (Feldman, 1973a). It may be useful for group workers to know also that peer groups are characterized by significantly lower levels of normative integration in midadolescence (modal age eleven to fourteen years) than in early adolescence (modal age ten years) or late adolescence (modal age fifteen years). Therefore the reputed "sturm und drang" of middle adolescence may not be so much attributable to the fact that youths adopt countercultural attitudes during that period as to the fact that peer group consensus is highly variable. Indeed, it is *non*normative rather than *counter*normative (Feldman, 1972). Finally, as illustrated below, various forms of group integration bear a direct and positive relationship to the group worker's capacity to generate prosocial behavior change among antisocial youths.

Evaluation of Treatment Implementation

One of the most distressing aspects of the group work literature pertains to the oft-repeated allegation that group treatment has "failed" *even when* it has not been implemented. For the most part this occurs because evaluators routinely assume that poor client outcomes *must* be due to the fact that the presumed treatment method was somehow deficient. In truth, however, the *group worker* may have been inadequate while the treatment method itself was effective. Recent research demonstrates that certain treatment methods tend to be inadequately applied by group workers (Feldman and Caplinger, 1983; Feldman, Caplinger, and Wodarski, 1983). Therefore, when client outcomes are poor, it may be unfair to conclude that the method itself was deficient (unless, of course, failure to apply the method was due to its complexity or the actual impossibility of operationalizing it). Distinctions must be made between the merits of a given treatment method and the individuals who try to implement it.

The extant research literature does little to assure group work supervisors that practitioners effectively implement their assigned treatment methods. This is so even when the theoretical and practice principles of the assigned methods are relatively clear. Therefore, periodic evaluations concerning the group worker's implementation of treatment ought to be conducted by independent judges, such as trained nonparticipant observers. Even if in rudimentary fashion practice principles now can be derived from contemporary group work treatises, transformed into observational codes, and evaluated in terms of the group worker's ability to deliver the specified interventions (for relevant examples, see Feldman, Caplinger, and Wodarski, 1983, 220–21; Wodarski, Pedi, and Feldman, 1974). It is necessary to expand and refine such procedures if group workers are to assess the results of their interventions more accurately and thereby advance the frontiers of practice.

Establishment of Control
and Comparison Techniques

Practice advances necessarily are impeded when the research methods of a profession are unable to clarify its key treatment processes. In group work this occurs because researchers frequently fail to create control groups or comparison groups for the particular treatment groups that are studied. While it may be expensive or cumbersome to create such groups, the researcher usually is obliged to do so. Many of the evaluation procedures available to caseworkers are inapplicable to group work research. Control groups or comparison groups are especially necessary when one wishes to determine whether or not an experimental treatment method is better than current treatment methods or even no treatment at all.

The literature contains few studies that attempt to determine whether a particular group work method works better than minimal group treatment or no treatment at all. Yet such studies are essential in order to ascertain whether or not a particular method of group work truly "makes a difference." The deficit in group work research is largely due to the difficulty of creating analogs for the "placebo" or "no treatment" situations that are prevalent in casework and single-subject research. Nevertheless, minimal-treatment approaches to group work can be devised for evaluative purposes so long as proper safeguards are set forth for clients, parents, and agency administrators.

In essence, minimal treatment methods do not engage the group worker in a particular training regimen. They merely require that the worker interact with group members in a spontaneous and minimally intrusive fashion. Detailed discussions of minimal treatment group work procedures and safeguards can be found elsewhere (Feldman and Wodarski, 1975, pp. 176–78). Finally, it should be noted that at least one of the principal assessment procedures of casework research is indeed applicable to group work, to wit, baseline procedures can be implemented with relative ease (see, for example, Feldman, Caplinger and Wodarski, 1983, p. 69). However, unlike single-subject research, it is more difficult, and sometimes impossible, to employ multiple baselines and treatment reversals in group work research.

Multiple Evaluation Strategies

Finally, it is germane to note that group workers now have access to a broader variety of evaluation techniques than in previous years. Although increased reliability can result from the use of multiple evaluation techniques, few group work studies employ more than a single mode of evaluation. Baseline periods, control or comparison groups, and nonparticipant observation techniques all can be utilized in the same study (see, for example, Feldman, Caplinger, and Wodarski, 1983). Relevant data about children's maladaptive behavior can be acquired from such diverse sources as parents, referral agents, group leaders, teachers, nonparticipant observers, and the children themselves (see, for example, Feldman, Stiffman, et al., 1982). Interjudge agreement from multiple observers can strengthen the researcher's confidence in a given set of findings. Likewise, evaluations from multiple sources can enable the practitioner to gauge the extent to which treatment-generated behavioral changes take hold in a variety of settings, such as the home, social service agency, peer group, and school. For the most part the expense and inconvenience entailed by multiple evaluation strategies are likely to be offset by the increased breadth, reliability, and validity of the ensuing information.

EVALUATION OF GROUP WORK INTERVENTION: THE CASE OF SCAPEGOATING

Two case illustrations will be employed in order to demonstrate how the systematic evaluation of group-level variables can contribute to the enhancement of group work practice. The first illustration pertains to a frequent phenomenon in social work groups, namely, scapegoating behavior. While the illustration is hypothetical, all of the data and trends reported therein are drawn from a sustained program of field research (cf. Feldman, 1967, 1968, 1969a, 1969b, 1969c, 1969d, 1972, 1973b, 1974, 1976b).

The target client in the case illustration is named Patrick, a twelve-year-old boy who belongs to a treatment group consisting of nine other youths of the same age and sex. Patrick is intensely disliked by them. In addition to overt instances of rejection and scapegoating by his peers, he earns an average rating of only 1.0 (the lowest possible) from his peers in response to the question, "How much do you like him?" This means that Patrick is "very much disliked" by all the members of his group.

Close scrutiny reveals that Patrick's behavior is indeed a serious problem for the group. He does not adhere to the norms of the group, contributes virtually nothing toward attainment of the group's goals, has very little ability to get the other group members to do what he wants, and, as might be expected, does not like the other boys in the group. In other words, he is poorly integrated into the group in normative, functional, social power, and interpersonal terms. The group worker's observations about Patrick's status in the group have been clearly confirmed, moreover, by the low scores he registered during a recent administration of the long-form normative integration, functional integration, social power, and interpersonal integration questionnaires. Indeed, Patrick's configuration of social attributes is the typical, or modal, one for youngsters who occupy the scapegoat position in children's groups.

How, then, should the group worker approach intervention? Is it true, as some theorists posit, that Patrick is a "provocative" youngster who actually "deserves what he gets" from his peers? If so, treatment should focus essentially, though not entirely, on Patrick's behavioral deficits. Thus the group worker should help Patrick to recognize the group's basic norms, appreciate them, and adhere to them. Patrick should be coached in order to build skills that enable him to contribute effectively to the group's goal attainment. Such skills should enable him to assist the group in meeting its goals, coping with internal tension or disharmony, and getting along with other groups. Respectively, these capabilities pertain to Patrick's skills at goal attainment, pattern maintenance, and external relations. The group worker should also help Patrick to develop constructive sources of expertise or influence that will enable him to move upward in the group's power structure. Finally, the worker should help Patrick to develop skills that will make him better liked by peers. The group worker should do everything possible to help Patrick like the other boys in the group and thereby initiate a constructive reversal in the reciprocal disliking processes that characterize groups with a scapegoat. In short, the worker should strive to increase Patrick's normative integration, functional integration, social power, and interpersonal integration within the group. The worker's success, or lack thereof, can be evaluated systematically about three or four weeks afterward by a repeat administration of the same questionnaire that the group members completed previously. If time is of the essence, the group worker or an independent observer can fill out the forms in lieu of the members.

But how can Patrick learn to like his peers when they are unanimous in their negative feelings about him? His efforts at friendship, compounded by serious deficits in skills and security, are bound to face a steep uphill struggle. And what if Patrick seems adept at discerning the norms in groups other than this one? That is, what if the norms in this particular group are unclear to *everyone*? Even worse, what if they are hidden from Patrick so that he has little hope of perceiving them accurately and thereby conforming to them? Put simply, what if the group itself is a large part of Patrick's problem?

At first blush the group worker is not very likely to accept this hypothesis. For one thing it means that he or she has not done a particularly good job of assessing the group and of working with it as a system. Furthermore, Patrick's deviant behavior stands out dramatically while the rest of the group seems to be rather "normal" in its comportment. The effect, of course, is one of "contrast." It is not easy for the worker to grasp fully how well or how poorly the remaining members get along with *each other*. For, rather than focusing on Patrick's relationships with nine other peers, this requires the worker to concentrate upon seventy-two additional dyadic relationships?

Nevetheless, the group worker may thoughtfully ponder the extent of his or her knowledge about scapegoating. The group work literature unfortunately provides only two or three pieces of published research about this topic. Hence it would be a dedicated worker indeed who ferrets it out. The worker, for example, may recall a somewhat dated article about the "emotionally disturbed child as the family scapegoat" (Bell and Vogel, 1968). If so, the thought might arise that Patrick's maladaptive behavior is due in some way to the tenuous relationship that exists among other members of the group. However, this possibility might be rapidly dismissed since there are obvious differences between a mother–father–child triad and a ten-person treatment group.

Perhaps, too, one of the darkest epochs in human history may pass fleetingly through the worker's mind. During World War II many persons contended that Jews, gypsies, and homosexuals were being oppressed ruthlessly in Nazi Germany because their social characteristics fitted the classic scapegoat profile. Whether right or wrong, it was argued that such persons did not adhere to the predominant norms of the larger German society, did not contribute much to Germany (especially after they had been formally or informally deprived of certain occupational and legal rights), did not possess enough power to influence other Germans significantly, and even did not appear to like the majority population. Perhaps these persons, too, "deserved what they got."

But, having been socialized in professional school to such values as group responsibility, personal liberty, individualization, diversity, and cultural determinism (cf. McLeod and Meyer, 1967; Feldman, 1971, 1973a), the group worker would be likely to reject this hypothesis. The worker might then recall that other commentators had argued even more trenchantly that the ruthless scapegoating in Nazi Germany was due to critical flaws in the larger society itself. Within Germany there had been political turbulence, economic chaos, and competing rivalries among various subgroups within the majority population. Perhaps the best way to bind together a fragile or disintegrating society is to divert its attentions toward a weak, visible, and seemingly recalcitrant minority. From this perspective, scapegoating may be due to basic deficiencies of the social system itself. But then the group worker might conclude that just as the treatment group is not a three-person family, neither is it a microcosm of Nazi Germany.

So how does the worker find out what role, if any, the group itself plays in the scapegoating process? Perhaps one of the more fruitful means entails the evaluation of relevant group-level variables, such as the extent of normative integration, functional integration, interpersonal integration, and power dispersion within the group. Employing the questionnaire and observational methods cited earlier, the worker can do this rather easily. If the results of previous research apply to the worker's own group, a number of important findings would emerge. First, Patrick's groupmates are not likely to exhibit much reciprocal liking for *one another*! Having had a graduate course in statistics, however, the worker may conclude that the group's level of reciprocal liking, or interpersonal integration, was unduly depressed because of the extremely low liking scores received by Patrick. Being circumspect, the worker might then eliminate all of Patrick's "liking" scores (both the ones he received from peers and the ones that he assigned to them) and then recalculate the mean interpersonal integration score for the remaining group members. To the worker's surprise and possible chagrin, it probably still will be found that the group members dislike each other, regardless of how they feel about Patrick.

Furthermore, the worker is likely to discover that the group is not effectively performing its goal attainment, pattern maintenance, and external relations functions or that these functions are not distributed equally among the members. Since a group member's influence is linked with his or her contributions to the group, the extent of power dispersion in the group is likely to be similar to its pattern of functional integration. Finally, the group members are likely to exhibit either very low norm consensus or, possibly, very high norm consensus (generated, in part, by the fact that they concur about Patrick's scapegoat status). In other words, the worker's evaluation of group-level variables is likely to reveal that the group *as a system* is characterized by low degrees of interpersonal integration, functional integration, normative integration, and power dispersion. Indeed, as indicated by the above-cited studies, this is the classic pattern for groups that engage in scapegoating.

What are the implications of such findings? First, the worker can benefit greatly from a dual-pronged approach toward intervention. That is, to gain maximum leverage upon scapegoating, the worker should direct his or her interventions toward *both* the individual and the group levels of analysis. The worker should not cease individual efforts with Patrick. However, there should be increased efforts to deal with the group's deficiencies as a social system. The vicious cycle of individual malfunctioning and group malfunctioning, which in essence feeds upon itself, can best be broken by intervening concurrently at both levels of analysis. Accordingly, the group worker should devise programs and activities that will help Patrick's groupmates to build better friendships with one another as well as with him.

Even more important, the worker should direct the group's energies toward challenging tasks that can be completed successfully and will enable the members to cope with internal and external stresses. In doing so, the worker should try to help each member to contribute equally and effectively to the performance of one or more of these group functions. As a salutary side effect, it is likely that power dispersion within the group will increase concurrently. Finally, the worker should help the members to clarify latent group norms, reach consensus about them, and act upon them in group activities. Employing the techniques cited above, the worker can later assess the respective levels of normative integration, functional integration, interpersonal integration, and power dispersion within the group. With skill, persistence, and a little bit of luck, the worker may find that the interventions with Patrick and his group will eliminate or substantially diminish the scapegoating problem. Concomitantly, the worker may begin to appreciate the utility of evaluating important group-level variables in the course of treatment.

EVALUATION OF GROUP WORK
INTERVENTION: TREATING ANTISOCIAL
YOUTHS IN PROSOCIAL GROUPS

The second case illustration focuses upon a continuing challenge to social group work, namely, the search for more effective ways of modifying the behavior of youths who have been referred to treatment because of their antisocial or delinquent conduct. In particular it concentrates upon efforts to treat small numbers of antisocial youths in groups that are composed essentially of prosocial youngsters. Like the previous illustration, the data in the hypothetical case are drawn from a sustained program of field research (cf. Feldman, 1978; Feldman and Caplinger, 1977, 1983; Feldman and Wodarski, 1975; Feldman, Wodarski, et al., 1972; Feldman, Wodarski, et al., 1973; Feldman, Stiffman, et al., 1982; Feldman, Gingerich, and Wodarski, 1977; Wodarski and Feldman, 1976; Wodarski, Pedi, and Feldman, 1975; Wodarski, Rubeiz, and Feldman, 1974). Since this research has been summarized elsewhere in considerable detail (Feldman, Caplinger, and Wodarski, 1983) the illustration appears in abbreviated form.

In the present instance suppose that the group worker is pondering how to treat Robert and Randy, two thirteen-year-old boys who have been referred for treatment because of their antisocial behavior. For a variety of reasons the worker has concluded that it will be extremely difficult to treat these boys in a group that is composed solely of youths who are referred for similar types of behavior. Among other things, such youths are likely to model deviant behavior for Robert and Randy and to reinforce them for engaging in antisocial behavior. Therefore, the worker decides to enroll Robert and Randy in a group at a nearby community center. The group consists of thirteen-year-old youths who are not known to be antisocial. The worker assumes that the latter youths will model positive behaviors for Robert and Randy and also that they will be more likely to reinforce Robert and Randy for behaving in a prosocial manner. However, because of a heavy caseload, the professional group worker chooses to lead only the group in which Robert is placed. The worker enrolls Randy in an identical group that is led instead by a college undergraduate who has no professional training in group work.

If this approach should be beneficial for either Robert or Randy, the agency administrator may wish to examine two additional questions. First, did Robert or Randy fare any better than similar referred youths who were treated in the usual fashion, that is, solely among antisocial peers? Second, did the behavior of the prosocial youths who were in Robert's or Randy's group become any worse than the behavior of similar prosocial youths who were not exposed to an antisocial youngster in the course of their group work experience?

To answer these questions, it is essential to compare the behavioral profiles of Robert and Randy with the behavioral profiles of antisocial peers who were treated in groups consisting solely of referred antisocial youngsters. It is essential also to compare the behavioral profiles of Robert's and Randy's groupmates with the profiles of prosocial peers in groups that consisted only of youngsters who were not known to have significant behavioral problems. In other words appropriate control or comparison groups are needed for both the antisocial and the prosocial youths in the mixed, or integrated, groups. In addition, as explicated elsewhere in this volume, the rigor of the group worker's evaluations can be enhanced by employing a baseline period, by evaluating the group members' proportionate behavioral profiles (rather than absolute frequencies of maladaptive behavior), by using a time-sampling observational system throughout treatment, and by acquiring evaluations about the boys' antisocial behavior from a large variety of independent sources, such as their parents, teachers, referral agents and the youths themselves (see Chapter 27).

If the group work treatment is effective, the worker is likely to discover that Robert and Randy became more highly integrated into their respective treatment groups than did youths in the purely antisocial groups. More important, the worker will note a significant reduction in their antisocial behavior. In the course of treatment Robert and Randy will adhere increasingly to the group's norms, gain greater social power, and grow to like, and be liked by, their peers. After evaluating the group as a system, moreover, the worker is likely to discover that such changes in the boys' behavior were anteceded by higher levels of normative integration and functional integration in the group. High interpersonal integration, in contrast, would not promote such changes. In fact, high interpersonal integration in antisocial groups is likely to deter treatment gains.

While both boys are likely to show clear signs of improvement, the relevant data probably will reveal that Robert fared much better than Randy in most respects. Although the boys' prosocial peers are likely to fare equally well, the experienced group worker will be better able than the inexperienced worker to enhance the group's normative integration and functional integration. Indeed, the supervisor's observations of both workers is likely to reveal that the untrained worker is less consistent and less thorough in implementing the prescribed treatment method. But even so, the prosocial peers in the mixed, or integrated, group are likely to offset the untrained worker's deficiencies. The important antecedents of prosocial behavior change are shaped, then, by the interactions between two key treatment variables, namely, the peer composition of the treatment group and the extent of the group worker's professional training.

Pertinent longitudinal research shows that group treatment with antisocial youths typically progresses through a series of phases. First, three fundamental variables (namely, the group worker's level of experience, the peer group's composition, and the type of treatment method employed) interact in order to influence the types of therapeutic interventions and program activities that will be implemented by the worker. Next, the worker's interventions and program activities shape the particular types of behavior that are manifested by the peer group. These include the extent of functional integration, normative integration, interpersonal integration, and power dispersion that emerges and also the overall patterns of prosocial and antisocial behavior within the group. Finally, the latter variable determines the behavioral outcomes of particular clients within the group, such as Robert and Randy.

In other words, the unique attributes of the group worker, the treatment method, and the peers in group treatment shape the group worker's interventions. Such interventions then influence the group as a social system. The peers in the treatment group then become able to promote desired behavioral changes on the part of particular target individuals. However, only by means of longitudinal evaluations of group-level variables and their interactions can the group worker hope to recognize, and ultimately refine, the quality of his or her practice with antisocial youths and other clients who are in need of treatment.

SUMMARY

This discussion examines seven different aspects of group work evaluation: definition of pertinent group-level variables; identification of longitudinal processes of group development; specification of relationships between group change and individual change; assessment of interactive relationships among group-level variables; evaluation of treatment implementation; establishment of control and comparison techniques; and multiple evaluation strategies. In conjunction with an analysis of related field research, the importance of these items is illustrated by the examination of hypothetical cases regarding group work practice with scapegoats and antisocial youths.

REFERENCES

BELL, NORMAN, AND EZRA VOGEL
    1968   "The emotionally disturbed child as the family scapegoat." In Warren G. Bennis et al. (eds.), *Interpersonal Dynamics: Essays* and *Readings on Human Interaction*. Homewood, Ill.: Dorsey Press, pp. 90–105.

CARTWRIGHT, DORWIN, AND ALVIN ZANDER (eds.)
    1968   *Group Dynamics: Research and Theory*. Third edition. New York. Harper & Row.

FELDMAN, RONALD A.
    1967   "Determinants and objectives of social group work intervention." In *Social Work Practice, 1967*. New York: Columbia University Press, pp. 34–45.

    1968   "Interrelationships among three bases of group integration," *Sociometry*, 31: 30–46.

    1969a   "Group integration and intense interpersonal disliking," *Human Relations*, 22: 405–14.

    1969b   "Group integration, intense interpersonal dislike, and social group work intervention," *Social Work*, 14: 30–39.

    1969c   "Group service programs in public welfare: Patterns and perspectives," *Public Welfare*, 27: 266–71.

    1969d   "Social attributes of the intensely disliked position in children's groups," *Adolescence*, 4: 181–98.

    1971   "Professionalism and professional values: A cross-cultural comparison," *International Review of Sociology*, 2: 85–97.

    1972   "Normative integration, alienation, and conformity in adolescent groups," *Adolescence*, 7: 327–42.

    1973a   "Professional values; A cross-cultural and cross-professional comparison," *International Review of Modern Sociology*, 3: 119–26.

    1973b   "Power distribution, integration and conformity in small groups," *American Journal of Sociology*, 79: 639–64.

    1974   "An experimental study of conformity behavior as a small group phenomenon," *Journal of Small Group Behavior*, 5: 404–26.

    1976a   "Normative Integration." In Orval G. Johnson (ed.), *Tests and Measurements in Child Development: Handbook II*. San Francisco: Jossey-Bass, pp. 1188–89.

    1976b   "Social power and integrative behavior in adolescent peer groups," *Journal of Group Process*, 6: 169–93.

    1978   "Delinquent behavior in the public schools: Toward more accurate labeling and effective intervention." In Ernst Wenk and Nora Harlow (eds.), *School Crime and Disruption*. Davis, Calif.: Responsible Action.

FELDMAN, RONALD A., AND TIMOTHY E. CAPLINGER
1977 "Social work experience and client behavioral change: A multivariate analysis of process and outcome," *Journal of Social Service Research*, 1: 5–34.
1983 "The St. Louis Experiment: Treatment of antisocial youths in prosocial peer groups." In James R. Kluegel (ed.), *Evaluating Juvenile Justice*. Sage Research Progress Series in Criminology. Beverly Hills, Calif.: Sage Publications.

FELDMAN, RONALD A.; TIMOTHY E. CAPLINGER; AND JOHN S. WODARSKI
1983 *The St. Louis Conundrum: The Effective Treatment of Antisocial Youths*. Englewood Cliffs, N.J.: Prentice-Hall.

FELDMAN, RONALD A.; WALLACE J. GINGERICH; AND JOHN S. WODARSKI
1977 "A behavioral approach toward the labeling of anti-social behavior," *Sociology and Social Research*, 61: 204–22.

FELDMAN, RONALD A., AND JOHN S. WODARSKI
1975 *Contemporary Approaches to Group Treatment*. San Francisco: Jossey-Bass.

FELDMAN, RONALD A.; JOHN S. WODARSKI; NORMAN FLAX; AND MORTIMER GOODMAN
1972 "Treating delinquents in 'traditional' agencies," *Social Work*, 17: 72–78.

FELDMAN, RONALD A.; JOHN S. WODARSKI; MORTIMER GOODMAN; AND NORMAN FLAX
1973 "Pro-social and anti-social boys together," *Social Work*, 18: 26–36.

FELDMAN, RONALD A.; ARLENE R. STIFFMAN; DEBORAH A. EVANS; AND JOHN G. ORME
1982 "Prevention research, social work and mental illness," *Social Work Research and Abstracts*, 18: 4–12.

FRANK, JEROME B.
1957 "Some determinants, manifestations and effects of cohesiveness in therapy groups," *International Journal of Group Psychotherapy*, 7: 53–63.

MCLEOD, DONNA L., AND HENRY J. MEYER
1967 "A study of the values of social workers." In Edwin J. Thomas (ed.), *Behavioral Science for Social Workers*. Glencoe, Ill.: Free Press, pp. 341–49.

THOMAS, EDWIN J.
1967 "Selecting knowledge from behavioral science." In Edwin J. Thomas (ed.), *Behavioral Science for Social Workers*. Glencoe, Ill.: Free Press, pp. 417–24.

WODARSKI, JOHN S., AND RONALD A. FELDMAN
1976 "Objective measurement of the independent variable: A neglected methodological aspect in community-based behavioral research," *Journal of Abnormal Child Psychology*, 1: 239–44.

WODARSKI, JOHN S.; STEVEN J. PEDI; AND RONALD A. FELDMAN
1975 "Labeling by self and others: The comparison of behavior among 'anti-social' and 'prosocial' children in an open community agency," *Criminal Justice and Behavior*, 1: 258–75.

WODARSKI, JOHN S.; GHASSAN RUBEIZ; AND RONALD A. FELDMAN
1974 "Program planning for anti-social boys, *Social Work*, 19: 705–13.

22

Evaluation of Client Outcomes in Groups

Sheldon Rose and Richard Tolman

GROUP WORKERS ENGAGED in attempts to bring about individual change must answer a fundamental question: "Did the group benefit the individual members?" Certainly this question is posed by funding sources, administrators, supervisors, group members themselves, and their significant others. A debate about the effectiveness of social work interventions, fueled by studies that purported to show that social casework was ineffective (Fischer, 1973; Wood, 1978; Reid and Hanrahan, 1982), has led to concern for accountability in the delivery of service to clients. This concern has resulted in greater emphasis on the use of empirical evaluation techniques to provide evidence for achievement in groups. Our purpose will be to present a framework for group workers that can guide their attempts to evaluate individual change. Although many evaluation techniques have been derived from the efforts of researchers, the main focus of this chapter is on techniques that can be utilized by group workers rather than the academic investigator. To this end we shall be concerned with such issues as minimal cost, level of intrusiveness, time requirements for application, and appropriateness to clients in a group.

BACKGROUND OF EVALUATION

Evaluation procedures are applicable in all groups. However, the principles and procedures of evaluation described in this article are designed primarily for groups in which members have identified specific cognitive, affective, or behavioral goals.

Purposes of Evaluation

Evaluation serves a number of purposes. First, it guides intervention on an ongoing basis. The worker determines whether or not progress is being made toward accomplishing individual goals. Evaluation is not only a pre–post process but a continuous one, which provides corrective feedback to the group worker as to the efficacy of his or her treatment strategies throughout the life of the group.

Second, evaluation enables the worker and client to decide the extent to which the goals of intervention have been achieved. A related purpose of evaluation is to determine whether or not the group intervention itself accounts for the client's improvement. Making causal inferences about the role of the group intervention in producing change requires consideration of evaluation design, a topic discussed later.

A final purpose of evaluation is to assist in determining how the information gathered from one individual or group as a whole can be used to guide the group worker's subsequent interventions with other groups. As we shall discuss in the following sections, evaluation can be structured in such a way that its usefulness for future work can be enhanced.

Phases of Evaluation

The evaluation process occurs throughout treatment. It begins prior to the first group session to establish a basis of comparison for later measurement. We refer to this as the *pregroup phase*. The *ongoing phase* continues throughout the program with systematic or informal observations, self-reports, weekly questionnaires, attitudinal measures, and so forth to provide feedback to the worker and the members as to ongoing progress. In the *termination phase*, as members complete the group, initial measurements are often repeated and exit interviews held. The final or *follow-up phase* occurs at some interval following the conclusion of the group or the termination of an individual. Measures are repeated and an interview completed in order to assess the maintenance of change and to determine whether any new problems may have arisen since termination.

To Quantify or Not to Quantify

Controversy about using evaluation techniques that require measurement has raged for years. Some have argued that human behavior of the type which social work practitioners must deal with is often too complex for quantification (see Karger, 1983), while others seem to argue that measurement is the only valid source of information for evaluation. We believe that part of the debate is based on a false dichotomy. In our view no single type of evaluation information should be used exclusively. Quantification of evaluation can be integrated with and enrich other nonquantified evaluation information such as subjective impressions of group process, underlying motives, and the cognitive and affective responses of clients to ongoing group stimuli.

Measurement of change has its advantages and disadvantages. Among the advantages is that quantification guides observation. In order to measure change one needs to structure carefully what is to be observed. In this process the group worker and client must assess what is the relevant information to be observed. This process can move one from a fuzzy problem to a clear statement of what is to be changed. For example, a client whose initial complaint is a general feeling of psychological discomfort and loneliness might be helped by the group to see the problem in more specific terms, such as feeling anxious when meeting new people. Specific outcomes to be measured may include the number of contacts made with new acquaintances, the number of negative self-evaluations in interpersonal situations, such as "this situation is horrible and impossible to deal with," the number of positive self-statements such as "this situation is uncomfortable but I can handle it," and ratings on a paper-and-pencil social anxiety measure. The goals would be derived from the measures used as well as the group discussion that would have followed.

This sharpening of observation by the measurement process also applies to self-evaluation by the client. For example, a group of depressed patients were asked to rate their subjective level of depression on a 1-to-10 scale three times daily throughout the treatment period and to describe the situations that immediately preceded the ratings. This quantification process facilitated the members' becoming more sensitive to minor fluctuations in their depression level and to cues that might otherwise have gone unnoticed, such as becoming aware that a slight increase in depression tended to follow an argument with a spouse.

Another advantage of measurement is that it makes comparisons easier and more systematic. Several types of comparisons are relevant: comparing the client with himself or herself at different time periods, comparing group members with each other, comparing the client to members of other groups, and comparing members to other populations. The value of these comparisons and the procedures for carrying them out are discussed in subsequent sections.

Measurement also has its disadvantages. One problem is that workers can make the error of reifying a measure; that is, equating a phenomenon with its measure. Once defined, it is possible to begin to focus exclusively on the measured behavior as the only relevant criterion of change and to exclude other important information from evaluation. Related to this is our experience that some clients may feel their concerns are made trivial by reducing them to numbers on several measures. This disadvantage can be overcome by balancing measurement as one source of information with other sources, such as professional intuition, unstructured observations, and informed opinions.

A second disadvantage of measurement is that the demands of measurement can structure treatment. If the group worker is committed exclusively to measurement as a source of information, only those problems that can be measured are selected for treatment. While we firmly believe that important aspects of all problems can in some way be measured, some are more conveniently quantified than others. Group workers need to be flexible in their inclusion of concerns in treatment. We believe it is possible to weave into the context of treatment measurement of some problems or aspects of problems, in addition to attending to other less explicitly defined concerns. The issue is not the ultimate existence of a phenomenon but rather under what conditions measurement aids the intervention process.

A related disadvantage of measurement is its cost in time and effort to the worker and the client. Measurement is generally not an easy or costless procedure. Treatment time is reduced to allow measurement to take place. Clients sometimes complain that we are more interested in the numbers than in them. In designing specific measurement efforts in a practice situation, the cost in time, effort, and intrusiveness to the client must be weighed against the benefits expected to be derived from that specific measurement effort. The concerns of the clients must be discussed and dealt with. If that is done, our experience has led us to the conclusion that the cost-benefit ratio of measurement is favorable. Quantitative data can apply a corrective to the perpetuation of unfounded hunches and our personal biases or expectations. Often we have been confronted with data that go against what we felt would be the outcome. Our clients, when asked to measure problem behaviors, have often found that problems they felt were quite extreme occurred much less often than they had believed. The next step at such a juncture is not to dismiss intuition or the data but rather to use the incongruity to spur efforts to rethink or probe more deeply. At other times data have served as a satisfying confirmation of our intuitive hypothesis based on nonquantitative sources of information.

Advantages of Evaluation in Groups

In the group, workers can observe directly the interactions among members as a sample of real-life interactive patterns. They can observe, for example, how a member deals with an attempt at domination by another member, with criticism and praise from other members, and with other forms of anger or group conflict. Of course, so much interactive behavioral data are available in a group that workers may require some assistance in the form of an observer with a formal observation schedule in order to systematize the collection of data. (The difficulties in developing such an observation schedule are briefly discussed in a later section.)

The group provides information about the individual's response to the group, such as attraction to the group, satisfaction with the group, attendance at group meetings, promptness at group meetings, participation in group meetings, and percentage of homework assignments completed. The data permit weekly evaluation of the ongoing group process, which in turn mediates a large part of treatment. (See Rose, 1984, for details on measurement of group process.)

The group provides an efficient training context for its members in the application of various evaluation behaviors. Clients learn together how to interview each other. They learn to role-play and to provide feedback to others about how well each has role-played. The members learn to model for each other appropriate evaluation behaviors. The group provides an opportunity to explore some topics that no individual alone might have been willing to open up.

The group provides multiple models for evaluation skills. Each person, as he or she provides information in the group, models for other members a way to communicate such information and a vocabulary for communication. In the same regard each member models a domain of concerns for evaluation. Members may discover new areas or aspects of problems, which will become targets of change.

Members also observe the ways in which others evaluate themselves. They may come to see negative self-evaluations as too harsh or unrealistic. In the same way the worker can use the client's behavior in the group for analyzing internal dialogues. For example, if a given client is particularly quiet at a session, the worker might ask him or her to analyze his or her thinking processes at that moment. Finally, the group often serves as a control on the group worker's value imposition in his or her selection and application of evaluation procedures. A group of people may more readily disagree with or criticize a social worker than a single client.

Limitations of Evaluation in Groups

The group worker is limited in what can be evaluated by the theme of the group. The theme—for example, child management skills, anger control, or assertiveness—represents an implicit contract with members. Although it protects members from the highly irrelevant contributions of individuals with a tendency to let their words wander, it also serves to deter the exploration of idiosyncratic needs or problems that dramatically deviate from the agreed-upon themes. Many group workers and group therapists are moving away from groups with limited themes in response to this limitation (e.g. Flowers, 1979; Lawrence and Sundel, 1972; Lazarus, 1981). Although the elimination of a central theme broadens the problems that can be legitimately evaluated, it increases the diversity and theoretically, at least, risks lowering the group attraction. Given limited resources, evaluation in thematic groups may be limited to common denominators rather than a full exploration of the idiosyncratic problems of each member. Instead of tailoring specific evaluation procedures for each member, it may be necessary at times to use standardized measures that evaluate a broad range of issues. For example, one broad measure used in a variety of groups is the SCL-90-R, a checklist of psychological symptoms, which measures diverse factors such as somatization, depression, and phobic anxiety (Derogatis, Lipman, and Covi, 1975).

The restricted time alloted to any one member at a given meeting is also a limitation on group evaluation. Thus relevant information from each member must unfold more gradually and often less systematically than in a treatment dyad.

Since the client is not trained in professional ethics, self-disclosure of intimate information cannot be guaranteed to be held in strictest confidence, even though clients are strongly encouraged to hold to this value. Although initial testing or individualized observations may be carried out without common knowledge of the group, much other material is discussed openly in the groups. For many groups, especially those focusing on highly emotional material, the concern for confidentiality may represent an important limitation not only for evaluation but for the entire group therapeutic approach. In fact, for this reason alone an occasional client has appropriately refused to participate when made aware of the potential difficulty of public exposure. In groups with an overt behavioral or cognitive focus, the problem seems to be not as great. For these the group may even provide a greater stimulus to self-disclosure than the conditions of the therapeutic dyad because of the strong modeling effect found in most groups.

In summary, although large problems are inherent in the evaluation process, these can be addressed. In our opinion the fruits of evaluation are sufficiently rich to warrant paying the costs of time, intrusiveness, and energy. Let us now look at the evaluation procedures commonly used with clients who are in groups. In some cases the procedures are applied uniquely to group clients. In other cases no differences between the individual and the group client can be noted.

MEASUREMENT PROCEDURES

Role-Play Tests

Role-play tests are used primarily where the target response is (at least in part) a response to an interactive situation. Most targets of change in groups fall into this category. Clients are asked to take part in a simulation of a real-life problem situation so that their response to the situation can be evaluated. The client is presented either on tape or by the tester with a description of a number of situations, one at a time. These situations are similar to ones they and others with similar problems have described in the individual interviews. Each client is asked to imagine being in the given situation and to give his or her verbal and motoric responses just as if the client were in that situation. Following the role-played response, the client is asked to describe affective and cognitive responses to the situation as well. The responses and sometimes the entire situation are either video- or audiotaped and later coded in terms primarily of social competency or other behaviors the client is trying to achieve. The data are used to determine what kind of situations each client has difficulty with and to evaluate changes following the group.

The clients are specifically asked to imagine themselves in each situation and then to rate the level of distress in each. In this way the worker can develop an anxiety index.

Clients are also asked to rate their satisfaction with their response. The satisfaction data are used to estimate whether the client perceives the situation to be at all problematic. Also, if the client seems to be satisfied with what appears to be ineffective responses or dissatisfied with seemingly effective ones, the problem may be cognitive as well as or instead of behavioral. The cognitive dimension needs to be evaluated as well.

Generally, each client is presented with anywhere from six to twenty-four situations. The stock of situations from which we draw is derived from a number of highly developed role-play tests for different populations. The most common role-play tests we have used are those developed by Berger (1976) for the elderly who are institutionalized; by Rosenthal (1978) for the female adolescent; by DeLange (1976) for women in general; by Bates (1978) for mildly retarded adults; by Edelson (1979) for adolescent children; by Schinke and Rose (1977) for self-referred outpatients; and by Rose and Hanusa (1980) for parents. Most of these particular tests have precoded scoring systems and have been developed following the recommendations of Goldfried and D'Zurilla (1969). We have been experimenting with asking clients to read all of the situations for their population in advance of the test and then selecting those most relevant to themselves. In permitting a choice we lose the standardization of content, but we gain the standardization of the level of relevance for the client. Where we have had both choice and standardized items, we found that choice items are more sensitive to before–after differences. Although often administered prior to and following treatment, role-play tests can be administered within the group as part of the group sessions. Following the test the group provides the individual with feedback as a form of group intervention. In this way ongoing evaluation data can also be collected. If pre–post individualized measurement is too costly, the in-group procedure may save time.

Role-play tests have severe limitations. Role-play skill can be confounded with the behavioral skills the test is designed to measure. The extent to which improvement on skills in a role-play test really reflects changes in real-life performance is unclear and has not been empirically established.

For this reason other tests should be used to evaluate outcome in addition to role-play tests (see Bellack, Hersen, and Turner, 1978, for criticism of the role-play tests).

Let us look at three items from an eleven-item role-play test developed by DeLange (1976, p. 197) for evaluating the outcome of assertion training groups for women.

1. Your boss comes up to you in the late morning and asks you—as he frequently does—to do a whole series of time-consuming jobs for him. He says to you: "You know this project has really turned out to be a big one! Our report to the city is due at the end of the week, and it's got to be typed up. Here's the correspondence for the day; make sure it gets done before you leave. Oh, and Susan—I've got this desk set that I need exchanged today. Can you run over to Manchester's and get the one I ordered? Here's the sales slip. I realize you may have to stay late, but we have to finish everything—O.K.?"

2. Last week your supervisor gave you your yearly evaluation. After reading it you think there are some points not favorable to you which are unjustified. You made an appointment to see him.

You are now in the interview and he has taken each point and justified his position without asking for or listening to your side. He now acts like the topic is closed. "Well, Jane, I'm glad you came in to clear these things up. I know these evaluations are important. However, we'll always try to give the employees the benefit of the doubt. You can work on these problems and improve by the next six months."

3. You are in a sporting goods store looking for a gift for a friend who loves to camp. You have thought about getting a camping heater but do not know what kinds there are or how they work. The man explaining them to you has been calling you "honey" and "sweetheart," generally talking in a condescending way. He has left you to answer a telephone call and now returns. "Sorry 'bout that. Now, sweetheart, have you made up your mind which one it will be?"

After each of the items is read to the client, she is asked to respond as if she were in that situation. A manual for rating the responses to all eleven items is found in DeLange (1976, pp. 175–198).

In summary behavioral role-play tests can be individualized for each client by permitting choice among items. The tests provide the clients with examples of situations that may be problematic to them. They provide the group worker with data on the range and adequacy of social coping skills, the stress experienced in various situations, and the cognitive and/or behavioral locus of the problem. But role-play tests are costly to apply and code in terms of group worker and client time, and they are insufficient in terms of validity to be the only measure. For these reasons, role-play tests are often supplemented with other measures, such as self-rating checklists and inventories.

Self-Rating Checklists and Inventories

Self-rating checklists and inventories are structured instruments designed to enable the client to report systematically on a specific target problem or on a general problem area. The specific checklist used depends on the theme of the group or on the specific target problem the client has identified. Although for most groups the same checklist is used for each member in order to provide intragroup comparison and comparison with similiar groups, often a checklist will be specific only to the member to whom it is given. Not all inventories or checklists are filled in by the clients themselves. Some are filled in by parents, teachers, or others in the client's world. With children, for example, we have asked teachers to respond to the Behavior Problem Checklist (Quay and Peterson, 1967) and the School Behavior Checklist (Miller, 1972). When working with teachers, most of whom have little time available for evaluation, brief checklists seem to be advisable.

Some examples of self-inventories commonly used in groups with specific themes are the following. With unassertive individuals, the Gambrill–Richey (1975) Assertion Inventory or Rathus (1972) has been used. For depressed individuals, the Beck Depression Inventory can be used (Beck and Beamesderfer, 1974). One of the more common inventories in evaluating the group treatment of problems related to anxiety has been the State–Trait anxiety inventory (Spielberger, Gorsuch, and Lushene, 1970). Hudson (1982) has developed a set of checklists, many of which can be used in groups. They have received extensive evaluation for reliability and validity.

Several disadvantages characterize the use of self-report checklists. Members may give socially desirable answers or may fall into a response set, that is, indiscriminately answering items in a similar manner. When checklists are used more than once, for example before and after the group, the second administration of the checklist may be affected by the first.

Despite these and other limitations, checklists are often the best way to access certain evaluation information. They are cost-effective and convenient, that is, the client can report information quickly and systemically. Second, some checklists have been carefully studied and have established reliability and validity. Third, clients may be willing to disclose more information on a checklist than they would in the group or in an interview with the leader.

Self-Monitoring

Self-monitoring, a method of observing one's own overt behavior, thoughts, or feelings, requires the client to record his or her own behavior at specified intervals or under specific conditions in a systematic manner (Eisler, 1976). If done systematically, and if there is evidence to assume reliability, the results of self-monitoring may be used to evaluate the progress and outcome of group treatment.

In groups self-monitoring is especially useful where external observational methods do not provide the private data necessary to assess cognitive behavior. For example, clients in self-control groups will often count their urges to indulge in an abused substance such as alcohol or other drugs, or food, as well as their overt and covert responses to that urge. In parent training groups, some parents will record the frequency and intensity of anger that they experience either periodically or during stressful situations. Others have kept track of self-"putdowns." An example of a self-monitoring form (Figure 22–1) used in a therapy group is described below. Members were asked to keep track of their stress three times daily by recording the average level of stress experienced during a time period as well as the highest stress level reached during that period.

Overt behaviors are also self-monitored, especially when the frequency of a given behavior indicates the severity of the problem. For example, in parent groups, parents may be asked to count their praise response to their children's behavior. In social skill groups, clients are asked to count the number of people they have approached in a week. In an anger control

Name _____

Please fill in day of week and date: e.g., Monday, Sept. 19

Instructions: Rate your highest distress and average distress for each period of time, on a scale of 1-10, with 1 being totally calm and relaxed and 10 the highest distress you could experience. Choose a consistent time to rate for each period every day, e.g., breakfast, lunch, dinner, and before bed.

DATE	Morning		Afternoon		Evening		comments
	highest	average	highest	average	highest	average	

Additional comments:

FIGURE 22–1. Self-monitoring Form

group, clients have counted episodes of their verbal and physical abuse of others.

Diaries and logs as used in groups refer to the extragroup activity of reporting in some detail situations encountered, behavior, thoughts, and/or feelings as they occur. Group members may be asked to keep a record of situations that elicit a problem behavior and their response to the situation. Early in the group, such records provide information as to how to go about addressing the problem. The diaries may provide the group session with structure, as sessions can be focused on dealing with problem situations members have recorded. In addition the diaries are useful as evaluation tools because they provide an ongoing record of the client's progress in dealing with problem situations. Patterns in response may be established, and the change in these patterns more readily noted, through the evaluation of the logs over time.

An example of a structured diary form is shown in Figure 22–2. The reader may notice that the form asks for a detailed description of a problem situation, the client's thoughts and feelings during the situation, and the client's response.

In another type of structured recording the emphasis is on cognitive evaluation. The client provides in her or his log a brief description of an event and then the thoughts that accompanied the event. Clients rate their degree of belief in the thoughts and attempt to change those that are self-defeating. Progress may be noted by decreased belief in self-defeating thoughts and less emotional distress associated with events that formerly elicited distress.

Self-monitoring is useful in that it extends evaluation to the natural environment. Clients are involved intensely, and the evaluation value derived from the logs comes from these naturalistic observations of the client. Because the data are obtained in an ongoing manner and in natural settings, self-monitoring may have greater validity than some other evaluation methods.

Unfortunately, often clients do not comply with extensive monitoring assignments. Care must be taken not to overwhelm the client with demands to monitor more than is reasonable. Clients are more likely to continue to bring in information if it is used in sessions. We have found that clients will quickly begin to decrease their record-keeping if we don't make use of the information on an ongoing basis. The information is useful not just as a pre–post evaluation device, though logs and diaries could be used this way, but rather as an ongoing guide to practice.

Self-monitoring is a behavior in its own right with which the client has had limited experience. As a result it must usually be shaped, as must any other behavior. Failure in self-monitoring is often due to inadequate definition of the monitored behavior, high expectations in the early phase of therapy, and inadequate training in monitoring or counting the behavior. Be-

FIGURE 22-2.   Structured Diary Form

Name:
Date:

Stress Diary Sheet

1. Describe your stress situation briefly.
   What happened? Where were you? At what point did you begin to experience stress?

2. *Subjective Units of Stress Scale*
   (circle one) How uncomfortable were you in this situation *before* you said or did something?

completely relaxed	1	2	3	4	5	6	7	8	9	10	highest distress

3. What did you do in the situation? How did you cope? (May be adaptive or mal-adaptive coping.)

4. What was your Emotional Response to this stressful situation? (anger, nervous, anxiety . . .)

5. Where did you experience the stress in your body? (heart rate, hands sweating, headache, sore shoulders, etc. . . .)

6. What else could you have done to reduce your stress?

7. Circle one. How uncomfortable were you in this situation *after* you said or did something?

completely relaxed	1	2	3	4	5	6	7	8	9	10	highest distress

cause of its unique structure the group lends itself to efficient training of clients in common self-observed behavior. The group worker can model the process of self-observation, and the members can provide each other with diverse examples. In addition the group provides opportunity for practicing self-observation with ample feedback from the client's peers as to the efficacy of their self-monitoring activity. Clients can also work in pairs to see that adequate definitions of the counted behavior occur. Ample peer reinforcement exists for those who appear to monitor carefully. The group also lends itself to monitoring of the self-observations. Since each member must report publicly to the group the results of his or her observations, group pressure usually exists to carry out the assignment and to be as accurate as possible in the recording. Some group workers provide incentive for monitoring by reserving an extra portion of group time for those who have successfully completed their ongoing monitoring assignments.

Goal Attainment Scaling

Goal attainment scaling is a practical technique to evaluate client progress (Kiresuk and Garwick, 1979). Unlike standardized measures described above, goal attainment scales are derived by the group worker and the members. Goals are specified for each individual, and then for each goal a scale is developed. Each goal describes the most favorable to least favorable outcomes that can be expected as a result of intervention. Generally the midpoint of a five-point scale is the "expected" outcome (see example below). Outcomes specified may be behaviors, thoughts, feelings, or changes in environment. In the following example one possible format of a goal attainment scale is presented. In groups most clients would have three to five such goals. In addition it would be possible to put group goals such as increasing the cohesion of the group on such a scale.

Goal Attainment Scale: An Example

PREDICTED OUTCOME LEVELS	INDIVIDUAL TREATMENT GOAL (MAKING FRIENDS)
Much less than expected -2	Talks to one group member on the playground for at least one minute.
Moderately less than expected -1	Talks to two group members on the playground for at least one minute.
Predicted or expected 0	Talks to one classmate (not a group member) for at least one minute.
Moderately more than expected $+1$	Talks to two classmates on the playground for at least one minute.
Much more than expected $+2$	Talks to and plays with two or more classmates on the playground for at least five minutes.

Goal attainment scales have several advantages. They are focused specifically on each individual. They provide specific criteria for determining whether a client has improved or deteriorated. Because changes are quantified, the rating scales offer some degree of intra- and extragroup comparability. In addition, in groups it is possible to involve the entire group in the process of establishing goals. Of course, there are threats to both reliability and validity, which several authors have pointed out, but the general conclusion has been in favor of goal attainment scaling's general usefulness (see Cytrynbaum et al., 1979, for an extensive critical review of goal attainment scaling).

Evaluation by Others

There are a number of ways in which significant others in the life of the group member can monitor the behavior of the client. These include highly structured direct observation outside the group and inside the group, problem checklists, and informal reports from significant others. Some of these are discussed below.

Observations outside the group. Most of the data collection procedures discussed thus far have depended on self-report or self-observations of the client. This gives rise to problems of both reliability and validity of the measurement process, such as social desirability and extreme response styles. One way to minimize these particular problems is the use of direct observation of the client in extragroup situations. Unfortunately, such procedures are quite costly and quite difficult. Simple observation systems, however, have generally been used in schools and in institutional settings where the clients are readily monitored by others. In these cases staff, family, or school personnel have been trained to look for highly specific target behaviors such as temper tantrums, cooperation with others, approach responses to other children, putdowns, and reinforcing statements. These behaviors may be counted or rated by the observers (see Rose, 1977, for more detail). Because of its cost, the need for careful definition, and the demand for careful and extensive observer training, direct observation is rarely used outside of the school and other institutional settings where groups take place (for those group workers who wish to explore this topic further and have the necessary resources see Rose, 1977).

Problem cards. Problem cards provide another method for systematically obtaining information about a member's progress in the natural setting from someone other than the client. This technique was proposed by Goodman and further developed by Flowers (1979), who applied it to trainees in a group. On each of two cards a client briefly describes a problem he or she is currently experiencing. The client also names someone who could judge the client's improvement in that area. The raters could be family members, friends, or any other person whom the client feels comfortable about asking for a rating. Whenever possible the client should work out his or her own contract with the rater. Training the group in negotiating a contract is often necessary.

Hazel, Schumaker, Sherman, and Sheldon-Wilgen (1981) have described the use of "Home Notes," a similar procedure in adolescent social skill groups. An example of a home note is shown in Figure 22–3.

Observations in the group.   Observation of interacting behaviors in the group is quite difficult. Although a number of complex observation

HOME NOTE

Dear _____ Mrs. Jones _____ :

The group discussed and practiced Accepting Negative Feedback this week. _____ Jim _____ has agreed to practice this skill with you three times this week. We would appreciate it if you would record what the practice situation was and how well the skill was performed. On the back is a Skill Sheet which shows the steps for doing this skill correctly. Please check your teenager's performance against these steps. For each of the three practice situations give a checkmark for a correct performance only if the teenager made no more than two mistakes during it. As a review, your teenager has also agreed to practice Giving Negative Feedback one time this week. Please sign the bottom of the form after the practices. It is very important to return this form at the next group session. Please help your teenager to remember to return it. Thanks for your help.

Situation	Performed Correctly?	Steps Omitted
1. *Accepted negative feedback from Mom for not cleaning his room*	✓	
2. *Accepted negative feedback from Mom for coming home late at night*	✓	*Did not ask for clarification*
3. *Accepted negative feedback from a friend for not calling her*	✓	
4. (Review Skill) *Gave his dad negative feedback for not letting him go to a party.*	✓	*Did not ask to talk to him*

Signed _____ Mrs. John Jones _____   Date _____ 2/3/81 _____

FIGURE 22–3.

schemes do exist, they have been used primarily by researchers rather than group work practitioners. What we have found useful is observation of member participation regardless of its quality. In this procedure the observer notes who is speaking every ten seconds. At the end of the meeting the totals for each person are counted and their percentages calculated. At the beginning of the next meeting these data are presented and, if necessary, can be discussed in terms of whether each person has made effective use of the group meeting. If the members note that a problem exists, the group will problem-solve around that issue.

The observers may be students, other agency staff, volunteers from previous groups, or members of the group who rotate the responsibility. Training takes about five to ten minutes prior to the meeting. In an earlier study (Rose, 1981) we found that participation measured this way was significantly correlated with outcome.

It is also possible to use the coding system from the role-play tests to evaluate role-plays as they occur in the group, provided that the precoded role-plays are used. Although we have limited experience thus far with this procedure, it seems to be an effective way of obtaining ongoing data about improvement in the social skills of the clients before the end of treatment. These role-play tests are identified above.

Occasionally, by using an observer in the group, we have measured isolated low-frequency behaviors. For example, in a social skills group we observed two children for the frequency of asking adults for help. In a parent group we observed positive statements and putdowns (in agreement with the parents) for all the members. In both cases a great deal of time had to be spent in defining the observation categories and training the observer. In general the interaction was too fast to obtain high-frequency behaviors without a larger investment in observational training than most group workers have time and other resources for (see Piper, Montvila, and McGihan, 1979, for an example of a more complex observation system used in a treatment group).

In order to slow down the interaction with children, the "freeze" technique has occasionally been applied. In this procedure a timer is set randomly but less than every ten minutes. When the timer goes off, the children are required to freeze in the position in which the bell catches them. The behavior that the child was performing at that moment is noted, and if appropriate the child may be reinforced. Children up to age fourteen like the technique, and it permits the worker to get a count at the end of the meeting on several target behaviors. One might use this procedure to ask the clients what they are thinking immediately prior to the ringing of the bell in order to evaluate cognitive phenomena.

In summary, observation is a highly useful but costly tool in the evaluation process. By slowing down the observation process and by using simple categories, observation in groups is gaining increasing numbers of adherents among group workers.

DESIGN

The design of one's evaluation activities is related to the types of questions the group worker can answer. In order to use evaluation data to guide intervention on an ongoing basis, one must gather data throughout treatment. If one wants to know the degree of change that has occurred from the start of intervention to the end, it is necessary to gather baseline data as well. A baseline is a series of observations taken prior to the start of intervention, which can then be compared to observations taken after intervention is completed. When examined together, the two sets of observations allow one to draw conclusions about the direction and magnitude of change that has occurred. Contrast this situation to taking data only at the completion of intervention. Measuring the level of a target problem at the completion of intervention allows one to make a judgment about whether the problem is at an acceptable level. Without baseline data one cannot judge whether or not the level is a change from where the client began. If one wants to make a judgment about whether the treatment itself accounted for improvement, as opposed to some other factor, then a more complex design must be used. Below are brief descriptions of designs that can be used to answer evaluation questions.

Pre-Post Design

In the pre–post design data are gathered prior to the start of intervention and then again at the completion of intervention. This design allows one to make a judgment as to the magnitude as well as the direction of change. However, because only a single measurement is taken before and after intervention, confidence in the inferences drawn from pre–post measurements is limited. Each measurement may be subject to influence from many factors (e.g. a worse day than usual, the client has a headache, an unclear instruction). One cannot be completely confident that the measurement reflects the actual level of the target being measured, be it a behavior, thought, or feeling.

The effectiveness of the pre–post design can be improved by taking multiple measurements in the baseline phase as well as in the postgroup phase.

The Repeated A–B Design

In a repeated A–B design, repeated measurement is taken throughout the baseline (A) phase and the intervention (B) phase. Because repeated measurements have been taken, the worker can make judgments about the magnitude and direction of change with greater confidence than with the pre–post design. In addition, when multiple measures are taken throughout the intervention phase, the worker can determine on an ongoing basis if the intervention is proceeding successfully. Adjustment in techniques may occur as a result of this information.

While the A–B design provides useful information, one cannot make causal inferences about the role of the group in bringing about the changes the client experiences. It is possible that an uncontrolled event occurring concomitantly with intervention may have produced the change. Campbell and Stanley(1963) refer to this as a threat to validity due to history. For example, in a group of children, one in particular improved dramatically from the pre to the post test. It was learned that his previously separated parents had reconciled during the course of group treatment. It was therefore unclear what the cause of improvement was.

In spite of its inability to provide evidence for causal inference about the intervention's contribution to change, the A–B design is a practical design for use in group treatment. The threats to internal validity are reduced when the design is used in a group setting because of the criteria of "successive implausible coincidences" (Carter, 1972); that is, when measures are taken on several group members and similar change occurs in all of them, it is less likely that the positive change can be attributed to factors other than the group, especially if change occurs at a similar point in time after the baseline measure. It is implausible that an improvement in a target behavior or problem would occur simultaneously for several group members if the group intervention did not have some role in the change.

B Only

Sometimes, because of the need to intervene quickly or other practical constraints, the group worker is not able to collect baseline information. In such a case measurement is still usefully collected. Repeated measurement after the start of intervention does not allow for comparison of the magnitude of change occurring from a baseline measure, but it does allow one to determine if improvement is occuring. Even a single measurement at the conclusion of the group will improve a decision about whether the problem is at a level to warrant termination or whether further service is advisable.

Designs That Permit Causal Interference

Several single-system designs allow for ruling out more threats to internal validity. Such designs enable the group worker to infer that the group intervention was responsible for change in target problems. Such designs are often difficult to implement in practice, however, and certainly no practitioner is likely to use them in all cases. There are times when a worker may choose a group to evaluate using a design that allows for causal inference. Inferential designs include the following:

- ABAB or reversal, withdrawal designs, where treatment is initiated and then withdrawn in order to examine its effect on the target behavior
- Multiple baseline designs, where intervention is initiated in phases across behaviors, clients, or settings (If behavior changes occur in each baseline following the initiation of intervention, then confidence is increased that the intervention is responsible for the changes.)
- Changing criterion designs, where successively more difficult levels of performance are required for access to reinforcement (If the behavior repeatedly changes in a fashion that resembles the changing criterion, then confidence is increased that the intervention [reinforcement] is responsible for the change.)

Further discussion of these and other designs can be found in several sources (Hersen and Barlow, 1976; Jayaratne and Levy, 1979; Bloom and Fischer, 1982).

A Case in Point

In this section we shall describe an example of evaluation procedures used in a ten-week stress management group. The members of this group were recruited by advertisement from the community at large. Although they came primarily for problems related to difficulties in managing stress, their concrete problems were quite diverse and in many cases quite serious. Although the tests and measures used in this group are different from those used in other types of groups, the evaluation program is not atypical of ones we use with children as well as adults. Prior to the first meeting each of the members in the group was interviewed in order to establish preliminary goals to be used in goal attainment scaling. Following the interview each person in the group filled in two paper-and-pencil checklists: the symptom checklist (SCL-90-R) (Derogatis, Lipman and Covi, 1975) and the Hassles Scale (Kanner et al., 1981). Two people in the group who complained of depression were also given the Beck Depression Inventory (BDI) (see Beck and Beamesderfer, 1974). One group member who had complained, among other things, of high blood pressure and who was attending the group with his physician's encouragement had his blood pressure taken. The specific targets for goal attainment scaling were determined based on the scores on the checklists named above, as well as self-observations to be carried out during the week. The specific goal attainment scales for one person involved his lowering the scale on the BDI and his increasing recreational activity. A second person aimed at reducing the severity of hassles as measured by the hassle inventory and increasing her assertion with a co-worker who was always imposing on her. A third person had as his goal the reduction of blood pressure (on both diastolic and systolic), and the reduction of the experience of anxiety on an anxiety self-report. This client also focused on reducing the intensity of hassles he was experiencing.

During the group sessions a postsession questionnaire was distributed to measure satisfaction and usefulness of the session for each individual. In addition questions were asked abut self-disclosure (see Rose, 1984, for more detailed descriptions of these measures and how they were used). Data were collected on the rate of assignment completion and participation since in previous studies these were found to be highly correlated with successful outcome (Rose, 1981). Thus they could be used to indicate whether a change in the program or renegotiation of goals might be considered. Other ongoing measures included a self-report scale for stress and a similar one for depression and anxiety, one of which was filled in three times a day by each of the members.

Finally, both at termination and three months after the group program, all members were retested on the checklists and inventories. Clients were interviewed in the group to determine the degree to which each of the goals was achieved and maintained.

The research design for most of the goals on the goal attainment scale, the inventories, and the checklist was a pre–post–follow-up design without a control group.

The cost of the evaluation activities was the equivalent of two sessions or eight hours of professional time. This came to an average of one hour per each group member beyond the cost of six professional hours per person for ten sessions. This time included the interviews, the giving of the measures and coding them, the review of the measures to determine the degree to which goals were achieved, and preparation.

CONCLUSIONS

Was the above evaluation program worth the effort put into it? The thrust of this article has been that failure to design such a program is by far the most costly approach of all. Without evaluation we lose vital tools to estimate our progress, our failures, and our successes.

At a sizable cost but still only a small proportion of the cost of treatment, evaluation can be a regular feature of a treatment approach. Of course, evaluation behavior like all other behavior has to be learned and practiced to be maintained. Agencies must set up structures and make resources available to their staff for the systematic collection of data. Even more important a program of review of the ongoing significance of these data must be incorporated into the program.

Perhaps with the advent of low cost personal computers the task of setting up a systematic data collection program will be facilitated. Certainly the storage and the recording process will be easier. Regardless of how convenient an evaluation program becomes, the endeavor will only retain clinical significance if data collection is combined with the intuitive formulations of the experienced group worker.

REFERENCES

BATES, PAUL, E.
   1978   "The effects of interpersonal skills training on the acquisition and generalization of interpersonal communications behaviors by moderately/mildly retarded adults." Unpublished doctoral dissertation, University of Wisconsin-Madison.
BECK, AARON T., AND A. BEAMESDERFER
   1974   "Assessment of depression: The depression inventory," *Modern Problems of Pharmacopsychiatry*, 7: 151–69.
BELLACK, ALAN S.; MICHEL HERSEN; AND SAMUEL M. TURNER
   1978   "Role play tests for assessing social skills: Are they valid?" *Behavior Therapy*, 9: 448–46.
BERGER, RAY M.
   1976   "Interpersonal skill training with institutionalized elderly patients." University of Wisconsin-Madison.
BLOOM, MARTIN AND JOEL FISCHER
   1982   *Evaluating Practice: Guidelines for the Accountable Professional*. Englewood CLiffs, N.J.: Prentice-Hall
CAMPBELL, DONALD T., AND JULIAN C. STANLEY
   1963   *Experimental and Quasi-Experimental Designs for Research*. Chicago: Rand-McNally.
CARTER, ROBERT
   1972   "Designs and data patterns in intensive experimentation." Unpublished paper, University of Michigan, School of Social Work.
CYTRYNBAUM, SOLOMON; YIGAL GINATH; JOEL BIRDWELL; AND LAUREN BRANDT
   1979   "Goal attainment scaling: A critical review," *Evaluation Quarterly*, 3: 5–40.
DELANGE, JANICE
   1976   "Effectiveness of systematic desensitization and assertive training with women." Doctoral dissertation, University of Wisconsin-Madison, School of Social Work.
DEROGATIS, L. R.; R. S. LIPMAN; AND L. COVI
   1975   "SCL–90: An outpatient psychiatric rating scale—preliminary report." *Psychopharmacology Bulletin*, 9: 13–28.

EDELSON, JEFFREY L.
1979 "A behavioral role play test for assessing children's social skills: Testing booklet." Unpublished manual, University of Wisconsin-Madison.

EISLER, RICHARD M.
1976 "The behavior assessment of social skills." In M. Herson and A. S. Bellack (eds.), *Behavior Assessment: A Practical Handbook*, New York: Pergamon, pp. 369–96.

FISCHER, JOEL
1973 "Is casework effective? A review," *Social Work*, 18: 5–20.

FLOWERS, JOHN V.
1979 "Behavioral analysis of group therapy and a model for behavioral group therapy." In Dennis Upper and Steven Ross (eds.), *Behavioral Group Therapy*. Champaign, Ill.: Research Press, pp. 5–38.

GAMBRILL, EILEEN D., AND CAROL A. RICHEY
1975 "An assertion inventory for use in assessment and research," *Behavior Therapy*, 6: 550–61.

GOLDFRIED, MARVIN R., AND THOMAS D'ZURILLA
1969 "A behavior-analytic model for assessing competence." In Charles D. Spielberger (ed.), *Current Topics in Clinical and Community Psychology*. Vol. 1. New York: Academic Press, pp. 151–96.

HAZEL, J. STEPHEN; JEAN B. SCHUMAKER; JAMES A. SHERMAN; AND J. SHELDON-WILDGEN
1981 *Asset: A Social Skills Program for Adolescents*. Champaign, Ill.: Research Press.

HERSEN, MICHEL, AND DAVID H. BARLOW
1976 *Single Case Experimental Designs*. New York: Pergamon Press.

HUDSON, WALTER W.
1982 *The Clinical Measurement Package: A Field Manual*. Homewood, Ill.: Dorsey Press.

JAYARATNE, SRINKIKI, AND RONA L. LEVY
1979 *Empirical Clinical Practice*. New York: Columbia University Press.

KANNER, ALAN; JAMES COYNE; CATHERINE SCHAEFER; AND RICHARD LAZARUS
1981 "Comparison of two modes of stress measurement: Daily hassles and uplifts versus major life events," *Journal of Behavior Medicine*, 4, no. 1.

KARGER, H. JACOB
1983 "Science, research, and social work: Who controls the profession?" *Social Work*, 28: 200–205.

KIRESUK, THOMAS J., AND GEOFFREY GARWICK
1979 "Basic goal attainment scaling procedures." In Beulah R. Compton and Burt Galaway (eds.), *Social Work Processes*. Homewood, Ill.: Dorsey Press, pp. 388–400.

LAWRENCE, HARRY, AND MARTIN SUNDEL
1972 "Behavior modification in adult groups," *Social Work*, 17: 34–43.

LAZARUS, ARNOLD A.
1981 "Multimodel group therapy." In George M. Gazda (ed.), *Basic Approaches to Group Psychotherapy and Group Counseling*. Third edition, Springfield, Ill.: C. C. Thomas, pp. 213–34.

MILLER, LOVICK C.
  1972 "School behavior checklist: An inventory of deviant behavior for elementary school children," *Journal of Consulting and Clinical Psychology* 38, no. 1: 134–44.
PIPER, WILLIAM E.; RUTA M. MONTVILA; AND ALAN L. McGIHON
  1979 "Process analysis in therapy groups: A behavior sampling technique with many potential uses." In Dennis Upper and Stephen M. Ross (eds.), *Behavioral Group Therapy*. Champaign, Ill.: Research Press, pp. 55–70.
QUAY, HERBERT C., AND DONALD R. PETERSON
  1967 *Manual for the Behavior Problem Checklist*. Champaign: Children's Research Center, University of Illinois.
RATHUS, SPENCER A.
  1972 "An experimental investigation of assertive training in a group setting," *Journal of Behavior Therapy and Experimental Psychiatry*, 3: 81–86.
REID, WILLIAM, AND PATRICIA HANRAHAN
  1982 "Recent evaluations of social work: Grounds for optimism," *Social Work*, 27: 328–40.
ROSE, SHELDON D.
  1977 *Group Therapy: A Behavioral Approach*. Englewood Cliffs, N.J.: Prentice-Hall.
  1981 "Assessment in groups," *Social Work Research and Abstracts*, 17: 29–37.
  1984 "The use of data in resolving group problems," *Social Work with Groups*, 7 (April): 23–36.
ROSE, SHELDON D., AND DARALD HANUSA
  1980 "Parenting skill role-play test." Madison: University of Wisconsin-Madison Interpersonal Skill Training and Research project. Mimeographed.
ROSENTHAL, LISA
  1978 "Behavioral analysis of social skills in adolescent girls." Unpublished doctoral dissertation, University of Wisconsin-Madison.
SCHINKE, STEVEN P., AND SHELDON D. ROSE
  1977 "Interpersonal skill training in groups," *Journal of Counseling Psychology*, 23: 442–48.
SPIELBERGER, CHARLES D.; RICHARD L. GORSUCH; AND ROBERT E. LUSHENE
  1970 *STAI Manual for the State-Trait Inventory*. Palo Alto, Calif.: Consulting Psychologists Press.
WOOD, KATHERINE M.
  1978 "Casework effectiveness: A new look at the research evidence," *Social Work*, 23: 437–58.

23

An Evaluation of Group Work Practice with AFDC Mothers

Elizabeth Navarre, Paul H. Glasser, and Jane Costabile

PROJECT GOALS

SOCIETY HAS BEGUN to return its attention to providing ways for those trapped in the lowest socioeconomic stratum to be upwardly mobile. Intervention at many levels is directed toward removing barriers to achievement and opening doors to fulfillment. The child in the AFDC family is particularly prone to school failure, and work with the mothers of such families is one of many measures needed to break the cycle of poverty and chronic underachievement. With many specific efforts under way, attention must be given to monitoring their effectiveness.

Evaluation studies are relatively new to social work practice. This chapter summarizes the result of one of the few studies evaluating the outcome of a group treatment project. Its importance lies not only in its demonstration of the effectiveness of a particular intervention process but also in the fact that it could be done using both objective measures of change and a control sample.

The project was developed and carried out over a four-year period, from 1962 to 1966, through the combined interests and cooperative efforts of The University of Michigan School of Social Work and The Michigan Department of Social Services.[1] Its focus was upon facilitating the healthy

This chapter is a revised version of the authors' report (April 1969) based upon research sponsored by Children's Bureau Grant D-16. The analysis is the responsibility of the authors, not of the Michigan State Department of Social Welfare or its staff. The original paper was given at the 96th Annual Forum of the National Conference in New York City on May 28, 1969.

[1]Department personnel cooperating with the project staff were Tom Cook, Ora Hinckley, Lynn Kellogg, Roger Lind, Frances McNeil, Winifred Quarton, Robert Rosema, June Thomas, Jeanne Walters, and Fred Wight.

development of children by improving the attitudes and behavior of parents toward their children through the use of group sessions. The setting was the Oakland County Department of Social Services, including the Oakland County Children's Division and the Oakland County Bureau of Social Aid. This county is an urban area contiguous to Detroit and has problems similar to Detroit's problems.

Project goals included multiple theory development, the provision of service, and field training of social group work students. This report will confine itself to a summary of the group work methods and techniques used, a review and interpretation of the statistical findings of the evaluation study, and some implications for future research and practice.[2]

DEMONSTRATION AND SERVICE

During the first eighteen months of the project the emphasis was on demonstration and service. The intent was to try out a variety of service patterns in the recruitment, composition, goal orientation, and leadership of groups. Toward the end of this period consistency in service patterns became a requirement, as the project moved into the pretesting and evaluation phases. The decision was made to recruit clients for the experimental groups from the Oakland County Bureau of Social Aid because of the much larger number of members available there than in the Children's Division. AFDC mothers who had one or more children who were having learning or behavioral difficulties in public school were recruited to groups, which met in a community agency or institution in their neighborhood. Workers focused group attention on parent–child interaction related to these school problems. Three subgoals were identified: (1) the provision of additional resources (clothing, medical care, etc.) related to the children's achievement and attendance in school, (2) changes in mothers' attitudes toward the school system, and (3) changes in mothers' attitudes toward their children's behavior and achievement in school. Throughout the three years there were twenty-one groups of this type, including the twelve groups in the experimental sample. There were other types of groups as well.

AFDC mothers whose children were having difficulty in school were chosen to be clients in the experimental groups only after considerable thought. Since almost all AFDC mothers have this problem, a large supply of potential clients would be available. Furthermore, selection of this goal orientation was very much in line with the project's original intent to "center its attention upon the prevention of emotional disturbance and/or delin-

[2]Other aspects of the project are summarized in the mimeographed Final Report dated January 1968. See also Glasser and Navarre (1965a, 1965b).

quency in children through group treatment of parents";[3] it was related to the prevention of intergenerational financial dependency and the 1962 Social Security Amendments on rehabilitation; and it was an area of great interest to both local and Central Office Department staff.

During the three demonstration years about five hundred clients attended group sessions, although a considerably larger number initially had been invited. The number of sessions held for each group in the experimental sample ranged from four to twelve, and the mode was six. Average attendance at each of these sessions was five; the meetings generally lasted about one and one-half hours. The groups were led by both agency-trained workers and a second-year student in the social group work program at The University of Michigan School of Social Work. All group leaders were supervised by a faculty member from the school, and much consultation was provided by the authors.

Members were referred to the groups by regular agency staff. Caseworkers listed names of clients within their caseloads who had relevant problems. They specified which clients had cars or were close to bus lines, and identified children by ages and school grades. They tried to screen out clients known to be unable to attend meetings because of work, illness, or some other reason. Following conferences between the group worker and the referring caseworker, home calls to describe the new service and extend invitations to attend were made by the caseworker, the group worker, or both. Clients were told that there were two purposes for the service: to aid them to get and give help in the resolution of problems held in common; and to assist the agency in finding out whether group sessions of this type are useful.

Customarily arrangements were made for clients to meet at a centrally located neighborhood facility, such as the public school or local recreation agency, so that many clients could walk to the meeting place. A week before the first group meeting clients received reminder letters, which briefly described the group purpose once again, gave specific directions to the site of the group session, and urged attendance. Thereafter mimeographed notices were mailed weekly. Often clients who failed to respond to the weekly notices were visited or telephoned. Seemingly, the greater the effort devoted to recruitment, the higher the attendance.

Throughout the history of the project recruitment, diagnostic and group leadership procedures were changed to make them more effective and more efficient. Those described in this report were generally followed in the third and final year of the evaluation study. They reflect careful thought concerning previous experiences with the integration of social science and practice theory.

[3]Quoted from original project proposal.

Often prior to the first meeting, but always before the second session, the group worker prepared for each client expected in the group a short diagnostic statement, based on record material, home visits, and his or her conferences with the caseworker. Specific behavioral goals related to the purpose of the group and the individual diagnostic evaluation were required as part of this statement. Further, prior to each group meeting, individual goals, group goals and intervention plans were prepared for that session. All of these formulations were in written form, serving as a basis for supervision, but also demanding considerable preparation for the rehabilitation process.

The problem-solving approach, developed out of the Bales material on social interaction, was used as one theoretical basis in all experimental groups (Bales and Strodtbeck, 1960; Bales, 1958). A second emphasis was the group work practice theory formulated at the University of Michigan (see Chapters 1 and 2). Individual difficulties and the concerns verbalized by clients were reinterpreted by the worker into a problem formulation relevant to the majority of group members. The group was then helped to move through the orientation (information gathering), evaluation (proposed alternate solutions), and control (reaching a decision) phases of the process, each member contributing ideas to and learning from others during every session. Each member was able to choose from among the multiple solutions proposed during the third phase and to make use of those most relevant to her situation.

This training in problem-solving was repeated a number of times during the history of each group. The women were asked to report the results of their attempts to try out new solutions. After a few successful experiences in the group, the worker explained the process the group had been through in easily understandable terms, and each client was asked to try out the process on a specified problem on her own and report back at the next meeting, at which time reports were discussed and evaluated. At the last group session the problem-solving process was reviewed, and group members were encouraged to continue using this rational approach to the difficulties they were experiencing.

Although the primary activity of all groups was discussion, a variety of other program techniques were used when appropriate. Tape recordings, films, pictures, stories, role-play, and so on were attempted to stimulate group members in a variety of ways. In order to orient themselves better to a particular problem, many groups invited outside resource people, particularly bureau and school personnel, to attend group sessions. Such contacts had intrinsic value in that they often led to more positive client perceptions of these authority figures in their lives.

Following termination of the group, workers prepared reports on each client, summarizing each woman's participation in the project and the degree to which individual goals were achieved. Next, steps for the caseworker were recommended. Once these reports were read by the client's caseworker and/or the casework supervisor, a conference was held between the group worker and one or both of these agency staff members. A group summary report was also written and made available to agency staff.

EVALUATION METHODS

In the first project year relationships between the local agency and the university were established, concepts of social group work in a public agency setting were developed, and the agency and the project staff explored various means of adapting to the needs of both organizations as well as to the needs of the clients to be served. No research was attempted during that year. In the second year the evaluation study was designed, and instruments were developed and pretested. The third year was spent in data collection. During the fourth and final project year the statistical analysis was performed, and preliminary drafts were written on all project activities.

Four types of populations were used in the research:

1. An initial sample of 158 mothers on AFDC known to be physically able to attend group meetings was selected for twelve experimental groups in Oakland County. Of these 158 mothers, 85 attended two or more meetings whereas 73 attended one or no meeting. The 85 AFDC mothers constituted the *experimental sample*. The time periods when data were collected for this sample will be described during discussion of each measure.

2. Comparisons between the 85 attendees and the 73 mothers who came to one or no meeting was made for social background data to account for selection bias. The group of 73 is called the "no treatment" group; no important differences between it and the experimental sample were found.[4]

3. A *control sample* of 27 mothers on AFDC from Washtenaw County who received no social group worker services during the study period was randomly selected. All of the clients were living in either the Ypsilanti or Willow Run school districts, areas similar to Oakland County. A six-month interval elapsed between the collections of before and after evaluation measures.

4. A second type of control sample was attempted in order to hold constant the content, focus, and goal orientation of the group. This

[4]Only one statistically different finding was noted. Twenty-one percent of the experimental grantees were mothers at the time of first marriage, while only 12 percent of the "no treatment" group reported this.

consisted of 25 parents who attended two groups in the Children's Division. Important differences between these parents and all of the others place great limitations on the meaningfulness of comparative findings, and therefore they will not be included in the discussion that follows.

POPULATION CHARACTERISTICS

The following description will focus on the experimental population; comparisons with the control group are presented when there is a statistically significant difference between the two groups.[5]

Thirty-four percent of the experimentals were black and 66 percent white. The picture reverses itself among the controls, with 63 percent black and 37 percent white. The median number of years experimentals were in school was 8.1. Sixty-five percent reported their normal occupation as unskilled service, and 80 percent reported no present employment. A larger proportion of controls were employed full time (15 percent) than experimentals (1 percent), because of the selection procedures in the experimental groups.

In the experimental sample 25 percent of the former heads of the house were employed in unskilled service, 34 percent in factory work, and 25 percent in skilled service. The occupational status of the family prior to AFDC was lower in the control population but not statistically significant. However, this difference is reflected in the AFDC grantees' reports of highest income ever earned: Six percent of experimentals reported less than $2,500; 31 percent $2,500–$5,000; 32 percent $5,000–$7,500; and 4 percent over $7,500. The controls reported significantly lower "highest incomes."

Median age for experimentals was 37.5 and for controls 40.2. Forty-two percent of the experimental group were thirty-five or under while only 17 percent of the control group were within this age category. The health of the controls was significantly poorer than experimentals (37 percent versus 14 percent reporting poor health). More controls than experimentals were never married (11 percent versus 3 percent), but fewer of them reported being married more than once (15 percent versus 25 percent). Seventy-nine percent of the experimentals were divorced.

The average number of children in experimental families was 4.5. About half of these mothers reported no illegitimate children in the family. Few of the children were removed from the home for delinquency or ne-

[5]T Test at .05 level of significance. The initial draft of this material was prepared by Yeheskel Hasenfeld, Lecturer, The University of Michigan School of Social Work, when he served as Research Assistant on the project one summer.

glect. The majority of mothers were Protestant; 22 percent more controls than experimentals belonged to fundamentalist sects.

A somewhat smaller percentage of controls than experimentals reported reason for grant as divorce or desertion (44 percent to 59 percent), but the reverse was true for the report of loss of employment (33 percent to 9 percent). Among experimental families the median number of children eligible for aid was 3.9; among control families, 3.6. The median number of years since the first AFDC grant was longer for controls than experimentals (5.8 to 4.2), and they had had contact with more social agencies (4.3 to 2.8).

In general the population of both groups is typical of AFDC grantees in urban Michigan. However, a difference of some importance between the experimental and control samples was racial composition. In addition, controls were older and had a longer history of deprivation than experimentals. Nonetheless, these differences proved to be unrelated to changes in clients' attitudes and behaviors as measured by our instruments.

FINDINGS

The group worker approaches the complexity of client problems on many levels simultaneously. As a reflection of the practice situation, a number of instruments were used to measure the effectiveness of the service in achieving change in its target population.

Worker Rating Form

The primary objective of the project was to achieve individual change in client attitudes, feelings, and behavior related to the purpose of the group. To test this objective a measure of movement that was individualized for each recipient's problems was needed. Also tapping the group leader's personal knowledge of progress within the group that might have been unmeasurable with any of the other testing instruments was desired. Therefore, group leaders were asked to rate each of the members of their groups on progress toward specific goals and on group participation.

The form required the worker to identify three major goals for each client drawn from her formulation of individual goals written earlier on the diagnostic statement. The worker then had to assess each member's progress toward each of these goals on a scale from 0 to 5. The member's participation was also ranked on a 0 to 5 scale by the group leader. These ratings were completed prior to access to any of the findings on the other evaluation instruments. A mean goal score was derived arithmetically for each group member. In addition, goals were categorized in terms of (1) handling children, (2) school problems, and (3) other. Although tests of coder consistency were performed with the data, awareness existed concerning the limitations of validity and reliability of this type of measure.

Differences in scores between the three categories were not significant. The mean progress score on "school problems" was lowest (2.04), while that on "other" was highest (2.88), and "handling children" was slightly lower (2.76). Goals falling into the "other" category tended to be specific and immediate, e.g. arrange a medical examination, so that achievement was likely to be rapid and easily noted by the worker. Mean goal scores were positively and significantly related to attendance ($p < .001$) and to anticipation scores ($p < .001$).[6] Participation scores were also related to attendance but not as strongly ($p < .05$).

Anxiety

In an exploratory study carried out during the second project year, it was found that one of the main difficulties of AFDC clients was a high level of generalized anxiety, which made it hard for these clients to find and mobilize energy to do something constructive about their problems (Glasser and Navarre, 1965a). For this reason the IPAT Anxiety Test was included to measure initial anxiety level as well as change in this factor over the demonstration period. Respondents were asked to complete this short form at their first group meeting. In administering this and other tests, a literacy problem was anticipated and so questions were read to the respondents while each had a form and a pencil before her; at that time, each was required to check the answers appropriate to her situation.[7] The test was given to each respondent a second time at the last meeting of the group.

The IPAT Anxiety Test had several advantages. It is brief and not stressful. The form has been extensively tested and found to be both reliable and clinically valid. Raw scores have been standardized by sex. The use of standardized scores for women was especially helpful since the sample was relatively small and only the female sex was represented.

The scale is designed to measure free-floating, manifest anxiety level, overt and covert, whether this be situationally determined or relatively independent of the immediate situation. In addition, five dimensions have been isolated by means of factor analysis: (1) defective integration, lack of self-sentiment; (2) ego weakness; (3) suspiciousness, paranoid-type insecurity; (4) guilt proneness; and (5) frustration tension. The last dimension was particularly important for this study since it includes situational fear.

---

[6] In all cases T Tests were used. Two-tailed tests were used for scores on the IPAT Anxiety and the Day at Home. One-tailed tests were used for all other measures.

[7] For a discussion of the problems in the administration and use of paper-and-pencil tests with lower-lower-class or welfare respondents, see Radin and Glasser (1965).

Scores for the final sten as well as each of the factors were computed for experimental and control groups, and differences in change scores between the two samples were analyzed. In addition, an analysis of the differences between before and after scores for each sample was performed.

As expected, scores on the before tests were high although within normal limits, with the mean of the experimental group somewhat higher than that of the control group. Upon comparing the difference (change scores) for the before and after tests, an interesting pattern emerged. On most dimensions, the anxiety of the experimental group was lowered. The changes in frustration tension and on the total sten just miss the .05 level of significance (.06 and .07). The change in the control group was more significant, but in the opposite direction, with significantly higher levels of frustration tension, overt anxiety, and total score. The difference in change scores between the two groups on total sten and frustration tension is highly significant ($p < .01$) because of this move in opposite directions.

These findings are somewhat difficult to interpret, especially since no known particularly stressful situation arose during the study period for the control group that might explain the higher score. General anxiety and frustration tension in particular may be cumulative for AFDC women, but this process was reversed through the group sessions in at least two ways: (1) The support provided by the worker and mothers for each other reduced anxiety, and (2) the positive changes that took place in their daily living experiences initiated by the problem-solving processes at the group sessions reduced anxiety. In addition, it seems likely that (3) high anxiety serves as both motivation to come to group meetings and motivation to change.

There is evidence for these three hypotheses. Before and after IPAT Anxiety scores were available for nine clients in the no treatment sample, who came to one or no meeting, and for a small number of clients in the second control sample (Children's Division) who also attended very few meetings. In both cases their anxiety scores increased on the total score and the frustration tension subscale. Additional evidence for this point of view will be presented subsequently.

Parental Attitudes

While the group sessions were focused on helping mothers help their children adjust better to school, one hoped-for by-product of this experience would be more positive general childrearing attitudes on the part of the mother. Thus a scale that measured both was wanted.

The Parental Attitude Research Instrument (PARI) developed by Schaefer and Bell has been used extensively for tapping general childrearing attitudes. However, studies clearly indicate that its findings lead to theoretically meaningful results primarily when the samples involve homogeneous upper-middle class families (Becker and Krug, 1965). Thus, by means of a variety of pretests it was adapted (Radin and Glasser, 1965).

By means of an item analysis three subscales were developed.

1. Fourteen items which are most class sensitive. Client movement was expected to be toward the middle class.
2. Ten items with which 45 percent or more of the disadvantaged mothers disagreed in pretests were added to test for acquiescence response set. The hope was that there would be no change on these items by the AFDC clients.
3. Eight items which showed the least class sensitivity were selected to provide a check on the first fourteen.

Finally, four other scales of five items each were added to test more directly the school adjustment attitudes of the mother: (1) Importance of School, (2) Fate Control, (3) Comfort with School, and (4) Mother's Responsibility.

This test was completed by respondents at the same time as the IPAT Anxiety was given, and in the same manner. Tests in differences between change scores for experimental and control groups, and between before and after scores were performed for each of the seven subscales.

The findings for the three subscales related to social class attitudes in childrearing practices provide little meaning for purposes of the evaluation of the group work method. Clients in the experimental groups significantly reduced the number of positive responses on all three subscales. Clients in the control sample significantly reduced their responses on the class-sensitive and least class-sensitive items. These scales did not provide the differentiated responses expected from their use in other studies.

Of the four school-related subscales, difference scores for Importance of School, Fate Control, and Comfort with School were not significant. The mothers of the experimental group changed toward taking greater responsibility for their children's achievement in school, although the change did not quite reach a .05 level of significance. Once again the control group changed in the opposite direction, leading to a significant difference ($p < .05$) between the change scores of the two groups.

Day at Home

Measures of change in behavioral interaction within the family are difficult to develop, and some of them, like observation schedules, are costly for samples of the size in this evaluation and have many technical problems. For this reason it was decided to adopt a scale that required mothers to report family behavior in the home subjectively.

The Day at Home Test was originally designed by P. G. Herbst (1952) for Australian families. Specific questions are asked concerning who performs tasks and who decides how tasks are to be performed in four family areas: (1) household maintenance, (2) child care, (3) economic activities, and (4) social activities. These questions were adapted to urban American lower-class culture. In addition, a fifth subscale was added that was concerned with school-related tasks. The simplicity of the tasks involved (for example, "Who turns on the radio?" or "Who decides when homework is to be done?") and the specificity of the questions provides partial solutions to several of the problems noted in the discussion of other instruments.

The ten subscales (five on task performance and five on decision) are scored by percentages of actions for each family member. The scoring techniques are rather complicated since they provide a map of family interaction, but they were adapted for IBM coding. The same types of statistical tests were carried out for each of these subscales and the total instrument as is discussed for the preceding measures. The procedure was administered individually to experimental respondents almost always prior to the first group session. Again, it was done orally by the group worker, usually in a home visit. The second phase was not repeated until approximately three months after the termination of the group. The purpose of the extra time period was to evaluate delayed reactions to the group experience. The second test was administered by the group worker, the regular agency worker, a former agency worker, or one of the members of the project staff.

Mothers, of course, bear the largest portion of task performance and decision within the family. Their total scores averaged two to three times the sum of all children's and others' in the household. In the experimental group, girls were second to the mother in both task performance and decision. In the control group, girls and boys were more equal on task performance though girls scored higher. Boys in the control group scored higher than girls in decision. The difference was found in school decisions and social decisions and may reflect a larger degree of autonomy in these areas accorded to teen-age boys. Seventy percent of the mothers in the control group had boys thirteen or older while only 32 percent of the mothers in the experimental group had boys in this age group. The proportion of mothers in each group with girls thirteen or over was less disparate.

A comparison of the before and after tests indicates that the mothers in the experimental group scored significantly higher on both task performance and decision, while the scores of both boys and girls were lower than in the initial measure. The scores of girls dropped significantly on childcare tasks, school-related tasks, and social decisions ($p < .05$). Boys' scores, already low, dropped significantly on childcare decisions ($p < .05$) and on social decisions ($p < .01$). The differences in mothers' scores were significantly higher in the same areas: childcare tasks, childcare decisions, school tasks, school decisions, and social decisions. There was only one significant change in the scores of the control group, but it should be noted that this change, as well as the majority of other changes, were consistently in the opposite direction from that found in the experimental group.

Participation in the group seems to have increased both the mother's task performance and her decision-making in the home. Since a large majority of the children (77 percent) were under the age of thirteen, this finding should be interpreted positively.

Pupil Behavior Inventory

Since behavioral change is an important measure of successful intervention, three measures of the behavior of the children whose mothers attended the rehabilitation groups were included in the study. The Pupil Behavior Inventory (PBI) was one of them.

The PBI was developed as a means of evaluating and classifying the behavior of pupils in the classroom situation. It was standardized for males on the junior and senior high school level and has proven valid and reliable for this group (Vinter et al., 1966). Essentially it measures the extent of the pupils' conformity to the behaviorial standards of the school. The ratings are made by the pupils' teachers on a standardized form of thirty-four short items. The teacher indicates the frequency of the indicated behavior for each item. Items are graded in such a way that the higher score always indicates the more conforming behavior or attitude, although the items are variously phrased in positive or negative fashion. Obviously the relationship between the pupil and the teacher is reflected in the ratings. However, it is also apparent that the relationship between the pupil and the teacher is a powerful factor in the student's success in school.

Previous research revealed five dimensions through factor analysis: (1) Classroom Conduct; (2) Academic Motivation; (3) Socioeconomic State; (4) Teacher Dependence; and (5) Personal Behavior. Statistical tests were performed for each of the factors and the total scale.

The tests were completed by teachers just prior to or during the week of the first group session. They were completed again by the same teachers at the end of the academic year. A number of problems developed in administration, however. Not all teachers of children whose mothers were in experimental or control groups could be located. Some teachers refused to fill out the form, and some filled it out incorrectly. In some cases there was a change in teachers. The sample of children is therefore very uneven. However, there is no reason to suspect a strong difference between the children included and those who were not, except for the group that dropped out of school.

Significant improvement between before and after scores was found only for the experimental group on the Classroom Conduct factor ($p < .01$). No significant changes were found in other factors, nor was there any significant change for the control group. It is interesting that the improvement was in that factor which is, perhaps, the most directly observable by the teacher.

School Grades and School Attendance

Information on grades and attendance was gathered from school records for the semester just preceding the beginning of the group meetings and at the end of the semester in which the meetings took place. Control sample school information was taken for two consecutive semesters during the year the experimental groups met. In addition to the sampling problems mentioned earlier, there were serious difficulties in comparing the records of the various school districts. Schools use different grading systems, different policies about giving grades in the early years of school, and different patterns in recording attendance. While efforts were made to compensate for these differences, results of this portion of the analysis have to be regarded as merely suggestive.

Grades in the various systems were coded numerically. The subjects were divided into academic (English, Arithmetic, etc.) and nonacademic (Shop, Domestic Arts, Physical Education, etc.), and a mean grade was computed for each category. Statistical differences within and between experimental and control groups were computed for the two categories. There were no significant changes in attendance or in grades for children of the experimental sample or those of the control sample.

Cross-Comparisons

When appropriate, cross-comparisons among the many variables were made for the following purposes: (1) to evaluate the effects of social background factors on client change and attendance patterns; (2) to discern consistency in patterns of change for particular clients among the many measures used; (3) to evaluate which types of changes may be most closely related to other types of changes in clients' attitudes and behavior.

It will be recalled that there were statistically significant differences between the experimental and control groups on a number of social background variables and that change scores on each of the instruments proved unrelated to these variables.

It was desirable to see the extent to which the IPAT Anxiety, the PARI, and the Day at Home tap similar or different problem areas. Little consistency was expected, because groups were planned and conducted to aid each member in reaching goals appropriate to her. While women shared many general problems, such as low income and children having difficulty in school, the details of these problems and the extent of difficulty experienced varied considerably among individuals. Only one correlation was found, this not easily explained, and may be accounted for by chance alone.[8] In addition, among the experimentals it was found that only eight of the fifty-six women who completed all sections of all three instruments changed in a negative direction on at least two of the three instruments; only seventeen had consistency on two of the three instruments in the directions predicted by our hypotheses. Among the control group the findings were similar: six of twenty-two had positive consistency and four had negative consistency.

This inconsistency probably is an indication that the worker was successful in individualizing the group somewhat differentially. Also this probably highlights the statistical significance of some of the change scores, for despite individualization the demonstration of change was achieved.

Returning to the hypothesis that anxiety may serve as a motivating factor in change, change scores were correlated on the PARI and Day at Home with initial (before) scores on the IPAT Anxiety. No significant correlations were found in the control group, or with the PARI in the experimental group. However, change scores on the Day at Home have high correlation with initial anxiety scores. Both Mother's Task Performance and Mother's Decision scores are positively correlated with IPAT Anxiety Total Sten ($p < .01$). The higher the initial level of anxiety, the greater the change score for the mother. Since anxiety is a bilateral factor, the question still remains: At what range does anxiety serve as motivation for change, and at what ranges does it prevent change because the client is either too comfortable or too anxious to take steps to work on her problems?

SOME CONCLUSIONS

The findings are impressive. Only a small number of all social work evaluation studies include control samples and use objective measures of change rather than worker rating forms or continuance in treatment alone as criteria for success (Briar, 1966). Studies of group work practice constitute a small minority of the total number of outcome or method studies in the profession (Schwartz, 1966). And as Scott Briar points out, the findings of the more, as well as the less, rigorous studies are indeterminate.

The typical number of sessions held for each group was only six. The clients' goals were particular, while necessity required the measuring instru-

[8]In the experimental group there is a negative correlation between attendance and Mother's Decisions on the Day at Home ($p < .05$).

ments to be more general. Despite these apparent limitations, the findings are not indeterminate. As expected, workers believed that their clients reached goals. But these beliefs were confirmed by many objective measures. Total sten and the subscale related to reality demands (frustration tension) showed statistically significant decreases on the IPAT Anxiety. The PARI revealed that mothers significantly increased their attitudes of responsibility toward their children's adjustment in school. The data from the Day at Home reinforce this conclusion. Mothers scored significantly higher in total task performance and decision-making in the home, and in the specific areas of childcare tasks, childcare decisions, school tasks, school decisions and social decisions. Finally, the PBI shows significant improvement in the Classroom Conduct factor.

Note that those measures most closely related to individual and group goals tended to reveal significant changes in the directions predicted. The practice implication seems clear: specificity and clarity of individual and group goals and the means to achieve them are requirements for effective group work practice.[9] Specificity is one reason why the establishment of the contract is so important in practice (see Croxton, Chapter 10, above; Frey and Meyer, 1965). In addition, this supports the emphasis of learning theory on specificity of methods and techniques, particularly when used in conjunction with other social science theory and practice wisdom (Thomas, 1967, 1968).

The demonstrable importance of clear and specific goals poses dilemmas for both practice and research, however. Most of the clients that social workers see have multiple, interrelated problems. How can priorities be set concerning which behaviors ought to be handled first, second, last or not at all? Or if the point of view is taken that one or more problems underlie many maladaptive behaviors, as was taken in this study (knowledge and ability to solve problems rationally), how can there be certainty that abstractions are correct—that is, directly related to the maladaptive behaviors? Further, researchers are often forced to use generalized measures, while the worker–client contract often specifies particular changes. Measured changes, even when positive—in the directions predicted—often do not tell which specific techniques were most or least effective, although they do give some suggestions and provide a framework for further study.

Why didn't more of the data show changes in the predicted directions? Already mentioned are the short-term nature of the groups and the problems of generalized measures and particular client goals. One must add that the PBI, and reports of school grades and attendance, were not directly related to the client population but to their children, that is, clients once re-

---

[9]For a summary of the social psychological theory on this issue, see Cartwright and Zander (1960) and Raven and Rietsema (1960).

moved from the target population. No direct intervention was attempted with the children of the AFDC mothers. For this reason the researchers were pleasantly surprised with the positive finding on the Classroom Conduct factor on the PBI.

The most positive findings were on the Day at Home, the test that asked the most specific behavioral questions of the population being treated. Data for the after measure were collected about three months after termination in order to evaluate delayed reactions to the group experience. There is considerable evidence that therapeutic intervention reverses a downward spiral of behavioral maladaptation and maladjustment (Frank, 1961; and Goldstein, 1962). Since data for all of the other measures were collected immediately after the rehabilitation process ended, it is possible that the full extent of the social group work experience was not tested. A follow-up study might have revealed more improvement.

FINIS

Evaluation studies are relatively new to social work practice. This report summarized the results of one of the few studies evaluating the outcome of a rehabilitation service using the social group work method. Its importance lies not only in its demonstration of the effectiveness of the intervention process but also in that it could be done using both objective measures of change and a control sample. We hope it will serve as a stimulant to others so that the quality of practice may be refined as a means toward helping more people more quickly.

REFERENCES

BALES, ROBERT F.
   1958   "Task roles and social roles in problem-solving groups." In Eleanor E. Maccoby, Theodore M. Newcomb, and Eugene L. Hartley (eds.), *Readings in Social Psychology*. Third edition. New York: Holt, Rinehart & Winston, pp. 437–47.
BALES, ROBERT F., AND FRED L. STRODTBECK
   1960   "Phases in group problem solving." In Dorwin Cartwright and Alvin Zander (eds.), *Group Dynamics: Research and Theory*, Evanston, Ill.: Row, Peterson, pp. 624–40.
BECKER, WESLEY C., AND RONALD S. KRUG
   1965   "The parent attitude research instrument: A research review," *Child Development*, 36, no. 2 (June).
BRIAR, SCOTT
   1966   "Family services." In Henry S. Mass (ed.), *Five Fields of Social Service*. New York: National Association of Social Workers, pp. 16–33.

CARTWRIGHT, DORWIN, AND ALVIN ZANDER
1960 "Individual motives and group goals: Introduction." In Dorwin Cartwright and Alvin Zander (eds.), *Group Dynamics: Research and Theory*. Second edition. Evanston, Ill.: Row, Peterson, pp. 345-69.

FRANK, JEROME D.
1961 *Persuasion and Healing: A Comparative Study of Psychotherapy*. Baltimore: The Johns Hopkins Press, pp. 207-14.

FREY, LOUISE, AND MARGUERITE MEYER
1965 "Exploration and working agreement in two social work methods." In Saul Bernstein (ed.), *Exploration in Group Work*. Boston: Boston University School of Social Work, pp. 1-11.

GLASSER, PAUL H., AND ELIZABETH L. NAVARRE
1965a "The problems of families in the AFDC program," *Children*, 12, no. 4 (July-August): 151-57.
1965b "Structural problems of the one-parent family," *Journal of Social Issues*, 21, no. 1 (January): 98-109.

GOLDSTEIN, ARNOLD P.
1962 *Therapist-Patient Expectancies in Psychotherapy*. New York: Macmillan.

HERBST, P. G.
1952 "The measurement of family relations," *Human Relations*, 5, no. 1 (January): 3-30.

RADIN, NORMA, AND PAUL H. GLASSER
1965 "The use of parental attitude questionnaires with culturally disadvantaged families," *Marriage and the Family* 27, no. 1 (August): 373-82.

RAVEN, BERTRAM H., AND JAN RIETSEMA
1960 "The effects of varied clarity of group goal and group path upon the individual and his relation to his group." In Cartwright and A. Zander (eds.), *Group Dynamics: Research and Theory*. Second edition. Evanston, Ill.: Row, Peterson, pp. 395-413.

SCHWARTZ, WILLIAM
1966 "Neighborhood centers." In Henry S. Maas (ed.), *Five Fields of Social Service*. New York: National Association of Social Workers, pp. 174-82.

THOMAS, EDWIN J.
1968 "Selected socio-behavioral techniques and principles: An approach to interpersonal helping," *Social Work* 13, no. 1 (January): 12-26.
1967 *The Socio-Behavioral Approach and Applications to Social Work*. New York: Council on Social Work Education.

VINTER, R. D.; ROSEMARY SARRI; D. VORWALLER; AND WALTER SCHAEFER
1966 *Pupil Behavior Inventory: A Manual for Administration and Scoring*. Ann Arbor, Mich.: Campus Publishers.

24

Beyond Group Work: Organizational Determinants of Malperformance in Secondary Schools

Rosemary C. Sarri and Robert D. Vinter

THE PUBLIC SCHOOL TODAY is required to educate every youth without regard to ability, interest, or prior preparation. There is general agreement that the school's primary goal is to prepare individuals to meet the knowledge and skill requirements for adult occupational roles. The public school is also expected to further its pupils' character development and preparation for responsible citizenship; and it is increasingly held responsible for aiding those who have been educationally disadvantaged by cultural, family, or community conditions. The emphasis on enhancing educational opportunities for all pupils has brought into sharp focus some familiar problems within elementary and secondary schools: underachievement and academic failure among those believed to be intellectually capable; pupil misconduct that disrupts classroom procedures and school discipline; and the tendency of youths to drop out before high school graduation.

A variety of approaches are being developed and tested to resolve these problems. A research and demonstration project, employing the use of group service methods to reduce malperforming behavior among junior and senior high school pupils, is reported here. The initial objectives of the project were to modify pupil behavior that curtailed effective learning and/or disrupted classroom procedures; to strengthen pupils' commitments to educational objectives and school completion; and to change or to propose

This chapter is a revised version of an article, "Group Work for the Control of Behavior Problems in Secondary Schools," published in *Innovation in Mass Education*, David Street (ed.) (New York: John Wiley & Sons, 1969), pp. 91–110. Principal support for the project reported here was provided by a curriculum development grant from the Office of Juvenile Delinquency and Youth Development, U.S. Department of Health, Education, and Welfare, in cooperation with the President's Committee on Juvenile Delinquency and Youth Development, and by a research grant from the National Institute of Mental Health, U.S. Public Health Service. The authors gratefully acknowledge the contributions in this project of their faculty colleagues, Maeda Galinsky, Frank Maple, and Walter Schaefer.

modifications in school practices that hampered effective education for malperforming pupils. As the project progressed over a three-year period, it became apparent that school organization, curriculum design, and staff behavior were even more important for pupil malperformance than initially expected. Such discoveries led to some modifications in the intervention approach.

THE PROBLEM IN PERSPECTIVE

Within limits, schools are seeking to increase pupils' motivation to achieve adademically, to ameliorate personal and social stresses that circumscribe student learning, and to cope with behavior that jeopardizes classroom processes. In order to perform its new roles, the school must develop special procedures for pupils who are inadequately prepared, insufficiently motivated, or unresponsive to classroom behavior standards. Some efforts center on changing curriculum or teaching procedures or introducing special services for pupils with particular problems, needs, or disabilities. But many defects still exist within the educational system for which adequate solutions have not been devised. As a consequence some pupils, particularly lower-class youth, are especially handicapped by prevailing educational conditions and practices. Because of its strategic role in the lives of all children, the school plays a less than optimal part in helping some children move into legitimate adult roles.

Increased demands upon many public school systems have produced problems, even crises, particularly in large cities: poor physical plants, pressures toward standardization, overcrowding, racial segregation, the lack of special or compensatory education for those most in need, and stable or decreasing economic resources in a period of increasing demand.[1] Students and parents are exerting pressures on schools to provide improved educational opportunities and to allow participation in decision-making about curriculum, personnel, and practices. Demonstrations, boycotts, and other forms of protest that have existed for several years at the college level, have increased in junior and senior high schools. Responses to such protests by boards of education and school personnel have often been piecemeal and inadequate.

If the new demands are to be met, even at a minimal level, the changes required are substantial. In view of past stalemates and the inadequacy of

---

[1] Elder (1966) presents data from a study of a "continuation school" on the West Coast that is particularly relevant for this demonstration effort. He points to the problem of links between the school's curriculum and meaningful adult vocational roles for its graduates and also to the importance of the school's public reputation.

change efforts, innovation strategies must attend to interrelated parts of the system that form the school and must include plans for phasing each specific change into the ongoing operations of the school. To achieve lasting, successful change, the strategy of "phasing in" may be as important as the substantive content of specific changes.

CONCEPTIONS OF MALPERFORMANCE

Standards for academic achievement and criteria of desirable conduct vary among schools and, to some extent, even within the same school. Types of malperformance such as underachievement, poor classroom conduct, and failure to adjust are not defined identically; and the pupil personality, performance, or ability at issue in one situation is not the same as that in another.

Second, curriculum, resources, teacher competency, student body, and organization vary widely among schools. Such variations create great differences in learning environments, in opportunities for achievement or adjustment, and in conditions that shape the meaning of the school experience.

Third, schools differ significantly in their procedures for identifying and coping with pupil malperformance. In one school students who manifest difficulty may become the targets for a full complement of remedial services. In another pupils who exhibit similar behavior may encounter relative indifference or find that, when attention is given, the result is a loss of status or privileges, perhaps leading eventually to exclusion from classes and even suspension from school.

The theoretical framework for the study of deviant behavior used here is similar to that of Cohen (1966), Lemert (1967), Freidson (1966), and Erikson (1964). *Malperformance* refers to behavior that violates valued norms in the school and/or community to the degree that if it persists, it will lead to assignment to a status having negative consequences for the person whose behavior is so defined. As Erikson suggests, the consequences of such labeling may have both a long- and a short-run nature.

Deviance is not a property inherent in certain forms of behavior but a property conferred upon these forms by the audiences that directly witness them. The critical variable in the study of deviants, then, is the audience rather than the individual actor, since the audience eventually determines whether or not any episode of behavior or any class of episodes is labeled deviant (Erikson, 1964). Given this concept of deviance, pupil malperformance may be viewed as social or interactional, in that it results from adverse interactions between characteristics of a particular student and conditions within a particular school.

Any type of malperformance must not be considered a unitary phenomenon or one inhering primarily in the attributes of the pupils, but rather as a result of the interaction between the school and the pupil. Pupil difficulties are social since they are manifested through interaction with other pupils, teachers, and the academic tasks of the curriculum. Their problems assume relevance only as they are assessed in terms of the social objectives and values of school personnel. "Deviant" behaviors originate in and are shaped by the pupils' social relations and their experiences in the school and elsewhere. Once the pupil has been identified as a deviant, this social recognition may affect the pupil's identity and self-image in a variety of situations. It may induce the pupil to seek compensatory approval through informal associations that support further deviancy. Finally, such identification has important implications for the manner in which the pupil is subsequently dealt with by the school, for the way in which the pupil's career is shaped, and ultimately for the pupil's life changes (Cicourel and Kitsuse, 1963).

Both the process by which malperformance is identified and the ways in which malperforming pupils are managed within the school are concerns in this chapter.

THE DESIGN FOR RESEARCH
AND DEMONSTRATION

Preliminary investigations revealed that the reduction of malperformance is complex and that effective strategies for intervention would require close observation of many facets of organizational behavior. Four main areas for research were delineated. The first was pupil characteristics, behaviors, and perspectives, assessed with particular reference to how these related to both educational achievement and malperformance. Second, in order to understand school organization and behavior, curriculum design, the behavior and perspectives of teachers and other staff members, and organizational mechanisms for defining and coping with malperformance and for processing pupils into different curricular tracks were studied. Third, study of the performance patterns of pupils over the three-year high school career provided opportunities to examine certain interactions between pupil characteristics and school practices. Last, the processes and outcomes of group service methods were evaluated.

Seven schools in five different communities were included in the major phases of the project. Contrasting communities were selected: a rural community with a kindergarten through high school program housed on a single campus; a middle-class college town; a small industrial community; a residential suburb of a large metropolitan area; and an industrial community adjacent to a metropolitan area. Some of the school systems had initiated contact with The University of Michigan School of Social Work because of concerns about behavioral misconduct and underachievement.

Information from the U.S. Census and from local school censuses was used to ensure variation in school district and community characteristics. Although three elementary schools were included in parts of the study, greater attention was directed toward the junior and senior high schools. The intervention strategy was designed primarily for male pupils. Only two of the experimental groups were composed of girls; consequently, generalizations for this population are very tentative.

Before a school was selected for inclusion, it was necessary that school officials agree to maintain the experimental service program, as it was designed, for a minimum of one academic year. In no case was this requirement difficult to meet. Arrangements were made for each school to employ one or more social workers to provide the group service as a part of its social work or special education program. The service program was conducted in each of the schools for more than two years. Since the termination of the project four of the five school systems have continued and expanded the effort.

In line with the interest in organizational change, it was believed essential that each school contribute to the development and support of the new program from the beginning. Far too often, innovations developed in demonstration projects are not adopted after a project ends, partly because special external resources are used to support the demonstration effort; little attention, if any, is given to assisting the organization to provide for the financial and other support of the endeavor.

Pupil Characteristics and Behavior

In all schools pupils were being identified and referred to receive special attention for underachievement and disruptive behavior; the introduction of group services apparently did not alter the schools' criteria for referral. Detailed information, collected about each pupil referred, included grades, intelligence and performance test scores, family background, and school behavior reports. Thus it was possible to gain some understanding of the different kinds of pupils and behaviors "produced" by each school's distinctive organization and patterns. Later an attempt was made to systematize the selection of pupils who received group service by using standardized referral procedures for teachers, examination of school records, and observation of pupil behavior within the school setting by the research staff. Many more pupils were referred than could be served in the groups. Pupils were screened out whom the research staff judged to be retarded, in need of intensive psychological or psychiatric treatment, or so handicapped that they could not participate in activities with their peers. Systematic screening procedures also helped in identifying problematic conditions that were similar for many students. Although variations existed within and among the schools with respect to the types of students referred for services, certain similarities emerged. Most students fell within the "average" range of intellectual ability, but nearly all were "underachievers" in relation to their capabilities. Most also manifested serious behavior problems, including disruptive conduct in the classroom or in other school areas; poor interpersonal relations with adults and peers; violation of school conduct norms, including frequent truancy and suspension; or withdrawn and isolative behaviors.

Control groups were established in each school system. Referred pupils were matched in pairs; one of each pair was then randomly assigned to a service group, and the other became a control who received whatever attention was customary within each school *except* the group service. A second type of control group was selected randomly from the total population, excluding the referred malperformers, in appropriate grade levels. Matching procedures were slightly modified in one school because of service requirements during one year of the study. In the latter situation experimental and control groups were "matched" after selection, because two natural peer groups were referred; it was decided to provide service to these groups and then to select their controls.

The design of the study called for the use of a series of before-and-after measures in addition to comparisons between experimental groups and both matched and random control groups. These measures permitted the identification of outcomes that could be attributed directly to group work service rather than to pupil maturation or factors of chance. At the same time the design allowed attitudinal and behavioral comparisons at a single point in time between malperforming pupils and a sample of the rest of the school population. During the second year of the project data were collected on approximately 400 pupils in the service, matched control, and random groups, all of whom were closely observed in the five school systems. Data were obtained on a slightly smaller number who were observed in the first year of the project. The demonstration phase took place between 1962 and 1965, with most of the data collection completed by 1964.

Three principal sets of before-and-after measures were used to evaluate change. First, an instrument was developed to inventory teachers' assessments of pupil behavior in five areas: classroom conduct, academic motivation and performance, socioemotional state, teacher dependence, and personal behavior (Vinter et al., 1966). A second set of measures was composed of objective indices of school performance: grades, attendance records, and performance scores normally collected by the schools. The third set was derived from pupils' self-reports of behavior and attitudes obtained in interviews and written questionnaires. Dimensions studied included educational goals and expectations; academic and social skills; attitudes toward teachers, peers, and parents; and reports of school experiences. All of these data were collected on all pupils in the experimental, matched control, and random control groups at the beginning and the termination of service. Matched pairs were used to develop change score differences for the evaluation.

The narrative records prepared by group workers were also used to evaluate change and to see what practitioner behaviors were associated with pupil change. These records were analyzed with reference to targets of change, means of influence, and modes of interaction.

The before-and-after measures of pupil change served as the primary means for evaluating the modifications effected by group services. Means for assessing the processes of change included systematic review of the practitioners' service records, independent interviewing of treatment groups in special group sessions, and direct consultation with service personnel. Practitioners were requested to obtain and record specific information about pupils during the period of treatment. With such information it was possible to assess elements of group processes and to identify some of the key factors in change. This particular phase of the design was important to gain somewhat greater knowledge about processes of change. Far too often evaluative studies of treatment programs have measured only outcomes, with processes of change remaining unknown or unidentified.

Some members of the research staff served as consultants to school personnel actually working with the groups. Planning and problem-solving conferences were held every six weeks with the practitioners to explore service procedures and examine preliminary study findings. Practitioners also undertook study and validation of project materials such as the practitioners' manual.

School Organization and Practices

This area of study comprised school conditions and practices, including school size, staffing, and resources; school goals; curriculum design; grading criteria; means of identifying, labeling, and handling misconduct and malperformance; classroom practices; and teachers' orientations and perspectives. These dimensions were assessed through several procedures; directly observing classroom and other activities in the school; reviewing documentary and file materials; interviewing school administrators, teachers, and special service personnel; and administering questionnaires to all professional personnel in the sample schools. In addition, extended observations were made of the daily cycle of school activities; of board, faculty, and committee meetings; and of informal activities among pupils and teachers.

Data feedback sessions were held periodically with school administrators during the latter phase of the study. These sessions provided additional information about school practices and, in particular, about executive behavior. Continued observation of the several schools permitted some knowledge of planned organizational changes as attempts were made to implement some of the recommendations from the study. Unfortunately, the project ended before many of these changes were developed to the point where they could be assessed adequately.

Pupil Careers

Study of pupil careers over a three-year period was completed in two of the senior high schools. Interest here was in identifying factors associated with curriculum placement, performance patterns including grades and test scores, and length of career. Grading practices were systematically analyzed. Other reward systems were also examined, although less systematically.

To accomplish the study of career patterns, all pupils were identified who entered the tenth grade in the fall of 1961 in the two schools. They were followed through the spring of 1964, when the majority completed the twelfth grade. Data abstracted from official files included grades, semester of and reason for leaving for those who did not continue, curriculum and changes in curriculum for each pupil, intelligence and performance test scores, sex, race, father's occupation, and extracurricular participation.

Group Services

In accordance with the initial intervention strategy, group services for malperforming pupils were provided in seven of the sample schools. Prospective group members were interviewed by the school social workers to review school difficulties, to explain why each had been selected for service and what would happen in the group, and to establish an initial "contract" for working together on specific problems. Workers frequently encountered resistance and skepticism in these interviews. Pupils often had had negative experiences in the school and frequently were doubtful that the school was really interested in helping them or in altering conditions that affected them adversely. The example of Bob White, a fifteen-year-old entering the tenth grade, is illustrative of initial contacts. The social worker reported:

> Bob was referred by his ninth-grade counselor for underachievement, rule breaking, and disruptive classroom behavior. He was on probation in the juve-

nile court for auto theft and stealing from a bowling alley. The counselor described him as one who elicited both adult and peer rejection. In the initial interview Bob expressed a desire to work on some of his problems. He was negative about his probation experience but did reveal some understanding about his situation and school achievement. He agreed to give the group experience a try but wasn't optimistic about his future.

Groups typically were composed of five to eight members, identical in sex and grade level. Sessions were held one or more times a week during school hours and in the school buildings. Additional after-school sessions were arranged according to workers' plans and group members' requests. The group sessions were the primary means of attempting changes, although individual services were provided, as necessary and whenever possible, by the same worker who conducted the group sessions.

Within the groups explicit recognition was given publicly to each pupil's difficulties and to the need for mutual assistance in resolving them. Emphasis was placed on mobilizing pupils' motivations for change and directing them toward improved academic achievement and appropriate school conduct. Workers deliberately sought to increase members' attraction to the group and to school, and they sought to help the students develop new skills and alternatives for coping more effectively with stressful school situations. One of the special advantages of working with such pupils in groups was assumed to be that powerful social forces can develop to support the desired changes rather than to encourage continued, covert deviance.

The researchers noted, as have many others, that pupils identified as underachieving and disruptive tended to seek each other out and to form associations that reinforced deviancy. A boy in one of the groups explained this tendency in these words:

> It depends on who you hang around with. Some guys' idea of fun is to see who gets the lowest grades, skipping school and classes, smoking in the bathroom. I started hanging around with guys like that. . . . The only reason me or anyone else did things like skip school was to make an impression on your friends. They'd think you're chicken otherwise. I feel if you can't get good grades, then brag about getting away with it.

The sessions clearly demonstrated the importance of identifying certain primary targets of change, i.e., specific academic skills and abilities; skills of social interaction with teacher and peers; and pupils' values, goals, and motivations. The means and opportunities for successful performance were insufficiently or inaccurately perceived by malperformers; some of their deficiency in academic skills could be improved within the group (e.g. study habits, efficient use of time, or test preparation), and their readiness for successful interaction with teachers and other school personnel could be improved. Social skills particularly were amenable to influence in the group sessions. Pupils' values, goals, and motivations often contradicted those supported by the school and frequently were the outcome of prior failures that resulted in pessimism and negativism toward school.

The workers often observed that legitimate opportunities for malperforming students were more limited than for other students. In some cases, workers intervened on behalf of the pupils with other school personnel. One tenth-grader's views were typical of malperformers' perceptions of their situation:

> If Mr. Owen [the principal] had believed I was not the one who provoked fights, he would not have kicked me out for three days. Maybe kids like me won't get too far because of our actions in school, and we don't get good grades. He didn't seem interested in helping—kicks kids out real easy. Seems like he's looking for some of us kids to be doing something.
>
> Should lower standards about getting on teams—lots of times you can't get high enough grades even if you try hard. Am not doing as good as I wanted to regarding grades—wanted to get into wrestling, but in the first marking period grades dropped, came up second period but not high enough and I had been trying real hard. I don't think it's fair—if you try hard enough should be able to get a good enough grade to do what you want to do. Don't know why got those grades—studied harder for tests but still dropped down. . . .
>
> [Regarding same chances as other kids of getting good grades:] No, long ago I might have. At Carr School I don't think they taught kids half as much as other schools did because when us Carr kids got to junior high other kids were twice as smart as us—due to bad teaching at Carr.

Activities of the groups were largely determined by the goals set by workers and members together. Problem-focused discussion predominated, but all groups engaged in other activities as well. Groups with younger members tended to engage in discussion less frequently. In teaching new academic and social skills, the workers employed simulation techniques and other procedures designed to improve study habits and test preparation and to increase their ability for requesting assistance from teachers and classmates, and for completing assignments. Pupils were coached or coached each other in test taking, report writing, and the like. The workers recognized that each of these acts was a complex behavior that subsumed several specific skills. When possible, attempts were made to define these skills so that generalizations could be made to other situations in and out of school.

Workers also became aware that the pupils' opinions about school materials and procedures had to be considered. Pupils often commented that required textbooks were dull and failed to "turn them on." A twelve-year-old boy asked, "Who wants to read *Elmer the Worm*—about a worm who talks to a boy?'' To encourage malperformers to join the mainstream of school life and associate with others, workers attempted to encourage and facilitate their participation in extracurricular activities.

The social workers deliberately attempted to create cohesive and viable groups but explicitly pointed out to the members that these groups were instruments to individual change. In a few cases, where the groups were most cohesive, problems were aggravated and few change goals were achieved. An effective solution, however, usually was changing the memberships of the groups.

The workers were able to guide the groups to create desirable change conditions. Similar demonstration projects have reported that workers relied almost exclusively on the peer group and deemphasized their own roles (McCorkle, 1958). That did not work successfully in this project. Observations and evaluations indicate that the workers tended to be more effective when they carefully structured the program of the group, using a variety of direct and indirect means of influence. The adult exemplified the roles he or she wished to have the members adopt even though the adult indicated acceptance of the problematic situations of the pupils. It appeared that a climate was created in which members felt free to discuss and explore problems without fear of ridicule or rejection. They then were encouraged to try out new patterns of behavior in the group before displaying them outside.

Although most pupils seemed to perceive the groups as rewarding and satisfying, they were continuously aware of the serious purposes of this experience and its relevance to school performance. This was accomplished partly by encouraging pupils to report incidents and difficulties that they were currently experiencing in the school—and for most students there was no lack of such reports. The worker then involved the group jointly in exploring the situation, in considering cause-and-effect sequences, and in discovering more appropriate responses that pupils might have made. Because all pupils had witnessed or participated in similar incidents, they were very effective in curbing each other's tendencies toward denial or projection and in proposing alternative ways for coping with situations.

Despite the positive findings about the intervention strategy, critical limitations were also exposed. The school social workers soon discovered that many problems could not be resolved successfully by changing the pupil's behavior or attributes. School conditions hampered the attainment of desired change goals, such as improved grades, increased participation in extracurricular activities, and reduced dropping out. Malperforming pupils could not be helped when they were isolated from school events. The practitioners needed to have knowledge of curriculum, of teachers and their practices, of classroom climates, and of general school conditions in order to understand the particular circumstances that contributed to each pupil's problems. In addition to providing direct services to group and individuals, the school social workers had to function as mediators and as consultants to teachers and other school personnel about the experiences and difficulties of particular pupils and of the malperformers in general. They also served as lobbyists in and out of school on behalf of malperformers, and they negotiated with families and agencies in the community.[2]

STUDY FINDINGS

Effects of the Demonstration Project

The results of the intervention were partially disappointing. Findings from the effort were evaluated at the end of each of the two years that it ran. The results after the first year indicated that there were no significant changes for either the experimental or control groups in grades received, absences, truancies, suspensions, or leaving school. Similarly, minimal change was observed among the random groups selected from the total population. One change-measuring instrument, the Pupil Behavior Inventory, showed some positive results for the experimental group. This instrument, described later, was designed to obtain teachers' ratings of pupil behaviors before and after the service program.

To understand what happened, it became apparent that more systematic and detailed information was needed about school practices and conditions. Procedures were then developed to study pupil career patterns, curricular design, teachers' perceptions and behaviors, and mechanisms for identifying and coping with various forms of deviancy in the school. The findings of these studies and how they were used to modify the strategy for reducing pupil malperformance will now be discussed.

Characteristics, Perspectives, and Behavior of Malperformers and Randoms

Intensive study of the pupils referred in each school provided new insights. Data in this section are presented for the sample of malperformers who were identified in their schools as pupils who needed additional atten-

---

[2]A set of principles for school practitioners who wish to employ this method of intervention was prepared in conjunction with the project by Sarri, Vinter, and Goodman (1965). Most of the social workers affiliated with the demonstration project engaged in each of these activities at one time or another, but among the different schools variations in emphasis were apparent. Apart from the direct work with service groups, no attempt was made by the project staff to achieve uniformity in role patterns among the school social workers.

TABLE 24-1.   Achievement, IQ, and Attendance Records of Malperformers and Randoms

Grade point average, first semester, of tenth grade

Malperformers	1.84
Randoms	2.63

Mean IQ

Malperformers	107
Randoms	107

Average number of single-period absences for year

	Excused	*Unexcused*	*Total*
Malperformers	3.9	2.4	6.3
Randoms	1.5	0.9	2.4

Average number of whole-day absences for year

Malperformers	11.5	1.3	12.8
Randoms	4.9	0.2	5.1

tion. These data are compared with similar findings for the random sample of pupils (referred to hereinafter as "randoms") selected from the total population (excluding malperformers) of each school.

Table 24-1 shows the marked differences in overall grade point average and in numbers of absences between the two groups. No difference in mean IQ test score was noted, however. Below-average academic performance therefore must stem from factors other than deficiency in intellectual ability. The important findings can be summarized in five generalizations.

1. *Malperformers placed as great an importance as randoms on achievement and success in school, as well as on long-term goals relating to employment and success in future life.* Frequently school personnel assert that malperformers are not committed to educational goals and are not interested in school. Contrary to these beliefs, the data in Table 24-2 indicate that malperformers continue to maintain a basic commitment to succeeding

TABLE 24-2.   Pupil's Attitudes Toward Educational Goals and Community Norms

PERCENTAGE SAYING ITEM IS IMPORTANT:	MALPERFORMERS	RANDOMS
Passing courses	76%	89%
Getting the most from school	57	68
Getting along with teachers	40	47
Going to college	67	70
Having a well-paying job when you are an adult	76	70
Having a steady job when you are an adult	92	94

TABLE 24-3. Reported Attitudes of Parents Toward School

Percentage Reporting That:	Malperformers	Randoms	Level of Significance
Parents are against dropping out[a]	90%	98%	N.S.
School performance is below parents' expectations[b]	84	28	< .001

[a]"What do parents think about kids dropping out of school?"
[b]"How are you doing in your school work as compared with what your parents expect?"

in school and that they value educational goals even when experiencing personal failure. Because none of the differences between malperformers and randoms was statistically significant at the .02 level, it can be inferred that the two groups are essentially alike in these basic attitudes.

Although data were not obtained directly from parents about their attitudes and values, boys were asked what their parents thought about school and their school performance. Parents of both groups were reported as being strongly opposed to their sons' dropping out of school (Table 24-3). Furthermore, malperformers reported much more often that their parents viewed their school performance as falling below parental expectations. Thus the academic problems experienced by these pupils were not the simple outcome of a lack of interest in school, intellectual ability, or parental concern.

2. *Malperformers engaged in a number of unacceptable activities more often than randoms. These were truancy, tardiness, leaving class, fighting, and being sent to the office.* Although malperformers were interested in and committed to educational goals, they reported that they did not put the same effort into school work as did the randoms. The findings in Table 24-4 reveal significant differences between malperformers and randoms re-

TABLE 24-4. Pupils' Behaviors in School[a]

Percentage Reporting:	Malperformers	Randoms	Level of Significance
Staying home when you could have come to school	57%	28%	< .02
Being late for class	80	54	< .01
Leaving class without a good reason	38	13	< .01
Getting into a fight	35	9	< .01
Being sent to the office	37	11	< .01

[a]"In the past two months how many times have you done each of the following things?" Figures are percentages of each group responding "one or more times."

garding the violation of school norms. The former reported that they frequently engaged in a number of unacceptable activities, such as truancy, tardiness, fighting, and skipping school, and they often created trouble for teachers in their classrooms. Over a period of time, they increasingly failed to conform to school standards of conduct.[3]

Whatever the psychological mechanisms involved, malperformers seemed to devalue many school norms and standards of conduct. This pattern may represent the gradual development of a general negative orientation toward the school as a crucial source of frustration and disenchantment. Of course, deviant behavior itself decreases the likelihood of achieving a high level because of negative teacher reactions and falling farther behind in class work as suspensions and other sanctions are imposed. In turn, low achievers may "try less hard" and thus get into further trouble. They also are likely to turn toward other boys in similar difficulty as referents in support of antischool attitudes and behavior.

3. *Marked differences between malperformers and randoms were noted in "acquired capabilities" such as study habits, classroom conduct, and perceptions of relationships with teachers.*

Malperformers more frequently stated that they did not try as hard, lacked study skills, failed to complete assignments, and found it difficult to ask teachers for help. Table 24–5 reveals consistent and large differences between the two groups of pupils in reports of their own behavior. Perceptions of teachers as unfriendly and not helpful seemed to be the result of repeated failure or continued difficulty in handling relationships with teachers. The findings in Table 24–6 illustrate malperformers' reports of their views of teachers. Malperformers also were likely to report lower degrees of self-confidence and self-control in their transactions with teachers. Often they responded impulsively and aggressively to requests and to difficult situations.

4. *Malperformers were often isolated from the mainstream of life in the school, but they were not isolated from peers.* Contrary to some observations, the findings indicate that malperformers were integrated into cohesive peer groups that supported behavior and attitudes largely inconsistent with conventional and acceptable norms. These peer groups exhibited much antisocial behavior in and out of school and provided encouragement for others to do likewise.

The findings in Table 24–7 reveal that malperformers often reported having as many friends as other pupils, but that they spent somewhat more time with these friends. They also generally reported that their friends were

---

[3]The candor and truthfulness of the malperformers' self-reports, as measured in these and other areas and validated by school records, lent credence to their statements about their own and parental attitudes.

TABLE 24-5. Pupils' Reports of Study and Classroom Habits

PERCENTAGE REPORTING THAT:	MALPERFORMERS	RANDOMS	LEVEL OF SIGNIFICANCE
I try as hard as most other students in my class to do well in school work.	40%	77%	$< .001$
I can't seem to read as well as most other kids in my class.	34	42	N.S.
I don't seem to get very much done when I study.	56	28	$< .01$
I find it hard to keep my mind on school work.	78	57	$< .05$
I can't seem to remember much of what I have studied.	60	30	$< .01$
It's hard for me to sit still for very long in classes.	55	34	$< .05$
I fail to complete homework assignments once a week or more.	72	49	$< .01$
When schoolwork is hard, I ask teachers for help.	31	58	$< .01$
I ask friends for help when school is hard.	27	55	$< .01$
The way I do in school isn't much to be proud of.	59	32	< 0.1
I try as hard as most other students to do well in my schoolwork.	40	76	$< .01$

experiencing difficulties similar to their own and that they were not part of the dominant social system. These friendships were highly valued, perhaps for compensatory reasons. In interviews with both groups of pupils, each group indicated little contact with the other; randoms, in fact, reported that they deliberately avoided associating with malperformers. The latter reported similar behavior, and it is not surprising that pupils experiencing similar difficulties and situations turn to each other and collectively adopt standards of conduct. The lack of support for positive achievement in school is demonstrated by the fact that malperformers asked their friends for help with school work less often than did randoms. These findings are similar to those of Polk and Richmond in a study of Oregon pupils. They suggest that students who fail are progressively shunned by achieving students, teachers, and the "system as a whole" (Polk and Richmond, 1966).

TABLE 24-6.   Pupils' Perception of Teachers

PERCENTAGE AGREEING THAT:	MALPERFORMERS	RANDOMS	LEVEL OF SIGNIFICANCE
Most of the teachers at this school are friendly.	69%	91%	<.01
The teachers here don't deserve the respect they demand.	53	23	<.01
I have a fair or poor reputation regarding schoolwork.[a]	77	37	<.01
I have a fair or poor reputation regarding behavior.	37	19	<.05

[a]"What kind of reputation do you have among teachers as far as your schoolwork (or behavior) is concerned?"

5. *Malperformers perceived that they had far worse reputations than randoms and that, at least in part, as a consequence of their school experience, they had few chances for success in school or adulthood.* Interviews with pupils, social workers, and counselors all pointed to the conclusion that malperformers were very pessimistic about the future as a consequence of their continued failure and lack of any positive reinforcement from the school. Table 24-8 clearly indicates their pessimism about success in school. When these findings are compared with those in Table 24-2, it is possible to see marked differences between goals and the perceived reality of their situations. It is not surprising, therefore, that malperformers turn away from desirable goals which they believe they have little likelihood of ever achieving and accept alternative standards that may violate school or community norms. They are caught in a spiraling situation of diminishing rewards and

TABLE 24-7.   Pupils' Perceptions of Peers

PERCENTAGE REPORTING THAT:	MALPER-FORMERS	RANDOMS	LEVEL OF SIGNIFICANCE
I have five or more friends.	66%	73%	N.S.
Friends hang around together a lot.	57	19	<.001
Friends take part in a lot of school activities.	29	55	<.01
Friends study a lot.	29	47	<.02
Friends are concerned about grades.	69	87	<.05
Friends look for a good time.	67	34	<.01
Friends have a reputation with teachers as good students.	37	60	<.05
Friends are concerned about behaving as teachers think they should.	20	51	<.01

TABLE 24–8.   Pupils' Attitudes Toward Future

PERCENTAGE OF PUPILS WHO:	MALPERFORMERS	RANDOMS	LEVEL OF SIGNIFICANCE
Expect to pass courses	24%	62%	< .001
Expect to finish high school	51	70	< .05
Expect friends to finish high school	42	64	< .05
Expect to have a good record when leaving school	16	53	< .001
Expect to have a steady job as an adult	28	60	< .01

increasing frustration and negative reactions. A tenth-grade student expressed his pessimism in these terms:

> I wanted a job out of school, but I wanted to get a good job. I dropped out in the fall. . . . I just didn't care. I wasn't getting good grades in the ninth grade. I figured out since I wasn't getting good grades then, it wouldn't change so I just didn't care.

It is reasonable, therefore, that these pupils will view the classroom as confining and classroom tasks as uninteresting. Thus any effort for successful change must be directed not only toward developing the necessary capabilities in the pupils but also toward providing sufficient positive rewards and opportunities in the system. As the findings became known to the practitioners, the group service project was increasingly focused toward the latter ends. The workers emphasized the need to narrow the gap between measured capability and performance; to stress the persistence of pupils' commitments to conventional values, including achievement and success; and to honor the students' desire to reduce the adverse consequences of being regarded and handled as deviants. Experiences within the group sessions offered some opportunity for success and for developing additional skills for classroom accomplishment. However, the crucial condition was the extent to which these pupils could find new opportunities for positive achievement and could be rewarded for improved performance in the classrooms. In this regard teachers apparently noted changes in pupils' behavior, but rewards such as grades showed little if any change.

Teachers' Perspectives and Ratings of Pupil Behavior

Information obtained from teachers indicated that at least two foci were needed for the group work services. Unfortunately, much of this information was not obtained until the demonstration effort was under way and therefore could not be used fully. Teachers regarded adequate pupil motivation as crucial to success. Three-fifths or more of the teachers in the schools reported that the single most important source of difficulty for most or all malperformers was their lack of motivation and interest in school. Motivation was thought to be an attribute that the pupil brought to school, and few teachers seemed aware that educational practices in school can contribute to it.

Because of their perceptions school personnel had difficulty accepting the study findings that revealed relatively high levels of commitment and aspiration among malperformers. Many (but not all) malperforming pupils were perceived as challenging the teachers' authority, and in some schools teachers were especially concerned about this problem. The findings about teacher perspectives indicate that greater emphasis should also have been placed on developing social skills relevant to the classroom and to pupil-teacher interactions.

That the work with the pupils had some positive effects, despite the weaknesses in the design of the intervention, is shown in the findings on the Pupil Behavior Inventory. Teachers' ratings of pupils before and after group work services indicated that impressive gains were achieved. Those in the service groups, as compared to matched controls, showed improvement in many areas of performance.

Statistical analysis of the ratings given the students led to the identification of five major dimensions of student behavior (Vinter et al., 1966): (1) *classroom conduct*: twelve items; for example, disrupts classroom procedures, teases, provokes other students; (2) *academic motivation and performance*: nine items; for example, is motivated toward academic performance, is alert, is interested in school work; (3) *socioemotional state*: five items; for example, appears generally happy, seems isolated, has few or no friends; (4) *teacher dependence*: two items; seeks constant reassurance, is possessive of teacher; and (5) *general socialization*: six items; for example, swears or uses obscene words, has inappropriate personal appearance. These dimensions indicate significant facets of pupil–teacher interaction patterns and can be regarded as sets of behavior about which teachers maintain expectations and toward which they focus judgments of pupils' conduct. Within these areas malperforming pupils apparently lacked sufficient skills and needed assistance in order to gain positive evaluation from teachers.

In Table 24–9 change scores are presented by dimension for the experimental and matched control groups in seven schools. The scores represent differences in ratings before and after the group services. A positive score means that the treatment groups showed more positive change than their matched controls. Comparison of difference scores across horizontal rows in the table shows variations among schools. The final columns on the right

TABLE 24-9. Change Scores Expressed as Differences Between Treatment and Control Group Scores, by School and Dimension, 1963–1964

	School[a]							Total Negative Values	Total Positive Values
Dimension	A T−C[b]	B T−C	C T−C	D T−C	E T−C	F T−C	G T−C		
Classroom conduct	−0.135	0.528	0.224	−0.259	0.542	0.243	−0.250	3	4
Academic motivation and performance	0.136	0.095	0.200	−0.568	−0.404	0.262	0.850	2	5
Socioemotional state	0.170	0.260	0.292	0.498	0.600	0.340	1.310	0	7
Teacher dependence	−0.127	−0.085	−0.100	0.770	−0.028	0.214	1.260	4	3
Personal habits	0.055	0.105	−0.067	−0.256	0.230	0.033	0.820	2	5

[a]School key: A = senior high school, B = senior high school, C = junior high school, D = junior high school, E = elementary school, F = junior high school, G = elementary school.

[b]T − C = Treatment group score minus control group score.

427

indicate that experimental groups, considered together, made progress during the time they received service on all dimensions except "teacher dependence." The negative scores obtained in several schools on this dimension require clarification. It was reported earlier that many malperforming pupils had considerable difficulty in soliciting help from teachers. One objective of the group service was to increase pupils' skills in relating to teachers and in seeking and using their help within the classroom. The negative change scores indicate that pupils in the experimental groups were perceived as becoming more dependent on teachers at the end of the year. In view of the objective these particular scores should be considered differently from the other negative change scores.

School Conditions and Practices

It has been asserted that interaction between certain aspects of the school and characteristics of the pupils accounts for malperforming behavior. To clarify this relationship, three aspects of the school will be considered: grading practices, sanctioning procedures, and patterns of dropping out.

Grading practices.   Because so little change was observed in the grades received by pupils in the experimental, matched control, and random control groups over the period of a year, grading practices were examined more systematically. In two senior high schools—hereafter referred to as Industrial Heights and Academic Heights—the grades received by all pupils entering the tenth grade were studied over a three-year period until the pupils either graduated, transferred, or dropped out of school. Important, relevant findings emerged (Schafer and Olexa, 1971). First, grades were observed to be important determinants of location in the curriculum independent of factors such as IQ and reading scores. Second, when grades were analyzed with controls for curriculum location, it was found that at both schools the distribution of course marks differed notably between college-preparatory and non-college preparatory tracks (Table 24-10). Although the performance of pupils could not be measured apart from the grading practices of teachers, the data clearly suggest that differences in course marks are to some degree a result of different grading standards. In other words, if two pupils performed at the same level when measured objectively, their chances of receiving good grades would be different in the two tracks. Some of the differences in scholastic rewards might be thought to reflect underlying differences in reading skill. If this were the case, differences in achievement between curricula should decline similarly across reading skill levels—but in fact every comparison revealed that pupils in the non-college-preparatory curriculum fared less well than those with comparable reading skills in the college-preparatory curriculum.

TABLE 24-10. Distributions of Course Marks by School, IQ, and Curriculum

| SCHOOL, IQ,[a] AND CURRICULUM | COURSE MARKS | | | | | | NUMBER OF CASES |
	A	B	C	D	E	TOTAL	
Industrial Heights							
High							
College-preparatory	20%	35	30	11	3	99%	(2102)
Non-college-preparatory	5	25	37	23	9	99	(363)
Low							
College-preparatory	3	19	39	29	10	100	(65)
Non-college-preparatory	2	13	34	40	10	99	(119)
Academic Heights							
High							
College-preparatory	27	35	28	8	2	100	(3553)
Non-college-preparatory	4	44	40	11	2	101	(166)
Low							
College-preparatory	7	25	43	19	5	99	(1946)
Non-college-preparatory	2	18	41	28	10	99	(1652)

[a]IQ cutting points are as follows: Industrial Heights, high, 109 and above, and low, 108 and below; Academic Heights, high, 109 and above, low, 108 and below.

It appears that there may be a universal grading scale in the high schools with an arbitrary devaluation of performance within the non-college-preparatory track. Since a large proportion of the malperformers were enrolled in the latter curriculum, the lack of any increase in their grades over time becomes more understandable. Pupils were aware of the differential opportunity patterns, and it is not unlikely that this knowledge affected their motivation to perform.

Sanctioning procedures. In addition to offering rewards and recognition to pupils for acceptable conduct or achievement, teaching personnel used a variety of negative sanctions to curb malperformance. Grades were, of course, the chief means for both reward and punishment. In the short run poor grades serve as negative judgments, and in the long run they curtail pupils' future opportunities. Sanctions often went beyond grades. Pupils were frequently exposed to a kind of double (or even triple) penalty. Those who performed below a certain standard received adverse grades and, as a direct consequence, might also be denied a wide variety of privileges and opportunities in the school. Also, in several schools policies explicitly provided for the arbitrary reduction of grades for smoking violations, suspensions, and other forms of behavioral misconduct not directly associated with academic performance. Pupils incurring these sanctions lost esteem among most of their classmates, were seldom chosen for minor but prestigious classroom or school assignments, and were excluded from participation in certain extracurricular activities. This process, in turn, often subjected pupils to negative parental responses, representing a third penalty.

The linking of secondary rewards and sanctions to grades may result in far more than reinforcement of academic criteria, since it denies the poor performer legitimate alternative opportunities for recognition and success. The pupil's motivation to continue trying and his or her commitment to educational objectives are thereby jeopardized at the very time when additional supports may be needed to stimulate effort. In these situations the underachieving pupil receives little support for his or her efforts to improve as continued failure subjects the pupil to new deprivations. School personnel seldom indicated an awareness of the negative consequences that could result when grading practices and sanctions for behavioral misconduct were interrelated.

Patterns of dropping out.   Perhaps the greatest determinant of adult role placement is whether or not a person graduates from high school; occupational and income ceilings are much lower for those who lack a high school diploma (Clark, 1962; Miller, 1960; Folger and Nam, 1964). Successful completion of high school is increasingly essential because of technological and bureaucratic demands in this society. Unfortunately many youths still leave school before they have completed the twelfth grade. And in this project the efforts of the social workers did not prevent several members of the target population from dropping out before graduation.

In both senior high schools dropouts tended to be disproportionately represented in the following categories: boys, Negroes, those from working-class families, pupils with lower IQ scores, those lower in reading test scores and in overall achievement, those with lower grade averages, and those in the general curriculum. The data in Table 24–11 report the percentage of all pupils who were dropouts in each of these categories in the two schools studied. Grade point average was the single factor most important in predicting who would drop out and who would not. Forty-one percent of the students at Academic Heights within the fourth quartile of the grade point average dropped out, as did 63 percent in the same quartile at Industrial Heights. Dropouts also tended to show greater decline and less improvements in grades than did graduates.

Several other studies have shown achievement to be associated positively with remaining in school until graduation. As one writer suggests, this is not difficult to understand: "It seems entirely reasonable that any normal person would seek to escape as soon as possible from any situation in which he persistently found himself branded as incompetent" (Hand, 1956).

TABLE 24–11. Percentages Who Were Dropouts Among Various Categories of Students

	DROPOUTS	
CATEGORY	ACADEMIC HEIGHTS	INDUSTRIAL HEIGHTS
Sex		
Boys	17%	24%
Girls	9	22
Race		
Whites	13	19
Negroes	38	27
Social class (based on father's occupation)		
Upper-middle	5	7
Lower-middle	11	11
Upper-working	20	15
Lower-working	32	31
IQ (quartiles)		
1 (high)	3	5
2	3	10
3	13	21
4 (low)	26	43
Reading score (quartiles)		
1, 2 (high)	3	13
3	8	26
4 (low)	25	24
Overall grade point average (quartiles)		
1 (high)	0	5
2	3	6
3	5	24
4 (low)	41	63
Curriculum		
College-preparatory	4	5
General	35	47

SUMMARY AND CONCLUSIONS

The findings from this study and demonstration effort provide substantial support for the proposition that pupil malperformance is most usefully viewed as a consequence of adverse school–pupil interactions. Both intraschool and interschool variations were noted in teachers' perspectives, in group services, in curriculum placement patterns and outcomes, in grading practices, and in pupil careers. The findings further indicated that pupil careers are shaped in part by motivations, capabilities, and skills that are influenced by the opportunities and responses of the school through which class groups and particular individuals pass. The school itself may maintain and even generate the very malperformance it seeks to eliminate by offering limited opportunity for educational attainment for some pupils, by judging pupils adversely because of attributes that are independent from their actions, by undermining existing motivation through unwise use of control practices, and by making it exceedingly difficult for the pupil "to find his or her way back" once the pupil has been labeled as a malperformer.

Many of the findings about organizational conditions and behavior were made subsequent to the intervention effort and therefore not available for use in it. Had they been available, much greater effort would have been directed toward modification of school policies and practices. As it was, the social workers tended to focus their main effort on providing group services to specified individuals. Limited positive results were thereby achieved. It is of interest, however, that since the formal conclusion of the project four of the five school systems have attempted to make organizational changes on the basis of the study findings.

As was indicated earlier, the design for this research and demonstration project provided for two series of conferences to be held periodically over a two-year period. One series was conducted with practitioners to review study procedures and to systematize their interventions as far as possible. In general the response of the practitioners was extremely positive, and they participated actively in reviewing preliminary findings and in using this knowledge to modify existing procedures.

A second series of conferences was held with school administrators—principals, superintendents, directors of special education, and so forth. The object of this series was also to review the study findings with reference to their implications for school policy and program design. These sessions were far less successful. Many administrators were reluctant to accept the findings as valid and reliable and maintained strong ideological perspectives about the causes of pupil malperformance. These views inhibited acceptance of the notions that school conditions contributed to malperformance and that basic policies and conditions needed reexamination.

The use of these conferences as a strategy for inducing organizational change proved to be less potent and far more time-consuming than anticipated. However, after the conferences concluded, administrators in three of the five systems reinstituted contact with project staff members, who then provided some consultation about changes in school policies and procedures. In one community a new senior high school was designed with a primary concern that conditions for the pupil in the general curriculum be improved. Modifications have also been made in grading practices and policies governing the application of negative sanctions. Changes in staff assignments have resulted, with some of the more effective teachers being assigned to develop and teach courses in the general curriculum.

In a second community utilization of the findings led to a demonstration project directed toward modifying the policies, rules, procedures, and practices that serve to identify and label pupils adversely or to reduce opportunities for certain pupils to participate successfully in the academic and social life of the school. A second objective was to provide an opportunity for pupils to participate in educational decision-making, and a third was to redesign existing curricula in light of study findings. The third school system has modified explicit policies and procedures that adversely affect malperformers.

It is now apparent that effecting innovation and change in today's public school is a complex and difficult task requiring attention not only to attributes of individuals in the system but also, and perhaps more importantly, to the behavior of the school itself. Findings indicate that planned change can be effected, but that no single technique is likely to succeed unless it is addressed to the complexity of the total situation.

REFERENCES

CICOUREL, AARON, AND JOHN I. KITSUSE
  1963 *The Educational Decision-Makers*. Indianapolis: Bobbs-Merrill.
CLARK, BURTON
  1962 *Educating the Expert Society*. San Francisco: Chandler Publishing Company.
COHEN, ALBERT H.
  1966 *Deviance and Control*. Englewood Cliffs, N.J.: Prentice-Hall.
ELDER, GLEN H.
  1966 "The schooling of outsiders," *Sociology of Education*, 39 (Fall): 324–43.
ERIKSON, KAI T.
  1964 "Notes on the sociology of deviance." In Howard Becker (ed.), *The Other Side*. New York: Free Press, pp. 9–22.
FOLGER, J. K., AND C. B. NAM
  1964 "Trends in education to the occupational structure," *Sociology of Education*, 38 (Fall): 19–33.
FREIDSON, ELIOT
  1966 "Disability as social deviance." In Marvin Sussman (ed.), *Sociology and Rehabilitation*. Washington: American Sociological Association, pp. 71–79.
HAND, H. H.
  1956 "Who drops out of school?" In W. O. Stanley et al. (eds.), *Social Foundations of Education*. New York: Holt-Dryden, p. 236.

LEMERT, EDWIN
  1967 "Legal commitment and social control." In *Human Deviance, Social Problems and Social Control*. Englewood Cliffs, N.J.: Prentice-Hall, pp. 67-71.
McCORKLE, LLOYD
  1958 *The Highfields Story*. New York: Henry Holt.
MILLER, HERMAN P.
  1960 "Annual income and life-time income in relation to education: 1939—1959," *American Economic Review*, 50 (December): 962-86.
POLK, KENNETH, AND LYNN RICHMOND
  1966 "Those who fail," Eugene, Oregon: Lane County Youth Project, unpublished.
SARRI, ROSEMARY C.; ROBERT D. VINTER; AND ESTHER GOODMAN
  1965 "Group work in the schools: A practitioner's manual," Ann Arbor: The University of Michigan, unpublished.
SCHAFER, WALTER, AND CAROL OLEXA
  1971 *Tracking and Opportunity*. San Francisco: Chandler Publishing Company.
VINTER, ROBERT D.; ROSEMARY C. SARRI; WALTER SCHAFER; AND DARREL VORWALLER
  1966 *The Pupil Inventory: A Manual for Administration and Scoring*. Ann Arbor, Mich.: Campus Publishers.

V

Group Work in Selected Fields of Practice

This section of the volume is intended to illustrate the principles provided in the first four parts. Seven selected fields of practice have been chosen for that purpose. The criteria for selection of the seven chapters included not only that they contribute useful examples of the University of Michigan model of group work practice but also that they reflect the social work profession's attention to a variety of fields of practice of importance today. That is one reason why six of the seven chapters are new to this edition. As noted earlier, the Michigan model is an open system of intervention. That permits considerable variety in how the model is used. Differences created by the nature of the problems of the members of the group as well as the goals and the organization of the agency under whose auspices the group meets are illustrated throughout these chapters. They should encourage the creative use of the material presented earlier in this volume.

The first selection, Chapter 25, by Sundel and Sundel, describes the use of time-limited groups with clients whose problems include job stress, marital discord, child management, depression, self-control, anxiety, and interpersonal difficulties with friends, families, work associates, and superiors. The approach combines the Michigan model with behavior modification theory to help members pursue specific intervention goals. After an intake interview with each client, there are generally eight group sessions with five to seven members and two individual follow-up conferences. The Sundels believe that time-limited groups provide more motivation for members to change quickly, lead to better organization of group time, help to make sessions more focused and goal-directed, and enable practitioners to treat more clients in need of aid.

Group members help each other establish behaviorally specific goals by indicating the undesired responses, their antecedents and consequences, and the measures of their strength in terms of response rate or duration, modeling the worker's examples. The eight sessions include the following four methods: (1) the development of norms to foster pro-treatment behaviors in the group; (2) education to behavioral principles of assessment and modification to be used in the change process; (3) problem-solving by members of the group, allowing each to move toward the achievement of his or her goals; and (4) behavioral training and practice of new behaviors in the group so that they may be used successfully in the social environment. The Sundels provide a session-by-session discussion of objectives and the procedures used to achieve them so that other professionals can make use of their approach. Using statistical analyses of member reports, time-limited groups are demonstrated to be successful with the large majority of clients who were included in them.

Chapter 26 by Garvin focuses on work with disadvantaged and oppressed groups. By social oppression the author means the ways social institutions damage people's identities, denigrate their life-styles, and deny them access to opportunities based on attributes they share with others. That includes not only minorities such as blacks, Hispanics, and Asian Americans but also many other groups such as the elderly, the poor, the handicapped, women, and gays and lesbians. The main purposes of work with such groups is to help their members (1) rediscover their self-worth and dignity, (2) overcome isolation, (3) learn to cope better with or to change the social institutions that oppress them, and (4) combine to increase their power so that they may exercise interpersonal influence through groups to struggle against oppressive institutions. In those circumstances the professional must serve as a broker and an advocate for members in negotiations with institutions in the community.

Groups composed of disadvantaged clients have varied and overlapping goals. Among them are (1) consciousness raising, (2) individualized treatment, (3) social action, (4) network linking and social support, and (5) development of skills and competence. The author describes the special problems of work with such groups throughout their development, emphasizing that at termination members must evaluate not only what they have accomplished but also what they have learned, and plan next steps in their move to achieve equality.

Ronald Feldman, in his view of group work with antisocial youths in Chapter 27, points out that such efforts have not been very successful. The reasons are as follows:

1. There is a conflict between the organizational requirements of custody and treatment, accentuated by overcrowding in many correctional facilities.
2. Teaching youngsters to adapt to institutional life may be dysfunctional in the environment to which they return.
3. Many institutions are schools for crime as antisocial peer group influences are much stronger than prosocial and treatment efforts. Since most community programs work with groups composed exclusively of youth labeled as delinquent the same problem is present.
4. The process of labeling young people delinquent or deviant militates against an increase in prosocial behavior. Since the large majority of youth display both prosocial and antisocial behavior, most of which is prosocial, such labeling is especially antithetical to the reduction of antisocial acts.
5. Most programs for delinquents are not initiated until it is too late, until they have deeply ingrained patterns of deviant behavior. Secondary prevention or primary prevention programs are rare.
6. Most group leaders are untrained subprofessionals.
7. For youth who have made gains in institutions there are few maintenance programs in their natural environments.
8. There is little research on the technology of group treatment for this population—the linkages between process and outcome.

Therefore, the author proposes early intervention, mixing prosocial and antisocial youths in the same groups in nonstigmatized agency settings under professional leadership. Prosocial behavior should be emphasized and supported and labeling avoided. Group maintenance programs for institutionally discharged youth together with primary and secondary prevention services need to be developed.

Although the emphasis in mental health and retardation is on deinstitutionalization at present, in Chapter 28 Churchill and Glasser point out that large numbers of patients and residents continue to live in hospitals and training schools. The recent emphasis on the civil rights of patients and residents and much stricter involuntary admission criteria have led most institutions to develop an integrated service plan for each client, and that together with the new medications have reduced the institutional populations. Increasingly the institutions are being seen as therapeutic milieus where the total environment may have a positive therapeutic effect.

Many types of groups have always existed in institutions, some used for social control as well as for treatment. Patients and residents are constantly influencing each other in groups even when their behavior may seem bizarre. Groups of varied sizes are useful in achieving combinations of the following goals: (1) present appropriate ego models, particularly that of the worker; (2) increase the social involvement of patients and residents, many of whom tend to isolate themselves; (3) provide clients with behavioral feedback; (4) enhance the self-esteem of patients and residents; (5) help the retarded and mentally ill to learn new knowledge and skills; (6) provide opportunities for institutional members to relearn forgotten social skills; and (7) provide support from appropriate old and new patterns of behavior and disapproval of deviant actions. To achieve those ends the group worker must have administrative support from all levels of institutional management.

As cancer is probably the most feared disease in America today, its diagnosis tends to isolate patients and their families. Chapter 29 by Galinsky discusses how group work can deal effectively with the problem. Groups can provide support to patients and their families, help them to share feelings not always easy to express, increase their coping skills in the many difficult hospital and home environment situations they must face, provide them with useful information about the illness and its treatment, and help all concerned deal with such existential considerations as life and death.

Referral agents such as physicians and nurses, as well as patients and their families, must understand the purpose and utility of such groups. It is not psychotherapy for mental problems but rather focused on here-and-now explorations of how to cope with external events. Friendship relations are easily established in such groups because of the common bond of illness, and there are opportunities for members to get out of the dependent role of patient as they learn to help each other.

To be effective the group leader must have dealt with his or her own feelings about illness and death and be empathic and knowledgeable about cancer. Since such groups are an enormous emotional drain on the worker, co-leaders are useful in helping each other deal with their feelings about the disease of cancer and its impact on patients and their families. In addition, if they are from different professions, each may have specialized knowledge useful to members. Individual conferences with members and/or their families and with other medical personnel often may be necessary. The mature, skilled leader doesn't let the group focus exclusively on complaints about hospital care and medical personnel or their negative and often frightening feelings about their illness but helps members to cope more effectively with the many reality problems they face.

Groups have been the preferred method of treatment for chemical dependency for many years now. In Chapter 30 Reed states that the reasons are the popularity of self-help groups run by former users, the fact that individual treatment approaches have not proved very successful because of the nature of client defenses, and the fact that most chemical dependency is initiated and supported by family and peer groups, making it natural to use groups to overcome the problem. Chemical dependency includes addiction to alcohol, drugs, and certain prescription medicines.

Groups can be used for prevention through education, not only of potential addicts but also of community agency professionals as well as distributors (physicians, bartenders, and so on). Secondary prevention through early referral by teaching family, friends, and key institutional personnel how to motivate alcohol and drug users to seek treatment is also gaining acceptance. Rehabilitation groups make use of the worker as a role model who emphasizes the development of more effective social skills by members so that they can deal more effectively with their reality problems. Group work frequently is done with family members of the abuser as well in order to support and sustain changes in the addict. More professionally trained group workers need to enter this important field of practice.

In Chapter 31, ending this section, Campbell writes with warmth and appreciation of the writing groups for the elderly with whom she has worked. Writing results in a real product, which for the aged can be a legacy for their children, friends, and relatives and at the same time can be a process of self-discovery and exploration. The group is a place where life's experiences can be validated, where learning about others and their problems can be put into better perspective, and above all where close, intimate friendships can be made when death and geography have separated many from their loved ones.

Each group of about twelve members with varied educational backgrounds from many parts of the country meets weekly. The first fifteen minutes are spent on catching up on personal news. Then each member reads a selection he or she has written during the week or tells a story instead. They write about the past as well as the present. The author notes that experience enhances writing, but writing enhances one's power of observation. With warmth and empathy members comment on each other's work, encouraging and learning from one another.

Experience has shown that each group needs a professional worker who provides a sense of continuity, helps the group over its low points, emphasizes individual strengths, helps new members gain acceptance, points out commonalities among members, and provides the perspective of another generation. At times it is only the worker who can deal with sensitive issues like the member who talks too long. The professional is also available for individual counseling. Campbell comments at the end that although the professional has much to offer the elderly in such groups, he or she also has the opportunity to learn much from the wealth of experience they provide.

25

Behavior Modification with Time-Limited Groups

Martin Sundel and Sandra Stone Sundel

THE CONFLUENCE OF THREE TRENDS during the past decade has contributed to a favorable climate for treatment of individuals in time-limited behavioral groups. First, the emphasis on accountability within the context of limited resources has fostered attempts to provide services to clients within brief time frames (e.g. Bloom, 1984; Budman, 1981). Second, increased attention has been directed toward development of a knowledge-based empirical approach in the helping professions (e.g. Bloom and Fischer, 1982; Fischer, 1981; Thomas, 1984). Third, human service professionals have become active in applying behavioral principles and techniques to group settings (Lawrence and Sundel, 1972, 1975; Lawrence and Walter, 1978; Rose, 1972, 1977, 1980; Sundel and Lawrence, 1970, 1974, 1977; Upper and Ross, 1979, 1980, 1981, 1985).

The purpose of this chapter is to present a time-limited behavioral group work model and describe selected applications. The main features of the model are reviewed, emphasizing the assessment, planning, intervention, and evaluation components. Various aspects of this model have been described in the literature (Lawrence and Sundel, 1972; Lawrence and Walter, 1978; Sundel and Lawrence, 1970, 1974, 1977; Sundel and Sundel, 1985, in press).

The model of group work presented here combines behavior modification principles and small group theory to pursue the specific goals of group members. In this model the client becomes a member of the group to solve a problem of concern to the person or significant others. The objective is to change the behavior of each member outside the group, where the behavior has been defined as undesired. Group functioning dimensions such as cohesiveness, leadership, or decision-making are addressed as a means to help participants achieve their goals. Attention to these group dimensions are secondary, although necessary, to the pursuit of individual goals (see Chapter 2 by Robert Vinter).

440

Client problems treated in this type of group have included job stress, marital discord, child management, depression, self-control, anxiety, and interpersonal difficulties with friends, families, work associates, and superiors. The treatment groups are voluntary and typically consist of five to seven individuals. The usual course of treatment in these groups involves one individual intake session and eight group sessions. Follow-up interviews are held one month and three to six months after termination of the group.

The group serves as the context in which the behavioral change goals of each member are pursued. The practitioner influences the activities and relationships of group members to facilitate the achievement of client objectives. The practitioner establishes group functioning goals to optimize appropriate participation of group members.

The time-limited behavioral approach structures group treatment in order to achieve the following client objectives and conditions for group participation:

1. *Treatment norms are established within the group.*

   a. Members are expected to attend every session.

Group members are told that they are expected to attend every session as a condition of treatment. Verbal agreement to comply with the rule is obtained from each individual during the initial interview and confirmed during the first group meeting. Attendance at every session is considered crucial to fulfilling the tasks required at each phase of the problem-solving process. Group members learn through didactic presentations by the practitioner as well as through personal and observational experiences, and each session builds on the knowledge and skills developed in the previous sessions.

   b. Group discussions related to clients' problems are considered confidential within the group.

Confidentiality within the group is a central ethical issue related to group treatment (Corey, 1981). In order for members comfortably to discuss sensitive or intimate problems in the group, they must be confident that these problems will not be discussed outside the group.

   c. Socializing among members outside of meetings is discouraged.

Members are told to refrain from socializing with other group members outside of meetings for the duration of the group. Discussing group meetings outside the group could create cliques or alliances that affect objective participation in the group. Other behavioral group treatment approaches, however, have allowed and even promoted contacts among group members both in and out of group meetings, such as the "buddy system" described by Rose (1977).

   d. Discussion of members' problems focuses on current events and observable data.

The focus of behavioral treatment is on present conditions rather than interpretation of early childhood experiences. The behavioral approach involves systematic client observation and recording of current target behaviors. This may involve self-monitoring as well as monitoring the behavior of others.

   e. Members are required to perform assignments outside the group.

   Performance of behavioral assignments structures activities between group sessions and gives the client practice in performing desired behaviors in the social environment.

   Enforcement of group norms.   The above treatment norms are provided as guidelines for optimal functioning of the group within this treatment model. Although the practitioner can enforce the norms with legitimate authority, pressure for compliance can also be exerted by group members in a cohesive group. The practitioner seeks to establish cohesiveness in the group by (1) engaging members in problem-solving activities that require member interaction to achieve individual goals (e.g. role-plays, discussions) and (2) providing social reinforcement, along with other group members, for performance of desired behaviors. As the group becomes cohesive, members are more effective in enforcing group norms (see Chapter 4 by Radin and Feld).

   2. *Members prioritize their problems.*

   The following criteria are used to help clients prioritize their problems and select one for immediate attention:

   a. The problem of immediate concern to the client and/or significant others (for example, family, friends, employer)
   b. The problem that has severe aversive or negative consequences for the client, significant others, or society if not handled immediately
   c. The problem that can be corrected most quickly, considering resources and obstacles
   d. The problem that requires handling before other problems can be treated (Sundel and Sundel, 1982, pp. 84–85)

   3. *Members help each other in the assessment of their problems, and in establishing behavioral change goals.*

Members apply their knowledge of behavioral concepts, learned in the group, to the analysis of each individual's problems. Vague, general statements made by a client are followed by requests for specification of target responses, antecedents, and consequences. Client data obtained outside the group are examined in terms of measures of response strength and controlling conditions. If an individual has difficulty identifying target behaviors and controlling conditions, role-plays are devised by the practitioner in which group members assume the roles of the client or significant others.

   After the client collects and presents desired assessment data, the group helps the client establish behavioral change goals. Various desirable behaviors and supporting environmental conditions are suggested and discussed.

Successful experiences of particular group members in similar circumstances can be used in formulating appropriate goals.

4. *Members contribute suggestions for change and solutions to each other's problems.*

An intervention plan is developed with each client based on the goals that are established. The practitioner encourages group members to offer suggestions for resolving each other's problems. This input from group members expands the range of interventions available to the clients. Clients may also be more amenable to acting on these suggestions because they are supported by other members of the group.

5. *Members participate actively in role-playing and educational procedures designed to teach problem-solving skills.*

After intervention plans are established for the clients, role-plays are devised to provide opportunities for them to practice desired behaviors in the group. Subgroups of two to four individuals may be formed to allow clients to practice desired behaviors in role-plays, while the worker and other members provide prompting, corrective feedback, and social reinforcement. For example, a client can learn assertive behaviors by role-playing increasingly difficult situations that require assertive behaviors. A client can learn how to decrease anxiety in stressful situations by role-playing difficult situations.

An educational component is included in this model to help group members efficiently work on problems in the course of group treatment and to help members apply this knowledge to new problems that may arise after the group terminates. The practitioner teaches assessment concepts to group members that show how a problem can be broken down into parts that are functionally related to each other. The concepts of reinforcement, extinction, and punishment are used to illustrate conditions influencing the performance of desired and undesired behaviors. A variety of examples are drawn from the group members' experiences to facilitate the learning of these concepts.

6. *Members provide social reinforcement and constructive feedback to each other.*

The worker shows group members how to provide social reinforcement in the form of praise, recognition, and encouragement for complying with group norms, actively participating in problem-solving activities, performing behavioral assignments outside the group, and reporting their data. Social reinforcement is also given for participation in role-plays and offering suggestions for appropriate behaviors. Constructive feedback is given by group members in the form of pinpointing behaviors that were performed appropriately as well as providing suggestions for improvement. This feedback is based on observations of the individual's behaviors in role-plays and the consequences they produce. Members are told to refrain from negative evaluations of the individual, accusations, or verbal attacks. The practitioner serves as a model for providing social reinforcement and constructive feedback for members throughout the course of the group.

OVERVIEW OF MODEL

This model is based on a treatment planning cycle with four components: assessment, planning, intervention, and evaluation. This logical, problem-solving framework requires systematically working through each phase of the cycle for each problem while managing the group process, an approach consistent with the model developed by Robert Vinter and his colleagues at The University of Michigan as represented in this volume.

The groups have been composed of men and women ranging in age from twenty to fifty-four. The groups described in this paper met for two and one-half hours once a week for eight consecutive weeks and were led by two workers. Other groups using this model, however, have been conducted by a single practitioner.

Time-Limited Focus

The model presented here is for an eight-week group treatment program. The model was designed to be time-limited for several reasons:

1. Clients are given the expectation that their problems can be resolved in the specified period of time if they follow the prescribed procedures. If no time limits are imposed, clients could remain in the group for an indefinite period without making significant progress toward problem resolution. The attractiveness of group membership and participation could outweigh the incentive for clients to solve their problems quickly.

2. Clients and practitioners are encouraged to organize their group time and to work on problem-solving activities between group sessions. Managing the group process is necessary in order to keep the group focused on problem-solving. If problems in group functioning (for example, clique formation or scapegoating) impede goal progress, practitioners actively intervene to refocus the group to prevent excessive time expended on group maintenance. Group members become highly task-oriented in order to spend a maximum amount of group time in goal-directed activities.

3. Practitioners can treat more clients. By treating clients' problems within a brief interval, practitioners become available to treat more clients than is possible with long-term groups. Time-limited groups also reduce the cost of individual treatment as well as the length of suffering.

4. The behavior modification approach typically involves highly focused, goal-directed sessions that systematically work through the treatment

planning cycle (Sundel and Sundel, 1982). Establishing a specific time limit for group treatment is consistent with this approach. Brief behavior therapy programs of up to 25 weekly sessions are frequently reported in the literature (e.g. Miller, 1980; Wilson, 1981; Sobell and Sobell, 1978). An upper limit of 25 weekly sessions has been reported for behavioral treatment groups and training groups, with the most frequent range between 10 and 18 sessions (Rose, 1977). More intensive treatment programs meeting more frequently during the initial weeks or days, however, might be appropriate for certain groups such as weight loss groups as suggested by Rose (1977).

Time-limited practice and short-term therapy are gaining wider acceptance in human service agencies such as child welfare and community mental health settings and are frequently preferred over long-term treatment (Bloom, 1984, Chapter 3; Budman, 1981; Garvin and Seabury, 1984, pp. 30–31; Mandel, 1981; Rush, 1982). Reviews of studies comparing psychotherapy outcomes have indicated comparable results for time-limited and time-unlimited therapies (Garfield, 1982, p. 615).

A time limit of eight weeks was established for the group treatment model, based on the practitioners' experience of the time required to teach group participants basic problem-solving concepts for assessing and treating their problems and evaluating the outcomes. The number of sessions could be varied, however, according to the characteristics of particular groups, such as size of group, length of sessions, number of leaders, and similarity of client problems.

Assessment

Intake. Prospective group members were interviewed individually to determine the appropriateness of group treatment for their problems.

Two basic criteria were used for client selection: (1) the client could contribute to problem-solving activities in the group and (2) the client would interact appropriately with other group members. Most suitable candidates for short-term group treatment included individuals who could talk about their problems, agreed to adhere to the proposed group norms, and agreed to help others solve their problems as well as work on solving their own.

Individuals with severe psychiatric impairment, such as clinical depression, or individuals who are suicidal or who exhibit extremely hostile or aggressive behavior, are less suitable candidates for this type of short-term group treatment (Corey, 1981; Lazarus, 1976). Their problems are more appropriately treated in individual sessions.

During the intake session the practitioner discussed the norms of the group and the prospective member agreed to follow the rules governing the group's operation. Clients were told that if they followed the prescribed procedures, it was likely that they achieve their goals within the period of group treatment.

The worker's objectives for intake were to obtain:

1. A verbal agreement from the client to follow the rules for group participation
2. A statement from the client indicating willingness to participate in group treatment
3. A behaviorally specific description of the client's problem
4. A statement of the client's goals for treatment

The following six procedures were used by the practitioners to achieve these objectives.

Procedure 1. Orientation to the initial interview. Prior to the intake interview each prospective group member completed a problem checklist (Sundel and Lawrence, 1974, pp. 341–42). The client was asked to specify relationships that were problematic and to describe the problem and the desired change. Using the checklist helped the worker focus the interview. It also helped to structure the way in which clients presented their problems.

Procedure 2. Establishment of an initial treatment contract. The initial treatment contract consisted of the practitioner's statement of the conditions of group participation (treatment norms) and the client's verbal agreement to abide by these conditions. In discussing the contract, the worker answered the client's questions and explained the rationale for the procedures that would be used during treatment. The conditions of the verbal contracts made with each client were discussed and reconfirmed during the first group meeting.

Procedure 3. Role induction. Teaching a client who comes for group treatment how to behave as a group member and what to expect from the worker and other group members is necessary to prepare the individual to assume the client role in the group. Role induction or socialization to the client role in psychotherapy has been discussed as an orderly social process requiring certain complementarity of behaviors and expectations (Lennard and Bernstein, 1970). Positive expectations regarding client role and behaviors have been associated with improved treatment outcomes (Gambrill, 1983, p. 91; Orlinsky and Howard, 1978).

Several expectations for the behavior of group members were established during the intake interview.

1. The problem selected for treatment was expected to improve during the course of the group.
2. The client was expected to abide by the norms stated by the practitioner for group participation: Members were expected to attend every session; group discussions of client problems were confidential; socializing outside the group was discouraged; the focus of group discussions of client problems was on current events and ob-

servable data; and members were expected to perform assignments outside the group.

3. The client was expected to participate actively in problem-solving both with regard to his or her problem and in assisting other group members.
4. The client was expected to acquire knowledge and skills in behavior modification concepts, recording, and measurement and to apply them in problem-solving.

Procedure 4. Description of problems in behaviorally specific terms. Clients frequently describe their problems in vague statements (for example, "My life is all messed up"). They often make assumptions about what causes their problems ("If only I were more attractive, I wouldn't be lonely"); or how they could be solved ("The only way to solve our family problems is to send our son away to school"). To avoid choosing interventions on the basis of faulty assumptions, the practitioner asked the client to specify the problem within the context of the person and circumstances involved. Examples of behaviorally specific descriptions include: "When the boss told me to explain my report, I trembled and answered in monosyllables." "When I say 'no' to my son, he runs into his room and slams the door."

The worker then asked the client to give recent examples of each problem. If the examples were inconsistent with the client's statement of the problem, the statement was revised to accurately depict the problem.

Procedure 5. Identification of problems to work on in the group. During the initial interview, the worker discussed each problem area with the client and encouraged the client to bring up others that might exist. The client and worker then narrowed down this list of problems to a few that would be appropriate to work on in the group. Criteria for establishing problem priorities were reviewed with the client (Sundel and Sundel, 1982, pp. 84–85).

Procedure 6. Discussion of treatment goals. The discussion of goals included what the client could reasonably expect to achieve in group treatment and the client's statement of behaviors and conditions the client wanted to alter.

Although behavioral specificity was attempted during intake, goals were not made final until the more detailed process of behavioral assessment took place during group meetings. The following example illustrates a tentative statement of a goal:

PROBLEM: When my boss asks me to explain my reports, I tremble and answer in monosyllables.

TENTATIVE GOAL: When my boss asks me to explain my reports, I will answer him with the facts, looking him square in the face.

RAC-S. In order to learn problem-solving skills, group members are first taught a method for assessing problem behaviors (Lawrence and Sundel, 1972; Sundel and Sundel, 1982). This method, referred to as RAC-S, includes the following components: (1) Response, (2) Antecedents, (3) Consequences, and (4) Strength. The specification of these four elements is required of each member during the assessment phase. A form for recording these data is provided (Sundel and Lawrence, 1974, p. 343). Assessment objectives, therefore, require each member to provide:

1. A clear definition of the problem, indicating undesired responses, their antecedents and consequences
2. Measures of the strength of problem behaviors, using response rate or duration data

For example, John complained that his wife didn't understand him. The workers and group members asked him to describe a typical incident, including what each partner said and did in that situation. The group continued to ask him questions until he specified his undesired responses (R), their antecedents (A), and their consequences (C).

One of John's problematic responses was that he continued to read the newspaper (R) when his wife asked him how his day had gone (A). As a result, she screamed at him until he put the newspaper down and yelled back (C). John was given an assignment to record the number and duration of such incidents during the next week (S).

Behavioral reenactment is a role-playing technique used to obtain RAC-S information regarding a client's behaviors in the problematic situation by observing the client role-play an incident that simulates the problem (Lawrence and Sundel, 1972, p. 40). This technique is used to obtain a more accurate picture of the client's verbal and nonverbal behaviors in problematic situations. For example, a behavioral reenactment of John's problematic situation revealed that he kept his head down and eyes focused on the newspaper when his wife asked him questions about work. There was a scowl on his face, and when he finally put the paper down he threw it on the floor. When presented with this feedback, John said he had not been aware of his negative nonverbal behaviors in the situation.

Goal-setting. After RAC-S assessment data are collected, treatment goals are formulated with each member. Group members contribute to the goal statements of others based on reported RAC-S data as well as on observations of the individual's interactions in the group and in behavioral reenactments. Although a goal might be stated initially in broad terms, it is delineated into behaviorally specific components including desired responses (R), antecedents (A), and consequences (C).

For example, John's goal stated that when his wife asked him questions about his work (A), he would put down the newspaper, look at her, and answer her questions (R). The potential positive consequences would be avoiding arguments and having pleasant conversations (C). This scenario should occur in the evenings when John comes home from work and sits down to read the newspaper. An alternative goal to be negotiated might be that when John arrives home from work (A), he asks his wife to allow him twenty minutes to read the newspaper in silence (R), after which he initiates pleasant conversation with her (C).

Planning

The intervention plan provides a framework for systematically carrying out the behavioral change program to attain the client's goals. This plan is designed to alter behaviors and their controlling antecedents and consequences, in order to move the client toward goal attainment. Without an explicit plan application of an isolated behavioral technique could be ineffective in achieving the client's goal.

Behavioral techniques can be classified according to their effects in altering response strength so that a response is acquired, increased, maintained, or decreased (Sundel and Sundel, 1982, pp. 198–99). Behavioral techniques are applied as interventions to influence the frequency, intensity, or duration of target behaviors. Some of these techniques can be combined to form treatment packages. For example, assertiveness training might include positive reinforcement, model presentation, and behavioral rehearsal.

In planning interventions certain factors are considered. These include cost, efficiency, client and environmental resources and barriers, and appropriateness and relative effectiveness of available techniques.

The eight-week group treatment model was designed to implement individual treatment programs for clients. The eight sessions were planned to include the following four methods:

1. *Development of group norms.* The practitioners establish rules for participation and model appropriate behavioral techniques to foster pro-treatment behaviors in the group.
2. *Education.* The practitioners teach basic principles of behavioral assessment and modification to participants and teach them how to apply these principles to their individual problems and circumstances.
3. *Problem-solving.* The practitioners direct the group in systematically assessing the problems of each member, formulating relevant goals, prescribing viable solutions, monitoring progress, and evaluating outcomes of interventions.
4. *Behavioral training and practice.* The practitioners teach group members how to perform desired behaviors using modeling,

prompting, shaping, behavioral rehearsal, corrective feedback, and reinforcement. Clients practice these behaviors in the group before trying them out in their environments. They also participate in behavioral training as models and significant others in role-plays, provide corrective feedback, and suggest alternative behaviors.

Intervention

To implement the intervention plan, clients are given instructions on how to perform appropriate behaviors in role-plays. Members practice these behaviors in the group, with feedback from the workers and other group members. Additional instructions, prompts, and cues are given to help shape these behaviors. Behavioral rehearsals allow members to practice desired behaviors in a controlled setting until they are well established.

An important advantage of the group is the availability of individuals who can serve as models in performing desired behaviors. Multiple models provide diverse examples of how desired behaviors can be performed and allow group members to imitate those models that are most acceptable. Another advantage is that group members provide reinforcement to each other for appropriate behaviors. This can be more effective than if only the workers were providing the reinforcement. The workers serve as role models for members by performing problem-solving behaviors, as well as by demonstrating how to provide instructions, cues, and positive reinforcement.

After members have demonstrated desired behaviors in the group, they are assigned to perform them in their social environments. Those tasks or behavioral assignments involve behaviors to be performed by the clients outside the group setting between sessions. They are used to provide continuity between the group setting and the clients' environments. They also help structure the time between group sessions so that group members can continue to work toward their treatment goals.

In order to accomplish individual goals, the practitioners take an active role in controlling group functioning so that all members have a chance to participate in problem-solving and group maintenance activities. Potential pitfalls include domination by one person, overworking one person's problem to the neglect of others, detailed discussion of irrelevant or tangential topics, inability of a member to focus on his or her problem, and noncompliance with group norms. Methods for handling such problems have been discussed elsewhere (Sundel and Lawrence, 1977; Sundel and Sundel, 1985).

Evaluation

Evaluating treatment progress is based on the extent to which the client's goals are accomplished. This is usually determined by observation of treatment-related behaviors in the group as well as client self-evaluation reports. The reliability of these reports can be increased by observations of the client's behaviors in the social environment.

Measures of the client's satisfaction with the results of the treatment program should be consistent with the client's attainment of the treatment goals. The practitioners discuss objective measures of progress toward goal achievement with the client and relate these measures to the client's personal satisfaction with behavioral change. Measures of client satisfaction are obtained throughout the behavioral change program so that both objective measures of goal progress and the client's perceptions of improvement can be compared. If the client's goals are achieved but the client is dissatisfied, this may indicate a failure to have established goals considered significant by the client. It might also mean that other problem areas need to be considered in the client's behavioral change program.

On the other hand a client who has difficulty achieving behavioral change goals may report satisfaction with the behavioral change program. Such an individual may be deriving sufficient social reinforcement from relationships with group members or practitioners to compensate for lack of goal progress. The practitioners should help such clients to evaluate progress toward attainment of treatment goals realistically and separate this evaluation from the clients' satisfaction with relationships in the group (Sundel and Sundel, 1982, Chapter 16).

Follow-up interviews are held with each group member individually. These sessions are designed to: (1) evaluate the extent to which treatment gains have been maintained; (2) provide additional interventions, if necessary, for the problems worked on during group treatment; (3) determine if additional treatment is necessary for problems not dealt with in the group or that developed after termination of group treatment; and (4) determine if the clients have applied the techniques they learned in the group to other problems.

Planning for Group Meetings

A significant feature of this behavioral group model is the attention given to planning the objectives and tasks to be accomplished during group meetings. In order for the co-leaders to coordinate their efforts effectively, they plan an agenda before group meetings and analyze the results of each meeting. A session-by-session plan specifies what is to be accomplished during meetings and interventions that could be used to achieve these objectives. Session plans are sufficiently flexible to allow the practitioners to respond spontaneously to unexpected events.

During the planning sessions the co-leaders discuss members' progress toward goal attainment as well as their functioning in the group. The activities and roles of each practitioner are specified, including who will begin the session, the kinds of role-plays to be structured, and the behaviors or techniques that will be modeled and reinforced. In discussing each member's progress and participation in the group, the co-leaders also plan intervention strategies for modifying member behaviors that impede individual or group functioning.

Co-leaders typically establish operating rules that govern their own behavior in group sessions. These rules include procedures for handling differences of opinion between them, structuring role-plays and assignments, and making educational presentations.

In treatment groups co-leaders have certain advantages over a single worker. While one worker assumes an active role in running the groups, the other attends to nonverbal behaviors of group members and helps manage the group process. The workers switch roles periodically so that each has a chance to observe the group process, as well as take the active role. The leader who is observing analyzes interactions among members and instigates changes to affect the group's functioning. If the active leader misses an important statement or nonverbal behavior, the other worker can pick up on it. Other benefits of co-leadership are that group members have (1) two professional role models in addition to the models provided by group members, (2) a second professional's perspective on their problems, and (3) an additional source of reinforcement. Because of the intensity of the two-and-one-half-hour group sessions and the considerable amount of information covered, it is advantageous to have compatible co-leaders to keep the group focused on productive activities while maintaining a cooperative group climate. In describing his model of behavioral group therapy, Flowers (1979) indicated that two leaders were required.

Session objectives and procedures.   The first two group sessions focus on problem identification and assessment of individual behaviors, establishment of problem-solving norms in the group, and presentation of basic principles of behavioral analysis. During sessions three and four behavioral assessments are completed for all members. Intervention plans are established and implemented for individuals whose assessments were completed in previous sessions. Sessions five through seven focus on behavioral training, and assignments are given for members to perform desired behaviors in their natural environments. Session eight is devoted to evaluating member achievements in regard to goal attainment and to scheduling follow-up meetings.

Some typical objectives for the sessions are given below. Specific applications of this approach with client groups have been described elsewhere (Sundel and Lawrence, 1977).

Session 1: Objectives
1. Members describe their problems in behavioral terms and give examples specifying undesired behaviors.

2. Each member identifies an undesired behavior to observe and count during the next week.

3. Each member participates in determining problem priorities for other members.

A summary of the procedures established to achieve these objectives include:

1. *Orientation.* Members are introduced to each other, the group's purpose is explained, and a description of the treatment approach is given. The rules for group participation are discussed.

2. *Educational.* The concept of response, or behavior, is taught. The workers teach group members the technique of specifying responses by demonstrating how to convert vague descriptions into observable, measurable statements.

3. *Confirmation or redefinition of client problems.* Members verify or revise their problem statements.

4. *Group tasks.* The practitioners and group discuss with each member the problem selected for treatment. Each member affirms his or her willingness to abide by the group norms stated by the workers. The workers model and reinforce appropriate participation.

5. *Assignment.* Members are assigned to observe and record the frequency of their problem behaviors on a data sheet and to report the results to the group.

The practitioners structure the first session to establish the clients' expectations for participation in the group. Group members are shown how to assume an active role in analyzing their problems as well as in helping other individuals to problem-solve. The task-oriented requirements for participation in the group are explained in relation to the time limits of each session as well as the overall program.

Session 2: Objectives
1. Each member reports data from the recording assignment.
2. Each member identifies target responses and their controlling antecedents and consequences, and devises a procedure to measure response strength.
3. Each member participates in assessment activities and provides appropriate social reinforcement to other group members.

Procedures:

1. *Data-gathering.* Members present measures of their target responses that they recorded since the last meeting. The data-gathering procedures and experiences of members are discussed. If clients have difficulty in carrying out the assignment, the workers and group analyze the difficulty and demonstrate correct procedures.

2. *Educational.* The workers teach the RAC-S behavioral assessment framework (Sundel and Sundel, 1982, Chapters 8 and 9), giving various ex-

amples that illustrate its application. The concept of positive reinforcement, particularly its role in maintaining problematic behaviors, is also taught.

3. *Group tasks*. The practitioners and group provide social reinforcement to members for completing assignments. Members discuss difficulties encountered in identifying and specifying target behaviors and in observing and recording them. Members participate in role-plays that allow the group to observe typical problematic behaviors.

4. *Assignment*. Members are assigned to record target behaviors and their frequency of occurrence, describe relevant antecedents and consequences, and report the results to the group.

Sessions 3 and 4: Objectives
1. Members report data from their assignments.
2. Each member presents examples of target responses and their strength (frequency and duration data), and controlling conditions.
3. Each member specifies a behavioral change goal and identifies examples of positive and negative reinforcement contingencies from his or her data.
4. Each member participates in prescribing intervention strategies for members who have provided sufficient assessment data.

Procedures:

1. *Data-gathering*. Members discuss the data they recorded regarding target responses and their strength, and relevant antecedents and consequences. If members experience difficulty, additional instructions are given until they demonstrate mastery of the recording assignments.

2. *Educational*. The workers teach members how to formulate goals based on RAC-S data. Positive and negative reinforcement contingencies are examined in relation to their role in maintaining target behaviors.

3. *Behavioral training and practice*. In role-plays, members demonstrate the behaviors they have agreed to perform outside the group. Appropriate behaviors are shaped in the group setting based on feedback from the practitioners and group members. This feedback is used by members in refining the behaviors to be performed outside the group.

4. *Group tasks*. The workers and group provide social reinforcement to members for completing assignments. The group examines the assessment data available for each member to help determine conditions that maintain target behaviors.

For example, Thomas rarely completed his class assignments before midnight. His data indicated that he engaged in highly reinforcing behaviors early in the evening that were incompatible with studying: removing his shoes, sitting down with the newspaper, and turning on the television.

After assessment is complete and a behaviorally specific treatment goal is formulated, the group develops an intervention plan to achieve the goal.

For example, in order to increase "studying between 6 P.M. and 10

P.M.,'' Thomas was told to study for thirty-minute intervals, after which he could read the newspaper for five-minute intervals.

5. *Assignments*. Members continue recording RAC-S data; they carry out behavioral assignments given by the workers and group.

Sessions 5-7: Objectives
1. Each member reports data from the assignments.
2. Each member evaluates progress toward goal attainment.
3. Members perform behavioral tasks and assignments designed to achieve their goals.
4. Group members participate in role-plays and give each other feedback on their performances.

Procedures:

1. *Data-gathering*. The practitioners and group discuss client data in relation to progress made in achieving treatment goals. If a member fails to make progress, assessment data are reviewed to corroborate controlling conditions. If controlling conditions have been correctly identified, alternative intervention strategies and techniques are developed and implemented.

2. *Behavioral training and practice*. Group members perform tasks in the group that are directed toward goal achievement. Role-play techniques including behavioral rehearsal, modeling, and role reversal allow members to participate in the behavioral change programs of their peers. In addition, members are given assignments to perform the appropriate behaviors rehearsed in the group in their natural environment.

3. *Group tasks*. Members provide feedback to each other in role-plays, offer suggestions, serve as role models, provide reinforcement to each other for completing tasks and assignments, and evaluate each other's progress toward goal attainment. The workers gradually fade out their role in directing all group activities, allowing the group to take a greater part in structuring behavioral rehearsals, suggesting assignments, and reinforcing appropriate and improved behaviors.

4. *Assignments*. Members carry out behavioral assignments given by practitioners and group.

Session 8: Objectives
1. Members evaluate their progress toward attainment of treatment goals.
2. Members describe procedures for maintaining their treatment gains.
3. Members arrange for individual follow-up interviews.

Procedures:

1. *Data-gathering*. An evaluation form is distributed to group members who are told to complete it (e.g. Sundel and Lawrence, 1974, pp. 344–46). The form includes a description of problems worked on in the group and instructs members to rate the extent to which their goals were achieved.

Each member presents evaluative data indicating goal progress, including examples of modified behaviors and conditions.

2. *Educational*. The workers discuss ways to maintain the changes achieved.

3. *Group tasks*. Members discuss their plans and summarize their experiences in the group. Members reinforce each other for treatment gains and encourage each other to follow through with the maintenance plans.

4. *Follow-up*. Members are scheduled to return individually for one month follow-up meetings. Additional follow-up meetings are to be arranged at that time.

RESEARCH FINDINGS

In an exploratory study using this model with three groups, fifteen of the seventeen (88 percent) group members rated their problems "much better" or "completely solved" six months after treatment. In addition twelve (71 percent) reported that they had successfully applied the behavioral concepts they learned in the group to other problems (Lawrence and Sundel, 1972; Sundel and Lawrence, 1977).

Lawrence and Walter (1978) used a controlled outcome study to test the group model further with clients in a family service agency and a community mental health clinic. These clients presented interpersonal problems with family members, acquaintances, and work associates. Forty-eight subjects were randomly assigned to two conditions: the behavioral group model or a no-treatment control group. The experimental condition consisted of four groups of five or six members. Each group was led by two workers. Subjects in the control group were placed on a waiting list until evaluation posttests were administered nine weeks later. The behavioral group model was implemented over an eight-week period. The control group then received the same treatment.

The behavioral group model was found to be more effective than no treatment ($X^2 = 12.60$, df = 1, p < .001) according to a problem rating form filled out by each client, as well as ratings by two judges. Changes from pretest to posttest were observed to be greater within the treatment group than within the control group on a number of other measures used (a behavioral problem-solving test, the Rathus [1973] Assertiveness Scale, and two social effectiveness tests). A three-month follow-up survey of treated clients showed that 74 percent of the clients sustained substantial improvement.

A STUDENT TRAINING METHOD

Lawrence and Sundel (1975) taught a course to social work graduate students at The University of Michigan in which the students participated in self-modification groups as part of their training in group treatment. They found this to be a viable alternative when field work opportunities for learning how to apply behavior modification in groups were unavailable because of either lack of trained supervisors or agency opposition to behavior modification. The students were taught this model by following the guidelines developed by Lawrence and Sundel (1972). The students were assigned to groups of five and six members who met outside class to work on preselected problems. The professors screened these problems to ensure that they were appropriate for the time-limited groups. Problems selected by the students included poor study habits, nail biting, forgetting names, overeating, smoking, and nonparticipation in class discussions. The groups met for two-hour sessions over a period of six to seven weeks. Group members rotated weekly in the roles of group leader, observer, and recorder. One of the professors consulted with the student leader for each week to help plan the next meeting. Weekly class lectures and discussions focused on topics that paralleled the issues and tasks to be addressed as the groups developed.

In one class of twenty-two students divided into four groups, Lawrence and Sundel (1975) reported the following results: Fourteen members achieved their behavioral change goals; five made significant improvements; and three failed to make significant improvements according to self-reports. The authors noted that the relatively poor performance of one group—two failures, three partial successes—was associated with poor attendance, disruptive behavior, and leadership difficulties.

Four years of experience using this student training model revealed the following to be among the most significant benefits for the students:

1. Opportunity to learn behavioral group treatment skills under the guidance of an experienced practitioner
2. Observing, experiencing, and handling a variety of group functioning problems similar to those encountered in client groups
3. Gaining a perspective on being a client in this kind of group
4. Firsthand observation of the effectiveness of the behavioral group model in obtaining desired behavior changes (Lawrence and Sundel, 1975, p. 83)

CONCLUSION

Over the past fifteen years the time-limited behavioral group treatment model has been applied in family service agencies, mental health clinics, psychiatric hospitals, and correctional settings. The model has also been adapted for use in developing assertiveness and other interpersonal skills in women's groups, community education courses, and government personnel seminars (S. Sundel and Sundel, 1980; Sundel and Sundel, 1985).

The following research questions regarding the group treatment model warrant further investigation: What is the relative effectiveness of the model with homogeneous and heterogeneous client groups and problems? What is the optimum composition of groups? What is the optimal number of sessions required to treat certain client problems or populations? What are the effects of co-leaders *versus* a single leader? What are the optimal agency conditions and characteristics that support time-limited behavioral group treatment? Answers to these questions can provide an agenda for the next decade of inquiry on this topic.

REFERENCES

BLOOM, BERNARD L.
    1984   *Community Mental Health: A General Introduction*. Monterey, Calif.: Brooks/Cole.
BLOOM, BERNARD L., AND JOEL FISCHER
    1982   *Evaluating Practice: Guidelines for the Accountable Professional*. Englewood Cliffs, N.J.: Prentice-Hall.
BUDMAN, SIMON H. (ed.)
    1981   *Forms of Brief Therapy*. New York: Guilford Press.
COREY, GERALD
    1981   *Theory and Practice of Group Counseling*. Monterey, Calif.: Brooks/Cole.
FISCHER, JOEL
    1981   "The social work revolution," *Social Work*, 26: 199–207.
FLOWERS, JOHN V.
    1979   "Behavioral analysis of group therapy and a model for behavioral group therapy." In Dennis Upper and Steven Ross (eds.), *Behavioral Group Therapy*. Champaign, Ill.: Research Press, pp. 5–38.
GAMBRILL, EILEEN
    1983   *Casework: A Competency-Based Approach*. Englewood Cliffs, N.J.: Prentice-Hall.
GARFIELD, SOL L.
    1982   "Eclecticism and integration in psychotherapy." *Behavior Therapy*, 13: 610–23.
GARVIN, CHARLES D., AND BRETT A. SEABURY
    1984   *Interpersonal Practice in Social Work: Processes and Procedures*. Englewood Cliffs, N.J.: Prentice-Hall.
LAWRENCE, HARRY, AND MARTIN SUNDEL
    1972   "Behavior modification in adult groups," *Social Work*, 17: 34–43.
    1975   "Self-modification in groups: A student training method for social group-work," *Journal of Education for Social Work*, 11: 76–83.
LAWRENCE, HARRY, AND CLAUDE WALTER
    1978   "Testing a behavioral approach with groups," *Social Work*, 23: 127–33.

LAZARUS, ARNOLD A.
1976   *Multi-Modal Behavior Therapy*. New York: Springer.
LENNARD, H. L., AND A. BERNSTEIN
1970   *Patterns in Human Interaction*. San Francisco: Jossey-Bass.
MANDEL, HARVEY P.
1981   *Short-Term Psychotherapy and Brief Treatment Techniques*. New York: Plenum.
MILLER, W. R., (ed.)
1980   *The Addictive Behaviors: Treatment of Alcoholism, Drug Abuse, Smoking and Obesity*. New York: Pergamon Press.
ORLINSKY, DAVID E., AND HOWARD, KENNETH I.
1978   "The relation of process to outcome in psychotherapy." In Sol L. Garfield and Allen Bergin (eds.), *Handbook of Psychotherapy and Behavior Change*. Second edition. New York: John Wiley & Sons.
RATHUS, SPENCER
1973   "A 30-item schedule for assessing assertive behavior," *Behavior Therapy*, 4: 398–406.
ROSE, SHELDON
1972   *Treating Children in Groups*. San Francisco: Jossey-Bass.
1977   *Group Therapy: A Behavioral Approach*. Englewood Cliffs, N.J.: Prentice-Hall.
1980   *A Casebook in Group Therapy*. Englewood Cliffs, N.J.: Prentice-Hall.
RUSH, H. JOHN (ed.)
1982   *Short-Term Psychotherapies for Depression: Behavioral, Interpersonal, Cognitive and Psychodynamic Approaches*. New York: Guilford Press.
SOBELL, MARK B., AND LINDA C. SOBELL
1978   *Behavioral Treatment of Alcohol Problems*. New York: Plenum.
SUNDEL, MARTIN, AND HARRY LAWRENCE
1970   "Time-limited behavioral group treatment with adults," *Michigan Mental Health Research Bulletin*, 4: 37–40.
1974   "Behavioral group treatment with adults in a family service agency." In Paul Glasser, Rosemary Sarri, and Robert Vinter (eds.), *Individual Change Through Small Groups*. New York: Free Press, pp. 325–47.
1977   "A systematic approach to treatment planning in time-limited behavioral groups," *Journal of Behavior Therapy and Experimental Psychiatry*, 8: 395–99.
SUNDEL, MARTIN AND SANDRA STONE SUNDEL
1982   *Behavior Modification in the Human Services: A Systematic Introduction to Concepts and Applications*. Second edition. Englewood Cliffs, N.J.: Prentice-Hall.
1985   "Behavior modification in groups: A time-limited model for assessment, planning, intervention and evaluation." In Dennis Upper and Steven Ross (eds.), *Handbook of Behavioral Group Therapy*. New York: Plenum.
In press   "A behavioral approach to time-limited groups," *Social Work with Groups*.

SUNDEL, SANDRA STONE, AND MARTIN SUNDEL
1980 *Be Assertive: A Practical Guide for Human Service Workers.* Beverly Hills, Calif.: Sage Publications.

THOMAS, EDWIN J.
1984 *Designing Interventions for the Helping Professions.* Beverly Hills, Calif.: Sage Publications.

UPPER, DENNIS, AND STEVEN ROSS (eds.)
1979, 1980, 1981 *Behavioral Group Therapy: An Annual Review.* Champaign, Ill.: Research Press.
1985 *Handbook of Behavioral Group Therapy.* New York: Plenum.

WILSON, G. TERRENCE
1981 "Behavior therapy as a short-term therapeutic approach." In Simon H. Budman (ed.), *Forms of Brief Therapy.* New York: Guilford Press.

26

Work with Disadvantaged and Oppressed Groups

Charles D. Garvin

OPPRESSION DEFINED

THE PURPOSE OF THIS CHAPTER is to describe how group workers can help members to cope with and struggle against social oppression. By social oppression we mean the ways that social institutions damage the identities, denigrate the life-styles, and deny access to opportunities to people based on attributes they share with others. To some degree all of us have had such experiences, and consequently the perspectives of this chapter are universally applicable. We shall, however, focus on group services to people whom we see as most severely suffering from being disadvantaged and socially oppressed. Examples that come to mind are such ethnic populations as blacks, Hispanics, native Americans, and Asian-Americans, as well as women.

Among those who experience social oppression are sexual minorities such as gay men and lesbians; age categories such as the elderly; handicapped people; populations that have been labeled "mental patient" or "offender"; individuals from "nontraditional" families; and the working and nonworking poor. This is an incomplete list. To extend it one can add members of many self-help groups that have formed to provide support for people who have been rejected by social welfare institutions.

The experience of oppression is devastating and has been well described by Goldenberg (1978). He wrote:

> Oppression is, above everything else, a condition of being, a particular stance one is forced to assume with respect to oneself, the world, and the exigencies of change. It is a pattern of hopelessness and helplessness, in which one sees oneself as static, limited, and expendable. People only become oppressed when they have been forced (either subtly or with obvious malice) to finally succumb to the insidious process that continually undermines hope and subverts the desire to "become." [p. 2]

The experience of members of the groups listed above attest to their social oppression. Gay men and lesbians are often denied employment or promotion; elderly individuals are not offered jobs for which they are fully qualified; handicapped people experience workplace discrimination and may find access to public facilities blocked; ex-offenders and ex-mental patients, in addition to these barriers, may be prevented from securing an education or positions in community organizations; single parents may find that schools, workplaces, and other pathways to independence are unnecessarily stressful because of rigidities in their schedules and policies. Poor people are stigmatized in educational and social institutions and can be caught for generations in a poverty cycle.

We have stressed ways that oppression blocks attaining skills and jobs because this is almost a common denominator for such groups. Those are only the most obvious consequences of being in an oppressed status. Social oppression may prohibit full access to many social institutions, may include rejection by peer groups, may deny one equal rights to adopt children or hold office, and may even cause a person to fear realistically for his or her safety, as the murder of a city supervisor in San Francisco because he was homosexual so tragically illustrates.

GROUP WORK AND EMPOWERMENT

Group work can be an effective means of serving members of oppressed groups for several reasons. These individuals often wish to join with others in a similar status in order to rediscover their self-worth and dignity. They may also seek membership in heterogeneous groups as a means of overcoming their isolation. In either case they may wish to enhance their ability to cope with or to change social institutions, and group experiences can provide training for this. Finally, and in many cases most importantly, they may recognize that a group possesses more power than a single individual to change an oppressive condition in either the service agency or in the larger environment.

In all of the above ways that groups can serve oppressed people, the key concept is *empowerment*. Solomon (1976) defines this as

> . . . a process whereby persons who belong to a stigmatized social category throughout their lives can be assisted to develop and increase skills in the exercise of interpersonal influence and the performance of valued social roles. Power is an interpersonal phenomenon; if it is not interpersonal it should probably be defined as "strength." However, the two concepts—power and strength—are so tightly interrelated that they are often used interchangeably. In any event, the transformation of the abstraction of power into an observable reality will be the dominant theme of the chapters that follow. [p. 6]

And we may add that this transformation of power will also be a dominant theme in this chapter. While Solomon primarily applies this concept to work with black people, we believe it is relevant to work with all victims of social oppression. Solomon presents an analysis of indirect and direct power blocks. She refers to three levels of indirect blocks. The first level includes negative evaluations that "become incorporated into family processes and prevent optimum development of personal resources." At the second level "power blocks occur when personal resources that have been limited by primary blocks in turn act to limit the development of interpersonal and technical skills." At the tertiary level "power blocks occur when limited personal resources and interpersonal and technical skills reduce effectiveness in performing valued social roles."

Solomon describes direct power blocks that can be experienced as blocks based on "negative valuation" that are applied directly by some social agent. Among the social agents that she discusses are health services, educational opportunities, and providers of material resources.

These kinds of blocks are encountered by all socially oppressed people, and it is the function of group work to help them to develop the kinds of power they need to struggle against them. This kind of focus is not new in social work, as the historical mission of the profession has been to help people to overcome obstacles to self-fulfillment. This has certainly been true of group work because of its social reform origins and its initial use in community centers and settlements with members who were oppressed by virtue of poverty, lack of education, and membership in stigmatized ethnic groups.

Group work lost some of this focus when it became more predominantly employed in psychiatric settings where the purpose of intervention was likely to be individual rather than social change. We favor some return to group work's earlier commitments, with the difference being the utilization of more effective interventions drawn from developments in practice as well as the social sciences.

AGENCY EFFECTS

The practitioner who seeks to offer group services to oppressed people must consider the effects of his or her agency setting. Many of our agencies themselves employ institutional forms of racism as well as institutional biases against members of other oppressed groups. Chesler (1976) in discussing institutional racism describes a number of forms of it in reference to blacks that we believe occur more generally. These forms are "blaming the victim"; focusing on the pathology of the victim; attributing blame to cultural values; using racism to maintain the *status quo*; and assuming members of the group are permanently dependent. The type of agency that welcomes the procedures and approaches we shall describe later is one that takes a social view of the problems of oppressed people. Such an agency does not confine its services to one-to-one or even group opportunities but provides support for the worker to function as an advocate and broker on behalf of clients. The worker is allocated time to contact other community agencies and is supported when she or he encounters conflict as a result of efforts to obtain entitlements for group members. The agency will also join in nonpartisan efforts to modify existing institutions and create new opportunities for the groups it serves.

The "ideal" agency for service to an oppressed group will support intervention technologies that are effective in enhancing empowerment. A principal feature of those technologies, as we shall more fully describe later, is their focus on developing the competence of individuals to cope with and seek to change aversive environments. Relevant ideas come from Maluccio's "Competence-Oriented Social Work Practice" (1981); Solomon's *Black Empowerment* (1976); Goldenberg's *Oppression and Social Intervention* (1978); Grinnell, Kyte, and Bostwick's "Environmental Modification" (1981); and Glasser and Garvin's "Organizational Model" (1976). An agency that employs group approaches focusing on internal psychological problems is likely primarily to "blame the victim."

The agency that operates in ways we have described also does not "colonize" the oppressed group but encourages its members to be fully involved at all levels of agency functioning. This includes the governing board, if it is not a public one, or at the highest policy-making level that remains within agency discretion to appoint members, if it is public. Members of the oppressed group will also be recruited for staff positions at all levels. The obvious consequence of this is that information regarding the group will be available, prejudicial attitudes in the agency will be modified, and role models will be available. Such evident agency openness will also be a boon when it comes to recruiting group members.

Some agencies that seek to serve members of oppressed groups will not operate in the aforementioned ways. The potential barriers can be removed as the agency prepares the way for such services. The agency should anticipate that if barriers to good service exist, it is likely that the group members, with the help of their worker, will work to alter agency conditions and should do so. Agency good faith is demonstrated when the agency is open to this.

GROUP PLANNING

When an agency expands its service to members of specified oppressed groups, it should begin with a needs assessment. This demonstrates that the agency wishes to know how such individuals define their needs and that it makes no assumptions. Such an assessment can be conducted by surveying members of the oppressed group in the agency's catchment area. Ideally, the survey should be conducted by staff members working with an advisory group comprising members of the targeted population. Another approach has been to arrange one or more "hearings" at which members of the groups can present their wishes for services.

This type of process led one agency to establish a group for former prison inmates who wished to support each other in coping with employment issues. The group also wanted to change the image of ex-offenders in the community. A university counseling center decided to reach out to gay and lesbian people. As a result of its needs assessment it established several "coming-out" groups, a conference for parents of homosexuals, a committee to respond to occasions when homosexuals were harassed, and a planning group for a gay social center. In another community the needs assessment identified a wide range of service deficits for the elderly. The agency consequently approached the central funding body with the recommendation that a new agency offering comprehensive services for the elderly, and particularly group services, should be formed.

Following the needs assessment, and when the types of group services to meet these needs have been ascertained, a period of agency preparation should take place. Unless the agency is largely composed of members of the specific oppressed population, a process of staff "consciousness-raising" should occur. This type of staff development includes meeting with representatives of the group, clarifying staff values, critiquing agency policies and procedures that embody discriminatory practices, and anticipating the challenges the agency will have to respond to as the program gets under way. One agency that wished to expand its services to the physically handicapped used such a process to learn about the problems handicapped people face in local businesses; sexuality and the handicapped; and the lack of understanding by teachers at all educational levels of how to approach people with such handicaps as blindness, deafness, and perceptual disorders.

After the type of service is determined and the agency is prepared, an active recruitment of prospective members should be conducted. This may require the agency to change its image in the community. The agency should seek publicity for its program in the media and should employ existing networks as well. An example of this was a new agency to serve homosexuals, which arranged interviews of its staff on local television and appearances before local homosexual groups. Posters on agency services were placed in gay bars and businesses. Physicians and other health services used by homosexuals were contacted as well as a local church that had been established by and for members of this population.

GROUP FORMATS

Group approaches will vary depending on the format chosen for the group. A variety of types of groups are appropriate, depending on the specific needs addressed. We now describe some of the formats that have been used to enhance empowerment. These types, however, are often combined in various ways in actual groups and are never as "pure" as we portray them.

1. *Consciousness-raising groups.* These groups are usually time-limited and help members to explore their views of their oppressed status, their reactions to the ways others respond to the status, how they wish to define their role, and their goals for personal and social change. Value clarification is an important component of such group experiences.

2. *Treatment groups.* While we have stressed that therapy groups often adopt a "blame the victim" posture, this does not deny that all the forms of treatment described throughout this volume may be required by oppressed people. By treatment we mean help in modifying one's dysfunctional behaviors, cognitions, or affects. Thus, for example, a homosexual who is fully committed to his or her sexual preference may wish help in improving the quality of relationships, feeling less depressed, or improving self-esteem. An agency that offers psychological services to such people, however, will employ staff who do not view homosexuality as a disease, who can help group members overcome their homophobia (fear of homosexuality in oneself and others), and who fully understand aversive social responses to homosexuality.

Analogously, while poor people will primarily need help in securing needed resources in the short run and economic justice in the long run, they may also require help with psychological problems. The issue is that individual as well as group treatment services are often geared to the more affluent and better educated members of society. Group treatment services for poor people should often be time-limited, should not pose transportation difficulties, should make childcare available during meetings, should be more acton- and less insight-oriented, should provide opportunity for members to "learn" how to function in treatment situations, should minimize social distance between staff and members, and should focus on contemporary concerns (Lorion, 1978). Group rather than individual treatment approaches are often more acceptable to poor people because of the support they experience from the presence of others who are similarly oppressed.

3. *Social action groups.* Engaging in action to change oppressive conditions will be helpful to disadvantaged people in several ways. In addition to the manifest purpose of the action, this activity will enhance members'

competence to cope with the environment, raise their self-esteem, and teach skills in working with others. A primary consideration for this type of activity is the selection of a project that is neither too insignificant nor too ambitious. Group workers in an earlier period were notorious for the fervor with which they sought stop signs on busy thoroughfares. In the 1960s, in contrast, social workers in their civil rights zeal led group members into rent strikes, welfare department sit-ins, and the like without adequate anticipation of the power of the establishment at least to procrastinate if not to retaliate. The voter registration drive of the 1980s, in contrast, appears to be a useful action that many client groups have supported with totally positive consequences.

4. *Network and support groups.* A frequent problem for oppressed people is their social isolation from others in a similar status. An important service, therefore, is to help them to make contact with each other so they can secure support in coping with the consequences of oppression as well as seeking changes in their situations. The role of the worker is to facilitate the ways oppressed individuals can communicate with one another in order to establish such groups. This has been done with the help of such community institutions as churches, schools, and trade unions as well as other social welfare agencies. The worker will usually work with an initial planning committee and will remain as a consultant and resource once the group is under way.

5. *Skill groups.* Agencies may also be helpful to oppressed people by training them in skills. Some of these skills are group leadership, social change, communications, and networking. In group leadership sessions members have been taught how to plan agendas, conduct meetings, and organize discussions. In social change groups members have been taught skills for lobbying, advocacy, use of the media, and even passive resistance. Communication skills, which can be useful in any skill-building situation, include techniques for presenting one's own "case" clearly as well as giving feedback to others on the clarity of their expression. Networking involves ways of identifying and contacting individuals and institutions, both professional and "lay," that can be helpful in attaining one's goals.

6. *"Mainstream" groups.* Nothing we have stated is meant to imply that oppressed people should always be isolated in groups with others in a similar status. Homogeneous groups are often valuable because of the support they provide, their central focus on reaffirmation of identity, and their potency in social change. On the other hand, for a variety of reasons an oppressed person may choose to join a group with others who are not oppressed in the same way. This can be useful for all concerned as members discover how oppression diminishes the oppressor as well as the oppressed and as all search for an understanding of the nature of a just society. An ex-

ample of this was a social group of adolescents that recruited a youth with cerebral palsy. One member later confided to the worker that he would never again use the word "spastic" in a pejorative way.

GROUP DEVELOPMENT

Pregroup Phase

Once the type of group format has been chosen as a consequence of a needs assessment and of negotiations between potential group members and the agency, a process is initiated that begins with the composition of the group and continues until the group terminates. Since the emphasis is on empowerment, the members or their legitimate representatives should be involved at each stage of the process. With reference to composition this means that individuals from the targeted population should participate in recruiting members. That does not deny the group worker the opportunity to use his or her expertise in the task but does require that it be shared. As members become familiar with the skills involved in creating groups, they will be able to employ them independently of professional workers on future occasions if they so wish. Occasionally, however, confidentiality issues regarding individuals will arise and will be respected.

An example was a project conducted in a prison setting. The worker began his group program in a traditional manner by conducting several groups for inmates. As members discovered the ways the groups could help them plan for their futures as well as cope with the prison as a system, a number of them volunteered for a group leadership training program. Graduates of the training became co-leaders with professionals, and ultimately a number of groups were conducted by two co-leaders, both inmates. Those leaders took charge of recruiting inmates for and composing groups. Future plans call for an inmate governing council for the program that will assume responsibility for initiating groups. It should be mentioned that this was not a specially designed prison setting. The worker did encounter opposition from prison authorities but gradually and over a period of time moved in the direction we have described, as each step was found to enhance the likelihood of prisoner rehabilitation.

Formation

As with any other type of group, one of the first tasks after the group has convened is the determination of individual and group goals. We believe that any type of group work activity must consider both types of goals. An additional ingredient is more relevant to groups for empowerment than other social work sponsored groups: Group and individual goals must also consider the effect on others who are in a similar social status to the members.

Oppressed people must understand the negative social and political implications if some individuals make gains at the expense of others. When one (or a few) poor people, ex-prisoners, or homosexuals become tokens, this can be used to deny opportunities to others, and the token becomes a representative of a group rather than an individual in his or her own right. It is also politically problematic for some individuals to take a position contrary to that of organizations that legitimately represent the oppressed group without their careful consideration of the consequences for all involved. For example, when several gay group members sought employment in a firm that was boycotted by the gay community, the energies of all concerned were placed in intracommunity struggles rather than in creating job opportunities.

Goals and means to attain them should be based on an assessment of individual competencies to cope with institutions as well as on institutional opportunities and barriers. The differences between this and traditional social work assessment is the emphasis on assessing social competence and related opportunity structures. Within this process, as Maluccio (1981) has pointed out, the member is viewed as a learner and the measure is of competence rather than of personality deficits. When presented in this way, we find that many forms of resistance to service are removed and cooperation between professional and member is more likely to be forthcoming, particularly if the type of agency preparation we described earlier has been achieved.

As we have shown, oppressed and disadvantaged people require ways of becoming personally more powerful as well as changing social institutions. Thus both the assessment and the related goal choices will reflect a dual focus on individuals and their environments.

Goal Attainment

During the group's goal attainment phases, several approaches are used for group sessions for empowerment as well as for social change. We shall emphasize empowerment in this section as strategies such groups can use to change their social environments are documented elsewhere in this volume (see Chapter 17).

One set of techniques that we referred to earlier is that for consciousness-raising. It includes asking members (1) to describe their life histories to each other so they can see ways in which past experiences led them to devaluate themselves and (2) to examine their current interactions to identify how they now respond to such experiences in powerless ways. A relevant concept here is "false consciousness," which refers to an acceptance of the values of one's oppressor to one's own detriment. Thus poor people may come to believe they are incompetent; homosexuals that they are evil; mental patients that they are incurable; and the handicapped that they do not have the same rights as others to an education or an intimate relationship. All of these myths must be challenged as part of the empowerment process. Values clarification (Simon, Howe, and Kirschenbaum, 1972) is another useful tool in this process. An example of this was a consciousness raising group for women who were patients in a psychiatric hospital (Adolph, 1983). The worker was able to help the members to make important steps toward rehabilitation when she facilitated their awareness that much of their dysfunctional behavior was their way of coping with their oppression as women.

A second set of techniques relates to *training members in social competence*, one type of which is assertiveness. This concept derives from the idea that all human beings have the right to express their needs, wishes, and feelings in ways that do not infringe upon the needs and rights of others (Lange and Jakubowski, 1976). Disadvantaged and oppressed people are often given the idea that their allegedly low status requires them to be compliant rather than assertive. Assertiveness training is therefore an important feature of empowerment. This training includes preliminary discussion of an assertive philosophy regarding the expression of one's needs. That is followed by the presentation of assertive models and an opportunity to rehearse assertive responses relevant to one's specific situation.

Other types of competencies to enhance empowerment are how to engage in constructive confrontation, how to express anger appropriately, how to negotiate, and how to present information to support one's position. Workers also teach members how to defend their rights more aggressively. This includes identifying vulnerable positions of others, eliciting help from people who have authority over an adversary, and threatening to employ legal action.

A third set of techniques pertain to *responsibility enhancement*. Sue (1981) points out that a distinction must be made between locus of control and locus of responsibility. Locus of control refers to attributions regarding the causes of events to either one's own actions or those of others. Locus of responsibility refers to the self-expectation that one should act to change situations as opposed to the expectation that others should act on behalf of oneself. We join Sue in the belief that it is functional for oppressed people to have an external locus of control and an internal locus of responsibility. In other words, oppressed people should not blame themselves for the personal consequences of social oppression but, nevertheless, should assume responsibility for changing their own circumstances as well as those of others in the same status. This distinction is made as workers help members to understand the historical and current roots of oppression while still expecting members to take action on behalf of themselves and their group.

When workers strive to help members empower themselves they should remind the members and themselves of the possibilities of repercussions: Pressure may be brought upon the agency to discontinue the group; the agency, itself, may not wish to face the political risks; the worker may be charged with unprofessional conduct for encouraging members to project blame; the other people in the member's network may seek to punish the member—to name only a few of the consequences we have encountered. There are clear reasons why social work has, at times, retreated to a psychological stance. Social change always meets with opposition, sometimes at considerable cost to all concerned. Thus a worker should help the members anticipate the likely consequences of their actions and to plan how these consequences will be faced. It is essential, moreover, that the worker guarantee the group that she or he will support the members to the fullest extent possible throughout the process, but that all face risks.

Termination

All the usual tasks of termination are undertaken in this type of group work, but some are particularly important. Since the mission is empowerment, and the full emancipation of members from oppression during the life of the group is inconceivable, members must be helped to take from this experience the strength they have acquired. This requires a full identification of what has been learned together with a plan as to the next steps. Many members, after an empowering experience in a group, will seek to affiliate with broader-based social action movements, and this can be facilitated and encouraged.

Since, as we have stated, opposition to change is expected, it is rare that all the group's goals will have been achieved; more often than we would like, efforts at social change meet with failure. Members, in that circumstance, must be helped to take the view—to paraphrase the old saying—that it is better to have struggled and lost than never to have struggled at all because of the experience of learning together with others, the comradeship enjoyed, and the identification of future challenges.

REFERENCES

Adolph, Marcelle
    1983   "The all-women's consciousness raising group as a component of treatment for mental illness," *Social Work with Groups*, 6, nos. 3-4 (Fall/Winter): pp. 117-32.
Chesler, Mark A.
    1976   "Contemporary sociological theories of racism." In P. Katz (ed.), *Toward the Elimination of Racism*. New York: Pergamon, pp. 21-72.

GLASSER, PAUL H., AND CHARLES GARVIN
  1976 "An organizational model." In Robert W. Roberts and Helen Northen
        (eds.), *Theories of Social Work with Groups*. New York: Columbia Uni-
        versity Press, pp. 75–115.
GOLDENBERG, IRA
  1978 *Oppression and Social Intervention*. Chicago: Nelson-Hall.
GRINNELL, RICHARD M.; NANCY S. KYTE; AND GERALD J. BOSTWICK, JR.
  1981 "Environmental modification." In Anthony N. Maluccio (ed.)., *Promot-
        ing Competence in Clients: A New/Old Approach to Social Work Prac-
        tice*. New York: Free Press, pp. 152–84.
LANGE, ARTHUR J., AND PATRICIA JAKUBOWSKI
  1976 *Responsible Assertive Behavior*. Champaign, Ill.: Research Press.
LORION, RAYMOND P.
  1978 "Research on psychotherapy and behavior change with the disadvan-
        taged." In Sol L. Garfield and Allen E. Bergin (eds.), *Handbook of Psy-
        chotherapy and Behavior Change: An Empirical Analysis*. New York: Wi-
        ley, pp. 903–38.
MALUCCIO, ANTHONY N.
  1981 "Competence-oriented social work practice: An ecological approach." In
        Anthony N. Maluccio (ed.), *Promoting Competence in Clients: A New/
        Old Approach to Social Work Practice*. New York: Free Press, pp. 1–26.
SIMON, SIDNEY B.; LELAND N. HOWE; AND HOWARD KIRSCHENBAUM
  1972 *Values Clarification: A Handbook of Practical Strategies for Teachers and
        Students*. New York: Hart.
SOLOMON, BARBARA B.
  1976 *Black Empowerment*. New York: Columbia University Press.
SUE, D. W.
  1981 *Counseling the Culturally Different: Theory and Practice*. New York:
        Wiley.

27

Group Work with Antisocial Youths

Ronald A. Feldman

GROUP WORK METHODS have been used with antisocial youths since the earliest days of social work. Group services have been offered to youths in closed correctional institutions (such as reformatories), residential settings (including psychiatric treatment centers and group homes), outpatient and community-based facilities (such as community mental health centers and juvenile courts), recreational agencies (such as neighborhood houses), and on the streets (in the form of detached group work programs for delinquent gangs). With only a handful of exceptions (e.g. Feldman, Caplinger, and Wodarski, 1983; Ross and Gendreau, 1980), however, the results of group work with antisocial youths have not been particularly encouraging. In fact, a substantial body of literature suggests that group programs for antisocial youths have failed miserably (e.g. Carney, 1977; Lipton, Martinson, and Wilks, 1975; Romig, 1978).

In the vast majority of instances group therapists have not been able to generate prosocial behavior change on the part of antisocial youths or to maintain behavioral changes that had been previously brought about in the treatment setting. However, in fairness—and with some degree of dismay— it must be noted that few systematic studies have appeared in the social work literature about the effects of group work treatment with antisocial youths. Rather, nearly all of the pertinent research appears in the criminology, psychology, and psychiatry literatures. It is probable that most of the group treatment programs reported therein were conducted by intervention agents who did *not* have professional training in social group work. Hence, to acquire a more accurate assessment of the effects of group work with antisocial youths, at least two tasks ought to be initiated in the near future. First, studies of group treatment programs that appear in allied literatures should be reviewed carefully in order to differentiate between interventions

This article was prepared with the assistance of research funds from the Center for Studies of Crime and Delinquency, National Institute of Mental Health (MH 18813), Office of Prevention, National Institute of Mental Health (MH35033), and the Youth Development Bureau, Administration on Children, Youth, and Families (290 PD 86517).

that can properly be cited as instances of social group work, on the one hand, and as examples of other therapies on the other. Second, group workers should systematically and comprehensively review the efficacy of their own efforts to deliver group treatment to antisocial youths.

Regardless of the treatment agent's professional affiliation, however, it is not particularly difficult to identify the key reasons for the lackluster results of group intervention programs with antisocial youths. Unresponsive social service agencies, outdated training programs, reified practice traditions, and inadequate knowledge about contemporary research all play a role. While the present discussion does not presume to address the former two concerns, it seeks, in part, to acquaint the reader with pertinent research about group work with antisocial youths, which in turn may lead to the modification of ineffective treatment practices.

TRADITIONAL APPROACHES TO
GROUP WORK WITH ANTISOCIAL YOUTHS

To comprehend fully the problems, as well as the vast potential, of group work with antisocial youths, it is necessary to examine the many dysfunctions of the traditional approaches that have been employed. In brief, these can be considered in terms of their organizational settings, small group contexts, timing of intervention, worker training, definitions of the "antisocial" youth, maintenance of behavioral gains, linkages among treatment technologies, and emphasis upon rehabilitation. Each of these issues merits separate consideration.

Organizational Settings

Group work programs that attempt to deal with antisocial behavior concentrate predominantly upon youths who already manifest deeply ingrained patterns of behavioral disorder. It is not surprising, therefore, that group workers concentrate upon rehabilitation more than prevention and, even further, that their practice efforts frequently take place in such organizations as correctional institutions, reformatories, and large residential centers. Ironically, however, the basic preconditions for effective group work treatment of antisocial youths often are absent in such settings.

In many, if not most, correctional settings, service delivery problems tend to arise because of inherent conflicts between the organization's custodial requirements and its treatment objectives. As a result staff friction is likely to occur, and treatment efforts may become fragmented or neutralized. Even more problematic is the fact that correctional institutions are drastically overcrowded, leading to countertherapeutic forms of social control among the inmates. When facilities are overtaxed, the need to control inmate behavior in the short run—rather than modify it in the long run—takes precedence within the institution. For example, the National Assessment of Juvenile Corrections has reported that only 26 percent of surveyed institutions for juveniles maintained the staff-inmate ratio usually recommended by the leading standard-setting organizations (Sarri, 1974). Similarly, Nagel (1977) has warned that America now has the highest prison population in its history and that the growth of inmate populations has reached crisis proportions. When correctional institutions are inordinately large, staff often relinquish the responsibility for social control, at least in part, to the inmates themselves. In doing so, they may inadvertently—or even purposely—delegate control powers to highly antisocial inmates and thereby legitimize countertherapeutic behavior within the institution. As a result genuine behavioral change may be difficult or impossible to achieve. And even if achieved, it may be impossible to generalize such change beyond the correctional institution or to stabilize it within the youths' natural communities.

Behavioral changes that are adaptive in an institutional setting may, in fact, prove to be maladaptive in more normalized environments. Indeed, this is documented by the fact that large numbers of youths recidivate quickly after release from a correctional institution. Goldman (1974), for example, has reported that 51 percent of the youths who were released from juvenile correctional facilities in New York state were reapprehended by the police within a year; an additional 18 percent were apprehended within the next two years. Similarly Kitchener, Schmidt, and Glaser (1977) found that 50 percent of the recidivists in their study committed a crime less than two years after release.

Even more relevant for group workers, however, is the fact that the peer group subculture within such institutions tends to militate against effective behavior change. In an important but little-known study, for example, Street (1965) has shown that inmates within such institutions tend to be isolated and insulated from one another. They rarely form solitary peer groups, even in order to resist the authorities who ultimately control their fate. Instead, the atmosphere is one of alienation, mistrust, and prisonization, all of which are formidable barriers to effective treatment. Even in a small detention home Duncan (1974) found that delinquent verbalizations occurred nearly twenty-two times more frequently than prosocial verbalizations. Moreover, delinquent verbalizations were accorded peer reinforcement in 98.3 percent of all cases while prosocial verbalizations were reinforced only about three-quarters of the time. In effect, the clients in such settings were encouraged to model deviant behavior for one another and to reinforce one another for antisocial behavior rather than prosocial behavior. In this respect, then, it is hardly a cliché to suggest that correctional institutions may serve more readily as "schools for crime" than as settings that promote positive behavior change.

Finally, even when prosocial behavior change is generated in such institutions, released youths often encounter a unique problem that works to their disadvantage: They become stigmatized as a result of being treated in an institution that reputedly houses "criminals," "delinquents," "perverts," or "maladjusted" youths. This often causes important work opportunities or other legitimate opportunities to be foreclosed. Even worse, as observed by Newton and Sheldon (1975), the more one's status as "deviant" is reinforced by others, the more one tends to view himself or herself as deviant and to behave accordingly. Likewise, Farrington (1977) has employed official records of juvenile delinquency to demonstrate that adverse public labeling leads to increased deviance on one's part. His data indicate that the effects of adverse labeling are cumulative and that youths who are first labeled before age fourteen suffer more persistent effects than those who are labeled at a later age.

Despite the formidable treatment barriers in institutional settings, it is obvious that group work programs will continue under their auspices. Among other things, they facilitate social control and protect the institution's public identity as a rehabilitation setting rather than as a purely custodial facility. But regardless of the evaluative criteria employed, the cost-benefit ratios of group work programs in such settings are bound to remain decidedly high. More optimum preconditions must exist for group work practice with antisocial youths.

Small Group Contexts

During the last two decades many social workers and juvenile justice officials have made valiant efforts to avert the problems entailed by delivering treatment in closed institutions. They have attempted group work in community-based settings such as group homes, youth development centers, work furlough programs, halfway houses, and various types of juvenile diversion programs. Clearly, group work programs in such settings are able to avoid a host of difficulties, including overcrowding, countertherapeutic social control processes, adverse institutional subcultures, severe problems in generalizing behavior change to the clients' natural communities, and excessive per capita costs.

Yet, to the surprise of many observers, community-based group treatment programs have hardly fared any better than their counterparts in closed institutions. While their per capita costs obviously are much lower, failures to generate long-term behavioral gains are roughly the same. Studies by McCord (1978), Koshel (1973), Romig (1978), Lerman (1975), and Wright and Dixon (1977) clearly demonstrate that community-based group treatment programs for antisocial youths have been far from successful.

Given the various advantages of such programs vis-à-vis the ones in closed institutions, what then accounts for their notable lack of success? In brief, their most critical deficiencies can be traced to some of the same factors that adversely affect the programs in closed settings. Essentially these pertain to the small group context in which service is provided. Even in community-based settings, for example, the traditional modus operandi results in groups composed in a manner that militates against effective treatment. Specifically, the treatment groups in such settings tend to consist entirely of youths who manifest significant antisocial problems. In fact, virtually all rehabilitative programs in group work tend to cluster together clients with similar symptomatologies. Thus, for instance, social workers establish groups for alcohol abusers, teenage mothers, discharged schizophrenics, and, of course, antisocial youths. It is presumed that such clients can help one another to develop effective coping skills or perhaps that economies of scale occur as a result of grouping together clients with similar symptomatologies. But, given the scant success of group work efforts with such populations, these assumptions are highly suspect. In fact, it is entirely plausible that the dysfunctions of this mode of group composition neutralize, or even surpass, its presumed advantages. What, then, would constitute a more productive means of composing treatment groups? This question will be examined shortly.

Timing of Intervention

The vast majority of group work programs for antisocial youths tend to serve individuals who already have highly deviant patterns of antisocial behavior. Accordingly, such youths tend to be in their midadolescent or late adolescent years. Yet, interestingly, a large number of longitudinal studies reveal that most youths who embark upon delinquent "careers" commit their first adjudicable offense at a relatively young age. In a study of 9,945 boys, for example, Wolfgang, Figlio, and Sellin (1972) found that the first officially recorded act of delinquency tended to peak at thirteen years of age. Large numbers of official offenses occurred even before that age. Farrington and West (1971) report that children who exhibit bad public school conduct at ages eight and ten—as stated by teachers—become either persistently aggressive youths or adjudicated delinquents by the age of fourteen. Hence it is obvious that many, if not most, group work programs for antisocial youths are geared toward clients who already have deeply ingrained patterns of antisocial behavior. In essence this means that such programs are engaged in tertiary prevention rather than secondary or primary prevention.

Longitudinal studies of antisocial youths reveal two further items of note. First, the initial antisocial acts of youths who eventually become delinquents are not of a very serious nature. Rather, they tend to be acts that occur frequently, or at high base rates, but are not exceptionally serious. Wolfgang, Figlio, and Sellin, for instance, found that 87 percent of recorded delinquent acts scored below 300 on their "seriousness" index. Almost one-third of the delinquencies were apprehensions for curfew violations, truancy, trespassing, or similar activities. Clearly their subjects engaged in relatively minor forms of antisocial behavior during the early stages of their delinquent careers. Similarly, a literature review by Conger, Miller, and Walsmith (1966) found that even in early grade school future delinquents generally are less well adjusted than nondelinquent peers of the same age, sex, intelligence quotient, socioeconomic status, residential background, and ethnic group membership.

In a now classic series of longitudinal studies with patients from a child guidance clinic, Robins (1966, 1972, 1974, 1978) likewise found that clinical evidence of antisocial behavior on the part of preadolescents predicted effectively to adult criminal behavior or psychopathology. Of youngsters who were referred to the child guidance clinic for antisocial behavior (N = 314), only 15 percent had no psychiatric illness as adults, as against 52 percent of the controls (N = 90) and 30 percent of the children who were referred for reasons other than antisocial behavior (N = 122). And, after completing a large-scale study of former juvenile delinquents, Lewis and Balla (1976) concluded that juvenile justice officials often ignored the lesser and more frequent offenses of juveniles only to find that such youths subsequently committed far more serious crimes, including murder, that required incarceration.

Second, longitudinal studies clearly indicate that large numbers of preadolescents first commit frequent, albeit minor, offenses but, if left untreated, progress toward increasingly serious forms of antisocial behavior. This hardly means that all such youths are at extreme risk for adult criminality. Rather, youths become increasingly at risk for more serious forms of misbehavior as they progress toward each successive "plateau" of a deviant career. Patterson (1982) and Loeber (1982), for example, have identified "career chains" among antisocial youths. They found that childhood noncompliance to parents leads to increased statistical risk for more serious forms of antisocial behavior. Each step in the career chain becomes more deviant or disruptive than the preceding ones. Frequent fights with peers, for example, are succeeded by teasing, then temper tantrums, and subsequently by serious antisocial acts. Likewise, lying to parents is associated with a greater statistical probability of uncontrolled running around with antisocial peers, which in turn progresses to higher at-risk status for stealing, and then for setting fires. In other words, serious antisocial acts that occur at a low base rate, such as assault or homicide, tend to be preceded by less serious misbehaviors that occur at a comparatively high base rate.

Somewhat similarly, studies by Zax et al. (1968) and by Westman, Rice, and Bermann (1967) demonstrate that children who are labeled as hyperactive or a conduct disorder seldom change for the better if left untreated. Follow-up studies of such children have found continued classroom misbehavior and poor peer acceptance (Riddle and Rapoport, 1976); sustained behavior problems and immature moral development (Campbell, et al., 1977); and persistent academic, interpersonal, and social difficulties (Mendelson, Johnson and Stewart, 1971; Minde et al., 1971). Cahalan and Room (1974) have reported similarly that adult alcoholism is predicted better by early antisocial behavior of a nonspecific type than by any other social characteristic. And, of course, the above-cited studies by Robins suggest that, even if diagnosed and treated at an early age, the antisocial behavior patterns of youths are likely to continue in exacerbated form into adulthood.

Finally, in this regard it is pertinent to note that self-report questionnaires from a random sample of 3,070 male and female subjects in French Canadian high schools revealed that 64.6 percent of the respondents had been involved in *more than one type* of delinquent behavior. In other words, during the early stages of antisocial behavior 77.5 percent of all the reported delinquent involvements were of a multiple and heterogeneous nature. In fact 46 percent of the youths had participated in four or more different types of delinquent behavior, including aggressive acting-out, drug abuse, petty theft, serious theft, vandalism, and arson. Among other things the diversity of early antisocial behavior among youths indicates that interventive programs in small group settings are especially promising, for it is in these settings that many such behaviors are likely to be first manifested and potentially remedied. This conclusion is further supported by the well-documented fact that many forms of high-base-rate antisocial behavior first occur in small group settings or in the company of peers (cf. Friday and Hage, 1976; Akers et al., 1979; Jessor, Jessor, and Finney, 1973; Radosevich et al., 1978; Biddle, Banks, and Marlin, 1980; Johnstone, 1978; Erickson and Jensen, 1977; Haney and Gold, 1973; Hirschi, 1969; Hindelang, 1976).

Leader Training

During the past two decades research concerning the ineffectiveness of professional intervention for antisocial youths has led to a variety of results. On the one hand, group workers have advocated increased rigor in research, more effective training programs, and greater attention to the quality of professional intervention. On the other hand, many administrators have decided to employ large numbers of subprofessional or nonprofessional personnel as group leaders. The latter trend was stimulated in part by early research findings which suggested that such individuals were nearly as effective as better paid professionals (cf., for instance, Carkhuff, 1969; O'Donnell and George, 1977; Poser, 1966; Alley and Blanton, 1976; Scioli and Cook, 1976). In recent years, however, few empirical data have been reported in support of this claim. Even more pertinent to the present discussion, no systematic field studies within the group work realm have attempted to address the question. Hence it is plausible that much of the presumed ineffectiveness of social group work may be attributable, in fact, to the inadequacies of relatively untrained subprofessionals. However, before one can recommend that professional training be regarded as a prerequisite for group work with antisocial youths, it is essential to acquire systematic empirical evidence regarding the particular efficacy of professionally trained group workers. This issue, too, will be examined shortly.

Definitions of the "Antisocial" Youth

Perhaps the most fundamental factor that militates against effective group work treatment inheres in the definitions of "antisocial" and "delinquent" behavior that are prevalent in the helping professions. This problem plagues not only group work but all criminal justice professionals regardless of their practice modalities. Specifically, societal problems such as juvenile delinquency and antisocial behavior tend to be defined in dichotomous terms. Both in clinical assessment and legal practice, youths are labeled in simple "either-or" terms. That is, they are judged to be either "delinquents" or "nondelinquents"; likewise, they are deemed to be either "antisocial" or "prosocial." Little recognition is given to the fact that the overwhelming majority of youths are neither "delinquent" nor "nondelinquent." Rather, the behavioral patterns of most youths represent the vast middle ground of behavioral variation that exists between the polar extremes.

As Schrag (1971) has commented, the practice of dichotomizing people into criminal and noncriminal categories is contrary to common sense and available empirical evidence. Indeed, after a major self-report study, Gold (1970) concluded that if any chargeable offense makes a youngster technically a delinquent, then by their own admission more than 80 percent of the teenagers in his random sample of "normal" youths were delinquent at the time of the study. For the most part social workers have taken little heed of Empey's (1969) assertion that traditional ways of viewing the delinquent must be changed in light of the fact that delinquent behavior is not merely an attribute or a characteristic of an individual. Since it now is obvious that delinquency and antisocial behavior are matters of degree, this fact must be recognized in ensuing diagnostic and intervention programs if group workers are to achieve success in treating antisocial youths.

A related concern pertains to a second noteworthy fact. That is, most youths who are formally adjudicated because of delinquent activity have been involved in serious misbehaviors that are enacted on a relatively *infrequent* basis. Although the mean incidences of some antisocial behaviors, such as rape and robbery, are very high for certain populations, only a handful of individuals exhibit such behaviors at a truly high rate. These are low-base-rate behaviors that are unlikely to constitute even one-tenth of 1 percent of any particular individual's total behavioral profile. The extremely low frequency of such behaviors poses immense problems for the assessment and prediction of antisocial behavior on the part of any given youth. Besides concentrating on high-base-rate behaviors, then, group workers should utilize evaluation procedures that enable them to perform a more comprehensive assessment of any particular client's behavioral profile.

Maintenance of Behavioral Gains

Despite—or perhaps because of—the somewhat gloomy portrayal of group work efficacy that has been depicted above, it is imperative to point out that the available reviews of group treatment with antisocial youths have not been unanimous in their conclusions. While the overall trends are consistent, occasional studies suggest that some group treatment programs have been effective in the short run. But, unfortunately, it is evident that clients' behavioral gains usually are not maintained for a lengthy period of time, such as a year or more beyond treatment. Reviewers frequently assert, therefore, that various group treatment programs have failed because the clients' behavioral gains were not stabilized beyond termination.

In my judgment, however, such a conclusion is not warranted. It is specious to assert that group efforts have "failed" so long as initial behavioral gains were, indeed, achieved. Rather, the failure inheres in the fact that social service agencies seldom provide maintenance programs for clients who have successfully completed a period of group work treatment. The supposition, naive as it may be, is that "once cured, forever cured." This stance, as well as the limited mode of group work practice that follows from it, is entirely at odds with one of the most fundamental assumptions of group work practice, namely, that human behavior and its remediation are a product of the ongoing interaction between an individual and his or her environment. The full burden for maintaining treatment gains is placed solely upon the previously malfunctioning client, even though it is widely acknowledged that he or she may face awesome environmental stresses upon the termination of treatment. Once treated successfully, group work agencies should continue to provide services for former clients. However, their services should shift from a focus on tertiary prevention to secondary prevention and, if feasible, to primary prevention.

Strengthening Linkages
Among Treatment Technologies

Another challenge that besets contemporary group work is the need to strengthen the linkages among available technologies of group treatment. Although group work texts have proliferated rapidly during the past decade, systematic formulations of treatment principles are still relatively rare.

Nevertheless, as indicated throughout the present volume, considerable progress has been made toward understanding the social, psychological, and behavioral foundations of small group intervention. To date, however, the respective merits of these perspectives have not been linked together in a systematic and coherent fashion. If this challenge can be met, group work practitioners are likely to make substantial strides in their ability to cope with a wide range of behavioral problems.

The deficiencies of current treatment technologies are exemplified, in part, by the fact that group work practice typically is evaluated only in terms of individual outcomes. While this represents the most essential aspect of treatment evaluation, it is hardly the sole one. Surprisingly, few studies of group treatment examine the extent to which the group worker actually implements his or her planned treatment strategies. Instead, group work tends to be viewed as an inscrutable "black box" whose effects and, indeed, whose very existence are inferred only from client outcomes. Yet without accurately gauging the extent to which group workers actually implement a given treatment technology, it is impossible to determine how, if at all, client behavioral outcomes are related to the worker's specific interventions.

Emphasis upon Rehabilitation

A final note pertains to an issue that has been briefly mentioned above; to wit, social workers typically do not provide services to youths until they exhibit obvious evidence of behavioral disorder. Hence, for the most part their efforts are limited to rehabilitation, or tertiary prevention, and they typically work with the most recalcitrant clients within any particular diagnostic category. Interventions occur at a relatively late stage in the youth's antisocial career, and therefore the client is less amenable to remediation than if treatment had begun at an earlier point. Nevertheless, group workers are well positioned to engage in primary or secondary prevention. Their active involvement in recreational programs, socialization activities, and neighborhood services enables them to diagnose incipient social problems at an early stage of development and thus to intervene earlier than other professionals. Nevertheless, few social service agencies have systematically and comprehensively directed their group work programs toward secondary and, especially, primary prevention with youths who are at high risk for antisocial behavior. To do so would result in more efficient utilization of available group work resources.

TOWARD EFFECTIVE GROUP WORK
WITH ANTISOCIAL YOUTHS

Although group work services for antisocial youths clearly are in need of improvement, the current situation is far from hopeless. On the contrary, the foregoing analysis points to several discrete and coherent strategies for developing more effective group work services for antisocial youths. Furthermore, a large-scale program of field research with more than one thousand boys has confirmed the efficacy of many of the recommendations that follow from the analysis. While passing reference to various aspects of the research appear below, the full details and results of the program are available elsewhere (Feldman and Caplinger, 1983; Feldman, Caplinger, and Wodarski, 1983).

Nonstigmatizing and Normalized Service Settings

The foregoing discussion has described the dysfunctions of traditional juvenile justice, mental health, and social service agencies that attempt to provide group work services for antisocial youths. Undoubtedly such institutions will remain an integral part of the American scene for many years to come. Indeed, in the absence of a drastic reformulation of the current approach toward juvenile justice, there will be a pressing need for rehabilitative, and even custodial, care for tens of thousands of youths. However, it is clear that better approaches can be devised and that these should reduce the need for treating youths in closed facilities.

In brief, increasing numbers of group work programs for antisocial youths ought to be offered in agencies that are nonstigmatizing and highly normalized. Specifically, such agencies should not carry the stigmata of being publicly identified as "correctional" or "mental health" agencies. Rather, they should be regarded by the public as mainstream social service agencies that typically provide services for "normal" clients. Even further, they should enable limited numbers of antisocial youths to interact with large numbers of prosocial youngsters under circumstances that do not differ greatly from the ones in their own neighborhoods.

Hence it is proposed that social work organizations such as neighborhood houses, community centers, and recreational agencies increasingly direct their group work programs toward antisocial youths. In doing so, however, it is imperative that they bring only limited numbers of antisocial youths into the agency so as not to jeopardize its nonstigmatizing public identity. They should do so in accordance with safeguards like the ones to be described later. While only small numbers of antisocial youths will be served by any given program, the efficacy of this approach, along with the ease with which it can be adopted by many agencies, indicates that its nationwide impact can be substantial. For the interested reader, the rationales for redirecting "traditional" social service agencies in this fashion are spelled out in fuller detail elsewhere (see Feldman et al., 1973; Feldman, Caplinger, and Wodarski, 1983).

Prosocial Small Group Contexts

In organizational settings such as the ones described above, it is proposed that treatment groups be composed in a manner that enables antisocial youngsters to interact frequently with potent prosocial role models and with other youngsters who are likely to reward or reinforce them for conventional behavior. Accordingly, one or two antisocial youths should be integrated into activity groups of six to ten prosocial peers. Laboratory studies demonstrate that group conformity pressures are most potent when the individuals who are targeted for behavior change are confronted by a unanimous majority of relevant others (cf. Asch, 1952). More important, however, recent field research demonstrates that antisocial youngsters exhibit significant diminutions in antisocial behavior and significant gains in prosocial behavior when they are treated approximately once a week over a nine-month period in activity groups that consist essentially of prosocial peers (see Feldman, Caplinger, and Wodarski, 1983, pp. 127–268).

Given the rationales for such an approach toward group work with antisocial youths, what, then, has militated against its ready adoption by large numbers of social work agencies? Perhaps the foremost factor is the fear that the prosocial members of integrated treatment groups will become antisocial because of their prolonged exposure to youths who have conduct problems. However, recent research demonstrates that they are unlikely to do so if all but one or two of the group members are prosocial and if the group worker has had graduate social work training (Feldman and Caplinger, 1983; Feldman, Caplinger, and Wodarski, 1983). It is important also to assure that treatment affords each member a broad range of opportunities to engage in recreational activities and to meet at least one or two hours a week over a period of nine months or more. Furthermore, the group worker must plan systematic interventions that aim to enhance the ability of the prosocial youths to serve as active change agents for their antisocial peers.

in addition it is essential that the youngsters who are referred to such groups not be labeled beforehand as "antisocial," "delinquent," or otherwise behaviorally disordered. In such conditions large numbers of referred youths seem to display nearly instantaneous reductions of antisocial behavior. Other youths exhibit marked behavioral gains after only a month or two of treatment. Furthermore, limited follow-up data indicate that the behavioral gains of the referred youths are retained even a year after the end of treatment (Feldman, Caplinger, and Wodarski, 1983, pp. 202–17). In large part the retention of such gains is due to the fact that they are generated in relatively normal settings that permit easy transfer of the newly learned behaviors to the youths' natural environments. Once treated, furthermore, clients do not encounter the usual forms of stigmatization associated with programs at mental health or correctional agencies.

Early Intervention

As explicated above, antisocial youths rarely begin their delinquent careers with an extremely serious deviant act. Rather, their antisocial behavior tends to begin at a relatively early age and to progress successively from one plateau of seriousness to another. Hence it is recommended that group work programs for antisocial youths be targeted toward individuals who are in the earliest stages of a deviant career, that is, who range in age from nine through thirteen years old. This suggests, furthermore, that group work interventions should concentrate upon high-base-rate behaviors even though they usually are less serious than low-base-rate behaviors such as assault and homicide. The small-group context will permit the social worker to intervene in a broad variety of situations, thus affording the possibility to cope with the diversity of early patterns of antisocial behavior.

Professional Training

Group work of the type proposed imposes great demands upon the social worker. Therefore it is hardly surprising that relevant field research (Feldman and Caplinger, 1977; Feldman, Caplinger, and Wodarski, 1983) indicates that group workers without professional training are unlikely to achieve significant gains when treating such groups of youths. In contrast, group workers with as little as one year of graduate social work training are likely to achieve very significant gains when treating antisocial youngsters in mixed, or integrated, groups.

Even more important, research demonstrates that professional social work training is especially useful when treatment groups are composed in the traditional fashion, that is, solely of homogeneous clusters of antisocial youths. Although trained group workers have great difficulty in generating behavioral gains on the part of antisocial clients in such groups, their clients' behavior does not deteriorate. When untrained leaders attempt to treat such groups, however, behavioral retrogressions can be expected. Indeed, field research shows that there is a pronounced interaction between these two variables, namely, the peer composition of the treatment group and the extent of professional training possessed by the group worker. Specifically, the combination of a professionally trained group worker and an integrated treatment group (consisting essentially of prosocial youths plus one or two antisocial peers) is more effective in bringing about behavior change than is either variable alone.

Comprehensive Behavioral Profiles

As noted above, several challenging problems confront both practitioners and researchers who are concerned about the accurate measurement of antisocial behavior. First, many forms of antisocial conduct are low-base-rate behaviors. Hence it is difficult, if not impossible, to assess the extent to which intervention reduces their incidence. Second, some youths who manifest high frequencies of antisocial behavior also display high frequencies of prosocial behavior (Caldwell, 1977). That is, in comparison with other youths, they generally exhibit more frequent activity of all types. Yet, the *proportion* of their total behavioral profile that is antisocial may not be any larger than for "normal" youths who are less hyperactive. Third, as noted above, antisocial behavior is not a dichotomous "either-or" phenomenon. Rather, it is a matter of degree.

To account for these crucial considerations, it is essential to evaluate clients' antisocial behavior in terms of its frequency and proportionate distribution. Time-sampling procedures should be employed throughout the course of treatment in order to enable the group worker to assess the proportionate distributions of prosocial, nonsocial, and antisocial behavior that are displayed by clients at any particular point in time (for operational examples of such a procedure, see Feldman, Caplinger, and Wodarski, 1983, pp. 78–86). It is a relatively easy matter, for example, to determine whether or not a youth's behavioral profile has improved from one in which 20 percent of his or her behavior was antisocial to one in which only 5 percent is antisocial. This approach is facilitated, moreover, by focusing on high-base-rate antisocial behaviors that are likely to occur in the early stages of a delinquent career. It is much more difficult, in contrast, to ascertain whether or not a youth has ceased low-base-rate behaviors of a more serious nature, such as assaults, rapes, and thefts.

Even further, many observers now agree that proper assessment of a client's mental health cannot be made without also paying due consideration to the client's various strengths (see, for example, Clausen, 1968; Werner and Smith, 1982). Hence it is recommended again that group work diagnoses, *in situ* observational systems, and posttreatment evaluations examine the proportionate, rather than the absolute, frequencies of clients' antisocial behavior. This procedure not only permits more comprehensive and discrete measurement of individuals' behavior change but also lends itself to the collection of data that reflect the overall configuration of behavioral patters within the group as a whole.

By the same token, it is essential for group workers to make concerted efforts to avoid either premature or adverse labeling of client behavior. Such propensities are especially likely on the part of preprofessional group leaders and in treatment groups that have many members or high worker turnover (Gingerich, Feldman, and Wodarski, 1977; Wodarski, Pedi, and Feldman, 1975). To avert such tendencies, group workers must employ precise, valid, and behaviorally specific diagnostic labels that are reviewed at frequent intervals in order to determine whether or not they still are accurate for the particular client(s) being treated. To the extent possible, such labels should denote the precise types of antisocial behaviors exhibited by youths, the seriousness of those behaviors, the frequencies of their occurrence, and their social context. A more detailed discussion of procedures that can promote accurate labeling of youths' behavior is set forth elsewhere (Feldman, 1977, 1978; Wodarski, Pedi, and Feldman, 1975). Suffice it to suggest that this crucial issue be addressed carefully and continuously in group work practice with antisocial youths.

Similarly, it is recommended that youths' comportment be evaluated in a broad variety of settings. This procedure facilitates assessment of the cross-situational consistency of their behavior. Reports about youths' behavior can be acquired from parents, teachers, group leaders, and referral agents, respectively, in order to gauge their behavioral patterns in such diverse environments as the home, school, group work setting, and referral agency. Furthermore, trained nonparticipant observers can be employed in order to corroborate such reports (for detailed examples, see Feldman, Caplinger, and Wodarski, 1983, pp. 78–90; Wodarski, Pedi, and Feldman, 1974, 1975).

Maintaining Behavioral Gains

As noted previously, some group work programs for antisocial youths have generated significant behavioral gains, which unfortunately were not maintained long enough to become stable components of the client's behavioral repertoire. Yet this problem reflects not so much upon the merits of the group treatment program as upon the paucity of follow-up programs that try to maintain the behavioral gains originally achieved. This represents a vast and relatively uncharted area for future group work practice.

It is proposed, therefore, that social work agencies increasingly offer programs that enable clients to maintain behavioral gains that were generated under their auspices. Such maintenance programs should take place in normalized and nonstigmatizing organizational settings and preferably among peers who do not have discernible behavior problems. Unlike rehabilitative group work, however, it may not be necessary to require that maintenance groups be led by professionally trained group workers. Pending requisite empirical data, it is plausible to assume that such groups can be led satisfactorily by preprofessional group leaders working under the close supervision of professionally trained group workers.

Integrated Treatment Technologies

Research suggests that group work techniques based upon social learning or behavior modification principles may be somewhat more effective with antisocial youths than techniques based upon more traditional social psychological principles (Feldman, Caplinger, and Wodarski, 1983, pp. 127–217). Moreover, certain program activities, such as team sports, are of considerable value in reducing youths' antisocial behavior and also in enabling their behavioral gains to generalize from the treatment setting to the natural environment (Feldman, Caplinger, and Wodarski, 1983, pp. 218–41; Wodarski, Rubeiz, and Feldman, 1974). However, few, if any, efforts have sought to integrate these important bodies of knowledge. In view of their recently documented efficacy for group work with antisocial youths, it is thus proposed that systematic efforts be initiated that seek to integrate, and thereby strengthen, the theoretical and practice linkages among these bodies of knowledge. As such efforts progress, it is recommended further that attention be paid to the extent to which assigned intervention modalities actually are implemented by group workers and therefore are responsible for subsequent changes, if any, in clients' behavior. A variety of nonparticipant observational schemas can be employed in order to acquire such data (see, for example, Wodarski, Pedi, and Feldman, 1974, 1975; Wodarski and Feldman, 1976).

Increased Emphasis on Preventive Intervention

Many of the considerations denoted above lead inexorably to the conclusion that group workers can greatly enhance the efficacy of their efforts with antisocial youths by concentrating increasingly upon programs of primary and secondary prevention. The available literature about delinquent careers, proportionate behavioral profiles, and normalized treatment settings all point to the potential efficacy of gearing group work interventions either toward preadolescents who are beginning to display antisocial behavior or toward youths who are at risk even though they do not yet exhibit clear symptomatology.

Nevertheless, many barriers militate against the proliferation of prevention programs in group work. Not the least of these are the difficulties of measuring the effects of preventive intervention and of enlightening skeptical administrators and board members about the economic and public relations value, as well as the human value, of prevention programs. Nevertheless, neither group work nor any other helping profession will achieve optimum use of its resources until it can substantially prevent, as well as remediate, behavioral problems on the part of its clients.

SUMMARY AND CONCLUSIONS

The available literature regarding group work practice with antisocial youths reveals that a variety of formidable barriers hinder effective treatment. They include dysfunctional organizational settings and small group contexts, inappropriate timing of intervention programs, inadequate worker training, faulty definitions of "antisocial" behavior, a paucity of programs that concentrate on the maintenance of behavioral gains, insufficient linkages among treatment technologies, and an undue emphasis upon rehabilitation.

To rectify these deficiencies, a number of recommendations are set forth regarding group work practice with antisocial youths. Among other things, it is recommended that group work treatment be provided in nonstigmatizing and normalized organizational settings and in prosocial small group contexts; interventions be directed toward preadolescents who are embarked upon the early phases of delinquent careers; professionally trained group workers be employed in rehabilitative group treatment programs; comprehensive behavioral profiles be used periodically to evaluate clients' prosocial and nonsocial behavior, as well as their antisocial behavior; specific group work programs be designed in order to facilitate the maintenance of behavioral gains; theoretical and practical linkages be wrought among such diverse knowledge bases as applied behavior analysis, social psychology, and group work programming; and increased emphasis be accorded to programs of primary prevention and secondary prevention. Available field research points to the efficacy of virtually all of these recommendations.

REFERENCES

AKERS, RONALD L.; MARVIN D. KROHN; LONN LANZA-DADUCE; AND MARCIA RADO-
    SEVICH
    1979　"Social learning and deviant behavior: A specific test of a general theory,"
        American Sociological Review, 44: 636–55.
ALLEY, SAM, AND JUDITH BLANTON
    1976　"A study of paraprofessionals in mental health," *Community Mental
        Health Journal*, 12: 151–60.
ASCH, SOLOMON
    1952　*Social Psychology*. Englewood Cliffs, N.J.: Prentice-Hall.
BIDDLE, BRUCE J.; BARBARA J. BANKS; AND MARJORIE M. MARLIN
    1980　"Parental and peer influence on adolescents," *Social Forces*, 58: 1057–59.
CAHALAN, DENNIS, AND ROBIN ROOM
    1974　*Problem Drinking Among American Men*. New Brunswick, N.J.: Rutgers
        Center of Alcohol Studies.
CALDWELL, BETTYE M.
    1977　"Aggression and hostility in young children," *Young Children*, 32: 4–13.
CAMPBELL, SUSAN B.; MICHAEL SCHLEIFER; GABRIELLE WEISS; AND TERRYE PERLMAN
    1977　"A two-year follow-up of hyperactive preschoolers," *American Journal of
        Orthopsychiatry*, 47: 149–62.

CARKHUFF, ROBERT R.
1969   *Helping and Human Relations: A Primer for Lay and Professional Helpers*. New York: Holt, Rinehart & Winston.
CARNEY, LOUIS
1977   *Corrections and the Community*. Englewood Cliffs, N.J.: Prentice-Hall.
CLAUSEN, JOHN A.
1968   "Values, norms, and the health called 'mental': Purposes and feasibility of assessment." In Steven B. Sells (ed.), *The Definition and Measurement of Mental Health*. Washington D.C.: U.S. Department of Health, Education, and Welfare, National Center for Health Statistics.
CONGER, JOHN J.; WILBER C. MILLER; AND CHARLES R. WALSMITH
1966   "Antecedents of delinquency, personality, social class and intelligence." In Paul H. Mussen, John J. Conger, and Jerome Kagan (eds.), *Readings in Child Development and Personality*. New York: Harper & Row.
DUNCAN, DAVID F.
1974   "Verbal behavior in a detention home," *Corrective and Social Psychiatry*, 20: 38–42.
EMPEY, LAMAR T.
1969   "Contemporary programs for convicted juvenile offenders." In *Crimes of Violence*. Volume 13 of *Staff Report to the National Commission on the Causes and Prevention of Violence*. Washington, D.C.: U.S. Government Printing Office.
ERICKSON, MAYNARD L., AND GARY F. JENSEN
1977   "Delinquency is still group behavior: Toward revitalizing the group premise in the sociology of deviance," *Journal of Criminal Law and Criminology*, 68: 262–73.
FARRINGTON, DAVID B.
1977   "The effects of public labeling," *British Journal of Criminology*, 17: 112–25.
FARRINGTON, DAVID B., AND DONALD WEST
1971   "A comparison between early delinquents and young aggressives," *British Journal of Criminology*, 11: 341–58.
FELDMAN, RONALD A.
1977   "Legal lexicon, social labeling, and juvenile rehabilitation," *Journal of Offender Rehabilitation*, 2: 19–30.
1978   "Delinquent behavior in the public schools: Toward more accurate labeling and effective intervention." In Ernst Wenk and Nora Harlow (eds.), *School Crime and Disruption*. Davis, Calif.: Responsible Action.
FELDMAN, RONALD A., AND TIMOTHY E. CAPLINGER
1977   "Social work experience and client behavioral change: A multivariate analysis of process and outcome," *Journal of Social Service Research*, 1: 5–34.
1983   "The St. Louis Experiment: Treatment of antisocial youths in prosocial peer groups." In James R. Kluegel (ed.), *Evaluating Juvenile Justice*. Sage Research Progress Series in Criminology. Beverly Hills, Calif.: Sage Publications, pp. 121–48.
FELDMAN, RONALD A.; TIMOTHY E. CAPLINGER; AND JOHN S. WODARSKI
1983   *The St. Louis Conundrum: The Effective Treatment of Antisocial Youths*. Englewood Cliffs, N.J.: Prentice-Hall.

FELDMAN, RONALD A.; JOHN S. WODARSKI; MORTIMER GOODMAN; AND NORMAN FLAX
1973 "Pro-social and anti-social boys together," *Social Work*, 18: 26–36.

FRIDAY, PAUL C., AND JERALD HAGE
1976 "Youth crime in post-industrial societies: An integrated perspective," *Criminology*, 14: 347–68.

GINGERICH, WALLACE J.; RONALD A. FELDMAN; AND JOHN S. WODARSKI
1977 "A behavioral approach toward the labeling of anti-social behavior," *Sociology and Social Research*, 61: 204–22.

GOLD, MARTIN
1970 *Delinquent Behavior in an American City*. Belmont, Calif.: Wadsworth.

GOLDMAN, I.J.
1974 *Arrest and Reinstitutionalization After Release from State Schools and Other Facilities of the New York State Division for Youth: Three Studies of Youths Released January 1971 Through March 1973*. Albany: New York State Youth Division.

HANEY, BRUCE, AND MARTIN GOLD
1973 "The juvenile delinquent nobody knows," *Psychology Today* (September): 49–55.

HINDELANG, MICHAEL J.
1976 "With a little help from their friends: Group participation in reported delinquent behavior," *British Journal of Criminology*, 16: 109–25.

HIRSCHI, TRAVIS
1969 *Causes of Delinquency*. Berkeley: University of California Press.

JESSOR, RICHARD; SHIRLEY C. JESSOR; AND JOHN F. W. FINNEY
1973 "A social psychology of marijuana use: Longitudinal studies of high school and college youths," *Journal of Personality and Social Psychology*, 26: 1–15.

JOHNSTONE, JOHN W. C.
1978 "Juvenile delinquency and the family: A contextual interpretation," *Youth and Society*, 9: 299–313.

KITCHENER, HOWARD; ANNESLEY SCHMIDT; AND DANIEL GLASER
1977 "How persistent is past-prison success?" *Federal Probation*, 41: 9–15.

KOSHEL, JEFFREY
1973 *Deinstitutionalization: Dependent and Neglected Children*. Washington, D.C.: The Urban Institute.

LERMAN, PAUL
1975 *Community Treatment and Social Control*. Chicago: University of Chicago Press.

LEWIS, DAVID O., AND DAVID A. BALLA
1976 *Delinquency and Psychopathology*. New York: Grune & Stratton.

LIPTON, DONALD; ROBERT MARTINSON; AND JUDITH WILKS
1975 *The Effectiveness of Correctional Treatment: A Survey of Treatment*. New York: Praeger Publishers.

LOEBER, ROLF
1982 "The stability of antisocial and delinquent child behavior: A review," *Child Development*, 53: 1431–46.

McCord, Joan
1978 "A thirty-year follow-up of treatment effects," *American Psychologist*, 33: 284–89.
Mendelson, Wallace; Noel Johnson; and Mark Steward
1971 "Hyperactive children as teenagers: A follow-up study," *Journal of Nervous and Mental Disease*, 153: 272–79.
Minde, K.; D. Lewin; Gabrielle Weiss; H. Lavigueur; Virginia Douglas; and E. Sykes
1971 "The hyperactive child in elementary school: A five-year controlled follow-up," *Exceptional Children*, 38: 215–21.
Nagel, William G.
1977 "On behalf of a moratorium on prison construction," *Crime and Delinquency*, 23: 154–72.
Newton, C., and R. G. Sheldon
1975 "The delinquent label and its effects on future behavior: An empirical test of Lemert's levels of deviance," *International Journal of Criminology and Penology*, 3: 229–41.
O'Donnell, John M., and Kathi George
1977 "The use of volunteers in a community mental health center emergency and reception service: A comparative study of professional and lay telephone counseling," *Community Mental Health Journal*, 13: 3–12.
Patterson, Gerald R.
1982 *Coercive Family Processes*. Eugene, Ore.: Castalia Publishing Co.
Poser, Ernest G.
1966 "The effects of therapists' training on group therapeutic outcome," *Journal of Consulting Psychology*, 30: 283–89.
Radosevich, Marcia; Lonn Lanza-Kaduce; Ronald L. Akers; and Marvin Krohn
1978 *The Sociology of Adolescent Drug and Drinking Behavior: A Review of the State of the Field*. Omaha: Boys Town Center for the Study of Youth Development.
Riddle, K. Duane, and Judith L. Rapoport
1976 "A two-year follow-up of 72 hyperactive boys," *Journal of Nervous and Mental Disease*, 162: 126–134.
Robins, Lee N.
1966 *Deviant Children Grown Up*. Baltimore: Williams & Wilkins.
1972 "Follow-up studies of behavior disorders in children." In Herbert C. Quay and John S. Wherry (eds.), *Psychopathological Disorders of Childhood*. New York: John Wiley.
1974 "Anti-social behavior disturbances of childhood: Prevalence, prognosis, and prospects." In E. James Anthony and Cyril Koupernik (eds.), *The Child in His Family: Children at Psychiatric Risk*. New York: John Wiley.
1978 "Sturdy childhood predictors of adult outcomes: Replications form longitudinal studies," *Psychological Medicine*, 8: 611–22.
Romig, Dennis A.
1978 *Justice for Our Children: An Examination of Juvenile Delinquency Rehabilitation Programs*. Lexington, Mass.: Lexington Books.

Ross, R. R., and P. Gendreau (eds.)
1980   *Effective Correctional Treatment*. Scarborough, Ont.: Butterworths.
Sarri, Rosemary C.
1974   *Under Lock and Key: Juveniles in Jails and Detention*. Ann Arbor, Mich.:
National Assessment of Juvenile Corrections.
Schrag, Clarence
1971   *Crime and Justice: American Style*. Washington, D.C.: Center for Studies
of Crime and Delinquency.
Scioli, Frank P., Jr., and Thomas J. Cook
1976   "How effective are volunteers? Public participation in the criminal justice
system," *Crime and Delinquency*, 22: 192–200.
Street, David
1965   "The inmate group in custodial and treatment settings," *American Sociological Review*, 30: 40–55.
Werner, Emmy E., and Ruth S. Smith
1982   *Vulnerable but Invincible*. New York: McGraw-Hill.
Westman, Jack; Dale Rice; and Eric Bermann
1967   "Nursery school behavior and later school adjustment," *American Journal of Orthopsychiatry*, 37: 725–31.
Wodarski, John S., and Ronald A. Feldman
1976   "Normative integration." In Orval G. Johnson (ed.), *Tests and Measurements in Child Development: Handbook II*. San Francisco: Jossey-Bass,
pp. 1188–89.
Wodarski, John S.; Steven J. Pedi; and Ronald A. Feldman
1974   "Objective measurement of the independent variable: A neglected methodological aspect in community-based behavioral research," *Journal of Abnormal Child Psychiatry*, 2: 239–44.
1975   "Effects of different observational systems and time sequences upon nonparticipant observers' behavioral ratings," *Journal of Behavior Therapy
and Experimental Psychiatry*, 6: 275–78.
Wodarski, John S.; Ghassan Rubeiz; and Ronald A. Feldman
1974   "Program planning for anti-social boys," *Social Work*, 19: 705–13.
Wolfgang, Marvin E.; Robert Figlio and Thorstein Sellin
1972   *Delinquency in a Birth Cohort*, Chicago: University of Chicago Press.
Wright, William E., and Michael C. Dixon
1977   "Community prevention and treatment of juvenile delinquency: A review
of evaluation studies," *Journal of Research in Crime and Delinquency*, 14:
35–67.
Zax, Melvin; Emory L. Cowen; Julian Rappaport; David R. Beach; and James
D. Laird
1968   "A follow-up study of children identified early as emotionally disturbed,"
Journal of Consulting and Clinical Psychology, 32: 369–71.

28

Small Groups in Large State Institutions for People Who Are Mentally Ill, Mentally Retarded, and Developmentally Disabled

Sallie R. Churchill and Paul H. Glasser

DEINSTITUTIONALIZATION HAS BEEN the central concept guiding the services provided to people who are mentally ill, mentally retarded, and developmentally disabled since the mid 1960s. The professional literature has focused primarily on the removal of persons from large state institutions and on the provision of services to those people in their local communities. Issues related to services to people residing in the large institutions have been eclipsed; the fact that the large institution is still an integral part of the continuum of care outlined by the community mental health concept seems to have been forgotten. Each year thousands of individuals are admitted to and reside in large mental hospitals (regional centers) and institutions for retarded and developmentally disabled (developmental centers). Can these individuals be helped, while they are in a large institution, so that they may return to their communities and live with an adequate degree of dignity and acceptance?

The use of group experiences within the large institution and the use of groups as linkages to the community resources are viable techniques for the modification of the behavior of both the mentally ill patient and the mentally retarded resident who are institutionalized in large state facilities. Group experiences can permit the mentally ill person to restore or improve the level of his or her social functioning so that he or she can behave in an acceptable manner in his or her community. Group experiences can permit the retarded individual to develop beginning social skills or to improve inadequate social skills so that he or she can function in a less restrictive environment.

The implementation of group techniques requires professional and administrative commitment of institutional staffs toward realizable goals and the conceptualization of improvement as behavioral change rather than

494

cure for the mentally ill person and the development of social and interpersonal skills which permit a greater, although somewhat limited degree of independent functioning for the retarded or developmentally disabled person. The institutionalized period must be viewed as temporary, and interventions must be directed toward the return of both patients and residents to the community as quickly as possible.

STRUCTURE OF LARGE
MENTAL HEALTH INSTITUTIONS

The potential of groups in these large institutions can be understood best when the characteristics of hospital structure in general are understood. Theoretically structure is an organized method of achieving goals. It has emerged over the years in an unplanned, utilitarian manner to meet the demands of society and the maintenance needs of the institution. The structure reflects the disparate values of care and custody, on one hand, and treatment, on the other, and as conflict between belief in the need for permanent lifelong care and temporary, brief, and revolving stays. The structure that has evolved in large hospitals and developmental centers generally is not a structure directed primarily toward the treatment of patients. Fragmented treatment programs do exist, but they are frequently subjected to curtailment of funding with each financial crisis. Treatment often is related to student training for professions or the research segments of the hospital. Some of this may be mitigated by increased emphasis, in law, on the civil rights of patients and residents and accountability for and documentation of patient and resident services.

Large hospital structure and the problems inherent in the structure have been the subject of extensive research and subjective evaluation. Perrow (1965) reviewed the literature on hospital structure and with some facetiousness identified six themes in the literature (while descriptive of the mental hospital, the themes can apply as well to large developmental centers): (1) Communication threads its way through virtually every description; it is always blocked. (2) Attendants and their illegitimate, abused power are the villains of nearly every piece. (3) Psychiatrists are castigated for being poor administrators, for being aloof from nurses, for clinging to the two-person model of treatment. (4) The business staff of hospitals hoard supplies and frustrate change. (5) The hospital structure is characterized as paranoid, granulated, and authoritarian. (6) Treatment goals are always displaced by custody. Apparently the hospital structure cannot be responsive to the treatment-oriented professional's interest in patients as isolated individuals. Such practitioners often are convinced that institutions exist for the benefit of the patient. They believe, in line with the so-called

Protestant Ethic, that hard, skilled work by the professional on behalf of the institutionalized client can effect a cure. Such beliefs create a dilemma; for they are neither true nor instrumental to patient change in a large institution. Workers need to pay attention to the institution as a social system and to locate where professionals may exert influence and foster changes within that system.

Both the mental hospital's and the developmental center's complex organizational structures have created enduring relationships that use energy in a patterned effort to change conditions of human beings in a predetermined way. The organizational task in each is the alteration of the behavior of human beings. Three sets of factors interact in the achievement of this organizational task: (1) cultural systems of goals, values, and beliefs; (2) treatment techniques employed to bring about change; and (3) arrangements to implement goals.

Thus, theoretically extant complex organizational structure has a tenacious grasp on the ongoing operations in any institution and is quite resistant to modification. However, substantial nationwide changes in the assigned functions of these hospitals and developmental centers over the last twenty years have been made with the implementation of deinstitutionalization. Perhaps there has been some dislodging of the old structure.

CHANGES IN INSTITUTIONS
WITH DEINSTITUTIONALIZATION

Five critical aspects of structural and functional changes forced upon the large mental health organizations by implementation of the deinstitutionalization concept will be discussed: (1) a decrease in the size and number of institutions has occurred; (2) admissions to both types of institution are viewed as temporary, and readmissions are common; (3) intensified concern with patient and resident civil rights, supported by law, create new structural roles in the institutions; (4) more restrictive laws modify involuntary admissions; (5) there has been a modification of the types or mix of problems residents and patients present. Other changes, which will only be mentioned, are reduction of funds, reduction of personnel, and increased demands for documentation of staff interactions with patients and of services provided.

Size

In the twenty-year period 1955–75, there was a 65 percent decrease in the population of state mental hospitals. However, admissions sharply increased. A trend toward short-term hospitalizations, coupled with several readmissions, was established (Bassuk and Gerson, 1978). In the fifteen-year period between 1967 and 1982 the number of mentally retarded persons residing in large state facilities declined by more than 33 percent (Lakin et al., 1982). In 1978 there were still 398 large state institutions serving either mentally ill persons or mentally retarded and developmentally disabled persons (Krantz, Bruininks, and Clumper, 1978).

Integrated Individual Service Plans

The goal for the institutionalized mentally ill person is to change his or her behavior so that he or she can function in society at least at a minimally acceptable level. The goal for the mentally retarded or developmentally disabled institutionalized person is to maximize his or her potential through habilitative services so that he or she may be able to live with dignity in a less restrictive environment.

Both types of institutions are mandated to use an integrated service plan for each patient admitted. This requires an orderly process of planning, initiated at the time of admission to the large institution and including predischarge planning. Predischarge planning implies that each patient will leave eventually the role of patient at discharge and become reintegrated into society. Plans may include use of intermediate steps, which involve less restrictive placements in the community or outpatient treatment while living at home or independently. Such planning must involve patients, therapists, and community resources (New York City Advisory Board Report, 1978).

Civil Rights

Three principal areas of patients' and residents' civil rights have been addressed by changes in laws and in institutional structure: (1) patients' and residents' rights to receive treatment and habilitation services; (2) the patients' and residents' right to refuse treatment or habilitation services; and (3) involuntary admission and readmission. Willetts (1980) comments that state advocacy programs for patients' civil rights are spreading throughout the country. She suggests that advocacy programs may be less necessary now, because with deinstitutionalization there are less use of involuntary procedures, fewer applicants for release through haebeas corpus, and a diminution in the absolute number of complaints relating to inadequate facilities and the denial of civil liberties.

However, Willetts stresses that institutionalized patients, once committed to hospitals as involuntary patients, quickly sink into the morass of potential abuse of their rights.

Involuntary Admission Criteria

Laws regarding involuntary admissions have become stricter. For example, Nebraska law (Luckey and Berman, 1981) restricts involuntary commitment to three situations: (1) an individual is found dangerous to him/herself; (2) an individual is found dangerous to others; and (3) an individual is found incapable of providing for one's own needs. The law provides procedural safeguards for the individual through the use of a multistage process with mandatory reviews at each stage. Implementation of this law had the result that more patients were referred for institutionalization by the legal system, with an increase in the number of admissions, accounted for by readmissions.

Mental Hospital Patients

Currently more of the mental hospital patients may be dangerous, and fewer may be chronically ill.

Whitmer (1980) reports that with the new commitment laws' emphasis on dangerousness as a criteria for involuntary commitment, many former chronic patients who had used long-term custodial care in mental hospitals during the 1960s have been shifted to the legal system. Once these people forfeit their treatment, they congregate in inner urban ghettos of ex-hospital patients, where their behavior compels police interventions. All too often they are sent to jail.

The length of mental hospital stays has been reduced significantly. But Reissman, Rabkin, and Struening (1977) reported that the results of treatment for patients hospitalized for an average of three to sixty days were not significantly different from those of patients with longer hospitalization. These results, true both at time of discharge and at a two-year follow-up, included reduction of symptoms, level of social functioning, global adjustment, and recidivism of hospitalization.

Kinard (1981) describes a unique group of discharged mental hospital patients who desire to return to the hospital. He says that this was unexpected, given the negative aspects of institutional life. It had been assumed that patients would rather live in the community. Based on a study of 176 patients who were discharged an average of one year, Kinard found that one-fourth desired to return to the hospital. These people had problems with self-image, relationship, and use of leisure time. While this represents a failure of community resources, it poses a challenge for hospital treatment.

Mentally Retarded and
Developmentally Disabled Residents

Thomas Mulhern (1978) cites that deinstitutionalization for mentally retarded and developmentally disabled persons is a movement away from custodial care to a model that emphasizes treating handicapped people in as nearly a normal fashion as possible. (Ideally this would be in small community-based facilities.) This is a move from total dependence toward maximum independence.

Increasingly complex management problems result from the competing and often conflicting demands of various regulatory bodies, budgetary committees, and community organizations. Deinstitutionalization is, however, a model of care in which emphasis is clearly on habilitation goals for each individual, goals that should be specified in an individualized treatment plan. Each treatment plan is based on an evaluation focusing on the resident's strengths and potentials, not on his or her handicaps.

Lam (1981), speaking of the mentally retarded and developmentally disabled, comments that only a minority of long-term patients can realize the expectations of the deinstitutionalization concept, that is, helping people become part of the mainstream of our society and normalization. The community treatment placements that receive the most attention are geared to the higher-functioning minority. However, 75 percent of the residents in the large residential centers are severely or profoundly retarded (Bruininks, Hill, and Thorsheim, 1982).

There has been a sharp rise in readmissions of the mentally retarded to large institutions. Thorsheim and Bruininks (1978) state that this relates to the lack of adequate community placements, community rejection, and the families' inability to cope with their family members who are mentally retarded. However, this does put the additional stress of "failure" on residents with low self-esteem and somewhat limited resources.

CHANGES IN VALUES, BELIEFS, AND GOALS

Mental Illness

During the twentieth century three aspects of the mental hospital patients' experience have been the focus of attention in mental hospitals: (1) the social and physical environment of the patient, (2) the internal dynamics of psychological functioning of the patient, and (3) the patient's behavior. Shifts in the attention given to one or another of these foci are related to both the beliefs and the values of the general population concerning mental illness and the development of therapeutic efforts among professionals in the mental health field.

At the turn of the century attention was focused on the social and physical environments of the mental hospital patient. The abuse of institutionalized patients by personnel and the deplorable physical conditions of hospitals received much attention. National, state, and local mental health societies and other organizations clamored for reform, and much was done to clean up and repair some of the hospital facilities and to eliminate the physical abuse of patients.

The influence of Freudian psychoanalytic theory began a new era in the 1930s. Various forms of psychosis were seen as illnesses rather than "the work of the devil." Emphasis was placed on changing the internal dynamics or psychic functioning of the patient in order to bring about change in the patient's behavior. Little attention was paid to the social and physical environment of the patient, except to prevent the abuses that had occurred earlier, since therapists thought that patients could handle their environment adequately once certain changes in their personalities had occurred.

The third trend can be seen as a refinement of the second and as one that is frequent in hospitals today. Emphasis is still on modification of the psychic functioning of the patient to enable him or her to handle his or her life in a better way, but greater recognition has been given to how the hospital environment itself can hinder the patient's progress in individual psychotherapy. In recent years the physical and social situation of the patient has been made as neutral as possible so that individualized therapy and training are not hampered by the institutional environment and to permit one-to-one treatment methods to be more effective. The degree of neutralization varies from one hospital to another; a custodial program is not always consistent with a neutral environment. While patients have had more positive experiences in recent years, negative experiences do continue to occur, although they are often rationalized as necessary to protect the patient from her/himself and others and to prevent his or her escape from the institution.

The fourth trend now frequently found is characterized by efforts to change the physical and social situation sufficiently to influence each patient's behavior. This approach requires changes in the organizational structure and in the daily living experiences of patients. Most of the changes take place in the context of the small group.

This trend is developing against a background of the relative lack of efficiency and effectiveness of individualized psychological treatment for the large numbers of mental patients in large hospitals. Up to the present only a small proportion of institutionalized clients have received individualized help. In the foreseeable future the number of therapists cannot possibly become sufficiently large to treat individually the increasing number of patients. Even when individualized treatment methods have been available, they have not always been successful. A large number of patients can be treated more quickly and successfully in the context of the group, particularly as changes are brought about in their daily living experiences.

A therapeutic milieu approach that makes maximum use of natural and formed groups within the institution can consider and incorporate individual differences among the client population. Some therapists believe that the changes in patient behavior produced in groups may be accompanied by changes in their internal dynamics and psychological functioning. In any case the environment is not neutral, as in the psychoanalytic approach, but it becomes an active and powerful force in the rehabilitation process.

The use of group situations to modify patient behavior to a socially approved and/or acceptable level of social functioning reflects the acceptance of new beliefs regarding the nature of mental illness and a change in the values and goals of treatment technologies. These new beliefs view mental illness and mental health in terms of a person's behavior. They do not address the question of cure but, rather, the question of restoration of appropriate social functioning. Since "the problem" is viewed as difficulty in behaving in a social milieu, the treatment laboratory logically becomes a social system (or a series of social systems) that simulates the arenas where problems occur and where corrected behavior must be manifest. The treatment locales should be selected group situations.

The goal of better social functioning means that patients must be allowed to become more independent and have increased opportunities for decision-making in regard to their own lives. Patients should be permitted to make decisions they can handle but should not be asked to take responsibilities beyond their capacities. Achieving such a balance is not simple, but efforts at patient government and the increasing patient advocate activities indicate that the danger lies in underestimating and underusing patient capacities rather than the opposite.

Mental Retardation and the Developmentally Disabled

There have been similar changes in the view of the function of institutionalization of mentally retarded persons. (Some of this change is reflected in the multiple names assigned to these people: feebleminded, moron, idiot, imbecile, exceptional, and so on.) Institutionalization was at one time a lifelong incarceration of the perennial child. Other views included (1) custody and control of the "dangerous feebleminded" or the sexually active retarded woman; (2) protective custody of individuals in a place where they could develop their low potential (if indeed they had any potential) under conditions of minimal stimulation and opportunities, free from unfair competition of "normal" people (Some of these persons could handle minimal responsibilities and maintenance tasks within the institutional walls.); (3) education utilizing behavioral modification techniques to train individuals for self-care and participation in more extensive in-house tasks; and (4) habilitation opportunities to maintain the person whenever possible, outside of the institution.

Most of these changes reflect evolving and interacting changes in many domains. Some of these are (1) gradual acceptance of the concept of the acceptability of and value of human beings who have handicaps, who are different, or who are not "normal" by families, professional persons, and society in general; (2) developments in medical science that helped (a) to maintain life which had previously been seriously endangered (e.g. antibiotics have minimized continuous life-threatening infections for persons with Down's syndrome and extended life expectancy into mature adult years), (b) to control serious seizuring behaviors that interfered with daily functioning, and (c) to reduce random or constant hyperactivity that prevented sufficient attention span for much learning to occur; (3) development of and acceptance of learning theory and teaching techniques of behavior modification, which enabled a wide range of mentally retarded to learn at least minimal self care-skills (this changed the belief that retarded persons could not learn or, even if the retarded person did learn some things, such learning was not valuable since what they learned was insufficient to permit the person to function as a "normal person"); (4) increased knowledge of learning/teaching, which utilized differentiated educational protocols and provided alternative routes for learning; and (5) increased use of due process in placement, so that children no longer left the hospital nursery for lifelong care based on the judgment and recommendation of a single physician.

However, the limitations cited earlier with regard to mental hospitals and individualized psychological treatment for large numbers of mentally ill patients apply also to individual habilitative efforts on behalf of residents of large developmental centers.

The therapeutic milieu and the socioeducational approach in the institution, which make use of natural and formed groups in the institution, can perform a viable helping function for the residents. The concrete experiential aspects of learning, critical to the learning process of many persons who are retarded, are more readily available in groups. The retarded person, when supported and rewarded for small behavioral learning and/or change, can become a peer model for his or her fellow patient. Learning is easier among peers who are "more like" one another than like the nonretarded worker.

Readmissions are most frequent because of the retarded person's lack of social skills, including a too limited ability to relate to other persons, lack of leisure time activities skills, and low self-esteem. The readmissions are not related to level of intellectual ability (Hill, Rotegard, and Bruininks, 1984). These difficulties are remedied only in interactive situations with other persons; they cannot be learned in the abstract. The small group seems the ideal treatment situation.

The goal of maximum functioning in the least restrictive environment demands that workers assess the assets and strengths of each individual. Efforts must be made to avoid underestimating the capacities of the person and underevaluating these capacities. Habilitation and educational efforts must be directed at maximizing these capacities on behalf of increasing self-concept, social skills, and leisure time skills so that each person can move toward his or her greatest level of independent functioning.

THE NATURE, THEORY, AND TECHNOLOGY
OF GROUPS WITHIN THE INSTITUTIONS

Cultural systems of goals, values, and beliefs constitute one set of factors relevant to the achievement of the mental institution's task of altering human behavior. A second set of factors concerns the nature and technology of groups.

Groups can be useful, very harmful, or just neutral. This is true in any setting: a school, a church, a community center, or a mental hospital. Groups may be used as tools. Their value depends on why they are used, how skillfully they are used, and how well they are constructed.

Group experience is an important part of human life, beginning with early family experiences, then in the play group, in school, on teams, in church, and so forth. Through group experiences individuals find acceptance or rejection, develop a self-image, learn, and practice reality-testing. Through group experiences people become social beings, learning how to deal with other people. For the patient in the institution groups can be laboratories where the tasks of social living can be reexperienced or relearned.

However, for many of the older retarded persons, the institutional placement has limited these normal group learning opportunities. Many mentally retarded adults were placed in institutions as infants. Isolation in cribs at an institution aborted the early group experiences in their families.

For those individuals who had handicaps limiting their mobility in the institution, social experiences were apt to be minimal. Physical care took precedence. Thus for those individuals who had difficulty in learning at a normal rate, opportunities for social learning were minimized rather than increased.

A great variety of patient groups exists within each institution at all times. The groups include those organized by the patients themselves, by the staff for specific therapeutic or training objectives, and by staff for administrative purposes. There is practically no time in the patient's hospital stay when he or she is not in a group. The patient sleeps, eats, idles, works, plays, walks, and waits in groups. Often much of his or her group experience has been imposed upon him or her for hospital convenience without thoughtful employment of the group as part of a patient's identified treatment opportunities.

Groups in mental hospitals and institutions for mentally retarded sometimes have had very negative effects on the life of the patient. This has been true when the focus was on the group itself, especially as a way to control patients and to force conformity to hospital procedures.

Groups formed by patients often constitute a way for patients to exercise control over one another. These groups can also have antitherapeutic effects. When patients are not permitted to have much responsibility or to participate in making decisions about their own lives, they often find informal means to assert power and authority. One example is a "sitters'" group composed of patients, each of whom has a special chair placed in a special position in the dayroom on the ward. During free time, when they are permitted in the dayroom, they maintain their positions in specific chairs. Even if patients are nonverbal and passive, they manifest their power in a variety of ways. First, if someone else sits in "their" chair, he or she will fight for his or her right to have the occupant removed. Second, they exercise power over staff. If the staff attempt to move chairs, the patients will move them back to their original positions. They may fight with someone who attempts to sit in "their" chair. The routine of the ward may be upset, and the staff must intervene. The "sitters'" group illustrates that such behavior can affect the therapeutic milieu of the ward and the achievement of treatment goals for individual patients. The staff must evaluate these informal interactions in terms of their potential effects.

Institutionalized clients usually experience social hunger. They are driven to find ways in which to have contact with others. Sometimes the types of relationships patients establish with each other seem bizarre. Even nonverbal interaction can signify a meaningful relationship. Such behavior is the way patients can have meaningful social contact despite their acute illness. It must be recognized that even in such interactions patients can influence each other. Groups can be most valuable when they exist for the needs of the group members; individual needs rather than group needs are the hospital worker's main concern.

One of the greatest problems incurred by patients and residents as they attempt to modify their behavior so they may be discharged is the difficulty of institutions tolerating the process of change. Much maladaptive behavior is expected when a patient or resident is admitted (or they should not be admitted!). Maintenance of the organization requires at least minimal compliance to behavioral standards. Too often it is a matter of compliance or noncompliance. Intermediate steps or small changes are often overlooked and viewed as continued noncompliance by the staff. Small group experience can provide, especially with the help of a worker, opportunities for a patient or resident to be supported, tolerated, and/or rewarded for small changes. Research has suggested that individuals are more accepting of correction by peers and more influenced by peer actions. Some institutions have instituted levels of behavior expectations associated with levels of privileges and movement toward discharge. These have been useful in control of behavior and—it is hoped—in helping the patient develop awareness of the effect of one's own behavior on what happens to oneself. This cannot replace the importance of the interpersonal gains of support for change by peers.

In viewing groups as a viable technology in the treatment of institutional patients three assumptions have been made: (1) Informal social processes exist among any inpatient population, and these processes affect the treatment and its outcome. (2) Social processes can be molded to enhance a patient's treatment experience and to improve the treatment outcome. (3) A patient's membership in different hospital groups significantly affects his or her response to treatment and its outcome. These assumptions have found support in a study conducted by Lamberger (1964). She studied four types of formal groups in a Veterans Administration mental hospital: occupational therapy groups, group therapy groups, sleeping groups on the ward, and recreation groups. She found that the more frequently persons interact:

1. The stronger their sentiment of friendship for one another is apt to be
2. The higher they will rank each other as having influence on the ward generally
3. The more likely they are to have a strong personal influence on each other

Observers of severely retarded clients may doubt that these people are able to relate in a meaningful way to one another. They may cite their lack of verbal communication or their lack of physical mobility. This belief may have brought about lack of relationships because all opportunities for relationships to develop had been denied. Handicapped people in institutions have unintentionally been forced into solitary confinement. When physical movement and use of other communication channels have been provided, even many profoundly retarded patients have developed as natural groups on a ward.

The concept of "group" becomes confusing unless it is recognized that groups occur at many levels of member involvement and that any group is an evolving social entity with a life of its own. Norma Lang (1972) conceptualized a paradigm that described three "ideal type" groups. Each "ideal type" group varies in terms of the social development and social skills required of the group members and the role and functions of the worker (nonmember leader). All three "ideal groups" occur normally in the population and are dependent on the developmental level of its members; each group has its counterpart in the world of retardation or pathology. The ideal groups are not discrete types. In fact groups may pass from one type to another as they move through the group developmental phases. Any group may move ahead or regress temporarily dependent on group stresses or motivation.

The first "ideal type group" is the allonomous group. It is composed of individuals who, while in the same location, have little spontaneous (positive or negative) interaction. Their skills are undeveloped (or regressed) to such an extent that they are unable alone to carry out social functions that allow a group to exist. Rather, they remain individuals within their own space or responding only to themselves. They cannot set up rules, plan activities, accept peer governance, and so on. A worker can carry on these functions as the central person to whom all members will relate. Members are then supported in interactions and guided in their participation. A group exists with the help of vigorous worker activity. Once the worker leaves any "group interaction" falls apart.

Allonomous groups are quite typical of early preschoolers; they are also typical of groups within institutions where residents are profoundly or seriously retarded or patients are severely withdrawn or regressed.

The second "ideal type," the allonatonomous group, is composed of individuals who have developed some basic social skills. These skills are sometimes weak, sometimes strong, sometimes available, sometimes unavailable. At times the members can manage the group's business easily, at other times their social skills are inadequate to the task. (Skills may be lost under stress or fatigue; specific skills may not have been learned.) The worker has a surrogate role with these groups; the worker permits the members to carry the responsibility for the group's work when it can and offers needed assistance when the group cannot. The worker's level of activity will then vary as necessary.

The allonatonomous group is the typical group of grade school youngsters, and perhaps typical of many adolescent or adult groups in the initial meetings. The allonatonomous group is also the type of group found in many hospitals and developmental centers with the less seriously disturbed patients and the mildly retarded resident. In fact, most formed therapeutic groups are of this type.

The third "ideal type group" is the autonomous group, wherein group members have mature social skills and can manage group business themselves. An autonomous group needs the help of a worker only as a resource person.

It is rather unusual for an autonomous group to exist in either type of institution. Sometimes this is a reflection of staff beliefs that patients or residents who are having difficulties in dealing with some parts of their lives are incapable of taking on mature behavior in other areas. That belief is reflected, at least in part, in resistance to self-governance groups on wards, or in the institution to self-help groups (such as Alcoholics Anonymous, Parents Anonymous) and to support groups (such as Recovery, Inc.) where ex-patients or ex-residents return to the institution to meet with patients and residents hoping to facilitate the transition experiences.

Research and clinical observation leave little doubt that clients and patients have strong influences on each other in a variety of ways in a variety of groups. Some groups are formed by the patients themselves, because they are located near each other on a ward or elsewhere in the hospital and have common interests and backgrounds (natural groups). These can be developed for therapeutic purposes. Other groups are specifically formed by professional staff with a therapeutic intent. For both types of groups these questions must be answered: Who should work with a group? Who should be in a group? What activities should take place? The purpose of the group should largely determine these answers.

Who Should Work with Whom?

The purpose of establishing a group or developing a therapeutic program with a natural group should be specific and clear. The residents selected to compose a group should be determined by the purpose of the group. Additionally, the assignment of a worker, staff member, or volunteer should be related to the purpose of the group. When it is clear what work must be done, then it can be known what skills or expertise a worker will need in order to help the members to work successfully in a group.

A worker who is to help a group become a therapeutic experience for a group member needs to have knowledge of deviant behavior and mental illness, learning processes and mental limitations, individual needs, and group processes. In addition, a group worker should have some understanding of what constitutes "normal" behavior, a point that is often overlooked despite the fact that the goal of the group frequently is to have patients achieve more "normal" functioning. He or she should be aware of the particular nature of deviant behavior of the group and what constitutes a stress situation for each member. He or she must know what behavior changes are desirable for each member and what barriers need to be surmounted in the efforts to change. Without such knowledge the worker may err in one of two directions. He or she may focus on the illness or retardation rather than on the patient's strengths or acceptable behavior and overestimate the limitations imposed on the patient by illness or retardation. Such limitations often appear to be greater than they really are, partly because many workers have difficulty identifying clearly the small gains and partial success that pave the way to important change. In the opposite direction, they assume that since the patient behaves adequately in many situations, the patient should behave acceptably most of the time. Neither stance is helpful, for both deny the patient's reality and cloud the areas where he or she needs help. All who work with groups in a mental hospital must understand that the treatment and the rehabilitation process are not straight-line processes. Improvement involves both forward and backward change. As certain problems are resolved, other problems may assume higher priority. Progress also may include periods where no change seems to occur.

"Work with groups" implies that a group itself is being worked with— things are being done for, done to, and done with a group. Any group should exist as a means of helping each member, not to be an end in itself. Depending on the purpose of the group, general goals for all group members or specific individual goals can be articulated. Remotivation, a technique designed primarily for nursing personnel, uses groups to expand horizons, create group interest, "build a bridge to reality," and promote interaction among people living on the same ward (American Psychiatric Association, 1963). Social group workers use groups as a means and a context for changes in individual behavior.

Paraprofessionals, paid or volunteer, can lead patient groups, particularly where the primary goal is to develop recreational skill or a special interest. Such workers may help patients maintain contact with reality, expand their experiential horizons, continue some contact with the outside community, and simply have fun—a rare commodity in any institution. Volunteers can arrange experiences away from the hospital for patients such as Project Transition, developed at Ypsilanti Regional Center, Michigan. In that program small groups of community women meet with small groups of patients for a few hours weekly. The meetings are at local churches or other community sites. Two categories of paraprofessionals should be considered more often than they are: ex-patients, who may be useful models to patients, particularly when they are able to share their success and past hospital experiences; and people who are from the same ethnic, racial, or social class group as the patients. People who are similar to patients' own reference groups can facilitate the patient's resumption of "normal" social intercourse.

Formed groups should be used carefully and selectively. Certain patients may need the specialized services of a highly trained group specialist before they are able to benefit from membership in a group led by a less trained worker. Some patients need a specialized service at the same time that they are part of a group led by a less trained technician. The purposes of the two groups may be quite different. Other patients may need to experience participation in a large group to enable them to invest in and tolerate a group experience before they can make use of a small group.

A recurrent problem is that many of the professionals within the mental institutions think that work with patients in groups is restricted to their domain, whatever it may be. Much energy has been expended on experiments by professionals to try out their methods with groups of patients in an effort to support an elitist view. The old bugaboo "status" plagues even professionals (remember George Orwell's *Animal Farm*, where "all animals are equal, but some are more equal than others"?). One therapeutic group is too often considered "more therapeutic" than another type of therapeutic group. Experience shows that professional groups latch on to what is considered high-status work and often drop their own unique professional skills. This simply narrows the treatment opportunities for patients. Mental hospitals, with their broad range of patient needs, must offer a breadth of group services. Currently psychologists and psychiatrists often use groups in order to help patients develop greater insight. Recreational therapists use various types of programs in small group and mass recreation settings to help patients reexperience pleasure in activity. In developmental centers speech therapists, educators, occupational therapists, and nurses duplicate the structural contest.

L. H. Levy (1978) writes of the current self-help movement, noting that while the effectiveness of such groups is viewed favorably, only 30 percent of the professionals said their agency would integrate such groups into their programs.

Size of Group

Small, medium, and large groups offer patients different kinds of experiences. No one size is necessarily more beneficial than another. Actually, many patients need experience in groups of various size. Small groups of four to eight members provide a setting in which patients are forced into greater interaction with one another. In large institutions, where lack of participation in viable decision-making is prevalent, small groups can offer opportunities for each patient to be involved in several roles and have a part in making decisions.

Large groups allow for anonymity. The roles are more formal. There is some opportunity for interaction among patients, particularly within subgroups in the larger group. In larger groups there is more task role differentiation.

What Can Be Achieved in Groups?

To achieve a reasonable degree of health, all people must be able to find a comfortable balance between being alone and being with others, and a comfortable balance between being like others and being unique. Often there is concern that individuals will get lost in a group. That can be avoided when the worker is aware that the focus in therapeutic groups should be on the individual. Groups are formed to help the clients. Incidentally, while group workers fully acknowledge the value of group experiences, they must be champions of meeting the needs of patient privacy. A group worker must ask, "When can the patient have the right to be alone?" In most institutions the answer is not very often.

What can be achieved in a group? Towey and his colleagues (1966) suggest seven principal values of groups in an article entitled "Group Activities with Psychiatric In-Patients." Many of these apply to developmentally disabled residents as well.

1. *The presentation of ego models.* Despite occasional gibes to the effect that the only difference between the patient and the staff person is that one goes home after eight hours and the other goes to bed, the staff generally is much healthier and more adequate than the patients. The distance between the patients, who are sick or retarded, and the staff, who is well or normal, is sometimes too great to allow patients or residents to identify with staff. They may feel defeated before they start in attempting such identification. Often healthier patients are closer to less healthy patients than they are to staff members. Groups can help bridge this gap between degrees of sickness and health or retardation and normalcy.

2. *Social involvement.* Patients and residents can sometimes be characterized as intensely self-centered, dependent, and passive. These nonhelpful roles are usually encouraged and sometimes enforced by institutional routines. The identification with other patients or residents in the protected environment of the small, rehabilitation-oriented group helps each member move out of these roles into social interaction and active involvement with others.

3. *Behavioral feedback.* In the security of a group, where the patient or resident has gained the feeling that other members can and do like him or her and where others also have problems, he or she can begin to learn how his or her behavior affects others. This is done without a sense of punishment for misbehavior. It arises from the desire of the individual to change in response to the greater acceptance of the people to whom he or she can relate.

4. *The enhancement of self-esteem.* Through the development of a sense of identification with the group, members are provided with opportunities for the enhancement of self-esteem. The group provides a sense of belonging, helps to reduce feelings of inferiority and isolation, and encourages members to test reality by reacting to others and perceiving how others react to them. These three characteristics are very important attributes for patients and residents, who tend to be perennial isolates or "outsiders," and for the person whose sense of identity is not intact.

5. *Learning new knowledge and skills.* In a group members can learn from each other as well as from the worker. Further, they can learn through the observation of others without making a public commitment. They can learn by applying the situations of others to their own circumstances, through analogy rather than confrontation. In this way they can learn that it may be safe to take a chance, to try new ways of handling and solving personal and social problems.

6. *Remedial social education.* Groups can provide opportunities to re-learn forgotten social skills. Contacts with the world outside the institution and ways of dealing with it can be reestablished through discussions, role-playing, trips to the community, and so on.

7. *The support and utilization of social hunger.* Through recognition of the intact portions of a patient's ego, groups can stimulate, nurture, and support social hunger. The normative system established through group relationships can be developed to provide approval for appropriate old and new patterns of behavior as well as to limit deviant behavior. Peer sanctions and limits often provide more effective controls for the character disorder than an outside authority affords. On the other hand, peer encouragement and approval often enable the withdrawn patient or resident to take a chance on interacting with others to satisfy his or her need for social involvement.

Group services can be highly successful in helping incoming patients and residents maintain the social skills they have on admission and in providing both a place for recovering and/or developing social skills and peer support systems as they move toward discharge. The latter can reduce the problems often experienced at the point of discharge where community attitudes and lack of community resources blunt the effectiveness of the deinstitutionalization efforts.

ADMINISTRATIVE SUPPORT

The final factors that must be considered in the achievement of institutional tasks—the change of patient behavior—are the administrative arrangements necessary to implement goals.

While most group programs can be instituted without many structural changes, the operation of a new group program needs the support of administrators. Peal (1965) indicates four ways in which the institutions' administration can aid new group programs. (1) Relatively protected meeting times must be arranged and preserved. A social work student went to the ward to meet with his group for the first time. The group had been carefully selected and balanced by the group worker on the basis of referrals from the ward psychiatrist. When he arrived he found one patient had been sent out on a leave of absence, one had gone on a work assignment, and one was at the dentist. Only two patients were available for the group session. (2) The administration must make provisions for the worker to have time to prepare for and hold the meeting. (3) The administration can support the patient's or resident's attendance at meetings when "pro"-*status quo* personnel sabotage a worker's efforts to hold meetings by preventing their attendance. (4) The administration must allow for failure or mediocre success of a new program and thereby provide protection for the worker who is wiling to take a chance with new techniques. Only when failure is acknowledged to be one of the possible and acceptable outcomes of an experiment is a social worker free to try new projects, free to move away from the safety of the tried and true methods. Acceptance of possible failure allows him or her to experiment to the ultimate benefit of patients.

Perrow (1965) states that the structure of an organization is basically influenced by its technology and, vice versa, an organizations' technology is basically influenced by the structure of the organization. It can be difficult to introduce new technique in an existing structure if the nature of the new concepts implies some organizational change. For example, the concept of the therapeutic milieu probably could not be implemented successfully within an authoritarian structure, since the therapeutic milieu approach demands a nonauthoritarian structure. If, however, the authoritarian structure itself were used to institute a therapeutic milieu, the program once started would introduce a series of changes in the authoritarian structure itself.

According to Perrow, the reasons for the depressing conditions of mental institutions do not lie in their structure, process, or goal commitment but in their technological limitations. He believes there is no valid treatment technology consistent with large mental hospitals.

However, the authors believe that group situations in which the patient can gradually reassume responsibility for decisions regarding himself or herself and in which he or she gradually increases his or her obligations for social living—which usually are denied to the mentally ill person—can provide a viable treatment technique for large mental hospitals. Such treatment depends upon the acceptance of patienthood as a temporary condition in which the patient modifies his or her dysfunctional behavior and from which he or she is permitted to reenter the community as a complete citizen. Likewise, we believe that group experiences in which a retarded person gains increased social skills increases his or her ability to live in a less restrictive environment and he or she too becomes a person living in the community experiencing the rights and freedoms he or she can manage.

REFERENCES

AMERICAN PSYCHIATRIC ASSOCIATION; MENTAL HEALTH SERVICE; AND SMITH, KLINE & FRENCH LABORATORIES
   1963 *Remotivation Technique*. Remotivation Project.
BASSUK, ELLEN L., AND SAMUEL GERSON
   1978 "Deinstitutionalization and mental health services, 1977," *Scientific American*, 238 (February): 46–53.

BRUININKS, R. H.; B. K. HILL; AND M. J. THORSHEIM
1982 "Deinstitutionalization and foster care for mentally retarded people," *Health and Social Work*, 7: 198–205.
HILL, BRADLEY; LISA ROTEGARD; AND R. H. BRUININKS
1984 "The quality of life of mentally retarded people in residential care," *Social Work*, 29 (May–June): 275–81.
KINARD, E. M.
1981 "Discharged patients who desire to return to the hospital," *Hospital and Community Psychiatry*, 32: 194–97.
KRANTZ, G. C.; R. BRUININKS; AND JANE CLUMPER
1979 *Mentally Retarded People in State Operated Residential Facilities Year Ending June 30, 1978*. Minneapolis: Minnesota University Department of Psyschoeducational Studies.
LAKIN, CHARLIE K.; GORDON C. KRANTZ; ROBERT H. BRUININKS; JANE L. CLUMPER; AND BRADLEY K. HILL
1982 "One hundred years of data on populations of public residential facilities for mentally retarded." *American Journal on Mental Deficiency*, 87 (July): 1–8.
LAM, H. P.
1981 "What did we really expect from deinstitutionalization?" *Hospital and Community Psychiatry*, 32: 5–19.
LAMBERGER, LINDA
1964 "Factors affecting friendship and power relationships among patients on an open psychiatric ward." Master of Social Work thesis, University of Michigan, Ann Arbor.
LANG, NORMA
1972 "A broad-range model of practice in the social work group." *Social Service Review*, 46: 76–89.
LEVY, L. H.
1978 "Self-help groups viewed by mental health professionals: A survey and comments," *American Journal of Community Psychology*, 6: 305–13.
LUCKEY, J. W., AND J. J. BERMAN
1981 "Effects of commitment laws on mental health system," *American Journal of Orthopsychiatry*, 51: 479–83.
MULHERN, T. J.
1978 *Training Staff of Development Centers*. Letchworth Village: New York State Office of Mental Retardation and Developmental Disabilities.
NEW YORK CITY ADVISORY BOARD TO THE DEPARTMENT OF MENTAL HEALTH, MENTAL RETARDATION AND ALCOHOLISM SERVICES: INTERAGENCY TASK FORCE ON PROBLEMS OF DEINSTITUTIONALIZATION AND THE CHRONICALLY MENTALLY ILL
1978 "Deinstitutionalization and the community: The interagency task force on the problems of deinstitutionalization and the chronically mentally ill," July 17.
PEAL, JAMES
1965 "Responsibility of administration to group therapy programs." State of Michigan, Department of Mental Health, Lansing (mimeographed).

PERROW, CHARLES
  1965 "Hospitals, technology, structure and goals." In James G. March (ed.), *Handbook of Organizations*. Chicago: Rand-McNally, pp. 910–71.
RIESSMAN, C. K.; J. G. RABKIN; AND E. L. STRUENING
  1977 "Brief versus a standard psychiatric hospitalization: A critical review of the literature," *Community Mental Health Review*, 2 (March–April): 1.
THORSHEIM, M. J., AND R. H. BRUININKS
  1978 "Admission and readmission of mentally retarded people to residential facilities." Minneapolis: Minnesota University, Department of Psychoeducational Studies (April), 58 pp.
TOWEY, MARTIN S.; WADE SEARS; JOHN A. WILLIAMS; NATHAN KAUFMAN; AND MURRAY CUNNINGHAM
  1966 "Group activities with psychiatric in-patients," *Social Work*, 11 (January): 50–56.
WHITMER, G. E.
  1980 "From hospitals to jails: The fate of California's deinstitutionalized mentally ill," *American Journal of Orthopsychiatry*, 50: 65–75.
WILLETTS, RUTH
  1980 "Advocacy and the mentally ill," *Social Work*, 25 (September): 372–77.

29

Groups for Cancer Patients and Their Families: Purposes and Group Conditions

Maeda J. Galinsky

DIAGNOSES OF CANCER can be devastating experiences for patients and their families. Cancer is perhaps the most feared disease in America today, not only because it can signify disability, deterioration, and death but also because it can leave patients isolated and lonely. Others may fear contamination, may be unable to deal with the illness or imminent death, or may not know how to relate to the person in the new role of cancer patient. They may avoid the patient or, when in contact, rule out any mention of feelings and reactions to cancer. Patients, too, frequently engage in avoidance behavior.[1] Furthermore, they may feel keenly the lack of understanding of those surrounding them as they come to grips with violent shifts in their life situations. The families of cancer patients may be stunned, anxious about the patient, and often too guilt-ridden and burdened to attend to their own needs. Both the patient and the family may feel that they are alone and that the healthier world cannot comprehend their situation. While some may seek out others in similar circumstances for support and help, many do not have access to other patients and their families. Even those who know other cancer patients may not know how to approach them to get the assistance they need and desire. Because group work can bring similarly affected persons together and break through the isolating effects of the disease, it is an ideal means by which to offer services to cancer patients and their families

[1]The loneliness, fears, distress, and stigma associated with cancer are portrayed in fiction and essay by writers such as Albert (1982), Solzhenitsyn (1968), and Sontag (1978); in personal accounts of life with cancer by Graham (1982) and Solkoff (1983); in the social science literature by Wortman and Dunkell-Schetter (1979) and Freidenbergs et al. (1982); and in the clinical practice literature by Arnowitz, Brunswick, and Kaplan (1983), Larsen and Kaiser (1978), McCloy and Lansner (1981), and Spiegel, Bloom, and Yalom (1981).

The author wishes to thank Janice H. Schopler for her continuing support and help; Patricia McGarry for her careful bibliographic work; and Dianne Wildman and Cheryl McCartney for their invaluable professional assistance during the writer's own experience with cancer.

in an atmosphere that fosters the discovery of common concerns and development of mutual aid.[2]

Groups with cancer patients and their families have been formed to meet a variety of needs. Groups have been organized for ostomy patients, for mothers of hospitalized children, for radiation patients, for spouses of mastectomy patients, for the terminally ill, for recent widows, and for patients in oncology or radiation clinic waiting rooms. The professional literature reflects an increasing use of groups. While there have been a few summaries and some evaluation data,[3] reports of cancer groups are mostly descriptive of work with a single group designed to meet the current and pressing needs of that group of patients or families.[4] Of course, the special needs of cancer patients may call for modification in the use of traditional group techniques and thinking about groups, or for attention to aspects of group conditions. What follows is an overview and examination of the purposes of groups with cancer patients and families and a discussion of the unique features of group work with this population.[5]

PURPOSES OF GROUPS

The service needs of cancer patients and their families lie in many spheres—psychological, interpersonal, familial, vocational, financial, and institutional. Group purposes that have been developed as a response to these needs fall into five distinct, but sometimes overlapping, categories: support, sharing feelings, coping skills, information and education, and existential considerations.[6]

[2]Groups are increasingly used in health care settings. For an examination of the goals and benefits of these groups, see Democker and Zimpfer (1981) and Northen (1983).

[3]Summaries of group work with cancer patients are found in Cohen (1976) and Fobair et al. (1982). Some evaluation research has utilized control or comparison groups (Bloom, Ross, and Burnell, 1978; Ferlic, Goldman, and Kennedy, 1979; Krumm, Vannatta, and Sanders, 1979; Spiegel, Bloom, and Yalom, 1981; and Vachon et al., 1979). Other data have been obtained solely from the treatment group (Johnson and Stark, 1980; Rudolph et al., 1981; Schwartz, 1977; Winick and Robbins, 1977; Wood and Tombrink, 1983).

[4]Illustrative references provided in the text are based on a review of the literature on cancer groups.

[5]Although professionally led groups are emphasized in this chapter, especially with social workers as leaders of cancer groups, it should be evident that self-help groups are an important source of aid and support to cancer patients.

[6]The five categories for group purposes were derived from the themes that appear repeatedly in the professional literature. Almost all of the groups described in the literature reported a concentration on more than one, and often three or four, of the five main purposes.

Support

As mentioned, the experience of cancer can be isolating and alienating. There is an immediate need for help and understanding, yet a widening gulf opens between the patient and those around her or him. Social support can serve as a potential source of strength and of adaptation to cancer (Bloom, 1982; Clark, 1983; Wortman and Dunkel-Schetter, 1979). Often assistance can best be provided by persons who have faced or are facing crises similar to those now confronting the patient and the family.[7]

Meeting with other cancer patients who understand what a diagnosis of cancer means and the feelings it evokes can provide a much-needed sense of support. They have been through the itching and burning of radiation, the humiliation of hair loss, the terror of waiting for test results. They have had to wait long hours for appointments and at times have met uncaring, sometimes hostile personnel in the hospital system.

What can patients give each other in the way of support? They can encourage their fellow sufferers to continue with treatment and keep going with work, family, and friends, and can take note of gains made by patients, however small, in rehabilitation and treatment. Because they know how difficult life can be in the throes of cancer, their encouragement is not idly given. Furthermore, they can share their own hopes for the future and support the patient's positive views. At the same time they can allow the patient to feel hopeless and helpless temporarily, since they know those feelings are inevitable in the course of treatment. When it is clear that the illness is terminal, they can offer comfort and solace.

Families also need support as they come to terms with the illness of a loved one. In addition to the anguish and helplessness associated with watching a relative react to a diagnosis and treatment of cancer, family members may face increased responsibility, financial difficulties, and a change of life-style. They may feel sorrow, anger, and guilt. They may be afraid for themselves as well as for the patient. Talking with others in like circumstances can help family members get through extremely trying times.

Sharing Feelings

Fear, shame, anxiety, loneliness, confusion, panic, anger, denial, sadness, depression, guilt, frustration, and devastation are commonly reported

---

[7]Most cancer groups stress support as one of their aims. See, for example, Arnowitz, Brunswick, and Kaplan, (1983); Euster (forthcoming); Ferlic, Goldman, and Kennedy (1979); Franzino, Garen, and Meiman (1976); Herzoff (1979); Johnson and Stark (1980); Kopel and Mock (1978); Ross (1979); Roy and Sumpter (1983); Vachon et al. (1979); and Yalom and Greaves (1977).

to be associated with a diagnosis of cancer. Patients and their families may think they are alone in experiencing such emotions and may be ashamed of having these feelings, or they may believe that stoicism and a brave front are virtues to be sought. The bottling up of these emotions may leave the individuals drained and isolated. For emotional stability it is important to express such feelings and to recognize them as acceptable and permissible. Groups are especially conducive to the sharing of such feelings.[8] One member's account of the emotional turmoil he or she is experiencing can trigger recognition and expression of similar feelings in another. When patients are unable to express their own emotions directly, they may gain release and comfort by hearing others' descriptions. Joint communication of feelings may not only enhance members' psychological health but also enable them to make, and act on, more facilitative decisions about medical treatment.

As members in the group interact, they have the opportunity to observe others' reactions to the cancer experience and to mark differences as well as similarities in feelings and actions. In the regimented and universalistic environment of the hospital or clinic, individuality should be encouraged by human service professionals. Furthermore, a sharing of feelings may help prevent social withdrawal, as members find that their feelings are not only respected but expected.

Coping Skills

New coping skills are required to handle the initial shock of having cancer and to manage long-term implications and demands of the disease and its treatment. Since the experiences most patients face are novel, they have no guidelines to follow. Demands for adjustment are many, and among the complex situations that patients and families encounter are chemotherapy and its effects; changed body appearance and functioning; what to tell children about the illness; managing physical weakness; how to preserve personal autonomy in the midst of medical control; where to get wigs; how to keep food down; how to get information from physicians and nurses; how to respond to others who awkwardly ask, or pointedly don't ask, about the illness; and how to continue to work. The list of new responses demanded can seem endless. Some of the adjustments, such as to the loss of hair, may appear relatively mundane and time-limited to those not afflicted; to the pa-

---

[8]Representative of groups that have the sharing of feelings as a goal are Arnowitz, Brunswick, and Kaplan (1983); Heffron (1975); Kopel and Mock (1978); Parsell and Tagliareni (1974); Ross (1979); Spiegel and Yalom (1978); Vachon et al. (1979); and Wellisch, Mosher, and Van Scoy (1978).

tient, however, they may be overpowering in their effects on self-image and life-style.[9]

Group members who have encountered or are facing similar crises can offer each other tested solutions and discover together new ways of responding. Patients and families can more easily trust the recommendations of those who are, like themselves, struggling to cope with the new and terrible intricacies of life with cancer or accept the help of the professional in the group context. Thus an individual who has successfully mastered the management of an ostomy can give practical advice, as well as hope, to someone newly diagnosed as having cancer of the colon. Two patients who are afraid to tell their children about having cancer may discover a way to do it through brainstorming. Or parents of terminally ill children may engage in a discussion of how to help the siblings of these children.

Families, too, have adjustments to make. Financial, interpersonal, and social alterations are likely to be called for. Since the focus of treatment and concern is often on the cancer patient alone, families may not find the patience and suggestions they need from others. Furthermore, the patient's treatment may have caused psychological or physical scars. Mastectomies, ostomies, and laryngectomies may be almost as difficult for families to adjust to as they are for the patient, especially since there is less social sanction and support for the family's negative feelings and behavior than there is for the patient's. Therefore, family members may find it helpful to meet with other families to share reactions and discover new coping skills.

An important task for both patients and families results from the unpredictable course of cancer. It is often difficult to detect when cancer has spread, and there is no way to tell with certainty if cancer, once treated, will recur—at least within a five- to ten-year period for most types. Use of the term "remission," rather than cure, is indicative of the status of the disease as viewed by the medical community. The task of learning to live with uncertainty, to continue daily living in a normal way when one does not know whether or not cancer cells are actively growing and multiplying, is a formidable challenge for patients and families.[10] They will benefit from the empathy and practical guidelines received in group sessions.

In addition to dealing with personal and interpersonal situations, patients and families must also cope with the harsh realities of treatment regimens and hospital routines. Institutional management demands new coping

[9]Groups that emphasize coping skills include those reported by Euster (1979, forthcoming); Franzino, Geren, and Meiman (1976); McCloy and Lansner (1981); Ross (1979); Spiegel (1979); and Vachon et al. (1979).

[10]Cognitive adaptation is noted by Taylor (1983) to be a critical factor in adjustment to cancer.

skills, such as arranging appointments with physicians, nurses, physical therapists, or social workers, or responding to possible impersonal treatment in the course of radiation therapy, x-rays, blood tests, and medical examinations. Getting from one part of the hospital to another can be a chore, and waiting in clinics can seem endless. Not only is assertive behavior often called for from persons who are not accustomed to dealing with bureaucracies in a forthright manner, but such behavior is required at a time when the patient and family are especially vulnerable and afraid of behaving in ways that might upset the patient's care. In the group setting members are able to commiserate with each other about the obstacles they face, discover new ways of maneuvering through the institutional maze, learn assertive behavior, role-play difficult interactions, and acquire methods of getting the information and services they need in a manner that respects their time and preserves their dignity.

Information and Education

Cancer patients and their families often lack basic information about the nature of the disease, the course of treatment, and its effects. Fearful responses to radiation therapy, chemotherapy, and surgery may then be magnified. When hospital personnel take the time to explain the status of the disease or the treatment recommended, they often use medical terminology that creates greater confusion. In addition, patients may be unaware of dietary and other life-style factors that can enhance or impede treatment and uninformed about activities in which they are free to engage. When cancer has affected genital areas, patients and spouses may not know what kind of sexual activity is either possible or permissible.

As patients and families meet in groups, information and education can be provided by qualified personnel who are attuned to the language of the lay person. Group leaders can give basic information or call in other professionals as specialized content is needed.[11] Members who ask questions or respond to the information given can be helpful to their fellows in stimulating further consideration of their own conditions. Orientation to the hospital and explanations about procedures and routines, sometimes forgotten in the hectic pace of responding to critical illness, are valuable additions to the educational function of groups.

In addition, patients and families may need to acquire an understanding of the social and economic changes they can expect and what they can do to facilitate adjustment to them. Roles are bound to be altered to some

---

[11]Discussion of groups that have as one of their purposes information and education can be found in Ferlic, Goldman, and Kennedy (1979); Johnson and Stark (1980); Kopel and Mock (1978); Krumm, Vannattas, and Sanders (1979); Rudolph et al. (1981); Schwartz (1977); and Wood and Tombrink (1983).

extent at work and at home, as patients cope with the illness and families, friends, and co-workers change their expectations. While some patients may be required by illness to decrease their activities, others who are more able to perform are forced into unwanted changes in their homes, jobs, and social situations by the stigma of cancer and the erroneous views others have about limitations of cancer patients. Financial problems may come with reduced incomes and increased medical expenses. Patients who are accustomed to being independent are put in a dependent role as a result of the medical care they require. Although education will not necessarily change the circumstances of patients and families, knowledge of what to expect can help individuals view their experiences and reactions as reasonable and enable them to take preventive action to avoid troublesome situations they might otherwise encounter. Moreover, access to particular information, such as how to apply for Social Security disability payments and medical insurance benefits, can be immediately helpful to those struggling to cope.

Existential Considerations: Facing Issues of Life and Death

Cancer patients and their families must come to terms, at some point, with the quality of life and the possibility of death. When those with whom they interact are uncomfortable, pretending that there is no current need to deal with questions of mortality, or when they insist on talking only about pleasant matters, the ill and their relatives may feel a sense of frustration and alienation. Yet patients often need to discuss existential issues of life and death and, in the case of the terminally ill, to come to terms with dying.

While health professionals in oncology may understand these needs, they may have neither the time nor the skills to help patients work through these issues, and indeed some may feel that attention to such topics will cause patients unnecessary pain or lead to loss of hope or the will to live. Furthermore, medical personnel who must repetitively face the death of their patients and come to terms with their own helplessness cannot be expected continuously to help patients and families deal with death and grief at the same time as they provide medical care.

Human service practitioners, trained in group work and in facilitating patients' and families' discussion of life with cancer or of imminent death, are particularly adept at fostering a climate wherein those delicate issues can be examined.[12] Patients find that they are able to talk about potentially painful topics and to face the threat to their lives, and can help one another

---

[12]Existential considerations have been cited less frequently as objectives of cancer groups than have the other four objectives. However, they are important in a number of groups. See, for example, Adams (1978); Corder and Anders (1974); Heffron (1975); Parsell and Tagliareni (1974); Roy and Sumpter (1983); and Yalom and Greaves (1977).

come to terms with cancer and, when necessary, death. The detoxification of death is seen as one result of attention to these issues (Spiegel and Yalom, 1978).

Families of patients can also find relief and assistance through discussion of their own reactions and fears. Some may feel guilty in talking about these concerns when the immediate danger is not directly their own. They may believe that others want to falsely reassure them or may be terrified of death and deny the seriousness of the patient's condition. If death does occur, family members may need further assistance from the group to accept the reality of their loss and to integrate the experience in their own lives. Sometimes group leaders find it helpful to bring patients and families together to discuss these existential issues.[13]

GROUP CONDITIONS

Particular features of groups with cancer patients and families merit attention: initiating the group, group purpose and structure, patient relationships, leader behavior, and group problems. While these groups, of course, have group processes and conditions common to all client groups, those group aspects that are most critical and sometimes unique to cancer groups are emphasized.

Initiating the Group

Essential to beginning the group is the involvement of health care personnel and the hospital administration, especially if the group is to take place in the context of the clinic or ward.[14] Because physicians and nurses are important sources of referral and support for the group, leaders need to explain carefully the purposes, activities, and benefits of the group and to work out procedures for accommodating to hospital schedules and getting patients and families to group meetings. Medical personnel may be initially resistant to the idea of patients interacting with one another for fear of their frightening or intruding on one another, developing a hostile attitude to

---

[13]While not paramount aims in most cancer groups the following purposes have also been identified: intrapersonal issues and family conflicts (e.g. Cohen, 1976; Euster, 1979; Ringler et al., 1981; Wellisch, Mosher, and Van Scoy, 1978); patient advocacy or institutional and social change, especially in self-help groups (e.g. Adams, 1979; Fobair et al., 1982; Herzoff, 1979); physical rehabilitation (e.g. Euster, 1979); assessment and referral (e.g. Herzoff, 1979; Kopel and Mock, 1978); discharge planning (Huberty, 1974); and provision of cognitive meaning (Schwartz, 1977).

[14]See, for example, Arnowitz, Brunswick, and Kaplan (1983); Fobair et al. (1982); Johnson and Stark (1980).

hospital activities or staff by joint complaining, or because they believe patient interchanges and expression of emotions will not assist, and may even harm, patients and families.[15] The data show that patients in cancer groups evaluate them as beneficial and that they gain information and learn to cope more effectively; these results can be presented to staff as support for group interventions.[16] Inclusion of health care professionals directly in the group is important. Physicians and nurses have often initiated and led or co-led patient and family groups; at other times they have provided information and education sessions as one part of a meeting or series of group meetings.

Recruitment of patients and families for cancer groups can be especially problematic (Barstow, 1982; Euster, forthcoming). In addition to staff reluctance to refer, one must pay attention to patients' schedules, families' unwillingness to leave patients for meetings, especially during periods of hospitalization, and patients' desire for privacy. Furthermore, some patients and families may be unfamiliar with groups and what occurs in them, and leaders may need to give them detailed explanations prior to their joining (Whitman, Gustafson, and Coleman, 1979).[17] Active outreach by leaders to secure group members, including advertising, has been suggested (Fobair et al., 1982).

The location of group meetings is another important factor to consider. Patients can be intimidated by the formal medical setting; one group found it helpful to meet in the community room of a department store (Schwartz, 1977). Because moving beyond the confines of the hospital may be impractical, leaders have been creative in finding meeting places on wards or in clinics, even holding meetings in clinic waiting rooms (Arnowitz, Brunswick, and Kaplan, 1983). Finding the most convenient time for group members can also be a problem. One group finally opted for a concentrated period on Saturday mornings (Barstow, 1982); other groups have been run with members entering or leaving as necessary for medical appointments (Herzoff, 1979; McCloy and Lansner, 1981). Groups vary as to how many meetings members attend, from as few as one to weekly sessions for more than a year, as to whether they are open-ended or have closed

[15]Careful interpretation of the benefits of emotional expressiveness may need to be given by the group leader who wishes to obtain the support of medical personnel. Bloom, Ross, and Barnett (1978) found that patients who received supportive treatment, including membership in a group, were more emotionally labile immediately after surgery; however, they also scored higher on a measure of self-efficacy two months later.

[16]Positive evaluation of cancer groups are reported in the studies cited in footnote 3.

[17]Schwartz (1977) suggests starting sessions with a formal presentation of educational material so that members are not threatened and can accommodate themselves to the group. This approach to beginning the group in a benign fashion is also recommended by Euster (1979), whose group of recently diagnosed mastectomy patients began each meeting with physical therapy exercises.

membership, and as to the length of time the group runs, with some groups planned for only a short time and some open-ended groups lasting as long as four or more years.

Cancer groups differ in their composition. Some groups have membership restricted either to patients or to families, while others have combined the two populations. Choice of members on the basis of type of cancer, such as breast cancer; stage of illness, such as the terminally ill; or type of treatment, such as radiation therapy, can also be determinants of group composition. At times it is believed helpful to have successfully coping "old-timers" present to serve as role models for newly diagnosed patients (e.g. Vachon et al., 1979). While no clear-cut rules about composition can be proclaimed, the purpose for which the group is formed seems to be the overriding consideration in determining composition.

Group Purpose and Structure

A clear statement of the purposes of the group is essential for recruitment, for easing of members' entry, for integrating new members in open-ended groups, and for composition and planning. As noted earlier, most leaders of cancer groups have stated that intra- or interpersonal learning, or what is traditionally billed as group psychotherapy, is not paramount as an objective; in fact, some workers think that a focus on "mental health" may be interpreted by some patients as an indication that they have mental problems or are deviant (Kleiman, Mantell, and Alexander, 1977; Schwartz, 1977). Therefore, clarity in communicating the purpose of the group to its members is especially important.

Opinions differ about whether the group should be highly structured, with preplanned topical sessions, or unstructured. There are numerous ways in which cancer groups have been organized. Some leaders have found it expeditious to plan the topics and focus of meetings carefully and let patients and staff know exactly what will occur each time, believing that necessary material will then be covered and patients will know what they are contracting for. Time is often allotted for discussion as well as presentation of material (Ferlic, Goldman, and Kennedy, 1979; Wood and Tombrink, 1983). Other leaders argue that groups should be kept flexible so that members can raise immediate and pressing concerns (Gustafson et al., 1978; Kopel and Mock, 1978). A variation that combines both directives involves a larger group meeting in which information is presented, followed by small group discussions in which concerns and questions can be raised. Some groups alternate structure, with planned topics in some meetings and open discussion in others. One open-ended group of mastectomy patients on a hospital ward spent Mondays, Wednesdays, and Fridays in spontaneous discussion and Tuesdays and Thursdays on structured topics (Euster, 1979). Still other group leaders are ready with planned agendas, which they are prepared to drop if patients raise other topics they wish to discuss.

Confidentiality is an issue in groups where the leaders maintain contact with professional staff. There is a question as to whether concerns and complaints of patients should be communicated beyond the group or whether strict in-group confidentiality should be maintained. In any event, members need to know how this issue will be handled.

Cancer groups differ from more traditional therapy groups in several aspects of their functioning. They are reported to be more focused on content than process (Spiegel and Glafkides, 1983), with relatively little confrontation and here-and-now interpersonal exploration (Fobair et al., 1982). They are also more committed to helping members cope with shared external events (Schwartz, 1977).[18]

Patient Relationships

Patients quickly establish relationships in cancer groups. The bond of illness serves to unite members and provides a basis of common feelings, interests, and experiences (e.g. Johnson and Stark, 1980; Parsell and Tagliareni, 1974; Spiegel and Yalom, 1978). Group formation is speeded as members discover the similarities involved in a diagnosis of cancer—the pain, the fears, the stigma, the treatments.

For many patients there is enormous relief in being able to express their negative reactions and feelings, some for the first time, to others who may share them. Relatives, friends, and health personnel may feel that it is inadvisable for patients to maintain other than a cheerful or optimistic demeanor. Patients may not wish to disturb or disappoint their loved ones. Furthermore, some patients find that others reject their attempts at communication about cancer and its personal impact. Relatives of cancer patients similarly find solace in discovering their guilt, their hostility, and their repugnance are shared by those in like circumstances.

The altruism and mutual aid evident in supportive groups have been cited as important ingredients in improving the tenor of patients' lives as they maintain some sense of mastery and reciprocity (e.g. Euster, 1979; Yalom and Greaves, 1977). After being required to be passive and receptive in their patient roles, having the opportunity to help fellow members may itself be therapeutic. The group experience provides a welcome opportunity

---

[18]Several authors have stated that there is a clear distinction between cancer groups and group psychotherapy (Kopel and Mock, 1978; McCloy and Lansner, 1981). However, since definitions of what constitutes group psychotherapy vary, and since cancer groups themselves differ in aproach, it is difficult to make a sharp differentiation between cancer groups and group psychotherapy.

for interpersonal competence (e.g. serving as role models in problem-solving) amid the breakdown of familiar roles and relationships and the dependency and loss of control inherent in the patient role. Although the interpersonal network in a cancer group may resemble the relationships formed in other types of groups, its impact may be more pronounced.

Patients in cancer groups often contact one another outside of the group for continued support, sustenance, and help (e.g. Johnson and Stark, 1980; McCloy and Lansner, 1981; Yalom and Greaves, 1977). Perhaps because the healthy do not want to share the burdens of the sick, especially when the disease is cancer, cancer patients need the repeated attention of their cohorts. Group members also visit, at home or in the hospital, members who have had setbacks in their fight against the disease (Spiegel, Bloom, and Yalom, 1981). Especially poignant interchanges may take place with group members who are dying. While outside contacts are often discouraged in traditional therapy groups, continued member interactions may be encouraged in cancer groups; because of the close bonds developed, patients may persist in seeing each other even after their formal association with the group has ended. Similarly, families and friends of patients who have died may continue to seek each other out for comfort and understanding.

Leader Considerations and Requirements

Because of the nature of cancer and its often fatal consequences, as well as the public myths and fears that surround it, leaders of cancer groups must deal with their own anxieties and fears about the disease and about death (e.g. Kopel and Mock, 1978; Yalom and Greaves, 1977). Leading cancer groups is especially demanding and challenging; workers need to be able to discuss their emotionally depleting experiences with colleagues and supervisors. Group workers must be able to face their own mortality and serve as role models of emotional expressiveness. While communicating to group members that they are not afraid of painful material, they must create a climate that encourages discussion of feelings. Leaders should strive to be empathic as well as knowledgeable and work to prevent a division between the healthy leader(s) and the ill members, which would be detrimental to the work of the group.

Leaders of cancer groups are often asked to be directive, to remain active, to set the stage quickly for patient interactions (Euster, forthcoming), and to provide openings for members to discuss difficult subjects (Whitman, Gustafson, and Coleman, 1979). Given that many cancer groups are open-ended, workers need to ease members' entry and exit (Galinsky and Schopler, in press; see also Chapter 6) as well as to help focus discussion. Since patients may attend a limited number of meetings, the leader must be ready to help them deal with emotionally charged content of the sessions. When groups are highly structured, the leader's role is by definition one of control as well as of facilitation.

Co-leadership and the participation of members of various professions are often recommended because of the personal drain of cancer groups and the need for different types of expertise. When information and education are group goals, medical personnel may attend several sessions. Clergymen may be invited to help members deal with existential issues. Social workers, psychologists, psychiatrists, and nurses trained in group methods and discussion of affect most often serve as primary leaders to help members deal with support, coping skills, and sharing of feelings. A partnership of social worker and nurse is a common form of co-leadership (Adams, 1976; Herzoff, 1979). Physical therapists, dieticians, recreational specialists, occupational therapists, and volunteers from self-help organizations may also be a part of the group team.

Group leaders must be ready to intervene directly with members beyond the boundaries of group meetings (Euster, forthcoming; Johnson and Stark, 1980; Kopel and Mock, 1978). Members who are upset or regarded as vulnerable in any way may need immediate individualized attention. This is especially true when discussion of pain, treatment, and death unleashes unaccustomed emotions or when difficult feelings such as guilt, blame, and anger have been expressed. Furthermore, professional medical staff who are not part of the group may need to be informed of the patient's emotional status or of negative reactions to care—provided, of course, the patient's consent has been obtained.

Special Group Problems and Considerations

A common topic of concern in cancer groups is the impersonal and insensitive care that patients and families sometimes encounter in the hospital setting. In fact, as mentioned earlier, part of the resistance of hospital personnel to the group method is based on the fear that patients and families will dwell on and escalate these complaints when they meet in a group. While displeasure about hospital treatment is often expressed in group discussion and is a permitted topic, leaders also note that it is important to move beyond a listing of unfortunate occurrences and reiteration of hostile feelings to other areas of members' concerns. In most cases, with skilled intervention of leaders and sufficient time for members to express what are often realistic complaints, groups do not stagnate in a frustrating repetition of these experiences. At times physicians or nurses may be invited to the group to talk with members about their perceptions. In other cases, changes in hospital procedures or interactions may be achieved through leaders' and members' actions outside the group.

Prolonged ventilation of members' personal responses to cancer is another problem that may be encountered, as is continued angry behavior, which often results in hostile responses from families, friends, and caregivers (Johnson and Stark, 1980; McCloy and Lansner, 1981). Leaders, while sensitive to special needs, must also consider the effects on the group of individual outpourings. Strong and excessive expression of emotions may be frightening and overpowering to other members. Furthermore, the development of a group climate that encourages undue attention to negative factors may be damaging to those who are striving to cope.

Members may find themselves overwhelmed by expressions of sad or fearful emotions. In a cancer group, which has a strong potential for emotional lability and the uncovering of disturbing feelings, leaders must create conditions of safety for members (Ringler et al., 1981). While articulation of feelings is to be encouraged, the pace of communication may need to build slowly, and the leaders must be attuned to those members who are having difficulty when events appear to move too rapidly for them. Sometimes it is necessary for the worker to protect reticent patients when group norms encourage open expression. Thus the leader has the task of assisting members in expressing intense feelings, while at the same time ensuring that the disclosure is not destructive to others in the group. Withdrawn or depressed members also require special leader interventions.

Patients or families in cancer groups often must deal with the death of members, an especially difficult and frightening experience. Sensitivity on the part of the leader is required to help members come to terms with this experience and to deal with their reactions. Termination may raise especially difficult issues when it involves the death of a member or a member's spouse (Euster, forthcoming; Spiegel and Yalom, 1978). Group workers must be attuned to signs of strain in members and need to encourage open responses and expressions of grief. Some groups have been formed for survivors of cancer victims to help them deal with the issues of grieving and living in the aftermath of death (Roy and Sumpter, 1983).

CONCLUSION

A review of the literature on cancer groups has shown that they are an important source of support, learning, and problem-solving for both patients and their families. These groups enable members to cope with the nature and consequences of cancer and the special reality it creates, as well as to master and integrate emotions and cognitions. Group members build upon their common plight to offer assistance and encouragement to one another. Together they face issues related to diagnosis and treatment, family and social relationships, finances and work, quality of life and death. Leaders of cancer groups have adapted group techniques to meet the individual needs of cancer patients and their families. Besides attention to group conditions and interactions, interventions are often required beyond the group sessions with group members and families and with participants in the health care team. Leading a cancer group is demanding and emotionally exhausting, requiring maturity, skill, and commitment to patients. A solid base in group work practice must be enhanced by a knowledge of cancer and its effects and a willingness to enter the world of the cancer patient and to learn from the experience.

REFERENCES

ADAMS, JEANETTE
   1979   "Mutual-help groups: Enhancing the coping ability of oncology clients," *Cancer Nursing*, 2: 95–98.
ADAMS, MARGARET A.
   1976   "A hospital play program: Helping children with serious illness," *American Journal of Orthopsychiatry*, 46: 416–24.
   1978   "Helping the parents of children with malignancy," *Journal of Pediatrics*, 93: 734–38.
ALBERT, GAIL
   1982   *Matters of Chance*. New York: G. P. Putnam's Sons.
ARNOWITZ, EDWARD; LYNNE BRUNSWICK; AND BARRY H. KAPLAN
   1983   "Group therapy with patients in the waiting room of an oncology clinic," *Social Work*, 28: 395–97.
BARSTOW, LINDA F.
   1982   "Working with cancer patients in radiation therapy," *Health and Social Work*, 7: 35–40.
BLOOM, JOAN R.
   1982   "Social support systems and cancer: A conceptual view." In Jerome Cohen, Joseph W. Cullen, and L. Robert Martin (eds.), *Psychosocial Aspects of Cancer*. New York: Raven Press, pp. 129–49.
BLOOM, JOAN R.; ROBERT D. ROSS; AND GEORGE BURNELL
   1978   "The effect of social support on patient adjustment after breast surgery," *Patient Counselling and Health Education*, 1: 50–59.
CLARK, ELIZABETH J.
   1983   "The role of the social environment in adaptation to cancer," *Social Work Research and Abstracts*, 19: 32–33.
COHEN, JEROME
   1976   "Exploring the current scene in group psychotherapy for cancer patients." In Catherine Cordoba and Patricia Fobair (eds.), *Cancer—and the Group Experience*. San Francisco: American Cancer Society, pp. 7–17.
CORDER, MICHAEL P., AND ROBERT L. ANDERS
   1974   "Death and dying: Oncology discussion group," *Journal of Psychiatric Nursing and Mental Health Services*, 12: 10–14.

DeMocker, Janice DeLa Hooke, and David G. Zimpfer
   1981   "Group approaches to psychosocial intervention in medical care: A synthesis," *International Journal of Group Psychotherapy*, 31: 247–60.

Euster, Sona
   1979   "Rehabilitation after mastectomy: The group process," *Social Work in Health Care*, 4: 251–63.
   Forthcoming   "Adjusting to cancer in an adult family member." In Howard B. Roback (ed.), *Group Interventions with Medical-Surgical Patients and Their Families*. San Francisco: Jossey-Bass.

Ferlic, Mary; Anne Goldman; and B. J. Kennedy
   1979   "Group counseling in adult patients with advanced cancer," *Cancer*, 43: 760–66.

Fobair, Pat; Catherine Cordoba; Constance Pluth; and Joan Bloom
   1982   "Considerations for successful groups." In *Western State Conference on Cancer Rehabilitation*. Palo Alto, Calif.: Bull Publishing Co., pp. 105–17.

Franzino, Mary Ann; John J. Geren; and Gregory L. Meimen
   1976   "Group discussion among the terminally ill," *International Journal of Group Psychotherapy*, 26: 43–48.

Freidenbergs, Ingrid; Wayne Gordon; Mary Hibbard; Linda Levine; Carol Wolfi; and Leonard Diller
   1982   "Psychological aspects of living with cancer: A review of the literature," *International Journal of Psychiatry in Medicine*, 13: 303–29.

Galinsky, Maeda J., and Janice H. Schopler
   In press   "Open-ended groups: Patterns of entry and exit," *Social Work with Groups*.

Graham, Jory
   1982   *In the Company of Others*. New York: Harcourt Brace Jovanovich.

Gustafson, James; Frederick Coleman; Allen Kipperman; Helen Whitman; and Roy Hankins
   1978   "A cancer patient's group: The problem of containment," *Journal of Personality and Social Systems*, 1: 6–18.

Heffron, Warren A.
   1975   "Group therapy sessions as part of treatment of children with cancer," *Pediatric Annals*, 4: 102–12.

Herzoff, Nancy E.
   1979   "A therapeutic group for cancer patients and their families," *Cancer Nursing*, 2: 469–74.

Huberty, David J.
   1974   "Adapting to illness through family groups," *International Journal of Psychiatry in Medicine*, 5: 231–42.

Johnson, Edith M., and Doretta E. Stark
   1980   "A group program for cancer patients and their family members in an acute care teaching hospital," *Social Work in Health Care*, 5: 335–49.

Kleiman, Mark Allen; Joanne E. Mantell; and Esther S. Alexander
   1977   "Rx for social death: The cancer patient as counselor," *Community Mental Health Journal*, 13: 115–24.

KOPEL, KENNETH, AND LOU ANN MOCK
  1978 "The use of group sessions for the emotional support of families of terminal patients," *Death Education*, 1: 409–22.
KRUMM, SHARON; PATRICIA VANNATTA; AND JUDITH SANDERS
  1979 "Group approaches for cancer patients: A group for teaching chemotherapy," *American Journal of Nursing*, 79: 916.
LARSEN, ROBERT, AND VIRGINIA KAISER
  1978 "The self-help process in a group of cancer patients," *Current Concepts in Psychiatry*, 4: 15–18.
MCCLOY, STEVEN G., AND ANITA S. LANSNER
  1981 "In the leper colony: Group therapy for cancer patients." In Jane Goldberg (ed.), *Psychotherapeutic Treatment of Cancer Patients*. New York: Free Press, pp. 246–60.
NORTHEN, HELEN
  1983 "Social work groups in health settings: Promises and problems," *Social Work in Health Care*, 8: 107–28.
PARSELL, SUE, AND ELAINE MURRAY TAGLIARENI
  1974 "Cancer patients help each other," *American Journal of Nursing*, 74: 650–51.
RINGLER, KARIN E.; HELEN H. WHITMAN; JAMES P. GUSTAFSON; AND FREDERICK W. COLEMAN
  1981 "Technical advances in leading a cancer patient group," *International Journal of Group Psychotherapy*, 31: 329–44.
ROSS, JUDITH W.
  1979 "Coping with childhood cancer: Group intervention as an aid to parents in crisis," *Social Work in Health Care*, 4: 381–91.
ROY, PHILIP F., AND HELEN SUMPTER
  1983 "Group support for the recently bereaved," *Health and Social Work*, 8: 230–32.
RUDOLPH, LAURA A.; THOMAS W. PENDERGRASS; JAMES CLARKE; MARY KJOSNESS; AND JOHN R. HARTMANN
  1981 "Development of an education program for parents of children with cancer," *Social Work in Health Care*, 6: 43–54.
SCHWARTZ, MARC D.
  1977 "An information and discussion program for women after mastectomy," *Archives of Surgery*, 112: 276–81.
SOLKOFF, JOEL
  1983 *Learning to Live Again: My Triumph over Cancer*. New York: Holt, Rinehart & Winston.
SOLZHENITSYN, ALEKSANDR I.
  1968 *The Cancer Ward*. New York: Dial Press.
SONTAG, SUSAN
  1978 *Illness as Metaphor*. New York: Farrar, Straus & Giroux.
SPIEGEL, DAVID
  1979 "Psychological support for women with metastatic carcinoma," *Psychosomatics*, 20: 780–87.

SPIEGEL, DAVID; JOAN R. BLOOM; AND IRVIN D. YALOM
   1981   "Group support for patients with metastatic cancer," *Archives of General Psychiatry*, 38: 527–33.
SPIEGEL, DAVID, AND MICHAEL CONSTANTINE GLAFKIDES
   1983   "Effects of group confrontation with death and dying," *International Journal of Group Psychotherapy*, 33: 433–48.
SPIEGEL, DAVID, AND IRVIN D. YALOM
   1978   "A support group for dying patients," *International Journal of Group Psychotherapy*, 28: 233–45.
TAYLOR, SHELLEY E.
   1983   "Adjustment to threatening events: A theory of cognitive adaptation," *American Psychologist*, 38: 1161–73.
VACHON, MARY L. S.; W. ALAN LYALL; JOY ROGERS; ANTON FORMO; KAREN FREEDMAN; JEANETTE COCHRANE; AND STANLEY J. J. FREEMAN
   1979   "The use of group meetings with cancer patients and their families." In Jean Taché, Hans Selye, and Stacey B. Day (eds.), *Cancer, Stress and Death*. New York: Plenum Medical Book Company, pp. 129–39.
WELLISCH, DAVID K.; MICHAEL B. MOSHER; AND CHERYLE VAN SCOY
   1978   "Management of family emotion stress: Family group therapy in a private oncology practice," *International Journal of Group Psychotherapy*, 28: 225–31.
WHITMAN, HELEN; JAMES P. GUSTAFSON; AND FREDERICK W. COLEMAN
   1979   "Group approaches for cancer patients: Leaders and members," *American Journal of Nursing*, 79: 910–13.
WINICK, LAWRENCE, AND GUY F. ROBBINS
   1977   "Physical and psychologic readjustment after mastectomy," *Cancer*, 39: 478–86.
WOOD, JANE DIVITA, AND JUDITH TOMBRINK
   1983   "Impact of cancer on sexuality and self-image: A group program for patients and partners," *Social Work in Health Care*, 8: 45–54.
WORTMAN, CAMILLE B., AND CHRISTINE DUNKEL-SCHETTER
   1979   "Interpersonal relationships and cancer: A theoretical analysis," *Journal of Social Issues*, 35: 120–55.
YALOM, IRVIN D., AND CARLOS GREAVES
   1977   "Group therapy with the terminally ill," *American Journal of Psychiatry*, 134: 396–400.

30

Group Approaches to the Prevention and Treatment of Chemical Dependency

Beth Glover Reed

GROUP WORK TECHNIQUES and approaches that draw on fundamental group principles have historically been staples of drug and alcohol programming. In fact, more explicit recognition of group concepts and strategies and the reasons why they are important and useful should enable planners and practitioners to apply them more consciously and effectively. As yet there has been little systematic research and evaluation on the effectiveness of various group approaches, partly because the chemical dependency field is relatively new and is rife with often competing ideologies.

The purpose of this chapter is to describe why group approaches have been so important in the chemical dependency field and to review briefly the many ways that group work concepts and strategies have been employed. Finally I shall discuss some theoretical and practical issues that must be addressed to develop our knowledge about the usefulness of group approaches in this important and burgeoning field.

Definitional unclarity and value dilemmas abound in the alcohol and drug literature. In this chapter I shall be concerned about all psychoactive chemicals, including alcohol, nicotine, caffiene, and prescribed and over-the-counter (OTC) drugs. Developing clear distinctions among different types of use and their consequences is very important in policy-oriented, prevention, or treatment practice. Experimentation behaviors, controlled social or medicinal use, misuse or problematic use (with negative physical and/or social consequences), and systematically defined dependency (e.g. compulsive and repeated use despite negative consequences) can signify different stages of use; can arise from different combinations of individual, group, and societal conditions; and are likely to indicate different degrees of seriousness and need different types of intervention. For this chapter, however, given space limitations, I have noted definitional distinctions only when they are crucial to the discussion. To simplify the language I shall use "chemical dependency" (CD) as a generic term to indicate various types of problems with alcohol and drug consumption (although the reader should note that in practice "dependency" is often used to define very specific types of diagnostic categories).

BACKGROUND AND RATIONALE
FOR GROUP APPROACHES

The use of chemical substances in ways deemed unacceptable by at least some components of a society has a long cultural history. The development of an addictions field that seeks to regulate the use of ingestible substances is of more recent origin. Until recently, to a large extent, those concerned about alcoholism have worked separately from those most knowledgeable about illicit drugs. Attention to use of licit drugs and other compulsive behaviors is a very new phenomenon. Thus the chemical dependency field is still very diverse, with different segments often having little knowledge of the data, assumptions, and practices of each other; in fact, contentious disagreements are not uncommon. No single theory or social intervention dominates the field (c.f. Burglass and Shaffer, 1983–84).

This complex and often confusing state of affairs derives partially from the relative newness of the field, the diverse frames of reference of individuals in a position to formulate theory, and the growing recognition that problems with use of, or dependency on, drugs and alcohol are usually multifaceted and multiply determined. Early moral weakness theories have gradually yielded to personality deficit theories (needing treatment rather than will power and penitence), although these have not held up in well-controlled research studies. More recently theorists have been conceptualizing CD as a physical syndrome incorporating social, environmental, and cultural factors well beyond the individual's control.

Throughout this evolution new patterns of chemical use have emerged, and there is increasing public recognition of CD and its consequences. Massive efforts have been made to coordinate and consolidate resource allocation and policy-making at the federal and state levels. To a large degree, however, the field is still characterized by a paucity of facts and few generally accepted paradigms.

Formal training in a single discipline tends to focus one in the domain of that discipline, while a comprehensive understanding of CD requires knowledge in a wide range of areas (e.g. physiological, psychological, sociological, legal, and cultural-political factors and processes). In fact, many would argue that professional and disciplinary training have to a large degree been irrelevant or have interfered with the development of useful knowledge and effective interventions with CD. Narrow perspectives, a general lack of knowledge about CD, and often negative stereotypes have combined to create a whole network of human service agencies whose staff have little training, skills, or interest in the detection and treatment of CD. As a result many of the prevention, outreach, and treatment models that have emerged have been developed by those with personal experience with CD, either as "users" themselves or as family members. Historically relatively few, often "maverick" professionals have espoused the CD field as a career and a primary intellectual interest. Development of advocacy groups, federal initiatives, and third-party payments for CD treatment are quickly changing this situation, but often without appropriate changes in professional training programs.

The interventions that have evolved, despite all of the above, most often include important group components. In fact those who are attempting to chronicle the state of the art in CD treatment often state that group work is the preferred or most widely practiced mode of treatment (e.g. Zimberg, 1982; Fuhrmann and Washington, 1984). Similarly, much primary and secondary prevention planning includes group approaches. The relative lack of professional involvement, however, and the highly ideological nature of the models that have developed have produced few attempts to compare and contrast different approaches or to evaluate their outcomes systematically. Often practitioners do not use a common language, so that similarities in approaches go unrecognized.

The consistent incorporation of group practices in widely diverse settings by people who have been largely operating on nonintersecting tracks probably results from a number of factors:

1. Self-help groups are leading components of the alcoholism and addiction fields and have been the most consistently successful in helping members attain and sustain abstinence or sobriety. In these groups those who are recovering help each other with support, instillation of hope, educational and other structured activities, techniques for enhancing perception of "reality," and the creation of alternative social and activity networks. The benefits of self-help groups are being increasingly recognized in many life and social problem areas. They can provide experiences not easily created in other forms of intervention, although some techniques and components from them can be and have been incorporated into other types of intervention programs. A worker who is knowledgeable and nondefensive about their benefits can often work very effectively in conjunction with such groups. In fact, CD programs often sponsor on-site Alcoholics Anonymous, Narcotics Anonymous, or Women for Sobriety meetings and/or mandate attendance in such groups as part of the treatment contract.

2. Great difficulties are inherent in working individually with someone who is chemically dependent. It is possible and sometimes desirable, but very difficult. Persons who have lost control of their chemical use and are experiencing negative consequences from that use are often either quite so-

cially isolated or heavily involved with others who also drink or use drugs. They usually rely primarily on the defense mechanisms of denial, rationalization, and projection and thus may have little systematic and conscious awareness of the consequences of their behavior, which is often highly manipulative and avoidant. There is great ambivalence about being "helped," and the expression of anger often alternates with strong dependency needs. Many authors discuss the ambivalence, primitiveness, and strength of transference that a group can help to dilute (c.f. Zimberg, 1982; Kanas, 1982) as well as the difficulties in combating often antitherapeutic "street codes" within the treatment setting (c.f. Brill, 1981).

3. Alcohol and drug use are most often socially transmitted and supported, even when there are also substantial genetic/physical and psychological risk factors present. Peer and social pressures often lead to first use; family, peer, and community norms help to determine what chemicals are available and what use patterns are acceptable; drinking and use practices and misuse remedies often are "taught" to neophyte users by others around them; and patterns of continued use are either reinforced by one's social milieu or, at minimum, not effectively challenged. Chemical use is part of a homeostatic balance—within the individual, the family, the peer group, the community, and the larger culture. Both reducing the incidence of use and misuse and trying to change already existing destructive patterns will be greatly facilitated by employing techniques that reduce the resistance to change from other components of the ecological system. Group and milieu techniques are important staples in this type of work with all social problems.

WAYS THAT GROUPS
HAVE BEEN USED IN THE CD FIELD

Prevention

Increasingly those concerned about prevention of destructive use of chemicals are recognizing that such behaviors usually result from a complex interaction of a number of factors related to the chemical itself, the individual's physiology and set (expectations, cognitive characteristics), and the environment (peer group, family, community, economic circumstances, and so on). Prevention strategies can either target the reduction of individual or societal risk factors or work to create options for support and alternative behaviors within the individual or the environment (Blane, 1982; NIDA, 1981).

Initially most prevention activity targeted youth and relied heavily on scare tactics about the dire consequences of all use (usually of particular chemicals). We have moved to an understanding that people of all ages and types can incur negative consequences from the use of many types of substances and, in fact, from many compulsive behaviors (e.g. eating disorders, gambling, workaholism). More recent educational strategies stress the development of well-informed and moderated fitness-oriented behaviors (c.f. Nowlis and Jackson, 1977). Many of these activities occur in groups, partly because more people can be reached in a cost-effective way and partly because the programs' designers are also interested in influencing the group and cultural norms and values that help define and regulate "appropriate" behavior. These group activities occur in preschools and K-12 classrooms (e.g. Adix, Kelly, and Rosenthal, 1984), via community meetings, and in outreach activities to settings where people of different types congregate (e.g. churches, senior citizens groups, social clubs, prenatal classes).

Prevention planners are using group approaches to help develop interpersonal communication skills, practice alternative forms of coping, clarify values, and facilitate making well-informed decisions. All such skills and behaviors are thought to reduce vulnerability to peer pressure by embedding all choices in a well-defined set of values and enhancing skills that will help individuals make healthy life choices within their peer culture. Similarly parenting training and other forms of values and communication training with family members increase families' flexibility and adaptiveness so that they can successfully negotiate necessary transition periods, within the family as a whole and for its individual members. Family theorists have proposed that some types of CD result from a family's inability to make some transitions (e.g. separation of adolescent children, Stanton, 1977).

Group skills are also useful for prevention planning and organizing within a community. Every community is unique on some dimensions; assessment and planning for relevant and possible prevention work is likely to require a range of resources and perspectives, often best accomplished in planning committees and task forces (Rothman and Reed, 1984). In some communities barriers exist among groups that could work together more effectively (e.g. parents, teenagers, police, human service workers, educators, ethnic community leaders). Group work techniques have been used effectively to develop communication linkages and coalitions across these barriers.

Group training strategies (including information dissemination, attitude examination, and discussion of alternatives) of those who regulate the supply of chemicals can reduce easy access to them and overindulgence. For instance, those concerned about dependence on sedative-hypnotic drugs among women have developed training programs for physicians in which they examine their prescribing practices, learn about signs and symptoms of CD in women, and develop alternative ideas about how to work differently with these patients. Similarly, sessions for bartenders have focused on how their promotion practices (e.g. two-for-one specials during after-work happy hours) promote overindulgence, the consequences for them if a customer engages in dangerous driving while intoxicated, and ways they can promote more responsible behaviors among customers, including how and where to refer them for assistance.

Other types of prevention activities use group techniques to work with those known to be more vulnerable to destructive use of chemicals—e.g. children of alcoholics (as children and as adults); women in life crises or transitions (e.g. battering situations, divorce or widowhood); people in chronic pain or chronically depressed or anxious (may self-medicate or have drugs prescribed in dependency-producing patterns); and the unemployed. These groups can be considered primary prevention activities for many participants for whom support and education about alternatives will forestall less adaptive coping patterns. They will also identify some already in trouble with chemical use before they suffer more severe consequences and need more extensive intervention. Such sessions always should include some assessment of negative consequences, and group leaders should be prepared to make appropriate referrals or provide more intensive services for those who need or desire them.

Secondary Prevention: Early Identification, Crisis Intervention, and Techniques for "Motivating" Treatment

Many of the activities mentioned so far have early intervention consequences. As individuals learn more about CD, its signs, and its consequences (especially if even minimal assessment and screening procedures are available), many will recognize incipient problems in themselves or others they know.

As our understanding of CD, its causes, and its consequences has evolved, there has been increasing attention to techniques designed to identify CD and intervene earlier in its progression to halt further individual and family deterioration and to reduce social costs. Many of them involve group activities and interventions of various kinds.

Previously practitioners felt that the decision to seek treatment was the individual's responsibility. Family and others aware of the problem could only wait until the individual "bottomed out," that is, suffered severe enough emotional, physical, or social life consequences to overcome the positive attractions of the chemical use and the resistance to the often massive life changes that would be necessary to sustain abstinence or sobriety. Increasingly we are understanding that CD interferes with individuals' ability to recognize the consequences of their behavior and that most seek treatment in response to external pressures. While the desire to gain control and stop hurting oneself and others is almost always present, the individual's attempts to do this alone often increase the denial and associated life difficulties (Bean, 1981). Family members, friends, and others who encounter the individual—e.g. the employer, health service, family service, and criminal justice workers—often do not know what to do, or for various reasons either try to ignore the CD or "help" the person they care about by protecting him or her from the consequences of the chemical use (e.g. overlooking poor job performance, making excuses, giving one more chance). These "enabling" behaviors, often well-intended, actually prolong the CD and thus make eventual negative consequences more likely and more severe (Johnson, 1973).

Secondary prevention interventions that involve group work include training programs for those in a position to encounter and recognize CD before a person finds his or her own way into a treatment program. Several types were described in the previous section. They generally include information and practice about how to recognize CD, why a person seldom voluntarily seeks treatment, and how to help him or her do so. This last often includes role-playing, strategy development, and problem-solving within the group. An emphasis is on how to use the "clout" that individuals and institutions have to "raise the bottom" (make likely negative consequences clear before they are inevitable or before all resources already are lost). Child protection workers, law enforcement and criminal justice staff, valued family members, and employers often control resources that can be powerful motivating tools to stop the slide into more and more destructive behaviors (e.g. the threat of job loss, imprisonment, or child custody problems).

The burgeoning employee assistance movement usually involves a heavy emphasis on CD detection and programming. It often relies heavily on group approaches not only in training for detection but also in joint union, management, and worker planning and coordinating teams. Many of these teams also have developed and implemented strategies to change workers' attitudes about chemical use and to enhance workplace conditions to create more workplace investment and less tendency to "drop out chemically."

Attention to special underserved populations also has led to group-oriented programming with people and in locations that had been of less concern when white men or inner-city men were the field's primary concern. As chemical use patterns have changed and new knowledge has developed about use patterns in women, youth, the aged, and various racial, cultural, and ethnic groups, we have begun to recognize that these groups often define problems differently, seek help from different sources, and even may encounter different consequences of CD (c.f. Reed, in press). Outreach attempts may target "indigenous helpers" in minority communities or work more closely with childcare, mental health, health, and family-oriented service networks where women often seek help for themselves or their families.

An explicit group strategy is the family constructive, coercive confrontation (Johnson, 1973; Liepman, Wolper, and Vazques, 1982). A group worker (often a recovering person or in conjunction with a recovering person) works with a family member or employer to identify key individuals who have knowledge and concern about a person's use of chemicals. These persons are asked to participate in team planning and then to present information about their perceptions of negative consequences deriving from the CD, with evidence, to the individual in question. Group cohesiveness and the development of an understanding of how group members together can effect change are important components of the process. Eventually the individual is told of their caring and their concerns, without blame or anger, and presented with what the group perceives to be viable treatment alternatives. The group process often changes the enabling networks surrounding the CD person sufficiently so that the ultimate meeting with the person of concern isn't necessary: The person decides that he or she needs help before the group has finished its preparations.

Group techniques also continue to be very important training and support mechanisms for the paid workers and volunteers who staff the crisis lines that are often an individual's first contact with a helping system. Group work concepts and skills also provide the framework for many peer outreach and counseling programs—in schools (elementary, secondary, and college level) and in various social organizations and communities.

Treatment and Rehabilitation

I have already alluded to the various self-help groups for CD and other compulsive behaviors. They all rely on group support and verbal interactions in a group setting to help change individual feelings and behavior. AA's twelve steps and structure have become models for many other self-help groups (see Kurtz, 1979, for a description of its origins). Any person who wishes to work effectively with CD should be knowledgeable about AA and other groups available in their area via attendance at open meetings, knowledge about the different types of meetings available locally (e.g. women's meetings, young people's, professional, gay), and contacts with self-help group members who can act as sponsors and supports for new members.

For those concerned about heroin, group therapy was first undertaken in institutional settings such as the Public Health Service hospitals at Lexington, Kentucky, and Fort Worth, Texas, and at Riverside Hospital in New York City, operated by the probation and parole systems. In ex-addict-directed therapeutic communities self-help techniques were combined with encounter group techniques designed to break through resistant defensive structures, ventilate hostility toward authority figures and others, and learn alternative means of problem-solving (Brill, 1981).

More recently a wide variety of group approaches have been adapted within CD treatment programs, including transactional analysis, gestalt, insight-oriented process groups, psychodrama, activity groups, and multiple family therapy groups. Groups for "special populations" or groups that focus on particular issues or topics (e.g. incest) are frequently used to provide support, education, a specialized focus, and skill building for those who are often minorities within a treatment program (both numerically and often in terms of societal status as well) or who have special needs or different cultural styles (c.f. Wedenoja and Reed, 1982; Harper, 1984; Wren, 1984; Stoltz, 1984; Doyle, 1982). In some programs participants are involved in more than one type of group: Issues particular to one's gender can be explored in all-women's and all-men's groups, for instance, while both women and men participate in other groups consistent with their progress through the stages of the treatment program.

Research that either compares various types of group strategies or examines the effectiveness of group rather than individual approaches is very sparse, and studies available so far have used such different measures and designs that results are not easy to compare (Anderson, 1982; Kanas, 1982; Solomon, 1982). In reading accounts of different types of groups in a variety of settings with quite different populations, however, one is struck by the many commonalities described. There appears to be substantial agreement among practitioners about the attributes of groups that work best with CD populations.

Most practice accounts state that it is preferable to work with CD persons in "homogeneous" groups (where everyone is CD), although there is increasing willingness to work with multiple types of CD in one group. The group leader's role often is described as more "transparent" than in many types of groups (e.g. Kanas, 1982) and as more directive, with explicit concern for modeling appropriate interpersonal skills and self-disclosure. Most group work in CD settings has substantial educational components, imparting information about CD, communication skills, family dynamics, and numerous other topics. Methods described are heavily present-oriented, including a focus on control of chemical use and making progress in a wide range of other life areas. Many groups encourage active involvement with many other types of resources within the community as well.

Many programs run open-ended groups for whomever is available to come. Others discuss selection criteria and stress the importance of screening out those less likely to benefit from group activities or who would be disruptive for the rest of the group. Some try to arrange their admission policies so they can work with a stable cohort of clients and family members for a period of time. Still others are developing different types of groups for different types of users—e.g. Flanzer's typology: (1) those socialized into a drug subculture, (2) those inadequately socialized, (3) those who are unsocialized into conventional values, and (4) those at a presocialization stage who need intense and basic socialization experiences. Flanzer has designed different group approaches for each of these types (Brill, 1981).

Some programs work with recovering persons at all stages of recovery together, using their different issues and perspectives as measures of progress and benchmarks for each other. Others have developed different types of groups for persons in different stages of recovery. Pittman and Gerstein (1984), for instance, describe three types: stabilization groups during the withdrawal period and some time thereafter (physiological, self-assessment, and educational focus), sustenance groups that rely more on member autonomy and work toward change in a number of life areas, and growth groups in which they work more with internal group process, interpersonal knowledge, and quality of life issues.

Whatever their form, there is substantial agreement about the uses groups have—among others, to help the CD person feel less alone and unique and to provide an opportunity to practice new and more effective social skills. Group approaches are felt to be especially useful in facilitating recognition and circumvention of rigid and unhelpful defenses since members will often recognize them in others before perceiving their own. Dependence on a therapist is diffused, and both support and presentation of "reality" are included. Group members are often urged to support each other outside of the group.

In addition to these group approaches with the CD person, programs are increasingly conducting multifamily groups for available family members (Kaufman and Kaufman, 1979; Wolper and Scheiner, 1981; Conner, 1984). In fact, many programs require some type of family involvement. These groups provide opportunities for families to receive support for change and to learn about CD, its impact on them, and how they may have enabled its continuation. They come to recognize the many similarities among CD families and also how theirs is unique. They help each other develop and practice alternative behaviors. These groups combine a knowledge of family dynamics with the development of supportive group norms and stages to facilitate change within families and help families understand and support the changes occurring within the CD member. Several therapists are likely to work with a multifamily group, often in different types of subgroups (e.g. spouses, sibs, parents).

FUTURE DIRECTIONS AND NEEDS

The CD field has been very likely to employ group approaches and will continue to provide many opportunities for group workers to do useful and innovative work, if they are sufficiently knowledgeable about chemical dependency and its ramifications. This knowledge should be incorporated into group work training programs much more than it usually is, since group workers will encounter alcohol and drug problems wherever they work. Similarly, those who work in alcohol and drug programs would benefit from training and supervision in a broad range of group techniques and theories.

If we are to understand more fully what types of techniques work with what problems in which individuals under what circumstances, however, we must also develop and implement well-designed research programs. At a minimum, careful description of current practices and their variations would be very useful.

Evaluation goals and techniques should include both the process and the organization of the group as well as a variety of outcome measures. Attention to progress toward abstinence or sobriety and a reduction of antisocial behaviors are necessary outcome measures but not sufficient if all the ways groups can be effective are to be assessed. Interpersonal functioning, social network and self-esteem changes, and new skill acquisition are all areas that could be included. Investigation of process measures would yield useful information about the impact of different leadership styles and group composition, for instance, and about different needs in different developmental stages of the group. There are great opportunities to develop new knowledge.

REFERENCES

ADIX, RUTH SMASAL; TERRY KELLY; AND DAVID ROSENTHAL
  1984   "Substance abuse prevention: A developmental skills approach," *Journal for Specialists in Group Work*, 9, no. 1: 32–37.
ANDERSON, SANDRA C.
  1982   "Group therapy with alcoholic clients: A review," *Advances in Alcohol and Substance Abuse*, 2, no. 2: 23–40.
BEAN, MARGARET H.
  1981   "Denial of the psychological complications of alcoholism." In Margaret H. Bean and Norman Zimberg (eds.), *Dynamic Approaches to the Understanding and Treatment of Alcoholism*. New York: Free Press, pp. 55–96.
BLANE, HOWARD T.
  1982   "Preventing alcohol problems." In Nada J. Estes and M. Edith Heinemann (eds.), *Alcoholism*. St. Louis: C. V. Mosby, pp. 77–89.
BRILL, LEON
  1981   "Group therapy." In Leon Brill, *The Clinical Treatment of Substance Abusers*. New York: Free Press, pp. 118–32.
BURGLASS, MILTON EARL, AND HOWARD SHAFFER
  1983–84   "Diagnosis in the addictions," *Advances in Alcohol and Substance Abuse*, 3, nos. 1–2: 19–34.

CONNER, DONNIE G.
  1984 "Multifamily educational groups in juvenile court settings with drug/alcohol offenders," *Journal of Specialists in Group Work*, 9, no. 1: 21-25.
DOYLE, KATHLEEN M.
  1982 "Assertiveness training for drug dependent women." In Beth Glover Reed, George M. Beschner, and Josette Mondanaro (eds.), *Treatment Services for Drug Dependent Women*. Vol. 2. DHHS Pub. No. (ADM) 82-1219. Rockville, Md.: National Institute on Drug Abuse, pp. 213-46.
FUHRMANN, BARBARA S., AND CRAIG S. WASHINGTON
  1984 "Substance abuse: An overview/tentative conclusions," *The Journal for Specialists in Group Work*, 9, no. 1: 2-6, 62-63.
HARPER, FREDERICK D.
  1984 "Group strategies with black alcoholics," *Journal for Specialists in Group Work*, 9, no. 1: 38-43.
JOHNSON, VERNON
  1973 *I'll Quit Tomorrow*. New York: Harper & Row.
KANAS, NICK
  1982 "Alcoholism and group psychotherapy." In E. Mansell Pattison and Edward Kaufman (eds.), *Encyclopedia Handbook of Alcoholism*. New York: Gardner Press, pp. 1011-21.
KAUFMAN, EDWARD, AND PAULINE KAUFMAN
  1979 "Multiple family therapy with drug abusers." In Edward Kaufman and Pauline Kaufman (eds.), *Family Therapy of Drug and Alcohol Abuse*. New York: Gardner Press, pp. 81-103.
KURTZ, ERNEST
  1979 *Not God: A History of Alcoholics Anonymous*. Center City, Minn.: Hazelden Educational Materials.
LIEPMAN, MICHAEL R., BENNET WOLPER; AND JAIME VAZQUES
  1982 "An ecological approach for motivating women to accept treatment for drug dependency." In Beth Glover Reed, George M. Beschner, and Josette Mondanaro (eds.), *Treatment Services for Drug Dependent Women*. Vol. 2. DHHS Pub. No. 82-1219. Rockville, Md.: NIDA, pp. 1-61.
NIDA (NATIONAL INSTITUTE ON DRUG ABUSE)
  1981 *Handbook for Prevention Evaluation*. Rockville, Md.: U.S. Department of Health and Human Services.
NOWLIS, HELEN, AND LURIA JACKSON
  1977 "Role of education and prevention." In S. N. Pradhan and S. N. Dutta (eds.), *Drug Abuse: Clinical and Basic Aspects*. St. Louis: C. V. Mosby, pp. 535-43.
PITTMAN, JOE F., AND LAWRENCE H. GERSTEIN
  1984 "Graduated levels of group therapy for substance abusers," *Journal for Specialists in Group Work*, 9, no. 1: 7-13.
REED, BETH GLOVER
  In press "Drug misuse and dependency in women: The meaning and implication of being considered a special population or minority group," *International Journal of the Addictions*.
ROTHMAN, JACK, AND BETH GLOVER REED
  1984 "Organizing community action to address alcohol and drug problems." In

Fred M. Cox, John L. Erlich, Jack Rothman, and John E. Tropman (eds.), *Tactics and Techniques of Community Practice*. Second edition. Itasca, Ill.: R. E. Peacock, pp. 115–29.

SOLOMON, SUSAN D.
1982 "Individual versus group therapy: Current status in the treatment of alcoholism," *Advances in Alcohol and Substance Abuse*, 2, no. 1: 69–86.

STANTON, M. DUNCAN
1977 "The addict as savior: Heroin, death and the family," *Family Process*, 16: 191–97.

STOLTZ, SANDRA GORDON
1984 "Recovering from foodaholism," *Journal for Specialists in Group Work*, 9, no. 1: 51–61.

WEDENOJA, MARILYN, AND BETH GLOVER REED
1982 "Women's groups as a form of intervention for drug dependent women." In Beth Glover Reed, George M. Beschner, and Josette Mondanaro (eds.), *Treatment Services for Drug Dependent Women*. Vol. 2. DDHS Pub. No. (ADM) 81–1177, Rockville, Md.: NIDA, pp. 62–136.

WOLPER, BENNETT, AND ZONA SCHEINER
1981 "Family therapy approaches and drug dependent women." In Beth Glover Reed, George M. Beschner, and Josette Mondanaro (eds.), *Treatment Services for Drug Dependent Women*. Vol. 1. DHHS Pub. No. (ADM) 81–1177. Rockville, Md.: NIDA, pp. 390–94.

WREN, DEBORAH F.
1984 "Group work with female alcoholics," *Journal for Specialists in Group Work*, 9, no. 1: 44–50.

ZIMBERG, SHELDON
1982 "Group therapy and psychodrama." In *The Clinical Management of Alcoholism*. New York: Brunner/Mazel, pp. 81–87.

31

Writing Groups with the Elderly

Ruth Campbell

FOR SIX YEARS Ellen* has been going to her "writing party" every Monday afternoon at an outpatient geriatric clinic of the University of Michigan Hospital in Ann Arbor. One Monday she'll read a story about threshing on the farm in southern Missouri when she was a child. Another day she'll read a letter she's just written to a relative back home recounting the memory of a Catholic man who long ago was shunned by the pious Baptists in that small country town. She is occasionally absent when she has one of her dizzy spells, which make her feel like a "drunk old lady." When she misses a meeting her friends call, encouraging her to try to come next Monday. Jane, one of the younger members of the group, picks her up each week along with Barbara. Barbara has been legally blind for the last few years but keeps selling articles to magazines and recently won a prize for best travel writing from the Mid-West Writers Association.

About sixty men and women have participated in two writing groups, which have been meeting weekly since 1978 at Turner Clinic. They gather to read to each other the memoirs, fiction, poetry, and essays they have written at home during the previous week. Each group has a membership of from fifteen to twenty members, ranging in age from mid-sixties to ninety, with the average being somewhere in the late seventies. There has been a remarkable amount of stability in group membership: More than half of the original members still attend regularly, with the new members added only as space opens up. The group leaders have been clinical social workers, graduate students, and volunteers. One group has had continuity in leadership; the other has had nine leaders in its six-year history. However, the groups have developed so that leadership is actually shared among the members with the group leader or facilitator.

The popularity of groups of this sort has spread widely in recent years. When Marc Kaminsky began doing poetry groups in senior centers in New York, he felt at first as if he were working in the dark; what he was doing could not be characterized as poetry therapy or poetry workshops. "They

*The names of all participants have been changed to conceal their identifies.

were quite definitely poetry groups. They were the place where we found the person in the poem and the poem in the person" (Kaminsky, 1978b, p. 210). Since then others have written of their experiences in conducting poetry and writing groups at nursing homes, senior centers, union halls, churches, and universities (Koch, 1977; Campbell, 1981, 1984; Kaminsky, 1984). The success of this type of group for the elderly may lie in its underlying assumption that despite the decline and loss present in aging, there are also positive changes, opportunities for creativity, growth, and wisdom. Dale Worsley (1984, p. 36) discovered as he listened to retired seamen ". . . the meaning, the peculiar and valuable meaning of life as a seaman, once communicated, became a huge affirmation."

The particular model of a writing group discussed here is intended to provide a starting point for others to adapt to their own settings, styles of leadership, and purpose. I believe writing itself is important, because a real product is produced that can be handed down as a legacy to children and friends, and because the writing becomes a process of discovery and self-exploration. It is also important, however, to consider the life history and reminiscence models of Meyerhoff (1978) and Ingersoll and Goodman (1980), among others.

The theoretical foundation for all of these groups comes from an interest in reminiscence and aging stimulated by Robert Butler's work (1963) on the "life review" process. The perspective gained through a review of the past events of one's life may be a way of achieving what Erikson and Erikson (1978) see as the task of old age—making sense of what has passed and coming to a kind of acceptance of it.

Meyerhoff and Tufte (1975, p. 543) also see reminiscing as a way of integrating one's life experiences: It "offers to the elderly the chance to be attended to, to be seen and recorded as having existed, and through this means, to integrate their historical experiences and thus construct and manifest a valuable identity, a personal mythology." Although researchers disagree on whether reminiscing is a normative and universal process in the elderly, writers such as Weinberg (1974) and McMahon and Rhodick (1964) urge relatives to encourage reminiscing behavior as a valuable contribution to family history and not to regard it as a sign of deterioration.

STRUCTURE AND FORMAT

Both groups meet weekly all year long, with an occasional week or two off. The continuity has been important, since it allows members to be absent when ill or on vacation, yet return to the group and be welcomed. Group size at any particular session varies, but twelve seems to be the most comfortable number, allowing each member sufficient time to read and talk. The format does not change; we begin with the first volunteer to read and proceed around the table. If someone has not written that week, he or she may say there wasn't enough time or there is a work in progress but as yet unready. Frequently those who have not written will have a good story to tell, usually stimulated by something one of the group members has said, or will bring a photograph or letter to share.

In the beginning we established the pattern of having each person read for five to ten minutes, followed by group discussion. Criticism tends to be mild: Some request it, others don't like it. In any case the group discussion is considered by most of the members to be as important as the writing. It is in the discussion that moral points are debated, scraps of history traded, and forgotten stories remembered. One person's story about her father can suddenly bring back another person's long-forgotten recollection from her own childhood.

At the first session the group requested weekly assignments. It soon became clear that people wanted assignments in order to have something to write about if they got stuck and to have an opportunity to demonstrate independence from me, the leader. There have been periods without assignments, but the members invariably ask for them. Sometimes the assignment is suggested by a member of the group. For example, after one woman wrote about a holdup at her office, others began telling stories about their experiences with thieves and burglars. That then became the assignment for the following week.

As the group developed, most people discovered what they wanted to do and undertook their own projects. An assignment often provided an escape from a long-term project or tickled someone's fancy leading to a new area of exploration.

The first assignments were chronological in order. Among the topics were: (1) When my parents were young, (2) Bring a photo of yourself as a child and write about it, (3) Describe your early teens, (4) Describe a "one-word feeling" without using that word—either real or fictional, (5) Marriage, (6) Something I never told anyone, (7) My favorite meal, (8) An awakening.

A time frame located strictly in the past is not possible. We jump from past to present. The first fifteen minutes of each session are devoted to catching up on the news, who is absent and why, what happened to members during the previous week. Groups such as these must respond to the fluidity of life, for although these people have lived full lives, their lives are not static and the process of writing is an evolving one, which takes place very much in the present. As Leon Edel (1969, p. 16) writes, there is evidence that "creation . . . is a work of health and not illness, a force for life and life-enhancement."

Sharing each other's writing leads to sharing tangible proof that what is being written is indeed true. When Ellen wrote a story about shooting a mad dog as a young girl on her family's farm, she also brought along a coke bottle cap with a perfect hole in the middle, ultimate proof of her accuracy. Bill brought in an old book written in French about his home town in Austria. Less dramatic items such as photographs, souvenirs, and postcards from trips, gifts and wild flowers are often shared, as each object takes on renewed meaning.

GROUP COMPOSITION

Unsurprisingly for a group in a university town, there is a larger percentage of group members with advanced degrees than one would expect in this age group. There are also several members who had to leave school early for economic reasons and who lack much formal education; however, their keen awareness and disappointment over not being able to continue in school led to a deliberate lifelong self-education. Therefore, the barriers between them and those with advanced degrees are insignificant. One woman who customarily prefaces her work with an apology for her lack of "book learning" is regularly shouted down by the group. This heterogeneity of background (note also that members represent almost every area of the country) contributes to the breadth and variety of the writing; it is a characteristic the group members find highly agreeable. The need for a more homogeneous group would arise when literacy is a problem or when language is a barrier between members (Bloom, 1984). Otherwise, different cultural backgrounds can be an advantage, presenting opportunities for members to teach and learn from each other and to discover the surprising universality of their diverse experiences.

GROUP PROCESS

When members called to register for the first session of the writing group, they were asked to bring in something they had written or to think about what they would like to write about while in the group. Most of them were able to do this, and it set a norm for group participation and created an atmosphere of anticipation. It was hard for some members just to read in front of strangers, but the risk taken in doing so made each person feel brave, and the praise lavished on each reader rewarded the effort. The assignment for the second session was "When my parents were young," which allowed members to talk about their parents rather than themselves and provided us with a variety of settings, from Nebraska to New York, Northern Michigan to Southern Indiana, even a glimpse of rural Germany. It seemed as if immediately members were willing to share personal stories, and from this willingness a feeling of trust and friendship quickly grew.

An observer of the Friday group writes:

> To observe the group beginning a session, an . . . important reason for attendance emerges: most have become good friends. In this room is a mood of warmth and familiarity—we might easily be sitting on a front porch exchanging news of family, friends and events. Someone asks after a member who has been absent due to illness. There is an update of her progress, and several plan to visit.

> "I like writing that has a touch of whimsy," comments Martha as her description of a bird watching class in high school in the 1920's rolls off her tape recorder. Her years in rural western Virginia have clearly shaped her love for birds, as she recalls each species encountered and their various foibles and tastes in food. The group murmurs with appreciation and another woman tells about the wildlife in her backyard pond. It would seem that, just as their experiences have enhanced their writing, so writing has expanded their powers of observation.

> We hear a story about early school years. A photo is passed around, and nearly all can distinguish the right face in the crowd of schoolchildren. A man, new to the group, reads several love poems written to his recently deceased wife. He now has over 100 poems, some of which he recites from memory. The exact dates are also recalled, as if each poem, and day, mark a profound stage of insight into his loss. The reading is received with quiet reverance, marking his formal acceptance into the circle. [Wunsch, 1984, p. C4]

A recent session of the Monday group begins when members who have been on trips are welcomed back. Elizabeth says she has to tell the group what happened when she returned to the small town in the Upper Peninsula of Michigan where she spent all her married life. She met a former student on the street who is now a teacher herself. "You were my inspiration, you are why I became a teacher," the woman told her. A few days later, in the course of conversation with another young friend, he told her, "You are our treasure."

"That's what people are like up there," she said. "It made me feel so good. I had to tell you."

Alice says she knows how Martha felt. Alice has just returned from her native New York City, where three times a day she met with different friends to celebrate her ninetieth birthday. Her eyes filled with tears as they brought out yet another birthday cake. "Don't cry into the cake," her friend told her. To be able to relive moments of triumph among an appreciative group of friends is a significant aspect of this group; the reason why members can refer to the group as a "family."

Muriel, who has joined the group in the past two months, starts the reading with a story about blue beads she received as a gift when she was five. "I loved them," she writes, but she soon lost them, only to discover her best friend wearing them. "Finder's keepers, loser's weepers," her best friend said. "Since that was the law where we lived," Muriel says, "I let it go, but I never forgot." She remained friends with this woman until she died. Her friend didn't remember the story when Muriel reminded her of it. But Muriel does. "I don't think I ever forgave her."

Everyone likes the story. We discuss making it part of a play we are thinking of writing. Jane says she has a pair of blue beads that sound just like the ones Muriel described, and she'll bring them in for Muriel to see. Muriel has cautiously inched her way into the group. At her first few sessions she sat with her chair pulled somewhat away from the circle. A few weeks earlier she told the group it wasn't what she had expected. "I thought there'd be more teaching of writing, more criticism," she said. Unknowingly she had touched on one of the sensitive issues of the group. The need for more criticism arises from time to time but it is always resolved with the general opinion that "we like it just as it is." Some group members have taken short-term writing courses to satisfy a wish for more instruction, but the group norm was expressed by several members in response to Muriel's remark: "We learn dialogue by listening to what Ellen writes; we hear Bob's piece and learn how to create a certain kind of mood; the teachers here know more grammar than anyone can teach us. We don't want instruction, we all teach each other."

The following week Angel expanded on this theme in a piece she wrote, and Muriel once more explained what she meant: "It's just that I'm a newcomer. You all know how to write. I don't."

I suggested that we revive a procedure we had used before—those who wanted a critique could ask for it and I or another group member could take it home over the weekend and make comments. This suggestion hung in the air. Others said Muriel's writing was fine.

When Muriel read her "blue bead" piece in this session, the group's enthusiastic response was a form of acceptance. They gave suggestions about how to adapt it in a play; they sympathized with her feelings; they responded generously and warmly to the effect she wanted to create. Her chair at this session was firmly within the circle. Although nothing was mentioned about criticism, the unspoken feeling was, "We take you seriously. You can write. You're one of us." To emphasize this, one of the group members said she'd drive Muriel to Martha's farewell party. When Muriel said it was too much of a bother, the entire group demurred, and she accepted the offer. To some degree this ritual of acceptance takes place with each new member, and the group leader must provide support for the new member as the process evolves.

The assignment that session was to describe a scene from the kitchen of your childhood. The topic appealed to many members. We heard about Lori's father washing dishes as her mother read to him from a novel. Martha recalled the day her baby brother arrived home from the hospital. She watched as he received his first at-home bath on the kitchen table and learned for the first time why boys are different from girls. After Jane sang "I'm Forever Blowing Bubbles" just as her uncle had as she sat on his lap waiting for supper, Alice remembered something that had happened in a kitchen in Germany, where she went as a young girl to visit relatives. She and her brother were told that if they ate their lima beans ("the biggest we'd ever seen"), they could have ice cream for dessert. They did, and the ice cream arrived, but dry ice had gotten into it and it was inedible. "To this day," she said, "I don't eat lima beans."

Elizabeth was so delighted at the many memories evoked by kitchens that she suggested the group's next book be called "It Happened in the Kitchen." There was some disagreement over this limitation, and the decision was postponed. Another writer that day read about the use of profanity in her childhood, which was "nothing like I hear now." Someone said, "My grandchildren are always saying, 'sorry Grandma.'" The session ended with Diane's reading of a story about a Mrs. Fall, who was sitting alone at a restaurant table when a young woman joined her, looked at her, and said, "Can I go home with you?" The story disguised as fiction was, Diane said after she read it, a true story. *She* was Mrs. Fall and the incident, a frightening one, had occurred that week. She asked for advice, and the session ended with her friends exploring the young woman's motives and reassuring Diane that by giving the woman agencies to call she had done what she could to help.

TERMINATION

The sadness inherent in ending a group is often a product of staffing demands rather than the needs of the group members. Our experience with the writing groups indicates that a one-year commitment from a leader is necessary in order to build trust, but the group itself can continue with many changes in leadership. The few times in which we have tried to keep the group going with only leaders from within the group were not successful. People dropped out, and there were misunderstandings, demonstrating that the facilitating role is important and that the group wants a younger person to be a part of it. The facilitator points out commonalities, emphasizes strengths in an individual where they are not immediately apparent, and helps the group over low points such as the illness or death of a member. However, the group itself is a strong unit and should be allowed to continue indefinitely with new leadership adding the perspective of another generation.

THERAPEUTIC BENEFITS

At the first meeting I passed out a sheet of paper stating the purposes of the group: (1) to encourage creativity; (2) to get a better understanding of one's own life; (3) to preserve and pass on memories; (4) to share one's own experience with others; and (5) to interpret what has happened and reflect on its meaning as time passes. Six years later I see that I only dimly understood the therapeutic benefits of such a group, benefits for the leaders as well as the group members. In the following discussion I shall list specific therapeutic outcomes, but I think it is important to recognize the fact that the group is not generally regarded as therapy by its members. They are writers who have come to share their writings with each other. They have become extended family; indeed, many of us know more about each other than our relatives know about us. A writing group may be classified in the group work literature as an "activity" group, but its advantage, particularly for people with many years of life experience, lies in its wide scope. It incorporates education, mutual support, history, and creativity. It contributes to the continuing growth of an individual and, most important, produces a product that others can receive and appreciate.

Harry R. Moody describes this position precisely:

> The moment we separate these two—poetry and truth—we start down a road that leads to the separation between "education" and "therapy." This false separation ends by condemning our deepest wish for meaning to a merely private sense of "life satisfaction," as the gerontologists would phrase it. . . . Can I ask, implore, petition and beg all social workers, therapists, historians and educators to remember this duality, to remember that "education" and "therapy" are never separated? Keep the duality in mind considering each of the methods of practice with older people. Poetry therapy, historical education, drama workshops, group work services all have their uses, but none can grasp the living reality of old age without this act of self-called life review. [Moody, 1984, p. 1965]

Outcome for Group Members

1. *Leaving a legacy.* Angel, at eighty-four, wanted to "write down information about my family and my husband's family for the benefit of our children and their children. I myself have often wished, during my later years, that I knew more about my elders. My own children seem to me strangely uncurious about their origins. When one is young, one is so busy

living actively that it doesn't often occur to ask while some of the elders are alive. I wanted them to ask, which they seldom did, but the time will come when they will want to know.'' Each Christmas she presents her children photocopies of her writings illustrated with old family photographs. The gifts are now eagerly anticipated and appreciated. The rewards of her activity have been more immediate than she expected.

Others have begun to explore their family history, filling in gaps of knowledge through research, visiting home towns, and talking to other family members. Laura is reconstructing her family's experiences from life in a weaver's village in Scotland and their journey to Canada as part of a utopian community, through their eventual settlement in Michigan. The role of the older person as historian, a traditional and revered role in many societies, is thus revived in a contemporary world in which technological innovation is often thought to have weakened the value of the knowledge of the elderly.

2. *Recording and validating a life.* Larry, a retired geologist, kept detailed diaries during a fascinating career, which included searching for oil in the wild lands of Mexico. But his children found his stories dull and overdetailed. With help from the group, the stories he distilled from the diaries are now exciting accounts. In one, money is dropped from an open-cockpit biplane into a Mexican jungle, the author's first and most frightening ride in an airplane. He writes of a colleague's exploits forty years ago as well as a horse thievery in 1981. He writes a fantasy, which the group applauds, on ''If I were a rich man.'' The group sees his childhood, his midlife, and his present life as an ongoing experience. They share his adventures with him.

John joined the group because his wife dragged him. A self-educated man who completed his high school diploma in his fifties, he felt he couldn't write. But he began recording his love of music, his feelings for an old chair he repaired, and especially his feelings for his wife. In the middle of reading an account on how he met his wife, she left the room in embarrassment, much to the amusement of the group. When John died in 1981, his wife, after a short absence, returned to the group buoyed by the fact that their marriage had been recognized and celebrated in the group and that the extent of her loss was understood by group members.

3. *Self-exploration.* Although only a minority of group members would accept the label ''therapy,'' it is clearly part of the group process. One man, for example, wrote about a woman he had loved when he was twenty—a woman who had rejected him for reasons he still did not understand. When he cried, so did many of the group members. As the group went over the circumstances, trying to find a clue to her behavior and suggesting alternate approaches he could have taken, the whole moment became immediate: He was twenty again, and we were back there with him. We knew this man had been happily married for many years (shortly after this incident, in fact, his wife became a permanent member of the group),

but our reliving the past with him offered comfort and reassurance, and revealed our mutual puzzlement.

Annette says explicitly that she "writes because I am a stranger to myself. What is it that makes me function? What are my good points, what are my hang-ups? I have a double dose, German and American. . . . Born of man and woman, I am aware of myself as a link to eternity, and that is what writing does for me. It is a key; it is a key that unlocks the door to truth and muted ecstasy."

4. *Achieving a goal/dream.* Some join the group because they have longed for years to write a book. Age acts as a kind of deadline. At seventy, how long can one keep putting off a dream? Publication in local papers, senior newsletters, and commercial magazines, as well as presentations to community groups and college classes, have given members a strong sense of achievement. When a book of writings from both groups was published in 1984, the writers felt the excitement of a completed project.

5. *Compensation for handicaps, both physical and emotional.* Three members of the group are legally blind. One uses a tape recorder, another works with a volunteer reader, and the third is a former secretary and types as she thinks (if the phone rings and interrupts her, she must begin all over again). Martha joined both groups two years ago, shortly after losing her sight. A former journalist (the Washington correspondent for a newspaper chain), she came to Michigan from a Southern city in rage and helplessness over the loss of her sight. Her husband was dead. She had grown up in Ann Arbor, and her only relatives, a brother and his family, lived here. Fiercely independent and very angry when she first joined the group, she refused all attempts by me or group members to help her with her tape recorder. When it didn't work and I jumped up to see what was wrong, she commanded me to go back to my seat, pulled the plug, and said she would fix it by the next session (she did).

Although she had made good friends in the group, after two harsh Michigan winters Martha decided to return to the Southern city she loved. With renewed confidence, she felt she could manage on her own with the support of her friends there. At a farewell party she said, "I am so indebted to you all. When I came here two years ago I was very depressed about my blindness. I thought I couldn't write any more; my typewriter was useless. You were all so patient with me when I struggled to learn to use this blasted machine. Because of the writing groups, I'm not depressed any more. I am so grateful to you." By the time she said her farewell we all felt we had learned an important lesson about managing with loss. She and the other blind members have permanently altered our attitudes toward those with visual handicaps.

Hearing problems are more difficult to handle in a group. Several members designate themselves as monitors and interrupt a reader with admonitions to "speak up, we can't hear you." One man with very severe hearing loss joined the group only occasionally to read what he had written. His writing, however, was published in local newspapers, which brought him letters from strangers and old friends, leading to a new outlet of communication.

Several people recovering from depression have been brought into the group, and after some hesitation, have been well accepted. The weekly structure of reading what one has written relieves the pressure of self-revelation; one can control the degree and amount of intimacy. One man began with very factual accounts of history and, with the encouragement of the group, eventually wrote funny personal tales of his adventures with sports. He became known in the group as an expert on games, and all questions on that subject were referred to him.

6. *Friendship/intimacy/acceptance.* "We are a very caring group," Sheila says, and this image is an important one for group members. One member says, "The group membership turned out to be so miscellaneous, such honest, genuine people and so sincere, that I never want to give it up. We are very different but perfectly integrated and I love every one of the others." For the elderly who must cope with multiple changes in health and housing, the loss of spouse and friends, a stable group whose members know a great deal about you is very important. Members who get sick receive cards and phone calls and return to the group when they are well. Birthdays are celebrated; vacations and trips are shared with group members.

ROLE OF THE GROUP LEADERS

As Ingersoll and Goodman (1980, p. 317) point out, in this kind of group the leader can act as a student as well as a helper. "This switch from the traditional expert/client role of most therapeutic modalities can be satisfying for both leaders and participants." Kaminsky (1978a, p. 31) also emphasizes how the use of reminiscence can revitalize the worker. "The illusory sameness which the common problems of old people present to us is transcended; and we perceive, and experience, what makes each particular client different and unique."

From the beginning the leaders made it clear that "we were also there to learn" (Kraus, 1984, p. 165). And learn we did. Bring in any flower or weed to these groups, and someone can identify it. Learn how all teachers had to retire once they were married and how to raise a baby animal who's lost its mother. The learning is not all confined to the past. The group writes letters to protest the way primary elections are being conducted and discusses the recent suicide of a high school student. For the younger leader it is an education; for the older group members it becomes an opportunity for two-way communication in which their experience has value.

The role of the leader is also important to help ease the transition of new members into the group. Entering such a tightly knit group is not easy. The new member, with the support of the leader, gradually becomes part of the group and, once accepted, no longer needs the active sponsorship of the leader. The leader also acts as a timekeeper, controlling the flow of the group and intervening when nonverbal cues indicate a need. The leader's role is also that of an appreciator (lavishing praise) and a mediator. Criticism in the group tends to be mild, for fear of offending. The leader is called on at times to say things that group members would rather not say for themselves, such as to keep people from talking too long. Often through the years members have sought out the leaders for counseling outside the group on health and family problems, home care information, bereavement, and other emotional issues.

Natural leaders also emerge from the group and are called on to take over when the "titular" leader is absent. As their expertise is needed, the former teacher is referred to on questions of grammar, the published writer on markets for publication, and the farmer on questions of nature.

For the group worker the lasting benefit of this kind of group is a glimpse of the potential of age and the nature of change throughout life. Particularly for those helping the elderly through physical and emotional crises, it is necessary to understand the grace that age can confer, the humor, the wisdom and the hope. Antonie Hermann's short poem illustrates the redemptive power of life (Hermann, 1984, p. 41):

Upon Reading the Book *My Mother–My Self*

Antonie Hermann

I washed the windows of my soul
With tears of guilt and sorrow,
Thus was revealed my tarnished goal
But, too, the promise of tomorrow.*

REFERENCES

BLOOM, JANET
1984   "Minerva's doll." In Marc Kaminsky (ed.), *The Uses of Reminiscence: New Ways of Working with Older Adults*. New York: Haworth Press, pp. 115-33.

BUTLER, ROBERT
1963   "The life review: An interpretation of reminiscence in the aged," *Psychiatry*, 26: 65-76.

CAMPBELL, RUTH
1981   "Report on arts and humanities cultural forums. *The Arts, the Humanities*

*Used with permission.

and Older Americans. Policy Symposium of Philadelphia, Pennsylvania, February, 1981. Washington, D.C.: National Council on Aging.

1984 "The aging experience as reflected in creative writing." In Stuart Spicker and Stanley R. Ingman (eds.), *Vitalizing Long-Term Care: The Teaching Nursing Home and Other Perspectives.* New York: Springer.

EDEL, LEON

1969 *Henry James: The Treacherous Years: 1895–1901.* Philadelphia, Penn.: J. B. Lippincott.

ERIKSON, ERIK, AND J. ERIKSON

1978 "Introduction: Reflections on aging." In Stuart Spicker, K. Woodward, and D. Van Tassel (eds.), *Aging and the Elderly: Humanistic Perspectives in Gerontology.* Atlantic Highlands, N.J.: Humanities Press.

HERMANN, ANTONIE

1984 "Upon reading the book *My Mother–My Self.*" In Ruth Campbell (ed.), *Never Say Never.* Ann Arbor: Turner Geriatric Services, University of Michigan Hospitals.

INGERSOLL, BERIT, AND LILI GOODMAN

1980 "History comes alive: Facilitating reminiscence in a group of institutionalized elderly," *Journal of Gerontological Social Work,* 2, no. 4: 305–19.

KAMINSKY, MARC

1978a "Pictures from the past: The use of reminiscence in casework with the elderly," *Journal of Gerontological Social Work,* 2, no. 4: 19–31.

1978b "What's inside you, it shines out of you." In R. Gross, B. Gross, and S. Seidman (eds.), *The New Old.* Garden City, N.Y.: Anchor Books.

KAMINSKY, MARC (ed.)

1984 *The Uses of Reminiscence: New Ways of Working with Older Adults.* New York: The Haworth Press.

KOCH, KENNETH

1977 *I Never Told Anybody.* New York: Random House.

KRAUS, CLAUDIA

1984 "Introduction." In Ruth Campbell (ed.), *Never Say Never.* Ann Arbor: Turner Geriatric Services, University of Michigan Hospitals.

McMAHON, A. W., AND P. J. RHODICK

1964 "Reminiscing: Adaptational significance in the aged," *Archives of General Psychiatry,* 10: 292–98.

MEYERHOFF, BARBARA

1978 *Number Our Days.* New York: E. P. Dutton.

MEYERHOFF, BARBARA, AND VIRGINIA TUFTE

1975 "Life history as integration: An essay on an experimental model," *The Gerontologist,* 15: 541–43.

MOODY, HARRY R.

1984 "Reminiscence and the recovery of the public world." In Marc Kaminsky (ed.), *The Uses of Reminiscence: New Ways of Working with Older Adults.* New York: The Haworth Press, pp. 157–66.

WEINBERG, JACK

1974 "What do I say to my mother when I have nothing to say?" *Geriatrics,* 29, no. 11: 155–59.

WORSLEY, DALE
    1984   "Snug Harbor: Workshops at the National Maritime Union." In Marc
            Kaminsky (ed.), *The Uses of Reminiscence: New Ways of Working with
            Older Adults*. New York: The Haworth Press, pp. 27–36.
WUNSCH, ANN
    1984   "They write for creative stimulation, enrichment," *Ann Arbor News*, June
            23, pp. C1, C4.

VI

Conclusion

32

Developments Influencing the Michigan Group Work Model and Future Directions

Martin Sundel and Paul Glasser

IN THIS FINAL CHAPTER we will examine the evolution of the University of Michigan group work model in relation to the knowledge bases, research findings, and developments that have shaped it. Attention is focused on the conceptual and practice influences of the behavioral approach, cognitive formulations, and social learning theory. The impact of program evaluation methods and small group research is discussed. Possible future directions for the model are explored.

The University of Michigan group work approach provides a comprehensive frame of reference for practice with groups. It has been developed, tested, elaborated, and refined over a period of more than two decades. The Michigan approach is an open system that allows for inclusion of new practice methods, diverse theoretical orientations, and research developments. The model draws heavily on the social and behavioral sciences and attempts to integrate knowledge that has been empirically validated. Recognized for its rigor and versatility, the model has applied concepts and research findings from small group theory, the social psychology of interpersonal influence, and personality theory, as well as prevailing practice wisdom, knowledge, and skills. The group worker using this approach also considers knowledge from sociobehavioral theory, sociocultural theory, program media and techniques, community organization, and organizational theory. The model has been used with diverse theoretical orientations such as behavioral, psychodynamic, ego psychological, and gestalt.

The group work model presented in this volume has evolved within a framework that encompasses the foci of both treatment and prevention. Described by its leading proponents and others as the preventive and rehabilitative approach, the model is widely referred to, both in the United States and abroad, as The University of Michigan group work model. The framework has allowed for study and elaboration of the elements of problem-solving in the treatment of individuals in groups, as well as the examination of various dimensions and processes related to different stages and phases of group development. A defining feature of the model has been its emphasis on the individual, with the group serving as both a means and a context for improving the functioning of its members.

Since the first edition of this volume was published in 1974, the conceptual breadth and rigor of the Michigan model have been evidenced by its application to new and varied settings. Unlike a number of other group work approaches, the Michigan model provides opportunities for empirical validation and allowance for change based on new concepts and research findings. This characteristic is evident in the updated revisions of chapters in this volume, as well as by the addition of new selections that are at the vanguard of group work practice. Furthermore, the frame of reference provided in this book is at a level that offers specific guidance and practice techniques.

The preventive and rehabilitative approach to social work with groups (as a forerunner to the Michigan model) was influenced by the writings of Fritz Redl, Marion Sloan, and Gisela Konopka (Reid, 1981, p. 205). Reid identified Robert Vinter, Paul Glasser, and Charles Garvin as the contemporary leading proponents of the approach. Robert Vinter is recognized as the originator of this systematic group work model with its strong social and behavioral science emphasis.

THE BEHAVIORAL APPROACH

Behavior modification or behavior therapy is based on the experimental foundations of learning theory, including the principles and methodology of operant conditioning, classical conditioning, and social learning (e.g. Bandura, 1969, 1977; Gambrill, 1977; Sundel and Sundel, 1982). The relevance of behavioral theory to group work was described in the first edition of this volume (Rose and Sundel, 1974; Sarri, 1974; Sundel and Lawrence, 1974). Over the past decade behavior modification with groups has witnessed tremendous growth in its application to diverse populations and problems (e.g. Rose, 1972, 1977, 1980; also see Chapter 21 herein by Ronald Feldman, Chapter 22 by Rose and Tolman, and Chapter 25 by Sundel and Sundel). Several edited volumes on recent research and clinical practice innovations with behavioral groups have been produced (Rose, 1980; Upper and Ross, 1979, 1980, 1981, 1985). Since 1980 Sheldon Rose and his colleagues and students at the University of Wisconsin School of Social Work have been publishing *Behavior Group Therapy*, a periodic newsletter on current developments in the field.

The behavioral approach has provided methodology and interventions related to more precise definition and assessment of the problems and concerns of group members. Speech and actions are delineated into measurable statements of verbal and nonverbal behaviors, and conditions influencing target behaviors are described in observable terms. The intervention plan is based on the goals formulated during assessment of the individual's problems, and intervention techniques and procedures are directed toward achievement of specific, measurable goals. Frankel and Glasser (1974) identified a variety of behavioral procedures that could be used in behavioral groups including modeling, behavioral rehearsal, systematic desensitization, structured discussion groups, and programmed instruction. To these others can be added, including relaxation training, social reinforcement, feedback, videotape techniques, assertiveness training, and behavioral assignments. Another important characteristic of the behavioral approach is evaluation based on specification of service delivery outcomes in behavioral terms.

In many respects the behavioral approach provided a compatible and natural extension to the Michigan group work model. The Michigan model called for specificity in describing individual problems, in formulating individual and group goals, and in prescribing and implementing program strategies and techniques. The empirical stance of the model emphasized evaluation of group process and outcome, an area in which substantial progress in design and technology has been witnessed during the past decade (e.g. Bloom and Fischer, 1982; Hudson, 1982; Rose, 1981; see Chapters 21 and 22 herein). The Michigan model was also open to practice innovations in the social and behavioral sciences, so that the empirically based behavioral techniques and procedures could be applied within its framework. Significantly, the behavioral approach has shown itself to be particularly relevant for use with individuals of low socioeconomic status and ethnic and racial minorities (e.g. Acosta, Yamamoto, and Evans, 1982; Rose and Sundel, 1974; Turner and Jones, 1982), a feature consistent with the Michigan model's focus on group services for disadvantaged and oppressed populations. The special effectiveness of behavior therapy techniques has been supported by numerous studies (Giles, 1983; Kazdin and Wilson, 1978).

Behavior modification with groups, as an extension of the Michigan model, is consistent with the contemporary ideal of the scientist-practitioner (Barlow, Hayes, and Nelson, 1984). According to this ideal the practitioner can contribute to the development of practice knowledge as well as use data-guided knowledge directly to help individuals with their problems. The sociobehavioral eclectic approach described by Thomas (1977b) appears compatible with the scientist-practitioner concept, since practitioners of this persuasion rely on techniques that have empirical support and can be operationalized for purposes of affecting change. Thomas influenced the application of sociobehavioral principles and techniques in group work at The University of Michigan (e.g. Rose, 1967).

Thomas considered the sociobehavioral approach to hold the greatest promise for social work, for it includes knowledge relevant to direct service from all behavioral science disciplines and social work practice, and contributions from other helping professions. Thomas (1977a) proposed the "BESDAS" model as an acronym for six characteristics of effective practice: behavioral targets, empirically based knowledge, specific intervention procedures, data-guided practice, accountable outcomes, and self-correcting practice. Recently he has presented a framework for a systematic methodology of intervention design for the helping professions (Thomas, 1984).

THE COGNITIVE CONNECTION

Although behavior modification and its powerful technology offer many advantages, the comprehensiveness of this approach has been questioned. Bandura's (1969, 1977) social learning theory influenced the movement in behavior therapy from radical behaviorism, exemplified by animal conditioning models, to more complex, cognitive formulations of human behavior and experience. A significant advantage of social learning theory has been its promise for integrating applied behavior analysis, classical conditioning approaches, and cognitive formulations in a comprehensive, testable framework (Wilson, 1980).

During the past decade a growing number of practitioners have considered the individual's cognitive and self-regulatory processes and activities to be a logical extension of the behavioral paradigm (Karoly and Kanfer, 1982). The cognitive therapies are based on the premise that disordered thoughts or beliefs produce disordered behaviors, and alteration of dysfunctional cognitions will diminish and often resolve psychosocial and emotional problems. The client is shown how to modify irrational, unproductive or self-defeating cognitions and replace them with more constructive expectations and self-appraisals.

An increasing number of therapists have combined behavioral and cognitive approaches (e.g. Beck, 1976; Cautela, 1966; Ellis, 1962; Lazarus, 1971, 1976; Mahoney, 1974; Meichenbaum, 1977). The outgrowth of this interaction has been the field of cognitive behavior modification or cognitive behavior therapy. Cognitive behavior modification was influenced by the method of rational emotive therapy developed by Albert Ellis (e.g. Ellis, 1962; Ellis and Harper, 1975), as well as by the work of Beck (Beck, 1963, 1976; Beck et al., 1979) primarily in the treatment of depression. Bandura's (1969, 1977) social learning theory was a significant force affecting the conceptual development of this movement. Cautela's covert conditioning (e.g. Cautela, 1971) and Meichenbaum's (1977) self-instructional methodology provided further extensions and elaborations of attempts to combine cognitive and behavioral approaches. Multimodal behavior therapy, developed by Arnold Lazarus (1971, 1976), is an example of the eclectic use of cognitive, behavioral, and social learning techniques.

The use of cognitive behavior modification with groups has been advanced by the work of Sheldon Rose and his colleagues (e.g. Rose, 1980). They have applied this approach to significant social problems such as adolescent pregnancy (Schinke, Blythe, and Gilchrist, 1981) and spouse abuse (Edleson, 1984). The cognitive influence in the field of behavior therapy has been growing rapidly (e.g. Kendall and Hollon, 1979; Wilson et al., 1984), including greater representation in behavioral group therapy (Upper and Ross, 1979, 1980, 1981, 1985).

Frankel (1984) performed a behavioral analysis of gestalt therapy, transactional analysis, and ego psychology in an effort to demonstrate that each of these therapies contains a practice technology that could be compatible with behavior therapy. Attempts to integrate cognitive approaches such as psychoanalytic therapy with behavior therapy are highly controversial (e.g. Arkowitz, 1984; Ledwidge, 1978), with critics arguing that data for empirical justification of cognitive methods are lacking (Latimer and Sweet, 1984). It can be concluded from the current *zeitgeist* that, depending upon one's point of view, cognitive influence among behaviorists is considered either a tremendous advance or a step in the wrong direction. For many the goal of developing a comprehensive framework for understanding and treating the complexities of human problems and life circumstances remains an elusive but worthwhile endeavor. Toward this end Garfield (1982, 1983) recommends that greater attention be given to (1) consumers' views of the significant factors in psychotherapy, such as certain characteristics of therapists, and (2) identification of common aspects of effective therapy, regardless of the theoretical orientation of the therapist.

Assertiveness training is a behavioral method used to help individuals express their opinions and feelings and to help them stand up for their rights in a responsible manner. Behavior modification groups are often used to train members in ways to modify nonassertive or overassertive behaviors and to teach them more effective interpersonal skills (e.g. Lange and Jakubowski, 1976; Sundel and Sundel, 1980). Various forms of role-playing techniques such as behavioral reenactment, role reversal, and behavioral rehearsal are typically used. Assertiveness training groups are usually designed to teach members how to discriminate between assertive and aggressive behaviors; how to examine and refute irrational, self-defeating cognitions; how to deal with anxiety related to interpersonal communication; and how to develop assertive responses in problematic situations. Exercises are often used to teach members how to attend to both verbal and nonverbal behaviors of others.

Social skills training, also called interpersonal skills training, has emerged as a broader rubric that encompasses a wide range of interpersonal behaviors, including assertiveness. Social skills training is designed to provide a comprehensive method to address cognitive, emotional, and behavioral difficulties of individuals (e.g. Bellack and Hersen, 1979). Social skills training is frequently used in homogeneous groups of individuals with interpersonal deficits such as deaf adults, elementary school children with classroom problems, or elderly men in nursing homes (e.g. Rose, 1980, pp. 152–218).

Assertiveness training and social skills training groups are often arranged in a wheel pattern of communication, with the practitioner as the hub and the group members as the spokes. Forsyth (1984) observes that this arrangement leads to one-on-one social skills or assertion training conducted in a group, with the practitioner playing a highly directive role. Some behavioral group therapists (Flowers, 1979; Rose, 1977) have indicated that the groups could be more effective if the members assumed a more active role in the training. Rather than conducting individual behavior therapy in a group, the practitioner can use the influence of group members to serve as models for desirable behaviors, to provide constructive feedback and social reinforcement, and to exchange mutually beneficial information. In a more precise way this mirrors the historical criticism by group workers that the practice of casework in a group does not exploit the advantages of the group.

PROGRAM EVALUATION
AND RESEARCH ON GROUPS

The rapidly growing fields of program evaluation and evaluation research (e.g. Posavac and Carey, 1980; Rossi and Freeman, 1982) have contributed to more rigorous attempts to evaluate human services. The use of single-subject research designs has become more prevalent as an attempt to integrate evaluation with direct practice methodology (e.g. Bloom and Fischer, 1982). These developments have also been evident in the evaluation of group work services (e.g. see Chapter 21 by Feldman and Chapter 22 by Rose and Tolman herein; Garvin, 1981; Toseland and Rivas, 1984).

Renewed interest has been shown in assessing the dimensions of a group as a whole using Bales's systematic multiple level observation of groups (SYMLOG). A SYMLOG field diagram provides a comprehensive method to assess the functioning of groups (Bales, 1980; Bales, Cohen, and Williamson, 1979). This method also has been used to facilitate the training of group workers. Various methods for assessing group dimensions and the group as a whole have been described elsewhere (e.g. Garvin, 1981; Rose, 1981; Toseland and Rivas, 1984).

Research findings from social psychology and group dynamics have been applied in the Michigan group work model, and recent advances in these fields can be exploited to improve group work services (see Chapter 4 by Radin and Feld herein). The emphasis on cognitive processes has become dominant in the field of social psychology. This focus on social cognition is evident in such prominent research programs as the Research Center for Group Dynamics, which is affiliated with the Institute for Social Research at The University of Michigan. The research center is directed by Robert Zajonc, one of the originators of cognitive social psychology. Zajonc and his colleagues have studied such problems as the effects of social context on cognitive performance, the bases on which causal attributions are made, and the ways in which information is processed to arrive at social judgments (Cannell and Kahn, 1984).

The Michigan group work model will continue to benefit from the development of new knowledge in social psychology and group dynamics. Some have complained that the flow and transfer of knowledge from basic research on groups to group practice is weak and that researchers and practitioners in these fields rarely exchange concerns and problems (e.g. Zander, 1979). Another view reflects that the goal of connecting group dynamics to group practice is so prodigious that a great deal more needs to be accomplished on the research side to satisfy the requirements of practitioners (Luft, 1984). Perhaps the transfer of knowledge from small group research to group practice can be accomplished at present only in "leaky buckets" that preclude a perfect fit in application of knowledge in the two fields. Greater interaction on this issue by researchers and practitioners, along with more effective means of disseminating research findings and practice innovations, might help to reduce this gap.

CONCLUSION

Current conditions in the human services seem favorable for extension of the Michigan group work model to new settings, as well as for continued research on selected group structures, processes, and other dimensions related to the model and its application. The growth of doctoral programs with direct practice emphases is a trend that promises to yield new generations of scholars and researchers interested in group work theory and practice. Renewed interest in concentrations by methods in schools of social work once again is evident in graduate and undergraduate courses in group work; moreover, such courses are offered to professionals through continuing education programs. Practitioners in many settings are rediscovering the values of the use of groups, often to carry out functions and tasks described in the early group work literature.

Current interest in prevention mirrors the settlement house philosophy of the past but is more sophisticated in its orientation. Concepts such as primary prevention, populations at risk, and other epidemiological factors can substantively enhance the knowledge base for group work practice. For example, Frankel and Sundel (1978) have suggested a framework for using these concepts to integrate group treatment goals with community action and social change.

A broader array of techniques has become available to make the group work method more effective and efficient, buttressed by conceptual developments and research findings as demonstrated by the selections in this volume. The ability to intervene with multiple clients at one time has become viewed increasingly, by both administrators and professionals, as a way to improve agency efficiency.

Interest in addressing societal needs through small groups continues as new movements and social changes pose heady challenges to the ingenuity and skill of group workers. Group workers can play a significant role in the development and application of community-based services, particularly for individuals in transition states. For example, the movement toward deinstitutionalization of residents of mental hospitals and institutions for retarded persons has created the need for responsive, effective, and efficient services and resources for these individuals and their families. Other community-based settings where group work services are in demand include youth homes for individuals on probation and parole and group homes for children placed there in lieu of large institutions. Neighborhood settlements and service organizations are rediscovering how groups can be used to prevent problems of depression, deal with family and individual crises, and aid in the treatment of emotional problems, not only with youth but also with the growing numbers of old people.

The group work approach presented in this volume will continue to evolve, we hope in a robust and flexible manner, so that it will be open to modifications, innovations, and adaptations required by differing social and environmental conditions. Changing demographics, blended families, domestic violence (abuse of children, spouses, partners and the elderly), health concerns, and poverty are among the conditions that will challenge skilled and knowledgeable group workers to make significant contributions to individual and societal progress.

REFERENCES

ACOSTA, FRANK; JOE YAMAMOTO; AND LEONARD EVANS
   1982 *Effective Psychotherapy for Low-Income and Minority Patients.* New York: Plenum.

ARKOWITZ, HAL (ed.)
  1984 *Psychoanalytic and Behavior Therapy: Is Integration Possible?* New York: Plenum.
BALES, ROBERT
  1980 *SYMLOG Case Study Kit.* New York: Free Press.
BALES, ROBERT; S. COHEN; AND S. WILLIAMSON
  1979 *SYMLOG: A System for the Multiple Level Observation of Groups.* New York: Free Press.
BANDURA, ALBERT
  1969 *Principles of Behavior Modification.* New York: Holt, Rinehart & Winston.
  1977 *Social Learning Theory.* Englewood Cliffs, N.J.: Prentice-Hall.
BARLOW, DAVID H.; STEVEN HAYES; AND ROSEMARY NELSON
  1984 *The Scientist Practitioner: Research and Accountability in Clinical and Educational Settings.* New York: Pergamon.
BECK, AARON T.
  1963 "Thinking and depression: 1. Idiosyncratic content and cognitive distortions," *Archives of General Psychiatry*, 9: 324–33.
  1976 *Cognitive Therapy and the Emotional Disorders.* New York: International Universities Press.
BECK AARON T.; A. JOHN RUSH; BRIAN F. SHAW; AND GARY EMERY
  1979 *Cognitive Therapy of Depression.* New York: Guilford.
BELLACK, ALAN, AND MICHEL HERSEN (eds.)
  1979 *Research and Practice in Social Skills Training.* New York: Plenum.
BLOOM, MARTIN, AND JOEL FISCHER
  1982 *Evaluating Practice: Guidelines for the Accountable Professional.* Englewood Cliffs, N.J.: Prentice-Hall.
CANNELL, CHARLES F., AND ROBERT L. KAHN
  1984 "Some factors in the origins and development of the Institute for Social Research, The University of Michigan," *American Psychologist*, 39: 1256–66.
CAUTELA, JOSEPH R.
  1966 "Treatment of compulsive behavior by covert sensitization," *Psychological Record*, 16: 33–41.
  1971 "Covert conditioning." In A. Jacobs and L. Sachs (eds.), *The Psychology of Private Events.* New York: Academic Press, pp. 109–30.
EDELSON, JEFFERY L.
  1984 "Working with men who batter," *Social Work*, 29 (May-June): 237–42.
ELLIS, ALBERT
  1962 *Reasons and Emotion in Psychotherapy.* New York: Lyle Stuart.
ELLIS, ALBERT, AND R. A. HARPER
  1975 *A New Guide to Rational Living.* Englewood Cliffs, N.J.: Prentice-Hall
FLOWERS, JOHN
  1979 "Behavioral analysis of group therapy and a model for behavioral group therapy." In Dennis Upper and Steven Ross (eds.), *Behavioral Group Therapy, 1979: An Annual Review.* Champaign, Ill.: Research Press, pp. 5–37.

FORSYTH, DONELSON
  1984 *An Introduction to Group Dynamics*. Monterey, Calif.: Brooks/Cole.
FRANKEL, ARTHUR J.
  1984 *Four Therapies Intergrated: A Behavioral Analysis of Gestalt, T.A., and Ego Psychology*. Englewood Cliffs, N.J.: Prentice-Hall.
FRANKEL, ARTHUR, AND PAUL GLASSER
  1974 "Behavioral approaches to group work," *Social Work*, 19 (March): 163–77.
FRANKEL, ARTHUR, AND MARTIN SUNDEL
  1978 "The grope for group: Initiating individual and community change," *Social Work with Groups*, 1, no. 4 (Winter): 399–405.
GAMBRILL, EILEEN D.
  1977 *Behavior Modification: Handbook of Assessment, Intervention and Evaluation*. San Francisco: Jossey-Bass.
GARFIELD, SOL L.
  1982 "Eclecticism and integration in psychotherapy," *Behavior Therapy*, 13: 610–23.
  1983 "Effectiveness of psychotherapy: The perennial controversy," *Professional Psychology: Research and Practice*, 14: 35–43.
GARVIN, CHARLES V.
  1981 *Contemporary Group Work*. Englewood Cliffs, N.J.: Prentice-Hall.
GILES, THOMAS R.
  1983 "Probable superiority of behavioral interventions–II: Empirical status of the equivalence of therapies hypothesis," *Journal of Behavior Therapy and Experimental Psychiatry*, 14: 189–96.
HUDSON, WALTER
  1982 *The Clinical Measurement Package: A Field Manual*. Homewood, Ill.: Dorsey Press.
KAROLY, PAUL, AND FREDERICK KANFER (eds.)
  1982 *Self-Management and Behavior Change: From Theory to Practice*. Elmsford, N.Y.: Pergamon Press.
KAZDIN, ALAN AND G. TERENCE WILSON
  1978 *Evaluation of Behavior Therapy: Issues, Evidence, and Research Strategies*. Cambridge, Mass.: Ballinger.
KENDALL, PHILIP, AND STEVEN HOLLON (eds.)
  1979 *Cognitive-Behavioral Interventions: Theory, Research and Procedures*. New York: Academic Press.
LANGE, ARTHUR J., AND PATRICIA JAKUBOWSKI
  1976 *Responsible Assertive Behavior*. Champaign, Ill.: Research Press.
LATIMER, PAUL R., AND ANDREW A. SWEET
  1984 "Cognitive versus behavioral procedures in cognitive-behavior therapy: A critical review of the evidence," *Journal of Behavior Therapy and Experimental Psychiatry*, 15: 9–22.
LAZARUS, ARNOLD A.
  1971 *Behavior Therapy and Beyond*. New York: McGraw-Hill
  1976 *Multi-modal Behavior Therapy*. New York: Springer-Verlag.

LEDWIDGE, BERNARD
1978 "Cognitive behavior modification: A step in the wrong direction," *Psychological Bulletin*, 85: 353–75.

LUFT, JOSEPH
1984 *Group Processes: An Introduction to Group Dynamics*. Third edition. Palo Alto, Calif.: Mayfield Publishing Co.

MAHONEY, MICHAEL
1974 *Cognition and Behavior Modification*. Cambridge, Mass.: Ballinger.

MEICHENBAUM, DONALD
1977 *Cognitive Behavior Modification: An Integrative Approach*. New York: Plenum.

POSAVAC, EMIL, AND RAYMOND CAREY
1980 *Program Evaluation: Methods and Case Studies*. Englewood Cliffs, N.J.: Prentice-Hall.

REID, KENNETH E.
1981 *From Character Building to Social Treatment: The History of the Use of Groups in Social Work*. Westport, Conn.: Greenwood Press.

ROSE, SHELDON D.
1967 "A behavioral approach to group treatment of children." In Edwin J. Thomas (ed.), *The Socio-Behavioral Approach and Applications to Social Work*. New York: Council on Social Work Education, pp. 39–54.
1972 *Treating Children in Groups: A Behavioral Approach*. San Francisco: Jossey-Bass.
1977 *Group Therapy: A Behavioral Approach*. Englewood Cliffs, N.J.: Prentice-Hall.
1981 "Assessment in groups," *Social Work Research and Abstracts*, 17: 29–37.

ROSE, SHELDON D. (ed.)
1980 *A Casebook in Group Therapy: A Behavioral-Cognitive Approach*. Englewood Cliffs, N.J.: Prentice-Hall.

ROSE, SHELDON D., AND MARTIN SUNDEL
1974 "The Hartwig Project: A behavioral approach to the treatment of juvenile offenders." In Paul Glasser, Rosemary Sarri, and Robert Vinter (eds.), *Individual Change Through Small Groups*. New York: Free Press, 1974, pp. 404–19.

ROSSI, PETER, AND HOWARD FREEMAN
1982 *Evaluation: A Systematic Approach*. Second edition. Beverly Hills, Calif.: Sage Publications.

SARRI, ROSEMARY
1974 "Behavioral theory and group work." In Paul Glasser, Rosemary Sarri, and Robert Vinter (eds.), *Individual Change Through Small Groups*. New York: Free Press, pp. 50–70.

SCHINKE, STEVEN; BETTY BLYTHE; AND LEWAYNE GILCHRIST
1981 "Cognitive-behavioral prevention of adolescent pregnancy," *Journal of Counseling Psychology*, 28: 451–54.

SUNDEL, MARTIN, AND HARRY LAWRENCE
1974 "Behavioral group treatment with adults in a family service agency." In Paul Glasser, Rosemary Sarri, and Robert Vinter (eds.), *Individual Change Through Small Groups*. New York: Free Press, pp. 325–47.

SUNDEL, MARTIN, AND SANDRA S. SUNDEL
  1982 *Behavior Modification in the Human Services: A Systematic Introduction to Concepts and Applications.* Second edition. Englewood Cliffs, N.J.: Prentice-Hall.
SUNDEL, SANDRA S., AND MARTIN SUNDEL
  1980 *Be Assertive: A Practical Guide for Human Service Workers.* Beverly Hills, Calif.: Sage Publications.
THOMAS, EDWIN
  1977a "The BESDAS model for effective practice," *Social Work Research and Abstracts*, 13 (Summer): 12–16.
  1977b "Social casework and social group work: The behavioral modification approach." In John Turner (ed.), *Encyclopedia of Social Work.* Seventeenth edition. Washington, D.C.: National Association of Social Workers, Inc., pp. 1309–21.
  1984 *Designing Interventions for the Helping Professions.* Beverly Hills, Calif.: Sage Publications.
TOSELAND, RONALD W., AND ROBERT F. RIVAS
  1984 *An Introduction to Group Work Practice.* New York: Macmillan.
TURNER, SAMUEL, AND R. L. JONES (eds.)
  1982 *Behavior Modification in Black Populations: Psychological Issues and Empirical Findings.* New York: Plenum.
UPPER, DENNIS, AND STEVEN ROSS (eds.)
  1979 *Behavioral Group Therapy: An Annual Review, 1979.* Champaign, Ill.: Research Press.
  1980 *Behavioral Group Therapy: An Annual Review, 1980.* Champaign, Ill. Research Press.
  1981 *Behavioral Group Therapy: An Annual Review, 1981.* Champaign, Ill.: Research Press.
  1985 *Handbook of Behavioral Group Therapy.* New York: Plenum.
WILSON, G. TERENCE
  1980 "Cognitive factors in lifestyle changes: A social learning perspective." In Park O. Davidson and Sheena M. Davidson (eds.), *Behavioral Medicine: Changing Health Lifestyles.* New York: Brunner/Mazel, pp. 3–37.
WILSON G. TERENCE; CYRIL FRANKS; KELLY BROWNELL; AND PHILIP KENDALL
  1984 *Annual Review of Behavior Therapy: Theory and Practice.* Vol. 9. New York: Guilford Press.
ZANDER, ALVIN
  1979 "The psychology of group processes," *Annual Review of Psychology*, 30: 417–52.

Index